A HISTORY OF

Christianity in Asia

VOLUME I

A HISTORY OF
Christianity
in Asia

VOLUME I:
BEGINNINGS TO 1500

Samuel Hugh Moffett

ORBIS BOOKS

Maryknoll, New York 10545

Acknowledgments are found on page 559.

The Catholic Foreign Mission Society of America (Maryknoll) recruits and trains people for overseas missionary service. Through Orbis Books, Maryknoll aims to foster the international dialogue that is essential to mission. The books published, however, reflect the opinions of their authors and are not meant to represent the official position of the Society.

Second revised and corrected edition, copyright © 1998 by Samuel Hugh Moffett. Published by Orbis Books, Maryknoll, New York, U.S.A.

This is a revised and corrected edition of the 1992 version of this book published by HarperSanFrancisco, a division of HarperCollinis Publishers.

Text design by Rick Chafian
Maps by Clyde W. Breitwieser

Manufactured in the United States of America.

Library of Congress Cataloging-in-Publication Data

Moffett, Samuel H.
  A history of Christianity in Asia / Samuel Hugh Moffett.—2nd rev. and corrected ed.
    p. cm.
  Includes bibliographical references and index.
  Contents: v. 1. Beginnings to 1500.
  ISBN 1-57075-162-6 (alk. paper)
  1. Church history—Asia.   I. Title.
BR1065.M63   1998
275—dc21   97-49236
                                                                      CIP

To Eileen,
my partner in Asia,
for all these happy years together

Contents

Part I: From the Apostles to Muhammad

SECTION ONE:
THE FIRST TWO HUNDRED YEARS

Part II: Outreach: The Ends of the Earth
(From Alopen to the Crusades)

Part III: The Pax Mongolica:
From Genghis Khan to Tamerlane

Acknowledgments

It would be impossible even to list the names of those who have helped me immensely along the way, but I do want to mention a few. For the financial grant that enabled me to begin this project I thank the Institute for Advanced Christian Studies, and for a study in which to pursue it, Dr. McCord and the Center of Theological Inquiry in Princeton. The Presbyterian church's Commission on Ecumenical Mission and Relations and its Program Agency gave me important and much appreciated study leaves at Cambridge University. My classes and faculty colleagues at the Presbyterian Theological Seminary in Seoul, Korea, and at the Asian Center for Theological Studies and Mission challenged me to turn to the history of the church in Asia; and at Princeton Theological Seminary a different set of students and colleagues taught me the importance of endeavoring to make that history intelligible to Westerners. I am immensely grateful to Speer Library at Princeton Seminary, to Firestone Library at Princeton University, and to the Cambridge colleges of Fitzwilliam and Westminster and the university library on that idyllic campus for the privilege of happy hours of study and research. In a more personal vein, I gratefully number the names of Mackay, Latourette, and Bainton among my mentors; and for technical assistance in this age of bewildering technological advance I must mention John Webster, Kate LeVan, Patricia Grier, and Brenda Williams. But to no one do I owe more than to Eileen, my wife, who century by century, figuratively speaking, encouraged me to come out of the past to write for the living.

Princeton, New Jersey
September, 1991

Introduction

The story of Christianity in the West has often been told, but the history of Christianity in the East is not as well known. The seed was the same: the good news of Jesus Christ for the whole world, which Christians call "the gospel." But it was sown by different sowers; it was planted in different soil; it grew with a different flavor; and it was gathered by different reapers.

It is too often forgotten that the faith moved east across Asia as early as it moved west into Europe. Western church history tends to follow Paul to Philippi and to Rome and on across Europe to the conversion of Constantine and the barbarians. With some outstanding exceptions, only intermittently has the West looked beyond Constantinople into Asia and given attention to the long, proud traditions of a Christianity that chose to look neither to Rome nor to Constantinople as its center. It was a Christianity that has for centuries remained unashamedly Asian.

The following survey of early Asian Christianity is undertaken with the hope that it may serve as a reminder that the church began in Asia. Its earliest history, its first centers were Asian. Asia produced the first known church building, the first New Testament translation, perhaps the first Christian king, the first Christian poets, and even arguably the first Christian state. Asian Christians endured the greatest persecutions. They mounted global ventures in missionary expansion the West could not match until after the thirteenth century. By then the Nestorian church (as most of the early Asian Christian communities came to be called) exercised ecclesiastical authority over more of the earth than either Rome or Constantinople.

One reason, of course, for the neglect of the Asian dimension in church history is the comparative paucity of available source materials on the Eastern roots of Christianity outside the Roman Empire.

The surviving documents are too slender a base to support some of the bold and contradictory statements made about these earliest Christians of the East.

One historian, for example, calls the Nestorians the greatest missionaries the world has ever seen.[1] Another dismisses them as "passionless" Christians embarrassingly obsequious to the politically powerful.[2] One selects A.D. 1000 as the date of the climax of Nestorian expansion and power.[3] Another takes the same general date as the time of the eclipse of Nestorianism in China.[4] The same kind of contradictions persist in theological arguments about early Asian Christianity. To some, Nestorians are heretics, condemned by the ecumenical councils. To others they are ancient and apostolic Asian Christians untainted by the perversions of Western Greek philosophy. And, of course, many have forgotten the Nestorians altogether.

Some of these apparent contradictions disappear under further examination. Nestorianism was not the only form of early Asian Christianity, and it was not an undivided continuum. In third-century Osrhoene it was vastly different from what it became in thirteenth-century China. In fact, third-century Nestorianism is not, properly speaking, Nestorianism at all.

A word, therefore, about my use of terms. If I speak of Nestorians before the fifth century it should be borne in mind that this name was not used by the Nestorian church until early medieval times. Their own name was the Church of the East. But East and West are confusingly relative terms, and since to most Christians the Eastern church means Eastern Orthodoxy, it seems best after the fifth century to use the less accurate but more prevalent name Nestorian.

The term "Asian Christianity" is also open to more than one interpretation. I will use it culturally, not strictly geographically. Bethlehem, Jerusalem, Antioch, and Armenia are all geographically in Asia, but politically and to a considerable extent culturally they belonged sooner or later to the West, that is, to the Roman Empire until the Muslim conquest. "Asian Christianity" as used in this work will refer to the churches that grew and spread outside the Roman Empire in ancient oriental kingdoms east of the Euphrates and stretching along the Old Silk Road from Osrhoene through Persia to China or along the water routes from the Red Sea around Arabia to India.

Chronologically this volume will cover only the early period, from the time of the apostles to the age of Western discovery, about A.D. 1500. The general outline is familiar. Before the end of the first century the Christian faith broke out across the borders of Rome into

"Asian" Asia. Its first roots may have been as far away as India or as near as Edessa in the tiny semi-independent principality of Osrhoene just across the Euphrates. From Edessa, according to tradition, the faith spread to another small kingdom three hundred miles farther east across the Tigris River, the kingdom of Adiabene, with its capital at Arbela, near ancient Nineveh. By the end of the second century, missionary expansion had carried the church as far east as Bactria in what is now northern Afghanistan, and mass conversions of Huns and Turks in central Asia were reported from the fifth century onward. By the end of the seventh century Persian missionaries had reached the "end of the world," the capital of T'ang-dynasty China.

But by then a cloud from the desert, Islam, was about to bring this first period of Asian church history crashing to a close. It was not the end, however. Out of Asia, after another six hundred years, came another cloud, a storm of Mongol nomads racing west, destroying all before them and threatening the very center of medieval Christianity in Europe, but paradoxically reopening Asia as far as China once more to Christian expansion.

This is the vast panorama these pages will try to unfold. No one author can do it justice. This one has been stretched far beyond his field of expertise. Yet there is value in an attempt to view this wide but little-known segment of a whole continent's history from the focused perspective of a single observer. So, acknowledging my great debt to the works of a host of specialists, to which the notes can only partially bear witness, I can only hope that this volume will be another small step toward restoring global balance to the study of church history.

NOTES

1. A. Mingana, "The Early Spread of Christianity in Central Asia and the Far East," in *Bulletin of John Rylands Library* 9, no. 2 (July 1925): 347.

2. J. Legge, *The Nestorian Monument of Hsi-An Fu* (London: Trubner, 1888), 54.

3. A. S. Atiya, *A History of Eastern Christianity* (London: Methuen, 1968), 265.

4. J. Foster, *The Church of the T'ang Dynasty* (London: S.P.C.K., 1939), 115f.

Preface to the Second Edition

The response to *A History of Christianity in Asia:* Volume I, *Beginnings to 1500* has been most gratifying. The first edition of more than 4000 copies sold out faster than expected. A translation into Korean is already in print, and a Chinese translation is in process. Its use as a textbook has brought requests for more copies from as far away as Uzbekistan. So I am very happy that this has opened the way for publication of this paperback edition by Orbis Books of Maryknoll, New York, in an agreement with HarperCollins. Orbis, with its Maryknoll missionary roots, is highly respected both for its high academic standards and for the global range of its books.

Most welcome, also, is the chance to make improvements. Typographical errors have been corrected and some revisions have been made thanks to helpful reviewers and readers. A tangled footnote here and there has also been clarified. A few additions were made possible. For example, I have added a little more of the remarkable and dramatic history of the ancient Armenian church, which I had too arbitrarily excluded from this Asian history because of its close ties to the Hellenistic world of the west. Also an effort has been made to indicate in at least one of the maps that the Nestorians were not the only surviving church body in Asia in 1500.

Volume II, *The 500 Years from 1500 to the Present* is in progress and Orbis Books will be publishing that also. Then this complex task of describing in two volumes the most influential faith the world has ever known, on the largest and most heavily populated continent on earth, will be as comprehensive as one chronicler can tell it.

Samuel Hugh Moffett
Princeton, New Jersey
November, 1997

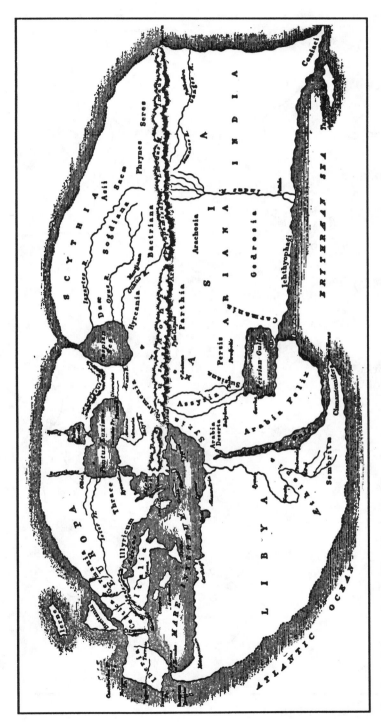

Strabo's Map of the World, A.D. 19

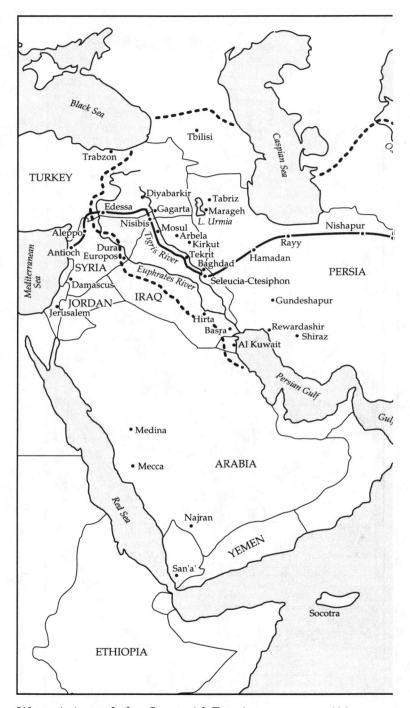

West Asia and the Sassanid Empire, ca. A.D. 600

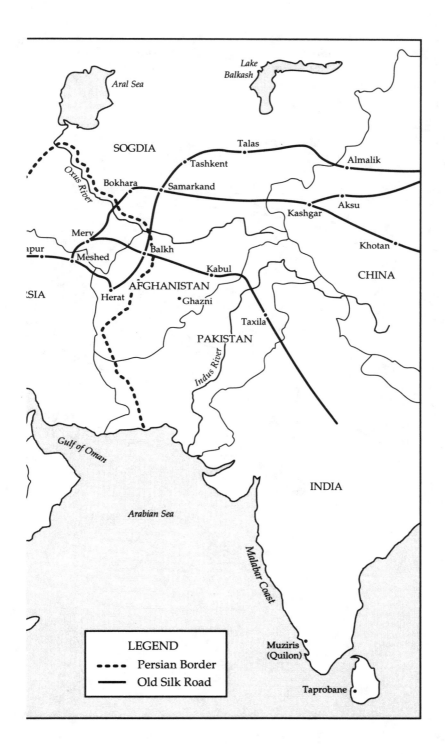

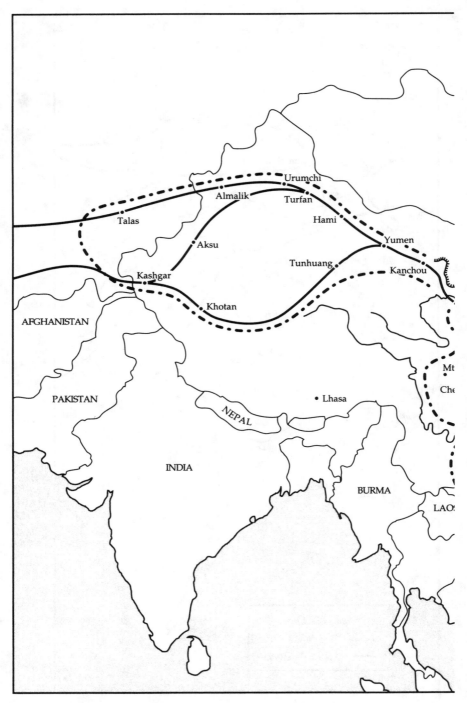

East Asia and T'ang Dynasty China, ca. A.D. 800

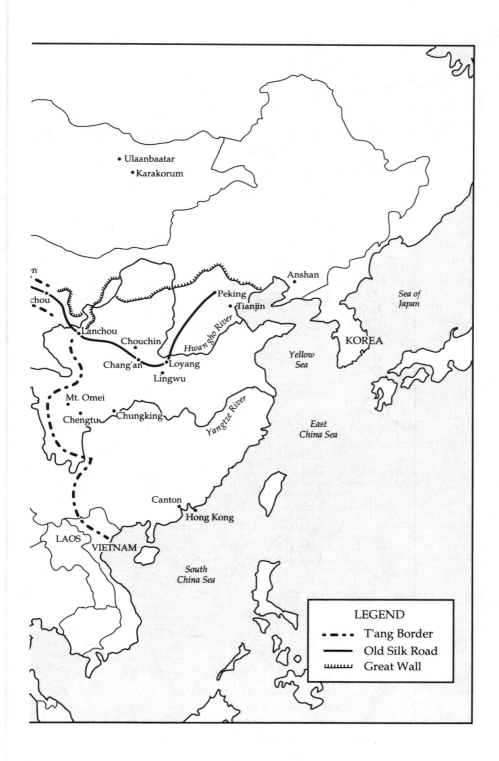

• Ulaanbaatar
•Karakorum

Anshan

•Peking
•Tianjin

Sea of
Japan

Lanchou
Chouchin

Hwangho River

KOREA

Chang'an
Lingwu

Loyang

Yellow
Sea

Mt. Omei

Chengtu
Chungking

Yangtze River

East
China Sea

Canton

Hong Kong

LAOS
VIETNAM

South
China Sea

LEGEND
- - - T'ang Border
—— Old Silk Road
⊔⊔⊔⊔ Great Wall

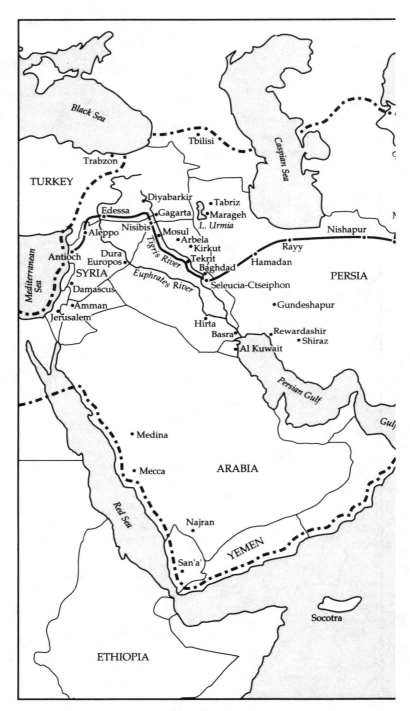

West and West Central Asia under Islam:
The Abbasid Caliphate, ca. A.D. 800

xxii

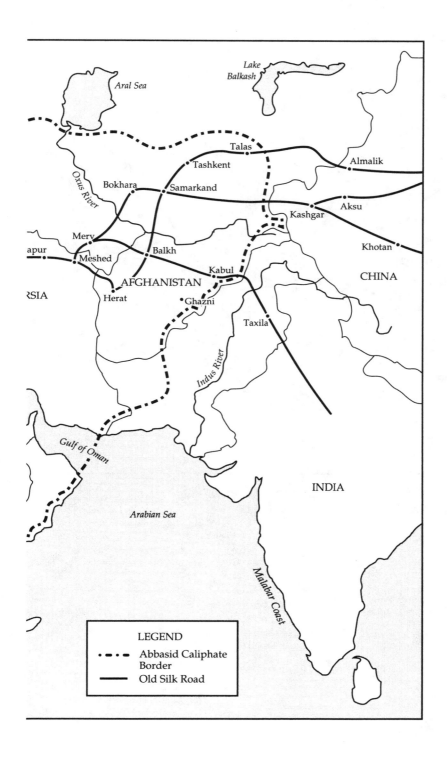

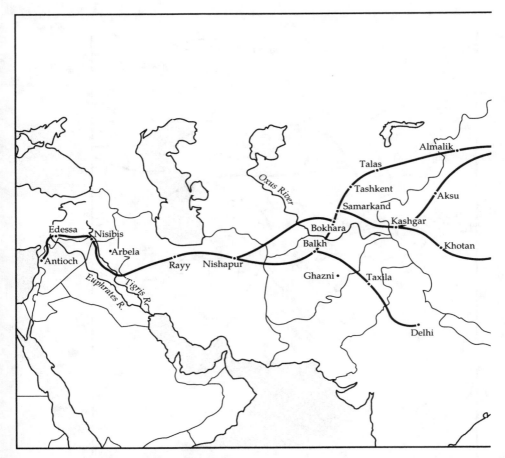

The Mongol Empire at its Greatest Extent,
under Kublai Khan, ca. 1260–1300

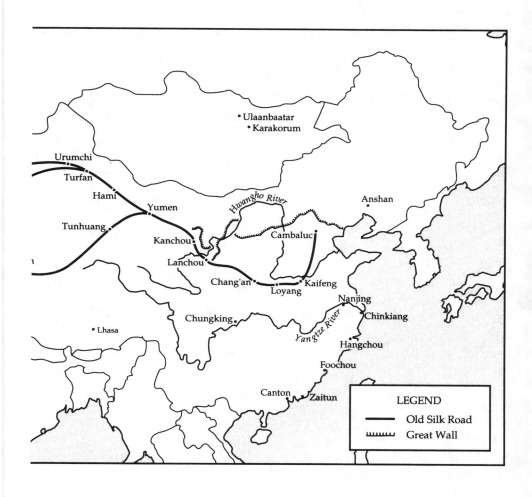

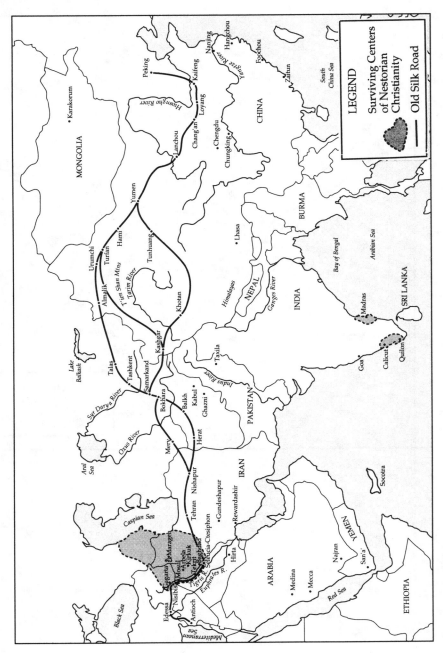

Asia, ca. 1500

PART I

From the Apostles to Muhammad

Chapter 1
Asia and the World
of the First Century

"Europe and Libya end at Asia. . . . Ctesias says that
India is not smaller than the rest of Asia, and
Onescritus that it is a third part of the inhabited
world. . . . [But] writers . . . do not describe [Asia]
on the far side of the Hypanis accurately, and
because of their ignorance and of its remoteness
magnify all things. . . . For example, the stories of
the ants that mine gold and . . . the Seres [Chinese]
who, they say, prolong their lives even beyond two
hundred years."

—Strabo, about A.D. 20, in his
Geographica, 2. 5.26; 15. 1.12, 37
(English translation by H. L.
Jones, Loeb Classical library)

IT was on a hill in Asia, at the far western edge of the continent, that Jesus said to his disciples, "Go ye into all the world and preach the gospel" (Mark 16:15). The New Testament, however, does not tell us what that little group, mostly fishermen, may have understood by the words "all the world." What was their perception of "the uttermost part of the earth" (Acts 1:8)? Luke, describing the crowd at Pentecost, speaks of "Jews . . . out of every nation under heaven" but mentions among the regions of Asia nothing more remote than three provinces of the Persian Empire, Parthia (northeastern Iran and southern Russia to the Afghan border), Media (south of the Caspian Sea, including modern Teheran), and Elam (now Khuzistan, east of the Persian Gulf). (Acts 2:5–11).

But unknown to the disciples, a fellow Asian of their own time, a Greek geographer from Pontus in Asia Minor, had recently capped a lifetime of study with the most successful attempt in the early history of Greek science to outline the bounds of the inhabited earth. It is true that none of the apostles would ever read Strabo. Even the scientists of that century tended to ignore him. But Strabo's *Geography*, appearing about A.D. 20, presented to the world of the apostolic church a better picture of the planet than its people had ever before possessed.

Its basic shape was startlingly modern, for the Greeks knew much that the Middle Ages forgot. Strabo's world was no flat-sided cube. It was a globe, with arctic and temperate zones, in size about twenty-five thousand miles around at the circumference. True, he knew only three continents—Asia, Europe, and Africa—but with remarkable prescience he conceded that there might be continents or other worlds unknown to him, for he remarked that the only land masses he could describe were too small for the size of the round world his astronomical measurements convinced him existed.

Land covered less than one-third of the surface of his sphere, measuring only seven thousand geographical miles from east to west and three thousand miles from north to south. Ireland was his farthest north, and he placed it above Britain. Spain was farthest west. To the east the world stretched across Asia to the southern tip of India; and the south disappeared in Africa beyond the Ethiopian Nile. The rest of his world was water. He simply filled in the remaining empty space with the uncharted sea on which the earth's three connected continents floated like an elongated, circular island.[1] (See the map on p. xvii.)

Half of Strabo's inhabited world was the continent of Asia. It reached from the Don to the Ganges, from Arabia to "the land of the Seres," China. He was the first Western writer to mention the Seres,[2]

4

yet it is surprising how little more of Asia he knew, really, than had already been opened to Western eyes three hundred years before by the conquests of Alexander the Great. He strangely distorted the shape of the continent, flattening out the southern coasts, squaring the edges, and thinning down the unknown north and far east. He frankly admitted that everything north and east of Sogdia (where modern Russia, China, and Afghanistan meet) was virtually a blank to him.[3]

Strabo divided Asia into two sections, one north of the mountains and the other south, but to do this, to make the continent fit his arbitrary pattern, he had to gather up all the great ranges of the roof of the world as we now know them—the Himalayas, Pamirs, Hindu Kush, and the Urals, the Altai, and Tien Shan mountains—and stretch them out in a thin wall across Asia straight east from the Taurus range in Persia to a distant sea where his mountain wall separated India from the land of the Seres. North of this wall were the wild nomads of the plains above the Black Sea, Scythians, Sarmatians,[4] and gold-ornamented Aorsi. Eastward along the valley of the Phasis River, which was a major trade route to the Caspian Sea, lived half-nomad Albanians and their more civilized neighbors, the Iberians. Beyond the Caspian Sea, which Strabo thought opened up into the "northern ocean" like a great narrow-mouthed bay, the Asiatic Scythians dominated the steppes with their hard-riding horsemen. Their eastern neighbors, the Saka, were already moving south through Bactria (Afghanistan) into northwest India. Strabo placed the Sacae north of the Jaxartes (Syr Darya) River; the Sogdians between the Jaxartes and the Oxus (Amu Darya); and the Bactrians, among whom sprang up one of the earliest Christian communities in central Asia, south of the Oxus, in what is now Afghanistan.

Asia south of Strabo's mountains was more familiar territory. Arabia, Syria, and Asia Minor were in the far west. Next, to the east, came Assyria and Parthian Persia, whose eastern provinces touched the borders of India. But of India itself beyond the Indus River, Strabo complains that he can learn nothing. Voyagers have ventured as far as the Ganges, he says, but they are too ignorant to give any worthwhile information.[5] Actually they were probably less ignorant than shrewd. His informants were the Arab and Greek-Egyptian mariners who at that time had a monopoly on Rome's rich commerce with the East, the same kind of sailors on one of whose ships, according to tradition, St. Thomas was carried to India and who quite understandably might be reluctant to share their navigational secrets with any who might try to break their monopoly. All they would tell Strabo was that the Ganges was the mightiest river on earth. So

Strabo's world, the world of first-century Rome, ended in India. Beyond the Ganges for seventeen thousand miles stretched the circling sea.

If that was the world as the best minds of the West saw it at the beginning of the Christian era, what a vastly deficient view of Asia the early Christians carried with them eastward. They were Asians themselves but they did not know Asia, not even as well as Strabo did. They were not in that respect, however, any different from other Asians of the time. There was no consciousness of Asia as a whole, nor did any one part as a rule know much more than the borders of the next part.

In many ways we know ancient Asia today better than it knew itself. First of all, we can see in retrospect four waves of empire that had swept across its broad expanse leaving, like tidal marks on the beach of the first century, four strands of civilization stamped upon its surface: Greco-Roman, Iranian (Persian), Sinic (Chinese), and Indian.

Greco-Roman Asia

It was in Roman Asia that Jesus Christ was born. A "decree from Caesar Augustus," the first Roman emperor, determined that the place of his birth would be Bethlehem, not Nazareth; and his disciples were first called Christians at Antioch "in the days of Claudius Caesar,"[6] the fourth emperor (Luke 2:1; Acts 11:26).

But Rome was an intruder in Asia, like Greece before it. The Romans were only accidentally, not intrinsically, Asian, despite the legends of their origin in Homeric Troy as recounted in Virgil's *Aeneid*. In fact, the Roman policy toward its holdings in Asia was to break off western Asia from the land mass of the continent and absorb it into the sea-centered Western world of the Mediterranean. To Roman eyes, Asia Minor, Syria, and Palestine were the eastern shores of the Great Sea. To the Parthians, however, these same lands were the western edge of Asia and belonged to Persia. The first seven centuries of church history, therefore, unfolded within the wider context of an imperial conflict between Persia and Rome that set East against West in mortal battle for control of what is now misleadingly called the Middle East.

Rome first fought Persia for control of western Asia at the battle of Carrhae in 53 B.C. and lost. The humiliation of that stunning defeat was one of the blows that toppled the Roman Republic and brought in the Empire. It was also the beginning of a seven-hundred-year war that neither empire finally won but that at least allowed Roman arms, with the aid of Greek culture, to keep the narrow Mediterranean rim of Asia more closely linked to the West than to the East.

In three short brilliant dynasties Rome stole the strategic Asian coastal corridor out of the Orient into the world of the West. The Julio-Claudian dynasty (4 B.C.–A.D. 68, from Augustus to Nero) established the empire. The Flavian dynasty (67–96, from Vespasian to Domitian) preserved the empire. And the Antonine dynasty (98–192, from Trajan to Marcus Aurelius and Commodus) brought in the empire's golden age.[7]

Even before he became emperor, Augustus, grandnephew and heir of Julius Caesar, had carved out the boundaries of Roman Asia. He avenged the defeat of the Romans at Carrhae and drove the Persians east into the Syrian desert. His people urged him to sweep on across Asia like a Roman Alexander. Wipe out Persia, they cried. Some would have had him push even farther, to India. But Augustus sensed, perhaps unconsciously, that Rome's power base was the Mediterranean and he persistently refused to be drawn into endless land wars. Having conquered Armenia he paused and, instead of pressing on, chose rather to force a treaty of peace in 20 B.C. on the hapless Parthian emperor, Phraates IV. It was an important date in history. It marked the beginning of a new era, the *pax Romana*, a hundred years of almost uninterrupted peace that Christian writers ever since Origen have hailed as a *praeparatio evangelium*, one of the ways in which God prepared the world for the coming of Christ and the establishment of the church.

That same treaty changed the pattern of church history also by fixing the boundary between Rome and Persia roughly along the course of the Euphrates River. As a result, from the beginning of the recorded history of Christianity, if any line of division is to be drawn between Asian and Western church history it falls most appropriately not at the western edge of the Asian continent and not at the Mediterranean, but at the Euphrates. It was there that East met West. West and north of that line, Asia Minor, Roman Syria, Judaea, and Armenia were all drawn sooner or later out of Asia proper into the history of Western Christianity. This was a separation, political and cultural, that as it turned out was eventually to divide the church and grievously affect the progress of Christianity in both the East and the West.

Augustus ruled his possessions in Asia by three categories of administrative organization, always with an eye on Persia, the enemy beyond.[8] First, he preferred to leave newly acquired territories to be ruled by native client-kings, local rulers who knew their own people and how to control them but who could in turn be controlled by Rome. One such was Herod the Great in Judaea. Then, as conquered areas became romanized or if vassal princes proved disloyal or unable to suppress rebellion, Rome would absorb the petty kingdoms into the empire as provinces. There were two kinds of provinces, imperial and senatorial. Next to the screen of client-kingdoms protecting the unstable border with Persia was a wall of *imperial* provinces with armies guarding the inner frontier: Galatia, Cilicia, Syria, and (by the time of the death of Augustus) Judaea which, for its intransigence, was reduced in rank from a kingdom to a province. Of all the imperial provinces Syria was by far the richest and most important in Asia. Its center, Antioch, became the bastion of Rome's military power in the East. It was also where the followers of Christ were first called Christians (Acts 11:26).

The other category was the *senatorial* province, located in those areas of Asia Minor most closely linked to the heart of the empire. They were romanized, unarmed, and stable. Such, under Augustus, were the province of Bithynia-Pontus on the north along the southern shore of the Black Sea and the province of Asia in the west (not to be confused with the continent of Asia). Asia was the closest of the provinces to Europe and was often mentioned by Paul in his Letters and by Luke in the book of Acts (1 Cor. 16:19; 2 Cor. 1:8; Acts 6:9; 16:6; 19:10). The province of Asia, like Judaea, had also once been a client-kingdom, Pergamum. Its greatest city was Ephesus.

From the viewpoint of the empire the most troubling areas in Roman Asia were the two sore spots of Armenia and Judaea. Armenia was the focus of unending trouble with Persia. It had always been more oriental than Greek or Roman. Traditionally, despite its fierce pride in its own independence, it had come to be regarded as a fief of the Parthian emperor's second son, and thus it was at first more a Persian than a Roman client-kingdom. Rome began to claim it as part of its own sphere of influence after a Roman victory in 69 B.C., in the days of the Republic, but only after three hundred years of tug-of-war between Rome and Persia did it finally turn Western, and then as much because of Western Christianity as of Roman power. Christian merchants are said to have been the first to introduce the new faith into the kingdom, but the "apostle to Armenia" was the great Gregory the Illuminator, who converted the Armenian king, Tiridates I (261–317) around the end of the third century. All Armenia, it is said, quickly became at least nominally Christian a decade or two before the conversion of Constantine. For this reason

Armenia is often called the first Christian nation, though such a claim, as we shall see, must be qualified.[9]

The other trouble spot was Judaea. No matter who ruled it for Rome, whether half-Jewish kings like the Herods or, after A.D. 6, Roman governors and proconsuls like Pontius Pilate, still it was always Jewish. Rome could find only two ways to keep the Jewish problem from getting out of hand: either give the Jews special privileges or wipe them out.

Up to about A.D. 64 Rome tried the first way. The Julio-Claudian emperors were unusually tolerant. Augustus legalized the exemption of Jews from military conscription. Tiberias, though he limited Jewish rights of worship in Rome, took care to avoid a clash with the Jews in the east and did not interfere with their religious observances in Asia. Roman emperors found it wise to keep their portraits off Roman coins in Judaea, in deference to the Jewish prohibition of images, and that was the only place in the world where the "rulers of the world" were so modest. Only the monster Caligula persecuted Jews. He ordered an image of himself erected in the Temple in Jerusalem, but his timely death in A.D. 41 before the statue could be erected averted an inevitable insurrection. His successor, Claudius, sensibly decreed that Jews were not to be forced into religious observances forbidden by their sacred laws. Even Nero's wife, whatever her other faults, was a protector of the Jews and came close, it was said, to embracing the Jewish faith. So up to the time of Nero, who ruled from 54 to 68, since Christians were considered Jews by the Romans, the church in Roman Asia enjoyed freedom from government persecution.[10]

But the next dynasty, the Flavian, went to the other extreme. When the "most favored nation" policy of the Claudians toward the Jews broke down in the last years of Nero and the Jewish War erupted in 66, Nero's general, Vespasian, began to tear the province of Judaea apart piece by piece. His campaign was interrupted by his sudden elevation to the imperial throne and as the new emperor he turned over the bloody climax, the destruction of Jerusalem in A.D. 70, to his son Titus. The Holy City fell. The last pocket of Jewish resisters perished on Mt. Masada, first killing their wives and children when the end was near, then themselves. With the fall of the Jewish state the flight of the refugees began, "the Second Diaspora," as it has been called. Many fled across the border into Persia and south into Arabia. Some, it is thought, went as far as India. Even in Roman Asia the Jewish faith survived. Unexpectedly, so also did some of their previous Jewish privileges, such as exemption from military service and emperor worship.[11] But the Temple was gone, and with it the Jewish state. Judaism as a faith began to crystallize into the close-knit, isolated Jewish communities of the Second Diaspora.

Christians, too, were scattered by the catastrophe but with a significant difference. Theirs was a living Messiah who had called them to a world mission and whose good news of the gospel was for all peoples. Instead of turning inward, they moved out across the world. Most of them were Jews, however, and as they went they found that the Jewish communities of the Diaspora were a natural, ethnic network for the beginnings of Christian advance. This was particularly true in oriental Asia. The surviving records of the earliest Christian groups in Asia outside the Roman Empire almost always have a strong Jewish-Christian tinge, as we shall see.

Iranian (Persian) Asia

Across the Euphrates, Jews and Christians alike found refuge from Roman violence in Persia, which is better called Iran today. Persians were only part of a larger Iranian whole that consisted of the Aryan tribes and peoples of a language grouping called Indo-European. They were spread in a wide band through western central Asia from the Ural Mountains north of the Caspian Sea to the Indus River, which flows out of the Himalayas into northern India. Their neighbors in the mist of prehistory had been Turko-Mongolian tribes on the east toward China and the Finns in the northwest toward Europe.[12]

In the time of Christ Iran was ruled by the Parthians (or Arsacids as they called themselves), the third in an impressive series of imperial dynasties that had made Persia the center of the world, surrounded by Rome to the west, China to the east, and India to the south.

The first dynasty, the *Achaemenids* (549–330 B.C.) were the Medes and Persians of the Bible. More ancient than Greeks or Romans, they have been called "the first Indo-European race to play a role in history" and the first nation "to create and administer an empire."[13] Their founder and first emperor, Cyrus II, the Great, freed the Jews from the Babylonian captivity, conquered Syria and Palestine, and brought much of Asia Minor into his empire. His successors completed the conquest of western Asia and by crossing into Europe to attack Greece set Asia against the West.[14] Had not the outnumbered Greeks checked the Persian advance at Marathon in 490 B.C. and again at sea ten years later, the Persians might well have orientalized all Europe and irreversibly altered the course of history.

The second dynasty, the *Seleucids* (312–238 B.C.), was Greek. As the heirs of Alexander the Great, conqueror of Persia, they turned back the flow of history and threatened for a time to westernize all Asia. These Greek rulers of a Persian empire carried the culture of Athens into central Asia as far as Afghanistan and across the borders of India. In fact, a Greek connection may have been as important as the Jewish one for the early Christian advance eastward. Edessa, Ecbatana, and even Taxila in India all had Greek military colonies. Greek trade routes from Antioch through Persia to Afghanistan and on to Patna on the Ganges remained open into the Christian era as inviting avenues of approach for Christian traders and evangelists.[15]

But the Greeks were too few and spread too thin in Asia. In the west their short-lived Seleucid dynasty lost its territories to the Romans (Asia Minor, Syria, and Judaea). In the east, even earlier, wild Asian warriors of a new dynasty had begun to push the Greeks out of central Asia back across the Euphrates.

This third dynasty, the *Parthians* (247 B.C.–A.D. 226), took Persia back from the Greeks and made it Asian again. It was in Parthian Persia and on its border with Roman Asia that Asian Christianity as distinguished from Western Christianity grew and began to develop a related but eventually separate existence.

The Parthians were a shocking contrast to the sophisticated Hellenistic Seleucids they displaced. Hard-riding, illiterate horsemen from the grassy steppes between the Caspian and Aral seas, they were the first mounted nomads, it is said, to vault directly to imperial power.[16] They rebelled against the Greek rule of the Seleucids about the middle of the third century B.C. and for the first hundred years remained independent and rebellious on the eastern Iranian plateau. Then under their first great king, Mithridates I, they broke out westward and startled the world by capturing the Seleucid emperor in Babylon in 140 B.C. Even China took note and sent an embassy to the Parthians about 100 B.C. to open the famous Silk Road for trade across Asia. But Rome, unwisely, was not impressed. In 53 B.C. Crassus, the colleague of Julius Caesar and Pompey, marched against the upstart Parthians for what he thought would be an easy victory and was routed in a defeat that shook Rome to its foundations. Near Edessa, at Carrhae, an army of Parthian archers under the command of a brilliant young general, Suren, from the Indian border, smothered the Romans under such hails of arrows that the famous Roman discipline broke down and the legions fled, committing the ultimate shame of abandoning their standards, the Roman "eagles." From that day on, as R. N. Frye points out, Western writers divided the world between Rome and Persia.[17] There is a possible link between that notable battle at Carrhae and the early evangelization of Asia. It has been suggested that another Suren, possibly a later relative of the hero of Carrhae, was the "king of India" who according to tradition brought Thomas to India on his mission to the East.[18]

Some have painted the Parthian period as an Iranian "Dark Age" between the golden age of the Achaemenids and the high Greek culture of the Seleucids, on the one hand, and the Persian renaissance of the Sassanid dynasty, on the other. That is partly true. To the Greeks, the Parthians remained warriors and barbarians to the end. But it was in their time and under their rule that the Christian faith moved beyond the Roman Empire into oriental Asia.

The weaknesses of the Parthians, in fact, may have been another preparation of the gospel like the Roman peace. Their relative lack of cultural identity, their nomadic indifference to all but war, the hunt, and tribal intrigue, the absence of a strong and predominant religion among them—all these factors, instead of impeding the progress of the Christian faith, seem to have given it better opportunity to plant in Persia some of the first roots of an Asian Christianity. Their capital, Seleucia-Ctesiphon, on the Tigris River north of old Babylon and just south of later Baghdad, became the ecclesiastical center of the Church of the East, which we call Nestorian.

The Parthians, like their enemies the Romans, screened their border with a patchwork of protecting client-kingdoms. Three of these vassal principalities figure prominently in the traditions of early Asian Christianity, Osrhoene, Adiabene, and Armenia. Osrhoene, with its capital of Edessa, guarded the crossings of the Euphrates at its great northern bend not far from the lower border of Armenia and sheltered what became the mother church of organized Asian Christianity.

Farther east the little kingdom of Adiabene stood on the upper waters of the Tigris River near old Nineveh. Its capital, Arbela (modern Erbil), was to become the center for Christian missionary advance into central Asia. A third protectorate state, Armenia, lay in the rough mountains north and east around Lake Van and Mt. Ararat. It was the most independent of the western border states, though it was usually ruled by kings related to the Parthian Arsacid emperors and had strong cultural ties and nominal political leanings toward Persia. It vies with Osrhoene for the title of first Christian nation in world history, but if that is true it was due to the missionary outreach of the church in the Roman Empire and therefore belongs more to Western than to Asian church history. The full story of the church in Osrhoene and Adiabene will be told later.

Sinic (Chinese) Asia

The third center of power in Asia at the time of Christ was China. Two hundred years earlier an empire builder, Ch'in Shih Huang-ti (221–210 B.C.), whose great tomb has recently been uncovered, took the China of Confucius, which was only a loose collection of quarreling, feudal states, and had hammered it into an imperial unity. He secured it against attacks from nomads outside the empire by building the Great Wall and tried to suppress dissent from within by rigid suppression of free thought. The burning of the books in his reign, however, forever stigmatized his name in the annals of succeeding Confucian generations. Nevertheless, his short, harsh Ch'in dynasty (221–207 B.C.) left to the later rulers of the Han dynasty (206 B.C.– A.D. 220) a unified empire, which they proceeded to mold into the shape it was to keep for the next two thousand years.

It is fruitless to speculate how history might have been changed had Christianity entered China with any effective impact in this crucial, formative period. China was not beyond reach in the apostolic age, as is sometimes supposed. It was precisely at that time, in fact, that China began to turn tentatively toward the West, reaching through all the barriers of central Asia—the endless wastes, the mountains, the marauding barbarian tribes—to open highways of trade with the world beyond. But there is no record that Christian missionaries ventured to traverse that Old Silk Road in the other direction, eastward to China, for another six hundred years. The later legend that St. Thomas pushed on beyond his mission to India into China is not to be taken seriously despite such later dubious references to apostolic missions as that in the Chaldaean breviary of the Malabar church: "By St. Thomas were the Chinese and the Ethiopians converted to the truth."[19]

As early as 128 B.C. the Han emperor Wu-ti sent an envoy, Chang Ch'ien, called "the Road-opener," to negotiate an alliance with the distant Yueh-chi tribe on the north of what is now Afghanistan. Like a landborne Columbus in reverse, this first Chinese explorer of the western regions returned with marvelous tales of rich lands beyond the barbarian steppes. The Chinese, alert and impatient for trade with the newly discovered West, flung open a road across the top of the world for caravans to come from as far away as the Indus River valley in southern Asia and the still farther borders of Greco-Roman Syria. This was about 106 B.C. For the first time in history Asia took on a semblance of continental unity, tied together at last by the long, thin thread of the Old Silk Road.[20]

But it was a very tenuous thread and one often broken. Not until 60 B.C. did China finally gain from the collapsing Hsiung-nu (Hun) "empire" firm control of the trade route along the scattered oases in the Tarim River basin through which all caravans had to pass. Commerce prospered until 6 B.C.,[21] but just about the time of Christ's birth there came a sharp break in Han-dynasty power. A usurper, Wang Mang, seized the throne, first as surrogate, then as ruling emperor from 1 B.C. to A.D. 23. Disorders broke out along the frontier and by A.D. 16, as recorded in the Chinese chronicles, "the Western Regions were broken up and scattered like loose tiles."[22] For the next sixty years, until the eighth decade of the Christian era, communication between China and western Asia was broken off. So it is quite true that in the first few decades of the apostolic church it would have been virtually impossible to reach China by land from Roman or Persian Asia.

However, perhaps as early as ten years after the death of the apostle Paul the road to the Far East was once again opened. The Han emperors had been restored to the throne in 23 B.C., but the early years of what is called their Later Han dynasty were occupied with domestic problems. It was not until a strong emperor, Ming-ti, came to power (A.D. 57–75) that China once again advanced into central Asia. The Silk Road at that time divided at Kashgar just east of the great Pamir mountain range that separates Afghanistan from China. One route led to the north around the Tarim River basin and was in the hands of the Hsiung-nu. Another went south through Khotan and was dominated by the Yueh-chi, who were attacking north India.

First the Chinese freed the northern route at Turfan, and then under one of the greatest figures in first century Chinese history, Pan Ch'ao, they brought the southern route through Yarkand and Khotan into their control. Pan Ch'ao was a member of an illustrious Han-dynasty family. His brother and sister achieved enduring literary fame as compilers of the *Annals of the Former Han,* and he as soldier-statesman and explorer was to dominate the history of central Asia for thirty crucial years, from 74 to 102. In a series of brilliant negotiations Pan Ch'ao managed, without war and with what for that age was only a minimum of violence (the beheading of Hsiung-nu ambassadors, for example), to persuade the tribal chiefs of Lop and Khotan to recognize Han authority. When he captured Kashgar, the strategic crossroads town where northern and southern silk routes converged, his work of pacification seemed complete. But at the moment of triumph, the death of the Chinese emperor in 75 threatened to undo all that Pan Ch'ao had accomplished. The new emperor was an isolationist and seemed content to let central Asia sink back into tribal chaos. One of his first acts was to recall his generals from the frontier.

So trusted, however, had Pan Ch'ao become among the tribes, that they begged him to stay and keep order. Defying the emperor's command he remained in Kashgar to guard the Silk Road. He wrote to the emperor warning him that the best defense for China was not to cower behind the Great Wall but to take the offensive against "the thirty-six kingdoms" of central Asia who threatened the peace. "Use barbarians to attack barbarians," he urged. Following his own advice Pan Ch'ao made friends wherever he could against his opponents, the Hsiung-nu. He cultivated the blue-eyed Wu-sun along the Ili River below Lake Balkash, the K'ang-chu (Sogdians) farther west below the Aral Sea, and the Kushan Yueh-chi, who had forged something of an empire of their own in what is now Afghanistan and had advanced south into India against King Gundaphar (Gon-dopharnes), who has been identified by some as the traditional patron of St. Thomas. The Yueh-chi helped Pan Ch'ao bring the entire Tarim basin under firm control by A.D. 87. For thus swinging central Asia again into the Chinese orbit the general was rewarded with the title "Protector General of the Western Regions," and caravan trade across Asia prospered once more.[23]

In 97 Pan Ch'ao sent a trusted envoy west from Kashgar to explore the regions beyond the high mountains where caravans disappeared on the long road to Persia and Roman Asia. The envoy, Kan-ying, penetrated the Parthian empire as far, apparently, as the head of the Persian Gulf and would have gone on to Roman Syria, which he called Ta-ts'in, had he not been dissuaded by the tall tales of the Persian and Arab sailors. "The sea is vast and great …," they told him. "With favorable winds it is possible to cross in three months, but if you meet slow winds it may take you two years."[24] They conveniently neglected to mention the easy overland route through the Arab city of Petra only sixty miles away. Perhaps they feared that a meeting between Rome and China might rob them of their profitable role as middlemen. At any rate, the Chinese ambassador turned back and returned to the Far East bringing tempting reports of the ten-to-one profits that might be reaped in Western trade and of Romans eager to communicate with China but blocked by Parthian greed. He may also have remarked on the existence of an alternative to the Old Silk Road, namely, the sea route to India known to the Arabs and by now to the Romans, but unknown in China. It would be useful knowledge should the land route through Parthian territory be closed by war or politics.

As the East explored the West, so also the West reached out in inquiry toward the East. The wide edges of the continent came closer together. Probably even earlier than Kan-ying's journey west, sometime in the first century A.D. a Macedonian trader named Maes Titianus sent agents east to reconnoiter the Silk Road to China. What route they took is uncertain but it was probably the northern road, for at a place called "the stone tower"[25] on the Chinese side of the Pamirs and at the edge of the Tarim basin they watched Syrian caravaners transfer goods to the camels of the Chinese or Mongols. It was the first recorded personal contact between subjects of Rome and China.

So the road was open. Even after Pan Ch'ao returned to China in 102 and Chinese control relaxed in central Asia, the "Chinese peace" of the East, like the *pax Romana* of the West, kept transcontinental trade flowing along the Old Silk Road.[26] It could have been another "preparation for the gospel." But though the road was open in those critical early years of the Christian church, it was Buddhist missionaries from India who used it, not Christians from Jerusalem or Antioch or Edessa, and the missionary faith that flowed along it, putting down deep roots in eastern Asia, was not Christianity but Buddhism. This may be why Buddhism, not Christianity, is now more often called the "most purely Asian of the great religions,"[27] and the "first of the missionary religions." It reached China according to Buddhist traditions, when its first foreign missionaries, Kasyapa Matanga and Dharmaratna (Chu Fa-lan) joined a Chinese embassy returning from a mission to the Yueh-chi and about A.D. 65 founded the White Horse monastery in Loyang.[28] More credible historically is the reported arrival of a Persian (Parthian) missionary in the second half of the second century (148). His name in Chinese was An Shih-kao.[29] This was four hundred years before the arrival of the first Christian missionary in China in the seventh century, who was also a Persian, as we shall see.[30]

Indian Asia

The last of the four great centers of power in first-century Asia was India. Here was the original home of Buddhism, the first of the missionary religions and the most successful, in Asia at least, until the rise of Islam. But in the time of Christ India was no longer an empire and Indian Buddhism was beginning to divide and slowly decline until it almost disappeared in its own home base, absorbed into all-embracing Hinduism.

India's great Maurya empire, founded about 321 B.C., once equaled in strength and perhaps surpassed for a time the Persian empire of the Greeks. There is high drama in the meeting of the founders of the two empires, Seleucus I of Persia and Chandragupta of India. One was the general and heir of Alexander the Great. The other may have been a distant relative by descent from the Buddha.[31] About 305 B.C. Seleucus marched east across the Indus River into the Punjab. Chandragupta stood to meet him with an army of half a million men and nine thousand elephants, and Persia and India hovered on the brink of a gigantic clash. But there is no report of any battle. Instead, the two reached an understanding, perhaps even a marriage alliance, with India receiving the better part of the bargain. Chandragupta accepted large tracts of Persian territory northwest of the Indus. Seleucus took back with him only a gift of five hundred war elephants.[32]

This was the beginning of an Asian counterthrust against triumphant Western Hellenism that, when linked to the revolt of the Parthians, brought down the Greeks and fought Rome to a standstill on the Euphrates. The height of Maurya power came in the reign of Chandragupta's grandson, the great Ashoka (ca. 274–236 B.C.), whose achievements were as much religious as political or military. It was in his reign that Buddhism came to its first flowering. With all the zeal of a new convert he convened the important Third Buddhist Council of about 250 B.C., which transformed Buddhism into a missionary faith seeking the conversion of all India.

But the Buddhist empire of the Mauryas fell apart after the death of Ashoka. The last of the dynasty was assassinated by an orthodox Brahman who took care to inaugurate his own minor dynasty with a Brahman horse sacrifice, not a Buddhist ceremony.[33] The end of the Maurya empire, which occurred about 180 B.C., ushered in the age of invasions, five hundred years of chaos and uncertainty before another Indian empire, the Gupta, could restore order to the subcontinent. Historically, it is just such periods of drastic change that seem most conducive to Christian expansion, and so it may have been, as strong traditions still assert, that in these troubled years an apostle brought Christianity to the great subcontinent.

But first came the Greeks. Though they had been stopped by Chandragupta from entering India a century and a quarter earlier, Alexander's generals carved out for themselves a little empire of their own on the Indian border in Bactria, which today we call northern Afghanistan and which then was the far eastern province of the Seleucid rulers of Persia. Unlike the sandy wastes into which much of it has now deteriorated, Bactria was then one of the richest, greenest pockets of Seleucid power and dominated the crossroads of Asia's inland trade routes. When the Seleucid emperors of Persia moved their capital from Babylon to Antioch they began to lose effective contact with their far eastern provinces, and about 250 B.C. the Greek governor-princelings broke away from the empire and set themselves up as kings of Bactria. The greatest of them was Menander (ca. 180–130 B.C.). Under his leadership the Bactrian Greeks turned south and east to conquer northern India (about the same time that their Parthian neighbors in central Asia were moving west to conquer Greek Persia). Menander's kingdom stretched from Kabul to the Indus River valley, and from there he marched on into India along the Ganges to claim as his own the remnants of the Maurya empire. His wealth and name were known even farther. Coins of Menander have been found as far away as Wales.[34]

But the Greeks in India vanished almost as quickly as they came. They might have hellenized India. Beginnings of hellenization can be seen in the traces of Greek style in Buddhist art, but the Greeks themselves as it turned out were more indianized than India was westernized. "In matters of the spirit," W. W. Tarn writes, "Asia was quite confident that she could outstay the Greeks; and she did."[35] Menander the Greek conquered much of India, but in the end, unsatisfied by Greek philosophy and probably long since having outgrown Greek paganism, he apparently turned Buddhist. A famous Buddhist text tells of the conversion. So completely were the Greeks being orientalized that, according to the *Milindapanha* (*The Questions of Milinda*, i.e., of Menander), even the Buddhist monk who argued the Greek king into the Buddhist faith was Greek, not Indian.[36]

After the Greeks came the nomads, wave after wave of them. Thirty years before the death of Menander, about 160 B.C., India began to feel the first stirrings of a mighty migration of wild horsemen from the northwestern borders of China, the hairy Hsiung-nu (the terrible Huns of the barbarian invasions of Europe).[37] Sealed out of China by the Great Wall and pushed west into central Asia by the Chinese, they met and defeated other tribes driving them farther inland. Like waves rippling across the grassy Asian steppes, the peoples of Asia's heartland began to move west and south. And according to tradition, it was in the dark days of these barbarian invasions from central Asia and about the time that they broke out onto the north Indian plains that the Christian faith came to India.

The Huns clashed first, near the end of the Great Wall, with the white-skinned nomads called Yueh-chi by the Chinese (and Indo-Scythians by the Romans).[38] The Yueh-chi had long been slowly moving east into Asia out of northern Europe, it is thought. Their clash with the Huns moving west was a significant turning in world history, for it has been marked as the end of a prehistoric movement of peoples from Europe into Asia and the beginning of an Asian advance into Europe that was to reach its climax in the fall of Rome to the barbarians.[39]

Defeated by the Hsiung-nu, the Yueh-chi retreated west leaving their chief dead, his skull polished into a drinking cup by the victors. The Yueh-chi clashed in turn with another tribe, the mysterious, red-bearded, blue-eyed Wu-sun, around the Issyk-kul basin[40] and were driven on still farther toward Fergana and Tashkent, where they found and attacked a great grouping of tribes called the Saka, "the Scythians of Asia," pushing them south toward India.[41]

It is almost impossible to reconstruct the unrecorded but re-membered waves of nomadic invasions that for a hundred years swept through the once-rich triangle of Asia now occupied by eastern Persia, Afghanistan, and northwest India and Pakistan. It would seem that the Saka, moving south toward the few Greek kingdoms that still survived below the Hindu Kush—in Kabul, Gandhara, and the upper Ganges—suddenly turned west and attacked the Parthian empire. Two Persian emperors died fighting the nomads about 130 B.C. and the Saka established such firm control over Persia's far eastern provinces that Sakastan (Seistan) still bears their name.[42]

Parthia struck back, however, under Mithridates II, and the hereditary Persian (Iranian) lords of the province, the powerful Suren family, regained control about a hundred years before the birth of Christ. Later, as the Persian monarchy weakened, the Suren and the Saka appear to have formed an alliance, throwing off their allegiance to the Parthian emperors and merging as an independent Partho-Scythian dynasty. In Indian annals they are called the Pahlavas, an unlikely combination of sophisticated Persians and nomadic Sakas, their names unknown to history until comparatively recent times. Moving down through the high passes toward India, they toppled the last of the Greek kingdoms.[43] And somewhere in India, an ancient tradition tells us, they encountered a Christian missionary.

Theirs was the dynasty ruling northern India in the time of Christ and of his disciple Thomas. Tradition has always connected Thomas with a mission to India beginning with the conversion of an Indian king. We shall therefore look more carefully at this Pahlava empire as we turn now to discuss the much disputed question of the apostolic origin of the Indian church.

NOTES

1. Strabo, *Geographica* 1. 1.20; 2. 5–18, 31–32. The most cited English edition is from the Loeb Classical Library (London, 1917).

2. Strabo, *Geographica* 15. 1.34, 37. He reported that the Chinese sometimes live to be more than two hundred years old. See also H. Yule, *Cathay and the Way Thither*, ed. H. Cordier, 4 vols. (London, Hakluyt Society, 1913–16), vol. 1:14n.

3. Strabo, *Geographica* 11. 12.1.

4. The latest wrinkle in the never-ending and inconclusive modern attempts to identify Britain's King Arthur makes him a Sarmatian, descendant of a military detachment brought by Rome from Asia to help in the conquest of the island.

5. Strabo, *Geographica* 15. 1.37.

6. A chronological list of Roman emperors is as follows: Augustus (27 B.C.–14 A.D.), Tiberius (14–37), Caligula (37–41), Claudius I (41–54), Nero (54–68), Galba (68–69), Otho (69), Vitellius (69), Vespasian (69–79), Titus (79–81), Domitian (81–96), Nerva (96–98), Trajan (98–117), Hadrian (117–138), Antoninus Pius (138–161), Marcus Aurelius (161–180), Commodus (180–192).

7. See the chronological list of Roman emperors in n. 6.

8. On the subject of Roman rule in Asia see D. Magie, *Roman Rule in Asia Minor to the End of the Third Century* (Princeton, NJ: Princeton Univ. Press, 1950) and T. Mommsen, *The Provinces of the Roman Empire*, 2 vols. trans. W. Dickson (London: Bentley, 1886), esp. 2:1–303.

9. The early historical sources for the conversion of Armenia are found in V. Langlois, *Collection des Historiens de l'Armenie*, 2 vols. (Paris, 1867–69), but it is difficult to separate fact from legend in them. Dating is uncertain. See also chap. 3, pp. 57ff. for another claimant to the title "first Christian nation."

10. See Mommsen, *The Provinces*, esp. 167, 188, 200.

11. For a thorough recent survey see E. M. Smallwood, *The Jews Under Roman Rule: From Pompey to Diocletian* (Leiden: Brill, 1976).

12. See E. D. Phillips, *The Royal Hordes, Nomad Peoples of the Steppes* (London: Thames & Hudson, 1965), 39ff., and R. Grousset, *The Empire of the Steppes: A History of Central Asia*, trans. N. Walford (New Brunswick, NJ: Rutgers Univ. Press, 1970), 5ff.

13. S. deVries, T. Luykx, and W. O. Henderson, *An Atlas of World History* (London: Nelson, 1965), 10.

14. Herodotus, *The Persian Wars,* trans. H. Cary (London: Ball, Bohn's Classical Library, 1894).

15. G. Woodcock, *The Greeks in India* (London: Faber and Faber, 1966), 48ff., 130ff.

16. Phillips, *The Royal Hordes,* 110.

17. R. N. Frye, *The Heritage of Persia,* 2d ed. (London: Cardinal, 1976), 208.

18. See chap. 2.

19. For traditions of the missions of Thomas, and even Bartholomew, to China, see Yule, *Cathay,* 1:101f.

20. See F. Hirth, "The Story of Chang K'ien: A Translation of Chapter 123 of the Shi-ki of Ssu-ma Ch'ien," *Journal of the American Oriental Society* 37 (1917): 89ff. The original translation from Ssu-ma Ch'ien's *Shih chi* is *Records of the Grand Historian of China Translated from the Shih chi of Ssu-ma Ch'ien,* by B. Wilson, vol. 2 (New York and London: Columbia Univ. Press, 1961), chap. 123, "The Account of Ta-yuan," 264ff.

21. There was one serious but short interruption in 42 B.C. when the Tibetans raided the route as far as the valley of the Wei. F. Taggert, *Rome and China: A Study of Correlations in Historical Events* (Berkeley, CA: Univ. of California Press, 1939), 105.

22. Pan Ku, *Annals of the Former Han, Ch'ien han shu,* trans. A. Wylie, "Notes on the Western Regions: Translation of Chapter 96, Part 2 of the *Ch'ien-han-shu,*" in *Journal of the Anthropographical Institute* 11 (1882): 112.

23. Grousset, *Empire,* 41–47; Taggert, *Rome and China,* 136–45.

24. Fan Yeh, *Hou-han-shu (Annals of the Later Han),* compiled about the middle of the fifth century. Its account of the West may well have been based on Kan-ying's report. A translation of the parts referring to the West is in F. Hirth, *China and the Roman Orient, Researchers into Their Ancient and Medieval Relations as Reported in Old Chinese Records* (Leipzig: Hirth; Shanghai: Kelly and Walsh, 1885), 39f., with commentary, 164ff.

25. Ptolemy, *Geographia,* book 1, chap. 2, 32ff. The page citations refer to the translation and edition by Edward Lutha Stevenson, *Geographia of Claudius Ptolemy* (New York: New York Public Library, 1932). Ptolemy at least extended Asia farther east than Strabo, 76f.

26. E. Chavannes, "Trois généraux chinois de la dynastie des Han" (Biographies of Pan Ch'ao, Pan Yung, and Liang K'in), in *T'oung Pao,* series 2, vol. 7 (1906): 210–69.

27. The phrase is from C. N. Parkinson, *East and West* (Boston, MA: Houghton Mifflin, 1963), 109.

28. This tradition is seriously disputed, but there is considerable agreement that Buddhism did indeed enter China between 50 B.C. and A.D. 50 along the Old Silk Road. See E. Zurcher, *The Buddhist Conquest of China* in vol. 11 *Sinica Leidensia* (Leiden: Brill, 1959; reprint, Taiwan), 22f.

29. Zurcher, *The Buddhist Conquest,* 32ff. An Shih-kao is the best known of the earliest-known Buddhist missionary team in Loyang. Besides An, it was formed of one other Parthian, three Yueh-chi, two Sogdians, and three Indians. Tradition describes An as a Parthian crown prince who resigned his rights to the throne when he gave himself to the vocation of religion and to the translation of the Buddhist scriptures into Chinese.

30. See chap. 15, pp. 291ff.

31. The Pali *Mahawanso* relates the Maurya to the Sakya, the tribe of Sakyamuni, who became the Buddha. E. J. Rapson, ed., *The Cambridge History of India,* vol. 1 (Cambridge: Cambridge Univ. Press, 1922), 470.

32. Rapson, *Cambridge History of India,* 1:431.

33. R. Thapar, *A History of India,* vol. 1 (Harmondsworth, Eng.: Penguin, 1966), 92. See also R. C. Majumdar, ed., *The History and Culture of the Indian People,* vol. 2, *The Age of Imperial Unity* (Bombay: Bharatiya Vidya Bhavan, 1951), 89, for other possible reasons for the fall of the Maurya empire.

34. G. Woodcock, *The Greeks in India* (London: Faber and Faber, 1966), 94f.

35. W. W. Tarn, *The Greeks in Bactria and India,* 2d ed. (Cambridge: Cambridge Univ. Press, 1951), 66f.

36. Tarn, *The Greeks,* 414–36. In another passage Tarn rather discounts the depth of Menander's conversion (268f.), feeling it may have been more political than religious. But Woodcock (*The Greeks in India,* 112ff.) takes a more positive view of the conversion, which is mentioned even by Plutarch. He quotes H. Zimmer, "If the Greek king was not himself actually a member of the Buddhist order, he was at least so great a benefactor that the community looked upon him as one of their own."

37. The identification of the Hsiung-nu with the Huns is widely accepted but still disputed. The Chinese described them as big-nosed and hairy, but to the Romans they looked Mongol. They were probably Turko-Mongolic people uniting as a nation sometime near the middle of the third century B.C. in "imperial Mongolia," the area that more than a thousand years later produced Genghis Khan. Religiously shamanist, they are known archaeologically for the Ordos bronzes out of which centuries later developed the Nestorian crosses of the Onguts in the Yuan dynasty. See Grousset, *Empire,* 19–29, and especially O. J. Maenchen-Helfen, *The World of the Huns; Studies in Their History and Culture,* ed. M. Knight (Berkeley: Univ. of California Press, 1973).

38. The nomads called Yueh-chi by the Chinese, Takhari by the Greeks, and Indo-Scythians by the Romans are now usually called Kucha (a dominant tribe among the Kushan). They were Asians, first appearing in Kansu but perhaps orginally from Thrace or western Russia, for Chinese sources call them white-skinned. Their language was Indo-European. By the first century B.C. they were probably racially mixed and dominated by Iranian tribes. They were the horsemen of the steppes who had invented the stirrup and revolutionized the art of war, though their enemies, the Hsiung-nu, also had

the stirrup in the third century B.C. Grousset, *Empire,* 27f.; Phillips, *The Royal Hordes,* 91, 111.

39. Grousset, *Empire,* 28.

40. Charpentier identifies the Wu-sun with the Asioi, a tribe Strabo listed among others as conquerors of the Bactrian Greeks. Some of the Wu-sun, along with the Saka and the Yueh-chi, may well have invaded Bactria. J. Charpentier, "Die ethnographische Stellung der Tocharer," *Zeitschrift der deutschen morgenländischen Gesellschaft* 71 (1917): 357–61. See also Grousset, *Empire of the Steppes,* 29.

41. The Sakas were Iranian nomads, kin to the Parthian tribes who had moved into Seleucid Persia about 300 B.C., but had remained on the steppes east of the Aral Sea and the Jaxartes (Syr Darya) River around Tashkent, Fergana, and Kashgar. They were called Scythians by the Greeks, "Asian Scythians" to distinguish them from the Black Sea tribes more properly called Scythians. Both are branches of the large Iranian Scytho-Sarmatian family of the northwestern steppes. The name "Saka" means "stag," a dominant motif in their art. Grousset, *Empire,* xxiii; H. W. Bailey, "Saka Studies: The Ancient Kingdom of Khotan," *Iran: Journal of the British Institute of Persian Studies* 8 (1970), esp. 68–69; Phillips, *The Royal Hordes,* 63.

42. Grousset, *Empire,* 29–32.

43. See Tarn, *The Greeks,* 344–47, and A. K. Narain, *The Indo-Greeks* (Oxford: Clarendon, 1957), 101–64.

Chapter 2
The First Missions
to India

"Remember, St. Thomas came to India when many
of the countries of Europe had not yet become
Christian, and so those Indians who trace their
Christianity to him have a longer history and a
higher ancestry than that of Christians of many of
the European countries. And it is really a matter of
pride to us that it so happened."

—Dr. Rajendra Prasad, President
of India, 1952–1962; quoted in
S. G. Pothan, *The Syrian Christians
of Kerala*

India and "The Apostle to Asia"

One of the oldest and strongest traditions in church history is that Thomas the apostle carried the gospel to India not long after the resurrection and ascension of Jesus Christ. It traces as far back as about the year 200 when a Christian in Edessa, on the great bend of the Euphrates River between Roman Asia and Persia, wrote a lively account of how the apostle had been sent out from Jerusalem to India protesting bitterly, a reluctant missionary, but one who preached fearlessly before kings and founded the Indian church. That early Christian romance, called the *Acts of Thomas*,[1] became the most popular of a number of similar apocryphal *Acts* that appeared in the third century, perhaps in answer to an insistent demand from a growing number of believers for more information about the original Twelve than is given in the canonical New Testament. Its importance in Asian church history is that it survives as the oldest narrative account of a church in Asia beyond the borders of the Roman Empire.[2] It makes strange reading today, with its incredible miracles and exaggerated asceticism, but the vivid picture it paints of Thomas as the "apostle to Asia" is a fitting introduction to the story of the church in Asia.

The Asian roots of the church, of course, lie deeper than such traditions and they do not begin with Thomas or with India. They begin with Jesus Christ, for Bethlehem is in Asia and so also is Golgotha. But when Jesus was born the little town of Bethlehem was ruled by Rome, and Rome was Western, so that part of Asia was drawn into Western church history. Paul's mission to the Gentiles moved the gospel still more decisively west in the histories, for there was a historian, Luke, accompanying Paul. No such contemporary historian recorded the gospel's eastward march, but there is no doubt that the gospel did move east even while Paul was opening a beachhead in Europe at Philippi. And however Western scholars may write their histories of the church, from time immemorial Asia has linked the church's expansion east to the missionary travels of the apostle Thomas.

The evidence for that link is traditional, of course, and only peripherally historical.[3] But the tradition is so ancient and the support so strong even in the normally skeptical twentieth century that it may be wise to admit that underlying some of the most improbable legends there often lies a foundation of fact.[4] So let us begin at the beginning with the legend itself.

The Acts of Thomas

The story opens impressively with the eleven apostles (Judas Iscariot not yet being replaced) gathered in Jerusalem to plan a strategy of obedience to the command of Jesus, "Go ye into all the world and preach the gospel."

> At that time we disciples were all in Jerusalem . . . and we divided the regions of the world that each one of us might go to the region which fell to his lot. . . . India fell to Judas Thomas, who is also Didymus [Twin]; but he did not wish to go, saying that through weakness of the flesh he could not travel, and "How can I, who am a Hebrew, go and preach the truth among the Indians?" . . . And . . . the Saviour appeared to him by night and said . . . "Fear not, Thomas, go to India and preach the word there, for my grace is with thee." But he would not obey and said, "Send me where thou wilt—but somewhere else! For I am not going to the Indians." (*Acts Thom.* 1:1)

Faced with such recalcitrance not altogether uncharacteristic of their fellow disciple Thomas, the others prayed for help and Jesus appeared in a vision. There happened to be in Jerusalem at that time, according to the story, an agent of the Indian king Gundaphar (Gundaphorus) looking for a carpenter to build a palace for the king, and in an ingeniously contrived solution to the problem of how to get a reluctant Thomas to India, the author has Jesus appear to the agent and offer to sell Thomas to him as the carpenter he needs.

> The Lord said to him, "Dost thou wish to buy a carpenter?" He said, "Yes." And the Lord said, "I have a slave who is a carpenter . . . "

It should be remembered that in some Asian traditions Thomas the Twin was twin brother to Jesus and therefore a carpenter and that in the New Testament all the disciples gladly called themselves "slaves of Jesus Christ."

> And when the sale was completed the Saviour took Judas who is also Thomas and led him to the merchant Abban. And . . . Abban . . . said to him, "Is this thy master?" And the apostle . . . said, "Yes" . . . But he [Abban] said, "I have bought thee from him." And the apostle was silent. On the following morning the apostle prayed . . . "I go whither thou wilt, Lord Jesus. Thy will be done." . . . So they began their voyage.

Their first stop on the journey was Adrapolis (Sandaruk, in the Syriac version). Its location is uncertain and not important if the *Acts of Thomas* is just a Syrian *Pilgrim's Progress,* an allegory. But many now take it more seriously as an imaginative but conscientious effort to reconstruct half-forgotten events that had actually occurred, the author believed, a century and a half before. If so, mention of the port city might refer to a provincial capital on the Nile route to India, Nomos Andropolites, or less likely to the Andhra territory on the Indian coast. At any rate, the account of the apostle's ministry in Adrapolis confirms a fact noted elsewhere, that in the earliest outreach of Christian missions the Jewish communities of the Second Diaspora were often the starting point for missionary evangelism in Asia. Thomas's first convert is a little Jewish flute girl at the king's court.

Another aspect of the apostle's mission in Adrapolis as reported in the *Acts* raises a question that will persist throughout the reading of the narrative. Can a story so full of miraculous fantasies be believed about anything? One example will suffice. Thomas is invited to the wedding of the king's daughter and is rudely slapped by a cup bearer. He turns on the man and tells him sharply that God may forgive him in the world to come, "but in this world . . . I shall see the hand that smote me dragged by dogs." This is no sooner said than the man is torn to pieces by a lion and a black dog picks up his right hand in its mouth and carries it into the banquet hall in triumphant vindication of the apostle's prophecy (*Acts Thom.* 1:6, 8, 9).

Thomas left Andrapolis in some haste, having angered the king by converting his daughter at her own wedding to a gospel of Christian virginity (*Acts Thom.* 1:11, 12). The ascetic emphasis is an often recurring theme in these early apocryphal *Acts* of the apostles.

At last he reached India and the realm of King Gundaphar. Here for a time the tale is at its best—apostolically artless and simple. Gundaphar set Thomas to the building of a royal palace and gave him a large amount of money for the project. But the apostle looked about at the countless poor around him and could not bring himself to give his life only to the providing of more luxury for the rich:

> [He] took it all [i.e., the building fund] and dispensed it, going about . . . distributing it and bestowing alms on the poor and afflicted, and he gave them relief. . . . But when the king came to the city he inquired . . . concerning the palace. . . . They said to him, "Neither has he built a palace, nor has he done anything else of what he promised to do, but he goes about the towns and villages, and if he has anything he gives it all to the poor, and he teaches a new God and heals the sick and drives out demons and does many other wonderful things; and we think he is a magician. But his works of compassion, and the healings which are wrought by him without reward, and moreover his simplicity

and kindness and the quality of his faith show that he is righteous or an apostle of the new God whom he preaches." (*Acts Thom.* 1:19–20)

When the king heard these things, the story continues, he shook his head and sent for Thomas. "Have you built my palace?" he asked. "Yes," said the apostle. "Then when shall we go and see it," the king asked. "Not now but when you die," said Thomas. Whereupon the frustrated ruler ordered him clapped into jail.

At this point the story returns again to fantasy. That night the king's brother died. In the abode of the dead he saw a beautiful palace and asked to live in one of the lower apartments. "No," said the angels. "This palace is one which that Christian is building for your brother." Startled, he begs leave to return and tell the king. Permission is granted for him to appear to his brother in a vision, and when at last Gundaphar is convinced that his palace has indeed been erected, not, however, on earth but in heaven, he brings the apostle out of prison and listens gladly to his preaching. Upon profession of conversion the king receives the three signs of admission to the Christian faith: anointing with oil ("the seal"), baptism ("the added seal"), and the Eucharist. Such details may tell us more about early third-century liturgical practice in Edessa than about what actually happened in first-century India, but at any rate this part of the story of the apostle's mission ends with great success: "And many others also, believing . . . came into the refuge of the Saviour" (*Acts Thom.* 2:22–27).

The final chapters of the *Acts of Thomas* close with the apostle's journey overland into other parts of India. He appoints a deacon to "preach Jesus" and take his place in the land of King Gundaphar. (*Acts Thom.* 7:66). Then he travels on to his final mission and death in the realm of King Misdaeus (Mazdai, in the Syriac), which tradition locates in Madras, in east India. There again the apostle's radical, ascetic teaching against marriage brings trouble. Some of the chief women of the kingdom, including the queen, are converted and in obedience to the new teaching faithfully shun the marriage bed. The king, understandably angry, accuses Thomas of bewitching them and orders his execution. He is led to a mount outside the city. The spears of the soldiers are poised to run him through as Thomas begins to pray, and he ends his apostolate as he had begun it long before in Jerusalem with the words of his great confession, "My Lord and my God":

My Lord and my God, my hope and redeemer and leader and guide in all the lands . . . I have fulfilled thy work and accomplished thy command. I have become a slave; therefore today do I receive freedom. (*Acts Thom.* 13:167; cf. John 20:28)

The Tradition Evaluated

Historians have not always been kind to this legend. Its fantasies do not inspire academic confidence. Besides, as was often pointed out, no king by the name of Gundaphar was known in Indian history. Of other kings there were plenty—Chandragupta, Ashoka, Menander. But no Gundaphar.

Then astonishingly in 1834 an explorer turned up a treasure of ancient coins in the Kabul Valley of Afghanistan. Many bore the pictures and names of forgotten kings and among them were some with a name stamped both in Greek and in an old Indian script. The name was Gundaphar, in various spellings.[5] Other discoveries followed fast, and Gundaphar coins were found from Bactria to the Punjab. The British Museum alone has thirty-three coins of King Gundaphar; the Calcutta Museum twenty-four. Further research has dated the coins as being from the first century A.D.[6]

Near the end of the nineteenth century more precise dating became possible when a stone tablet was discovered in the ruins of a Buddhist city near Peshawar bearing six lines in an Indo-Bactrian language. Deciphered, the inscription not only named King Gundaphar, it dated him squarely in the early first century A.D., making him a contemporary of the apostle Thomas just as the much-maligned *Acts of Thomas* had described him. The inscription reads, in part: "In the twenty-sixth year of the Great King Gundaphara in the Samvat year three and one hundred, in the month of Vaisakh ..." There is some disagreement in identifying the year referred to, but the general consensus is that the "*samvat* year 103" refers to a numbering system beginning in 58 B.C. (the "Vikama era"), which would set the inception of Gundaphar's reign in A.D. 19. He would still have been ruling, therefore, in 45 or 46, very near to the traditional date of the arrival of Thomas in India.[7]

So as far as history can be pieced together from the ambiguous evidence of the coins and from the even rarer inscriptions, it would seem that the Greek Bactrian kingdoms on India's northwestern borders from Kabul to the Ganges did not fall directly into the hands of the migrating Yueh-chi nomads but were first conquered by Saka warriors (eastern Scythians) whom the Yueh-chi were driving before them.[8] It is plausibly suggested that when Parthian rule of Persia weakened in 88 B.C., the Suren princes of the eastern Persian provinces threw off their allegiance to the empire, allied themselves with the vigorous Saka newcomers, invaded and conquered northwest India, and ruled for a time as an independent Partho-Scythian dynasty called the Pahlava (Parthian) dynasty in Indian histories.[9]

It is at this point that Gundaphar emerges into the light of history not as the figment of some credulous Edessan Christian's pious imagination but as the most powerful king to rule the Indian north in the stormy years between the end of the Maurya empire and the rise of a Kushan dynasty in the Punjab about A.D. 70. Gundaphar's territory stretched from Kandahar in eastern Persia (now southern Afghanistan) to the Punjab and probably as far north as Kabul. His capital is thought to have been Taxila. If it is true that he was of the princely house of the Suren, as E. Herzfeld has conjectured,[10] this would help to explain why the warlike but simpler Saka might accept a Persian alliance and a Parthian king, for the Suren were no weak, provincial governors but the greatest nobles in the Persian Empire, second only to the royal family. They had the hereditary right of crowning the emperor at royal investitures. Their greatest triumph had been the defeat of the Roman general Crassus at Carrhae in 52 B.C. by a Suren general who rode to war with a harem of two hundred wives, a baggage train of one thousand camels, and a personal army of ten thousand horsemen.[11] The fact that the Persian emperor instead of rewarding his victorious general had jealously put him to death could further explain the break with the empire by the Suren, their alliance with the Saka, and the rise of a Gundaphar as king of India.

All such reconstructions of the shadowy Saka-Pahlava relationships are tentative,[12] but two important facts are clear. The first is that there was a king in India named Gundaphar in the first half of the first century. The beginning of his reign in A.D. 19 has been called "one of the few fixed dates" in this chaotic period.[13] The other important established fact is that this Gundaphar was the dominant ruling figure in the swirling mixture of races, religions, and rulers in a time of violent political change in northwest India. For a time there in the first century A.D. he was perhaps even more powerful than his contemporaries, the Persian emperors.[14] But it is a return to fantasy to speculate, as some scholars have done, that Gundaphar was Gaspar, first of the Wise Men who came from the East with gifts for the Babe of Bethlehem.[15]

The question to ask is not whether Gundaphar went to Bethlehem but whether Thomas went to India. Proof of the existence of a King Gundaphar does not guarantee the historicity of accounts of Thomas preaching in India, however much it may enhance the credibility of the Thomas tradition. Positive assurance of the apostle's

Indian mission is as elusive as proof of the generally accepted mission of Peter to Rome.

But there is another important line of support for the tradition that must not be discounted, namely, the abundant evidence now available that travel back and forth between India and the Roman Empire was far more commonplace in the first century than some earlier skeptics had once thought possible. The visit of a trade agent from an Indian king to Jerusalem and even a voyage to India by an apostle would have been not at all unusual. Strabo did not exaggerate when he reported that on a visit to Egypt about the time of Christ he found as many as 120 ships a year sailing for India from the Egyptian head of the Red Sea.[16] Among the surviving documents of the first century, in fact, is a mariners' manual, *The Periplus of the Erythraean Sea,* written by an Egyptian Greek about A.D. 60, which corresponds closely to the traditional date for Thomas's mission (between 50 and 72). With the precision of one who had made the voyage himself, the author of the *Periplus* describes the route in detail, with a wealth of helpful hints on winds and tides, harbors and flourishing markets, and local tribes and rulers.[17]

India was quite possibly more open to direct communication with the West in the first two centuries of the Christian era than in any other period of history before the coming of the Portuguese fifteen hundred years later. E. H. Warmington describes the time as an age of new discoveries and enterprises. Roman peace and prosperity encouraged traders to turn east both by sea and by land—by sea through Greek and Arab middlemen and by land through Jewish, Syrian, and Armenian traders. The main channel for trade was the sea because of Roman-Persian wars along the land routes. For travelers from Alexandria the first stage was usually a week's journey up the Nile by riverboat, then overland by camel to Myos Hormos six or seven days (or somewhat longer to Berenice). The voyage from there to India in the time of Christ could take months crawling along the Arab and Persian coast for fear of the open sea.

But about A.D. 40 an epoch-making discovery revolutionized the journey. A navigational secret closely guarded from the Romans by Arab and Parthian sailors was betrayed to the West by a Greek mariner, according to the *Periplus*. It was the secret of the monsoons, winds blowing steadily for months at a time in one direction across the Arabian Sea. In the summer they blew toward India, in the winter back toward the Red Sea. From May to September, therefore, ships needed no longer to hug the shore but could sail before the wind across the ocean all the way to India. The whole trip, including the three weeks from Alexandria to the Red Sea, could now be accomplished in about ninety-four days, and larger ocean-going ships could replace the little coastal craft used hitherto. Some had as many as seven sails, and averaged between 200 and 300 tons.[18] (The Mayflower of the Pilgrims in 1620 was only 180 tons). Indian poems, very old, speak graphically of waves curling from the bows of the great "Yahvana" (i.e., Greek and Roman) ships entering Kerala ports on the Coromandel coast.[19]

From India the ships brought back peacocks and ivory, pepper and spice, Kashmir wool and precious jewels to such an extent that the emperor Tiberias complained about the cost of Eastern luxuries. In the other direction, the ships carried slaves and wines, coral, glass, and British tin from the Mediterranean to India. Perhaps about A.D. 50 one such ship also carried a Jewish Christian missionary, a carpenter, to India, for carpenters are mentioned in documents of the time as being much in demand in the East. Greek carpenters were brought, for example, to build a palace for a king in the southern Tamil kingdom of the Chola people.[20]

"Even if we cast aside as unhistorical every allegation of fact in the stories of St. Thomas," writes Warmington in his classic treatise on Roman trade with India, "we must at least admit that they reflect voyages habitually taken to India." In the Thomas tradition he finds echoes of three distinct stages through which that commerce developed. First was the discovery of the monsoons, as reflected in the apostle's voyage to the Indus or to some point on the west coast of India under Andhra control ("Andrapolis"). This is the North Indian tradition of Thomas's mission. Second was the discovery, after A.D. 40, that by sailing "off the wind" a great circle route to the south would bring ships to the rich Malabar Coast. This fits the South India tradition of a landing close to Cranganore about A.D. 51. Finally, "when that same tradition brings him (Thomas) overland from Malabar to the Chola coast, we have an echo of inland penetration of Greek merchants, possibly to Madura, Aragaru, and so on, as appears from the discoveries of coins, from Tamil poems, and from details in Ptolemy's Geography."[21]

Of course, it is one thing to say that Thomas could easily have gone to India and quite another to leap to the conclusion that he actually did so. Nevertheless there is another line of evidence that has been adduced for just such a conclusion. This is the testimony of the early church fathers, and it is true that a satisfying number do refer to Thomas as the apostle to India. However, the witness of the church fathers is clouded by the fact that there are two divergent lines of tradition among them. Early documents from Syria confirm the tradition of the Acts of Thomas that the apostle went to India. But

Christian writers in Egypt from about the same time report a different tradition, that Thomas went to Parthia. Moreover this theory, the Parthian tradition, is the one followed by Eusebius, called "the father of church history."[22]

The Syrian line specifically locates Thomas in India. The Syriac *Didascalia Apostolorum*, for example, which may have been written in Edessa as early as 250, speaks of how the early churches collected the testimony of the apostles who had gone out to spread the gospel to the world: James in Jerusalem, Mark in Egypt, Peter in Syria and Rome, and Thomas in India:

> India, and all its countries, and those bordering on it even to the farthest sea, received the Apostle's Hand of Priesthood from Judas Thomas, who was guide and ruler in the Church which he built there . . .[23]

St. Ephrem the Syrian, writing about a hundred years later, confirms the tradition of Thomas in India.[24]

In Egypt, on the other hand, the Alexandrian tradition places the mission of Thomas not in India but in Parthian Persia. Like the Syrian tradition, it also can be traced back to the third century, to Origen (d. 251), whom Eusebius quotes,[25] and to the *Clementine Recognitions.*[26]

It would appear that of the two traditions the Syrian has a slight edge in credibility if only for the fact that the eastern church in Syro-Persia, which might well have been tempted to claim for itself the apostolic origin offered it by the Alexandrian writers, modestly ceded Thomas to India, and claimed in the Didascalia, not one of the Twelve but an evangelist named Addai from a lesser circle of disciples, the Seventy who are mentioned by Luke (Luke 10:1–24). This tradition makes Addai the apostle to Edessa and Addai's disciple Aggaeus the pioneer in Persia.[27]

Actually, the two traditions are not necessarily contradictory. If Gundaphar was a Parthian Suren, as seems possible, a mission to India might loosely but not incorrectly be referred to as a mission to Parthians. But the evidence of these two traditions in the statements of the church fathers on Thomas in India are too scattered, too ambivalent, and too late to be taken as contemporary evidence.[28]

We must turn therefore to the Indian church itself for the most insistent and enduring tradition that Thomas was indeed, as far-off Edessa acknowledged him to be, "the apostle to India." For centuries the Christian communities of southwest India have proudly called themselves "Thomas Christians." The evidence is oral and traditional. It is not the tangible, datable documentation of written sources that historians prefer. But the songs and poetry of a living community handed down from generation to generation sometimes strike closer to the truth of ethnic and religious origins than manuscripts and mutilated inscriptions.

There is, for example, a Kerala wedding song, the *"Thomas Rabban Pattu"* ("Song of Thomas"), which dates the apostle's arrival to A.D. 50. It has been traced in writing, it is said, back to 1601 (or 1101) and beyond that date to an oral narrative handed down in one family line for forty-eight generations.[29] Another song, the better known *"Margam Kali Pattu,"* was put into writing in 1732. This locates the apostle's building of a king's palace in the Chola kingdom of south India. Whether or not these old Indian poems represent a reworking of the story from the *Acts of Thomas* or are an independent memory of very ancient church history is debatable, but in either case the variations and additions they give to the story are important.

The general consensus of local Indian traditions is that Thomas came first to south India, not to the Punjab of King Gundaphar. He landed on the Malabar Coast near the ancient port of Muziris, which is mentioned in the *Periplus* as the major southwestern port of the peninsula. The date was A.D. 50 or 52. He founded seven churches, usually named as Cranganore (two miles from his landing on the island of Malankara), Quilon, Paravur, Kokkamangalam (or Godhamangalam), Niranam, Palayur, and Cayal. In these towns he is said to have set up seven crosses, "the crosses of St. Thomas." He built a palace for the king that turned out to be a heavenly not an earthly mansion, as in the *Acts of Thomas*. Thousands were converted—6,850 of the Brahman caste, 2,590 Kshatriyas, and 3,780 Vaishyas, not to mention 2 kings and 7 village chiefs whom he ordained as bishops and leaders of the church. He preached both west and east and even beyond the borders of India into China, according to the *"Margam Kali."* And it was in the east that he died, at Mylapore near Madras where his tomb is held in reverence to this day.[30]

An interesting difference between the local traditions and the Syrian version is that in India Thomas's martyrdom is attributed not to royal resentment of his persuasively ascetic and celibate Christianity but to the enmity of the Brahmans and the powerful opposition of the Indian religion. The Indian story of the apostle's confrontation with Hinduism contains one of the most charmingly unbelievable of all his miracles. It happened, according to the song, near Pelayur in Kerala. A group of Nambudiri Brahmans were performing their ritual ablutions in the water of a temple basin. The apostle was watching them throw water into the air while they chanted their prayers. "Why do you do that?" he asked. "It is our sacrifice to the gods," they said. "Why don't your gods accept it, then? It keeps falling back on you," said Thomas. The Brahmans were indignant. "Who can make water stay up in the air?" "I can," said Thomas, and when they asked him to prove it, he said he would but only if they would promise to be baptized if he succeeded. They agreed, and the saint threw the water up and it caught and hung in the sunlight glittering like diamonds.[31]

In the end, however, the enmity of the Brahmans prevailed. A group of them ordered Thomas to worship the goddess Kali in her sacred grove. The apostle refused, and as he made the sign of the cross the grove burst into flames before their eyes. Angered, they speared him to death with a pointed stake.[32] He is buried, the story continues, on a hill outside Madras. On this point the Indian version agrees with the Syrian. Marco Polo visited the site in the thirteenth century and reported that even the dust of the shrine near Madras was believed to have curative powers; and seven hundred years before Polo, Gregory of Tours (ca. 540–594) wrote of a great monastery in India where a lamp burned day and night by the body of St. Thomas though no one fed it oil.[33]

There is a difference, of course, between tradition and history. Can we say with any certainty that Thomas was in truth the planter of the church in India? Few have dared to answer that question with an unequivocal yes or no. Given the difficulty of proving a negative answer and an equal hesitation to accept unwritten traditions without some reservation, most opinions range from "possible" to "probable," with a discernible trend toward the latter position since the discovery of the Gundaphar evidence and the renewal of interest in oral tradition as a source of history.[34]

A secondary question is whether the apostle's mission, if historical, was to northern or to southern India.[35] The Syrian tradition, as in the Acts of Thomas, suggests a northern base in the Punjab of King Gundaphar and is favored by those historians who see in the Gundaphar discoveries some contemporary supporting evidence for the tradition.[36] But, as proponents of the southern theory point out, all that the evidence can prove is that there was once a Gundaphar, not that there was even a hint of Christian mission in his realm. The deities on his coins are pagan—Zeus, Athena, a winged Victory.[37] No ancient crosses have been found in the north to indicate the presence of an early Christianity, and no ancient Christian community has survived there to claim an apostolic origin.

The south Indian tradition, on the other hand, has the strength of a living community behind it and of ancient communal memories with the supporting testimony of copper plate inscriptions and stone crosses dating back at least to the seventh or eighth century, as we shall see in a later chapter.[38] It lacks only what the north India theory has in its Gundaphar coins, that is, contemporary though indirect evidence from the first century. The nearest the south India theory comes to contemporary archaeological evidence is the discovery, in 1945, of a Roman trading station south of Madras dating to before A.D. 50 and containing a size of brick apparently not used after the end of the first century A.D. but similar to those in the tomb of St. Thomas at Mylapore.[39]

The consensus of the majority is that both theories are reasonable and, far from being mutually exclusive, can be interpreted as strengthening each other.[40] It is not implausible to believe that after preaching in Gundaphar's kindgom in the north, Thomas moved on as all traditions affirm, to preach the gospel to other kingdoms as well, the kingdoms of southwestern and southeastern India, until at last he was put to death, perhaps near Madras. If, as seems quite possible, he was the apostle to India at all, it is satisfying to believe with considerable reason that he was the apostle to all India.

The Mission of Pantaenus (ca. 180 or 190)

About a hundred and twenty years after the traditional date of the martyrdom of Thomas, a second Christian mission is reported to have reached India. The great church in Alexandria, center of Egyptian Christianity, sent its most famous scholar, Pantaenus, head of the theological school in that city, "to preach Christ to the Brahmans and philosophers there," wrote Jerome in the fifth century.[41]

Pantaenus is a remarkable figure. Born a Jew and thoroughly trained in Greek philosophy—probably in Sicily, for Clement calls him "the Sicilian bee" in recognition of his diligent study habits—he was converted to the Christian faith and moved to Alexandria. There his scholarship won him appointment as principal of the catechetical school for the training of the priesthood. He was soon acknowledged as the greatest Christian teacher of his age. Among his disciples were Clement of Alexandria and Origen. In background he was a Stoic with a mixture of Pythagorean Platonism, but his fame in Christian studies was as expositor of the Scriptures. Jerome, the Bible translator, acknowledges his debt to the many commentaries of Pantaenus, none of which unfortunately survive; and Clement pays tribute to him as his last but best teacher.[42]

Strangely, this great teacher owed to an illiterate bishop his rise to prominence. Bishop Demetrius of Alexandria and Pantaenus were an oddly assorted pair. The bishop was a countryman, a rustic layman who could neither read nor write; he even had a wife, which ordinarily would have disqualified him for high church office. But his predecessor had been told in a vision on his deathbed, it is related, that the man chosen by heaven as the next bishop would appear the next day bringing a present of grapes. Precisely on schedule the unsuspecting Demetrius showed up carrying bunches of grapes from his farm and was taken almost by force, hastily ordained, and thrust against his will upon the throne of St. Mark as the twelfth patriarch of Alexandria. Surprisingly, he ruled the Egyptian church long and well for forty-two years and built the catechetical school attached to his cathedral into a world-famous center of learning under three great masters, Pantaenus, Clement, and Origen.[43]

Sometime after the startling accession of Demetrius, which is dated by some as in 179, by others as 189 (the dating depends on the year accepted for the death of St. Mark), a deputation from India reached Alexandria. Impressed by the erudition of Pantaenus, according to Jerome, they asked Demetrius to send him to India for discussions with their own Hindu philosophers, and it is to the credit of the good bishop that he judged the Christian world mission to be no less urgent a priority than the advancement of Christian learning. Without hesitation he took his most famous scholar from the theological school and sent him as a missionary to the East.[44] Eusebius gives this early account of the mission:

> [Pantaenus] displayed such zeal for the divine word that he was appointed as a herald of the Gospel of Christ to the nations of the east and was sent as far as India. . . . It is reported that among persons there who knew Christ, he found the Gospel according to St. Matthew which had anticipated his own arrival. For Bartholomew, one of the apostles, had preached to them and left with them the writing of Matthew in the Hebrew language which they had preserved till that time.[45]

There is a shock hidden in that rather matter-of-fact statement. The Egyptian church would not have noticed it, for Eusebius was simply following the Alexandrian tradition, which had never, apparently, associated the apostle Thomas with India. The surprise, of course, is the mention of Bartholomew as the pioneer to the East. In one way it is a welcome independent confirmation of the Indian church's ancient and apostolic origin, but it seems to take away the apostolate from Thomas and give it to the lesser-known Bartholomew. If, as the church in India has always claimed, Thomas was its great founder, why did Pantaenus hear no mention of him there?

And what was Bartholomew, who was, according to tradition, "apostle to Armenia" and missionary to Arabia and Persia, doing in India with a Hebrew Gospel of Matthew?

Perhaps because of this slight to the memory of Thomas some Indian church histories tend to downplay the mission of Pantaenus. The mention of Bartholomew they explain either by relegating him to a secondary role in the Bombay area after the ministry of Thomas,[46] or they ingeniously suggest that Pantaenus, having difficulty with the language of the Thomas Christians he encountered, misinterpreted their references to *Mar Thoma* ("Bishop Thomas") as *Bar Tolmai* (the Hebrew name of Bartholomew).[47] Other Indian writers agree with the flat denial by a few Western historians that Pantaenus ever reached India. This rests on the assumption that Eusebius and Jerome simply confused India with Arabia or Persia as was often done by classical writers of the time.[48]

But the visit of Pantaenus to India is not to be dismissed so lightly. He may not have been "the first historical missionary to India," as some have called him,[49] for that implies too sweeping a judgment in favor of the evidence for Pantaenus and against the evidence for Thomas. But there are indirect, presumptive indications from the period of his mission that tend to support the later references to his journey.

Pantaenus's pupils and successors, Clement and Origen, for example, write about India as if they knew more of that land than passing myths and in no way confused it with Arabia and Persia. They speak of Indian Brahmans and "gymnosophists," and Clement writes discerningly of the difference between "Sarmanae" and "Brahmans," describing the former in terms that suggest the hermits or holy men of India.[50] This is the kind of information that they might have learned from Pantaenus himself. Moreover, Jerome would seem to be quite clearly pointing to India proper and not to Arabia when he speaks of Pantaenus preaching "to the Brahmans."[51]

The fact that Pantaenus was probably Jewish lends another touch of authenticity to the narrative. It explains his particular attention to the Hebrew copy of the Gospel of Matthew he is said to have brought back to Alexandria.[52] Jewish colonies are known to have existed in India from very early times. The Bene-Israel, at Kalyan near Bombay, traces its beginnings back to the period of the Second Temple, about the time of Christ. The arrival of Jewish immigrants farther south along the Malabar Coast at Cochin may have been not much later, perhaps at the time of the destruction of the Temple, A.D. 70, or in 136 when Jerusalem was torn down stone by stone in the reign of Hadrian.[53] So there were already Jewish colonies in India when Pantaenus is said to have arrived, and perhaps they were even there as early as the time of Thomas. The *Acts of Thomas* mentions a Hebrew flute girl on the route to India, though she was more likely a slave than a colonist. If there were, as the tradition asserts, Hebrew or Aramaic[54] copies of the Gospel in circulation as early as that, it is not unreasonable to imagine a Jewish missionary using one in his evangelistic work, for it was in the apostolic missionary tradition to preach first to the Jewish community.

As to whether the apostle in this particular case was Bartholomew as Pantaenus understood it or Thomas as most Indian Christians would insist, the evidence is too slight for a firm conclusion. Suffice it to say that the overall evidence for an apostolic presence in India overwhelmingly favors Thomas. Even Jerome, who is one of the two earliest sources for the mention of Bartholomew, seems elsewhere, when writing to Marcellus, to acknowledge the primacy of Thomas:

> He [Jesus] was present in all places with Thomas in India, with Peter in Rome, with Paul in Illyria, with Titus in Crete, Andrew in Greece, with each apostle and apostolic man in his own separate region.[55]

So the tradition remains and grows stronger with the years that already before the end of the second century the Christian church had been planted halfway across Asia in India, first by the apostle Thomas, not Bartholomew, and was then strengthened by the visit of the theologian Pantaenus from Egypt.

NOTES

1. Two modern translations are available: A. F. J. Klijn, *The Acts of Thomas: Introduction, Text and Commentary* (Leiden: Brill, 1962) and G. Bornkamm, "The Acts of Thomas," in E. Hennecke, *New Testament Apocrypha*, vol. 2, ed. W. Schneemelcher, English edition by R. M. Wilson (London: Lutterworth, 1965). Klijn, using the surviving Syriac text, stresses the essential orthodoxy of the writer; Bornkamm, working from a Greek text, deduces heavy Gnostic-Christian influence. Both the surviving texts are from a lost Syriac original. See also M. R. James, "The Acts of Thomas," in *The Apocryphal New Testament* (Oxford: Clarendon, 1924), 364–438.

2. The Abgar legend, claiming even earlier sources, would place the earliest Christian church outside the empire in Edessa (see chap. 3, p. 49), but it can be traced no further back than the Syriac *Acts of Thaddaeus*, probably written at the end of the third century, several generations after the *Acts of Thomas*.

3. On tradition and Thomas see, for example, A. M. Mundadan, *Sixteenth-Century Traditions of St. Thomas Christians* (Bangalore, India: Dharmaram College, 1970); Podipara J. Placid, *The Thomas Christians* (London: Darton, Longman and Tidd, 1970); and B. H. Streeter, *The Primitive Church* (New York: Macmillan, 1929), chap. 1.

4. The Thomas tradition is accepted by almost all Indian Christian writers and by an increasing number of secular historians as well, e.g., R. Thapar, *A History of India,* vol. 1 (Harmondsworth, Eng.: Penguin, 1966), 134, "not beyond belief"; A. L. Basham, *The Wonder That Was India,* 3rd ed. (London: Fontana-Collins, 1971), 345, "the story in its main outline is not impossible"; H. G. Rawlinson in *A Cultural History of India,* ed. A. L. Basham (Oxford: Clarendon, 1975), 432 "apparently based on a kernel of historical fact"; E. J. Rapson, *The Cambridge History of India,* vol. 1 (Cambridge: Cambridge Univ. Press, 1922), 579, "The Legend of St. Thomas has thus [i.e., by archaeological discoveries] been furnished with an historical setting which is chronologically possible"; and even the often critical K. M. Panikkar, *Studies in Indian History* (Bombay: Asia Publishing House, 1963), 13, referring to the south India tradition,"Though there are a few scholars who still claim that this is only a legend . . . [many of the facts] go a long way to confirm the truth of the tradition."

5. The explorer was Charles Masson, a deserter from the British army in India who also passed as James Lewis, according to Stephen Neill. He received a royal pardon and brought back more than fifteen hundred ancient, historic coins. S. Neill, *A History of Christianity in India,* vol. 1 (Cambridge: Cambridge Univ. Press, 1984), 27f.

6. The first scholar to connect the coins with Thomas was M. Reinaud in 1848. The name on the coins appears in many spellings, in Greek as Gondopharou, Gondapharou, and Undopherrou; and in the Indian script as Gudaphara and Gudapharna. See P. Gardner, *The Coins of the Greek and Scythic Kings of Bactria and India in the British Museum* (London: British Museum Trustees, 1886), xiii–xiv, 103–106, 174; and V. A. Smith, *Catalogue of the Coins in the Indian Museum in Calcutta,* vol. 1 (Oxford: Clarendon, 1906), 36–38, 54–56; and A. E. Medlycott, *India and the Apostle Thomas, an Inquiry with a Critical Analysis of the Acta Thomae* (London: David Nutt, 1905), 3–10. Medlycott's book is a detailed and perhaps too vigorous defense of the Thomas tradition.

7. The text of the inscription on the stone, which is now in the Lahore Museum, is given in S. G. Pothan, *The Syrian Christians of Kerala* (Bombay and London: Leaders Press, 1963), 13. Authorities tend to agree that the "*samvat* year 103" refers to the Vikama era. See F. W. Thomas, "The Date of Kaniska," *Journal of the Royal Asiatic Society* (London: 1913): 636; Rapson, ed., *Cambridge History of India,* vol. 1, 576; W. W. Tarn, *The Greeks in Bactria and India,* 2d ed. (Cambridge: Cambridge Univ. Press, 1951), 348ff.; and J. F. Fleet, "St. Thomas and Gondophares," *Journal of the Royal Asiatic Society* (London: 1905): 223–36. The major challenge to the dating comes from J. Van

Lohuizen-De Leeuw, "The 'Scythian' Period" (doctoral diss., Leiden, 1949) who places the end of Gundaphar's reign at 10 B.C.; but her dating is not widely accepted. See G. M. Moraes, *A History of Christianity in India*, vol. 1 (Bombay: Manaktalas, 1964), 22–24.

8. See chap. 1, p. 15. According to this theory, it was some time later in the first century A.D. that the Kushan dynasty of the Yueh-chi displaced the Pahlava dynasty.

9. A. K. Narain gives the most satisfying summary of the numismatic evidence in *The Indo-Greeks* (Oxford: Clarendon, 1957), 101–64, but argues that the Saka came independently from the northeast via Kashgar, Tashkurgan and Gilgit into the Swat valley. Most authorities prefer to place the invaders on the easier route from the west, that is from Sakastan via the Bolan pass. See Rapson, ed., *Cambridge History of India*, 560; G. Woodcock, *The Greeks in India* (London: Faber and Faber, 1966), 123f. Tarn thinks they first came up the Indus River from the west coast, in his *Greeks in Bactria and India*, 321f. It is possible that there were two conquests, one by the Saka chief Maues about 85 B.C. and another by the later Pahlavas.

10. E. Herzfeld, "Sakastan," in *Archaeologische Mitteilungen aus Iran*, vol. 4 (Berlin; 1931–32): 101 n. 25.

11. See chap. 1, p. 11; chap. 3, p. 47. On the Suren, see T. Mommsen, *The Provinces of Rome*, vol. 2, trans. W. Dickson (London: Bentley, 1886), 6–8.

12. Another view is that the Saka and Parthians remained enemies and that the Saka, after taking the Indus Valley from the Indo-Greeks, were in turn conquered by the Parthian Suren. The succession of names of rulers on the coins is a confusing mixture of Saka and Pahlava: Maues is Saka, Vonones is Parthian; Spalirises, Azes, and Azilises perhaps Saka; and Gundophares again Parthian. See Tarn, *Greeks in Bactria and India*, 346f., 494, 498f., 501; and S. Konow, "Kalawan Copper-plate Inscription of the Year 134," *Journal of the Royal Asiatic Society*, new series, 63 (London, 1932): 955.

13. Tarn, *Greeks in Bactria and India*, 494ff.

14. Tarn, *Greeks in Bactria and India*, 501.

15. "Gutschmid tries to show that Gaspard (or Casper), one of the three kings of the Christian legend, is identical with Gondophares." Gardner, *Coins of the Greek and Scythic Kings*, xliii.

16. Strabo, *Geographica* 2. 5.12.

17. *Periplus Maris Erythraei*, trans. W. H. Schoff (London: Longmans, Green, 1912).

18. E. H. Warmington, *The Commerce Between the Roman Empire and India*, 2d ed. (London: Curzon; New York: Octagon, 1974), 6ff.

19. Moraes, *History of Christianity in India*, 37, quoting from the *AganaNuRu*.

20. Warmington, *Commerce*, 61.

21. Warmington, *Commerce*, 83, 45ff.

22. Eusebius, *Historia ecclesiastica* 3.1.

23. The Syriac *Didascalia Apostolorum,* ed. and trans. W. Cureton, in *Ancient Syriac Documents* (London, 1864; reprint, Amsterdam: Oriental Press, 1967), 33. For the dating of the manuscript (fifth century) and the writing (third century), see 147n, 166n; and A. Mingana, "The Early Spread of Christianity in India," *Bulletin of the John Rylands Library,* 10, no. 2 (July 1926): 16.

24. G. Bickell, *St Ephraemi Syri Carmina Nisibena* (Leipzig: Bruckhaus, 1866), 163f.

25. Origen *Commentary on Genesis* 3, quoted by Eusebius, *Historia ecclesiastica* 3.1.

26. Syriac *Didascalia,* ed. Cureton, 34.

27. Syriac *Didascalia,* ed. Cureton, 34. Luke gives no names of the Seventy, and some manuscripts read "seventy-two."

28. Two other writers supposedly from the third century are sometimes quoted as giving even earlier witness to Thomas in India than those cited above. They are Hippolytus (d. 239) and Dorotheus of Tyre (end of third century). But the identification is probably spurious and the dates doubtful, so the authors are ususally styled Pseudo-Hippolytus and Pseudo-Dorotheus. See W. R. Philipps, "The Connection of St. Thomas the Apostle with India," reprint from *Indian Antiquary* 32 (Bombay: 1903); 145ff.

29. Manuscripts in the Mannanam monastery, translated into Italian by Fr. Rocca, "La leggende de S. Tomaso Apostolo," *Orientalia Christiana,* 32, 89 (Rome; 1938); 169ff., cited by A. M. Mundadan, *Sixteenth-Century Traditions of St. Thomas Christians* (Bangalore, India: Dharmaram College, 1970), 60–63; and L. W. Brown, *The Indian Christians of St. Thomas* (Cambridge: Cambridge Univ. Press, 1956), 49–50. Brown questions the antiquity of the song, noting that its vocabulary is not always seventeenth century and that years are given in Christian reckoning introduced by the Portuguese.

30. Mundadan, *Sixteenth-Century Traditions,* 61ff., 81ff.; and Brown, *The Indian Christmas,* 52ff. See also L. K. A. Ayyer, *Anthropology of the Syrian Christians* (Ernakulam; Cochin Government Press, 1926), 13–16.

31. As retold in Peter Bamm, *The Kingdoms of Christ: The Story of the Early Church,* tr. by C. Holme (London: Thames and Hudson, 1961), 224; Pothan, *The Syrian Christians of Kerala,* 14f. Potham's version, probably more accurate, has the water drops taking the shape of a flower.

32. Brown, *The Indian Christians,* 51.

33. On the site of the tomb at Mylapore, a suburb of Madras, see Mundadan, *Sixteenth-Century Traditions,* 2–37. On Polo see Henry Yule, trans., and H. Cordier, ed., *The Book of Ser Marco Polo* (London: Hakluyt Society, 1903), 11; 353f.; Gregory of Tours *De gloria martyrum* 32 (in Migne, *PL,* series 71, col. 733).

34. For bibliography on the subject see Mundadan, *Sixteenth-Century Traditions,* xix–xxiv; Fr. H. Hosten, who lists and annotates 283 books and articles

in his Antiquities from San Thome and Mylapore (Madras 1936); also the bibliography in Moraes, *History of Christianity in India;* and Brown, *The Indian Christians.* For an example of an unqualified no, see R. Garbe, who says, in effect, "There are no traces of Christianity in India before the fourth century," in his *Indien und das Christentum* (Tubingen, 1914), 339–79. For a more recent and equally emphatic yes, compare Panikkar, "The mission of the apostle to the Kerala coast . . . is now generally accepted [as having taken place] in A.D. 52." in his *Studies in Indian History,* 13.

35. See Mundadan's four categories of opinion on St. Thomas and India as outlined by E. R. Hambye in "St. Thomas and India," *Clergy Monthly* 16 (1952): (1) Some deny any Indian apostolate; (2) some support the north India apostolate and deny the southern; (3) some support the southern theory and are uncertain about the northern; and (4) some combine both northern and southern theories. See also the St. Thomas Christian Encyclopaedia, 2 vols., Trichur, India, 1982, 2: 1-12.

36. Advocates of the northern theory include A. Philipose, *The Apostolic Origin and Early History of the Syrian Church of Malabar* (1904); T. K. Joseph, "Constantine and Indias," *Journal of Indian History,* 28 (1950); and Brown, *The Indian Christians.* G. M. Rae, *The Syrian Church in India* (Edinburgh, London: Blackwell, 1892), treats both theories as reasonable.

37. Joseph, argues unconvincingly that the so-called Gundaphar symbol on the coins is a Christian symbol, a chalice ("Constantine and India," 2).

38. See chap. 22, p. 498ff. Advocates of the southern theory include Mundadan, *Sixteenth-Century Traditions;* Panikkar, *Studies in Indian History;* Pothan, *The Syrian Churches of Kerala;* E. Tisserant, *Eastern Christianity in India* (Westminister, MD: Newman Press, 1957); and many others.

39. George Schurhammer, *Franz Xaver, Sein Leben und seine Zeit,* vol. 2 (Freiburg, 1963), 547–79.

40. Among those who accept a dual ministry for Thomas in India are: Medlycott, *India and the Apostle Thomas;* J. N. Farquhar, "The Apostle Thomas in North India" and "The Apostle Thomas in South India," *Bulletin of the John Rylands Library,* 10, 11 (1926, 1927); Juhanon Mar Thoma, *Christianity in India and A Brief History of the Mar Thoma Syrian Church,* 4th edition (Madras: K. M. Cherian, 1968); and Moraes, *History of Christianity in India.*

41. Jerome, *Epistola LXX ad Magnum oratorem urbis Romae* (in Migne, *PL,* chap. 22, col. 667).

42. Clement of Alexandria, *Stromata* (in *Ante-Nicene Fathers,* vol. 1 [New York, 1903], 301).

43. J. M. Neale, *A History of the Holy Eastern Church: The Patriarchate of Alexandria,* vol. 1 (London: Masters, 1847), 16ff.

44. Jerome, *Liber de viris illustribus;* see also E. de Pressensé, *The Early Years of Christianity,* 2, *The Martyrs and Apologists* (New York: Nelson and Phillips, 1870), 271.

45. Eusebius, *Historia ecclesiasticae* 5.10.

46. Moraes, *History of Christianity in India,* 43–45, argues that Bartholomew's assignment to "India Felix", mentioned by Byzantine writers, refers to Kalyan, near Bombay, which may be translated "happy" in English, "felix" in Latin. He places Bartholomew in the Deccan at the same time that Thomas was in the Punjab. See also A. C. Perumalil and E. R. Hambye, *Christianity in India: A History in Ecumenical Perspective* (Aleppey, India: Prakason Publications, 1972); and H. Heras, S.J., *The Two Apostles of India* (Trichinopoly: Catholic Truth Society, 1944).

47. Pothan, *Syrian Christians of Kerala,* 19.

48. For the very real confusion between India and Arabia often seen in Roman writers, see Warmington, *Commerce,* 13. For denials of Pantaenus's connection with India, see J. L. Mosheim, *Ecclesiastical History,* trans. A. Maclaine (New York: Harper and Brothers, 1879), vol. 1, "Second Century," part 1, chap. 1:3, 51f.; and A. Mingana, who says, "It will be a matter of surprise if any responsible writer will ever mention in the future Pantaenus in connection with India proper" ("The Early Spread of Christianity in India," 17).

49. Rae, *Syrian Church in India,* 65; and George Smith, *The Conversion of India* (London: John Murray, 1893), 11.

50. Clement, *Stromata,* 15.

51. Jerome, *Epistola LXX ad Magnum oratorem urbis Romae.*

52. Some have denied that Pantaenus was Jewish (Valesius, Dupin) but most accept the implication of Clement that he was. See Neale, *History of the Holy Eastern Church,* 18 and note.

53. See Moraes, *History of Christianity in India,* 38ff., 44; and Warmington, *Commerce,* 59, 131f.

54. Brown, in his *The Indian Christians* (79n), suggests that it might have been a Pahlavi translation in Aramaic script. The question of the possible existence of a Hebrew Matthew at so early a date prompted E. J. Goodspeed to comment on the reference in Eusebius, "A very perplexing statement!" (*The Twelve* [NY: Collier Books, 1972], 97f).

55. Jerome, *Epistola LIX ad Marcellam.*

Chapter 3
The Church of the East: The Syrian Period

"What shall we say of the new race of Christians whom the Messiah has caused to arise in every place and in all climates by his coming? For lo, wherever we may be, we are all called Christians after the one name of the Messiah. On one day, the first of the week, we assemble ourselves together. . . . Wherever they are, and in whatever place they are found, the local laws cannot force them to give up the law of their Christ."

—Bardaisan of Edessa, ca. 196, in
his *Dialogue on Fate*

"The first bishop which the country of Adiabene had was, according to the doctor, Habel, Mar Pkidha on whom the apostle Addai personally laid his hands. He was the son of a poor man named Beri, who was in the service of a *Magi*."

—Msiha-zkha, in *Sources Syriaques*
(Mingana), sixth century

The Abgar and Addai Tradition

About the year 370 Ephrem the Syrian, a fiery and ascetic theologian of Edessa, wrote a hymn remarkable for the way it emphasized a link between the two earliest centers of the Asian church, India and Edessa. The hymn celebrated the arrival of the bones of St. Thomas brought from India at the request of the church in Edessa. Received with great honor after their long journey across the continent, the sacred relics were magnificently enshrined in a silver chapel. To honor the occasion, Ephrem wrote:

> "I stirred up death", the devil howled . . .
> "But now I am struck all the harder.
> The Apostle whom I slew in India
> Has overtaken me in Edessa."[1]

But why bring the bones of Thomas to Edessa?[2] The answer to that question turns the focus of Asian church history in its earliest years from India to an equally ancient center of Asian Christianity, the little kingdom of Osrhoene and the city of Edessa which was its capital.

Osrhoene was one of a string of small buffer states along the turbulent border that separated the two mighty, warring empires of Rome and Persia. Edessa is today called Urfa, a dusty town in eastern Turkey just north of the Syrian line, about halfway between Damascus and Mt. Ararat. It stood at the great northern bend of the Euphrates River, some 475 miles northeast of Jerusalem, where two ancient Asian caravan routes met and crossed. One was the Old Silk Road running east from Roman Antioch to the Persian border at Edessa 200 miles away and from there stretching on for endless miles across Asia to India and China. The other caravan road crossed it north and south from the mountains of Armenia down through Arabia to Egypt.

At the strategic junction of these two highways was Edessa. Abraham passed through there on his way to Canaan, though that was long before it became Osrhoene. Abraham's father died in Harran, only twenty-five miles from Edessa, and there Isaac found his wife Rebekah.

Centuries later, when Alexander the Great's general, Seleucus, became emperor of Persia and established himself as the first of a dynasty of Greek rulers of that oriental empire, he changed the name of the principal city in that area from the Syriac Orhay to the Greek Edessa but the city's independence as the capital of a separate state dates to the defeat of the Greek Seleucids in 130 B.C. when the

Parthians pushed the Greeks back across the Euphrates into Asia Minor and recovered Persia for the Persians (Iranians). The new Parthian dynasty protected its border with a ring of vassal kingdoms, the most important of which in the west was Osrhoene. For the next three and a half centuries a line of Arab kings in Edessa managed to play the Persians against the Greeks and then against Rome before finally losing their independence to the Romans in A.D. 214.[3]

In the first century before the birth of Christ, as Greek power passed to Rome in the West and Rome pushed east against Persia into Asia, Edessa found itself caught between the two empires in an agonizing seven-hundred-year war. Struggling to survive, it leaned sometimes one way, sometimes the other, but for the most part its culture remained Persian even when Roman victories dictated temporary shifts of loyalty from East to West.

Osrhoene was never quite trusted by Rome. Its eighth king, Abgar II (reigned 68–53 B.C.), for example, gave to Edessa a reputation for Arab perfidy mentioned by Roman writers for generations. When Crassus, the partner of Julius Caesar, marched arrogantly against Persia and was routed in the disaster at Carrhae, he accepted the offer of Abgar to act as his guide into Persia. But the shrewd Arab, preferring Persian rule to Roman, instead of leading the legions down the Euphrates River valley, which would have been the logical route to the Persian captial, diverted them into the terrible Syrian desert. There near Edessa, as we have noted,[4] an army of Parthian archers under the command of the Suren, a young general from the Indo-Persian border, fell on the lost and exhausted Romans and annihilated them. It was a strange quirk of history that thus brought together a King Abgar and a Suren in a decisive battle fought two or three generations before another Abgar and another Suren, King Gundaphar of India,[5] were linked by different traditions and in different ways to the ministry of the apostle Thomas.

We have already noted Gundaphar's link with Thomas as described in the third-century *Acts of Thomas*. The connection between the apostle and a king or prince of Osrhoene has more impressive but no less debatable credentials. According to Eusebius, writing about the year 324, it was Thomas who sent the first recorded Christian mission across the Roman border into Asian Osrhoene. He tells how the apostle asked one of his disciples, a man named Thaddaeus (or Addai, in Syriac), "one of the Seventy" mentioned in Luke 10:1, to answer a request for healing by the king of Edessa, Abgar V, called "the Black."[6] The fact that the usually reliable Eusebius adduced as evidence of this mission two highly questionable documents has not improved his reputation as a historian. The first, he said, was a letter from Abgar to none other than Jesus Christ; the second was Jesus' answer, and both letters, he claims, were found in the city archives of Edessa.

Eusebius quotes Abgar's letter as follows:

> Abgar Ukkama, the toparch, to Jesus the Good Saviour who has appeared in the district of Jerusalem, greeting. I have heard of you and your cures . . . [and] I decided that it is one of two things, either that you are God and came down from heaven to these things, or are the Son of God. . . . For this reason I write you to hasten to me and to heal the suffering which I have. Moreover I heard that the Jews are mocking you, and wish to ill-treat you. Now I have a city very small and venerable which is enough for both of us.

Jesus replied, according to Eusebius, that though he could not come himself he would send one of his disciples to the king after he had finished his work on earth:

> Blessed are you who believed in me, not having seen me, for it is written concerning me that those who have seen me will not believe in me, and that those who have not seen me will believe and live. . . . I must first complete here all for which I was sent . . . and when I have been taken up, I will send to you one of my disciples to heal your suffering and give life to you and those with you.[7]

The two letters of course are apocryphal. They were, in fact, declared spurious by Rome as early as the sixth century.[8] But copies of the supposed letter of Jesus were treasured for centuries and were used as charms to ward off evil not only in the East but as far away and as late as medieval Europe.[9] Edessa in particular cherished the legend as proof of its own link with the apostolic age through St. Thomas, a connection that was reinforced by the echo in the letter of the Lord's words to his doubting disciple: "You have believed me because you have seen me; blessed are they who believe in me not having seen me" (John 20:29). But though the Edessenes venerated Thomas as the commissioning apostle of the mission to Osrhoene, they traced the beginnings of their Christian faith not to the apostle but to his disciple, the missionary Addai.

The full tradition of Addai's mission is recounted in great detail in a Syriac document that, in an earlier version, may have been the source of Eusebius's abbreviated account. *The Doctrine of Addai*[10] written between 390 and 430, tells how Addai came to Edessa and in the apostolic missionary manner first sought out the Jewish community, lodging with "Tobias the son of Tobias." The king heard of his arrival, sent for him, and was miraculously healed. The next day he ordered all his people to assemble to hear Addai explain the source of his great powers and tell "the history of the coming of Christ," and "all the city rejoiced in his doctrine." So goes the legend.[11]

But even in the legend, the conversion of Edessa was not quite so sweeping as some of the rhetoric implies. A closer scrutiny of the narrative shows four groups singled out for mention as supporting the new faith, but to different degrees. In the intimation that not all the various segments of the population responded in the same way or with the same motives perhaps we have a memory of what really happened when Edessa first heard the gospel. The date was probably not so early as the legend claims but could possibly have been before the end of the first century.

The first group was composed of the nobles of Osrhoene and members of the royal family. According to *The Doctrine of Addai,* they proceeded to urge the building of a church and helped to furnish it and endow it with gifts. But their support was not unanimous, for it was one of the king's sons who first persecuted the church. The second group were the pagan religious leaders. The record says that the chief priests themselves tore down the altars of the old religions. A revealing admission, however, indicates that here too the conversion was not complete, for though the altars of Nebu and Bel (the gods of the sun and the moon) were destroyed, the "great altar" in the center of the city was spared.

The third group, it is said, were Jews "skilled in the law and prophets, who traded in silks," and these became disciples. But it is evident that not all Jews believed, for when Addai died it is noted that it was not just the Christians who mourned him, but that "Jews and pagans" also grieved over him. The most fervent support of the new teaching came from the fourth group, the common people, according to *The Doctrine of Addai.* They believed in great numbers and of their own free will, as the narrative explicitly states, for the king did not "compel any man by force to believe in Christ." The "force of the signs constrained" them, says the document, not royal coercion.[12]

This traditional account continues with the death of Addai, who died peacefully and was buried with great honor by King Abgar. He passed on the position of "Guide and Ruler" of the church to his disciple Aggai, a maker of silk robes and tiaras for the king. A deacon, Palut, was made presbyter. Under Aggai the church grew and prospered. It was said of Aggai that "instead of gold and silver he enriched the Church of Christ with the souls of believers" whose pure lives and care for the poor and the sick so commended them to the people of Edessa that "even the priests of Nebu and Bel" found that they now had to share equally with the Christians the honor and respect of the city.[13]

But it was also in the time of Aggai that the church faced its first direct persecution. When the good king Abgar the Black died, he was succeeded by his son, an unbeliever, who ordered Aggai to stop his preaching and get back to his former business of making royal robes and tiaras. The king demanded that he make him a new head-dress. Aggai replied, "I will not leave the ministry of Christ . . . and make the headband of the evil one." Whereupon the angry prince sent men to kill him in his own church by breaking his legs. The martyr died before he could ordain a successor.[14]

Thus ends the earliest known account of the first Christian mission east into Asia across the Roman border. It faces the church historian with the impossible task of seeking to determine how much of it is fact and how much fiction, for unlike Zen Buddhists, who look upon the disentangling of myth and event as a violation of the unity of truth, Christians root their truth in history. But the documentation for the history of that first-century Edessene Christianity, though more adequate than for India's Thomas Christians in the same period, is still so slim that, as F. C. Burkitt once observed, "We are in much the same position as if we had to reconstruct the course of the Reformation in England from a series of English Bibles (Tyndale to King James), together with a few tales taken out of Foxe's *Book of Martyrs*."[15]

THE TRADITION EVALUATED

Nevertheless, after the legendary chaff has been winnowed out of the strange story of Addai, Aggai, and King Abgar, some grains of fact seem to remain as a reasonable reconstruction of the beginnings of the church in Edessa.

First, it is not at all unlikely that Edessa was evangelized by a missionary named Addai. The Addai traditions were as persistent in the early church of Mesopotamia as the Thomas traditions were in India. By the end of the fourth century Addai was commonly accepted by Syrian writers both Eastern and Western as the founder of their church. The fact that so strong a center as Edessa was content with one of the lesser-known Seventy[16] rather than with one of the original Twelve supports the view that the historicity of Addai's mission was too well known to be easily set aside. He seems to deserve the honor tradition has given him as the father of the Church of the East which we call Nestorian.[17]

Second, it is not unreasonable to believe that the scattering of the first-century Christian community in Jerusalem by persecutions could easily have led to a very early beginning of a mission to Edessa, perhaps even as early as the latter part of the first century. A phrase in King Abgar's letter to Jesus, spurious though the document is, refers to the harassment of Christians in the Jewish capital and offers refuge in Osrhoene. This suggestion in the Abgar tradition of a connection between persecution in the West and opportunity in the East is completely consistent with the known history of the period. Already as early as the death of Stephen, about 37, there was a flight of believers, particularly among the martyr's Hellenistic-Jewish colleagues. As they fled, they evangelized and carried the gospel as far south as the Egyptian border and north as far as Antioch and Cyprus. Antioch was more than halfway to Edessa, and it would have been natural for some among the dispersed evangelists to move east along the Old Silk Road to find refuge and hearers among the many colonies of the Jewish Diaspora in Persia. Acts 11:19 records that at first they preached "to no one but Jews only," and the largest Jewish community outside Jerusalem was not in the West but in the East, in Babylon.[18]

Another possible date for the beginnings of missions to the East is the seventh decade of the first century. The siege of Jerusalem from 68 to 70 again forced a scattering of Christians from the city. The Jewish leadership of the church found refuge northeast across the Jordan at Pella, just below the Sea of Galilee.[19] It proved difficult for them to return to Jerusalem since for the next sixty years the Holy City was in ruins and in fact never regained its position as the center of the church. In Roman Asia its place was taken by Antioch, which was strongly Western and Hellenistic, the third most important city of the Roman Empire. But outside the empire, in Asia the earliest center seems to have been Edessa, where, unlike Antioch, the church was for some time more Jewish-Christian than Hellenistic-Christian. It may have been from Pella that an evangelist, perhaps the Galilean Addai, made his way north up the caravan route that led through Damascus and when he reached Edessa stopped to plant a church there.

The Jewish nature of Edessa's early Christianity is the third feature of the traditions that seems historically accurate. Legend makes Addai a Jew, born in Galilee at Caesarea Philippi (Paneas) "whence the river Jordan comes out." In Edessa he begins his ministry among his fellow Jews, and the Jews of the silk trade were among his first converts and church leaders.[20] The *Doctrine of Addai*, which relates these Jewish details, cannot be dated much before the fourth century and must be treated as a questionable source of information about first-century Edessa, but its credibility on this point is confirmed by a discovery in 1909 of a remarkable document that quite possibly pushes back our direct knowledge of Christians in Osrhoene to as early as A.D. 80 or 100. It is called the *Odes of Solomon*.[21]

The *Odes of Solomon* may well be, as J. H. Charlesworth says, "the earliest Christian hymnbook,"[22] and if indeed the work comes from Edessa, as some think, then we now possess not only the first known hymnbook of the church, but Christian hymns written in Asia in Syriac almost as soon as the church was planted outside the Roman Empire. Scholars still argue, but there are grounds for believing that its forty-two psalms or odes give evidence of being written for a church composed mostly of Jewish Christians living not far from Edessa toward the end of the first century (though some say early second).[23]

The poems give a clear and moving picture of a community at worship, rising early before dawn to begin the day in prayer, hands outstretched in the early Christian fashion to form the shape of the cross. This is how one of the odes (42:1–2) depicts it:

> I extended my hands and approached my Lord,
> For the expansion of my hands is His sign.
> And my extension is the common cross
> That was lifted up on the way of the Righteous One.[24]

The Jewishness of the community as reflected in the *Odes* is as open and unaffected as their Christianity. They claim Christ as God's promise of salvation to the offspring of Israel. Their salvation is "the circumcising by the Holy Spirit," and their hymns are in the familiar poetic mold of the psalms of David (*Odes Sol.* 21:12–13; 11:2–3). One particularly vivid instance of their innate Jewish spirit is a trace of hesitance about the propriety of accepting Gentiles as Christians. In the tenth ode, for example, the hymn writer puts into the mouth of Christ an almost apologetic defense of a Christian love so broad that it encompasses even the Gentiles and draws them into his church:

> And the Gentiles who had been dispersed were gathered together,
> But I was not defiled by my love (for them)
> Because they had praised me in high places. (*Odes Sol.* 10:5)[25]

This emergent broadening of the church is an indication of an early date, very different from the tinges of anti-Judaism that began to mar some of the later Syrian-Christian writings.

Despite an implied Christian hesitance about non-Jews, the hymn clearly indicates that here in a very Jewish Christian community Gentiles were welcomed into the Christian fellowship and made an integral part of it. In this first-century Jewish church, the Jewishness of the gospel had already been refined and transformed by an evangelistic love reaching out to both Jews and Gentiles with a message of grace that transcends "the law." So it is that the poet takes the words of the Psalmist, "In his *law* will I meditate day and night" (Psalm 119:97), and recasts them in *Ode* 40:6 as a Christian hymn of love, not law (italics added): "Let our hearts meditate in his *love* by night and by day."

It would not be wise to think that we can reconstruct from the *Odes* the theology of the church in Edessa in that very early period. A hymnbook is not a systematic theology and much about the nature and origin of the hymns remains an enigma. Nevertheless some conclusions seem fairly clear despite the rise and fall of conflicting interpretations.

All in all the *Odes* are generally orthodox, not heretical. As H. Chadwick observes, their language is the "language of pietistic enthusiasm" and if its exuberant imagery is stripped away it contains nothing "incompatible with an orthodox estimate of the nature and destiny of man."[26] Scriptural quotations and allusions abound, drawn from most of the canonical books of the New Testament and much of the Old, with references from the Gospel of John leading all others by far.[27] The benediction is emphatically trinitarian. (*Odes Sol.* 23:22), though in the *Odes* the Holy Spirit is often spoken of as feminine, as was common in the early East. Sometimes this makes for a symbolism of the Trinity that falls strangely on Western ears, as in *Ode* 19:1–2:

> A cup of milk was offered me
> And I drank it in the sweetness of the Lord's kindness.
> The Son is the cup,
> And the Father is He who was milked;
> And the Holy Spirit is She who milked Him.[28]

The Christology of the *Odes* is expressed in more familiar terms. Christ is the preexistent Son who humbled himself and redeemed his people by his death and resurrection. Some passages echo the great hymn of Philippians 2:6-11 and the prologue to John's Gospel, as in these lines from *Ode* 41:12–15 (see also *Odes Sol.* 17; 31; 42):

> His Word is with us in all our way
> The Saviour who gives life and does not reject (us).
> The Man who humbled Himself,
> But was exalted because of His own righteousness . . .
> And light dawned from the Word
> That was before time in Him.

The Messiah in truth is one.
And He was known before the foundations of the world,
That He might give life to persons forever by the truth of
  His name.

Some have seen traces of docetism in the imagery of the hymns[29] but, if so, they are more accidental than purposeful, and the references to the incarnation are unmistakable. The Gnostics of that day might easily accept a preexistent Son, but not the real birth and death, which the *Odes* so graphically celebrate. "So the Virgin became a mother . . . and she laboured and bore the Son . . . and she did not require a mid-wife" (*Odes Sol.* 19:6–10).[30]

Whatever weakness may underlie a supposed tendency toward docetism in the hymns, there is no Gnostic dualism to dilute the Christians' confidence in the total lordship of the Creator God and in the completeness of his victory in Christ. "Everything is of the Lord," the *Odes* declare; "nothing shall be contrary and nothing shall rise up against Him" (6:3, 5). Evil has been overcome (22); the light shines to drive away the darkness (21:3).

Out of this confidence springs a joyful missionary spirit that vitalizes this "first Christian hymnbook" with a vision of the gospel of the knowledge of God so holy and so all-embracing that it is described as a proclamation "written by the finger of God" and shot out "like an arrow" from heaven into all the regions of the earth. (*Odes Sol.* 23:5–22). Changing the metaphor, it flows down, strong and broad like a river to cover the surface of the whole world:

(The Lord) was zealous that those things should be known
  which through His grace has been given to us . . .
For there went forth a stream, and it became a river great and
  broad . . .
And it filled everthing.
Then all the thirsty upon the earth drank. (*Odes Sol.* 6:6–11)

The hymn then closes with a benediction upon the missionary-servants of the Lord who carry the life-giving water to the dying:

Blessed therefore are the ministers of that drink,
Who have been entrusted with His water.
They have refreshed the parched lips . . .
(The) living . . . who were about to expire,
They have held back from death . . . (*Odes Sol.* 6:13–15)

The *Odes* abound with such references to a vigorously evangelistic Christian mission that, thoroughly Jewish though it was, kept the community from a Jewish withdrawal into an inner-oriented ethnic community.

The reference in the quotation above to "the ministers of that drink" is typical of the tantalizingly ambiguous allusions to church organization in the early east Syrian church. There is no hint of an episcopal hierarchy. The argument from silence, of course, is never convincing, particularly in hymns, which are rarely required to sing of bureaucracies, but what the *Odes* do say about church ministries in first-century Edessa (if the dating and location are correct) points to an order much more loosely defined than the bishop-presbyter-deacon formula found in Edessa in the third century. The *Odes* speak simply of an order in which missionary and preaching urgencies predominate over the organizational and supervisory.

The nearest approach to a systematic list of ministries is found in *Ode* 12:4:

The interpreters of His beauty,
And the narrators of His glory.
And the confessors of His purpose.
And the preachers of His mind,
And the teachers of His works.

It has been variously suggested that the "interpreters" were Bible teachers or perhaps those who interpreted charismatic prophecies, the "narrators" were readers of the Bible lessons, and the "confessors" were evangelists. But this must remain conjecture. The clearer significance of the list is rather its suggestion of a very primitive evangelistic and missionary situation more like that of Paul's Letters to Corinth and Ephesus than 1 and 2 Timothy and Titus.[31]

There is an ascetic rather than an ecclesiastical air to the *Odes* somewhat akin to that of the Dead Sea Scrolls,[32] but breathing of rigorous Christian mission rather than of Qumran's withdrawal from the world. The church is a community of believers called to a covenant of war not so much against the world as *for* the world against the darkness. Initiation is through the "crown" of baptism; and here again a striking picture of the primitive church emerges— believers in white robes were prepared for the solemn ceremony that marked them as Christians; crowns of leaves, green with "living water," were placed symbolically on their heads as the initiates came near the baptismal waters (*Odes Sol.* 1:1–5; 9:8–11).[33] Their victory was in Christ, whom not even the darkness of Sheol could hold, who made a congregation of the living from among the dead, and who placed his name upon their heads "because they are free" (42:11–20).

In summing up what we may reasonably deduce from these earliest evidences of Christianity in Asia outside the Roman Empire, it is well to underscore again the inconclusive nature of the sources. The first-century Christians of the *Odes of Solomon* are fragments and shadows, and the dating of the hymns is still debatable. The "Thomas" Christians of India may be even older than their sister "Syrians" in the church of Edessa, as oral tradition suggests, but they remain undocumented by history until at least the fourth century. The Abgar legends of Osrhoene, likewise, can be traced back in manuscript no further than the fourth century. If a King Abgar was converted, as tradition claims, it is most improbable that he was the Abgar the Black of the famous letters. For stronger evidence than that of a Christian king in Edessa, we must wait another century or more.

But caution should not make us too skeptical. We cannot deny the unshakable conviction of the next generation of Asian Christians that their roots stretched back to the beginnings of the apostolic age, to a Thomas in India, or an Addai in Edessa. We can find traces of the first outreach of the gospel through its Jewish channels along the trail of the Diaspora into east Syria and Mesopotamia. We can rejoice in the outpourings of praise and simple happiness that permeated their earliest hymns with the "exultation of the Lord" their Savior (*Odes Sol.* 41). We can admire their openness in outreach and the outward missionary surge of their faith as they broadened the fellowship into gentile Asia. They "bridged rivers," and "uprooted . . . forests and made an open way" for the grace of the Lord to "spread over all the surface of the earth" (*Odes Sol.* 6).

By the end of the first century, as tradition contends, it is quite possible that there were indeed Christians in Asia from the Euphrates to India, and that Edessa, "the blessed city," had become the center of an early Asian Christianity so vigorous that it had already begun to penetrate eastward into the Persian Empire.

"The First Christian Kingdom"

Not until the second century, and the latter part of the second at that, does Asian church history move much beyond the realm of tradition. It is then that the churches of Edessa in eastern Syria and Adiabene in Mesopotamia begin to take clearer form in the writings of their first incontestably historical figures, that radically dissimilar pair of second-century theologians Tatian the ascetic and Bardaisan the hedonist. Heresies and sects multiply. Even secular history begins to take notice of the Christians. A church building is erected in Edessa without negative reaction from the authorities. It is publicly said in Edessa that the Osrhoene king himself has become a Christian. These are the first solid evidences of an organized Christian church in Asia beyond the borders of Rome.

Syrian tradition honors Edessa as the capital of history's first Christian kingdom, Osrhoene. The tradition may well be true, but if so, it was surely not as early as the legend reported by Eusebius of the conversion of Abgar the Black would have us believe. It is inconceivable that in the earliest days of Christianity a king could have become a Christian and no notice of it appear until the time of Eusebius, almost three hundred years later. But it is quite likely that a later Abgar did become a Christian, still early enough (a hundred or more years before the time of Constantine) to merit the title of "first Christian king."

Abgar VIII (called the Great) ruled Edessa a century and a half after the death of his ancestor, Abgar the Black.[34] He came to the throne in 177, at a time of political agony for that vulnerable little kingdom as it balanced its independence on the tightrope border between two world empires. In the first century when tradition relates that Addai had planted the church there, Osrhoene was an Asian client-kingdom of Persia. In the second century the power balance was tipping toward the West. The Roman emperor Trajan marched into Persia in 116, capturing the Parthian capital of Seleucia-Ctesiphon and sacking and burning Edessa for aiding the Persians. But after Trajan's death, Rome chose to draw its border back to the Euphrates and Persia resumed its supremacy in Osrhoene for the next forty years or more. Edessa's attachment to Persia, however, was never again quite the same. The central power of the Parthian dynasty had so declined that a Roman historian described it with some accuracy as a collection of eighteen kingdoms.[35] One of them was Osrhoene. But even when the Parthians mounted a temporarily successful invasion of Roman Syria through Edessa in 163, the king of Edessa so distrusted Persia's ability to keep its gains that he fled the city and took refuge with the retreating Romans. Three years later Marcus Aurelius threw back the Parthians and the Osrhoene king was rewarded by the return of his throne. From that time on Edessa became more and more Roman.

It was as a client-king of Rome, then, that Abgar VIII ruled Edessa for thirty-five years. He was called a "friend of Rome," but there are evidences that at heart he was pro-Persian. He rebelled at least once, and his mind was still more oriental than Western. At a time, moreover, when Rome was persecuting Christians, Osrhoene was a prime example of the Parthian policy of religious tolerance. In fact, Abgar is better called a friend of the Christians than "friend of Rome." Perhaps more than a friend. There are signs that have persuaded some, but not all, historians that the king actually became a Christian.

There is no doubt about the fact, for example, that in his reign the church in Edessa made remarkable progress and felt safe enough to become, for the first time, highly visible architecturally. The earliest documented record in history of a church building as such comes from Edessa in the time of Abgar VIII. For the first two hundred years Christians, as far as we can tell, met in homes. It was dangerous to be too conspicuous under a persecuting government. But sometime before the year 200 the Christians of Edessa came out of the shadows. The account for the year 201 in the records of the city, the *Chronicle of Edessa,* mentions "the church of the Christians" as matter-of-factly as it refers to the great palace of King Abgar the Great:

> In the year 513 in the reign of Septimius Severus [i.e., A.D. 201] and the reign of King Abgar . . . the spring of water that comes forth from the great palace . . . overflowed on all sides. . . . [The waters] destroyed the great and beautiful palace of our lord king and removed everything that was found in their path—the charming and beautiful buildings of the city, everything that was near the river to the south and north. They caused damage, moreover, to the nave [or shrine] of the church of the Christians. In this incident there died more than two thousand persons.[36]

It is also apparent that some of the king's contemporaries thought of him as a believer. The strongest evidence of his conversion is a statement by one of the city's most famous citizens, Bardaisan of Edessa. Bardaisan not only moved in the highest court circles, he is said to have been educated with the king when both were youths. In his *Book of the Laws of Countries* (also called *Dialogue on Fate*), he wrote:

> In Syria and Edessa there was the custom of self-emasculation in honour of Tar'ata, but when king Abgar had come to the faith, he ordered that every man who had emasculated himself should have his hand chopped off. And from that day to this no one emasculates himself in the territory of Edessa.[37]

Tar'ata was a mother goddess, the favorite deity of the neighboring city of Mabbog (Hierapolis) and popular also in Edessa. Her frenzied pagan rites featured the bloody castration of male worshipers outside her temple.[38] The fact that Bardaisan publicly linked the prohibition of this grisly ceremony with the Christian faith of the king in the king's own lifetime gives weighty support to the view that Abgar did become a Christian.

This is corroborated in the writings of the historian Sextus Julius Africanus, who visited Edessa in 195 in the company of the Roman emperor Septimius Severus and left a vivid record of life in the upper levels of Osrhoene society. Of King Abgar he says, he was a "holy man."[39] He did not specify "Christian" holy man, but it was an unusual remark for a Roman historian to make about an Edessene king, whom Romans rarely admired. And since it was made by a Christian historian, the description would be an unlikely characterization of a pagan monarch. Taken together, the two statements by Bardaisan and Julius Africanus seem to be reasonable enough justification for accepting the fact of at least a nominal conversion to Christianity on the part of the king of that small, troubled state. At the worst, wise politics might have suggested it as a shrewd gesture of deference to an increasingly important and aggressive segment of the population.[40]

What kind of Christians, in what kind of a church, had made such a mark on Edessa by the second century that a king himself, for whatever reasons, might turn Christian? Tradition, as we have seen, traces the growth to the witness of the first missionaries from the apostolic age and to the faithfulness of their successors. The earliest Syrian histories of the church and the martyrologies reconstruct a succession of bishops from Addai to the time of Bardaisan and beyond, bishops who promoted missionary outreach, organized the true church, and protected the faith against heretics. But there are some puzzling discrepancies between what tradition affirms and what little can be pieced together from the earliest surviving records.

Nothing written by Christians in the Church of the East before the end of the second century, whether by the writer of the *Odes of Solomon,* by Tatian, or by Bardaisan, mentions a bishop. There is no mention of a bishop in the *Chronicle of Edessa* before the early fourth century. The *Acts of Thomas* (early third century) has an apostle and a deacon, but no bishop. The first mention of a church officer corresponding to a bishop is in the *Doctrine of Addai,* but that is no earlier than late third or fourth century. It calls the first-century missionary Addai the "Guide and Ruler" of the church in Edessa and though it ascribes to him the functions of a bishop, such as appointing officers, teaching the Bible, and instructing Christians in "the ordinances and the ministry," it does not use the word "bishop":

He . . . built churches in other villages . . . and established in them deacons and presbyters, and he taught persons to read the Scriptures . . . , and he taught the Ordinances and the Ministry without and within. After all these things he was seized with that disease of which he departed from the world. And he called for Aggaeus before the whole assembly of the Church, and he . . . made him Guide and Ruler in his own place. And Palut, who was a deacon, he made him presbyter; and Abshelama, who was a scribe, he made him deacon.[41]

A succession of leadership from Addai is plausible, but after Aggai the continuity of authority becomes obscure. The *Doctrine of Addai* states that when Aggai was killed, he died too suddenly to ordain his elder, Palut, as "Guide and Ruler" to succeed him. Palut therefore

went to Antioch, and received the Hand of Priesthood from Serapion, Bishop of Antioch, which Hand Serapion himself also received from Zephyrinus, Bishop of the city of Rome, from the succession of the hand of Priesthood of Simon Cephas, which he had received from our Lord.[42]

Now there is no possible way of fitting such a Roman apostolic succession into a time frame that would bring a Palut, consecrated by Serapion, within range of Addai and Aggai, whether we date those pioneers to the middle of the first century, as the tradition does, or more probably to the end of that century. Serapion was not bishop of Antioch until 190.[43] Palut is described as being made elder by Addai. That would make him well over one hundred and twenty years old by the time of Serapion. But Palut does seem to have been a genuine historical figure. In the fourth century, orthodox Christians in Edessa were called "Palutians."[44] If we place Palut in the late second, rather than than the late first century, as leader of the Edessene church, the ecclesiastical pattern in the passage, particularly its suggestion of a transition from Edessene church independence to at least a nominal acceptance of the authority of Antioch, could be fitted into the period of Abgar the Great. Serapion and Zephyrinus belong to about the same period. Zephyrinus was pope from 198 to 217 and was in Rome when Abgar was received there on a lavish state visit to the capital.[45] The unknown author of the *Doctrine of Addai*, writing much later, may well have garbled his chronology and tried unsuccessfully to weave together the mission of a first-century evangelist (Addai) with the possible beginnings of an episcopal church organization after the middle of the second century (perhaps under Palut) and, in the third century, the gradual rapprochement between the church in Edessa and the Roman/Antioch church when

Rome's military expansion drew Osrhoene out of its Eastern orbit into the West. But by that time, it was too late to make believable the consecration of a bishop of Edessa by Serapion of Antioch.[46]

So speculative is this kind of theorizing about lists of bishops and lines of apostolic authority that it is not surprising to find that many scholars simply sweep it all away as an exercise in futility. The boldest and most influential rejection of the whole Addai-Palut-Abgar tradition is that of the New Testament scholar W. Bauer in his *Orthodoxy and Heresy in Earliest Christianity* (1934).[47] Discounting the conversion of even a late second-century King Abgar, his ingenious and carefully argued thesis is that the first Christians in Edessa were not of the orthodox variety at all. They were heretics, probably the followers of the excommunicated Marcion, he suggests. As for the orthodox, though he concedes the existence of a Palut, he insists that there is no reliable evidence of organized orthodoxy as a major factor in Edessa until the Edict of Toleration by Licinius and Constantine in 313 made Christianity legal in the Roman Empire. (Edessa had become a Roman colony in 214.)

Not all of this upside-down revision of the older histories is quite convincing. There is no more documentary support for the priority of Marcionites in Edessa than for the traditional view,[48] and tradition has deeper roots and manages to persist longer than most revisionism. But in one important area the scholarly Bauer rightly corrected the traditional picture of Edessa, "the blessed city." All through that early period Edessa, though revered as the mother church for eastward expansion, was a city awash with heresies. It was Bauer's "pioneering monograph" that forced renewed recognition of the fact, as one reviewer conceded, "that Catholicism or orthodoxy took much longer to shape itself than is commonly supposed, and that centrifugal [heretical] tendencies in the first three centuries were probably stronger than the later church liked to admit."[49] A revealing comment by the famous Bishop Marutha of Maipherqat, perhaps at the end of the fourth century, laments the persistence of heresy. Speaking of the church in his own surroundings near Edessa, he described it as like a "single ear of wheat on a huge field full of weeds which the Devil has sown full of heretics."[50]

It is quite true, for example, that the earliest reference to Christianity in the *Chronicle of Edessa*, apart from mention of the birth of Christ (2 or 3 B.C., according to the *Chronicle*), is a notice of the heretic Marcion, whose apostasy it dates at A.D. 138.[51] Marcion was not from Edessa. He was a rich shipbuilder from the shores of the Black Sea in Asia Minor who came to Rome and was gladly received by Christians there, no doubt partly because of the large gifts he made to the church. His welcome quickly cooled, however, when he began to teach some strange-sounding doctrines. The God of the Old Testament, he said, was not the God and Father of the Lord Jesus Christ, but rather an evil god, more like the devil and the sworn enemy of the true God. He could not be the true God because he created the world, and matter is evil. Jesus Christ was sent to earth by the true God, without birth and without a material body, said Marcion, to destroy the false god, the Demiurge, whom he cast into hell. But Christians must beware of his evil influence and rigidly control their bodies so that their souls may finally reach heaven.

To support his wrenching reconstruction of apostolic teachings, Marcion pruned away from the New Testament anything that would tend to contradict him. He had already thrown away the Old Testament and was left with a "Marcionite canon" consisting of ten Epistles of Paul (excluding the pastoral Epistles) and a shortened and mutilated Gospel of Luke. For such shocking unorthodoxy he was excommunicated.[52]

Cast out of Rome, Marcion carried his heresy with him. The Marcionites, according to Tertullian, poured out of Rome like swarms of angry wasps masquerading as gentle honeybees.[53] They must have come very early to Edessa, for theirs was the heresy Bardaisan of Edessa as an eager convert first determined to attack in defense of his new faith. That was perhaps about 179. But if any heresy at all was dominant in the early days of the church in Edessa, it was probably not Marcionism. The most persuasive and bewilderingly variegated of all the early heresies was Gnosticism, and Gnosticism also had roots in Edessa. One of the oldest surviving pieces of Gnostic literature ever discovered, the *Gospel of Thomas*, from the Nag Hammadi cache of manuscripts, is thought by some to be of Edessene origin, written possibly as early as the second half of the first century,[54] thus forging another ancient but apocryphal link between "the blessed city" and the doubting disciple.

Gnosticism appears in so many guises that it is difficult to form a simple, satisfactory definition of it.[55] The best one-sentence description is perhaps that by Plotinus more than seventeen hundred years ago. The Gnostics, he wrote, "think . . . very well of themselves, and very ill of the universe."[56] Simon Magus (Acts 8:9–24) has been called the first Gnostic, and traces of anti-Gnostic warnings appear in the later books of the New Testament, especially 1 John and the pastoral Epistles (1 John 4:2–3; 1 Tim. 6:20; 2 Tim. 2:16–18; and perhaps passages in Colossians). In general Gnosticism is faulted by the orthodox for four major doctrinal errors:

1. Matter is evil.
2. The world, therefore, was not created by God but by an anti-god.
3. Salvation is by knowledge of a special revelation beyond that of the Old Testament and the apostolic witness.
4. Human beings are divided into three classes: the spiritual (*pneumatics*), who are certain of salvation; the material (*somatics*), who cannot be saved; and a middle class of *psychics*, who can go either way.

The *Gospel of Thomas*, whether or not it was written in Edessa, may well serve as a sample of the kind of Gnostic teachings circulating among some who called themselves Christians in that city. It is a short collection of 114 "secret sayings" of Jesus attributed to Judas Thomas the Twin, as the apostle was known in Edessa. It is probably the best known of a library of Gnostic texts found in the Egyptian desert in 1945 by two peasants digging for fertilizer and was so miraculously preserved that the story of the Nag Hammadi hoard reads like a suspense novel.[57] The sayings are a curious mixture that can be separated into three categories. The first are authentic words of Jesus found also in the canonical Gospels but often embedded in unfamiliar settings, such as:

> Jesus said, "If those who lead you say . . . 'See, the Kingdom is in the sky,' then the birds will precede you. If they say . . . 'It is in the sea,' then the fish will precede you. Rather the Kingdom is inside of you, and it is outside of you. When you come to know yourselves, then you will become known."[58]

Most of the parallels are with Matthew and Luke.

The second category consists of sayings that ring true, such as the unfamiliar words in the saying above, or that might conceivably be words of the Lord as remembered by his disciples but not recorded in the New Testament. But third, there are less acceptable sayings that are quite inconsistent with the Jesus of the Bible. At least 14 of the sayings are radically unorthodox, like the 114th:

> Simon Peter said to them, "Let Mary leave us, for women are not worthy of life." Jesus said, "I myself shall lead her in order to make her male, so that she too may become a living spirit resembling you males. For every women who makes herself male will enter the Kingdom of Heaven."[59]

The emphasis on the secret meaning of the "sayings," which gives an elitist and esoteric tone to this apocryphal Gospel, marks it as Gnostic, though it is more orthodox than most of the other Nag Hammadi material.[60]

It is more orthodox, too, than what we know of some of the other queer and colorful Gnostic cults that swirled through Edessa. A teacher named Quq, who may have come to the city about the time of Bardaisan's conversion, around 179 perhaps, gathered a group of followers whom he taught to believe in the existence of a "light-world even before God" and the formation of the cosmos through seventy aeons brought forth by the Father and Mother of Life. The Quqites preserved most of the Old Testament, unlike the Marcionites, but interpreted it in Gnostic terms. Tradition connects them with the Samaritans, especially in their horror of defilement by contact with anything dead.[61] The most bizarre and repellant of the Gnostic cults were the Ophites. They celebrated the Eucharist with snakes, for to them the serpent in the Garden of Eden was not the enemy of man but a friend, offering the human race liberation from the evil, material God of the Old Testament.[62]

Such a ferment of Christian teaching, aberrational as well as orthodox, is a fact of church history as old as the days of the apostles and not limited to Edessa. It led, of course, eventually to the ecumenical councils beginning with Nicaea in 325, which with varying degrees of success reached a consensus based on apostolic authority in creed and canon to distinguish orthodoxy from heresy. But even before the consensus the line between true and false doctrine, though never quite so sharply marked as ecclesiastical hindsight has assumed, was also not so completely undiscernible as some would like to maintain. There have been times when church tradition read the future back into the past; but more often it was the tradition that carried the essential truths and vitalities of the past into the future, and what was thus carried forward, whether it is called "the Great Church," or "orthodoxy," or simply "the instinct for the Centre in early Christianity,"[63] has left clearer and more verifiable traces in history than the smudged footprints of the cults.

A prime example of the existence of a Christian "center," with a power to attract and organize as well as with a vulnerability to distortion, is the life and teaching of Bardaisan of Edessa, who was easily the most conspicuous and controversial Christian in the second-century Church of the East.

BARDAISAN OF EDESSA

Sportsman, nobleman, poet, philosopher, and friend of King Abgar the VIII, Bardaisan (in Latin, Bardesanes) was born in Edessa about 154. According to the traditional biography, his parents were Persian refugees fleeing into Osrhoene to escape the consequences of some palace conspiracy. One report states that after his birth his parents were forced to flee again, this time across the Euphrates into Roman territory to Mabbug, and that he was educated there by a pagan priest. It is more likely, however, that he grew up in Edessa where, according to Epiphanius, he was educated with the young prince who became King Abgar.[64]

When he was twenty-five (perhaps about 179) Bardaisan happened to pass by the church of the Christians, which Addai was believed to have founded, and heard the "bishop" Hystaspes explaining the Scriptures. He believed and was baptized. He proved to be a zealous convert and was soon made a deacon, earning a reputation for himself as a defender of the faith against the heretics in which Edessa abounded. His high position at the court of the king must have quickly marked him for leadership in the church. He excelled in everything he touched.

Julius Africanus, on his visit to Edessa in 195 accompanying the Roman emperor Septimius Severus, gives a lively description of Bardaisan's reputation as an archer in a city already famous for its archery. He watched Bardaisan demonstrate his skill before the emperor. A young man was ordered to stand with his shield held out in front of him while Bardaisan pumped arrow after arrow swiftly into the shield "like a painter with a brush" outlining the man's portrait, "the gleam of the eyes, the junction of the lips, the symmetry of the chin."[65]

But it was in the world of thought, not in sport or war, that Bardaisan made his lasting mark. F. C. Burkitt has called him, with some overstatement, "the only original thinker which the Syriac church helped to mould."[66] Perhaps he was too original. The first objects of his crusade against heresy were the Marcionites, for which Eusebius the church historian commended him. But in the eyes of most of the early church fathers he avoided one heresy, Marcionism, only to fall into another, Gnosticism. Eusebius remarks that "though he thought he had changed to orthodox opinion, . . . in fact he did not completely clean off the filth of his ancient heresy."[67]

To the Western fathers who condemned him, Bardaisan's "ancient heresy" was Valentinian Gnosticism.[68] Valentinus was a Christian who came to Rome from Alexandria and Cyprus about the same time that Marcion came from Asia Minor. He did not offend the church by teaching so bluntly as Marcion that the Old Testament must be rejected, and he accepted God as the creator of the world. But he too, like Marcion, felt deeply that matter was in some way evil or defiled. To reconcile evil matter with a good, creating God he began to spin a web of speculative philosophy, part Platonic, part Indian pantheism, part Christian, that soon carried him beyond the accepted limits of Christian thought. His God was no mere Trinity, but a thirty-headed Pleroma, the sum total of all spiritual existence. Of the thirty aeons or divine attributes that form this spiritual world, the first eight represent the essential being and nature of God. Their names are Profundity and Silence, Mind and Truth, Logos and Life, Ideal Man and Church. Each pair is linked, male with female. That is the upper end of the Pleroma. These higher aeons formed the spiritual world. At the lower end of the Pleroma was the aeon Wisdom (Sophia). When Wisdom developed an inordinate passion for knowledge she had to be rebuked. A Demiurge was formed who was not really a part of the divine Pleroma. He created the lower, material world and the man Adam. But a seed of the spirit was planted in Adam and to draw this bit of the spirit back into the higher world, a new pair of aeons was produced by Mind. The two aeons were Christus and the Holy Spirit, from whom came the last of the aeons, Christ the Savior. He came down into the lower world in what seemed to be a human body but was purely spiritual and saved all who would receive his perfect knowledge of the mysteries of the truth. Thus was the high God separated from responsibility for creating evil, and thus were the elite, the knowing ones, the Gnostics, to be saved.[69]

How much of this *gnosis* that Valentinian is accused of propagating is actually to be found in Bardaisan? A Western contemporary of his, Hippolytus (d. ca. 235), explicitly labeled him a Valentinian of the eastern school.[70] But Hippolytus, living in Rome, may not have known much about the Syrian East. More damaging were the attacks of Ephrem the Syrian a generation later in Bardaisan's own Edessa. Ephrem accused him of dividing up the Godhead, if not into thirty beings like Valentinus, at least into six. He said that Bardaisan taught a sexual concept of the Trinity (reminiscent of the paired aeons of Valentinus) and that he denied the resurrection of the body, like most Gnostics.[71] But was Bardaisan really "the last of the Gnostics," to quote the title of a nineteenth-century German book about him?[72]

Fortunately we are not left to judge him solely by the evidence of his critics. His most important work survives, and whether he wrote it himself or his disciple Philip wrote it for him, it is now generally agreed that *The Book of the Laws of Countries*, also called *The Dialogue on Fate*,[73] represents Bardaisan's own thought. Judged by this work he does not seem to be so much a Gnostic heretic as an unconventional theological pioneer, writing before orthodoxy had been systematized in the great creeds, a man who was sometimes right and often wrong, but who was at least trying to do for the Christian faith in Asia what Clement of Alexandria and the apologists sought to do in the West, that is, make the gospel intellectually meaningful in the Iranian intellectual and religious circles in which he moved at the court of Edessa.[74]

Even Ephrem, his great assailant, admitted that Bardaisan seemed orthodox on the surface. There is such a reasonable sound to the man's writings, he complained, that common people do not see the "madness" beneath.[75]

On the orthodox side Bardaisan contended stoutly for the unity of God against the aeons and demiurges and dilutions of divinity by which Gnostics and Marcionites explained the problem of evil in God's creation. "He who has power over everything is One," said Bardaisan. But his One God is also Three. Bardaisan was trinitarian, though his Trinity is a primitive one, antedating the full development of that doctrine in the creeds. He speaks of the Father, the Holy Ghost (the "Mother of Life"), and their Son, the "Word of Thought."[76]

Also orthodox is Bardaisan's insistence that God's work of creation is good and that matter is not evil. Here again he differs sharply from the Gnostics. Humans, says Bardaisan, are created in the image of God and are greater than the stars and equal to the angels, free in their own will to sin or to refrain from sinning. At one time, Bardaisan admits, he was intensely interested in the astrology of the Chaldaeans and believed that human fate was fixed by the stars. But now, he says he knows that all power is in the hands of God and that humans are not the slave of celestial forces. Such powers may influence their material fortunes, as do all the laws of nature, but the human will and spirit are free.[77]

This is the great theme of his *Dialogue on Fate:* human freedom. Freedom comes from the spirit. In the thought of Bardaisan, the soul is not the prisoner of the body, as Marcionites and Gnostics taught, but is joined to the spirit and the body at birth, and from the spirit the soul receives the gift of freedom. Though misused by Adam and therefore now partially limited in all human beings, the gift of freedom is restored by the coming of Christ. God made all people free and commands them to do nothing they cannot do. Even sex is not sin, but good. It is in fact purifying.[78] Unlike the Gnostics and even most Syrian Christian writers of the early centuries, Bardaisan's theology was a theology of freedom and not of ascetic restraint.

There was nothing unhealthy in this championing of normal human relationships against the abnormalities of the radical ascetics. Bardaisan was neither a Gnostic (in the accepted sense) nor an astrologer. His theological weakness, it would appear, lay rather in another direction—syncretism. He may not have been quite so heretical as Ephrem the Syrian believed, but neither was he orthodox in the traditional pattern. His root error, as seen from an orthodox position, would seem to be not so much any particular doctrine but rather the whole philosophical and cosmological foundation of his worldview, a view he had derived from outside Scripture and into which he tried to fit his new Christian worldview. He did not reject the Old and New Testaments, like the Marcionites, nor did he claim any special revelation for himself, like Mani after him. Neither did he teach a hidden, esoteric doctrine from other secret revelations, like the Gnostics and some of his own later followers.[79] For Bardaisan, truth was open to all and could be found by rational inquiry.

But what his reason was able to find in the Christian truth by this process—his Christology, for example, his sense of sin, and his understanding of God and salvation—was rendered inadequate and deformed by his attempt to fit Christian teaching into an overarching cosmology derived from too many and too diverse a collection of non-Christian sources.

To summarize his worldview: above is God and below is darkness. In between are the four pure elements, white light, red fire, blue wind, and green water. When chance disturbed the primeval harmony of these pure elements, darkness entered the mixture and evil came into the world. Only the coming of Christ, "the First Thought" (the Logos), was able to restore order in the resulting chaos.[80]

Christ is not, however, in Bardaisan's thought, the great turning point in the cosmic process, for salvation had already begun long before at the moment of creation (cf. Eph. 1:4). And Bardaisan's description of the process of salvation before the incarnation sinks into unscriptural fantasy. Out of the Holy Ghost (the Mother) came two daughters, the earth and sea. Ephrem further accused Bardaisan of teaching that out of the sexual union of the Father and the Mother came Christ, the Son of Life, who is also the Word of Thought, the Logos. This Logos passed through Mary (*per*, not *ex virgine*) and found its lodging in Jesus of Nazareth. This, of course, is docetism. But Bardaisan goes yet further. The Father and the Mother, that is, God the Father and God the Holy Spirit, are also the Sun and the Moon. And salvation and human freedom come from the knowledge of the Logos, the Son of Life, which the Moon receives from the Sun and sends into the world.[81]

In this confusing mixture of astrology, cosmology, and theology are the seeds of Bardaisan's downfall. In the end, his inquiring mind yielded to the besetting sin of the syncretist, that is, a willingness to so adapt the faith to prevailing cultural norms that it loses its Christian integrity. Oriental astrology, Hellenistic philosophy, traces of Gnosticism, Persian magic, and Greek science all fought with the Christian faith to find a place within his system. He may have thought he was using secular and pagan learning only to make the gospel intelligible to an unbelieving world, but the Greek and Persian lions did not lie down as peaceably with the Christian lamb as he seemed to expect, and the ill-matched combination brought on him the condemnation of the church. He was finally "expelled from the community of the orthodox," according to Jacob of Edessa (seventh century), and his biography adds that 'Aqi, the successor of "bishop" Hystaspes who had converted him, banned his teachings and his followers in Edessa. Despite their excommunication, however, Bardesanites continued as a separatist sect in Edessa for another hundred and fifty years.[82]

Actually, his excommunication may not have been quite so ecclesiastically formal as the biography, which was written much later, implies. There is another tradition that Bardaisan was not forced out of the city but left Edessa voluntarily to go as a missionary to Armenia, where he died.[83] Another possibility is that he left Edessa for political reasons, as a Persian nobleman resenting and fleeing from the Roman takeover of Edessa. In his lifetime Edessa slipped out of ancient Asia into the world of the West. Bardaisan's friend, King Abgar VIII, had Parthian sympathies and during the Parthian uprising in Mesopotamia of A.D. 194 joined the king of Adiabene in an attack on the Romans at Nisibis. He was soundly defeated and Edessa was placed for a while under a Roman procurator. When the Parthians again attacked Syria three years later, this time Abgar prudently chose the Roman side and was rewarded with a state visit to Rome that has been described as the most lavish since Nero's welcome of an earlier king of Armenia, Tiridates, to Rome in 66. Even his name was changed, and Abgar must have smarted under the extravagant Roman name of Lucius Aelius Aurelius Septimius. But when he died in 212, King Abgar VIII was still a "king of the Persians" to the Romans. The end of the dynasty and of Edessa's independence came very quickly. His son, Abgar IX, was invited to Rome, suddenly seized, chained, and treacherously deposed.[84] It may have been then that Bardaisan, the proud, highborn Edessene, left the city for exile. In 214 Edessa was made a Roman colony. Bardaisan died about 222. And in Persia, the shattered Parthian dynasty fell to a new line of rulers, the Sassanids, in 225.

The Assyrian Christians of Arbela

But by then, Edessa was not the only center of growth in Asia outside the Roman Empire, even if we exclude India. As a matter of fact some scholars argue that Edessa itself may have received the Christian faith not through a missionary from Jerusalem but from farther east in Asia, from Arbela. So from Edessa on the Euphrates let us look back now to Arbela on the Tigris in the first two Christian centuries.

Four hundred miles east of Edessa across the rich northern Mesopotamian plain lay another small Persian border kingdom, Adiabene. Its capital, Arbela (modern Erbil), was about fifty miles east of the Tigris, guarding the northeastern passes along the river as Edessa guarded the northwest frontier along the Euphrates, and, like Edessa, Arbela was one of the earliest Christian centers in oriental Asia. One theory, as we have noted, holds that the faith came first to Adiabene and from there was carried back west to Edessa.[85] Tradition and geography both count against this view but it is true that a very early report, handed down by the first-century Jewish historian Josephus, asserts that a king of Adiabene had become a convert to Judaism. He says that King Ezad of Arbela, while still crown prince and while visiting an Arab kingdom on the Persian Gulf, was converted by a Jewish merchant. Returning to Arbela, he found that his mother, Queen Helena, had also accepted the Jewish faith. This was in A.D. 36, which would make Ezad a contemporary of Abgar the Black, the legendary Christian king of Edessa.[86]

Such a conversion from paganism to Judaism early in the first century could have made Arbela a natural center for precisely the kind of Jewish Christian mission that was the earliest pattern of Christian expansion into Asia. But the Christian tradition of the evangelization of Adiabene mentions no such link with an earlier Jewish base. The earliest Christian accounts, rather, trace the mission to Adiabene to two disciples of Addai, the first missionary to Edessa. One account (the Syriac *Doctrine of the Apostles*) credits it to Addai's successor, Aggai[87]; another (the *Acts of St. Mari*) to a missionary named Mari.[88] A still later local tradition, recorded about the sixth century, states that Addai himself confirmed the first "bishop" of Adiabene, a man named Pkidha, in 104.[89]

The same sixth-century *History of the Church of Adiabene* (which is also called *The Chronicle of Arbela*)[90] gives a much disputed line of succession of bishops from 104 to about 511 in the form of biographical sketches of twenty "bishops." The first, Pkidha, is said to have been born as a slave of a Zoroastrian master but was converted by seeing the missionary Addai from Edessa raise a young girl to life as she was being carried to her grave. Thus this chronicle bypasses both of the earlier traditional apostles of Adiabene, Aggai and Mari, and links the beginning of church organization directly to Addai and Edessa.[91] All three traditions should be viewed with caution, but there is nothing unreasonable about placing the beginning of the evangelization of Adiabene at the turn of the first century or accepting that someone named Pkidha was its first convert. A first-century episcopacy in Adiabene is more debatable.

In Semsoun, the second "bishop," if the account is to be believed, the church in Adiabene found its first martyr. Zealously evangelistic, he converted so many people that the fire-worshiping Zoroastrians seized, tortured, and beheaded him. The Arbela *Chronicle* dates the event "after [Trajan's] defeat of Chosroes, king of the Arsacids," presumably referring to Roman victories in 116. Here, and in other accounts of early martyrdoms, inconsistencies abound, but tradition is at least reasonable in placing them in the early second century if they occurred at all.[92]

Semsoun's martyrdom in Arbela is dated in 117 or 123, and the deaths of Sharbil, Babai, and Barsamya, the first martyrdoms in Edessa under Rome, are attributed to 112. The names may be mythical. The tortures are hard to believe. Sharbil, for example, the converted chief priest of the idols of Edessa, is successively bent back and flogged on his belly, hung up by one hand, branded with flames between the eyes, burned slowly with candles, blinded with iron nails, constricted in an iron chest, suspended upside down, burned with red-hot brass balls under his armpits, hung on a tree, sawed in two, and finally beheaded—all the time preaching steadily to his tormentors![93] But it is not hard to believe that there may well have been martyrdoms in that time of spreading persecution under Trajan. What could be more unbelievable yet unquestionably authentic than the chilling letter of Pliny the Younger to Trajan in 112 in which that cultured Roman humanist coolly describes how he dealt with Christians in Asia Minor. He rather regretted the unpleasant duty of executing them, but that was the law. The Christians died more bravely than he expected and this piqued his curiosity. So to find out more, he casually tortured two young girls, deaconesses in the Christian community, to press them for further information.[94]

Very soon the new law on compulsory emperor sacrifices under which Pliny acted was enforced in Edessa, as the *Acts of Sharbil* states. But Semsoun's martyrdom in Arbela, farther east, is quite

properly not attributed to Roman law, for the Roman armies soon
retired from Mesopotamia. There the persecutors were Zoroastrians.

It must be questioned, however, whether the Persian persecutions actually began that early. The Parthian dynasty was religiously
tolerant. The blood of the martyrs was soon to run deep in Persia,
but authenticated martyrdoms there are probably not to be found
until after the fall of the Parthians and the rise of the Sassanians
in 225.

TATIAN THE ASSYRIAN

The first verifiable historical evidence of Christianity as far east in
Persia as Adiabene comes to light only after the middle of the second
century with the life and work of Tatian (ca. 110–180). This remarkable biblical scholar, linguist, and ascetic was born of pagan parents
in the ancient Assyrian territory of northern Mesopotamia (modern
Iraq). About 150, having come to Rome for study, he became a pupil
of that firm defender of orthodoxy Justin Martyr, who was the earliest of the church fathers to insist that the "memoirs of the apostles"
were of equal authority with the writings of the Old Testament
prophets. He was nevertheless surprisingly gentle with Jewish
Christians who still felt they must keep the whole law, so long, he
said, as they did not insist that all Christians must do so.[95]

When Justin was scourged and beheaded about 165 in the persecutions of the usually humane Emperor Marcus Aurelius, Tatian
opened a school of his own. But some time about the year 172 he
shook the dust of the West off his feet and returned to his own
Assyria. All evidence points to Arbela or somewhere near it east of
the Tigris "in the midst of the Rivers" as the center of his work
during the remaining years of his life. There he apparently once
more opened a theological school or perhaps simply a self-sustaining
Christian community and through it proceeded to stamp his own
stern image on the character of eastern Syrian and northern Persian
Christianity for years to come.[96]

No two people could be more unlike each other than Tatian of
Assyria and Bardaisan of Edessa, Asia's first theologians. The lonely
recluse and Bible translator of Adiabene and the jeweled courtier and
inventive philosopher of Osrhoene had little in common. But of
the two it was Tatian whose influence longest endured, for Tatian
brought the Bible, not philosophy, to the Church of the East.

The church in Asia east of Rome already had the Old Testament,
of course, thanks to its Jewish-Christian roots. But it was Tatian who

brought to those Judaic roots the good news of the written Gospels. On the foundation of the record of the mighty acts of God through Israel he placed the cornerstone, the revelation of the saving work of God in Jesus Christ.

But neither the Old Testament nor the Gospel record of the Syrians was quite like that of the Western church. Their Old Testament was not the Septuagint Greek version used by Christians in the Hellenistic world, nor was it the original Hebrew text. The Syrian churches used the Aramaic version of the Palestinian synagogues. This was a paraphrase that added to the text numerous explanations and illustrations.[97]

Tatian's version of the Gospels was also different in form from that in which they appear in our New Testament. As we all know, in the fluid years of early church growth the New Testament did not take shape all at once. The earliest books were probably the Gospel of Mark and some of Paul's Epistles, written from about A.D. 60, not long after the death of Jesus. By 100 the New Testament was substantially complete.[98] But it was still not gathered together into a single authoritative whole, which is why the personal testimony of the apostles who had actually seen and heard Jesus was considered so important. As the apostles died, followed by their disciples who had heard directly from the apostles' lips the words of Jesus, others arose claiming to be disciples also, but with contrary teachings like Marcion, or with different scriptures and strange gospels like the Gnostics. It suddenly became of extreme importance for the churches to know which writings contained the real teachings of Jesus and the apostles.

The process by which the twenty-seven canonical books came to be recognized as the New Testament began about the middle of the second century and was completed in the West by the end of the fourth century. The Synod of Hippo Regius in 393 and of the Synod of Carthage in 397 made official what most Western churches by then had already accepted.[99] But in the East, where the churches outside the Roman Empire were imperceptibly beginning to separate from the West, the process took longer.

As late as the beginning of the sixth century some of the books accepted in the West, like 2 Peter, 2 and 3 John, Jude, and Revelation, were still not generally read in most Eastern churches.[100] On the other hand, some apocryphal books not recognized in the West as apostolic were widely popular in the East, such as the *Acts of Thomas* and, to a lesser extent, the *Gospel of Thomas*. When Tatian came back from Rome to his homeland he found the East full of such dubious and apocryphal "Gospels" and "Acts." He set about, therefore, to produce an authentic life of Christ in Syriac, translated from the four canonical Gospels as he had studied them in Rome, a work he may have already begun before he left the West. It was not, however, a direct translation of the original Greek Gospels. Instead, he arranged it as a harmony of the Gospels and called it the *Diatessaron*, which means "through Four."[101] So for the first few centuries of the Asian church, its most widely used New Testament collection of the apostolic Scriptures began not with the four separate Gospels but with Tatian's convenient arrangement that wove together as consecutive history the four parallel accounts of Matthew, Mark, Luke, and John. There is some dispute as to which is the oldest translation of the Gospels from the original Greek. Some say the Old Syriac separate Gospels. Some say the Old Latin. But an emerging conclusion by many scholars is that the earliest of all was Tatian's *Diatessaron*, about A.D. 170.[102] This would mean that the first translation of a major section of the New Testament into any language was made in Asia.

It is a measure of the importance of Bible translation in the growth of the church that it was not until Tatian took the Gospels out of what he considered to be their imprisonment in the Greek language of Roman Asia and put them into Syriac, the language of the common people in the villages, that Christianity began to spread outside the Greek-speaking cities into the Asian countryside.[103] Syriac, the language of Edessa and Adiabene and the Euphrates Valley, was a form of Aramaic similar to the language of Jesus. It was this Syriac, not Palestinian Aramaic, moreover, that was the language of the whole Syrian and Mesopotamian world, the trading *lingua franca* of the ancient Asian Middle East. It became the ecclesiastical language of the church of the East as Latin became the language of the Western church. It was the literary cutting edge for missionary expansion into Asia.

Tatian was emphatically and unashamedly Asian. "I am an Assyrian," he said proudly in his *Address to the Greeks*,[104] the only one of his writings to survive in its entirety. The whole thrust of that work is a recapitulation of all the ways in which Asia (the whole non-Greek world, in fact, for he includes ancient North Africa) excels the West. Where did the Greeks learn their astronomy? he asks. From Babylon (in Asia). Their alphabet? From the Phoenicians (also Asia). Their poetry and music? From Phrygia (Asia Minor). Their postal system? From Persia. "In every way the East excels," said Tatian (to summarize and paraphrase his argument), "and most of all in its religion, the Christian religion, which also comes from Asia and which is far older and truer than all the philosophies and crude religious myths of the Greeks."[105]

TATIAN AND THE ENCRATITES

There is no doubt that Tatian's pride in his own Asian heritage and his devotion to authentic Bible translation make him worthy of all praise as one of the earliest Asian church fathers, but he is not beyond criticism. He is also remembered for an exaggerated emphasis on the merits of radical asceticism, an emphasis that deeply affected the character of the early Eastern church. Western theologians who attacked it named it as the heresy of Encratism. The word means "self-control" but as used in this connection it signifies abnormal self-denial and an insistence on the separation of Christians from the world because of the belief that matter is evil, which taints it with a touch of Gnosticism.

According to his opponents in the Western church, such as Jerome, Tatian was therefore a heretic. There are hints even in the *Address to the Greeks* that he did indeed regard the world of matter as evil. The "ignorant soul" without the light of the Logos, he says, "if it continues solitary . . . tends downward toward matter, and dies with the flesh." And again, "Matter desired to exercise lordship over the soul" and "gave laws of death to man."[106] Some see Encratite emphases also in his translation of Gospel texts in the *Diatessaron* and perhaps even additions to the text from outside sources.[107] But it is in the writings of his Western opponents who accused him of heresy (the Asian church did not) that he is charged with expressing even more extreme positions in works that have not survived. It is in these writings that he is said to have forbidden the eating of meat, the drinking of wine, and even the joys of marriage. Jerome, for example, writes:

> Tatian . . . the very violent heresiarch of the Encratites, employs an argument of this sort: "If any one sows to the flesh, of the flesh he shall reap corruption"; but he sows to the flesh who is joined to a woman; therefore he who takes a wife and sows in the flesh, of the flesh he shall reap corruption.[108]

Tatian has been defended from the attacks of his Western critics on the grounds that ascetic self-denial is thoroughly scriptural and that even if he did carry his renunciation of the world further than the scriptural norm, his position was not at all abnormal judged by

Asian religious ideals. His orientalizing of the Christian faith, writes
P. Carrington, was no more of a distortion than his opponents' hellenizing of it.[109] That may be partly true, but if his opponents'
accusations are also true, it is difficult to defend so radical a condemnation of material things that he should begin to wonder
whether a God who would create the world of matter could really be
the supreme God. And Tatian is further accused of going so far in
his revulsion against sex that he expressed some doubt, apparently,
as to whether Adam was really saved or that Jesus could be a physical descendant of David.[110]

For reasons such as these his opponents labeled Tatian "the
father of the Encratites," the radical ascetics of the Syrian deserts and
mountains. Whatever their motives, good or bad, whether they were
zealously eager to follow biblical patterns of self-denial or were led
astray by a less than Christian desire for merit or by philosophic (and
Gnostic) distrust of the world of physical matter, the Encratite hermits quickly became the popular models of sainthood in the Syrian
church.

Ascetic monasticism, in fact, may actually have originated in
Syria rather than in Egypt, as is usually stated. Athanasius (ca. 295–
373) called St. Antony of Egypt "the founder of asceticism." But it
was not until 270 that St. Antony renounced the world for the lonely
life and fought against demons in the desert, whereas Tatian, the
father of the Encratites, lived a whole century earlier. The solitary
recluses of the Syrian wastes were even more fanatical than their
Egyptian counterparts. They chained themselves to rocks. They bent
their bodies under iron weights. They walled themselves up in
caves. The earliest of them, according to later tradition, was Atones
(or Aones) who is said to have lived like a wild beast in the caves
near Edessa, by the well where Jacob met Rachel. The only food he
allowed himself to touch was uncooked grass.[111]

The same tone of abnormal self-denial runs through the *Acts of
Thomas*, which is as important for the way it mirrors the popular faith
of early Syrian Christians in Edessa at the end of the second century
as for the clues it gives to the history of the Thomas Christians in
India. This is how it describes Thomas:

> Continually he fasts and prays, and eats only bread and salt and drinks
> water, and he wears one garment whether in fine weather or foul, and
> takes nothing from anyone for himself, and what he has he gives to
> others. (*Acts Thom.* 2:19–20; 9:104)

According to the same account, Thomas the apostle behaves much
like the later Encratites. He considers marriage sinful. He is invited

to sing at the wedding of a royal princess and his song speaks so persuasively of the only "incorruptible and true marriage," which is union with God and not with man or woman, that the royal bride and groom renounce the joys of married life and consecrate themselves in perpetual virginity to Jesus Christ, the Heavenly Bridegroom (*Acts Thom.* 1:5–16).

Encratism, as described in such apocryphal *Acts* of the apostles, was an old heresy. It was much like what Paul condemns in 1 Timothy 4:1–6:

> The Spirit has explicitly said that during the last times there will be some who will desert the faith and choose to listen to deceitful spirits and doctrines that come from the devils . . . ; they will say marriage is forbidden, and lay down rules about abstaining from foods which God created to be accepted with thanksgiving by all who believe and know the truth. Everything God has created is good . . .

Nevertheless, it was just such an unorthodox asceticism, tainted by its apparent link with Gnostic heresy, that spread from Syria and Egypt and persisted well into the fourth and fifth centuries. Irenaeus, writing about 185, found it as far west as Gaul and blamed it on Tatian, the Easterner,[112] for it was in the East that it put down its deepest roots and appeared in so many forms that it is often difficult to distinguish between what was considered orthodox and unorthodox in the asceticism of the Eastern church.

Asceticism and Asian Missions

Not all the discipline of the early Asian church was centered on separation and withdrawal from the world. There was a missionary dynamic also in its faith that sent believers out into the pagan world to preach the gospel. And though Edessa of Osrhoene was traditionally the first base of missionary expansion to the East, Arbela of Adiabene was also to become a major center for missions beyond Mesopotamia into eastern Persia and central Asia.

In the very earliest Christian documents of the East, the call to ascetic self-denial is almost always associated with the call to go and preach and serve. This seems to have been the most striking difference between Syrian and Egyptian saint-ascetics. Egypt, more solidly agricultural, valued stability and tended to withdraw from outside contacts and movements.[113] Its saints ignored the world and retreated to their caves and cells. Syria, on the other hand, with its travel and trading traditions, stressed mobility and outreach. Its ascetics became wandering missionaries, healing the sick, feeding the poor, and preaching the gospel as they moved from place to place. R. Murray describes them as "homeless followers of the homeless Jesus on . . . ceaseless pilgrimage through this world."[114]

In the traditions of the first missionaries of the East there is the same note of wandering mission, of moving out across the world for Christ. Thomas in India gives thanks that he has become . . . an ascetic and a pauper and a wanderer for God (*Acts Thom.* 6:60–61; 12:139, 145, and *passim.*). And Addai refuses to receive silver and gold from the king of Edessa, saying that he has forsaken the riches of this world "because without purses and without scrips, bearing the cross upon our shoulders, we were commanded to preach the Gospel in the whole creation."[115] The *Gospel of Thomas*, that mixture of tradition and nonconformity found in Egypt but attributed to Edessa, exhorts the faithful to "become wanderers," perhaps as a call to mission. It declares that traveling and healing are higher calls than fasting, praying, and giving alms. And it quotes the Lord's call to missionary action—"The harvest is great but the laborers are few"—and repeats it again with a dramatic twist, "Many are round the opening but nobody in the well" (*Gos. Thom.* 9, 112, 77, 78).

The early traditional histories name Addai, Aggai, and Mari as the first missionaries to the farther east. The *Doctrine of the Apostles* relates that Addai was the pioneer who planted the church in Edessa, in Nisibis (Soba), and in Arabia and the borders of Mesopotamia. His disciple, Aggai, is credited with the apostolate to "the whole of Persia of the Assyrians and Armenians and Medians, and of the countries round about Babylon, the Huzites and the Gelai [i.e., on the Caspian Sea], even to the borders of the Indians, and even to the country of Gog Magog."[116] Another line of tradition centers around the missionary, Mari, another disciple of Addai.[117]

Perhaps Aggai and Mari were both early missionaries to Persia beyond the Tigris, though the accounts are unreliable and the sweeping geographic references must be treated with caution. There is something appealingly believable, however, about the story of Mari. In the tradition, this disciple of Addai, the disciple of Thomas, was, like the doubting apostle himself, a reluctant missionary. Sent out from Edessa "to the regions of the east," he became discouraged and begged the church at home to release him from his mission and allow him to return. But the church ordered him to persist. So obediently but grudgingly he set himself to the evangelization of Persia and set off on an arduous series of missionary journeys that brought him almost to India. There, when as he said he "smelt the smell of the Apostle Thomas," he felt at last that he had done his duty and had gone far enough.[118]

There is even more reliable evidence than the reports of those questionably accurate early histories that before the end of the Parthian dynasty the Christian faith had not only penetrated Persia but had moved beyond into the steppes of central Asia. In what has been called "the oldest document in Syriac literature relating to Christianity in central Asia," a "memorable sentence" from Bardaisan's *Book of the Laws of Countries,* written about 196, he mentions Christians living as far to the east as Bactria, which is now known as northern Afghanistan.[119] From Mesopotamia to Persia, and before the end of the second century to the Turkic tribes of the heartland of Asia, the faith was unquestionably spreading across the great continent of the East as vigorously as it moved westward into Europe.

By the year 225, as the Parthian dynasty fell before the Persian Sassanids, Christian missionaries had planted communities of the faith from the Euphrates to the Hindu Kush and from Armenia to the Persian Gulf. The *Chronicle of Arbela* reports that by that time there were already more than twenty bishops in Persia, with jurisdictions from the mountains of Kurdistan in the east to the Caspian Sea in the west. "Churches multiplied, monasteries increased and on every mouth could be heard words of glorification," it said.[120]

That report may not be completely reliable, but independent historical evidence supports the assertion of extensive Christian penetration of Persia by 225. The monument of a Christian bishop, Abercius of Hierapolis in Phrygia Salutaris (Asia Minor), erected perhaps as early as the middle of the second century and not discovered until the nineteenth century, gives remarkable contemporary proof of the spreading presence of Christians beyond the Euphrates. The bishop composed his own unusual epitaph centering around his great journey west as far as Rome and east to Nisibis. "I saw the Syrian plain and all the cities, [even] Nisibis, having crossed the Euphrates. Everywhere I found people with whom to speak (i.e., Christians)." An expanded version of the epitaph tells how he met the great Bardaisan in a delegation of Christians, distinguished from all the rest by his noble bearing. The language of the bishop is guarded, for the age of persecutions was not over, but he mentions celebrating the sacraments with those he met, referring to the Eucharist symbolically in terms of "the Fish" and the chalice.[121]

This early presence of a Christian community in Nisibis between Osrhoene and Adiabene is more than another evidence of Christianity's missionary flow eastward. It suggests the possibility that Arbela, the capital of Adiabene, if not prior to Edessa as a Christian center, could well have been an independent focus for a missionary thrust in all directions throughout the Persian Empire.[122]

In less than two hundred years after the death of Christ, Syrian Christians were beginning to carry the faith not just across the Asian borders of Rome, and not into Persia alone, but out across the continent toward the steppes of the central Asiatic nomads and the edges of the Hindu Kush.

NOTES

1. Ephrem the Syrian, *Carmina Nisibena XLII,* Latin trans. G. Bickell (Leipzig: Bruckhaus, 1866), 163.

2. T. K. Joseph raises the question in "The Tomb of St. Thomas," *Kerala Studies,* 44, cited by G. M. Moraes, *A History of Christianity in India,* vol. 1 (Bombay: Manaktalas, 1964), 46.

3. J. B. Segal's *Edessa, the Blessed City* (Oxford: Clarendon, 1970) gives extensive documentation on Osrhoene's rulers, history, and culture.

4. See chap. 1, p. 11.

5. On Gundaphar as a Suren, see E. Herzfeld, "Sakastan," *Archaeologische Mitteilungen aus Iran* 4 (Berlin: 1931–32): 101n. 25.

6. Eusebius, 1.13.6–10. Abgar V reigned twice: first from 4 B.C. to A.D. 7 as thirteenth king (or toparch) and again from 13 to 50 as fifteenth king. Segal, *Edessa,* 15n.

7. Eusebius, *Historia ecclesiastica* 1.13. His direct source was probably an earlier Syriac document, perhaps the apocryphal *Acts of Thaddaeus,* written about the end of the third century, which contains the letters "from the Book of Records which is at Edessa." Segal, *Edessa,* 62 n. 3.

8. In the so-called Gelasian decree. See E. Hennecke, *New Testament Apocrypha,* vol. 1, ed. W. Schneemelcher, trans R. M. Wilson (London: Lutterworth, 1963), 49.

9. The letter of Jesus Christ was translated into all the languages of Christendom. It was engraved on church archways. It appeared on the city gate of Philippi as early as the fifth century. It can be seen in an old service book dating back to Saxon times, which is still preserved in the British Museum and in which the letter holds a position of honor immediately after the Lord's Prayer and the Apostles' Creed. See W. Cureton, *Ancient Syriac Documents* (London: 1894; reprint, Amsterdam: Oriental Press, 1967), 154ff.; Segal, *Edessa,* 73–78.

10. This work exists in two manuscripts. An early fifth-century manuscript was discovered by Cureton in 1848 and published in 1864, as cited above. A more complete but later manuscript from the Imperial Public Library of St. Petersburg dates to the sixth century and was translated and edited by

George Phillips as *The Doctrine of Addai the Apostle* (1876). The date of writing is estimated on the basis of its reference to the legendary picture of Jesus at Edessa, which was not known before 390, and because it accepts the use in Edessa of Tatian's *Diatessaron,* which was replaced in the Syrian church by the separate Gospels after the Council of Chalcedon in 431. See L. J. Tixeront, *Les Origines de l'église d'Edesse et la légende d'Abgar* (Paris: Maisonneuve et Ch. LeClerc, 1888), 10ff., 120–35.

11. Cureton, *Doctrine of Addai,* in *Ancient Syriac Documents,* 12.

12. Cureton, *Doctrine of Addai,* in *Ancient Syriac Documents,* 13–15, 21.

13. The date is variously estimated at A.D. 45 (Cureton, *Ancient Syriac Documents,* 162) and 50, which is probably more accurate (Segal, *Edessa,* 15). The new king, Ma'nu V, reigned from 50 to 57, according to Segal.

14. Cureton, *Doctrine of Addai,* in *Ancient Syriac Documents,* 13–15, 21. As the *Doctrine of Addai* describes the church's organization, Aggai was "Guide and Ruler," Palut became presbyter, and Abshelama the scribe was made deacon.

15. F. C. Burkitt, *Early Eastern Christianity* (London: Murray, 1904), 40f.

16. On the Seventy, see B. M. Metzger, "Seventy or Seventy-Two Disciples?" *Historical and Literary Studies: Pagan, Jewish, and Christian* (Leiden: Brill, 1968), 67–76. Eusebius says "Seventy"; many Syriac sources say "Seventy-two."

17. Besides the mention in Eusebius (*Historia ecclesiastica* 1.13) and the *Doctrine of Addai,* he appears in the Syriac *Acts of the Apostles,* the *Chronicle of Arbela,* and the *Acts of Sharbil.*

18. W. H. C. Frend, *Martyrdom and Persecution in the Early Church* (New York: New York Univ. Press, 1963), 99, 114f.

19. Eusebius, *Ecclesiastical History* 3.5. But see G. Ludemann, "The Successors to Pre-70 Jerusalem Christianity: A Critical Evaluation of the Pella Tradition," in E. P. Sanders, ed., *Jewish and Christian Self-Definition* (Philadelphia: Fortress, 1980), 161–73.

20. Cureton, *Doctrine of Addai, Ancient Syriac Documents,* 3, 8, 14.

21. J. R. Harris, *The Odes and Psalms of Solomon: Now First Published from the Syriac Version* (Cambridge: Cambridge Univ. Press, 1909; 2d ed., rev., 1911); and "An Early Christian Hymn-Book," *Contemporary Review* 95 (1909): 420ff.

22. J. H. Charlesworth, *The Odes of Solomon: The Syriac Texts Edited with Translation and Notes* (Oxford: Clarendon, 1973; reprint with corrections and added indices, Missoula, MT: Scholars, 1977), 1. The original language, most now agree, was Syriac. See H. Chadwick, "Some Reflections on the Character and Theology of the Odes of Solomon," in P. Granfield and J. A. Jungmann, eds., *Kyriakon,* vol. 1 (Munster: Aschendorff, 1971), 266n, citing J. A. Emerton in favor of a Syriac original but noting W. Bauer's preference for a Greek origin.

23. A first-century date is favored by Charlesworth, *Odes of Solomon,* 49, 62;

as well as by R. H. Charles, "A Church Hymnal of the First Century," *The Times Literary Supplement* 430 (London: 7 April 1910): 124; E. A. Abbott, "Light on the Gospel from an Ancient Poet," *Diatessarica*, 9 (Cambridge: Cambridge Univ. Press, 1912); M. Testuz, *Papyrus Bodmer X-XII* (Cologny-Geneve: Bibliotheque Bodmeriana, 1959), 58; and others. A. F. J. Klijn, *Edessa, Die Stadt des Apostels Thomas: Das Alteste Christentum in Syrien* (Giessen: Neukirchener Verlag des Erziehungsvereins, 1965), dates the *Odes* "beginning of the 2nd century" (42ff.). J. Quasten also prefers a second-century date, "most probably in the first half of it" *Patrology*, vol. 1 (Utrecht-Antwerp: Spectrum, 1950), 160–68. H. J. W. Drijvers dates it in the third century, reading it as anti-Marcion (cf. *Studies in Gnosticism and Hellenistic Religion*, Quispel Festschrift (Leiden, 1981). The place of origin is also debated. Testuz, dealing only with Ode 11, sees it as of Essene origin; but see J. de Zwaan, "The Edessene Origin of the Odes of Solomon," in R. P. Casey, ed., *Quantulacumque: Studies Presented to Kirsopp Lake* (London and Baltimore: Waverly, 1937), 285–302. Segal, *Edessa*, 35n. 3, also doubts the Edessene origin. Selections from five of the odes were known since 1812 as part of the *Pistis Sophia*, but much remains unknown about them. See F. M. Braun, "L'Enigme des Odes de Salomon," *Revue de Theologie et des questions religieuses* 57 (Montauban: Imprimerie Cooperative, 1957): 597ff.

24. There is also a reference to daybreak prayers in 15:1. Quotations are from Charlesworth's translation. He comments on the parallel between Ode 15 and the younger Pliny's comment to Trajan (*Epistolae* X96) that Christians in his part of Asia Minor gathered before sunrise to chant a psalm of praise to Christ (*Odes of Solomon*, 68, n.). On the form of prayer, see D. Plooij, "The Attitude of the Outspread Hands (Orante) in Early Christian Literature and Art," *Expository Times* 22 (Edinburgh, 1912): 199–203, 265–69.

25. See Charlesworth's note, "*Odes of Solomon*," 49, citing R. H. Charles, "A Church Hymn," "Such a sentiment . . . belongs to the Palestinian communities where Judaism was still dominant, and to the first rather than to the second century when Gentile bishops were elected to the See of Jerusalem itself."

26. Chadwick, "Some Reflections," 268. In his defense of the essential orthodoxy of the *Odes* Chadwick sides with F. M. Braun, *Jean le theologien et son evangile dans l'eglise ancienne* (Paris: Libre Lecoffre, 1959), 232f.; and J. Danielou, "Odes de Salomon" in *Dictionnaire de la Bible*, suppl. 7 (1960); 677–84; and stands against such as Alfred Adam, *Lehrbuch der Dogmengeschichte*, vol. 1 (Gutersloh, 1965), 142–46.

27. From about fifteen Old Testament books and twenty-two New Testament books. Charlesworth, *Odes of Solomon*, 170ff.

28. Charlesworth comments, "In Syriac 'Holy Spirit' is usually masculine, in Aramaic usually feminine . . . and in Greek neuter" (*Odes of Solomon*, 83). The *Odes* share with the early Jewish-Christian gospel the idea that the Holy spirit is feminine.

29. Charlesworth credits P. Baffitol, *Revue Biblique* (1911), with being the first

to detect traces of docetism in the *Odes;* see Charlesworth, *Odes of Solomon,* 176. For a strong docetic passage: "I was not their brother, nor was my birth like theirs" (*Ode* 28:17).

30. The implied formula is the orthodox *ex virgine,* not *per virgine* as a Valentinian Gnostic might have described it. Charlesworth, *Odes of Solomon,* 177.

31. See Charlesworth's note on the verse (*Odes of Solomon* [1973 ed.], 62), citing 1 Corinthians 12:27; Ephesians 4:11; 1 Timothy 3:2, 8; 2 Timothy 5:17; and Titus 1:5.

32. See Testuz. *Papyrus Bodmer X–XII,* 56f.; and also his *Papyrus Bodmer VII–IX* (1959).

33. See also A. Voobus, *History of Asceticism in the Syrian Orient,* vol. 1, in *CSCO,* vol. 184, Subsidia Tomus 14 (Louvain, 1958), 62f, 90f.

34. See pp. 47ff. I rely largely on Segal's *Edessa.* He lists the kings from *Abgar V, the Black* (4 B.C.–A.D. 7 and 13–50) as follows: Ma'nu V, 50–57; Ma'nu VI, 57–71; Abgar VI, 71–91; interregnum, 91–109; Abgar VII, 109–16; interregnum, 116–18; Yalur and Parthamaspat, 118–22; Parthamaspat alone, 122–23; Ma'nu VIII, 139–63; Wa'el bar Sahru, 163–65; Ma'nu VIII again, 165–77; and *Abgar VIII, the Great,* 177–212 (Segal, *Edessa,* 15).

35. Pliny, 6. 12.

36. *Chronicle of Edessa,* ed. I. Guidi, *Chronica minora,* 1 (*CSCO, Scriptores Syri,* ser. 3, vol. 4 [1903], 1–11). The translation is quoted from Segal, *Edessa,* 24f. The *Chronicle* was compiled probably in the sixth century, but it incorporates some very early portions, such as this. See L. Hallier, *Untersuchungen über die Edessenische Chronik mit dem SyrischenText und einer Übersetzung* (Leipzig: Hinrichs'sche, 1892), 9.1.

37. H. J. W. Drijvers, ed., *The Book of the Laws of Countries: Dialogue on Fate of Bardaisan of Edessa* (Assen: Van Gorcum, 1965), 59.

38. See Segal, *Edessa,* 46f.

39. Julius Africanus *Kestoi* ("Embroideries"). Only fragments of the work survive. The text is in M. Thevenot, *Veterum Mathematicorum Opera* (Paris, 1693), 300ff.; G. Syncellus, *Chronographia,* 1.676, 13th ed. (Bonn, 1829).

40. There is still, however, considerable difference of opinion among scholars as to the historicity of the king's conversion. Among those who accept it are Burkitt, *Early Eastern Christianity,* 26f.; A. Fortescue, *The Lesser Eastern Churches* (London: Catholic Truth Society, 1913), 32; the two translators of the Syriac *Doctrine of Addai* manuscripts, W. Cureton and G. Phillips; Tixeront, *Les Origines,* 10; H. Lietzmann, *History of the Early Church,* 4 vols., trans. B. L. Wolf (London: Lutterworth, 1937–51), 2:260 and H. Chadwick, *The Early Church* vol. 1, *Pelican History of the Church* (Harmondsworth, England: (Pelican), Penguin, 1967), 61. Some of the above (e.g., Lietzmann, Chadwick) confuse Abgar VIII with Abgar IX. See Segal, *Edessa,* 14 n. 1, citing *Yale Classical Studies,* 5 (1935), 150. But R. Duval reviews the same

evidence in his *Histoire politique, religieuse et literaire d'Edessa jusqu'a premiere croisade* (1892) and brings a negative verdict. So also more emphatically, W. Bauer, *Orthodoxy and Heresy in Earliest Christianity* (Philadelphia: Fortress, 1972), 4–8. Segal, *Edessa*, 69f., leans toward an undogmatic negative: "He may have been well disposed towards the Christians; he need not have actually adopted the new religion." See also A. von Gutschmid, *Untersuchungen über die Geschichte des Konigreiches Osrhoene* (Memoires de l'Academie imperiale des Sciences de S. Petersburg, ser. 7, vol. 35.1, 1887), 1ff.

41. Cureton, *The Doctrine of Addai*, in *Ancient Syriac Documents*, 18. The first use of "bishop" in the East is in an untrustworthy fourth- or fifth-century martyrology, the *Acts of Sharbil* (Cureton, *Ancient Syriac Documents*, 71).

42. Cureton, *The Doctrine of Addai* in *Ancient Syriac Documents*, 23.

43. Eusebius, *Historia ecclesiastica* 6. 11, 12.

44. Ephrem of Edessa objected that the orthodox should be called simply Christians, and only the heretics be identified by the names of their founders. See K. McVey, *Ephrem the Syrian: Hymns* (New York: Paulist, 1989), 27.

45. Segal, *Edessa*, 14. But Zephyrinus could not have consecrated Serapion.

46. There are other shadowy traditions of a succession of leaders of Edessa's church, including names such as Hystaspes, the "bishop" who converted Bardaisan, and 'Aqi, who is said to have excommunicated him, and an Iani, who was even earlier. See F. Nau, *Une Biographie Inedite de Bardesane l'Astrologue* (Paris, 1897), 5–7; and Segal, *Edessa*, 86. The attempt to trace a succession is even further confused in the *Acts of Sharbil* and the *Martyrdom of Barsamya*, which tell of a Roman persecution in Edessa in 104 in which Barsamya, "Bishop of Edessa," is condemned for converting a pagan high priest, Sharbil. Barsamya's episcopate is grandly tracked through Abshelama, to Palut, to Serapion, to Zephyrinus, to Victor, and so on back to Peter. See Cureton, *Acts of Sharbil, Ancient Syriac Documents*, 41–72.

47. W. Bauer, *Rechtglaubigkeit und Ketzerei im altesten Christentum* (Tubingen, 1934). The English translation of the 2d ed., by R. A. Kraft, G. Krodel, et al. (Philadelphia: Fortress, 1972), updates the valuable appendices by G. Strecker. The first chapter, pp. 1-43, is on Edessa.

48. Bauer, *Orthodoxy and Heresy*. See appendix 2 in the English translation for reactions to Bauer's thesis. The most extended attack was by H. F. W. Turner, *The Pattern of Christian Truth: A Study in the Relations Between Orthodoxy and Heresy in the Early Church* (London: Mowbray, 1954). A. A. T. Ehrhardt, "Christianity Before the Apostles' Creed," *Harvard Theological Review* 55 (1962): 73–119, is more sympathetic but still critical, notably of the view that Marcionites founded east Syrian Christianity.

49. Moffatt, in *The Expository Times* 45 (Edinburgh, 1933–34), quoted in appendix 2 of the English translation of Bauer, *Orthodoxy and Heresy*, 293. Other recent scholars who acknowledge a debt to Bauer's emphasis on the heresies include: H. J. W. Drijvers, in "Quq and the Quqites," *Numen* 14 (Leiden,

1967): 104–29; and Klijn, *Edessa, Die Stradt des Apostels Thomas,* and *The Acts of Thomas* (Leiden: Brill, 1962), 30ff. Helmut Koester used the phrase "pioneering monograph" in "Introduction to the Gospel of Thomas" in *Nag Hammadi Library,* James Robinson, ed. (San Francisco: Harper & Row, 1977), 117.

50. Voobus, Asceticism, 1:161.

51. Guidi, ed., *Chronicle of Edessa,* 1f.

52. For an introduction to Marcion, see J. F. Bethune-Baker, *An Introduction to the Early History of Christian Doctrine to the Time of the Council of Chalcedon* (London: Methuen, 1933), 81–84; and A. von Harnack, *Marcion, das Evangelium vom fremden Gott,* Neue Studien zu Marcion in Texte und Untersuchungen, vol. 45, 2d ed. (Leipzig: Heinrichs, 1924). See also English translation by J. E. Streets and J. D. Bierma, *Marcion: The Gospel of the Alien God* (Durham, NC: Labyrinth Press, 1990.)

53. Tertullian, *Adversus Marcionem* iv. 4.5.

54. Jean Doresse, who was the first to study the manuscript, suggests an Edessene origin in the first or second centuries, in his *The Secret Books of the Egyptian Gnostics . . . with English Translation and Critical Evaluation of the Gospel According to Thomas,* Eng. trans. P. Mairet (London: Hollis and Carter, 1960). H. Koester attributes it to Syria, Palestine, or Mesopotamia "possibly as early as the second century." G. Quispel dates it 140 in "Gnosticism and the New Testament" in J. P. Hyatt, ed., *The Bible in Modern Scholarship* (London: Kingsgate, 1965), 253 passim.

55. The literature is immense. Good introductions include F. C. Burkitt, *Church and Gnosis* (Cambridge, England: University, Press, 1932); R. M. Wilson, *The Gnostic Problem* (London: Mowbray, 1958); R. M. Grant, *Gnosticism and Early Christianity* (New York: Columbia University Press, 1959); K. R. Rudolph, *The Nature and History of Gnosticism* (San Francisco: Harper & Row, 1982).

56. Cited by A. D. Nock, "Gnosticism," in *A. D. Nock: Essays on Religion and the Ancient World,* ed. Z. Stewart (Oxford: Clarendon Press, 1972), 2: 943.

57. The standard text in English is the translation by T. O. Lambdin, in Robinson, ed., *Nag Hammadi Library,* 117–30. Numberings in different editions and translations vary. For the story of the discovery, see Robinson's introduction, and Doresse, *The Secret Books.*

58. Robinson, *Nag Hammadi Library,* 118.

59. Robinson, *Nag Hammadi Library,* 130.

60. Doresse, *The Secret Books,* 348f.; Quispel, "Gnosticism and the New Testament," 253ff.

61. Drijvers, "Quq and the Quqites," 104.29. He rejects Harnack's contrast of Quqites as Gnostic Christian Jews and Bardesanites as gentile Christian Gnostics.

62. Bethune-Baker, *Christian Doctrine,* 85f. See also F. Legge, *Forerunners and*

Rivals of Christianity from 330 B.C. to A.D. 330. vol. 2 (1915; New Hyde Park, NY: University Books, 1964), 25–82.

63. The phrase is James Moffatt's, *The First Five Christian Centuries of the Church* (London: Univ. of London, Hodder and Stoughton, 1938), 78. For more on the process of an emerging Christian sense of orthodoxy in the early church see E. P. Sanders, ed., *Jewish and Christian Self-Definition,* vol. 1, *The Shaping of Christianity in the Second and Third Centuries* (London: SCM, 1980), esp. the articles by R. A. Marcus "The Problem of Self-Definition: From Sect to Church," and J. Pelikan, "The Two Sees of Peter," and A. H. Armstrong, "The Self-Definition of Christianity in Relation to Later Platonism." In the latter, Armstrong points to three features of Christianity that contributed to the development of a "normative self-definition": the emancipation from Judaism, the rejection of Gnosticism, and the sense of missionary vocation.

64. The traditional biography of Bardaisan is found in several variants: the earliest (tenth century) is by Agapius of Mabbug in his *Kitab-al-'Unwan,* ed. A. Vasiliev, PO 7 (Paris, 1911), 518. This was copied with additions in the twelfth century by Michael the Syrian in his *Chronicle,* trans. and ed. Nau, *Une Biographie Inedite de Bardesane l'Astrologue.* Another biographical sketch by Bar Hebraeus in his *Chronicon Ecclesiasticum* (thirteenth century) is based on that of Michael. The best recent study of Bardaisan is H. J. W. Drijvers, *Bardaisan of Edessa,* trans G. E. van Baaren-Pape (Assen: Van Gorcum, 1966). See his criticisms of the traditional biographies, 186ff., 217ff.

65. Segal, *Edessa,* 32. The reference is to Julius Africanus *Kestoi.*

66. Burkitt, *Early Eastern Christianity,* 157.

67. Eusebius, *Historia ecclesiastica,* 4.30, 3. Eusebius indicates that Bardaisan was first a heretic (Valentinian), then orthodox, then somewhat heretical again. Epiphanius (*Panarion* 56) states just the opposite, that he was first orthodox and later became Valentinian. The Eastern fathers imply a gradual drift into unorthodoxy. See Drijvers, *Bardaisan,* 167–185.

68. Drijvers, *Bardaisan,* citing Eusebius, Epiphanius, Hippolytus, Augustine (*De Haeresibus,* c.35), etc.

69. This summary follows Bethune-Baker, *Christian Doctrine,* 88ff.

70. Hippolytus, *Bardaisan Philosophoumena (Refutatio)* 6. 35, cited by Drijvers, 167f. Hippolytus calls Bardaisan "Ardesianes."

71. Drijvers, *Bardaisan,* 127–61, lucidly summarizes the extensive and abrasive comments of Ephrem against Bardaisan.

72. A. Hilgenfeld, *Bardesanes, der letzte Gnostiker* (Leipzig: Weigel, 1864). A long list of other scholars who have classified Bardaisan as a Gnostic includes Lipsius (1863), Harnack (1894), R. Duval (1900), della Via (1920), and G. Widengren (1952). Widengren, however, emphasizes correctly the Iranian syncretistic character of Bardaisan's "gnosticism." See Drijvers again, *Bardaisan,* 1–59, for a review of the scholarship on Bardaisan.

73. Drijvers, *Book of the Laws*. For much of the analysis of Bardaisan's thought I am indebted to this translation of the *Dialogue on Fate* and to the same author's biography, *Bardaisan*.

74. See H. H. Schaeder, "Bardesanes von Edessa in der Überlieferung der griechischen und syrischen Kirch," in *Zeitschrift für Kirchengeschichte* 51 (Stuttgart, 1932); 21–74. Schaeder sees Bardaisan essentially as a Christian humanist, not a Gnostic.

75. Ephrem the Syrian, *Hymnen contra Haereses*, ed. E. Beck, *CSCO* (1957), 75.1:11.

76. Bardaisan's trinity appears not in the *Book of the Laws*, but in his hymns, which survived only in quotations from his enemy, Ephrem. See Drijvers, *Bardaisan*, 143ff. The quotation on the unity of God, however, is from Drijvers, *Book of the Laws*, 28, 30.

77. Drijvers, *Book of the Laws*, 26, 32. "And now it is evident that we men are led in the same way by our natural constitution, in different ways by Fate, but by our liberty each as he will."

78. Here Bardaisan's own words, as given in the *Book of the Laws*, must be supplemented by Ephrem's references to his teaching in his *Prose Refutations* and *Hymns*. See Drijvers, *Bardaisan*, 152–57. On his attitude toward sex, see 190, 226.

79. Drijvers, *Bardaisan*, 110f. Barhadbesabba 'Arbaia was the only one to accuse the Bardesanites of having other revelations. See F. Nau, *La premiere partie de l'histoire de Barhadbesabba 'Arbaia*, trans. and ed. from Syriac in *Patrologia Orientalis*, vol. 23 (Paris, 1932).

80. Drijvers, *Bardaisan*, 137–43.

81. The cosmology here summarized is described by Ephrem in *Hymn* 55. Drijvers, *Bardaisan*, 143–52, maintains the reference is to Bardaisan; but H. H. Schraeder, in his "Bardesanes," 61, is not so sure and thinks the teaching may have been that of Bardaisan's son or later followers.

82. W. Wright, ed., "Two Epistles of Jacob of Edessa," *Journal of Sacred Literature*, N. Series, 10 (1867): 430–60. The biography mentioned is that of Michael the Syrian (twelfth century).

83. Moses of Khorene, *Histoire d'Armenie* 2. 66.

84. Segal, *Edessa*, 14ff.

85. Segal, *Edessa*, 65, 69. See also his reviews of E. M. Yamauchi's *Gnostic Ethics and Mandaenan Origins*, and A. F. J. Klijn's, *The Acts of Thomas*, in *Bulletin of the School of Oriental Studies* 36 (London, 1973): pt. 1, p. 135, and 27 (London, 1965): 143–45, respectively.

86. Josephus, *Antiquities* 20.17ff. See Jacob Neusner, "The Conversion of Adiabene to Judaism," *Journal of Biblical Literature* 83, no. 1 (1964): 60–66.

87. Cureton, *Doctrine of the Apostles, Ancient Syriac Documents*, 34.

88. J. B. Abbeloos, ed., "Acta Sancta Maris, Assyriae, Babyloniae ac Persidis seculo I Apostoli . . .," in *Analecta Bollandiana*, 55 (Brussels: 1885): 43–138.

89. A. Mingana, ed. and trans., *Sources Syriaques*, vol. 1, *Msiha-zkha, Texte et Traduction* (Leipzig: Harrasowitz, 1907), 77f., often referred to as the *History of the Church of Adiabene* or the *Chronicle of Arbela*.

90. Mingana, in his *Sources Syriaques*, gives it the subtitle *Histoire de l'Eglise d'Adiabene*; C. E. Sachau's German translation is titled *Die Chronik von Arbela* (1915). The manuscript itself had no title and the first lines were missing.

On the date and authenticity of the Arbela *Chronicle* (or *History*), attributed by Mingana to a Syrian, Msiha-zkha, Prof. Sidney Griffith guided me to an article by Khalil Samir, *Alphonse Mingana, 1878-1937, Occasional Paper No. 7*, (Birmingham, Eng.: Selly Oak Colleges, 1990). Cf. sharp criticisms of Mingana by J. M. Fiey, "Auteur et date de la chronique d'Arbels" in *L'Orient Syrien*, 12 (1967), 265-302. See also more positive comments by S. P. Brock in *Bulletin of the John Rylands Library*, 50 (1967), 200; and a defense of the accuracy of the parts of the *Chronicle* to 340 AD by W. G. Young, *Patriarch, Shah and Caliph* (Rawalpindi, India: Christian Study Centre, 1974), 8-11; and J. Neusner, "The Conversion of Adiabene to Christianity," *Numen*, 12 (1966), 144-150; and W. Hage, "Early Christianity in Mesopotamia: Some remarks concerning the authenticity of the Chronicle of Arbela," *The Harp*, 1, 2 & 3 (Kottayam, India: 1988), 39-46.

91. The episcopal succession is given as follows: Pkidha (104-114), Semsoun (120-123), Isaac (135-148), Abraham (148-163), Noh (163-179), Habel (183-190), Abedhmsiha (190-225), Hiran (225-258), Saloupha (258-273), Ahadabuhi (273-291), Sri'a (291-317), Iohannon (317-346), Abraham (346-347), Maranzkha (347-376), Soubhaliso (376-407), Daniel (407-431), Rhima (431-450), Abbousta (450-499), Joseph (499-511), Huana (511-?). Mingana, *Sources Syriaques*, 157f.

92. The text uses a Sassanian name for a Parthian king, perhaps as a generic term for "emperor." Both the Adiabene and Edessene martyr stories are equally confused on names and dates (see Mingana, *Sources Syriaques*, 1:79ff.).

93. Cureton, *Acts of Sharbil, Ancient Syriac Documents*, 41–63. The date of the persecution is given as "the fifteenth year of . . . Trajan Caesar" (i.e., 112), and "the third year of King Abgar the Seventh" (111), and "the year 416 of the . . . Greeks" (104–105).

94. Pliny the Younger, *Letters* 10. 96.3–4, 8.

95. Justin Martyr, *Dialogue with Trypho*, esp. 47, 48 and *First Apology* 67. Christians, he said, in his *Apology*, read the "memoirs of the apostles" along with the "writings of the prophets" at their Sunday services.

96. Strangely, no early Syriac writers mention Tatian but his influence was pervasive, notably in Syriac use of his *Diatessaron*, and his reputation as a pioneer ascetic. On his life see G. Bardy's article in *Dictionnaire de Theologie Catholique*, vol. 15 (pt. 1, 1946), cols. 59–66.

97. Voobus, *History of Asceticism* 1:8. See also his *Peschitta und Targumim des Pentateuchs: Neues Licht zur Frage der Herkunft der Peschitta aus den altpalesti-*

nischen Targumim. Handeschriftenstudien, in Papers of the Estonian Theological Society in Exile, 9 (Stockholm, 1957).

98. F. F. Bruce, *The New Testament Documents,* 5th ed. (Leicester: Inter-Varsity, 1960), 12ff. Cf. P. R. Ackroyd and C. F. Evans, eds., *The Cambridge History of the Bible* (Cambridge: Cambridge Univ. Press, 1970), 1:332ff.

99. Bruce, *New Testament Documents,* 21–28.

100. Bruce, *New Testament Documents,* 26.

101. For the history of the text see B. Metzger, "Witnesses to Tatian's Diatessaron," in his *Chapters in the History of New Testament Textual Criticism* (Grand Rapids: Eerdmans, 1963), 97–102; and "Recent Contributions to the Study of the Ancient Versions of the New Testament," in Hyatt, ed., *Bible in Modern Scholarship,* 352–55.

102. "There can be little doubt that the first form of the gospels in Syriac was the *Diatessaron,*" say Ackroyd and Evans, eds., *Cambridge History of the Bible,* 1:34. B. Metzger, *The Text of the New Testament,* 2d ed. (Oxford: 1968), 69, 72, 89–92, dates the *Diatessaron* about 170, the Old Syriac at the "close of the second or beginning of the third century," and the Old Latin, "last quarter of the second century." But Altaner opines that Tatian used an Old Syriac translation already in existence. Berthold Altaner, *Patrology,* English translation by H. C. Graef (New York: Herder & Herder, 1958), 128. See also A. Voobus, *Early Versions of the New Testament . . . ,* in Papers of the Estonian Theological Society in Exile (Stockholm, 1954). See extensive bibliography in Quasten. *Patrology,* vol. 1 (Utrecht-Antwerp, 1950), 225–28.

103. Burkitt, *Early Eastern Christianity,* 12.

104. Tatian, *Address to the Greeks* 42. English translation in *The Ante-Nicene Fathers,* vol. 3 (New York: Scribner, 1903).

105. Tatian, *Address to the Greeks* 1, 21, 29, 31–34.

106. Tatian, *Address to the Greeks* 13, 15.

107. Voobus, *Early Versions,* 5f., 20f., which sees Tatian weaving into his gospel harmony "extracanonical traditions borrowed from the Aramaic Gospel according to the Hebrews." See also his analysis of Encratite passages in the *Diatessaron* in his *History of Asceticism,* 1:39–45.

108. Jerome, *Commentary on Galatians.* See also Irenaeus *Adversus haeresas* 1. 28.1; and Tertullian *De ieiunio adversus psychicos (On Fasting)* 15f.

109. P. Carrington, *The Early Christian Church* (Cambridge: Cambridge Univ. Press, 1957), 164.

110. Irenaeus *Adversus haereses* 3. 23.8, as cited by Voobus, *History of Asceticism,* 1:36.

111. Sozomen, *Ecclesiastical History* 6. 33.

112. Irenaeus, *Adversus haeresus* 1.

113. R. Murray, *Symbols of Church and Kingdom: A Study in Early Syriac Tradition* (Cambridge: Cambridge Univ. Press, 1975), 29.

114. Murray, *Symbols*, 28n, attributing the suggestion to A. Guillemont, "Le depaysement comme forme d'ascese dans le monachisme ancien," *Annuaire de l'École Pratique des Hautes Études, Sect. Sc. Rel.*, 77 (1968–69): 31–58.

115. Cureton, *Doctrine of Addai, Ancient Syriac Documents*, 7.

116. Cureton, *Doctrine of the Apostles, Ancient Syriac Documents*, 34. See also A. Mingana, "The Early Spread of Christianity in Central Asia and the Far East," *John Rylands Library Bulletin*, vol. 9, no. 2 (July 1925): 302.

117. Abbeloos, "Acta Sancta Maris."

118. Abbeloos, "Acta Sancta Maris," esp. xxxii.

119. "Nor do our (Christian) sisters among the Gilanians and Bactrians (Kushans) have any intercourse with strangers." Drijvers, *Book of the Laws*, 61. See A. Mingana's comments on the significance of the quotation in his "Early Spread of Christianity in Central Asia," 301.

120. *Msiha-zkha*, in Mingana, *Sources Syriaques*, 103, 106ff. The names of seventeen of the bishoprics are given. Nisibis is specifically mentioned as not yet having a bishop.

121. The monument was discovered by W. M. Ramsay in 1883. Its inscription is more to be trusted than the fourth-century *Life of Abercius*, which expands the description of his journey with such details as the meeting with Bardaisan. The text of the inscription is in Quasten, *Patrology*, 1:172, who remarks that it is "the queen of all ancient Christian inscriptions," the oldest monument of stone mentioning the Eucharist.

122. See Murray, *Symbols*, 8ff.

Chapter 4
The Sassanid Revolution and the Church

"Imagine my joy when I heard that the fairest districts of Persia are full of those men on whose behalf I am speaking, the Christians. . . . Because your power is great, I ask you to protect them."

—Constantine the Great to Shah
Shapur II, according to
Theodoret

ABOUT the year 226 a revolution so changed the course of Persian history that, slowly at first, then with increasing momentum, the country's scattered groups of Christians were caught up in the changes. In that year the Parthian kings of Persia were defeated by a new dynasty, the Sassanids, a strong line of monarchs who ruled the empire for the next four centuries.[1] This marks a transition in Asian church history from the Syrian period to the Persian era.

The language of the church remained Syriac, but its organizational center shifted east to the Persian capital of Seleucia-Ctesiphon. Its theological center moved across the border from Edessa to Nisibis. As its ties with the Roman and Greek West accordingly loosened, it forged new bonds in the East with India's Thomas Christians, and before the end of the dynasty it reached out in a missionary advance that carried Christianity into the heart of China.

While the Persians were rising to new heights of imperial power, Rome slipped into a long century of embarrassing decline. Shortly before the Persian revolution, in about 214, Rome had stripped the kingdom of Osrhoene of its independence and seemed about to embark on a new age of expansion eastward. Instead, Rome weakened and Persia moved west. Looking back on the third century, later Roman historians marked Alexander Severus, who became emperor in 222 at the age of thirteen, as the last great Roman emperor for a hundred years. Rome's humiliation ended only when again a strong emperor, unexpectedly a Christian, emerged to bring back pride and power to the throne of the Caesars.[2] But from the early third century to the age of Constantine at the beginning of the fourth century, no other emperors on earth could match the wealth and might of the Sassanid shahs of Persia.

Rome and the Sassanid Shahs

This shift in world power from West to East, from a humbled Rome to the easy arrogance of the new Iranians, is nowhere more dramatically portrayed than on the triumphal rock carvings of Shapur I hewn in gigantic relief at Bishapur about A.D. 260. The Persian "shah-of-shahs" sits in victory astride his battle charger, three Roman emperors at his feet. One (Gordian III) lies dead, trampled beneath the horse's hooves. Another (Philip the Arab) kneels before the Persian, pleading for mercy with arms outstretched. The third (Valerian) is simply held contemptuously by the wrist like a little boy pulled along behind the conqueror's war horse.[3]

Another monument from that time also still survives, a monument to a different spirit. Northwest about eight hundred miles from the great rock figures at Bishapur, a small Roman garrison town once stood on the west bank of the Euphrates River, Dura-Europos. About 250 as the legions fell back before Shapur's advancing Persians, Rome abandoned the fort and the Persians destroyed it. For seventeen centuries its crumbling ruins lay open to the sun and the wandering Bedouins. Then in 1920 a British military detachment digging trenches uncovered a part of the ancient city wall that had collapsed, burying and preserving a narrow strip of the town much as the ashes of Vesuvius had in a much larger way covered Pompeii. Archaeologists carefully removed the fallen wall. A small building they uncovered proved to be unusually significant. It was a Christian church, the first complete church building that has ever been found. It was in remarkable condition. Sometime apparently between 230 and 250 a small group of Christians in that border town had taken a private home, perhaps the house-church in which they had been meeting, as was the Christian custom, and had remodeled it to serve specifically as a church. Because the town was Roman and because Christians were persecuted under Rome, they left the outer rooms plain and undecorated as before, to avoid attracting unfriendly attention. But they had completely transformed an inner room into a chapel. In the very front, beneath a central arch, was a low stone baptistry where new Christians were brought to enter the water as a sign of their dying to sin and rising again in new birth.

The most spectacular discoveries of all were the paintings on the wall, primitive but clear, not of an oriental monarch destroying his enemies as at Bishapur, but of a Good Shepherd who gives his life for his sheep and of a King who conquers death. The pictures are of Christ carrying the lost sheep and of the three Marys coming to the empty tomb.[4]

Those fragile paintings of the Christians at conquered Dura-Europos, which have lasted as long as the rock-wall carvings of the Persian shah, are a reminder that not all conquest is by force of arms, and that even as Shapur's armies were moving west, little congregations of Christians were moving east, spreading down the Euphrates across Persia and deeper into Asia.

Although the Sassanian revolution did indeed bring radical change into the life of the church in Persia, there was for the first hundred years at least little outward alteration in the church's situation. The monument at Bishapur was a nationalist exaggeration of the new surge in Iranian power. The hot-blooded Persians were capable of blinding bursts of conquest, as when Shapur I in 260 swept through Edessa and burned Antioch, but they found difficulty in sustained campaigns and detested winter warfare. What they won, they could quickly lose, and they soon lost Edessa again back to the Romans. The unstable border in this period usually followed a line running between Edessa and Nisibis, with Nisibis falling on the Persian side. But though Edessa was now politically Roman, its closest ties in culture and religion were still with the Syriac-speaking peoples of Persian Mesopotamia or of the east Syrian countryside, not with the Greek-speaking cities of Roman Syria. Edessa thus remained for some time the continuing center of Syriac Christianity on both sides of the border.

It is important to remember that the Roman-Persian border did not yet divide Christianity into East and West. The sense of Christian unity was still strong, though that unity was more spiritual and cultural than ecclesiastical and political. So in spite of the external changes that began to sweep around the Church of the East with the coming of the Sassanids, its feeling of fellowship with the churches of the West remained unbroken. As Bardaisan, one of the most Persian of Edessa's early Christians had said, unity in Christ is stronger than any differences of race or nation. The Christian faith had produced a "new race":

> What shall we say about ourselves, the new race of Christians whom Christ has raised up in all cities and all countries by His own coming? We are all called Christians, by the one name of Christ, wherever we may be found. On the day of Sunday we come together, and on the appointed days we fast . . .[5]

Church Life in Third-Century Persia

A book written in this period, the Syriac *Didascalia Apostolorum* (*The Teaching of the Apostles*), gives the earliest detailed description that has come down to us of how the "new race of Christians" met and worshiped and ordered their affairs in these years when East met West on the Roman-Persian border. It is the oldest manual of church order extant, written about 225–250 by a bishop living between Edessa and Antioch who was probably Jewish and perhaps also a medical doctor. Though written on what was normally the Roman side of the border, it circulated in Persia where it was used by Aphrahat, for example, in the next century. In a most revealing way it opens a window on the life and practice of the early Eastern churches, for its purpose was to give simple instructions to church officers and members on Christian conduct and worship.[6]

On Sunday, the first day of the week, they were to assemble themselves without fail at the church, for if they were not there, by their absence they would "rend and scatter (Christ's) body." The bishop, who sat on a throne at the eastern end of the sanctuary, was pastor, preacher, teacher, and judge. At his side sat the presbyters (elders). A deacon acted as usher, showing each believer to his or her place, the men in front, the women behind them, and the young on the side if there was room. If not, they stood. Young women with children had a separate place along with aged women and widows. The deacons were also charged with keeping order.

> And let the deacon see that each of them on entering goes to his place, that no one may sit out of his place. And let the deacons also see that no one whispers, or falls asleep, or laughs, or makes signs.[7]

If this seems too harsh and rigid an ordering of the social pattern for a Christian fellowship, it was warmed and balanced by the book's instructions to the bishop on how to treat visitors. If a rich man or a high official enters the church, the bishop is told to take no notice of him but to go on with his preaching, offering the visitor no special seat in the congregation unless in Christian love one of the brethren wishes to offer him his seat.

> But if a poor man or woman should come . . . and especially if they are stricken in years, and there be no place for such, do thou, O bishop, with all thy heart provide a place for them even if thou have to sit upon the ground.[8]

The integrity of the *Didascalia* is unnecessarily weakened by its bungling attempt to claim direct apostolic authorship at the Council of Jerusalem (Acts 15), but the light it throws on other aspects of third-century Christian life and thought in the East is invaluable. Its theology is straightforward, biblical, and orthodox. There are only minor variations from the New Testament norm, such as an overemphasis on the efficacy of baptism and the distinction between greater and lesser sins committed after baptism.[9] But the teachings are consciously rooted in the Bible and enjoin the faithful study of the Scriptures. The author shows an acquaintance with almost all the New Testament books with the exception of Hebrews and a few of the pastoral Epistles such as 2 Timothy, Titus, and Jude. He blesses marriage and approves the grateful use of all God's good material creation, thus opposing both Gnostic heretics and Encratite extremists. He is particularly concerned about the problem of the Judaizers and sharply distinguishes between the now abrogated ceremonial laws of "the Second Legislation" (the *deuterosis*) and the eternally valid law given to Moses on the Mount. In fact he condemns the former with its "purifications, sprinklings, baptisms and distinction of meats" even more severely than does the apostle Paul. "Sufficient for the faithful," he concludes, "is the circumcision of the heart."

The *Didascalia* also strikes a blow against a form of superstitious, popular Christianity that seemed to be spreading in the third century as church growth quickened and attracted followers only half-converted from their pagan backgrounds. Some Christians seemed unable or unwilling to give up all their old habits and sins at once. To ease their consciences they rationalized themselves into thinking they could wash away the stain of each sin after it was committed by being baptized again. Against this pernicious practice the *Didascalia* flatly stated that there can be only one baptism. Willful sins, it said, are not blotted out by mere repetition of the act of baptism, for though the impenitent sinner should "bathe in all the seas and oceans and be baptized in all the rivers, still he cannot be made clean." Repentance, it insisted, remains the condition for forgiveness.[10]

The life of the Christian family in those early days was disciplined and serious. There is more than a tinge of the puritan in the *Didascalia*. The Christian man, as much as the Christian woman, is warned against overadornment and fussing with his hair or trying to improve the looks of his face. The men did not shave, and the women wore veils in public. Marriage demanded complete fidelity from both partners. If a spouse died, second marriages might be allowed, especially for widows, but a third marriage was considered a shame. As for the raising of children, viewed from our permissive age the advice of the *Didascalia* sounds almost cruel. Teach them a craft, it counsels, to keep them from idleness and debauchery. "Give them no liberty to set themselves up against you, their parents." See that they do not get together with others of their own age, for that leads to carousing, mischief, and sin; and marry them early to save them from the temptations and fierce heats of youth.[11]

But it would be a mistake to judge that age by ours and to call its Christians humorless and grim. Theirs was neither the cruelty of the pagans around them, nor the narrowness of most of the heretics they condemned. It may seem odd that a bishop holding to rules as strict as those described above could nevertheless hotly rebuke some groups with whom he differed as "puritans and sticklers for holiness"[12]; but in fact the orthodox, who were beginning to call themselves "catholic," were the moderates of their time. On the one hand they were gentler and more tolerant than Tatian or the *Acts of Thomas* in accepting the delights of food and work and conjugal love as

God's good gifts to his people. But on the other, they were more biblically based, more self-disciplined, and more aware of the needs of the poor and the imprisoned, the orphaned and the widowed, than the highborn Bardaisan. They shared what they had, whether much or little, with those who had less.[13] Compared with some of the writings of the Western church in that same period, such as those of Tertullian or Hippolytus, there is a softer tone to the *Didascalia*.[14] Through all its righteous denunciations of sin there runs like a countermelody the sweet note of God's forgiving love:

> Judge strictly, (but) afterward receive the sinner with mercy and compassion when he promises to repent. Do not listen to those who desire (to put to) death, and hate their brethren and love accusations. . . . But help them that are sore sick and exposed to danger and are sinning. . . . How abundant are the mercies of the Lord. . . . Even sinners He calls to repentance and gives them hope.[15]

The Sons and Daughters of the Covenant

The *Didascalia* thus seems to represent a moderating viewpoint in the Eastern church on an issue that at times threatened to divide it. This was the issue of radical asceticism. In one form, such as the Encratism attributed to Tatian and traced by some modern scholars to Jewish sects like the Essenes of Qumran and the community who produced the Dead Sea Scrolls, the ascetic movement was attacked as a heresy.[16] In another form it appeared as a call to a purer life, a Christian life as "sons and daughters of the Covenant," which took an uneasy but honored place as a movement within the church eventually leading on to organized monasticism. A little later, the same type of radical asceticism, but with variations, was called Messalianism and declared heretical.

The note of irritation that can be detected in the Syriac *Didascalia* toward "puritans and sticklers for holiness" is a sign of an emerging critical difference of opinion in the Eastern church about the call of the ascetics to withdrawal from the world. The desert saints not only attracted great popular reverence for their dramatic piety, they also drew followers and disciples who wanted to emulate their example; thereby they faced the church of the third and fourth centuries with the practical problem of how to find a place within the "body of Christ," the church, both for ordinary, family Christians, on the one hand, and, on the other, for the solemn, strenuous athletes of the faith who took literally the command to give up all and follow Christ. It oversimplifies the situation to portray it in the familiar terms of a division between mainline, "Great Church" Christianity and cell-group sectarianism. For one thing, it is difficult to determine from the few surviving documents which of the two emphases represented the mainstream of Christianity in eastern Syria and Mesopotamia in that early period.

Some argue that the earliest churches in the East were so dominated by the ascetic ideal that it was precisely the "puritans" and holy celibates who constituted the church, while less committed Christians with their families and their possessions were only loosely attached to it as a fringe of adherents.[17] There is no doubt that the Eastern church, far more than the Western, was strongly influenced by an ideal of celibacy and sexual abstinence as the marks of the complete Christian. It was not a question of extramarital sex. All Christians would have agreed that was forbidden. But even marital union was often considered at best a falling away from the ideal and at worst a sin. In the *Acts of Thomas* it is a "deed of shame," a "partnership of corruption," and "filthy intercourse."[18]

The asceticism of the East set aside its disciples from other Christians more by this single cultural difference—the prohibition of marriage—than by any other practice, though it also laid down strict rules of poverty and went so far in its abhorrence of wine that some insisted on celebrating the Lord's Supper with water—bread and water, not bread and wine. It was sexual abstinence, however, that was the ascetic's ideal, the mark of the complete Christian. A. Voobus has called attention to an early surviving Syrian sermon, preserved only in the Greek, that illustrates this all too vividly. The preacher sees a host of pure virgins wearing crowns of everlasting life and entering the holy city singing the song of their triumph over sin. They dance with the angels before the throne of Christ, their bridegroom. They are the pure ones. But there is a darker side to the vision. Outside the gate is a group of women weeping bitterly. They are the married women and too late they have discovered that by marriage they have excluded themselves from paradise.[19]

By the third century, if not before, this rigorous and exclusive interpretation of the meaning of Christian discipleship began to take shape as an organized movement in the church. Those who chose the harder, more dedicated way were called Covenanters, or "Sons and Daughters of the Covenant" (in Syriac, *benai-* and *benat-qeyama*).[20] In the fourth century the outlines of its discipline become clearer. It was a company of the totally committed—celibate, single-minded, and separated, those who had taken the vow to be warriors for God against the world, the flesh, and the devil. The word most characteristically used of them is "singleness," with all its overtones of virginity of body, commitment of the heart, and mystic union with the Single One, Christ, the only-begotten.[21]

Sometimes converts who were willing to add this higher vow of covenanted separation to their profession of faith as they came forward for baptism were singled out for special commendation.[22] It is even possible that in some ascetic communities only the Children of the Covenant were eligible for baptism. But it stretches the evidence to argue, as some have done, that the covenanting ascetics *were* the church in its earliest and purest form[23] and that ordinary Christians who chose to live both as citizens in the world and as members of the church represented a later deterioration of the original Christian life-style who deserved no more than a second-class status in the fellowship. The New Testament supported no such double standard, nor did the church order of the Syriac *Didascalia* in the third-century church; and by the next century it became clear that, while the Asian church might still highly respect the radical ascetics, they were not to be considered the only models of the Christian way.

Popular though the movement had become by the fourth century, the East's two greatest theologians of that period, Aphrahat the Persian and Ephrem the Syrian, both of whom may have been at one time Sons of the Covenant, nevertheless wisely refused to limit the full rights of the Christian community to the "single ones."[24] Singleness as total commitment is a praiseworthy virtue and indeed is demanded of the Christian, they taught. But when singleness is defined as a complete separation, it not only divides the sexes, it may split the church. Sometimes it simply became absurd, as when a Syriac Christian document of unknown origin, probably from the fourth century, entitled *On Virginity* attempted to counsel believers on the problems entailed in observing the traditional "kiss of peace" in congregational worship without breaking the vows of chastity and separation. The solution, seriously proposed, was to wrap the right hand carefully in one's robe before extending it modestly for a filtered kiss.[25]

Such extremism did not commend itself to the more moderate. S. P. Brock quotes the shocked reaction of a couple of Christian parents in Antioch about 380 when their son left home to join the monks in the desert. "Incomprehensible! He is the son of respectable, upper-middle-class parents with a good education and excellent prospects for a steady, comfortable life, yet he has left home and gone off to join a lot of dirty vagrants."[26] And Ephrem the Syrian, less shocked and not without a touch of admiration, but also with sadness, described the ascetics with unflattering realism. They lived with animals, he wrote, ate grass like the beasts, and perched on rocks like birds, wild, scraggle-haired, dried up, and clothed only with dirt.[27]

Missionary Outreach

But it would be a mistake to ignore the other side of the ascetic movement. Monastic spirituality was not always a separation *from;* it could also be a separation *to.* Two Christian obligations, missions and reform, often combined to rescue the movement from passive spiritual introversion, and to both missionary outreach and internal reform the ascetics, even more than other segments of the church, proved conscientiously responsive.

The ascetic communities became the major dynamic for missions in Asia from the third century on, continuing the work of the "wandering missioners" of the first two centuries.[28] In the same document, *On Virginity,* which portrays so starkly the extremes of separatism, legalism, and superstition in the movement, there is also an underlying motif emphasizing the importance of the roles of the missionary as evangelist and pastor. The ascetic is under obligation to "traverse the cities and villages as traveling missionaries, expanding the gospel and strengthening the small communities."[29] His mission is described not as withdrawal but as an advance against the forces of error and darkness. It springs from a disciplined, missionary decision "to go forth," as one document of the times phrased it, "from his home and his relationship, to depart into other regions and to throw himself into the combat of the war of death."[30]

From the third century on, as east Syrian and Persian converts responded to the missionary challenge, the edge of the church in Asia moved steadily eastward beyond the Tigris and "slowly but surely worked to diminish the immense influence of the priests of the hundred and one primitive cults of central Asia, the most important of whom were the mobeds of Zoroastrianism and the wizards of shamanism."[31]

Tradition also records evidences of a missionary expansion to the southeast in early fourth century Persia that brought together, however tenuously, the two oldest centers of Christianity in Asia outside the Roman Empire, Syro-Mesopotamia and India. About the year 300, according to the Nestorian *Chronicle of Seert:*

> In the time of Sahloupas (Shalupa) and of Papas (Papa), the two metropolitans of the Orient, and of Stephen, partriarch of Rome . . . David (or Dudi), bishop of Bassarah (al-Basra) . . . left his see and departed for India where he converted a multitude of people.[32]

A quarter of a century later, a list of bishops who signed the creed of the Council of Nicaea in 325 included one who signed himself "John the Persian, of the churches of the whole of Persia and in the great India."[33] His identity is a puzzle, as is also the location of his bishopric. Eusebius, who was also present at Nicaea, confirms the presence of a bishop from Persia at the council.[34] Some speculate that John was perhaps the bishop of Rewardashir (or Rev-ardashir), the ranking see of the province of Fars, on the land route to India. If so, the two bishoprics, Basra and Fars, would indicate early missionary connections from Persia to India both by land through Rewardashir in southeastern Persia and by sea through Basra on the Persian Gulf.

Already by the year 340 "the way to India was strewn with bishoprics" and monasteries, says Mingana.[35] They were the stepping stones of a Christian advance into southern Asia from Persia to India that antedated later waves of Christian refugees, fleeing possibly from the great Persian persecutions of Shapur. Such travelers to India may have used Christian monasteries on the shores of the Persian Gulf as havens of rest on their perilous journeys. This network of missionary monasteries began at Basra, seat of the third-century missionary bishop David, and with Rewardashir on the east side of the Gulf, which became the ecclesiastical link with the church in India. The next step was perhaps the "monastery of St. Thomas in India" on the Arabian Sea, which was reported to be the home of as many as two hundred Nestorian monks. Farther down the Gulf was the monastery of "the Black island," probably one of the islands near Bahrain. Farther still was the island of Socotra where the presence of Christians is noted as early as, and probably earlier than, the middle of the fifth century.[36] The road to India was opening up for reunion between those who called themselves the converts of St. Thomas in India and the church reputedly founded by his disciple Addai, in Edessa.

NOTES

1. The beginning of the dynasty is dated somewhere between 224 and 226. Its emperors (to 425) are listed as follows by R. N. Frye, *The Heritage of Persia*, 2d ed. (London: Cardinal, 1976), 300:

Ardashir (224/6?–240)	Varahran II (276–293)
Shapur I (240–272?)	Varahran III (293)
Hormizd I (272–273)	Nerseh (293–302)
Varahran (Bahram) I (273–276)	Hormizd II (302–309)

Shapur II (309–379)   Varahran IV (388–399)
Ardashir II (379–383)   Yazdagird I (399–421)
Shapur III (383–388)   Varahran V (421–439)

2. Modern historians would not rate Alexander Severus so high nor some of his successors before Constantine so low, but the *Augustan History*, chief Roman source for the third century exalts Alexander above all. See S. Perowne, *Caesars and Saints: The Evolution of the Christian State, A.D., 180–313* (London: Hodder and Stoughton, 1962), 124ff.

3. This interpretation of the monument is R. Ghirshman's, in *Iran: Parthians and Sassanians,* trans. S. Gilbert and J. Emmons (London: Thames and Hudson, 1962), 151–61.

4. On the Dura-Europos discoveries see P. V. C. Baur, M. I. Rostovtzeff, et al., *The Excavations at Dura-Europos* 10 vols. (New Haven, CT: Yale Univ. Press, Yale, 1929–52); and M. I. Rostovtzeff, *Dura Europos and Its Art* (Oxford: Clarendon, 1938).

5. Adaptation of W. G. Young's translation in *Handbook of Source Materials for Students of Church History* (Madras: Christian Literature Society, 1969), 19. English translations vary. See also the epigraph on the title page of chapter 3 for Drijver's translation of this quote, H. J. W. Drijvers, ed., *The Book of the Laws of Countries: Dialogue on Fate of Bardaisan of Eddessa* (Assen: Van Gorcum, 1965), 59.

6. R. H. Connolly, *Didascalia Apostolorum: The Syriac Version Translated and Accompanied by the Verona Latin Fragments* (Oxford: Clarendon, 1929). For author, place, and date, see lxxvii–xcl. He dates it before the Decian persecution, i.e., before 249, which is earlier than any other such manual unless, of course, the more homiletical *Didache* is also considered a manual. Cf. Altaner, *Patrology,* 56f., who dates it "in the first decades of the third century"; and J. C. J. Sanders, "Autour de la Didascalie," *A Tribute to Arthur Voobus: Studies in Early Christian Literature and Its Environment, Primarily in the Syrian East,* ed. R. H. Fischer (Chicago: Lutheran School of Theology, 1977), 47–54. Zahn also dates it early third century. Though written in Greek, it was quickly translated into Syriac and circulated widely among the Eastern churches.

7. *Didascalia Apostolorum,* chap. 12 (Connolly, 120).

8. *Didascalia Apostolorum,* chap. 12 (Connolly, 122–124).

9. *Didascalia Apostolorum* (Connolly, liv, lvii, lxxii).

10. *Didascalia Apostolorum* (Connolly, lxix–lxxv); chaps. 24, 26 (esp. 214, 216, 233, 254).

11. *Didascalia Apostolorum,* chaps. 2, 3 (Connolly, esp. 8–11, 20, 26,) and chap. 22 (193ff.).

12. *Didascalia Apostolorum,* chap. 23 (Connolly, 195).

13. *Didascalia Apostolorum,* chaps. 4, 8 (Connolly, 32, 78 and *passim*).

14. As noted by Connolly, *Didascalia Apostolorum,* liv.

15. *Didascalia Apostolurum*, chap. 6 (Connolly, 43–44, 48, 50).

16. A. Voobus, in particular, links the Syrian ascetics with the Qumran community, *History of Asceticism in the Syrian Orient*, vol. 1, in *CSCO*, vol. 184, Subsidia Tomus 14 (Louvain, 1958), 100ff. But S. P. Brock doubts any direct link, "Early Syrian Asceticism," *Numen* 20 (Leiden, 1973), 7f. See also S. Jargy's description of the different theories in "Les 'fils et filles du pacte' dans la littérature monastique syriaque," *Orientalia Christiana Periodica* 17 (1951): 304–20.

17. See F. C. Burkitt, *Early Eastern Christianity* (London: Murray, 1904), 50f.; and his article "Syriac-Speaking Christianity," *Cambridge Ancient History*, 12:499; and more recently A. Voobus, *History of Asceticism*, 1:69ff., who states, "All the available sources (up into the third century) are unanimous in their testimony that the fundamental conception around which the Christian belief centered was the doctrine that the Christian life is unthinkable outside the bounds of virginity." He cites Harnack, Ficker, and Plooj as generally agreeing (p. 184).

18. M. R. James, *"Acts of Thomas,"* in *the Apocryphal New Testament* (Oxford: Clarendon, 1924), 117, 124, and *passim*.

19. Voobus, *History of Asceticism* 1:67f., 73, citing "Une curieuse homelie grecque inedite, sur la virginite," ed., D. Amand and M. C. Moons, *Revue Benedictine* (Maredsous), 68 (1953): 35ff.

20. The exact translation of the Syriac is argued. See Brock, "Early Syrian Asceticism," in *Numen* 20 (1972), 7.

21. The Syriac word is *ihidayuta*, which in adjectival form can be translated "only-begotten," "single," "solitary," and later "monastic." See R. Murray, *Symbols in Church and Kingdom* (Cambridge: Cambridge Univ. Press, 1975), 12–16.

22. Murray, *Symbols*, 14–16. Murray cites a fifth-century Monophysite work, *The Testament of Our Lord Jesus Christ*.

23. A. Voobus argues that the early Syrian church regularly reserved baptism for the unmarried alone. See his *Celibacy, A Requirement for Admission to Baptism in the Early Syrian Church*, Papers of the Estonian Theological Society in Exile (Stockholm, 1951). Murray is less dogmatic but is inclined to agree (*Symbols*, 15f.). The argument turns on whether some passages in later writings can be identified as earlier, embedded material.

24. As Voobus (*Celibacy*, 174 and *passim*) and Murray (*Symbols*, 12) both recognize. The problem is to reconcile statements by both theologians approving marriage with other statements endorsing abstinence from marriage.

25. Pseudo-Clementine, *De virginitate*, 2. 2, cited by Voobus, *Celibacy*, 82.

26. Brock, "Early Syrian Asceticism," in *Numen* 20 (1972), 1.

27. A. Voobus, "A Letter of Ephrem to the Mountaineers," in *Contributions of the Baltic University* 51 (Pinneberg, 1947).

28. See chap. 3, pp. 77ff.

29. Voobus, *History of Asceticism*, 1:97.

30. Voobus, *History of Asceticism*, 1:86. Voobus is quoting a Syriac document surviving in an Armenian translation.

31. A. Mingana, "The Early Spread of Christianity in Central Asia and the Far East," *Bulletin of the John Rylands Library*, vol. 9, no. 2 (July 1925): 299.

32. *Chronique de Seert*, ed. and trans. Addai Scher, in *PO* (Turnhout, Belgium, 1971), tome 4, fasc. 3, no. 17, pp. 236 (26), 292 (82).

33. Gelasius of Cyzicus, *Historia Concilii Nicaeni*, in Migne, *PG*, vol. 75, col. 1342ff. His collection of the acts of the council was probably not from the official records of Nicaea.

34. Eusebius, *Vita Constantini* 3. 7.

35. Mingana, "The Early Spread of Christianity in Central Asia and the Far East," 5–8.

36. Mingana, "The Early Spread of Christianity in Central Asia and the Far East," 6, 20, 22.

Chapter 5
The Clash of
Religions: Christian,
Zoroastrian, and
Manichaean

"Ardashir, the first King of the Persians . . . issued
an edict that Fire Temples be set up in honour of
his gods; and that the Sun, the great god of the
whole universe, should be honoured with special
veneration. He was the first to assume the title of
King of Kings and god. By taking for himself the
honour due to the gods, he added blasphemy
to injustice."

—Msiha-zkha (6th c.), *Sources
Syriaques*, 108 (Mingana)

IT was not only the Christians who thought of themselves as a "new race," a fresh, expanding force in history. In Persia, the revival of Zoroastrianism was much more obvious than the rise of Christianity. The Sassanid dynasty, which had come to power in 225, considered itself to be not a new race so much as an old and honored race revitalized with an old but true religion. The new Persian emperors were Zoroastrians. They claimed descent from the royal Medes and Persians of the Achaemenid empire of Cyrus the Great and from the priests of the royal fire temples at Istakhr. Zealous to restore the glories of ancient Persia, which had been dissipated first by the Greeks of Alexander in the fourth century B.C. and then by barbarous Parthians from central Asia in the third century B.C., they adopted a religious policy pointedly opposed to the soft Greek syncretism of the Parthians they had supplanted. In the reign of the two conquerors who established the dynasty, Ardashir I (A.D. 225–240), who captured Nisibis from the Romans, and Shapur I (240–272) who sacked Antioch, the new rulers not only reasserted Persia's military power but began to forge an alliance of state and religion that eventually spelled the end of the three hundred years of toleration that Christians had enjoyed in Persia ever since their first traditional missionary beginnings there. To the Sassanians, national glory demanded a return to Zoroastrianism, the national religion of Persia's golden age.

The change did not come all at once, however. The first shah, Ardashir, destroyed some pagan temples in Armenia and began to build fire temples with a Zoroastrian zeal that may have made Christians apprehensive, but there were no persecutions and only a few hints of the nationalizing of Zoroastrianism that was later to become so serious a threat to minority religious groups. The first hint was Ardashir's appointment of a high *mobed* or *magi*,[1] named Tansar, as religious adviser to the shah and chief priests of the Zoroastrian clergy. It was Tansar, the new chief priest, who urged the centralizing of all the empire's fire temples under the authority of the central "royal fire" and the prohibition of independent temples.[2]

How far the Zoroastrianism of the Sassanians resembled the ancient faith they thought they were reviving no one knows. Little can be said about the origins of that ancient religion with any certainty except that Zoroaster has always been revered as the Iranian prophet of Persia's heroic age. Tradition dates him in the seventh century B.C., about a hundred years before Confucius and two hundred years before the Buddha. Recent scholarship points to a much earlier date, probably before 1000 B.C.[3] His teachings were handed down orally for over a millennium or more before they were finally collected into a sacred book, the *Avesta*. It is conjectured that this was done in a Sassanian reaction to the spread of the Christian Scriptures in western Asia. At any rate, in the long process of transition from oral tradition to written word much of the original teachings of the prophet may well have been altered or obscured. Very early the *magi* of the Medes seem to have added elements of a more popular religion that combined astrology, the distinctive practice of exposing their dead to the sun and the birds rather than to the darkness of the grave, and rituals of magic (hence the derivation of the word "magic" from *magi*).

But however much of the *Avesta* is later addition to Zoroaster's lyric search for truth,[4] there was a religious power in its mystic, cosmological dualism of two warring gods in eternal conflict and in its high ethical demand that the good people of the realm must follow the good god, Ahura-Mazda (or Ormuzd), and worship him in fire. Their reward is eternal life; but the evil ones, possessed by Ahriman, the god of darkness, will be punished in "the house of lies."

The Zoroastrian temples in which the sacred fires of the god of light always burned were tended by village priests, the *mobeds*, called *magi* by the Greeks and Romans. Above the village *mobeds* there developed a network of higher-ranking regional *mobeds*, like bishops, and the whole was headed by a chief priest (*mobadan-mobed*, or *archimagus*). Under the Sassanian emperors this high *mobed* became one of the most powerful men in the realm, and it was with this powerful, highly organized state religion that the little Church of the East eventually found itself in direct conflict. Fortunately, however, unlike Buddhism, which came from farther east and confronted Zoroastrianism where it was strongest, on the Median steppes, Christianity came from the Syrian West and grew in the Mesopotamian provinces of Persia where the state religion was weakest. For the first hundred years of the new dynasty, Christians, though harassed by the *mobeds*, were not often persecuted by the state.

The first shah, Ardashir, passed on to his son, Shapur I, his ideal of an empire stabilized and united by a truly Persian religion. His dying charge may not be genuine, but it became a governing tenet of imperial Sassanian policy for the next four hundred years:

> Never forget that as a king you are at once the protector of religion and of your country. Consider the altar and the throne as inseparable; they must always sustain each other. A sovereign without a religion is a tryant; and a people who have none may be deemed the most monstrous of all societies. Religion may exist without a state, but a state

cannot exist without religion; and it is by holy laws that a political association can alone be bound.[5]

If so strong a commitment to a state religion can really be dated back to Ardashir I in the early third century, it is somewhat surprising to find little evidence of any persecution of minority religions like Christianity during the reigns of the first eight Sassanian monarchs. Except for a few years during the rule of the fifth shah, Varahran II (276–293) the Persian churches grew and multiplied in peace. They seem to have enjoyed as great a measure of religious toleration under the officially Zoroastrian early Sassanids as they had under the easy-going Parthians. Several reasons may be conjectured to account for this.

In the first place, the stronger kings like Ardashir and Shapur I were too busy fighting Rome (Byzantium) to be overly concerned about small religious groups like the Christians so long as they were no threat to national stability. Jews and Christians, often persecuted by Rome, were presumably loyal to Persia. Large numbers of them were refugees from Roman intolerance. The Jews, on the whole, were even more willing than Christians to accept governmental restrictions based on Zoroastrian religious practices, such as those on the use of fire. At the Jewish school in Nehardea in southern Mesopotamia, its famous leader Mar Samuel taught that "the civil law of the government is as valid for the Jews as their own law," and from that time on, about 260, Jews were largely untouched by persecution.[6]

A second factor that may have made the Persian government more tolerant in practice than its theory of a religous state might suggest is that the Sassanian rulers were not strictly orthodox. They favored a controversial variant cult within Zoroastrianism called Zurvanism, which has been described as a "creeping monotheism" undercutting the radical dualism of the popular orthodoxy.[7] The dilemma of dualism is its "truncated metaphysics." Each of its two gods is conditioned by the existence of the other, and neither is, therefore, the ultimate ground of being. As C. S. Lewis once observed, if evil is as substantive and self-consistent as good, "if Ahriman (evil) existed in his own right no less than Ormuzd (good), what could we mean by calling Ormuzd good except that we happened to prefer him?"[8] The Sassanid shahs, if they were, as many scholars believe, professed or secret Zurvanites, may have felt a sympathetic affinity toward Christian monotheism, which could explain why so many of them, though officially Zoroastrian, at one time or another were reported to be crypto-Christians.[9] Such reports were, of course, either wishful thinking on the part of Christians or political attacks by their enemies. But the fact remains that the first Sassanid century was a time of continued expansion of a Persian church largely unopposed by the government.

But already before the end of the reign of Shapur I in 272, a shadowy, fanatical organizing genius behind the throne was dreaming of putting sharper teeth into the Sassanid vision of a union between the ancient Zoroastrian faith and the new imperial power of the Persian state. This dark eminence was Kartir, who succeeded Tansar as the second chief priest of the Zoroastrian clergy. His was a name lost to history until four battered rock inscriptions were rather recently discovered and deciphered in southern Iran.[10]

Kartir appears in the inscriptions as a priest and teacher of no great importance under Shapur I, apparently restrained from attacking heretics by Shapur's tolerance for minority religions.[11] But when the great Shapur died, the rise of Kartir was sudden and complete. In swift succession he was elevated to the nobility, made chief priest, chief judge, and custodian of the royal fire at Istakhr. It was probably Kartir, and not Tansar, who finally organized the loosely knit Zoroastrian priesthood into a tight hierarchy. Fiercely missionary, he ranged the whole empire to convert the heathen and combat foreign faiths. At first, however, his wrath was directed more against Zoroastrian schisms than against older, alien religions.

The first to feel the pressure were the Manichaeans. In the first year of Shapur I (about 241) a burning young prophet named Mani stood up at the palace gates to interrupt the festivities celebrating the shah's accession to the throne. Like a John the Baptist he began to proclaim a strange and severe new faith. His religion, like his blood, was an uneasy mixture.[12] On his mother's side he was a descendant of the old Parthian royalty but on his father's side he was a world-denying "baptist" ascetic. He had been raised by his father in one of the strictest of the Jewish or Jewish-Christian baptizing sects of the desert. At age twelve he had visions; at twenty-four he began to preach in Persia and not long thereafter went on to India to convert the world. "My hope," he said, "will spread to the west and to the east . . . in every language . . . in every city."[13] For a while it appeared that his hope might well be realized. Having established a religious community in India, he returned to Persia and was well received at the imperial court, but his dream of a worldwide faith embracing the best of all religions soon clashed with the narrow but more intense zeal of the Zoroastrian hierarchy. Superficially similar but "inevitably hostile" is how E. G. Browne has described the two faiths: "Zoroastrianism was national, militant, materialistic, imperialist; Manichaeanism cosmopolitan, quietist, ascetic, unworldly."[14] Both claimed Persia and both eventually lost Persia, but the first losers were the Manichaeans.

Sometime between 273 and 276 Mani was seized and crucified. His skin was peeled and stuffed and hung on one of the gates of Seleucia-Ctesiphon. His followers were slaughtered throughout the realm. But he was not forgotten. For eight hundred years the gate on which his body hung was still remembered as the Gate of Mani. Not all of his disciples died. Untold numbers fled, many of them into central Asia where, as the tenth-century Arab author of the *Fihrist* noted, they were the first religious community other than shaman- ists to occupy the lands beyond the Oxus.[15] Crossing the Oxus Riv- er near Balkh into what is now Afghanistan they spread along the Old Silk Road to China, outracing the Persian missionaries of the Christian faith to the borders of China, perhaps wandering as far as Chang'an (Ch'ang-an), the T'ang capital.

There is little in the teaching of Mani to account for its aston- ishing capacity for missionary growth. Perhaps a clue lies in the fact that in an age of many developing religions it seemed to be able to combine, in different proportions for different regions, what was most appealing religiously to the cultures it penetrated. It has been described as "Christianized Zoroastrianism,"[16] but it was much more. It was a blend of many beliefs: Zoroastrian dualism, Gnostic cosmology, Jewish-Christian asceticism, Buddhist philosophy, Hindu habits, and Babylonian gods and myths. Mani borrowed from them all. "As a river joins another river to form a mighty current, so these ancient books (of the older religions) have joined one another in my writings," he said.[17]

The basic motif, however, was a Zorostrian dualism: Light against Darkness. In the world of matter Darkness holds prisoner particles of the Light. The Power of Light has always yearned to redeem the elements of Light held in the demon grip of the human body and from time to time has sent prophets of truth to proclaim the way of liberation: Adam, Noah, Abraham, Zoroaster, Buddha, and Jesus. The last and greatest of all was Mani. Mani taught that the way of salvation is the way of the ascetic. The body must be broken and subdued, for only so can the particles of Light break free to return to the home of Light.

Associated with this call to self-denial were all manner of pro- hibitions, some borrowed from the Buddhists. It was forbidden to kill, to have sex, to uproot vegetables, to eat meat or drink wine. Even milk was taboo, and believers were not supposed to change their clothes more than once a year or use medicines. Water was not to be used for washing or baptizing; it could only be drunk. The reasons for this last bit of legalism afford a glimpse into the curious worldview of the Manichaeans: running water was too sacred to use in such ways, for it was one of the five sacred elements; and rainwater was too vile, for it was the excretion of the demons of the air.[18]

Such a bewildering maze of laws and prohibitions was too much for most of his followers, and Mani, recognizing the difficulty, allowed for two classes of believers in a manner reminiscent of some Jewish or Gnostic sects or perhaps borrowed in part from Syrian Christian distinctions between Sons of the Covenant and family Christians. In the first class were the *elect*. They were to keep themselves pure from all the darknesses of manual labor and from physical contacts or pleasures. They had power to forgive the sins of the second class of believers, the *auditors*. The regular confession of sins in Manichaean practice is claimed by some scholars to be the origin of the confessional in medieval Catholicism. Since the pious elect were enjoined against all forms of common labor, they were fed and served by the auditors. "Sick dogs," Ephrem the Syrian called them, "who refuse to do any work."[19] The elect worshiped on Monday, for the common auditors the sacred day was Sunday.

Mani claimed to be an apostle of Jesus Christ, like Paul. Many of his doctrines had a Christian sound. He spoke at length of God and the devil, heaven and hell, the final judgment and the life everlasting. But when he announced that he had come as the Holy Spirit promised by Jesus, it began to appear to Christians that he had moved beyond the orbit of the historic faith as handed down through the church. But such deviations from orthodoxy by the Manichaeans were not always that obvious. Their chameleonlike ability to appear more Christian than the Christians (and more Buddhist than the Buddhists and more Zoroastrian than the Zoroastrians) makes it difficult to distinguish their surviving records from Christian documents, especially in some of the manuscript fragments found in central Asia that date back to the period when the two rival faiths were spreading east across the continent among the nomadic tribes along the Old Silk Road in Chinese Turkestan. There Manichaean communities survived to the thirteenth century.[20]

The ease with which Manichaeans took on Christian language and the consequent confusion of them with Christians may have been one of the primary causes of the first, short persecution of Christians in Sassanian Persia. In the reign of Varahran (Bahram) II, who ruled from 276 to 293, the Manichaean heretics were attacked for a second time by Kartir and his *mobeds*. It was in this persecution that Mani's successor, Sisin, was seized and run through with a sword. Then, perhaps because some Manichaeans claimed to be Christian to escape persecution or perhaps simply because the fanatical Zoroastrians did not know the difference (or did not want to know it), Christians too began to feel the edge of the sword.[21] One of Kartir's inscriptions complains of the threat of false religions to Persia's true faith and boasts of wiping them all out:

> In province after province, place after place the worship of Ormuzd (Lord of Light) and of the gods rose supreme. . . . The doctrines of Ahriman (Lord of Evil) and of the demons were dispersed and utterly destroyed. And Jews, shamans, Brahmans, Nazareans, Christians, Maktaks and Manichaeans (Zandiks) . . . have been annihilated in the Empire.[22]

The Syriac *Acts of the Martyrs*[23] calls this "the first persecution" of Christians in Persia. Even a queen was not spared. Varahran II, who is said to have been favorably disposed toward Christians at the beginning of his reign, had married "because of her astonishing beauty" a Christian, the daughter of Byzantine Romans captured by Shapur I. But when he asked her, "What is your religion?" and she replied, "I am a Christian and I serve my Lord Jesus Christ, and I confess God his father," he was perturbed. "Abandon your religion in favor of mine," he said. "Worship the Sun and the Fire and honour the Water . . . and [I will] make you chief queen in my realm." She refused, and according to the story of her martyrdom, which of course like so many of the martyr stories is a mixture of tradition and history, she was stripped, flogged, tortured, and paraded naked around the city in chains, but "the people of God gathered beside her," and with radiant face and "her mouth filled with laughter" she went to her death (though the manuscript at this point is incomplete).[24]

But brutal though this time of trouble was for the Persian church, it must be borne in mind that the persecution under Varahran II was only a comparatively minor interruption of almost a century and a half of religious peace for Christians in that early Sassanian period.

NOTES

1. The terms *mobed, herbad,* and *magi* are often used interchangeably of the Zoroastrian priesthood. *Mobed* seems to emphasize the priestly function, *herbad* the teaching function. *Magi* (singular *magus*) is the Greek and Latin

word for Zoroastrian priests, as in Matthew 2:1, where it is translated as "wise men," and is popularized in Christmas pageants as "kings."

2. See M. Boyce, *The Letter of Tansar* (Rome: Instituto Italiano per il Medio ad Estremo Oriente, 1968), and *Zoroastrians: Their Religious Beliefs and Practices* (London: Routledge and Kegan Paul, 1979), 102f., 107f. The historicity of the *Letter* from the Shah's adviser is much debated but Boyce makes a good case for the argument that it contains a core of third-century credible history. Arguing against this view are A. Christensen, *L'Iran sous les Sassanides*, 2d ed. (Copenhagen: Levin and Munksgaard, 1944), and J. P. Asmussen "Christians in Iran," *Cambridge History of Iran*, vol. 3 (Cambridge: Cambridge Univ. Press, 1983), 923-48.

3. Some say as early as 1700 to 1500 B.C. See A. Shapur Shahbazi, "The Traditional Date of Zoroaster Explained," *Bulletin of the School of Oriental and African Studies* 40 (London, 1977), pt. 1. H. W. Bailey, *Zoroastrian Problems in the Ninth Century Books* (Oxford; Clarendon, 1943, reprint 1971), xix; and Boyce, *Zoroastrians*, 18.

4. The epic verses of the *Gatha*, at least, probably trace back to Zoroaster.

5. Cited by F. J. Foakes-Jackson, *History of the Church . . . to A.D. 461*, 4th ed. (Cambridge; Hall, 1905), 548. Echoes of the same concept are found in the *Letter of Tansar*, 33f. Both may be from later sources.

6. Frank Gavin, *Aphraates and the Jews* (Toronto: Trinity College, 1923), 29.

7. R. C. Zaehner, *Zurvan, A Zoroastrian Dilemma* (Oxford; Clarendon, 1955) 12, 25. See also Boyce, *Zoroastrians*, 69ff.

8. C. S. Lewis, "Evil and Good," in *The Spectator* 166 (7 February 1941): 141ff. He concludes, "the difference between the Christian and the Dualist is that the Christian thinks one stage further and sees that if (the archangel) Michael is really in the right and Satan really in the wrong this must mean that they stand in two different relations to somebody or something far farther back, to the ultimate ground of reality itself. . . . Dualism . . . is only a half-way house."

9. For example, Varahran II in the early period, Yazdagird I in the middle period, and Chosroes II (Khusro) in the final period; the last was so often pro-Christian, though not actually Christian, that it has been conjectured that the royal house might well have become Christian but for the Islamic invasion. See M. L. Chaumont, "Les Sassanides et la christianisation de l'empire iranien au IIIe siecle . . .," *Revue de l'Histoire des Religions* 165 (Paris, 1964), 188; W. A. Wigram, *A History of the Assyrian Church A.D. 100–640* (London: SPCK, 1910), 85f.; W. G. Young, *Patriarch, Shah and Caliph* (Rawalpindi, India: Christian Study Center, 1974), 76f.

10. M. L. Chaumont, "L'inscription de Kartir a la 'Ka'bah de Zoroastre," in *Journal Asiatique* 248 (Paris, 1960): 339–80, and her "Les Sassanides et la christianisation de l'empire," 165–202. The two inscriptions at Naqsh-i-Rustam were not found until about 1939.

11. In his own inscriptions, Kartir claimed to have been given authority over all the priests of the realm, but Shah Shapur's inscription simply describes him as "*herbad*," or priest and teacher. See Boyce, *Zoroastrians*, 97f., 109–110. Shapur's protection for Mani and perhaps his friendship with the prophet are noted by Chaumont, "Les Sassanides," 79.

12. The classic sources for Mani and Manichaeanism are the ninth-century Syriac *Eskolion* by Theodore Bar-Choni (ed. Pognon, 1899), and the tenth-century Arabic *Fihrist* (ed. Flugel, 1871). But Manichaean studies were revolutionized by almost continuous manuscript discoveries in central Asia, Egypt, and the Middle East in the twentieth century. The Turfan manuscript discoveries were published by F. W. K. Miller, et al.; those in Egypt by C. Schmidt and H. J. Polotsky. H. Ibscher published an edition of the *Kephalaia* I (a Coptic source) in 1940. Manichaeanism's own canonical literature survives only in titles and fragments. See Gherardo Gnoli, "Manichaeanism: An Overview," in *Encyclopedia of Religion* (New York, London: Macmillan, 1987); and H. Ch. Puech, *Le Manichéisme. Son fondateur, sa doctrine* (Paris: S.A.E.R., 1949).

13. Quoted by H. Lietzmann, *A History of the Early Church*, trans. B. L. Wolf, vol. 2, 2d ed. (London: Lutterworth, 1950), 270.

14. E. G. Browne, *A Literary History of Persia . . .*, vol. 1 (London and Leipzig: T. Fisher Unwin, 1909), 154, 161.

15. Cited by Browne, *A Literary History of Persia*, 163f. The *Fihrist*, written about 987 by Muhammed B. Ishaq, relied on an eighth-century Zoroastrian author, Ibn ul Mugaffa, for Sassanian history (see Browne, *A Literary History of Persia*, 1:76).

16. Browne, *A Literary History of Persia*, 154.

17. C. Schmidt, ed., *Kephalaia* (Stuttgart, 1935), 2, cited by A.Voobus, *History of Asceticism in the Syrian Orient*, vol. 1 in *CSCO*, vol. 184, Subsidia Tomus 14 (Louvain, 1958), 112.

18. Voobus, *History of Asceticism*, 1:115–124, contains vivid descriptions of the ascetic practices of Manichaean monks and nuns.

19. Ephrem the Syrian, *Contra haereses* 2.

20. See J. G. Davies, "Manichaeaism and Christianity," in *Encyclopedia of Religion*. On Turkish texts from central Asia (including Christian, Manichaean, and Buddhist), see A. von Gabain, "Vorislamische altturkische Litteratur," in *Handbuch der Orientalistik*, series 1, vol. 5 vol. 1 (Leiden/Koln, 1963), 207, esp. 216, 222ff.

21. Chaumont, "Les Sassanides, 199, citing the *Chronicle of Seert*, ed. and trans. Addai Scher, in *PO*, t. 4, p. 238.

22. Chaumont, "L'inscription de Kartir," 347. She suggests that the "shamans" were Buddhist missionaries, but the word could also refer to shamans from Persia's Turkic minorities in the central Asiatic regions. S. P. Brock interprets "Nazareans" as native Persian Christians, and "Christians"

as perhaps referring to believers of Greek origin captured in the wars and resettled in the east. "Nazarean" was a common Syriac designation of a Christian, S. P. Brock, "A Martyr of the Sassanid Court Under Vahran II: Candida," in *Analecta Bollandiana* (Bruxelles, 1978), t. 96, fasc. 1–2, p. 167. The meaning of "Maktak" is obscure.

23. *Acts of the Martyrs* (Syriac). According to the *Chronicle of Seert* the author was Marutha, bishop of Maipherqat in the early fourth century, who was deeply impressed by the courage of the Persian martyrs. Scholars today see it as a composite by many different authors. See G. Wiessner, "Untersuchungen zu einer Gruppe syrischer Martyrakten aus der Christenverfolgung Schapurs II," doctoral diss., Wurzburg, 1962.

24. "The Martyrdom of Qndyr." See S. P. Brock's translation and introduction of this sixth-century manuscript, "A Martyr of the Sassanid Court," 167–81. The basic document is historically credible, but attributed quotations and details are almost certainly not contemporary description. Chaumont tentatively dates this first persecution between 286 and 291 ("Les Sassanides," 198f.).

Chapter 6
First Steps Toward a National Persian Church

"The weakness of early Syriac thinking about the
Church centres, perhaps, on the little-developed
doctrine of the Holy Spirit. . . .
It is strange how little stress we find, at least in our
early Syriac literature, on the unity of the whole
Church . . ."

—R. Murray, *Symbols of Church
and Kingdom . . . in Early Syriac
Literature.* (1975, 344f.)

THERE is very little reliable evidence of a developed episcopate in Persia until much before the year 300. It is apparent from the evidence in other parts of the Persian border regions, notably Edessa and Arbela (Adiabene), that ever since about the end of the second century the church had slowly been moving in the direction of greater centralization of authority and that in the third and fourth centuries the process accelerated. What had once been a collection of congregations and preaching points, each apparently independent but knit together by a common loyalty to Jesus Christ, became in the first half of the fourth century a nationwide community, with no single head but with graded church structures (bishops, priests, and deacons) separated geographically but in communication with each other. This network of recognized ecclesiastical command attempted a partially successful national synod (the Synod of Seleucia) in the early fourth century, but not until almost a hundred years later did the movement develop a workable, organized national unity. It was only with the first Persian synods of the fifth century, beginning with the Synod of Isaac in 410, that national authority was established and given to the bishop of the capital city, Seleucia-Ctesiphon.

This change is startling when one compares the swirling mixture of Christian groups in second-century Edessa, for example, with the ordered edicts of Seleucia-Ctesiphon in 410. But the process by which this transformation took place is nowhere made clear, and the judgment of M. J. Higgins is correct that even then "the Persian church never actually achieved unity." In these early centuries it was always plagued by schism.[1]

In the New Testament church authority clearly rested with the apostles, an authority they partially delegated to presbyters and bishops for leadership in the churches that the apostolic missionary witness established. At first, it would seem, the two terms "bishop" and "presbyter" (or "elder") were used interchangeably of this local leadership, as in the churches of Crete (Titus 1:5–9). In Macedonia, for example, a single congregation might have more than one bishop (Phil. 1:1) and it has been argued that the churches in the West, as in Rome and Philippi, were still ruled at the end of the first century by a collegium of presbyters (or bishops) with their deacons. But in Asia Minor by that time the situation had already changed or had been different from the beginning. The epistles of Ignatius of Antioch, written about 110, portray churches in which the bishop was supreme, a ruling officer and a spiritual authority higher than either presbyter (priest, elder) or deacon.[2]

What of the churches across the border in Persia? The evidence is too scanty to permit dogmatic conclusions, but this much at least should be noted. No document so far found dating to before 200 mentions a bishop. Later historians, however, labored to fill the gaps with unbroken lines of episcopal succession back to the apostles.[3]

It is not impossible that these traditional histories preserve genuine material even from before 200, as we have seen.[4] The years of relative toleration under the late Parthians and early Sassanid emperors would have furnished opportunity for visible, organized Christian leadership to emerge. However, though the evidence is more reliable in the third century, it is difficult to prove the existence of bishops in eastern Syrian and Mesopotamia before the year 300. Even in Edessa the first bishop in the Chronicle of Edessa (c. 550) is Qona, who is reported to have begun the building of the great Cathedral there in 313.[5] The important center of Nisibis had no bishop before 301, and the first bishop mentioned by name there, James of Nisibis or perhaps Babu (it is uncertain which was first), was not a metropolitan and therefore had authority only in his own congregation.[6]

Tiridates and the Conversion of Armenia

An important parallel to the rise of the Persian church is the conversion of Armenia and the founding of an ancient church that outlasted the Nestorians. Tradition traces its beginnings to the Apostle Thaddaeus, though history credits it to Gregory the Illuminator, who converted King Tiridates the liberator of Armenia from Persian rule. The story is dramatic. In 218 a brother of the Parthian Persian emperor became king of Armenia. Ten years later the Parthian dynasty fell and Armenia's king became an enemy of Persia. Persia had him assassinated but the assassin's son Gregory is said to have been saved. The king's son Tiridates also escaped and was prepared to free Armenia by the Roman Emperor Diocletian. Meanwhile Gregory was preparing to return to Armenia as a missionary. The two returned together with Gregory being asked to become the king's secretary without his knowing Gregory's ancestry. A pagan feast welcomed them. The king worshiped first, and Gregory was asked to follow. He rose to say, "I am a Christian. I do not worship figures made of gold, iron, or wood." Imprisoned, he was exposed as the son of the murder of Tiridates' father and thrown into a pit to die. But he did not die and the king fell sick. The king's sister sent for the saint who would not die. Gregory healed the king. Gregory goes to Rome to become a bishop and returns to baptize the king, probably in 303, which makes Tiridates the first verifiably Christian king in history, or at least, "the first king of a Christian state which has kept its identity through the centuries" (see H. Nersoyan, A History of the Armenian People, [New York: Armenian Church, 1963], pp. 19-41).

A Chronology of the Fourth-Century Persian Church*

ca.	270	First priest ordained in Seleucia-Ctesiphon
ca.	285	Papa bar-Aggai consecrated bishop, Seleucia-Ctesiphon
ca.	290	Brief persecution under Shah Varahran II of Persia
	298	Rome defeats Shah Narses of Persia, takes Nisibis
ca.	300	Aphrahat born (perhaps earlier)
	301	Conversion of king of Armenia, Tiridat I
ca.	306	James consecrated first (?) bishop of Nisibis
		Birth of Ephrem the Syrian, Nisibis
	309–379	Shapur II, shah of Persia
ca.	311	Conversion of Constantine the Great, Rome
	314	Death of Tiridat I of Armenia
	314/5	Persian Synod against Bishop Papa (Synod of Seleucia)
		Simon bar-Sabba'e, bishop of Seleucia-Ctesiphon (?)
	326/7	Death of Bishop Papa
		Catholicate of Simon bar-Sabba'e (326/7–344/5; 18 years)
	335	Shapur II campaigns in Armenia, repelled by Constantine
	337	Death of Constantine the Great; Roman Empire divided
		Shapur II wars against Rome (337–350)
		Aphrahat's *Demonstrations*, Part I
	340	The Great Persian Persecution (340–363; 379/83(?)–401)
	344	Martyrdom of Catholicos Simon bar-Sabba'e
		Catholicate of Shahdost (344–345)
	345	Aphrahat's *Demonstrations*, Part II
	345/6	Catholicate of Barbashmin (345–346)
	346–364	Twenty-year (?) vacancy in the Catholicate
	350	Ephrem the Syrian helps Nisibis repel Persian attack
	363	Shapur II defeats Julian the Apostate of Rome; Nisibis restored to Persia
		Ephrem the Syrian leaves Nisibis for (Roman) Edessa
	364/5	Catholicate of Tomarsa (365/5–372/3; 7 or 8 years?)
	372/3	Catholicate of Qayuma (372/3–379/80?; 7 years)
	379/80	Persecution renewed (379/90–401/2)
	380–402	Twenty-two-year vacancy in the catholicate

* The dates are only tentative and derived from many sources. Particularly helpful are M. J. Higgins, "Chronology of the Fourth-Century Metropolitans of Seleucia-Ctesiphon," *Traditio* 9 (1953), which revises earlier date listings such as in A. R. Vine's *The Nestorian Churches* (1937), 80ff., which in turn uses B. J. Kidd's collation in *Churches of Eastern Christendom* (1927), 416, which systematizes data from J. S. Assemani, *Bibliotheca orientalis* (1719–1728) and from J. Labourt, *Le Christianisme dans l'Empire Perse* (1904). See also J. E. T. Wiltsch, *Handbuch der Kirchlichen geographic und Statistik* (Berlin: H. Schultz, 1846).

The Episcopacy of Papa and the Synod
of Seleucia

It was not tradition but pragmatic and sometimes sordid ecclesiastical and political developments that eventually elevated the bishop of the Persian capital, Seleucia-Ctesiphon, to headship over all the Church of the East (later called the Nestorian church). As late as 270 the small group of Christians in the capital had no bishop, much less a catholicos (or patriarch). In that year, according to the disputed account in the *History of the Church of Adiabene*, the Christians of Seleucia-Ctesiphon begged Shaklupa, "bishop" of Arbela, who was visiting them, to choose and ordain their first priest, which he did.[7] About twenty years later, perhaps between 280 and 290, the two bishops of Arbela and Susa, deciding that it was now fitting that the capital city should have its own bishop, elevated its priest, Papa bar-Aggai, to the rank of bishop.[8]

At least one of the two consecrating bishops, Miles of Susa, was soon to regret it. Papa the Aramaean, as he was called, became the storm center of the first major power struggle to threaten the unity of the Church of the East. Finding himself bishop of the royal city and overcome with "intolerable pride" (as it seemed to bishops from older centers of the faith), he brashly proposed that even the bishoprics whose incumbents had so recently elevated him to the episcopacy, Arbela and Susa, now be made subordinate with all others to the bishopric of the capital, thus for the first time creating a national head for a church in which all bishops had been considered equal. The result was uproar.

At a council presumably called about 315 and named the Synod of Seleucia, although no official records survive save in references from later councils, Papa met humiliating defeat. Led by Miles, bishop of Susa, which was a more ancient royal city than Seleucia-Ctesiphon, the gathered bishops bluntly rejected Papa's pretensions to supremacy. In his youth Miles of Susa had taken seriously the challenge of Jesus to the rich young ruler and had given away his entire inheritance to feed the poor, taking up for himself the hard life of an ascetic. Now he pointedly reminded the ambitious Papa that the gospel calls to servanthood, not supremacy. At that point Papa lost his temper. Angrily he pounded a copy of the Gospel placed before the assembled synod. "Speak, Gospel, speak!" he cried, as if daring it to strike the real sinners. "You are here as a judge in our midst. Then how can you not cry vengeance for justice when you see even honest bishops drawn away from truth, not just the perverted?" But as he struck the Holy Word, according to this later record, he fell paralyzed by a stroke—a judgment on his sacrilege, his opponents gravely observed, and they promptly deposed him. Even his own delegation from Seleucia-Ctesiphon, perhaps tired of his arrogance, deserted him, and his archdeacon, the later martyr Simon bar-Sabba'e, was made bishop in his stead.[9]

It was a shabby beginning to the organization of the church in Persia, but not unique. Rivalry for high position has troubled the church since the days of the apostles (Matt. 20:20–28), and factionalism is an endemic structural weakness in human organizations since time began. But whatever the weakness of his motives or his methods, there was an almost inevitable logic to Papa's proposal of a national church with clear lines of authority. What alternatives are there to recognized leadership and organized structure? At any rate, time was on the side of the movement toward centralization. Alarmed at the threat of permanent schism when Papa angrily refused to accept deposition, the bishops began to fumble their way to a compromise. The details are obscure, but it seems to have included the pro forma restoration of Papa as bishop of the capital, the voluntary resignation of Simon bar-Sabba'e, his archdeacon who had been made bishop in his place, and an agreement that Simon would be promised the right of succession after Papa's death.[10]

By the same sort of working compromise, Papa's proposal of primacy for the bishop of Seleucia-Ctesiphon eventually came to be accepted, if not as an apostolic right at least as a practical necessity for contact between a minority church and a highly centralized, non-Christian monarchy. The bishopric in the capital was too new to claim direct apostolic tradition, and its bishop commanded too little reverence from his Persian colleagues for the primacy to be anything but an arrangement of convenience at first. Aphrahat, writing a generation later, is still scathing in his condemnation of the arrogance, greed, and ostentation of the bishop of Ctesiphon—"this brother of ours, with his tiara and his evil reputation among his fellows."[11]

But in an empire power flows to the capital, and perhaps it was wise counsel from the bishop of Edessa that averted a schism and persuaded the fractious Persian clerics to accept a nominal head. Later documents refer to "Western bishops" (that is, west Asian bishops) as playing a decisive role in this first organizational crisis in the Church of the East. They were said to have supported Papa's bid for supremacy and to have secured his reinstatement, and this alleged fact was later used to prove the dependence of the Persian church on Western lines of apostolic succession. The argument was embellished by the invention of an early legendary journey undertaken by candidates for the position of bishop of Seleucia-Ctesiphon in 190 to seek apostolic consecration from the bishops of Antioch and Jerusalem, but there is no contemporary evidence to support such assertions.[12]

If there indeed was any Western influence in the compromise that averted a schism in the Persian church at that time, it came probably from Edessa and Nisibis, not Antioch and Jerusalem. In the eyes of the Persian bishops Edessa was still the mother missionary church and still more Persian than Roman whatever the fortunes of war had done to it. As for Antioch, it is unlikely that a Persian church forming a national organization in the Persian Empire would accept official ecclesiastical legitimacy from Rome's main military base in Asia at a time of intense hostility between the two empires. Persian kings, whose favor the church was beginning to cultivate, were not likely to forget that only a half century earlier a patriarch of Antioch had been captured as an enemy and imprisoned in exile on the eastern Persian plains.[13]

Tradition records that Bishop Papa lingered on half paralyzed by his stroke but clinging tenaciously to an episcopal primacy, real or imagined, for twelve years before he died about 327.[14] He was succeeded, as promised at the stormy Synod of Seleucia, by Simon bar-Sabba'e whose family influence with the throne, it was hoped, might protect the church from the increasing hostility of the Zoroastrians. It did not. It did not even save his own life, as we shall see, for he was martyred in the Great Persecution. But by his martyrdom the good bishop may have done more to establish the national authority of his diocese than all the ecclesiastical strategies of his predecessor, Papa, or all the political maneuverings of his well-placed relatives. The death of the martyrs, and Bishop Simon bar-Sabbae's death in particular, wiped the slate clean for a while of the petty bickerings of church politicians and gave Persia's Christians a martyr and a hero to follow in the pain-filled years that ensued, years that saw the church as a national organization virtually destroyed.

Jacob of Nisibis and the Beginnings of Monasticism

While the bishops were sometimes praying and sometimes quarreling their way toward a national unity, at the other end of the ecclesiastical spectrum a very different quest for a satisfying organizational structure was occurring where it might be least expected. The radical ascetics, with much the same mixture of piety, necessity, and fractious human behavior displayed by their bishops, were beginning to move out of their separate, isolated orbits into community. The fourth century saw the rise in Persia of organized monasticism.

Tradition relates the beginnings of communal monasticism, as distinct from separatist asceticism in the Church of the East, to Jacob of Nisibis. We have already noted how the missionary movement in Syria and Persia drew most of its strength and personnel from the dedicated wanderers and the solitaries and puritans of the Sons and Daughters of the Covenant. Other ascetics responded to another call as compelling as the call of the regions beyond. Jacob (or James) of Nisibis did not go to far mission fields. The fifth-century historian Theodoret describes how Jacob at an early age chose the life of an ascetic. He cast off the world and went up into the woods and mountains around Nisibis. He wore no clothes and used no fire and his only protection from the elements was a cave in winter.[15] In this he differed little from other solitaries of the rocks. But about 306, unable in good conscience, apparently, to reject a plea from the church in Nisibis, he returned to the world and to the church in the world to become the first bishop of Nisibis.[16]

He is the earliest historical example of one of the finest traditions of the Eastern church. Time and again, when the church needed them, the greatest of the ascetics put the call to service above the claims of separation. Purified by prayer and privation they moved beyond the compulsions of self-discipline to the no less demanding task of reviving and leading the church. In 325 the name of Jacob of Nisibis appeared on the list of subscribers to the acts of the Council of Nicaea.[17] If he did attend that first great ecumenical council, as that would suggest, then the man who came down naked from the mountains of Nisibis to serve the church sat with a crowned emperor, Constantine, at one of the turning points of church history and played his part in the ecumenical movement of his time to purify and unite the church. The creed of Nicaea became an ecumenical creed, accepted equally by the churches of the West and the Church of the East (which was later to receive the name "Nestorian").

It was about the same time, according to tradition, that Jacob brought to Nisibis, which was then temporarily in the Roman Empire, a holy man from the Nile Delta, Mar Augin (or Awgen), to introduce the disciplines of the Egyptian monks to Syria and Mesopotamia. As an enthusiastic, newly converted pearl fisher from the mouth of the Nile, Augin had become a disciple of St. Pachomius, the celebrated founder of organized monasticism in Egypt at the monastery of Tabbenisi on the Nile about 320. Recent scholarship, however, questions the story of Mar Augin and the whole theory of

Egyptian origins of Syrian monasticism, for in Syria the movement had already developed tendencies toward ascetic community life tracing more to Antioch than to Egypt.[18]

On the Persian side of the border, as we shall see in the life of Aphrahat the Persian, a conscious effort was also being made to bring the spiritual values of the ascetics back into the Christian community. One way to make communities out of the "solitaries" was by calling them to a larger Christian goal, a mission beyond the pursuit of personal spiritual gain through physical sacrifice and hardship into the greater challenge of service to the poor and evangelism to the unconverted. This began to transform their caves and retreats into outreaching centers of sacrificial service for the church of Christ and for the world. Classically this is described as the gradual transition from the original pattern of a solitary anchorite's cell to a second stage, a loose collection of such cells into what was called a "laura," in which the independence of each ascetic could still be recognized and respected but might be combined with and strengthened by association with other like-minded and independent souls. The next step was a transition from the "laura" to the "coenobium," that is, from a collection of independent cells into a unified monastery where hermits and anchorites became monks, and monks could become missionaries. Still subject to their vows of self-denial, they now began to live as a monastic community under one roof and under one controlling authority, that of an abbot or a bishop.[19]

It is impossible to fix a precise date for the emergence of organized monasteries in eastern Syria and Persia. If the Mar Augin legend is true, the earliest monastery in east Syria could have been founded by him north of Nisibis about 330.[20] The yet more famous monastery on Mt. Izala was built on the site where he is said to have retired late in life, after he had sent out seventy disciples to found seventy other monasteries.[21] In Persia the beginnings of coenobitic monasticism are attributed to Aphrahat and his mountain bishopric of Mar Mattai north of Mosul around the year 340.[22] By the end of the fourth century monasteries were active throughout the Persian south, from the islands of the Persian Gulf to the desert of Anbar, that is, from Bahrain and the "black island" of the monastery of St. Thomas, to Piruz Shapur and Beit Katraye.[23]

Another way of bringing the spiritual power of the pious ascetics back from their far retreats to enrich the spiritual life of the church in the towns was to make a place for them in the ordinary congregations of believers. But how could such radically different life-styles and ideals of Christian vocation coexist in one church family without exploding? Just how awkward this could be and what prickly inconsistencies it involved becomes apparent in the works of Aphrahat the Persian, who began to write just about the time that Jacob of Nisibis died.

Aphrahat the Persian

Very little is known of Aphrahat's life, although he was the greatest Eastern theologian of the early fourth century and, in some respects, notably in the irenic way he conducted himself in theological disputes with the Jews, the most admirable of all the Christian thinkers of his time, East or West. His only surviving work, the *Demonstrations*, written between 336 and 345, is a remarkable blend of straightforward biblical teachings, deep and disciplined personal piety, a pure, classically Syriac literary style, and an unexpectedly "powerful, independent mind," as Neusner describes it.[24] Yet within two hundred years his name had disappeared, his writings were mistakenly attributed to his friend, Jacob of Nisibis, and not until the tenth century was he rescued from oblivion.[25]

Like Tatian, Aphrahat (in Latin, Aphraates) was an Assyrian, a northern Mesopotamian from the regions around Adiabene. He was apparently a convert from Zoroastrianism, and he writes as one who has taken the vows of singleness as a Son of the Covenant.[26] But there are hints in his writings that he too, like Jacob of Nisibis, had answered the call of the church and left the life of a solitary to become a bishop, the bishop of Mar Mattai (St. Matthew, a monastery high on a mountain crag on the east side of the upper Tigris River).[27] Later it became the seat of the metropolitan of Nineveh, second-highest prelate in the Nestorian hierarchy, but in Aphrahat's time it was probably still only a backwater diocese.

Aphrahat's *Demonstrations*, written under the pen name the "Persian Sage," are a series of short treatises, twenty-three in number.[28] They are the most important surviving source of information on Christian attitudes and thought patterns in the Persian church in the first half of the fourth century. The first ten chapters (written in 336/7) deal with ten specific aspects of Christian life and doctrine ranging from faith, fasting, and prayer to wars, Sons of the Covenant,[29] pastors, and humility. In the second section of thirteen chapters (written in 344), eight are written "against the Jews," which despite that description were doctrinal, not racist, in their texture but do indicate that the Eastern church, so Jewish in its early years, was now more strongly stressing its differences with the Judaism from which it had sprung.

Some have called Aphrahat anti-Semitic. True, he is severely critical of the Jewish legalisms of the synagogues and of the Jews' rejection of Jesus as the promised Messiah, but he is equally critical of his fellow Christians for falling away from their own early ideals and enthusiasms. He denounces the arrogance of Christian bishops in the capital at Seleucia-Ctesiphon and the self-indulgence of church members in the Persian cities.[30] He even detects with dismay hints of the relaxation of ascetic disciplines among the Sons and Daughters of the Covenant.[31] It is in his instructions to them that we are given the first clear picture of the severity of their religious vows. The Christian life of the "Covenanters," or "Solitaries," or "Monks," as they are variously called, must be a life of unrelenting warfare between believers and the devil. Satan will tempt them with all the enticements of the world's luxuries and pleasures. Then it is, says Aphrahat, that they must be ready to flee to the desert. The most dangerous instrument of Satanic temptation has always been women, from Eve to Delilah to Jezebel. The safest path for men, therefore, is to renounce the love of a woman and to live alone for Christ. As for women, their highest calling is to espouse virginity and thus rob the devil of his tool for temptation.[32]

But as a bishop, Aphrahat wisely recognizes that this will not be possible for all Christians. He knows, as a student of Scripture, that marriage is instituted by God and therefore good.[33] So Christians may marry. But if they do, he adds in another of his *Demonstrations*, it might be best to marry before baptism,[34] presumably so that the water can wash away the stains of sinful passion, which even the marriage relationship can arouse.

Such a summary is overharsh if it leaves an impression only of denunciation of Jews, contempt for women, and distortion of biblical teachings on marriage and baptism.[35] True, Aphrahat's theology was not always clear and consistent, his asceticism was exaggerated, and his Old Testament exegesis and arguments against the Jews were sometimes more subjective than exact. But beneath the rigor of his disputations and exhortations is a gentle Christian soul, "a serene, sweet-natured man . . . , a lover of the Church who grieves over arrogance and the abuse of authority."[36]

For example, though it is true that most of the second part of the *Demonstrations* is, in subject matter at least, sharply opposed to Jewish beliefs, there is no hate there. His differences are theological, not personal, and he makes every effort to show his respect for Jewish beliefs. He even couches the Christian creed with which he closes his first homily in such Old Testament terms that the change of a single word, it has been pointed out, would make it a completely Jewish creed.[37] In fact, the Jewish scholar J. Neusner remarks, "What is striking is the utter absence of anti-Semitism from Aphrahat's thought. While much provoked, he exhibits scarcely a trace of pervasive hatred of the Jews characteristic of the Greek-speaking churches of the Roman Orient, indeed of his near-contemporary John Chrysostom. . . . Though hard-pressed he throughout maintains an attitude of respect. He must be regarded as an example of the shape Christianity might have taken had it been formed in the Semitic-Iranian Orient, a region quite free of the legacy of pagan Greco-Roman anti-Semitism."[38]

Why did Aphrahat devote so much of his *Demonstrations* to the problems of Jewish-Christian dialogue? It was not the Jews who were harassing Christians, but the Zoroastrians. So would it not have been more relevant, given the times in which he lived, to deal at greater length with the agonizing position of Christians in pagan Persia caught in a war against Christian Rome?

Only one of the *Demonstrations* concerns the resumption of war once more between Rome and Persia. The Persian attack had been launched by Shapur II, who first marched north and west in 335 and again after the death of Constantine in 337. Aphrahat wrote as the war's devastations were beginning to be felt throughout Mesopotamia from the Persian capital in the south to the mountains of Armenia in the north. His homily was a message of comfort for his people, reminding Christians of how often in biblical times God in his mercy brought good out of evil. It was also a message of hope, but here Aphrahat was on dangerous ground both politically and exegetically. The political danger lay in the fact that he was a Christian Persian writing in Zoroastrian Persia, and however carefully he sought to soften the direction of his argument, the clear implication remained that he expected a victory for Christian Rome. Exegetically he faltered by trying to base this hope on a shaky and premature interpretation of the prophecies of Daniel. He predicts victory for Rome, "the fourth beast," over "the ram," Persia.[39]

He did well to write no more than he did on the war, for as a prophet he failed. As it turned out, after twenty-eight years of fighting and destruction the final battle ended in a disaster and the death of a Roman emperor. And by then the emperor, Julian, was no longer a Christian. The peace of 363 was a triumph for Persia, pagan Persia. Aphrahat was neither the first nor the last Christian writer to misread Bible prophecy, but at least he ended his homily on a sure and certain note: even the conquerors, he concludes, shall fall in their appointed time, but in the meantime let Christians "be earnest in imploring mercy that there may be peace upon the children of God."[40]

A more immediate problem than the rumble of distant wars was the major concern of Aphrahat in his *Demonstrations*. This was an issue that particularly troubled the churches of Adiabene, the problem of the relation of the Christian faith to its parentage in Judaism. From very early times Adiabene in the northeast, along with Edessa and Nisibis in the northwest and the capital area around Seleucia-Ctesiphon in the south, had been major centers for the Jews of the Syro-Persian Diaspora beyond the Euphrates. In the frontier client-kingdom of Adiabene where Aphrahat lived and worked, Judaism had won its most spectacular successes as a missionary faith. Before the Christian gospel had ever penetrated that far east, back in the first century A.D. a king of Adiabene and his mother and much of the nobility in Arbela, the capital, had been converted from paganism to the Jewish faith, as we have already seen.[41]

It was in the Jewish communities of the Diaspora in the East that Christian expansion outside the Roman Empire first put down roots, but the Jewish response to Christian evangelism was not always a glad welcome. Where strong rabbinical schools had been founded, as in Nisibis and Seleucia-Ctesiphon, church growth was slow and the church was late in organizing. But in Edessa and Adiabene, which had no such strong rabbinical centers, the rise of the Christian communities began early and they continued to flourish. This was especially true in Adiabene,[42] for though the royal family had adopted Judaism as early as A.D. 36, no school of rabbis was apparently formed there, and when early in the second century the king was forced to flee Arbela into Armenia by Trajan's successful invasion of 116, large numbers of Jews began to convert to Christianity. Jewish Christians in turn evangelized Gentiles, but as late as the beginning of the fourth century, about the time of the conversion of Aphrahat, Jewish Christians probably still outnumbered Gentiles in the church of Adiabene.

It may have been this shift in numbers from Jewish-Christian to gentile in the ethnic mixture in Adiabene Christianity that drew Aphrahat's attention to the need for clarification of the issues that distinguished Christians, whether Jewish or gentile in origin, from those who remained in the Jewish faith. Or perhaps he sensed the danger that Christians facing persecution in their own minority faith because of an imagined Roman connection might be tempted to return to the greater safety of the politically more favored Jewish community. For unlike that of Christians, the loyalty of the Jews to

Persia was not suspect. Their distrust of Rome had been tested and not found wanting ever since the destruction of Jerusalem in A.D. 70. Still a third possibility is that Aphrahat may simply have felt the need to warn Christians not to be swept away by zealous Jewish evangelists who could argue persuasively from the Bible that only the Jews were "the people of God."

At any rate, whatever the reasons, the major part of his *Demonstrations* is a remarkably even-tempered but firm and unequivocating exposition from the Jewish holy books themselves of the truth of the Christian faith and the fulfillment in Jesus Christ of all that is promised in the Old Testament to the Jews.[43] He treats Judaism as it was actually practiced and taught in the Diaspora, not as it was sometimes distorted by Christian apologists. He is realistically unsparing of cherished Jewish hopes. Prophecy does not guarantee the restoration of the Jews to Jerusalem, for the prophecy, he says, was already fulfilled in the return from Babylon.

His arguments are sometimes "disingenuous," as some have pointed out. His own Christian theology is not always clear. He does not quote the Nicene Creed and seems unaware of the crucial distinctions that were beginning to be made in Roman Asia and the West concerning the exact shape of the deity of Christ. Aphrahat, rather,* stands squarely on direct readings from the whole Bible, which for him is the final authority for all of life and belief. Throughout the *Demonstrations* Aphrahat quotes from most of the Old Testament books using the Peshitta, the Old Testament of the Palestinian synagogues with Jewish exegesis. He quotes from the Apocrypha (Tobit, Ecclesiasticus, Maccabees). In the Gospels, he uses Tatian's *Diatessaron*, significantly including the disputed last twelve verses of Mark which contain the Great Commission. For the rest of the New Testament he generally follows the canon of the Syriac Peshitta, which became the official version of the Church of the East and which omitted the four shorter "catholic Epistles" and the book of Revelation.[44]

In defending the doctrine of the deity of Christ he argues that though Jewish scholars say that God has no son, both their Old Testament and the Christian New Testament call the Messiah Son and God as no other man was ever the Son or called God:

> While we grant . . . that he [Jesus] is a man . . . [yet] we honor and call him God and Lord . . . God, Son of God, the King, son of the King, Light of the Light, Creator and Counsellor, Guide and Way, Redeemer, Shepherd, Gatherer, Pearl and Lamp. With many names he is called. . . . For us it is certain that Jesus is God the Son of God, and in

him we know the Father, and he has restrained us from all other worship.[45]

Add to this soaring statement on the finality of Christ the concluding verses from Aphrahat's homily on faith written not long before the Great Persecution of 340, and the two together could stand as a fitting creed for the church in Asia as it lived and believed in the early fourth century:

> Now this is faith:
> When a man believes in God the Lord of all
> Who made the heavens and the earth and the seas and all that is in them,
> And made Adam in His image,
> And gave the law to Moses.
> Who sent of His Spirit in the Prophets,
> Who sent His Messiah into the world;
> And that a man should believe in the resurrection of the dead,
> And in the sacrament of baptism,
> This is the faith of the Church of God.
> And that a man should separate himself from observing hours and Sabbaths and moons and seasons,
> And divinations and sorceries and astrology and magic,
> From the fornication and revelling and vain doctrines which are instruments of the Evil One,
> From the blandishments of honeyed words, from blasphemy and from adultery.
> These are the works of the faith which is based on the true Rock which is Christ,
> On whom the whole building is raised.[46]

NOTES

1. M. J. Higgins, "Chronology of the Fourth-Century Metropolitans of Seleucia-Ctesiphon," *Traditio* 9 (New York, 1953): 90.

2. Literature on the development of the episcopacy is immense and controversial. See D. Stone, *Episcopacy and Valid Orders in the Primitive Church* (1910); B. H. Streeter, *The Primitive Church* (1929); K. E. Kirk, ed., *The Apostolic Ministry* (1946); W. Telfer, *The Office of a Bishop* (1962); and H. Lietzmann, *History of the Early Church*, trans. B. L. Wolf, vol. 2 (London: Lutterworth, 1950), 57–68.

3. No bishops are mentioned in the *Gospel of Thomas, Gospel of Philip, Odes of Solomon*, Bardaisan's *Dialogue on Fate*, Tatian's *Address to the Greeks*, or even the *Acts of Thomas* (early third century). The *Didascalia* (early third century) clearly outlines a bishop's duties, but it is from west of Edessa.

4. For Edessa, the *Doctrine of Addai* (fourth or fifth century) see chap. 3, pp.

59f.; and for Arbela, the *History of the Church of Adiabene,* which is also known as the *Chronicle of Arbela* (sixth century), see chap. 3, p. 70 n. 89.

5. *Chronicle of Edessa,* ed. L. Hallier as *Untersuchungen über die Edessenische Chronik mit dem Syrischen text und einer Übersetzung* (Leipzig: Hinrichs'sche, 1892), 93. The *Chronicle's* list of bishops is: Qona 313, Aitallaha 324, Abraham 345–360, Barse 361–378, Eulogios 379–387, Kure 387–396 (in whose time the sarcophagus of St. Thomas was transferred to a memorial chapel, and Huns invaded the Roman Empire), Silvanus 398, Pekida (398–409), and Rabbulas 411/2–435 (see Hallier, *Edessenische Chronik,* 93–110 *passim*). The later traditional succession of bishops of Edessa as given in Bar Hebraeus (thirteenth century) is Addai, Aggai, Palut, Abselama, Barsamya, Tiridate, Bouznai, Saloula, Abda, (Gouria, Abda), Yazni, Hystaspe (who baptized Bardaisan), and Agai—these all preceding the bishops named above in the *Chronicle,* which is historically more reliable but which is oriented more to secular history in the early years. Then Bar Hebraeus follows a listing of bishops chronologically paralleling that of the *Chronicle:* Qona (Yona), Aitallaha, Abraham, Eulogius, Rabbula . . . There are many questions about both listings.

6. Elia Bar Sinaiya's *Chronography* (ed. L. J. Delaporte, in *Bibliotheque de l'École des Hautes Études, Ministere de l'Instruction Publiques Sciences, Historiques et Philologiques* [Paris: Honore Champion, 1910], 64) places Babu first and states that the bishop was not a metropolitan. The *Chronography* is from about 1010. But Voobus, in his *History of Asceticism, CSCO,* vol. 184, Subsidia t. 14 (Louvain, 1958), 1:142f., gives reasons for thinking that James was the first bishop.

7. A. Mingana, ed. and trans., *Sources Syriaques,* vol. 1, *Msiha-zkha* (Leipzig: Harrasowitz, 1907), 112.

8. The later traditional line of succession in Seleucia-Ctesiphon, as reconstructed by J. A. Assemani (largely from Amri and Bar Hebraeus) is as follows: Thomas, Addaeus, Achaeus (Aggai), Mares, Abres (ordained by Simeon Cleophas, bishop of Jerusalem), Abraham (sent to Seleucia from Antioch, d. ca. 152), Jacobus, Achadabuas (d. 220), Schiaclupha (Shaklupa, d. 244), Papa, Simeon. Assemani, *De Catholicis seu Patriarchis Chaldaeorum et Nestorianorum, Commentarius Historico-Chronologicus* (Rome, 1775), 1–9.

9. This account of the Synod of Seleucia comes from the proceedings of the Synod of Dadiso (Dadyeshu) of 424, as edited and translated by J. B. Chabot, in *Synodicon Orientale ou Recueil de Synodes Nestoriens* (Paris: Klincksieck, 1902), 285–98, esp. 290f. This record favors Papa's side of the case; but an account of the same council from the point of view of Bishop Miles of Susa agrees with it in all major particulars. See P. Bedjan, "The Acts of St. Miles," *Acta Martyrum et Sanctorum,* vol. 2, *Martyres Chaldaei et Persae* (Paris, 1890–97), 260ff., in Syriac. Higgins, "Chronology of Fourth-Century Metropolitans of Seleucia-Ctesiphon," 59, 89–92, critically analyzes the varied sources on the Synod. He gives "primacy" to the contemporary minutes of the Synod of Isaac in 410, and of Dadiso in 424 (p. 76). He finds the "Acts of Miles"

132 FROM THE APOSTLES TO MUHAMMAD

hagiographical but accurate in chronology and "truthful in essentials." Of the later histories and chronologies—the *History of the Church in Adiabene* (ca. 550), Pseudo-Elias of Nisibis (ca. tenth century), the *Chronicle of Seert* (ca. 1036), Bar Hebraeus (1286), Amri ('Amr ibn Matta, ca. 1350), and Sliba (Saliba ibn Johannan, ca. 1350)—after noting their varying accounts of the affair and describing their biases, he concludes, "full confidence can never be reposed in anything affirmed by them, whether singly or unanimously" (p. 92).

10. It is not unlikely that the account of the controversy as preserved in the records of the later Synod of Dadyeshu (424) smooths over some of the sharpness of the divisions and ambitions involved. For example, it claims perhaps correctly that Simon was made bishop against his will by the anti-Papa bishops. Chabot, *Synodicon Orientale,* 291, and see W. A. Wigram, *A History of the Assyrian Church* A.D. *100–640* (London: SPCK, 1910), 53–55.

11. Aphrahat, *Demonstrations* 14.

12. The earliest references to "western bishops" in the affair are in the Acts of the Synod of Dadyeshu (424) in remarks made by Bishop Agapit of Beit Lapat. Since that synod actively promoted closer relations between the Persian and Roman churches, the bishop's recollection of history may have had a pro-Western slant. See Chabot, *Synodicon Orientale,* 289–94. J. Labourt, *Le Christianisme dans l'Empire Perse sous le dynastie Sassanide, 224–632* (Paris: Lecoffre, 1904, 125n) has doubts about the complete trustworthiness of the Acts of the Synod, but Higgins ("Chronology," 94–98) vigorously defends its historical reliability. References to the legendary journey to Antioch and Jerusalem at the end of the "episcopate of Bishop Jacob" of Seleucia-Ctesiphon are much later, as in the histories of Mari Ibn Suleiman (twelfth century) and Bar Hebraeus (thirteenth century). The apocryphal correspondence allegedly brought back on this trip from Western patriarchs affirming the primacy of Seleucia-Ctesiphon in the East cannot be dated earlier than the fifth or sixth centuries. See Wigram, *Assyrian Church,* 41ff.; and Assemani, *De Catholicis,* 5f.

13. The capture of Bishop Demetrius of Antioch is reported by Mari Ibn Suleiman's *Book of the Tower (Liber Turris),* a twelfth-century record of the lives of the patriarchs of Seleucia-Ctesiphon.

14. Higgins, "Chronology," 54–61.

15. Theodoret of Cyrus, *History of the Monks (Historia Religiosa),* in K. Gilbert, *Bibliotheca der Kirchenvater,* 2d ed., 50 (1926). P. Peeters questions the details of Theodoret's account in his "La Legende de S. Jacques de Nisibis," *Analecta Bollandiana,* vol. 38 (Brussels, 1920), 291f., but Voobus defends the general picture Theodoret gives, *History of Asceticism,* 1:141–43, 151.

16. See n. 6 above. For a more recent critical study see J. M. Fiey, "Nisibe: metropole syriaque orientale et ses suffragants des origines a nos jours" (*CSCO,* vol. 388, subsidia 54 [1977]). Ephrem the Syrian gives the order of Nisibene bishops as Jacob, Babu, Walages, Abraham (K. McVey, *Ephrem the*

Syrian: Hymns [New York: Paulist, 1989], 8). Elia bar Sinaia (d. 1049) puts Babu first.

17. Voobus, *History of Asceticism,* 1:142

18. S. P. Brock points out that though many Syrian sources do credit Augin with introducing monasticism into Syria, in fact "Mar Awgen is never mentioned in any source, Syriac or Greek, that can be dated earlier than about the ninth century." He traces indigenous Syrian monasticism to the Lucan tradition of Antioch, as, for example, Luke's version of the Beatitudes emphasizing physical externals, "Blessed are the poor," in contrast to Matthew's "Blessed are the poor in spirit" ("Early Syrian Asceticism," *Numen* 20 [Leiden, 1973], 3ff.).

19. For the monasticism of Persia see E. A. W. Budge, *The Book of Governors: The Historia Monastica of Thomas, Bishop of Marga* A.D. *840,* vol. 1 (London, 1893), intro., cxxiiff.

20. H. B. Workman, *The Evolution of the Monastic Ideal . . .,* (London: Epworth, 1913), 113 and n. He observes that Assemani dates the foundation before the Council of Nicaea (325), others in 333.

21. A. S. Atiya, *A History of Eastern Christianity* (London: Methuen, 1968), 291.

22. Workman, *Monastic Ideal,* 113.

23. A. Mingana, "The Early Spread of Christianity in India," *Bulletin of the John Rylands Library,* 10, no. 2 (July 1926): 6. For an old but thorough study of the literature on early monasticism, see M. Heimbucher, *Die Orden und Kongregationen der katholischen Kirche,* 2d ed., 3 vols. (Paderborn: Schoningen, 1907).

24. The phrase is quoted from Jacob Neusner, who rejects the frequent characterization of Aphrahat as imitative and unoriginal. See his *Aphrahat and Judaism: The Christian-Jewish Argument in Fourth-Century Iran* Studia Post-Biblica, no. 19 (Leiden: Brill, 1971), xi.

25. Perhaps he dropped from sight because the West suspected him of Nestorian heresy, though he was too early for that, of course. It was a Nestorian, Bar-Bahlul (ca. 963), who rediscovered him. (See J. Gwynn's introduction to his translation of selections from Aphrahat's *Demonstrations,* in *Nicene and Post-Nicene Fathers,* 2d series, vol. 13 (Grand Rapids: Eerdmans, 1983), 152–56.

26. Aphrahat, *Demonstrations* 6. esp. 4–8.

27. Budge, *Book of Governors,* cxxxvff.

28. Aphrahat, *Demonstrations.* The standard text is *Aphraatis Sapientis Persae Demonstrationes,* ed. Parisot in *PS,* vols. 1, 2 (Paris, 1894–1907), translated into "rather unreliable Latin," according to R. H. Connolly, "Aphraates and Monasticism," *Journal of Theological Studies,* 6 (1905): 522n. All but five of the Demonstrations are also now translated into English by various authors including Gwynn, *Nicene and Post-Nicene Fathers,* 13 (1956); Neusner, *Aphrahat*

and Judaism; Hallock, *Journal of the Society of Oriental Research* 14 (1930), 18–32; and R. H. Connolly, *Journal of Theological Studies,* 6.522–539, as follows: 1. Faith (by Gwynn), 2. Charity (Hallock), 5. Wars (Gwynn), 6. Monks, i.e., Sons of the Covenant (Gwynn), 8. Resurrection (Gwynn), 9. 10. Pastors (Gwynn), 11. Circumcision (Neusner), 12. Paschal Sacrifice (Neusner), 13. Sabbath (Neusner), 15. Distinctions among Foods (Neusner), 16. The Peoples [and] the People, i.e., the Church (Neusner), 17. The Messiah (Gwynn, Neusner), 18. Against the Jews and On Virginity (Neusner), 19. Against the Jews (Neusner), 21. Persecution (Gwynn, Neusner), 22. Death and the Latter Times (Gwynn). The five not so translated are: Fasting, Prayer, Penitents, Rebuke to Clergy and Church, and Almsgiving.

29. The title of *Demonstrations* 6, translated "Monks" in Latin, is better rendered "Sons of the Covenant" from the Syriac *benai qeyama.* The Covenanters were premonastic ascetics, both men and women. See chap. 4, pp. 97ff.; and also E. J. Duncan, *Baptism in the Demonstrations of Aphraates the Persian Sage* (Washington, D.C: Catholic University of America, 1945), 84–103.

30. Aphrahat, *Demonstrations* 14.

31. Aphrahat, *Demonstrations* 7.

32. Aphrahat, *Demonstrations* 6. See also 14.1 and 18 ("Against the Jews, and On Virginity").

33. Aphrahat, *Demonstrations* 8.

34. F. C. Burkitt based his conviction that the third-century church reserved baptism only for the celibate on this passage (*Early Eastern Christianity* [London: Murray, 1904], 127), but Connolly argues, with reason, that this particular section of *Demonstrations* (7. 20) is addressed not to catechumens in general, but to those who intended to take the subsequent stricter vows of the Covenanters. (See his "Aphraates and Monasticism," 529ff.). He holds that paragraphs 1–16 of this chapter are addressed to all penitents but that paragraphs 18–25 are written to the Sons and Daughters of the Covenant and may simply mean "that those who have already set their heart on matrimony are, by that very fact, disqualified for membership of the higher grade of Christians and are free to marry at once" before baptism. Compare a similar attitude in Tertullian's *De Baptismo,* 18, written about 200: "For no less cause must the unwedded be deferred (from baptism) . . . until they either marry, or else be more fully strengthened for continence . . ."

35. On Aphrahat's teachings on baptism, see Duncan, *Baptism.* Duncan points out that though Aphrahat does emphasize the power of baptism to remit sins, he acknowledges that "in reality its [i.e., the remission's] efficacious cause is the Holy Spirit," as in *Demonstrations* 6 (pp. 14–17). There, the baptism of the spirit is related to the baptism with water, but the water itself is not regenerative, and the Spirit can be grieved and depart.

36. The quotation is from R. Murray, *Symbols of Church and Kingdom* (Cambridge: Cambridge Univ. Press, 1975), 29.

37. H. L. Pass, "The Creed of Aphraates," *Journal of Theological Studies* 9 (Oxford and London, 1908): 267–84.

38. Neusner, *Aphrahat and Judaism,* 5.

39. Aphrahat, *Demonstrations* 5. esp. 5–6, 10, 24, arguing from the book of Daniel 7 and 8 and Luke 14:11. Aphrahat does not name the two empires but the identification with Rome and Persia is clear. Ultimate victory, he wisely added, will be with Jesus the "mighty champion."

40. Aphrahat, *Demonstrations* 5.

41. See chap. 3, p. 70. The king was Izates I who, according to Josephus, was already a Jewish proselyte when he ascended the throne of his border kingdom. See a chronology in J. Neusner, *A History of Jews in Babylonia,* 5 vols. (Leiden: 1966–70), 1:61–67. Jesus himself once noted that the Pharisees were no less zealous in evangelism than his own disciples (Matt. 23:15).

42. On the Jewish school in Nisibis, see Neusner, *Jews in Babylonia* 1:48ff., 122ff., and 180, where Neusner writes, "What Edessa was to the Christians, Nisibis was to Tannaite Judaism." On Seleucia-Ctesiphon, where the Persians created a "head" for the Jewish communities of the empire, see pp. 103–121; and for schools in the south, pp. 39–41, 52–53, and 173–77.

43. Aphrahat, *Demonstrations* 11, 12, 13, 15, 16, 17, 18, 19, 21, 22, 23.

44. See Gwynn, *Nicene and Post-Nicene Fathers,* 13:162; F. Gavin, "Aphraates and the Jews" (Toronto: Trinity College, 1923), 14, 67–72; and especially Neusner, *Aphrahat and Judaism,* 199–214, for a list of Scripture references.

45. Aphrahat, *Demonstrations* 17. Neusner, in *Aphrahat and Judaism,* notes that Aphrahat's argument on Christ's deity is unusual in that it begins with references to other men called god in Scripture, such as Moses and Solomon, rather than with the usual clear distinction between Jesus and all others (p. 130f.). But for a more complete reconstruction of a Christological creed pieced together from Aphrahat's writings, see R. H. Connolly, "The Early Syrian Creed," *Zeitschrift für die neutestamentliche Wissenschaft und die Kunde des Urchristenthums* (1906): 202–23.

46. Adapted from Aphrahat, *Demonstrations* 1. 19. It was Burkitt who called this passage the "Creed of Aphraates" (*Early Eastern Christianity,* 84f.). Pass, in "The Creed of Aphraates," points out that with the change of one word, from "*sent* His Messiah" to "*will send* His Messiah," this would stand as a Jewish creed. But this was perhaps purposeful on the part of Aphrahat who was addressing Jews as well as Christians, and therefore wrote his *Demonstrations* in Jewish thought patterns to which he gradually added distinctively Christological passages. Pass's argument that the original actually was Jewish is unconvincing. See R. H. Connolly, "On Aphraates' Hom. 1:19," *Journal of Theological Studies* 9 (Oxford and London, 1908): 572–76.

Chapter 7
The
Great Persecution
(340–401)

"[Shapur II] fell into a violent rage [against Shim'un],
gnashed his teeth, and struck his hands together,
saying: 'Shimun wants to arouse his disciples and his
people to rebel against my Empire. He wants to
make them slaves of Caesar, who has the same
religion as they have: that is why he disobeys my
orders!'"

—Bedjan, *Acts of the Martyrs and
Saints*, 2:143. Translated by W. G.
Young—*Handbook*, 278

APHRAHAT'S ninth *Demonstration* is called "On Persecution." It draws attention to a bitter turn of events in his lifetime that tragically affected the Persian church. The great new fact of the fourth century for the church in Persia was not the relationship of Christianity to Judaism, nor the beginnings of monasticism, nor even the emergence of a national church organization. It was the great persecution that fell upon the Christians in Persia about the year 340.

It is somewhat strange that Aphrahat scarcely mentions the two major causes of this persecution. The first was the conversion of Constantine. The fact that Rome was now Christian was never far from his thoughts, as is obvious in his veiled references to Rome in the fifth *Demonstration*, "On War," written in the year that the first Christian emperor, Constantine, died. But as a Persian Christian, writing in a Persia that for centuries had been at war with Rome, he had good reason to mute any emphasis on the Christianization of the Western empire. It was clearly Rome's Christianity, not the second cause, Persia's Zoroastrianism, that triggered the outbreak of what is called the Great Persecution. Though the religious motives were never unrelated, the primary cause of the persecution was political. When Rome became Christian, its old enemy Persia turned anti-Christian.

Up to then the situation had been reversed. For the first three hundred years after Christ it was in the West that Christians had been persecuted. In the East they were tolerated. The martyrdoms in Edessa were Roman, not Persian, and they began with the decree of a Roman emperor, Trajan (reigned 98–117), under whose authority occurred the legendary deaths of Sharbil, Babay, and Barsamya in Osrhoene. It was Rome that first made Christianity there illegal.[1]

Again near the end of Roman persecution, it was the decree of another emperor, Licinius, that caused the better attested martyrdoms of Shamona, Guria, and Habib the deacon. This was about 309, just two years before Galerius, Constantine, and Licinius in 311 signed Rome's first Edict of Toleration. In that year, says the record, Licinius "made a persecution" in Edessa and ordered sacrifices to Jupiter. But Habib, a simple village deacon, knew his Christian duty. He went about encouraging the faithful "to stand fast in the truth of their faith," and when his resistance became known he gave himself up to save his fellow villagers. He was tortured and burned for his Lord.[2]

That was the last of the great Roman persecutions. Looking back two hundred years later, the Easterner Mar Jacob, bishop of Sarug (452–521), celebrated the martyrdom of Habib as the beginning of a new age. In his *Oration on Habib the Martyr* he wrote:

Then ceased the sacrifices and in the congregations there was peace. The sword was sheathed, nor Christians any more laid waste. With Sharbil it began, with Habib ended in our land. From that time until now, not one has it slain: since he was burned, Constantine, the chief of victors, reigns and now the Cross the emperor's diadem surmounts.[3]

Beyond Edessa to the east across the Persian border there was no such rejoicing. For two hundred and fifty years Persia had been a refuge for Christians from Roman persecution. The Parthians were too religiously tolerant to persecute, and their less tolerant Sassanian successors on the throne were too busy fighting Rome, as the *History of the Church in Adiabene* thankfully observed.[4] Moreover, as long as Roman emperors considered Christians to be enemies of Rome, Persian emperors were inclined to regard them as friends of Persia.

It was about 315 that an ill-advised letter from the Christian emperor Constantine to his Persian counterpart Shapur II probably triggered the beginnings of an ominous change in the Persian attitude toward Christians. Constantine believed he was writing to help his fellow believers in Persia but succeeded only in exposing them. He wrote to the young shah:

I rejoice to hear that the fairest provinces of Persia are adorned with . . . Christians. . . . Since you are so powerful and pious, I commend them to your care, and leave them in your protection.[5]

It was enough to make any Persian ruler conditioned by three hundred years of war with Rome suspicious of the emergence of a potential fifth column. Any lingering doubts must have been dispelled when about twenty years later Constantine began to gather his forces for war in the East. Eusebius records that Roman bishops were prepared to accompany their emperor "to battle with him and for him by prayers to God from whom all victory proceeds."[6] And across the border in Persian territory the forthright Persian preacher Aphrahat recklessly predicted on the basis of his reading of Old Testament prophecy that Rome would defeat Persia.[7]

Faced with what seemed to be a double threat, a threat not only to national security but to the national religion as well, Persia's priests and rulers cemented their alliance of state and religion in a series of periods of terror that have been called the most massive persecution of Christians in history, "unequalled for its duration, its ferocity and the number of martyrs."[8] The description is probably true, though the traditional accounts may exaggerate the numbers and usually fail to mention that the persecution was not concentrated in one long forty-year outburst of hate but occurred in at least two shorter but no less tragic periods of madness separated by an interval of comparative peace.

The persecutions began in 339 or 340,[9] in the reign of Shapur II, who ruled Persia for seventy years (309–379), longer than any shah before or since. It was an age of wars and persecutions, of the clash of empires and the revitalization of the Persian nation, of the Christianization of Rome and the disintegration for two generations of the Persian church.

But to look back forty years, as the third century ended and the fourth began, it had then been the Persian Empire not the Persian church that seemed about to disintegrate. In 298 the Roman Caesar, Galerius, had humiliated Narseh of Persia, Shapur II's grandfather, in a defeat so crushing that Persia lost all of northern Mesopotamia including Nisibis and five Persian provinces east of the Tigris north of Adiabene. Emboldened by the defeat, Arab tribes attacked Persia from the west and north. At one point the Arabs even captured the capital, Seleucia-Ctesiphon, and a Mongol tribe called Khitans began to move out of central Asia across the Bactrian border into Iran. The shah was helpless. Powerful nobles disowned Narseh's son, Hormizd II, and threw him into prison. Then, whether to preserve the dynasty or to ensure its fall, they held a crown over the womb of the deposed shah's pregnant queen and designated the powerless embryo his heir. The baby was born a few months later and proclaimed king of kings, Shah Shapur II. Surprisingly he survived. At age sixteen he took the government into his own hands and faced down the great nobles. Before he was twenty he moved brutally against the marauding Arabs, ordering his soldiers to puncture the shoulder blades of all prisoners so that they could never take arms against him again. This gave him the name of "Shoulder-piercer." Next he flung his armies east against the Kushans and captured Bactria. Finally, when still under thirty, he set out to avenge his grandfather's humiliation by Rome. He was determined to win back what Persia had lost—the great border fortress of Nisibis and the five provinces across the Tigris.

In 337 Constantine the Great died in the midst of preparations for his war as protector of Christians against pagan Persia. To Shapur the time seemed favorable for counterattack. The great Constantine was dead, his empire divided among his three sons. Light Persian cavalry crossed the border before the year was over; then their main armies besieged the strong walled city of Nisibis. The siege failed and Shapur withdrew; the historian Theodoret piously recorded that the prayers of its saintly bishop, James, saved the city by calling down a plague of flies to confuse and stun the Persians.[10]

It is little wonder, then, that when the persecutions began shortly thereafter, the first accusation brought against the Christians in Persia was that they were aiding and abetting the Roman enemy. "There is no secret which Simon (Bar-Sabba'e, bishop of Seleucia-Ctesiphon) does not write to Caesar to reveal," the Zoroastrians whispered into the ear of the shah. Shapur II's response was to order a double tax on Christians and to hold the bishop responsible for collecting it. He knew they were poor and that the bishop would be hard-pressed to find the money. The shah's order, preserved in one of the anonymous accounts of the martyrdoms, illustrates the absolute, arbitrary power of the Persian emperor:

> When you receive this order of our godhead, which is contained in the enclosure herein despatched, you will arrest Simon, the chief of the Nazarenes. You will not release him until he has signed this document and agreed to collect the payment to us of a double-tax and a double tribute for all the people of the Nazarenes who are found in the country of our godhead and who inhabit our territory. For our godhead has only the weariness of war while they have nothing but repose and pleasure. They live in our territory [but] share the sentiments of Caesar our enemy.[11]

Bishop Simon refused to be intimidated. He branded the tax as unjust and declared, "I am no tax collector but a shepherd of the Lord's flock." Then the killings began. A second decree ordered the destruction of churches and the execution of clergy who refused to participate in the national worship of the sun. Bishop Simon was seized and brought before the shah who, it is said, had known him from his youth. He was offered rich gifts to make a token obeisance to the sun, and when he refused, as his accusers expected, they cunningly tempted him with the promise that if only he alone would apostasize his people would not be harmed, but that if he refused he would be condemning not just the church leaders but all Christians to destruction. At that, the Christians themselves rose up and refused to accept such a deliverance as shameful. So on Good Friday, according to the tradition (but more likely on September 14), in the year 344, he was led outside the city of Susa along with a large number of Christian clergy. Five bishops and one hundred priests were beheaded before his eyes, and last of all he himself was put to death.[12]

For the next two decades and more, Christians were tracked down and hunted from one end of the empire to the other. At times the pattern was general massacre. More often, as Shapur decreed, it was intensive organized elimination of the leadership of the church, the clergy. A third category of suppression was the search for that part of the Christian community that was most vulnerable to persecution, Persians who had been converted from the national religion, Zoroastrianism. As we have already seen, the faith had spread first among non-Persian elements in the population, Jews and Syrians. But by the beginning of the fourth century Iranians in increasing numbers were attracted to the Christian faith. For such converts church membership could mean the loss of everything— family, property rights, and life itself.

The Syriac *Acts of the Martyrs* tells the story of a boy from a noble family who became a Christian. His name was Saba Gusnazdad. He told his mother of his change of heart but did not dare to tell his father. After the father died, however, it could be hidden no longer. An uncle came to attend the family sacrifices and ceremonies that would be observed for the installation of Saba as the family head. The mother made excuses. "The boy is too young," she kept saying. But all to no avail, and when the uncle finally discovered the real reason for the delay, he denounced the boy as a Christian and claimed the headship and family fortune for himself.[13]

Converts from the national faith had no rights and in the darker years of the persecutions were often put to death. The major agents in the slaughter were the Zoroastrian clergy, the *magi* or *mobeds*, but sometimes Christians suspected the Jews and accused them of acting as informers. This anti-Jewish note in some accounts of the persecution may be a later addition to the record, but it is true that the Jewish minority suffered less than the Christians in the harassment of religious minorities, and Sozomen, the fifth-century historian, reports the tradition that in the death of Bishop Simon's two sisters, the informers against them were Jewish. Shapur II's queen was a Jewish proselyte, according to Sozomen, and when she fell mysteriously ill it was said that her Jewish friends persuaded her that the Christian bishop's sisters, who were both ascetic Daughters of the Covenant and therefore considered oddly different from the pleasure-loving non-Christian Persians, had used witchcraft to cast a spell on her in retaliation for their brother Simon's death. The *magi* seized the two women, sawed them in two, and superstitiously directed that the sick queen be carried in her litter between their bleeding, severed bodies to cast off the evil Christian curse.[14]

The martyrdom of Simon and the years of persecution that followed wiped out the beginnings of the central national organization the Persian church had only so recently achieved. As fast as the Christians of the capital elected a new bishop after Simon, the man was seized and killed. The names of two of them have survived. A

Bishop Sahdost may have succeeded Bishop Simon in the catholicate (as the position of head bishop came to be called), and Bishop Barbashmin after Sahdost's death. Sahdost lasted not much more than a year, and Barbashmin probably not much longer.[15] Then for twenty years or more the position was left vacant. Elevation to the catholicate meant instant death.

Inflaming the anti-Roman political motivation of the government's role in the persecutions was a deep undercurrent of Zoroastrian fanaticism and hatred of other religions. The zealots' hatred and the type of charges they customarily hurled against Christians can be seen in the following passage from one of the *Acts of the Martyrs* that quotes a royal decree:

> The Christians destroy our holy teachings, and teach men to serve one God, and not to honour the sun or fire. They teach them, too, to defile water by their abolutions; to refrain from marriage and the procreation of children; and to refuse to go out to war with the Shah-in-Shah. They have no scruple about the slaughter and eating of animals; they bury the corpses of men in the earth; and attribute the origin of snakes and creeping things to a good God. They despise many servants of the King, and teach witchcraft.[16]

Sometime before the death of Shapur II in 379 the intensity of the persecution slackened. Tradition calls it a forty-year persecution, lasting from 339 to 379 and ending only with Shapur's death, but the worst seems to have been over at least a decade before his death. Perhaps it was the great Persian victory and the crushing defeat and death of the invading Roman emperor Julian in 363 that brought a period of peace to the church in Persia. Julian "the Apostate," who had renounced the Christianity of his uncle, Constantine the Great, became emperor in 361. He had already defeated the barbarians along the Rhine. Now, dreaming of becoming a second Alexander, he marched east with a great army down the Euphrates toward Seleucia-Ctesiphon. Outside the capital he easily defeated a Persian army and sent it reeling to safety within the city walls. Roman victory seemed imminent but the impression was illusory. Julian's Armenian allies deserted him. As Christians they were not inclined to die for an apostate emperor. His Arab supporters had also left him, offended by his Roman pride and stingy pay. Moreover, on the course of their march the Romans had tried and failed to reduce by siege a whole string of Persian walled fortresses. So instead of besieging Seleucia-Ctesiphon Julian decided to consolidate his resources by a temporary withdrawal. It was a retreat into disaster, a march toward the "appointment at Samarra" that was his death.

Shapur's Persians poured out of their citadels to harass the line of march; Roman supplies ran out, and at Samarra, about one hundred miles north of Seleucia-Ctesiphon, Julian was caught by surprise in a minor skirmish and struck by a javelin. The Christian historians Theodoret and Sozomen record the tradition that as he lay dying, he threw some of his own blood at the sky, crying, "O Galilean, thou hast conquered."[17]

Shapur forced a hard peace on the shocked, defeated Romans. He won back all that his grandfather Narseh had lost: the five provinces beyond the Tigris and, highest prize of all, the famous walled city of Nisibis. Multitudes of prisoners from the recaptured border territories were uprooted and resettled farther east in Persia, especially in Isfahan and Susiana. They included almost a hundred thousand Christian families, according to Moses of Chorene, adding not only to the numbers of Christians in Persia, but also perhaps bringing liturgical manuscripts and their sacred books. Voobus believes that it was through this influx of refugees and captives that the four separate Gospels of the Western canon came into circulation in Persia and gradually replaced Tatian's harmony of the Gospels, the *Diatessaron*.[18]

It was at this time that Ephrem the Syrian (ca. 306–373), who had helped to rally the defenders of Nisibis against an earlier Persian assault, chose to leave with the departing Romans. The city had been Roman all his life and Christian Roman at that. It had been captured by Rome less than ten years before he was born, and he was five or six when Constantine the Great became a Christian. So Ephrem was almost sixty when the treaty of 363 gave the border fortress back to Persia, and as a famed and open opponent of the return of pagan rule he had little choice but to take advantage of the peace treaty's guarantee of safe passage across the border into Roman territory for all the city's Christians. The Great Persecution was still raging in the empire of the shah so Ephrem went west and the Church of the East lost its best-known theologian, Bible expositor, and hymn writer. He spent the last ten years of his life in Edessa as a refugee. Tradition relates that he lived in a cave and earned a living for a while as a bath attendant. He steadfastly refused all offers of high position but probably taught for a while at the famous School of Edessa and wrote prolifically and testily on everything from the heresies of Bardaisan, Marcion, and Mani to the scientific theories of his day. Though he thundered against heretics and unbelievers, Ephrem had a tender heart for the poor. A disastrous famine swept Edessa and peasants were dying in the streets. Only Ephrem was concerned enough and trusted enough to shame the rich citizens of the town into giving up some of their hoarded wealth for relief of the destitute. He is credited with the founding of one of the first Christian hospitals in the East, a hasty, rough construction but a building with three hundred beds. When he died he asked to be buried not with the bishops and the rich, but with the poor.[19]

The conflicting traditions and histories of those troubled times make it impossible to date the ending of the great terror. It is believed that some time after the defeat of Julian, when fear of a Roman invasion subsided, Shapur II may have issued a decree of toleration in some limited form for Christians,[20] and when he died in 379 a weaker succession of Persian kings became more concerned about the rising rival power of their feudal underlords and the appearance on the northern borders of hordes of White Huns (Hephthalites) pouring out of central Asia than with continuing the war against Rome or the persecution of Christians. There are reports of outbreaks of violence under his immediate successor, Ardashir II, but that shah ruled only three years, and oppression diminished again under Shapur III (383–388), who concluded another peace with Rome.[21]

It is possible that it was in this period of comparative quiet, either before or after the death of Shapur the Great (Shapur II), that the Persian church managed to restore for a time the succession to the episcopate in the capital, Seleucia-Ctesiphon. There are shadowy references to the election of a head of the church, Bishop Tomarsa (or Tamuza), and of a Bishop Qayuma after him, to end the vacancy in leadership that followed the martyrdom of Bishop Barbashmin. Then, according to the records of the Synod of Dadyeshu in 424, there followed another long and paralyzing vacancy in national leadership, which was later called the catholicate. But neither the facts nor the dates are clear.[22]

The persecutions, it would seem, had never really ended. Like smouldering coals, hatreds and fanaticism were always just beneath the surface of the volatile social order, as Wigram describes it, flaring up from time to time, then "flickering out" again, but persisting up into the first years of the fifth century.[23] It is said that in Bishop Qayuma's time the persecutions were still so intense that when he was asked as an old man of eighty to accept the perilous position of leader of the church, he accepted only because, as he said, "I am going to die soon anyway, and I had rather die a martyr than of old age."[24]

When at last the years of suffering ended around the year 401, the historian Sozomen, who lived near enough to that time of tribulation to remember the tales of those who had experienced it, wrote that the multitude of martyrs had been beyond enumeration.[25] One estimate is that as many as 190,000 Persian Christians died in the terror. It was worse than anything suffered in the West under Rome, yet the number of apostasies seemed to be fewer in Persia than in the West, which is a remarkable tribute to the steady courage of Asia's early Christians.[26]

NOTES

1. Tradition places these first martyrdoms in the reign of Trajan, but some scholars believe that if they were historical at all they occurred in the great Roman persecutions of 250. See chap. 3, pp. 71f.

2. *The Martyrdom of Habib the Deacon,* in William Cureton, ed., *Ancient Syriac Documents* (London, 1864; reprint, Amsterdam: Oriental Press, 1967), 72–85.

3. *Oration on Habib the Martyr,* in Cureton, *Ancient Syriac Documents,* 95f.

4. A. Mingana, *Sources Syriaques,* vol. 1 (Leipzig: Harrasowitz, 1907), 106, 109.

5. Theodoret, *Ecclesiastical History* 1. 24. Sozomen's *Ecclesiastical History* gives an inaccurate summary of the same letter and dates it wrongly.

6. Eusebius, *Life of Constantine,* 4:56.

7. Aphrahat, *Demonstrations* 5. esp. 5, 6, 24. See chap. 6, pp. 127f.

8. L. C. Casartelli, "Sassanians," *Hastings Encyclopedia of Religion and Ethics* 11:203.

9. The traditional date is 340, but the Persian and Roman calendars overlap near the beginning or end of the year.

10. Theodoret, *Ecclesiastical History* 2. 26.

11. Cited by J. Labourt, *Le Christianisme dans l'Empire Perse sous le dynastie Sassanide, 224–632* (Paris: Lecoffre, 1904), 45f.

12. Sozomen, *Ecclesiastical History* 2. 9–10; and Labourt, *Le Christianisme,* 46– 68. The primary source is the *Life of St. Simon Barsabai* (in Syriac), ed. P. Bedjan, in *Acta Martyrum et Sanctorum,* vol. 2, *Martyres Chaldaei et Persae* (Paris and Leipzig, 1891), 130ff. The quotations are from p. 136. See also P. Peeters, "La date du martyre de S. Symeon, archevêque de Seleucia-Ctesiphon," in *Analecta Bollandiana* vol. 61 (Bruxelles, 1938), 118ff.

13. A. Voobus, *History of Asceticism,* vol. 1, *CSCO,* vol. 184, subsidia t. 14 (Louvain, 1958), 223f., citing Bedjan, *Acta Martyrum,* 2:642ff.

14. Sozomen, *Ecclesiastical History* 2. 12. On the role of the Jews, see A. Fortescue, *The Lesser Eastern Churches* (London: Catholic Truth Society, 1913), 46n.

15. M. J. Higgins, "Chronology of the Fourth-Century Metropolitans of Seleucia-Ctesiphon," *Traditio* 9 (1953): 45–92f., gives convincing reasons for dating the death of Bishop Simon Bar-Sabba'e at 344 and the catholicate of Sahdost as beginning in 344/45 and extending to an unknown date. He notes that all the chroniclers say that Barbashmin held office for seven years, but "they were all wrong," he states. Labourt, *Le Christianisme*, 72f., dates Sahdost's death as 342 and Barbashmin's as 346.

16. *Acts of Aqib-shima*, in Bedjan, *Acta Martyrum* 2:351, quoted by W. A. Wigram, *History of the Assyrian Church* A.D. *100–640* (London: SPCK, 1910), 64f.

17. Theodoret, *Ecclesiastical History* 3. 20; Sozomen, *Ecclesiastical History* 6.

18. Moses of Chorene, cited by J. Neusner, *History of the Jews in Babylonia*, 5 vols. (Leiden: 1966–70), 4:16ff.; and A. Voobus, *Studies in the History of the Gospel Text in Syriac CSCO* [128], subsidia t. 3 (Louvain, 1951), 30. See also Ammianus Marcellinus *Rerum Gestarum Libri* 20. 6, 7, an important Roman source on the wars with Shapur II.

19. This Ephrem is not to be confused with another, lesser-known Ephrem who was patriarch of Alexandria in the tenth century. There is no definitive edition of his complete works, though there is an extensive eighteenth-century collection of his writings by J. S. Assemani et al. (Rome, 1732–46). His hymns are carefully edited by K. McVey, with introduction, *Ephrem the Syrian: Hymns* (New York: Paulist, 1989). See also *Selections*, ed. J. Gwynn in *Nicene and Post-Nicene Christian Fathers, op. cit.*, Ser. II, vol. xiii, pp. 2 (1898); and O. Bardenhewer, *Geschichte der altkirchlichen Literatur*, 4 (1924), 343–75. On his life and work see J. B. Segal, *Edessa, The Blessed City* (Oxford: Clarendon, 1970, 87ff. and *passim*; and H. Waddell, *The Desert Fathers* (London: Constable, 1936), 189f. citing St. Basil's *Vita S. Ephraem* (C. vi, *Vit. Pat.* I) and *Paradisus Heraclidis* (C. xxviii).

20. Higgins, "Chronology," 92.

21. Shapur III earned the reputation of being "a just and merciful man." Wigram, *History of the Assyrian Church*, 83, citing al-Tabari (ed. Noldeke, p. 71).

22. Later traditions (Bar Hebraeus in 1286, and Amri about 1350) relate the episcopate of Tomarsa to the time of Shapur III, and that of Qayuma to near the end of the century. This conflicts with what would seem to be the more contemporary testimony of the Synod of Dadyeshu (Dadiso) about a twenty-three-year vacancy immediately before the catholicate of Isaac, which began in 401/2. Higgins, "Chronology," leans toward a theory of two vacancies, one before 379, during which Tomarsa and Qayuma might have briefly held office, and a longer vacancy from 379 to 401/2. A. R. Vine, *The Nestorian Churches* (London: Independent Press, 1937) gives a more traditional list adapted from Assemani, Labourt, and Kidd, as follows: Simon Bar-Sabba'e died 341; Sadhost 341–342; Barbashmin 342–346; vacancy 346–383; Tomarsa 383–392; Cayuma 395–399; and Isaac 399–410 ("first catholicate

410"). For the records of the Synod of Dadyeshu see J. B. Chabot, *Synodicon Orientale ou Recueil de Synods Nestoriens* (Paris: Klincksieck, 1902), 292.

23. The major collection of sources for the Persian persecution is Bedjan, *Acta Martyrum et Sanctorum, op. cit.*, published in seven volumes (1890–97), of which volume 2, subtitled *Martyres Chaldaei et Persae*, and volume 4, which contains additional lives of Persian saints and martyrs, are pertinent to this period. But the text is in Syriac. Some of the manuscripts edited by Bedjan may have been the source for Sozomen's accounts. The collection is the principal source for Labourt's history of the period in French, and for Wigram's in English. See Wigram, *History of the Assyrian Church*, 76–86, esp. 82; and Labourt, *Le Christianisme*, 43–82.

24. Bar Hebraeus, *Chronicon Ecclesiasticum* 2.

25. Sozomen, *Ecclesiastical History* 2. 14. Writing about 443 Sozomen states that the names of well-known martyrs alone would make a list of sixteen thousand.

26. Casartelli, "Sassanians," 11:203.

Chapter 8
The Reorganization of the Persian Church

"By the word of God we define: That Easterners cannot complain against their patriarch to the western patriarchs; that every case that cannot be settled in his presence must await the judgment of Christ . . . [and] on no grounds whatever can one think or say that the Catholicos of the East can be judged by those who are below him, or by a patriarch equal to him . . ."

—Synod of Dadyeshu; at
Markabta, Persia, A.D. 424

T HE paper-thin peace with which the fifth century opened so promisingly at the end of the Great Persecution was torn apart almost as soon as it began. In tragic fact, the fifth century proved to be one of the most tumultuous and bitter hundred years in all history. In the West it began with the sack of Rome by the barbarians and ended with the last of the Roman emperors. Alaric the Goth seized Rome in 410; and in 496 Odovacar the German deposed the puppet Caesar, Romulus Augustus, to end the western Roman Empire.

In the East[1] a no less terrible wave of invaders swept out of central Asia. In the summer of 395 the White Huns of what is now Afghanistan and southern Russia crossed the Don near its mouth, broke through the Caucasus Mountains into Persia, and threatened the Byzantine provinces of eastern Syria like a chill new wind sweeping west out of Asia against the ancient empires of Rome and Iran. R. N. Frye notes that Greco-Roman historians described the first millennium B.C. in central Asia as the period of the Scythians, the next five hundred years after Christ as the time of the Huns, and, after the Huns, the second half of that millennium as the age of the Turks and the Mongols.[2]

The Huns themselves may well have had Mongol origins.[3] For hundreds of years the slow, remorseless advance of nomads across the measureless plains of Asia had pushed other wandering tribes before them, driving the Scythians (the Saka) into India to end the kingdom of Gundaphar in the first century A.D. and then, three hundred years later, pressing the Goths into Italy to ravage Rome. Now the dreaded Huns themselves came to paint death across the upper edge of Persia and as far south as Osrhoene. A Christian Syrian poet, Cyrillona (Qirilona), writing about 396, shuddered as they passed:

> The North is depressed and full of wars;
> And if Thou be neglectful, O Lord,
> They will again lay me waste.
> If the Huns, O Lord, conquer me . . .
> If their swords lay me waste . . .
> If Thou givest up my cities unto them,
> Where is the glory of Thy holy church?[4]

As if in at least a partial answer to his prayers, the horsemen of the Huns swept past the Christians in the south and moved west to ravage half-Christianized Europe from the Danube into France and northern Italy, spreading death and destruction until the final defeat of Attila in 451. Persia was spared for a time and in the years of peace that marked the first two decades of the century the Persian church recovered from persecution and reorganized into an effective, functioning national body that in this fifth century for the first time came to be called Nestorian.

The barbarian invasions produced at least one beneficial result, a pause in the centuries of warfare between the imperial powers. Except for a short interruption in 420 there was peace between Rome and Persia for fifty-six years, from Shapur III (383–388) to Varahran V (421–440). It was in this interlude of international detente that the Persian church was able to restructure its national organization. These years were memorable as the first period of organized, working harmony between the Church of the East (that is, the church in Asia outside the Roman Empire) and the Church of the West since the rise of the Sassanian empire in 226. It was also the last such period of ecumenical unity. The fifth century was not only an age of worldwide wars that spanned the continents; it was also the century of the Great Schism. Before the century closed, the unity of Christendom had been permanently broken into three parts; the church of the West (Rome and Constantinople), the church of the East (Persia), and the church of Africa (Egypt and Ethiopia).

The Synod of Isaac (410)

The history of the church is often written as much by events outside it as within. A hundred years earlier, when Bishop Papa bar-Aggai set his mind to shape a national organization for the Persian church, a centralized structure seemed desirable and even necessary to deal with the increasing centralization of the empire. But the outbreak of hostilities with Rome made it impossible. Pagan Persia could not tolerate an independent national Christian organization within the empire while it was fighting Christian Rome. Only after peace was made with Rome and the persecution of Persian Christians ended, did the church find the opportunity it needed to reorganize and complete the unification begun under Papa. In the short space of fourteen years at the beginning of the fifth century the Persian bishops called three general councils or synods and swiftly and efficiently formed themselves into a nationwide church. They still called it the Church of the East.

Three sometimes competing, sometimes complementary interests dominated the process of organization: first, the achievement of a consensus among the Persian bishops, second, the long arm of the

Persian government, and third, the distant but watchful concern of the patriarchate of Antioch representing the Western church. Out of the interweaving of the powers and influence of these three bodies there emerged the independent Persian church, recognized for the first time as ecclesiastically supreme in the East under a catholicos (patriarch), the bishop of Seleucia-Ctesiphon. But though now autonomous, the Persian church proceeded to accept without question and with only minimum modifications the creed and customs of the Western church as laid down by the Council of Nicaea in 325, a council that up to then it had virtually ignored. Furthermore, though independent ecclesiastically, the church began to recognize that it could never be completely free from the temporal power of the state, and in this context the fact that the state in Persia, unlike Rome, was non-Christian became increasingly significant as the century unrolled.

The first Persian church council[5] after the persecutions was the Synod of Isaac, which met in 410, the year that Alaric the Goth burned Rome. It was a year of stunning grief in the Christian West, but of celebration for Christians in the East. How often joy in one empire was mirrored by agony in the other.

While Christians in the Mediterranean were shocked by the fall of Rome, across the border in Persia the forty bishops of the Church of the East who had been called to the synod in Seleucia-Ctesiphon were celebrating victory. The cause for celebration was an edict of toleration by Shah Yazdegerd I, issued probably in 409 since the synod convened in January 410. Yazdegerd's edict was as significant for the Asian church as the better known "Edict of Milan" was for the Western church almost a century earlier in 313 under Constantine. It was not so enduring, but both edicts officially ended great persecutions. The first words in the records of the Eastern synod were in praise of Yazdegerd, "King of kings, victorious," who

> gives peace and repose to the congregations of Christ and permits the servants of God publicly to exalt Christ . . . who has dissipated the shadow of oppression of the whole company of Christ; who has, in effect, ordered in all the empire that the temples destroyed by his fathers should be magnificently rebuilt . . .[6]

Later historians, Persian and Arab, were not as pleasantly impressed by Yazdegerd as the Christian bishops. His name in their histories was "Yazdegerd the Wicked," for though his reign brought twenty years of peace and prosperity to the nation, Zoroastrians and Moslems alike have never forgiven him for pursuing a policy of peace with the enemy, Rome, and for being a friend of the Christians.

Yazdegerd I, who permitted the calling of the Christian synod, came to the Persian throne in 399 and, despite the temptation to attack Rome from the east while barbarians spoiled it on the north, kept his empire free from war with the West until he died. The most effective agent in promoting peace between Persia and Rome (or Byzantium as we should now begin to call the eastern Roman Empire to distinguish it from the fading western Roman Empire, which from this time on has little to do with Persia), and in improving relations between the shah and his Christian subjects, however, was not the Persian shah but the Roman ambassador to Persia, a Mesopotamian bishop, Marutha of Maipherqat (modern Meiafarakin). The title of ambassador then referred not to a fixed post but to temporary assignment as head of a political mission, and Bishop Marutha may have represented Constantinople on as many as three such important missions, in 399, in 406, and again in 410, the year of the synod.[7] He was so successful in making peace between the two empires that when the Byzantine emperor Arcadius died in Constantinople in 408 leaving a seven-year-old son, Theodosius II to inherit the throne, he is said to have appointed the old enemy, the Persian shah, in this case Yazdegerd I, as guardian for the boy against the dangers of a Byzantine palace coup.[8]

One tradition says that it was the bishop-ambassador's medical skill that first won him the confidence of the Persian king, and W. A. Wigram therefore calls Marutha "the first medical missionary."[9] But all that the contemporary fifth-century historian Socrates says of this is that Marutha cured Yazdegerd of a violent headache the Zoroastrian *magi* had been unable to relieve and that he did it by prayer. Socrates adds that the jealous Zoroastrians plotted to drive Marutha from the kingdom by concealing an agent under the sacred fire in the temple where the shah regularly worshiped. As Yazdegerd approached, the hidden agent called out from the fire as instructed, "Remove the king. He has sinned and imagines that a Christian priest is loved by God." But the plan backfired. The wise Marutha uncovered the fraud, told the king, and was thereafter all the more trusted. Socrates adds that only the death of Yazdegerd in 420 "prevented his making an open profession of Christianity."[10]

This is not likely. It may have seemed so in the west, where Christians were always hoping for an Eastern Constantine to rise in Persia and make their world Christian. It may even have seemed so to the Zoroastrian extremists to whom any detent with Christian Rome smelled of apostasy and surrender. But it is highly doubtful that any Sassanian emperor in a realm already unified by a national religion ever at any time gave serious thought to conversion to the Christian faith.

Bishop Marutha was equally effective whether as an ambassador from the Western to the Eastern church or representing a Byzantine emperor to a Persian shah. His diocese of Maipherqat in the Kurdish mountains northeast of Edessa was just across the border on the Roman side. Its relationship to the mother church, Edessa, made him welcome to the Persian bishops, and he in turn became deeply impressed with the courage of the Persian martyrs. In fact he took back home with him from his ambassadorial visits in Persia so many relics and mementos of the martyrs that the name of his city was changed from Maipherqat to Martyropolis.[11]

He came to Persia at a most strategic time. The Eastern church, still dazed by the years of persecutions, was fumblingly rebuilding its decimated national organization. Sometime in the episcopate of Qayuma, who had accepted the authority only because he expected to die a martyr, peace came before martyrdom, and the reluctant bishop begged to be released from his burdensome responsibilities. "I would have been glad to die as bishop," he is reported to have said, "but I am too old to rule."[12] A younger man, Isaac, was elected to take his place in 401. But no sooner did the church once more have a vigorous head than jealousy consumed some who had been passed over for the honor. Isaac was accused before the shah of irregularities in office—not by Zoroastrians but by Christians, to their shame and to the humiliation of Isaac, who was thrown into prison. It was at this point that the Western bishop, Marutha, is said to have stepped in to use his influence with the shah. He quickly secured the bishop's release and was granted permission to have a council called to restore peace and order in the Persian church.[13]

The result was the complete vindication of Isaac. He not only presided over the historic council, but saw it confirm officially what had hitherto only been accepted somewhat irregularly in practice, the primacy of the bishop of Seleucia-Ctesiphon as "catholicos and archbishop of all the Orient . . . whose Chastity [i.e., holiness] shines more brilliantly than any bishops of the Orient who have preceded him." By the end of the century the term "catholicos " as used in Persia and east Syria came to be the equivalent of patriarch and implied the independence of the Church of the East and its coequality with the great and ancient sees of Jerusalem, Antioch, Alexandria, and Rome.[14]

In 410, however, this was still more implicit than expressed. It did not yet mean schism between East and West and was not even recognized as the beginning of a long process of gradual separation. The key role played by the West at this Eastern Synod was generously acknowledged. At the request of Bishop Isaac, Marutha, the bishop from across the border, opened the meeting with the reading of a letter he had brought from the "Western bishops," notably the patriarch of Antioch and the bishops of Amida and Edessa. He was received as an "apostle (and) messenger of peace whom God in his mercy sent to the east . . . , mediator of peace and concord between east and west."[15] Skilled in secular as well as ecclesiastical negotiations, Marutha had already wisely showed the letter first to the shah and had secured his powerful support for efforts to improve relations between the churches of the two empires.

The gist of the letter was contained in three requests that could bring Eastern and Western church practices and doctrines into harmony. First, it urged that there be only one bishop permitted in a diocese and that he should be properly consecrated by three other bishops. Second, it pled for agreement on the dates of Christmas and Epiphany, Lent, Good Friday, and Easter, so that the churches everywhere might be unified in their observance of the same holy days. And third, it recommended that the Persian synod adopt the canons of the Council of Nicaea, including the Nicene Creed. The requests were unanimously approved. The catholicos Isaac, speaking as chief of the Persian bishops, pronounced an anathema on any dissent, and all the bishops after him "with one accord" agreed.[16]

This was the first time that the Church of the East had adopted an official creedal standard of doctrine. Only one Persian bishop, it is thought, had attended the First Ecumenical Council at Nicaea, Jacob of Nisibis. The "creed of Aphrahat" was personal and unofficial. Now East and West were united by one authoritative confession of faith, orthodox and ecumenical:

> We believe in one God, the Father Almighty, Maker of all things visible and invisible—and in one Lord Jesus Christ, the Son of God, the only-begotten of the Father, that is of the substance of the Father; God of God and Light of light; true God of true God; begotten not made, consubstantial (*homo-ousion*)[17] with the Father: by whom all things were made, both which are in heaven and on earth: whom for the sake of us men, and on account of our salvation, descended, became incarnate, and was made man; suffered, rose again the third day, and ascended into the heavens, and will come again to judge the living and the dead. We also believe in the Holy Spirit.
>
> But the holy Catholic and Apostolic church anathematizes those who say "There was a time when he was not," and "He was not before he was begotten," and "He was made from that which did not exist," and

those who assert that he is of other substance or essence[18] than the Father, or that he was created, or is susceptible of change.[19]

The synod then drew up twenty-one canons regulating the government of the church, adjusting the Western rules of the Council of Nicaea to its own Eastern requirements with a freedom that underlined its sense of friendly independence of the West. The canons leave no doubt of the supreme authority of "the Great Metropolitan, the Catholicos of Seleucia-Ctesiphon." Without his approval no bishop's election was legitimate.[20] Below him the hierarchy was graded into two classes of bishops, metropolitans and regular bishops. In the highest rank, that of metropolitan (i.e., archbishop, or bishop in a major city usually with authority over a whole province) were the following five bishoprics: Beit Lapat (Gundeshapur) on the great plains of Khuzistan, which had been built and settled by Roman captives among whom were many Christians; Nisibis, which had become the theological center of the Persian church since its cession to Persia by Rome in 363; Prat de Maishan (Wahman Ardashir) in the far south between the junction of the Tigris and Euphrates rivers and the Persian Gulf (near modern Basra); Arbela (Erbil), capital of Adiabene, which was to become a missionary center of the Persian church; and Karka or Beit-Selok (modern Kirkuk) between the Tigris and the Iranian plateau east of Adiabene, which was soon (about 448) to become famous as the site of a mass martyrdom.[21]

There is an early Syriac document, sometimes described as the Marutha collection on east Syrian church order, which, if authentic, gives a listing of the lower orders in the Syrian church about the time of the Synod of Isaac (410). It adds immediately below the bishop the church office of chorepiscopos, or bishop's assistant, with duties of supervision of rural churches and monasteries. Next in rank is the presbyter (priest), followed by the office of reader. These ordained offices in the church were supposedly read by Marutha to the eastern Synod and accepted as canonical. In similar passages, five additional offices or positions in the church are described: deacon, exorcist, deaconess, singer, and acolyte.[22]

One significant omission in the canons of the Synod of Isaac may have influenced the subsequent history of the Persian church as much as all the other regulations combined with the exception of the creed. There was no canon stipulating the method of electing the catholicos. Whether this was by design or disregard is difficult to say, but the practical result was to leave the highest office in the church open to the political manipulations of a non-Christian government. The church is never free from political pressures no matter how clearly it writes its own laws of governance, but given no clear alternative in the regulations of the Persian church, when the shah chose to nominate a candidate he favored, it was virtually impossible to resist his formidable will.

The point was made clear even before the synod adjourned. As they neared the end the delegates were summoned before the grand vizier and the general of the armies. There they were informed that Bishop Isaac of Seleucia-Ctesiphon had been appointed by the shah "Chief of all the Christians of the Orient." No one pointed out that the synod had already done this in naming Isaac as catholicos. No one objected to the usurpation by the state of the responsibility of the church. Such lines of distinction belonged to a later age and were never quite defined in Asia. It is doubtful that the bishops even sensed a problem; more likely they were simply happy that the shah had graciously duplicated their own action. They had already dutifully recorded in the minutes of the synod the fulsome prayer:

> We all with one accord implore our merciful God that he will lengthen the days of the king victorious and illustrious, Yazdegerd, King of Kings, that his years be prolonged for generations to come, and for ages and ages.[23]

So the council adjourned, praising God for peace in the church and peace in the world. It was no mean achievement they celebrated, a peace at many levels: peace among the bishops, peace from persecuting emperors, peace between the great powers, and a new awareness of peace and unity between the Christians of East and West. It was also, though they did not know it at the time, a peace so fragile it could not last.

The first of the calamities that fell upon the church in fifth-century Persia was self-inflicted, another power struggle in the church. Next came a renewal of persecution by the Persian government. Finally, and worst of all, a violent theological controversy raged across the whole face of Christendom from North Africa and Europe into western Asia, wreaking havoc in the churches and irreparably destroying the unity of the church. The brief working fellowship forged at Seleucia-Ctesiphon at the Synod of Isaac in 410 was unable to survive this succession of calamities.

The Synod of Yaballaha (420) and Further Persecution

The first problem, strife among the bishops, was relatively minor and nothing new. When Bishop Isaac died soon after the close of the first synod, perhaps in 412, two saintly ascetics followed him on the throne of the catholics, Akha (or Ahai) from 412 to 415 and Yaballaha I from 415 to 420.[24] Yaballaha had been a missionary to pagan parts of Persia from which he returned to build a monastery on the Euphrates. There he hoped he could spend his days perpetually praising God in the singing of songs and hymns.[25] Instead, he was abruptly plucked from his retreat, thrust into office, and sent on a dazzling diplomatic mission to Constantinople where he was favorably impressed with his contacts with the church in the West. His return to the East must have depressed him. Back in Persia he found himself face to face with what seems to have been another ugly threat of schism, though the small church synod he called in 420 to avert an open break tactfully glossed over the exact nature of the problem.[26] At this second synod, as at the first, a bishop/ambassador from the West was present, Acacius of Amida, a city in Byzantine territory just across the border on the upper reaches of the Tigris River, near the diocese of the previous ambassador, Marutha. It was probably at the suggestion of Acacius that the Persians, who ten years earlier had adapted the canons of the Council of Nicaea to Persian practice, further strengthened their ties with the West by recognizing five more or less important Western councils as authoritative.[27] But pro-Western momentum in the Persian church was not to continue much longer.

By this time a more dreaded problem than internal differences threatened the peace of the church. In the last year of his reign, probably some time in 420, Yazdegerd I, Shah-in-Shah, friend and patron of the church for twenty years, turned against his friends the Christians. There is no reason to believe that his about-face was anything but pragmatic, as in all probability had also been his earlier friendship. When Persia's best interests called for detente with Christian Rome (or Byzantium) the Christians were valuable allies to the shah, but in times of war or open friction they were feared as untrustworthy. Now, however, the situation was different. It seemed to be national problems rather than foreign threats that lay behind a new wave of persecution.

In Constantinople a young and unagressive emperor sat on the throne, Theodosius II (408–450). His immediate concern was not Persia but the pressure of northern barbarians on his borders and their seepage into the empire itself. Germanic Goths inside his boundaries were as much a danger as the Asiatic Huns advancing against him from without; and the Huns in turn, under their remorseless chief Attila, were more to be feared than the old enemy Persia.

As for Persia, without Roman aggression to worry about and with the Huns moving away to attack the West, Shah Yazdegerd's attention turned to his domestic problems. He sensed a growing restlessness among his feudal nobles, who scented weakness and opportunity for their own ambitions as the emperor neared the end of his long reign. Equally dangerous was the open resentment of the Zoroastrian state hierarchy at the favoritism he had shown to Christianity. In the face of a possible rebellious coalition of power-hungry nobles and jealous high priests, suddenly his friendship with Christians in his realm had become a political liability, not an asset.

About 420 an alarmed Zoroastrian high priest came before Yazdegerd to complain that Christian evangelism was inducing mass apostasy from the state religion. The Christian cause was not helped by some arrogant attacks on fire temples by sincere but fanatical Christians, the most violent of whom were often converts from Zoroastrianism. The shah could scarcely ignore open desecration of the state temples and the disruption of religious peace in his realm.[28] He empowered the Zoroastrian clergy to persuade apostates from the national religion to renounce their conversion to Christianity and return to the faith of the empire "not, however, by death, but by fear and a certain amount of beating."[29]

At first the persecution was limited to converts as the king had commanded, but once unleashed, the thirst for retaliation and vengeance could no longer be contained. Yazdegerd I died in the first year of the persecution and his successor, Varahran V (421–439, known as Bahram in Arabic sources), continued the persecution. He had reached the throne only through the support of the Zoroastrian clergy against a rival claimant and was quite willing to repay his debt to them by declaring an empirewide campaign against Christians. He even demanded that the Byzantine emperor, Theodosius II, refuse refuge in the West to Christians fleeing the persecutions in Persia and that he promptly return all such to their proper punishment in Persia. Insulted, the Byzantines invaded Persia, attacking Nisibis, and an inconclusive war raged for months, which only added to the difficulties of the Persian Christians.[30]

A church historian of that period, Theodoret, has left us a description of the three or four years of this fifth-century persecution that suggests that though it was probably not as massive as the persecutions under Shapur II, it may easily have been the most cruel:

> It is not easy to describe the new kinds of punishment that the Persians invented to torment the Christians. They flayed the hands of some, and the backs of others. In the case of others again, they stripped the skin

of the face from the forehead down to the chin. They tore their bodies
with broken reeds, causing them exquisite pain. Having dug great pits,
they filled them with rats and mice and then cast the Christians into the
pits, first tying their hands and feet so that they could neither chase the
animals away or place themselves beyond their reach. The animals
themselves having been kept without feed, devoured these Christian
confessors in the most cruel way.[31]

Two contrasting attitudes toward war on the part of border bishops in this conflict between Byzantium and Persia are worth noting.
When the Persians attacked Erzerum (Theodosiopolis) in Roman Armenia, its bishop rallied the defense, rushed to the walls, blessed a
huge mechanical stone thrower (ballista) in the name of St. Thomas,
and aimed and fired it personally at the enemy, killing a high Persian
noble. His was not an uncommon, patriotic reaction among Byzantine Christians facing the pagan invaders. It was the kind of example, however, that only confirmed Persian distrust of Christians
on their side of the border. Very different was the example of his
brother bishop, Acacius of Amida, who as an emissary of the Western churches to the Persian synod of Yaballaha a year or so earlier
had come to hope for better relations between Christians of East and
West. At the sight of Persian prisoners in pitiable condition in Roman war camps he personally ordered the gold and silver vessels
and jeweled ornaments of his church's treasury to be sold for their
ransom and saw that the captives were safely restored to their own
country.[32]

When the war ended in 422, it may have been this generous
gesture of Acacius that speeded the negotiations for peace and
brought an end to persecution in Persia. The peace treaty contained
the remarkable stipulation that freedom of religion was to be granted
on both sides of the border, for Zoroastrians in the Byzantine Empire
and for Christians in Persia.[33]

The peace was short-lived. When Varahran V died in 439[34] massacres of Christians once again swept the country under his son,
Yazdegerd II (439–457). As usual, persecution of Christians once
more coincided with war against Constantinople, for Yazdegerd
opened his reign by declaring war against Byzantium. The war was
short and inconclusive, however, for Yazdegerd was more preoccupied with Huns in the east than with Romans in the west. But persecutions continued, fueled more by Zoroastrian angers, perhaps,
than by political expediency. This was the third of the fifth-century
persecutions, the first being that of Yazdegerd I in 419–420 and the
second that of Varahran V from 420–422. The most severe years of

persecution in this third outbreak were 445 to 448 in Persia and 454 to 456 in Armenia, which Yazdegerd dreamed of reclaiming for Persia by stamping out the Christian faith with the utmost ferocity. When the whole of Christian Armenia rose in revolt, even the Armenian patriarch was put to death.

The most appalling of the slaughters that marked the renewal of persecution in Persia occurred in northern Mesopotamia in 448. This was the frightful bloodletting at Kirkuk (Karka, of Beit Selok) which was one of the original metropolitanates, beyond the Tigris and east of Arbela. There on a mound outside the city masses of Christians were systematically butchered for days—10 bishops and an incredible 153,000 believers until at last (if a later chronicler can be believed) the chief persecutor, a man named Tamasgerd, sickened of it all and was so moved by the faith of the dying that he confessed Christ on the spot and joined his own victims in a martyr's death.[35]

The Synod of Dadyeshu (424) and the Independence of the Asian Church

Between the persecutions of Varahran V and Yazdegerd II a short interim of calm gave opportunity for the church to hold a third general council, the Synod of Dadyeshu (Dadisho) in 424.[36] It did not meet in the capital, perhaps for fear of renewed persecution, but in Markabta of the Arabs. The organization of the church was again in shambles. In the short, sharp persecution just ended, one catholicos, Mana (420), had been abruptly deposed and banished by the shah for failure to rebuke Christians who burned a fire temple.[37] Another, Dadyeshu (421–456), had been thrown into prison accused of being pro-Roman. For a while a pseudo-catholicos, Farbokt,[38] supported by an unholy alliance of anti-Christian Zoroastrians and rebel bishops, almost succeeded in capturing control of the organization of the church. When the persecution ended the true catholicos, Dadyeshu, was released from prison but, bruised by his sufferings and weary of badgering by power-hungry bishops, would have nothing more to do with the administration of the church and sealed himself off in a hermit's cell in the northern mountains to mourn the spiritual fall of the church of God. Only the combined pressure of thirty-six penitent and weeping prelates persuaded him to come down and preside over the reform council that one of his metropolitan bishops, Agapit of Gundeshapur (Beit Lapat), had called.

The Synod of Dadyeshu at Markabta proved to be one of the most significant of all the Persian councils. The first synod (of Isaac in 410)[39] had declared the catholicos of Seleucia-Ctesiphon to be supreme among the bishops of the East. This third synod, of Dadyeshu, added that he was the equal of any patriarch East or West and subject to none. The assembled bishops—six metropolitans and thirty conventional bishops from all over Persia—threw themselves at the feet of the reluctant Dadyeshu and vowed him allegiance in terms that unequivocally set apart the church in Asia as free in Christ under its own head, the catholicos, not opposed to the West but equal in rank and authority to any Western patriarchate. The synod declared:

> By the word of God we define: That Easterners cannot complain against their patriarch to the western patriarchs; that every case that cannot be settled in his presence must await the judgment of Christ . . . [and] on no grounds whatever can one think or say that the Catholicos of the East can be judged by those who are below him, or by a patriarch equal to him; he himself must be the judge of all those beneath him, and he can be judged only by Christ who has chosen him, elevated him and placed him at the head of his church.[40]

This was not an act of schism, as some have interpreted it.[41] The declaration of Markabta was a declaration of independent equality, not of ecclesiastical separation. Doctrinally the church was still united, East and West, by the creed of Nicaea. Ecclesiastically it was still one, bound together by common acceptance of the rules of the church councils. Only four years earlier, at the second council, the Synod of Yaballaha, the Persian church had accepted the canons of a whole string of Western councils,[42] and the Synod of Dadyeshu did not now repudiate them.

What distinguishes the Synod of Dadyeshu from the previous Persian councils is that it claimed for the Church of the East all the rights of a patriarchate. Clearly specified among these rights was the privilege of independent administration—not of heresy, or of separation, but of freedom from outside jurisdiction. Western bishops, it declared, had no "rights" in the East. For the first time no Western bishop was present at the council, though a friendly one was in Persia at the time, one who had been invited to the second synod in 420. Acacius of Amida had come to Persia from across the border as the personal guest of the shah to be thanked for the unusual act of Christian charity we have already noted, the ransom of seven thousand Persian prisoners of war.[43] But this time he was not invited to the council of bishops. The slight was probably not deliberate. The war was over, and the Synod of Dadyeshu (whose name, appropriately, means "friend of Jesus") was neither anti-Western nor schismatic. It was simply independent, and this was nothing new. So were the other patriarchates.

There is no reliable evidence of the church outside the Roman Empire in Asia ever acknowledging the supremacy of Antioch, much less of Rome or any other Western patriarch. There is little difference between Eastern and Western practice in this regard at that time. The First Ecumenical Council (Nicaea, 325) in its sixth canon had expressly recognized the independence of jurisdiction, each in his own sphere, of the great bishops (later recognized as patriarchs) of Rome and Alexandria, though in the fifth century Rome unsuccessfully appealed to a false version of this canon that contained a spurious clause, "*Ecclesia Romana semper habuit primatum*" ("The Roman church always had primacy").[44] The Second Ecumenical Council (Constantinople, 381), in its third canon, added the bishopric of Constantinople to patriarchal rank, second only to Rome, but without jurisdiction over the metropolitans of Asia and Pontus, who were independent as before. But the Fourth Ecumenical Council (Chalcedon, 451) in its twenty-eighth canon gave Constantinople jurisdiction over Pontus, Asia (i.e., Roman Asia), and Thrace and explicitly recognized that the ecclesiastical supremacy of Rome had been based on its political supremacy, not on divine origin, and that the "new Rome" (Constantinople) was now therefore entitled to the same privileges. It was at this point that Rome unsuccessfully challenged the new canon by appealing to its erroneous version of the Nicene sixth canon.[45]

The Synod of Dadyeshu thus merely made explicit what had long been recognized in practice and was to become even more clear at the Council of Chalcedon. To the Persian bishops in the synod in 424, the Christians of the West were brothers in Christ, not separated brethren. They were honored friends and trusted advisers, but their jurisdiction as ecclesiastics ended at the Persian border. Persian Asia was beyond Western control not by schism, but as a matter of patriarchal privilege. Schism, indeed, was soon to come, but when it did, it came from the West, from Antioch and Alexandria, not from the East.

NOTES

1. W. G. Young's chronological chart of Persian patriarchs (Catholici) and shahs of this period in his *Patriarch, Shah and Caliph*, p. 206f., is a useful reference here and for the chapters that follow:

Patriarch (Catholicos)	Shah
Isaac I (Ishaq), 399–410	Yazdegerd I (Yazdagrd), 399–420
Ahai, 411–414	
Yaballaha I (Yab-alaha), 415–420	Varahran V (Bahram), 420–438
Dadyeshu I (Dad-ishu'), 421–456	
	Yazdegerd II, 438–457
Babowai, 457–484	
	Peroz (Firoz), 459–486
Acacius (Aqaq), 485–495/6	Vologases (Walgash), 486–488
	Kavad (Quabad), 488–531
Babai, 497–502/3	
Silas (Shila), 505–521	
	Chosroes I (Khusrau), 531–579
Mar Aba I, 540–552	
Joseph (Yusuf), 552–556/7	
Ezekiel, 567 elected	
570–581 consecrated	
	Hormizd IV (Hurmizd), 579–590
Yeshuyab I (Ishu'-yab), 582–595	
	Chosroes II, 590–628
Sabaryeshu I (Sabr-ishu), 595–604	
Gregory I, 605–609	
Vacancy, 609–628	
Yeshuyab II, 628–646	Ineffective Shahs, 628–651
Maramama, 647–650	Arab conquest, from 636
Yeshuyab III, 650–658	

2. R. N. Frye, *The Heritage of Persia*, 2d ed. (London: Cardinal, 1976), 255.

3. There are three major theories about the origins of the Huns: Mongolian, Turkish, and Finnish. A generation ago the theory of Mongol origin was generally accepted, but it is disputed now once more. See O. J. Maenchen-Helfe, *The World of the Huns* (Berkeley: Univ. of California Press, 1973), 51ff., 358–375, who suggests that by the time they appeared on the borders of Europe the Huns were a Mongol-Europoid mixture.

4. Cf. the prose version of the poem, trans. O. J. Maenchen-Helfen, *World of the Huns* (Berkeley: Univ. of California Press, 1973), 56.

5. The "Synod" or Council of Seleucia in about 315, which deposed Papa, is sometimes called the first of the Persian councils, but since it left no contemporary records it is usually not listed as equal to the official synods.

6. The full records of the Synod are given in J. B. Chabot, ed. and trans. *Synodicon Orientale ou Recueil de Synodes Nestoriens* (Paris: C. Klincksieck, 1902), 253–75 (French translation and notes). The quotation is on p. 254.

7. J. Labourt, *Le Christianisme dans l'Empire Perse sous le dynastie Sassanide, 224–632* (Paris: Lecoffre, 1904), 88 n.

8. Many historians are skeptical about this alleged guardianship, but equally careful historians accept it as reasonable. See A. A. Vasiliev, *History of the Byzantine Empire*, vol. 1, 2d ed. (Madison: Univ. of Wisconsin Press, 1958), 96.

9. W. A. Wigram, *History of the Assyrian Church* A.D. *100–640* (London: SPCK, 1910), 88 n. 1.

10. Socrates, *Historia ecclesiastica*, in *Nicene and Post-Nicene Fathers*, second series, vol. 2 (Grand Rapids: Eerdmans, 1983), 7:8. The church historian was a contemporary of these events.

11. Labourt, *Le Christianisme*, 87 n. 89. Some attribute to Marutha the authorship of a number of the *Acts* of the Persian martyrs (p. 52f.).

12. The tradition is late (Bar Hebraeus, *Chronicon Ecclesiasticum* II, 47) and its historicity uncertain. See chap. 7, pp. 146f. nn. 22, 24. Labourt questions the historicity of both Tomarsa and Qayuma (*Le Christianisme*, 86), but they are listed in the eleventh-century. Nestorian history, the *Chronicle of Seert* (ed. A. Scher, *PO* tome 5, fasc. 2, 305f., 313).

13. J. B. Chabot, *Synodicon Orientale*, 292.

14. "Catholicos" was originally used in the Roman Empire in a secular sense of the emperor's minister of finance. It was first used as title of the head of a national church in Armenia. In the Persian Empire it appears as the title of the bishop of Seleucia-Ctesiphon in the martyrologies such as the *Acts of Shimun*. The Synod of Isaac used it of the patriarch of Antioch. P. Bedjan, *Acta Martyrum et Sanctorum*, vol. 2, *Martyres Chaldaei et Persae* (Paris, 1891), 134, 267, etc.; and Chabot, *Synodicon Orientale*, 255. A. Fortescue, *The Lesser Eastern Churches* (London: Catholic Truth Society, 1913), 2:48f., argues unconvincingly that the title implies dependence on the Antiochene patriarchate and thence on Rome. But see Wigram, *Assyrian Church*, 90–94.

15. Chabot, *Synodicon Orientale*, 255.

16. Chabot, *Synodicon Orientale*, 258–60. The West requested that Lent be observed for a full forty days within a period of seven weeks.

17. In Syriac, *bar ithutha.*

18. The Greek *hypostasis* is translated in Syriac as *qenuma*. No distinction was made between substance and essence (*ousia* and *hypostasis*), and the distinction between the two that was winning acceptance in the West (i.e., using *hypostasis* as "person") was not accepted in the East, a fact which was to cause later needless controversy. See Wigram, *Assyrian Church*, 98; and J. F.

Bethune-Baker, *An Introduction to the Early History of Christian Doctrine to the Time of the Council of Chalcedon*, 3d ed. (London: Methuen, 1933), 170, 235ff.

19. This is the translation by A. C. Zenos of the text in Socrates, *Ecclesiastical History*, 1:8 (*Nicene and Post-Nicene Fathers*, vol. 2).

20. *Acts of the Synod of Isaac*, canons 5, 6 in Chabot, *Synodicon Orientale*, 263f.

21. *Acts of the Synod of Isaac*, canon 21 (Chabot, 271). The bishop of Beit Selok was metropolitan of the province of Beit Garmai.

22. Date and authenticity are questionable, but probably not far wrong. The original source on the Vatican documents is in J. S. Assemani, *Bibliotheca Orientientalis Clementino-Vaticano*, vol. 3, 2 (Rome, 1728), 808–56. See O. Braun, *De Sancta Nicaea Synodo*, in *Kirchengeschichtliche Studien* 4, 3 (Munich, 1898); and A. Voobus, *Asceticism*, vol. 1, CSCO, 184, subsidia t. 14 (Louvain, 1958), 212ff., 276ff., 280f.

23. Voobus, *Asceticism*, 260f., 258.

24. The date of Isaac's death and Akha's succession is uncertain. Wigram gives reasons for placing it in 412 (*Assyrian Church*, 107); but Labourt and others put it in 410 (*Le Christianisme*, 99f.).

25. Labourt, *Le Christianisme*, 100.

26. Labourt, *Le Christianisme*, 100.

27. The councils thus recognized, along with Nicaea (325), were Ancyra (314), Neo Caesarea, Antioch (341), Gangra (343), and Laodicea (365?). The records of the synod, which were signed by only eleven Persian bishops, are in Chabot's *Synodicon Orientale*, 276ff. On the list of western councils recognized, see 278 nn. 1–6.

28. A church council in the West (in Elvira, Spain, in the late third century) wisely refused the title of martyr to anyone who had brought punishment on himself or herself by attacking pagan shrines, noting "there are not cases of such conduct in the gospel nor did the apostles ever behave thus." J. Moffatt, *The First Five Centuries of the Christian Church* (London: Univ. of London Press, 1938), 105.

29. Wigram, *Assyrian Church*, 114.

30. Labourt, *Le Christianisme*, 109–18.

31. Theodoret, *Historia Ecclesiastica*, V, p. 38. Theodoret's church history covers the years 322–427/8 and was published in 449. He was bishop of Cyrus from 423 to 458.

32. Wigram, *Assyrian Church*, 119.

33. Labourt, *Le Christianisme*, 118.

34. Varahran (also known as Bahram Gur) was immortalized by Omar Khayyam: "And Bahram that great hunter—the wild ass/Stamps o'er his head but cannot break his sleep."

35. Wigram, *Assyrian Church*, 138, citing *History of Karka* in Bedjan, *Acta Martyrum et Sanctorum*, 2:510–31. See also Labourt, *Le Christianisme*, 126ff.

36. The minutes of the synod are given in Chabot, *Synodicon Orientale,* 43–53 (Syriac text) and 285–98 (French translation).

37. The details of Mana's election and deposition are obscure. See Labourt, *Le Christianisme,* 119.

38. Chabot, *Synodicon Orientale,* 287; and Labourt, *Le Christianisme,* and Wigram, *Assyrian Church.* Farbokt is also sometimes named Marabokt.

39. The numbering of the councils is arbitrary. If the "Synod" of Papa, 315, is included, the Synod of Isaac would be second, not first. But no minutes of the 315 synod survive. Some lists include five of the Western synods (Ancyra, Nicaea, Antioch, Gangra, and Laodicea) recognized by the Synod of Yaballaha in 420 (see n. 27 above) and number the Synod of Isaac as the sixth synod. The numbering used here begins with the first officially *recorded* synod in 410, that of Isaac, and excludes Western synods.

40. Chabot, *Synodicon Orientale,* 296.

41. See, for example, Fortescue, *Lesser Eastern Churches,* 51: "From 424 we must date the independence of Persia from Edessa and Antioch. This involves, of course, independence from Antioch's superior at Rome; so, from the Catholic point of view, it seems that we must date the Persian Church as schismatical since the Synod of Markabta." But this reads into the fifth century an uncontested acceptance of the primacy of Rome, which did not then exist.

42. Wigram rightly questions the wisdom of so wholesale an adoption of 180 untested church laws by the Synod of Yaballaha. Many were irrelevant, and some mutually inconsistent. The catholicos Yaballah, though not opposing the action, hinted at the time that "it might be well to keep (our) own rules before binding (ourselves) to observe so many new ones." *Assyrian Church,* 111f.

43. Fortescue, *Lesser Eastern Churches,* 50 n.

44. B. J. Kidd, *History of the Church to A.D. 461,* 3 vols. (Oxford: Clarendon, 1922), 2:116ff.

45. Kidd, *History of the Church,* 3: 332ff. See F. Mourret and N. Thompson, *History of the Catholic Church,* vol. 2 (St. Louis and London: Herder, 1935), 593, for a Roman Catholic view of this "irregularity."

Chapter 9
The Great Schism

Earthly things have little interest for me. I have died
to the world and live for Him. . . . Farewell desert,
my friend . . . and [farewell] exile, my mother, who
after my death shall keep my body until the
resurrection. . . . As for Nestorius—let him be
anathema! . . . And would God that all men by
anathematizing me might attain to reconciliation with
God. . . .

—Nestorius, *The Bazaar of
Heracleides*

WHAT finally divided the early church, East from West, Asia from Europe, was neither war nor persecution but the blight of a violent theological controversy, that raged through the Mediterranean world in the second quarter of the fifth century. It came to be called the Nestorian controversy, and how much of it was theological and how much political is still being debated, but it irreversibly split the church not only east and west but also north and south and cracked it into so many pieces that it was never the same again. Out of it came an ill-fitting name for the church in non-Roman Asia, "Nestorian."

The dimensions of the schism can best be appreciated by comparing the church of 325 after the First Ecumenical Council, Nicaea, with the same Christian world a century and a quarter later in 451 after the Fourth Ecumenical Council, Chalcedon.

Both councils were called to repair deep theological divisions. In 325 the problem was Arianism, which denied the full deity of Christ. In 451 the question was more complicated and concerned the relationship of deity and humanity in the nature of Christ, as we shall see. But where Nicaea united the holy, catholic church against the defeated Arians, Chalcedon was unable to prevent the splintering of Christendom.

For a good many years even the earlier council, Nicaea, seemed doomed to failure. Scarcely had that council adjourned before the Christian unity it had achieved began to crumble. A violent Arian reaction spread through the Roman Empire. Constantine the Great's own son and successor in Constantinople, Constantius, was Arian. A triumphal missionary expansion of Arianism among the Teutonic tribes, spearheaded by the saintly "apostle to the Goths," Ulfilas (311–383), began to separate barbarian Europe, which was rapidly converting to Arianism and seemed about to overcome the orthodox, catholic empire.

Then the orthodox center itself began to disintegrate. The great patriarchates of Rome, Constantinople, Antioch, and Alexandria were torn apart by jurisdictional jealousies that were too easily translated into doctrinal divisions.

At the beginning of the fifth century, in 404, the infamous affair of the deposition and exile of Chrysostom of Constantinople split Rome away from communion with its three sister patriarchates,[1] and the church's internal resentments intensified. What should have been a spreading flame bearing light and warmth from the center to the ends of the earth turned instead into a wheel of fire spinning out of control and casting off blazing masses of incendiary countermovements. For a short period at mid-century, just after Chalcedon, every major political power center in Europe was Arian.[2] The far west (Spain and Gaul) remained Arian even longer. The far east (Persia, India, and east Syria) was Nestorian. Africa and the Near East (Egypt, Ethiopia, Syria, and Armenia) turned Monophysite. It was only a little more than a hundred years since Nicaea had unified the church, but to the orthodox it must have seemed that the heretics were winning the world. And the worst of the damage was done in just two decades, between 430 and 450.

The Nestorian Controversy

The theological entanglements of the period belong mainly to Western church history, but they impinge so significantly on the later development of Asian Christianity that they must be reviewed here. The landmarks are the great Christological statements of the first four ecumenical councils: Nicaea, 325; Constantinople, 381; Ephesus, 431; and Chalcedon, 451.

The first two, which condemned Arianism, were not a major issue in non-Roman Asia. The Church of the East, in fact, was largely ignorant of the Nicene Creed as late as the early fifth century, though it adopted it readily enough when it was presented at the Synod of Isaac in 410.[3] "Christ is truly God," declared Nicaea against Arius, the presbyter from Egypt who had described the Lord more as a demigod, a being created by God rather than coeternal with him.[4] "Christ is truly man," the second council, Constantinople, added, repeating on behalf of Syria and Asia Minor what had already been said at Nicaea but with an enlarged emphasis on the humanity of Christ.[5]

Then at the beginning of the fifth century the early church's quest for ever more precise theological definitions of the apostolic teaching on the person and work of Christ took a new turn. It became embroiled in a bitter argument between the theological schools of two of the great patriarchates, Alexandria and Antioch, on a vexing, unanswered question raised by the statement in the Nicene Creed that Christ is God and that he is also man. In that case, said some Christians, he must be two persons, one divine and one human. Then what becomes of his unity? Is he a split personality? On the other hand, if he is only one whole person, how can one contain two wholes ("wholly God and wholly man")?

The school of Alexandria, led by its strong-minded, hot-tempered patriarch, Cyril, put its emphasis on the unity of the person of Christ. But in order to preserve the oneness it was difficult not to weaken either his deity or his humanity, for "complete God" and "complete man" strongly implies duality of person. Cyril's explanation of the two natures seemed to Antioch to weaken the humanity of Christ and to stress his deity as of higher significance. The Alexandrian school, strong on the doctrine of redemption, genuinely and naturally defended the deity in Christ's nature, for only a divine Christ could save sinners. But in so doing, the Alexandrians ran the risk of losing some of the historic authenticity of Christ's human nature.[6]

The school of Antioch took precisely the opposite emphasis, and it was from this school that Nestorian theology derived. Its great strength was its insistence on the historic, human Christ. Antioch was as much interested in redemption as Alexandria but linked this with an equal concern for Christian ethics. It had long been known for its care for the poor and hungry. It was perhaps natural, therefore, for Christians in Antioch to emphasize Christ's humanity, for only a completely human Christ could be an ethical and moral example to Christian men and women.[7] In any such contrast made between the two schools, however, it must be remembered that neither Alexandria nor Antioch denied that Christ was both God and man. Both prided themselves on their orthodoxy. The difference was a matter of emphasis.[8]

The father of Antiochene (and therefore of Nestorian) theology was a well-born native of that city, Theodore, known to history as Theodore of Mopsuestia (350–428). His youth had been erratic. At first he was attracted to the cynical sophism of a famous rhetorician, Libanius, who taught his pupils to dismiss Christianity as a pack of "ridiculous and contemptible absurdities."[9] Surprisingly, the young Theodore was converted to the faith his teacher despised and, as is sometimes the case in such things, veered to the other extreme. Influenced by a fellow student, the later-famous John Chrysostom, who had also left the company of Libanius to follow Christ,[10] Theodore renounced the world and turned to radical asceticism. But he was no more fit for the lonely life of a monk than for that of a dilettante philosopher. He longed for marriage. Chrysostom guided him to an alternative: the life of a scholar-bishop. Here at last he found happiness, combining the busy human demands of diocesan administration with the scholastic challenge of a pioneering approach to Bible study and exegesis. In 392 he was made bishop of Mopsuestia, a town north of Antioch on the road to Tarsus, and ruled the church there for thirty-six years. His fame spread as an expositor of the Scriptures, and to this day he is called "the Interpreter" by the east Syrians. Theodore taught that the basic principle of biblical exposition was to concentrate on what the Bible actually said and to avoid the temptation to read into it one's own herme-neutical interpretations. "He limited his attention to the literal sense of Scripture," is how Socrates, the church historian who was a younger contemporary of Theodore, described it.[11] This was a sharp contrast to the allegorical style of Origen, so popular in Alexandria, which opened the Bible to often capricious interpretations by attach-ing two or three levels of meaning to every text. Theodore was also more careful than most not to overemphasize the prophetic and ty-pological allusions of the Old Testament. He accepted only four psalms as specifically messianic (Pss. 2; 8; 45; and 110). At one critical point, however, he left himself open to serious criticism. To some in the West, his doctrine of sin was more Pelagian than Augustinian. Perhaps Eastern bishops like Theodore, aware of Augustine's Man-ichaean past, read into Augustine's doctrine of original sin a hint of the Manichaean heresy with which they had to contend, namely, that human nature is basically evil because it is linked to the world of matter. At any rate, in Theodore's view sin was more a weakness than a disease or a tainted will. Weak definitions of sin will produce weak doctrines concerning the Savior from sin, so his opponents in the next generation thought and condemned him, as we shall see, along with his pupil, Nestorius, for allegedly teaching that Jesus was only "a man indissolubly united to God through the permanent in-dwelling of the Logos."[12]

But that came later. In his own lifetime the crowds chanted, "We believe as Theodore believed; long live the faith of Theodore."[13] It was only after he died that the smouldering theological volcano erupted and clouded his name for centuries, though now the cloud is lifting in the light of recent reappraisals of Theodore's essentially pre-Chalcedonian orthodoxy.[14]

The eruption, when it came, was touched off by Theodore's friend, Nestorius, who became the central figure in the most crip-pling controversy ever to divide the early church. Nestorius was born in Germanicia in the Euphrates district of the patriarchate of Antioch. Not much is known of his early life save that he entered a monastery near Antioch out of which he was often called upon to preach in the city's cathedral church. He was a powerful speaker and began to win fame as a highly popular preacher. He may have stud-ied for a while under Theodore of Mopsuestia. In 428 he was sud-denly appointed to one of the highest posts in all Christendom, that of patriarch of Constantinople. His opponents later sneeringly sug-gested that only his beautiful voice and fluent phrases could account for the unexpected promotion of this fairly obscure priest to the ecclesiastical throne of Eastern Rome, but when they complained to the emperor, Theodosius II coldly replied that good preaching was at least better than the bribes, violence, slander, and quarreling that was all they had to offer in his stead:

> (You) monks did not agree with the clergy: the clergy were not of one mind: the bishops were divided: and the people in like manner disagreed.[15]

On his journey to Constantinople to take up his new post, Nestorius stopped in Mopsuestia to visit Theodore, who warned him to be careful, be moderate, and respect the opinions of others.[16] It was good advice, but Nestorius did not heed it. Carried away by zeal at his consecration as patriarch in April 428, he cried out, "Give me, O Emperor, the earth purged from heretics, and I will give you heaven." So saying he launched a drive against the Arian heretics and closed their only chapel in Constantinople.[17] Other crusades followed swiftly; but suddenly, in an ironic twist of fate, Nestorius the heresy hunter found himself accused of heresy.

The trouble began when Nestorius celebrated the birth of Christ in a series of Christmas sermons and turned his attention to a popular phrase used in the West but not in Antioch to describe the Virgin Mary. In Constantinople she was called "the Mother of God" (in Greek, *theotokos*, or "God-bearer"), and this grated on the ears of an Antiochene schooled to defend the complete humanity of Jesus Christ. Others had already questioned the use of the title, and with the best of intentions Nestorius sought to mediate in the dispute:

> When I came here, I found a dispute among the members of the church, some of whom were calling the Blessed Virgin Mother of God, while others were calling her Mother of man. Gathering both parties together, I suggested that she should be called Mother of Christ, a term which represented both God and man, as it is used in the gospels.[18]

But the phrase Nestorius was criticizing for its loose theology had all the emotional popularity of a religious slogan, and his objection to the sacred words brought his enemies down on him like wolves. This was the opportunity that his rival, Cyril, the patriarch of Alexandria, had been hoping for. Cyril had two reasons for seeking the downfall of Nestorius. The first was political. Up to the end of the fourth century Alexandria had been the greatest patriarchate in the world next to Rome. But the Second Ecumenical Council (Constantinople, 381) had declared that Rome and Constantinople were equal, though Rome, of course, had the precedence of antiquity. So to the anguish of Cyril, Alexandria had been demoted below Constantinople. Added to this political enmity was the long-standing theological rivalry between the school of Antioch and the school of Alexandria.

On Easter Sunday in 429, Cyril publicly denounced Nestorius for heresy. With fine disregard for anything Nestorius had actually said, he accused him of denying the deity of Christ. It was a direct and incendiary appeal to the emotions of the orthodox, rather than to precise theological definition or scriptural exegesis, and, as he expected, an ecclesiastical uproar followed. Cyril showered Nestorius with twelve bristling anathemas. The Antiochenes countered with twelve equally angry counteranathemas against the bishop of Alexandria. These were attributed to the milder Nestorius but are now known not to be written by him.[19] As tempers mounted, a Third Ecumenical Council was summoned to meet in Ephesus in 431 to make peace among the warring patriarchs. All it produced was more war.

Ephesus, 431, was the most violent and least equitable of all the great councils. It is an embarrassment and blot on the history of the church. The council was called by the authority of the emperor, who favored Nestorius, but Cyril stole it away from him. When he received word that the patriarch of Antioch, who also sided with Nestorius, would arrive late and was asking the council to wait for him and his bishops, Cyril, who had brought fifty of his own bishops with him, arrogantly opened the council anyway, over the protests of the imperial commissioner and about seventy other bishops. Nestorius refused even to attend and later wrote this graphic, biased but accurate description of the proceedings:

> They acted . . . as if it was a war they were conducting, and the followers of the Egyptian (Cyril) . . . went about in the city girt and armed with clubs . . . with the yells of barbarians, snorting fiercely . . . raging with extravagant arrogance against those whom they knew to be opposed to their doings, carrying bells about the city and lighting fires. . . . They blocked up the streets so that everyone was obliged to flee and hide, while they acted as masters of the situation, lying about, drunk and besotted and shouting obscenities . . .[20]

So tense was the situation that a guard was flung about the house in which Nestorius lodged to prevent his murder. At Cyril's bidding the council proceeded obediently to vote two hundred to nil to excommunicate Nestorius. John of Antioch, with forty bishops, arrived too late to do anything but declare the result illegal and hold a countercouncil that excommunicated Cyril.

Confronted by an impasse that threatened to tear his Byzantine empire apart, Theodosius II reluctantly decided to defuse the situation by accepting the deposition of both the rival partriarchs, Nestorius and Cyril. They were arrested and imprisoned, but the two men reacted to the sentence in quite different ways. Cyril promptly bribed his way back to power. He bought the favor of the emperor's adviser, the grand chamberlain, with a present of fourteen oriental rugs, eight couches, six tablecloths, four tapestries, four ivory benches, six leather benches, and six ostriches and ran the church of Alexandria into debt to the amount of around three million dollars by today's reckoning.[21] Nestorius, on the other hand, who was often tactless and extreme but always honest and sincere, accepted the verdict with only a quiet protest at its injustice. He went obediently into exile, first to his old monastery near Antioch and then, in 435, as the opposition to him hardened, on to Petra in Arabia. Finally, so greatly was his influence feared, he was moved far out into the Egyptian desert. There he died about 451—to the Western church a heretic, to the Persian church a hero and a martyr, but to himself neither a heretic nor a hero. Near the end he wrote:

> Earthly things have little interest for me. I have died to the world and live for Him. . . . As for Nestorius—let him be anathema! . . . And would God that all men by anathematizing me might attain to reconciliation with God. . . . Farewell desert, my friend . . . and [farewell] exile, my mother, who after my death shall keep my body until the resurrection. . . . Amen.[22]

The Church of the East never accepted the judgment of the Council of Ephesus in 431. It remains the only one of the first four ecumenical councils rejected by Nestorians, and they may well have been right. Its legality is questionable.[23] Its conduct was disgraceful. And its theological verdict, if not overturned, was at least radically amended by the Council of Chalcedon thirty years later, which evened up the battle of the anathemas by excommunicating Cyril's successor in Alexandria, Dioscurus.

"Nestorianism" Examined

For fifteen hundred years Nestorius has been branded in the West as a heretic,[24] and for most of that time, from what the West knew about him the condemnation seemed just. His writings were burned; only fragments survived. His image as left to history was that created by his enemies. Then, dramatically, in 1889 a Syrian priest discovered an eight-hundred-year-old manuscript of a Syriac translation made about 540 of Nestorius's own account, in Greek, of his controversies and his teachings. It had remained hidden for centuries disguised under the title *The Book* (or *Bazaar*) *of Heracleides*, but the author was unmistakably Nestorius.[25]

Judged by his own words at last, Nestorius is revealed as not so much "Nestorian" and more orthodox than his opponents gave him credit for. Luther, for example, after looking over all he could find of his writings decided that there was nothing really heretical in them.[26] Opinions about him still differ widely, for his theological writing is difficult and often obscure.[27] But some points are clear. He took his stand firmly on the historical Christ as revealed in the Gospels. He was not at ease with technical and semantic theological distinctions. He was absolutely convinced that he was biblically orthodox. At no time did he deny the deity of Christ, as was charged against him. He merely insisted that it be clearly distinguished from Christ's humanity. Nor did he deny the unity of Christ's person, which was the most enduring of the charges against him. It was on this point that he was officially condemned. His opponents, the Alexandrians, maintained that by separating Christ into two "natures" (*keyane* or *keiane* in Syriac, *physis* in Greek)—"true God by nature and true man by nature" was how Nestorius put it[28]—he destroyed the real personality of the Savior, deforming Christ into a creature with two heads. Nestorius answered, "The person (*parsopa* in Syriac, *prosopon* in Greek) is one . . .," and "There are not two Gods the Words, or two Sons, or two only-begottens, but one."[29]

The problem lay partly in his choice of words. Nestorius used the Greek word *prosopon* to refer to Christ's person as the basis of Christ's unity. But *prosopon* is a weak word, used only once in the New Testament to refer to people as "persons" and more often meaning "presence" or even mere "appearance." His opponents insisted on the use of the stronger word *hypostasis* ("substance," or "real being," as in Heb. 1:3) for Christ's person as one being, incarnate. That, said Nestorius, is too strong—for *hypostasis*, like *ousia*, if used of Christ's unified, essential being confuses the fact that there is still a distinction between his humanity and his deity.[30]

There is a subtle distinction between "two natures" (Dyophysitism, which is what Nestorius and the school of Antioch taught) and "two persons," which is how Alexandria interpreted the phrase, as if Nestorius were teaching "dyhypostatism." By insisting that one person (*hypostasis*) can have but one nature (*physis*), Alexandria sought to make the teaching of Nestorius heretical.[31] But what Alexandria said he taught was not what Nestorius actually taught, even in his earlier works, and clearly not in the *Book of Heracleides*, his last work.[32] As early as Ephesus he struggled to find a way to express the essential unity of the person of the incarnate Christ without denying the essential reality of both the humanity and deity of the Savior and without surrendering the all-important truth that there is an ultimate, basic distinction between deity and humanity.

> The divine Logos was not one, and another the man in whom he came to be. Rather, one was the *prosopon* of both in dignity and honour, worshipped by all creation, and in no way and no time divided by otherness of purpose and will.[33]

This doctrine of the unity of the person (*prosopon*) of Christ[34] in two natures may have rested on the use of a word too weak to support the theological weight it was required to bear, but it was in no sense heresy.

Nor was Nestorius guilty of another serious charge against him, the heresy of adoptionism. Alexandria complained that the Christ of Nestorius was only a man, a man who was so good and so obedient that he earned for himself an adoptive "sonship" into divinity.[35] But to Nestorius, the incarnation was not a man earning deity, but an act of God's grace best described as in the Bible, in Philippians, as God emptying himself, "being born in the likeness of men" (Phil. 2:7). The divinity and the humanity, he goes on to say elsewhere, are one *prosopon*, the deity by *kenosis* (emptying), the humanity by exaltation.[36]

The fault, if there is one in the Nestorian "heresy," concludes A. Grillmeier, was neither a theology of a two-headed Christ, nor of a Jesus who earned his way into Godhead, but rather a failure to take the church's ancient tradition of the *communicatio idiomatum* seriously enough.[37] That tradition, as old as Origen and Athanasius, held that whatever is said either of Christ's human nature (for example, that he suffered) or of his divine nature ("in the form of God") or by whatever name he is called (Son of God or Son of man) is said of one and the same person who was and is both God and man. Had Nestorius recognized that traditional concept as acceptable, he need not have balked at calling Mary "Mother of God" and there might possibly never have been a "Nestorian controversy."

But violence and emotions had run too high at Ephesus. Between the councils of Ephesus in 431 and Chalcedon in 451 came twenty unhappy years of angry theological argument and intense political and ecclesiastical intrigue. The theological world hardened into three crystallized positions. On the right were the victors at Ephesus, the Alexandrians, ultraconservatives ready to defend the deity of Christ even at the risk of his real humanity. They were soon to be identified as Monophysites (from *mono,* meaning "one," and *physis,* meaning "nature"). Their leaders were the patriarchs of Egypt, Cyril and his successor, Dioscurus. On the left were the Dyophysites (from *duo,* "two", and *physis,* "nature"), soon to be called Nestorians after their exiled patriarch. They seemed more liberal than their opponents in that they defended Christ's humanity against obliteration by his deity but were less than precise in their theological definitions. Their leader (in the absence of Nestorius) was John, patriarch of Antioch.

In the center emerged a peace party characterized not so much by theological position as by a desire for unity. It was composed of a coalition of political and ecclesiastical moderates determined to save both church and empire from the perils of religious division. Their first step was to negotiate a theological truce in 433 between Alexandria and Antioch. Alexandria would drop its twelve anathemas against Antioch and accept "two natures" in Christ as taught in the Bible.[38] But this represented theological surrender for the implacable Cyril and was predictably unacceptable to the Alexandrian right wing. On the other hand the compromise also stipulated that Antioch, in turn, must accept the popular phrase "Mother of God" for the Virgin and assent to the excommunication of Nestorius. And this, of course, was ecclesiastical humiliation for John and unacceptable to loyal Nestorians. Nevertheless, under great pressure, the leaders agreed. "Behold again we are friends," wrote John of Antioch to Cyril of Alexandria,[39] and for a while at least it seemed that the shouting and the curses might be forgotten.

But the peace fell apart at the edges. On both sides the leaders failed to carry their partisans with them into the compromise, and when the leaders died—John of Antioch in 442 and Cyril of Alexandria in 444—the truce collapsed.

First to rebel were the Monophysites in Egypt. The accidents of succession gave Antioch and Alexandria two very unequal patriarchs after the deaths of John and Cyril. The Monophysites in Alexandria found in Cyril's successor, Dioscurus, a champion every bit as strong and stubborn and even more unscrupulous than Cyril without the saving grace of Cyril's theological insight and acumen. He could parade shamelessly with his mistress in the streets of Alexandria and at the same time rally the faithful with shouted repetitions of Cyril's formula for anti-Nestorian orthodoxy, "One nature after the union," referring to the undivided human and divine in the incarnate Christ. He utterly rejected the compromise of 433.[40] By contrast, at Antioch, the successor of John was a mild and ineffectual man named Domnus.

A power struggle at the Byzantine court at the time further turned the tide in the West against the Nestorians and in favor of the extreme Monophysites. Emperor Theodosius II was a retiring soul more interested in old manuscripts than in affairs of state. He "reigned but never ruled," as one church historian has observed.[41] Three jealous and powerful court favorites dominated him—two women and a eunuch. His wife, Eudocia, was sympathetic in religious affairs to the Nestorians. His sister, Pulcheria, was anti-Nestorian, but more orthodox than Monophysite. The eunuch, Chrysaphius, was a gross and wily court chamberlain, willing to support whichever side promised him financial or political advantage. He favored the compromise of 433 in the interests of religious peace but was equally willing to support whatever other settlement might bring him wealth and power if the peace failed. By 444 Dioscurus became patriarch of Alexandria; Pulcheria had been forced into retirement; Eudocia had fled to exile in Jerusalem, tainted by a palace scandal; and the unprincipled Chrysaphius was in control.

The Monophysites happily discovered in him a powerful ally, aided by his godfather, a Greek monk named Eutyches, who was as fanatical an opponent of the Nestorian Dyophysites as any Alexandrian. Dioscurus, Eutyches, and Chrysaphius persuaded the pliant Theodosius to call an ecumenical council at Ephesus in 449. There Dioscurus, as supremely arrogant as Cyril at the earlier Ephesus in 431, trampled not only on his old enemy, Antioch, but on the whole moderate center, both Rome and Constantinople. Flavian, patriarch of Constantinople, who had accused Eutyches of falling into the already condemned heresy of Apollinarius, that is, of denying that Christ had a human soul, and who had failed to bribe the powerful Chrysaphius, was deposed by the council. So also was Domnus of Antioch and his theologian, Theodoret of Cyrus, whose penetrating criticism of Monophysite theology in his book the *Eranistes* had dismissed Monphysite theology as a "patchwork of old heresies." The council did not even read the *Tome* of Pope Leo I, a statesmanlike theological position paper that Rome had prepared with great care as a possible bridge to peace between the warring schools. The Monophysites were ecstatically triumphant. But as Leo, who is called "The Great," later wrote to Pulcheria, the church had been betrayed by a "Council of Robbers," and by that name the Second Council of Ephesus has been known ever since.

As it turned out, the victory of the "Robbers" was a flimsy one. In less than a year, with one small turn of fate, it collapsed. Emperor Theodosius II fell off his horse and died. His sister, Pulcheria, swept back into power, executed the miserable Chrysaphius, and, disillusioned with Alexandria's grasp for power, withdrew her former support of the Monophysites to encourage a coalition of the moderate centrists under Leo the Great at Rome. As angry reaction spread across the empire against the wholesale condemnations pronounced by the "Robber Council," a great council of bishops was called to repudiate it; this council took its place as the Fourth Ecumenical Council, Chalcedon, 451.

Chalcedon was the greatest of the early church's seven ecumenical councils.[42] Only the first, Nicaea, can compare to it in importance. And Chalcedon was at least a partial victory for Nestorius. Had he lived another year he might well have rejoiced to hear the Chalcedonian Creed declare: "Christ has two natures." That was precisely what Antioch stood for and what Alexandria denied. Now it was the Alexandrians' turn to be banished and to be branded with the stigma of a heresy of their own, Monophysitism.

But the victory fell to neither side, Antioch or Alexandria. The full Chalcedonian formula was that Christ is "one person in two natures, human and divine." "One person" (defined as *hypostasis* and *prosopon*) contradicted Nestorius.[43] And "two natures" (*physis*) refuted Alexandria. As for the relationship of the two natures, which had been the heart of the controversy, even Chalcedon was unable to define it. It could only confess its faith that the two are not destroyed by the union in the one person but are preserved "without confusion, without change, without division, without separation."[44]

The general consensus of scholarship today would probably agree with A. R. Vine's observation that Nestorius was the better man but Cyril the better theologian and that, though the Third Ecumenical Council of Ephesus was a shabby affair, Chalcedon was probably right in recognizing that Nestorius's "*prosopic* union" was "not strong enough to bear the strain" of maintaining the essential unity of the person of Christ. The council, therefore, may well have been justified in clarifying and extending rather than reversing the verdict of Ephesus. The West, at least, was satisfied with Chalcedon, but not so Egypt and, to a lesser extent, Persia.

NOTES

1. See L. Duchesne, *Early History of the Christian Church*, vol. 3, trans. Jenkins (London: Murray, 1924), 73.

2. See J. Moffatt, *The First Five Centuries of the Christian Church* (London: Univ. of London Press, 1938), 142.

3. See above; pp. 155f.

4. See the summary in J. F. Bethune-Baker, *An Introduction to the Early History of Christian Doctrine to the Time of the Council of Chalcedon,* 3d ed. (London: Methuen, 1933), 155–72; or J. N. D. Kelly, *Early Christian Creeds,* 3d ed. (New York: McKay, 1972).

5. Bethune-Baker, *Christian Doctrine,* 187–89.

6. R. V. Sellers points out that Cyril's theology rests, on the one hand, on Athanasian orthodoxy but, on the other, on the theology of Apollinarius with whose heresy it is often wrongly confused, *Two Ancient Christologies: A Study in the Christological Thought of the Schools of Alexandria and Antioch in the Early History of Christian Doctrine* (London: SPCK, 1954), 1–106. B. J. Kidd points out that Cyril never spoke of the humanity of Christ as *physis, History of the Church to* A.D. *461,* 3 vols. (Oxford: Clarendon, 1922), 3:206.

7. Sellers, *Two Ancient Christologies,* 107–201. See also I. A. Dorner, *The Development of the Doctrine of the Person of Christ,* Div. 1, vol. 1 (Edinburgh, 1891), 25.

8. Sellers, *Two Ancient Christologies,* 116ff., shows that the Antiochene "Nestorians" cannot be accused of neglecting the importance of redemption and soteriology.

9. Socrates, *Ecclesiastical History,* in *Nicene and Post-Nicene Fathers,* second series, vol. 2 (Grand Rapids: Eerdmans, 1983), 3, p. 23.

10. Socrates, *Ecclesiastical History,* 8, p. 2. When Libanius was dying someone asked him who would take his place. "It would have been John (Chrysostom)," he said, "had not the Christians stolen him from us."

11. Socrates, *Ecclesiastical History,* 6, p. 3.

12. The phrase is H. B. Swete's description of Theodore's Christology, in *Theodore of Mopsuestia on the Minor Epistles of St. Paul,* 2 vols. (Cambridge, 1880–82), 1: 81ff. It is cited by Bethune-Baker, *Christian Doctrine,* 259n, who, however, in general defends Theodore's orthodoxy; see pp. 256–60.

13. Cyril of Alexandria, *Epistolae* 69, cited in Bethune-Baker, *Christian Doctrine,* 257 n. 2.

14. See A. Grillmeier's analysis of Theodore's Christology in *Christ in Christian Tradition,* vol. 1, *From the Apostolic Age to Chalcedon* (451), 2d ed. rev., trans J. Bowden (London and Oxford: Mowbray's, 1975), 421–39. "This [i.e., Theodore's Christology] was as far as theology could go before Chalcedon's distinction between *physis* and *hypostasis,*" he writes (p. 436f.), noting Theodore's careful use of such biblical analogies as the unity of husband and wife (Matt. 19:6) and of body and soul in one person (Romans) to illustrate but not explain the unity of the divine and human in Christ. See also R. A. Greer, *Theodore of Mopsuestia: Exegete and Theologian* (Westminster MD: Faith Press, 1961).

15. This was the emperor's reply to his critics as recorded by Nestorius years later in his *Apology,* the *Bazaar of Heracleides* (pp. 279-81); cited by J. F. Bethune-Baker from an anonymous translation from the D. Jenks manu-

script. See his *Nestorius and His Teaching: A Fresh Examination of the Evidence* (Cambridge: Cambridge Univ. Press, 1908), 6f. n. 3. See also Socrates, *Ecclesiastical History*, 7, p. 29.

16. Kidd, *History of the Church*, 3:192

17. Kidd, *History of the Church*, 3:192.

18. Nestorius, in a letter to John of Antioch, December 430, cited by F. Loofs, in a collection of early fragments entitled *Nestoriana* (Cambridge: Cambridge Univ. Press, 1912), 29.

19. See "Die sogenannten Gegenanathematismen des Nestorius," in *Sitzungsberichte der Bayrischen Akademie der Wissenschaften* (Munchen, 1922), book 1.

20. Bethune-Baker, *Nestorius*, 39, quoting from the anonymous translation of the *Bazaar of Heraclides* referred to in n. 15 above. This translation (by R. H. Connolly) predates the Bedjan edition. Cf. the same passage in G. R. Driver and L. Hodgson, *Nestorius, The Bazaar of Heracleides* (Oxford: Clarendon, 1925), 266f., from the Bedjan edition.

21. The whole shameful list of bribes is painstakingly recorded and preserved in *Bibliotheca Casinensis*, I. ii, p. 47, cited by Kidd, *History of the Church*, 3:258. Kidd estimated the debt in 1922 at 60,000 pounds sterling.

22. Nestorius, the *Bazaar of Heracleides*, as translated by F. Loofs and quoted in portions in his *Nestorius and His Place in the History of Christian Doctrine* (Cambridge: Cambridge Univ. Press, 1914), 17, 19. Cf. the same passages in Driver and Hodgson, *Nestorius*, 329, 378–80 *passim*. Bedjan text, 451, 519ff.

23. See however, I. Riker, *Studien zum Concilium Ephesinum . . .*, vol. 4 (Oxenbrunn, 1934), for a painstakingly thorough defense of the verdict, if not the conduct, of the council.

24. As late as 1951 the condemnation by the Council of Ephesus was confirmed by a papal encyclical (Pope Pius I, "Sempiternus Rex Christus," in *Acta Apostolicae Sedis*).

25. The best report of the discovery and the most thorough critical study of the text and its history is L. Abramowski's *Untersuchungen zum Liber Heraclidis des Nestorius* (*CSCO* Subsidia 22, whole no. 242, 1963). The Syriac text was edited by Paul Bedjan in 1910 (Nestorius, *Le livre d'Heraclide de Damas*, Paris). An English translation with introduction and notes by Driver and Hodgson, *Nestorius*, was published in 1925 based on the Bedjan edition. L. I. Scipioni, *Nestorio e il concilio de Efeson* (Milano, 1974), defends the authenticity of a part of the *Bazaar* (Book I, part I, pp. 7–86 in Driver and Hodgson), which Abramowski attributes to a "Pseudo-Nestorius" sometime between 451 and 470.

26. Loofs, *Nestoriana*, 21.

27. See Grillmeier, *Christ in Christian Tradition*, 1:559–68, for a survey of the literature in his appendix, "The Nestorius Question in Modern Study"; and A. R. Vine, *An Approach to Christology: An Interpretation and Development of*

Some Elements in the Metaphysic and Christology of Nestorius (London: Independent Press, 1948), 36–46. Of the major critical assessments: J. F. Bethune-Baker, F. Loofs, R. Seeberg, R. V. Sellers, E. Schwarz, L. Abramowski, and A. Grillmeier all more or less clear Nestorius of the charges of heresy, though Abramowski and Grillmeier both note his points of weakness. L. Hodgson, I. Rucker, B. J. Kidd, and L. J. Tixeront consider Nestorius's theology as at best weak and at worst heretical, agreeing (as does Grillmeier to a point) with Chalcedon's condemnation of Nestorius. P. Bedjan and F. Nau are completely anti-Nestorian.

28. Nestorius, *Book of Heracleides,* 79 (Driver and Hodgson, trans.; in Bedjan, p. 116).

29. Nestorius, *Book of Heracleides,* 23, 47 (Driver and Hodgson; Bedjan, pp. 34, 69).

30. "If we say 'one ousia,' the hypostasis of the God Logos becomes confused with the 'changeableness of the fleshly (hypostasis),'" as Severus quotes from a fragment of the *First Apology* of Nestorius (*Ctr. Gramm.* II., p. 32, cited by Abramowski, *Untersuchungen,* 216 n. 19). The major concern, as always, with Nestorius was "lest on account of the divinity it should not be believed that he was also man" (Nestorius, *Book of Heracleides,* 91 [Driver and Hodgson; Bedjan, p. 132]).

31. See Grillmeier, *Christ in the Christian Tradition,* 1:478–83. It is true, however, that in 612 the phrase "two hypostases" became official Nestorian doctrine, but not in quite the same sense that the phrase was being used in Alexandria a hundred and fifty years earlier. See "The Creed of the Bishops of Persia Which Kosroes Requested . . .," in L. Abramowski and A. E. Goodman, *A Nestorian Collection of Christological Texts,* vol. 2 (Cambridge: Cambridge Univ. Press, 1972), 90–100.

32. The earlier works are collected, mostly, in Loofs, *Nestoriana.*

33. Loofs, *Nestoriana,* 224, cited in Grillmeier, *Christ in the Christian Tradition,* 1:461.

34. "One prosopon of the two natures" is how Nestorius put it. *Book of Heracleides* (Driver and Hodgson), p. 219.

35. Grillmeier, *Christ in the Christian Tradition,* 1:467, 515.

36. Nestorius, *Book of Heracleides* (Driver and Hodgson, trans.), 164f., 246f.

37. Grillmeier, *Christ in the Christian Tradition,* 1:518, 559, who notes that this was also Luther's chief condemnation of Nestorius (in *Luther-Werke,* T. 50 [Weimar, 1914], 590, citing the passage 581–592). Interestingly enough, it was a Calvinist, J. Bruguier of Lille, who as early as 1645 was the first theologian in Europe to come to the defense of Nestorius's orthodoxy (*Disputatio de supositio, in qua plurima hactenus inaudita de Nestorio tamquam orthodoxo . . .,* cited by Grillmeier). See also Bethune-Baker, *Christian Doctrine,* 293f.

38. See Bethune-Baker, *Christian Doctrine,* 272.

39. A. Fortescue, *The Lesser Eastern Churches* (London: Catholic Truth Society, 1913), 74, citing *PG* 67, p. 247.

40. On Dioscurus see the French translation by F. Nau of his "Life" by Theophistus in *Journal Asiatique*, ser. 10, vol. 1 (1903): 5–108, 241–310.

41. Kidd, *History of the Church*, 3:49.

42. It was also the largest of the largest of the seven, with as many as six hundred bishops attending. The seven ecumenical councils were: Nicaea, 325, on Arianism; Constantinople I, 381, on Apollinarianism; Ephesus, 431, on Nestorianism; Chalcedon, 451, on Eutychianism; followed by three lesser councils, Constantinople II, 553, on the "Three Chapters Controversy"; Constantinople III, 680–81, on Monothelitism; and Nicaea II, 787, on iconoclasm.

43. The full phrase was "One and the same Christ, Son, Lord, Only begotten, made known in two natures [which exist] without confusion, without change, without division, without separation; the difference of the natures having been in no way taken away by reason of the union, but rather the properties of each being preserved, and [both] concurring into one Person (*prosopon*) and one *hypostasis*—not parted nor divided into two persons (*prosopa*) . . . ," as translated by R. V. Sellers, *The Council of Chalcedon* (London: SPCK, 1953), 210f.

44. Sellers, *Council of Chalcedon*, 210f.

Chapter *10*
The Controversy
Spreads into Asia

"The holy Theodore interpreted the Scriptures in Greek, and Mar Hiba, bishop of Edessa translated (them) into Syriac, together with other men trained in the divine Scriptures."

—Anonymous manuscript

"As he [Narsai] arrived at the church of [Edessa], he found there Persians; he asked them whether it would be possible for them to carry for him his books—for this was his entire treasure; . . . they were very glad (to help) and taking care carried all his books as far as Nisibis."

—Barhadbesabba *Histoire* II, cited
by A. Voobus *CSCO*, vol. 266,
subsidia tomus 26 (1965),
pp. 17, 45

THE Nestorian controversy we have been describing was a Western, not an Asian dispute. The unity of the Roman Empire was as much of an issue in it as the unity of the church. It revolved around the powers, political and ecclesiastical, of the Roman cities of Antioch, Alexandria, Constantinople, and Rome. Its central figure was Nestorius, the bishop of New Rome, Constantinople, and a man of Antioch. His great antagonist was Cyril, bishop of Alexandria. But its major victor was the bishop of old Rome, Leo I, whose authority both theological and ecclesiastical was strengthened by the acceptance of his guidelines for a theological compromise at the Council of Chalcedon,[1] which, though it reunified the churches in the West, tragically separated them from vast parts of Asia and Africa.

But that came later. Throughout most of the Nestorian controversy's stormy course the Church of the East was protected by the Persian border from direct contact with the theological storm center. From about 420 to 457 the Persian church was more preoccupied with its own problems of survival under the Zoroastrian persecutions of Yazdegerd I, Varahran V, and Yazdegerd II than with the angry quarrels of Western theologians.

Persia might well have escaped involvement altogether and might possibly have remained an innocent and untouched bystander, to the immense enrichment of the whole church, had it not been for its historic attachment to Edessa as its mother church. Edessa was now firmly Roman, and this was the connection that finally drew the Persian church into the controversy and fatefully drove the Christians of Persia into separation from the church of the West.

Edessa, Rabbula, and the Monophysites

In 411 or 412 a strong-minded Syrian named Rabbula from near Aleppo was appointed bishop of Edessa by Antioch and ruled there for almost a quarter of a century. His instincts were sound. He found Edessa crowded with churches, so instead of building more in order to enhance his reputation as a churchman, he chose rather to encourage the building of hospitals for the sick and the poor. Only where there were no churches did he instruct his priests to build them, and once built, he told them, they were to be kept clean and in repair. His rules for the clergy were strict and simple. No meat or wine unless they were sick. No involvement in lawsuits. No association with heretics or demon worshipers. No lenience toward adultery. And on a more positive note, priests were to "care for the poor and seek the cause of the oppressed without showing favour . . . (and to) hold all landowners in the respect that is their due without showing them favour or oppressing the poor."[2]

Rabbula was adamant against heretics, whether they were Bardesanites, Arians, Marcionites, Jews, Borborians who mixed sex with religion, Sadducians who reveled in visions, or Mesallians who built their gospel on such a literal interpretation of the Sermon on the Mount that many of them gave up all useful work to spend their waking hours in continual prayer, thereby ending up, not surprisingly, as beggars. Edessa teemed with heretics, and Rabbula vigorously attacked them all, driving them by the thousands, it is said, into the orthodoxy of his own church.[3]

Rabbula also played an important role in the Eastern churches' traditional emphasis on Syriac translations of the Scriptures. He has been credited with a part in the production of an authorized Syriac translation of the New Testament, the Peshitta, which replaced both Tatian's *Diatessaron* and the various texts of Old Syriac "Separate Gospels." This was completed some time before the schism of 431, and therefore was acceptable to both Nestorians and Monophysites. For two hundred years the Syrian and Persian churches had recognized Tatian's harmony of the Gospels as the preferred version, but early in the fifth century, a number of bishops like Theodoret of Cyrus on the upper Euphrates and Rabbula of Edessa opposed the use of the *Diatessaron* and favored a new, authorized Syriac New Testament, based on the old Syriac "Separate Gospels" (the "Mepharreshe") of which different versions were in circulation. Rabbula is said to have made his own private translation of the New Testament from the Greek into Syriac and was probably eager to bring the Eastern form of the Gospels into harmony with that of the West.[4]

At one critical point, however, Rabbula did more to divide the Syrian churches than to unify them. Edessa's natural leaning in the Nestorian controversy was toward Antioch and Nestorius. Its prestigious theological school held the commentaries of Theodore of Mopsuestia to be definitive in the interpretation of the Bible, and Nestorius was his disciple. But Rabbula, after some initial and uncharacteristic hesitation, sided with Cyril of Alexandria. Once committed, he threw himself into the fray with all his energy. In 431, the year Nestorius was condemned at the Council of Ephesus, Rabbula called his own council to meet at Edessa and cast into the flames the writings of Theodore, castigating him as the father of the Nestorian "heresy."[5] By 435 or 436, when Rabbula died, he may have largely freed the church in Edessa from the fringe sects but he had so thoroughly polarized his Christians into two warring camps, Nestorians against Monophysites, that Edessa was more dangerously divided than ever.

This became obvious when Rabbula was succeeded by a leader of the party he had so vigorously condemned. Hiba (or Ibas), who was bishop of Edessa from 435/6 to 457, was Nestorian in his theology. In fact he had reportedly been exiled with others by Rabbula's Edessene council in 431, having incurred that theologically belligerent bishop's wrath by translating into Syriac the works of the "pre-Nestorian Nestorians," Diodore of Tarsus and Theodore of Mopsuestia. The triumphant return of Hiba to Edessa as the new bishop brought the Nestorian party back into power, but only barely. In popular support, the two groups were almost evenly divided and rivalry was fierce.

Adding to the divisiveness was the fact that by the middle of the fifth century there were now three theological schools in Edessa: the School of the Persians, which was the oldest and most prestigious of the three schools; the School of the Syrians, which was probably anti-Nestorian and perhaps orthodox in the Chalcedonian sense but perhaps also seeking a compromise with the Monophysites; and the School of the Armenians, who were by now moving toward Monophysitism.[6]

In 449 excited Monophysite mobs took to the streets against Hiba shouting, "To exile with the companion of Nestorius" and "To the mines with Hiba." The governor of the city, alarmed for Edessa's peace, gave in to the pressure and threw the bishop into prison. The tide seemed to be turning sharply in favor of the Monophysites, and later that same year the notorious Robber Council of Ephesus, shamelessly dominated by the anti-Nestorians of Dioscurus of Alexandria, condemned Hiba and deposed him. His life-style as much as his theology may have contributed to his fall, for he loved sports and good living as much as he loved his books and was taunted as "the jockey bishop" by his adversaries. This second exile lasted only two years but he complained bitterly about the way he had been tossed about from prison to prison more than twenty times to prevent rescue by his angry friends.[7] It was only after the church in the West regained some semblance of stability at the Council of Chalcedon that Hiba's condemnation by the Robber Council was repudiated and he was restored to his bishopric.

The stormy episcopate of Hiba at Edessa had one unanticipated but disastrously far-reaching side effect. It carried the abrasive Christological disputes of the Western churches across the Roman border to trouble the church in Persia. In the intervals of peace between the smoldering wars of this period (Rome and Persia had gone to war four times within a hundred years)[8] large numbers of Persian students were able to cross into Roman territory to study the Bible and theology in Edessa's great School of the Persians.

The origins of that school are traced by some as far back as the time of Bardaisan, about 200, and by others with more likelihood but some uncertainty to Ephrem the Syrian, who is assumed to have taught there after moving to Edessa when Nisibis fell to the Persians in 363. The school probably existed before Ephrem, but its first known master was Qiore, in the early fifth century. The head of the school in Hiba's time was Narsai (Narses), a scholar from Kurdistan in the Persian mountains, who had come as a boy to study in Edessa. He was assisted by another Persian, Marun of Dilaita, an Assyrian from near Mosul.[9]

Persian students coming to Edessa from their theological isolation in Mesopotamia were inevitably caught up in the school's spirited defense of Nestorius and of his teacher Theodore of Mopsuestia, known as "the Interpreter" and expositor of the Holy Scriptures. They were taught to reject as unjust the anathemas pronounced against Nestorius by the two "Monophysite councils," Ephesus, in 431, and the Robber Council, also at Ephesus, in 449. Students educated in the School of the Persians at Edessa were soon to rise to high positions in the Persian church. They included a patriarch, Acacius; a bishop of Nisibis, Barsauma; and Narsai, who was to lead the school into exile in Nisibis.

Hiba himself, who had taught at the school before becoming bishop, contributed to the spread of Nestorian sentiment across the border. However, he never publicly proclaimed himself a Nestorian. In fact, at the Council of Chalcedon as the price of his reinstatement as bishop of Edessa, he was forced to assent to the excommunication of Nestorius, which had been pronounced at Ephesus. But in a famous and controversial letter to a Persian bishop, "Mari of Ardarshir," he had unguardedly revealed his true sentiments. The letter spoke frankly of his bitterness at the Monophysite troublemakers in his diocese, his resentment at the injustice done to Nestorius by Cyril and the Council of Ephesus, and his attachment to the "Nestorian" phraseology of Theodore of Mopsuestia on the critical question of the divine and human in the person of Christ.[10]

Hiba of Edessa managed to stem only for a brief interval the mounting wave of Monophysite emotion in the eastern Roman empire of Byzantium. Twice Edessa's Nestorians were sent fleeing across the border into Persia, first in 449 when the Robber Council condemned Bishop Hiba and with him a brilliant young scholar of the school, Barsauma,[11] and again in 457 when Hiba died and was succeeded by Nona, a bishop who favored the Monophysites.

Chalcedon and Schism in Africa

By this time the Monophysite tide within the empire was becoming irresistible and was beginning to turn separatist, particularly in Egypt where the theological and ecclesiastical differences were magnified by nationalist passions. It was as much the political breakup of Byzantine control over the provinces,[12] as the theological arguments of Monophysites against Dyophysites (whether orthodox or Nestorian) that led Egypt into the first great schism.

Constantinople in the last half of the fifth century was, in effect, ruled by Germans and Isaurians, not by the imperial aristocracy, and Alexandria felt culturally and politically as well as theologically superior to such barbarians. When Chalcedon humiliated and deposed the Egyptian patriarch Dioscurus and forced a Byzantine Chalcedonian patriarch, Proterius (452–457), onto the throne of the great Cyril, Egypt exploded, resulting in the first permanent schism of the Christian church. The Egyptian Monophysites elected a rival patriarch, Timothy Aelurus, nicknamed Timothy the Cat. This rupture marks the establishment of the Egyptian church as a separate, independent entity commonly called the Coptic church, since "Coptic" is the ancient Greek word for "Egyptian."[13] In 457, the year that Hiba of Edessa died and was succeeded by a Monophysite, mobs of Egyptians took to the streets of Alexandria, cornered the orthodox patriarch Proterius in a church, killed him, and burned his bloody body in triumph.

It might have been expected that as Africa turned Monophysite, separating from the West into the Coptic churches of Egypt and Ethiopia, the Asian churches that had been estranged by the Nestorian controversy would turn back toward fellowship again with Constantinople and Rome. Persia, Byzantium, and papal Rome were all Dyophysite theologically and in opposition to Alexandria's Monophysite formula that though there were "two natures" before the union, one divine and one human, Christ had only "one nature" after the incarnation. But as in Egypt, so now in Asia politics and history even more than theology moved the church toward greater schism rather than to reunion.

The politics of empire in Constantinople dictated that Monophysite Egypt was more important economically and strategically to the survival of Byzantium than the scattered Nestorian communities under pagan Persian rule in an enemy empire, more important, indeed, than even the maintenance of church unity with Rome, for by now Constantinople had replaced Rome as the seat of Roman civil power. The last Roman emperor in the West was brushed off his throne by the barbarians in 476. So the overriding concern of Constantinople for the half century after Chalcedon was to preserve the unity of the Eastern empire at whatever cost, by theological compromise with the separatist Monophysites if necessary, even if that meant schism with Rome in the West or repudiation of Nestorians in Asia.

The decisive role in this development was played by an Isaurian tribal chief from southern Asia Minor named Zeno.[14] The threatened emperors of Constantinople had watched with alarm how easily the barbarians had swallowed Rome. Aware of the rising numbers of barbarian mercenaries (mostly German) in their own armies, they looked about for ways to avert the same kind of disaster in the East. Emperor Leo I (ruled 457–474) conceived of a plan to bring in a detachment of Isaurians from Asia as an imperial bodyguard, thus providing a balance to the power of the Germans. The Isaurians were at least citizens of the empire and therefore technically not barbarians.

But as it turned out, the Isaurians were quite as capable of dominating the Eastern throne as the Germans were of beginning to dominate the West. Zeno the Isaurian married the daughter of Emperor Leo I in 468 and was promoted to commander of the army of the east, headquartered in Antioch. There he came under the influence of a heterodox churchman, Peter the Fuller, who had been expelled from Constantinople for Monophysite sympathies. By this time that heresy, triumphant in Egypt but long opposed in Antioch, was spreading up into Syria. Ever since 433 when the patriarch of Antioch, John, had reluctantly accepted the condemnation of Nestorius as the price of communion with his fellow patriarchs in Rome and Alexandria, the Syrian Christian community had become more and more confused and divided. They were emotionally supportive of their own Nestorius but felt compelled by political pressures and by theological arguments that sounded almost Monophysite to renounce Nestorius and stand loyally with the orthodox center. The Syrians were in the center of the storm.

The Council of Chalcedon only made the situation worse. A. S. Atiya has remarked that the compromise worked out at Chalcedon was a paradox. "It praised Cyril though it denounced his theology, whereas it condemned Nestorius while supporting Diophysitism."[15] Still confused after Chalcedon, Antioch drifted toward Monophysitism. Extremists like Peter the Fuller charged that the real heretics were his orthodox opponents in Constantinople and Antioch, whose rejection of the Monophysite formula "One nature after the incarnation" was nothing else but a denial of Christ's true deity. With Zeno's powerful support Peter drove the orthodox patriarch out of Antioch and took his place. Even when the orthodox Chalcedonians twice counterattacked and succeeded in exiling him for heresy (in 471 and 477), Peter kept climbing back again and again to ecclesiastical power.

As for Zeno, he rose even higher. In 474 he was crowned emperor in Constantinople. Since he had supported the Monophysites in Antioch, one condition of his enthronement was that he accept the Chalcedonian faith, and to this he assented, at least nominally. Almost at once, however, he was reminded of the power of the Monophysite party on which he had just turned his back. A usurper, Basiliscus (475–476), aided by Monophysite support, swept Zeno off the throne into exile, and in gratitude the new emperor issued an imperial encyclical[16] affirming the two anti-Nestorian councils of Ephesus and condemning the anti-Monophysite Council of Chalcedon. In that same year, 476, the year that old Rome lost its last Roman emperor to heretically Arian barbarians, the New Rome, Constantinople, found on its throne an emperor championing another heresy, Monophysitism. Three of the four eastern patriarchs signed the heretical encyclical, Timothy the Cat in Alexandria, Peter the Fuller in Antioch, and Anastasius in Jerusalem.[17] Only Acacius, patriarch of Constantinople (471–489), refused to sign, thereby remaining in communion with Rome, though a major reason for his loyalty to Chalcedonian orthodoxy might have made the pope uneasy. The Council of Chalcedon in its twenty-eighth canon had made Constantinople's patriarchate equal in authority, at last, to Rome, and Acacius's own interests demanded that he oppose any threat to the rulings of that council.

The tenuous unity between Constantinople and Rome was soon broken however. When Zeno returned to power in 477 and drove out the usurper Basiliscus, he was convinced by his experience of exile that the survival of the Eastern empire depended on reaching an accommodation with the Monophysites in Egypt. Acacius, the patriarch in Constantinople, was also eager by now for a settlement and was more concerned that the peace terms preserve the authority of Chalcedon than that they please Rome. With the help of Acacius Zeno issued an edict of union, called the *Henoticon*, in 482.[18]

The *Henoticon* was an ecclesiastical and theological compromise, with something for everyone except the Nestorians and the pope. It brought rejoicing to Alexandria and Constantinople, restoring the religious unity of the Eastern empire lost after Chalcedon. On the Monophysite side it recognized the condemnation of Nestorius and approved the harsh anathemas of Cyril of Alexandria. To satisfy the orthodox in Constantinople, it denounced the radical Monophysite heresy of Eutychus, who had taught that Christ had two natures before the incarnation but only one nature after the union. Also, while the *Henoticon* did not reaffirm Chalcedon, at least it did not specifically repudiate it as Zeno's encyclical had done six years earlier, and this pleased Acacius.

But Rome was outraged. There was no reference to Leo's *Tome*, which had been the theological cornerstone of Chaldecon and a symbol of Roman leadership. The *Tome* was replaced by Cyril's *Anathemas*, and in Roman eyes the *Henoticon* made Constantinople officially Monophysite. So in 484 Pope Felix III excommunicated both Acacius and the emperor Zeno, and Acacius promptly replied by excommunicating the pope. The schism between the two Roman capitals was complete. It lasted for thirty-six years. But it solved nothing.

The Persian Church Becomes Nestorian

Blessedly separated from the raging ecclesiastical wars in the West by the Persian border, the Church of the East was still largely untroubled and not yet divided from Rome and Constantinople by the Christological controversy. But it was beginning to hear of the controversy through the schools of Edessa, and ultimately that controversy was destined to cut off the Asian church outside the Roman Empire from communion with Western Christendom. For the moment, however, the catholicos (patriarch) in Seleucia-Ctesiphon was not only beyond the jurisdiction of the Western churches with their imperially imposed encyclical and *Henoticon*, he was also too busy with the problems of Christian survival under a pagan emperor and too vulnerable to charges of friendship with the Roman enemy to seek involvement in a theological quarrel so serpentinely linked to the politics of Western emperors.

The Persian emperor reigning when Zeno came to the throne of Constantinople was Peroz (457–483), son of Yazdegerd II. He was considered a friend of the Persian Christians because of his admiration for Barsauma, archbishop of Nisibis, though he was not above persecuting Christians in Armenia. He had won the respect of his people by bringing them safely through a parching, seven-year drought that completely dried up even the mighty Tigris River, but in foreign affairs and military ventures he brought Persia nothing but disaster. In the east, toward central Asia, he aroused the enmity of the Hephthalite (or White) Huns,[19] who were becoming as much of a threat to Persia from the east as Rome was in the west. Arrogantly condescending toward the nomad hordes, Peroz promised their chief a Persian princess in marriage as a peace offering. But, instead, he sent one of his female slaves dressed as a princess in court robes. The Huns never forgot the insult.

His entire reign was spent, it seemed, in waging losing battles. Twice he was defeated by the White Huns. The second defeat was particularly humiliating. He was forced to sue for peace by prostrating himself before the very barbarians he had so insulted. Then the Kushans[20] attacked around the southern end of the Caspian Sea. The Armenians, who had been forced by Peroz's father, Yazdegerd II, to renounce the Christian faith and convert to Zoroastrianism then rebelled against the weaker son. And finally, perhaps to wipe out the memory of his earlier humiliation at the hands of the White Huns, Peroz unwisely marched against them again and was ingloriously slain near Balkh in what is now northern Afghanistan.[21]

BARSAUMA OF NISIBIS

The outstanding figure in the church in Persia during the reign of Peroz was not the church's titular head, the catholicos Babowai (450–484), but Barsauma, the controversial metropolitan (archbishop) of Nisibis, who is charged, at least by Monophysite chroniclers, as being almost single-handedly responsible for leading the Church of the East into what they denounced as the Nestorian heresy.[22] Barsauma was born about 415 in the northern Assyrian regions of the Mesopotamian Valley. He studied as we have noted,[23] in Edessa at the School of the Persians. There, under the influence of Bishop Hiba he was attracted to the Nestorian "two-nature" side of the Christological argument against the "one-nature" Monophysites. The violent wave of Monophysite reaction that swept Edessa after the death of Hiba in 457 sent the leading Persian scholars of the school flying to safety across the border and probably only hardened Barsauma's convictions against the Monophysites.

In Nisibis, the fortress city on the Persian side of the border some forty miles from Edessa, he rose rapidly to ecclesiastical power. Nisibis ranked third in the episcopal hierarchy of the Church of the East, after the capital, Seleucia-Ctesiphon, and Beit Lapat.[24] But the ambitious and restless Barsauma, not content with high position in the church, accepted military-political powers also as commander or inspector on the Persian-Roman border.[25] Monophysite historians (Simeon of Beit Arsham in the sixth century, Michael the Syrian in the seventh, and Bar Hebraeus in the thirteenth) charge that he misused his military power to massacre Monophysites and to force his own Nestorianism on the unwilling patriarchs Babowai and Acacius (485–496). "The wild boar" was Simeon's name for him.[26]

Contemporary records of the Persian synods, however, do not substantiate the charge. There is no doubt that the powerful border bishop quarreled bitterly with both patriarchs and coveted the primacy for himself. But politics and church order, not theology, were the major points of contention. The Persian church at that time was in no sense leaning toward Monophysitism. Its sympathies were with the followers of Nestorius, and the only Monophysites then penetrating Persia were in isolated pockets like Tagrit and the monastery of Mar Mattai near Mosul.[27]

The struggle for power that racked the Persian church in the last half of the fifth century was more a personal rivalry between the patriarch Babowai and his unruly archbishop Barsauma than a theological dispute between Nestorians and Monophysites. The contest between the patriarch and the bishop, despite the higher rank of the former, was most uneven. Barsauma had the ear of the king himself, while Babowai, a convert from Zoroastrianism, lived in fear for his very life. Ever since the edict of Yazdegerd I conversion from the national religion had been a punishable offense even during the occasional intervals of toleration. Theoretically, the sentence was death, but the extreme penalty was rarely exacted. Usually a lesser punishment was inflicted. Babowai spent seven years of his eleven-year patriarchate in prison.[28]

It would seem that the patriarch and the archbishop clashed first on the thorny question of episcopal celibacy. The East was more ambivalent on this than the West. Its ascetics were more radical than Western monks, but its priests were more free and were not required to take the vow of celibacy for ordination. Whether this omission also applied to bishops is not clear. Traditionally bishops were expected to be celibate, and Babowai, a strict disciplinarian, tried to enforce this understanding. But Barsauma had taken a wife. His opponents branded her a concubine, and Western bishops from across the border, glad to embarrass a Nestorian foe, used the fact to discredit him. They complained to his patriarch in Seleucia-Ctesiphon. Barsauma hotly defended himself. The union was legal, he insisted, and quoted St. Paul, "It is better to marry than to burn" (1 Cor. 7:9). Babowai sided with the judgment of the Western bishops and wrote a personal letter to them to justify his failure to take action against the archbishop, asking them to persuade the emperor Zeno to intercede with the shah for an end to harassment and for greater freedom for the church in Persia. "We are enslaved under an impious government," he wrote, "and unable to enforce discipline in the Persian church as severely as we would like."

It was a dangerous letter. It not only criticized the government, it asked for foreign intervention. Sensing his danger, the patriarch tried to smuggle it secretly across the border hidden in a hollow cane. Unfortunately for him, the very man he was accusing, Barsauma, intercepted the letter at the border and lost no time, according to Monophysite historians, in exposing his antagonist to the king. Babowai was charged with treason, condemned to death, and hung up by his ring finger—the finger that bore the ring that had sealed the fatal letter—until he died.[29]

Barsauma, confidently expecting to be elected patriarch and indisputably master of the church in the interim, quickly called a church council in Gundeshapur (Beit Lapat) in 484 to give official approval to the marriage of bishops, to honor the memory of Theodore of Mopsuestia, and to issue a Nestorian confession of faith against the intrusion of Monophysite doctrine from the West where Zeno's *Henoticon* had just legitimized an anti-Nestorian position.[30]

But Barsauma's triumph was short-lived. His hopes were dashed by the sudden death of his patron, the shah Peroz, in battle against the Huns. The new shah, Vologases (or Balash, 484–488), was desperate for peace at any price in the East. He is reported to have been forced to accept terms promising tribute to the Huns for two years, a supreme humiliation for proud Persia. So, recognizing that it was no time to offend Byzantium by the appointment of the anti-Roman Barsauma as head of the Persian church, thereby adding trouble with the West to trouble in the East, he bypassed the powerful but controversial archbishop and chose instead another former student from the School of the Persians, Acacius, a man of a more ecumenical temperament.

Acacius ruled as patriarch from 485 to 496 and acquitted himself well. His first assignment from the new shah was a mission of appeasement to Constantinople.[31] In the emotionally surcharged atmosphere of the Byzantine court he managed to satisfy the Western hierarchy of his orthodoxy without compromising his own Nestorian leanings[32] by the simple expedient of agreeing to repudiate, if he could, his old rival Barsauma, the symbol of all that was anti-Byzantine and anti-Monophysite in the Persian church. His mission's success left Constantinople and Seleucia-Ctesiphon still in communion with each other despite the former's schism with Rome and the latter's widening breach with Monophysite Egypt and Syria.

THE SYNOD OF ACACIUS (486)

Back again in Persia the new catholicos vigorously reasserted his authority as patriarch. He had already reduced to quick submission the troublesome Barsauma, who no longer had a king to support him. Now Acacius hurried north with only one bishop and forced Barsauma to repent publicly before a group of his own bishops for his defiance of the late catholicos Babowai and to confess the illegality of his independent synod at Beit Lapat the year before. The penitent archbishop promised to accept whatever judgment a regularly called general synod might soon pronounce upon him.[33]

The next year, 486, the catholicos Acacius convened the Fourth General Synod of the Church of the East. Barsauma did not attend. Pleading the pressure of emergency military duty and probably fearing humiliation, he begged to be excused in a lively letter that complained about military pressures from plundering Arabs and suspicious Romans, and rather grudgingly assented in advance to any decisions the Synod might choose to make concerning the marriage of bishops and a new confession of faith.[34]

The Synod of Acacius[35] marked another major step in the separation of the Asian church from the West. Its first action was to draw up a "true, apostolic and orthodox" confession of faith that in effect repudiated both the Monophysitism of Africa and Roman Syria and the Chalcedonian orthodoxy of the West. On the one hand, it contained no reference to the Creed of Chalcedon, which was becoming the standard of Western orthodoxy, and, on the other, it condemned the creeping spread of the "blasphemy against the incarnation" among Eastern monks and ascetics. That "blasphemy" was Monophysitism, which, with its mystic emphasis on the divine Christ, had strong appeal to Christians zealous to renounce this world for a higher spiritual life, but which to the Persians seemed to deny his equally real humanity.

The first canon of the council defined its doctrine of the Trinity. It was thoroughly Nestorian. Of the Godhead, it confessed: "one divine nature only, in three perfect persons (*qenuma*), one Trinity, true and eternal of Father, Son and Holy Spirit . . ."

Even more explicitly Nestorian was its creedal statement on the incarnation and the nature of Christ. To the Nestorians, the failure of the Monophysites to distinguish properly between the divine and human sides of Christ's person opened them to the charge of teaching that the unchangeable and almighty God had changed his nature and that he had suffered not as the incarnate, human Son, but as the eternal, impassable Deity on the cross. The Synod of Acacius bluntly anathematized this as heresy. Though it accepted the orthodox and catholic Chalcedonian formula that Christ was in "two natures, different yet united in one person," it went on very explicitly to deny the possibility of suffering and change in deity:

> (Christ had) two natures, divine and human . . . without confusion in their diversity . . . (yet with) perfect and indissoluble cohesion of the divine with the human. And if anyone thinks or teaches that suffering and change inheres in the divinity, and if, when speaking of the unity of the person of our Saviour, he does not confess that He is perfect God and perfect man, let him be anathema.[36]

A second canon guarded further against Monophysite schism by reasserting the authority of the bishops over the monks and hermits who, it was feared, showed some tendency toward heresy. It forbade these ascetics to wander indiscriminately through the villages.

But most revolutionary of all was the third canon. It struck both against the radical ascetics of the East and against the canon law of the West. It specifically affirmed the rights of all Christians to marry, whether they be laymen, ordained priests, or even bishops. There had never been a rule against married priests in the Asian church but "ancient custom" decreed, as the canon admitted, that while married men might be ordained and be allowed to continue in the marriage relationship, it was improper for a priest to marry after his ordination. It was this tradition that Barsauma's dissident council at Beit Lapat had abrogated earlier to the horror of his Monophysite and orthodox opponents. But now an official general council made that abrogation the official rule of the Church in the East, though it should be noted that the next general council, the fifth meeting in 496, specifically pointed out that all else done at Barsauma's council was repudiated and only this one canon of that council was to be recognized.[37]

A number of reasons were given for this important decision. The first was scriptural. The canon quotes Paul's advice to Timothy: "If anyone aspires to the office of bishop, he desires a noble task. Now a bishop must be above reproach, married only once . . ." (1 Timothy 3:1–2). A second reason was moral. It was conceded that the application of so strict a rule as celibacy to those not called to a life of asceticism but ordained to the diaconate in preparation for ministry in the church had led to widespread abuse and immorality. Another scriptural injunction was quoted, the same used by Bishop Barsauma in his own defense when he had been criticized for doing what they were now making legal, that is, marrying a wife. He had pointed to 1 Corinthians 7:9, "It is better to marry than to burn."

Still a third reason may have been cultural. The canon itself speaks of the derision in which the celibate clergy were held by the Persians. That contempt, while it may have been directed at the clergy's failure to keep the rule, may also have been a natural scorn of anything so foreign and unnatural as a rule against marriage. Persians considered celibacy a cause of weakness in the empire. "The virtue of virginity irritated the Persians," remarks Voobus dryly.[38] Zachary the Scholastic, a fifth-century church historian, mentions the desire to conform to Persian culture as one of the underlying motives leading the Nestorians to change the church's tradition.[39] The social fabric demanded it, and the nation expected it. A later Nestorian historian, Mari ibn Suleiman, asserted that it was the Persian shah who insisted that Barsauma marry as proof of his loyalty to Persian ways.[40]

At any rate, whatever the reasons may have been, the third canon was a distinct and recognized break with the church order of the West, and because of this the Synod of Acacius and the year 486 are sometimes described as marking the final break of the church of Persia with the rest of Christendom.[41] But the schism was not yet quite complete.

As a matter of fact, the three ranking Persian prelates at the time of the synod, Acacius of Selecuia-Ctesiphon, Papa of Beit Lapat, and Barsauma of Nisibis, though each represented mutually divisive major movements in fifth-century Christendom, were nevertheless all held by that synod within the unity of the church and not separated from it. Papa was Monophysite in his sympathies[42] and second in rank to Acacius, who was Nestorian, but pro-Byzantine. Barsauma was also Nestorian, but anti-Byzantine. But both Papa and Barsauma affirmed the unity of the Eastern church and submitted to the authority of its catholicos, Acacius; and Acacius in turn stood loyal to the ancient and apostolic unity of Christendom. This he had publicly demonstrated on his mission to Constantinople when he declared his solidarity with the patriarch of the Eastern Roman capital. The pattern at the end of the fifth century between Christianity in Asia and the West was not schism, but diversity in unity.

THE SCHOOL OF NISIBIS

The West, however, proved to be less tolerant than the East of such diversity, and the unity was too fragile to survive the mounting tensions. The emperor Zeno in Constantinople had issued his *Henoticon* in 482 in an attempt to impose theological unity on the church for the sake of national unity. In 489 he took a further step in the same direction. At the urging of the strongly Monophysite bishop of Edessa, Qura (or Cyril, 471–498), whom Nestorians called "the Mad Dog," Zeno ordered the last foothold of Nestorianism in his empire closed, the famous School of the Persians. Its director, Narsai (or Narses, d. ca. 503), had already been hounded out of the city earlier.[43] Now all the remaining teachers were expelled. It was a shortsighted action. It only briefly placated the Monophysites, which was its purpose, but it permanently shut the Western church's door into Nestorian Asia.

For generations the School of the Persians in Edessa had been one of the most effective channels of intellectual communication and Christian ecumenicity between East and West. Persian Christians came there not only to study the Bible and the Greek church fathers, but also to learn of Greek philosophy and logic. The Nestorian scholar Probus had translated Aristotle's *Hermeneutics* and probably part of the *Organon* before the middle of the fifth century.[44]

Narsai and Barsauma[45] welcomed the refugees warmly. They found an old camel caravanserei near the church for a campus, and with Barsauma as promoter and supporter and Narsai as scholar and director, the school was reorganized in Persia as the School of Nisibis.[46] Considering the distinguished heritage and resources the refugees brought with them, it is little wonder that the School of Nisibis quickly became the most famous center of learning in Asia and brought new life and learning surging into the Persian church. Students came from afar, wrote the Nestorian chronicler of Arbela, "to draw spiritual milk and to drink from the sweet waters of orthodoxy."[47]

The glory of the school was in its spiritual discipline and Bible study. Scripture was the heart and center of the curriculum, as the surviving *Homilies* of Narsai plainly show.[48] In them, and therefore undoubtedly in his teaching, he took up the great overarching themes of the Bible—creation, the Fall, the history of the patriarchs, Moses, David, and above all the life and work of Jesus and the mission of his apostles. Within this framework of general biblical knowledge the students were given systematic training in the exegesis of Bible passages after the manner of the great "Interpreter,"

Theodore of Mopsuestia, whose sober, literal textual interpretations were always the Nestorian model. Homiletics was not neglected but it was based on hermeneutics, that is, the careful interpretation of the biblical text. So important was the study of the Bible considered that the only title given to the director of the school was *mepasquana,* which means "interpreter" or "exegete" of the Scriptures. Voobus notes the following tribute to Theodore, "the Interpreter," by Narsai:

> It is proper to call him the doctor of the doctors. . . . His meditation became for me as a guide toward the Scriptures; and he has elevated me toward the understanding of the books of the Spirit.[49]

In several significant respects, however, the Bible of the Nestorians differed from the Western canon. Their Old Testament omitted the book of Chronicles, and though they had replaced Tatian's *Diatessaron* with the four canonical Gospels, their New Testament, in its fifth-century form, the Peshitta, lacked 2 Peter, 2 and 3 John, Jude, and Revelation.[50]

The rules of the school as drawn up by Narsai in 496 still survive and underscore another strong emphasis in Nestorian theological education, namely spiritual discipline. The School of Nisibis was more than a school of the Bible or a theological seminary; it was a close-knit Christian community. In some ways it more resembled a monastery than a school. The twenty-two canons of the school's statutes[51] give a vivid picture of how incoming students were required to leave the life of the world, take vows of celibacy for at least as long as they were enrolled, and were even apparently expected to turn over all their possessions to the community of "brothers."

They roomed together in small cells in groups of three or more. Studies began at cockcrow and continued on until nightfall. Tuition was free, but there is more than one way of paying for an education. At Nisibis they worked for it. During the long vacation from August to October the students were sent out to labor and earn their keep.

Discipline was strict. A long list of prohibitions governed student conduct. Witchcraft, heresy, theft, falsehood, and of course immorality were all forbidden, along with "causing confusion in the school." The penalty for such offenses was immediate expulsion and there was no appeal to outside authority, either civil or ecclesiastical. Like some monasteries, the school enjoyed independence even from the jurisdiction of the bishop.[52]

One rule is particularly significant. Students were specifically forbidden to cross the border into Byzantine Roman territory. The Western contamination the school feared they might pick up there was probably as much theological as political, for Byzantium was then in the hands of Monophysites, heretics as they appeared to Nestorians. But there was also a political factor involved. The school authorities may well have deemed it expedient to keep their Christian students from even the appearance of collaboration with Persia's old enemy, Christian Rome.

The Persian church lived always under the shadow of political suspicion, as an incident in the life of Narsai shows. On one occasion he allowed a criticism of a military incursion of the shah into Arabia to creep into one of his homilies. The shah was defeated, and when his attention was called to the allegedly disloyal remarks of the Christian his anger boiled, and severe punishment might have fallen upon the Christians had not Narsai deftly and quickly produced another sermon into which he managed to weave some glowing tributes to the glory and might of the Persian Empire.[53]

But if the glory of the school was a spiritual discipline based on the study of the Scriptures, an important note should be added as to the practical application of this in the life of the church. Its theology was also a missionary theology; despite all necessary concessions to government control, the church's sense of mission could not be allowed to be stifled. No other explanation of the subsequent astonishing expansion of Nestorian missions is satisfactory. The roots of this are found quite explicitly in Narsai, the first great teacher at Nisibis, whose theology effectively combined doctrines of creation, salvation, and a universal mission patterned after two biblical models, Peter to the Jews and Paul to the Gentiles.[54] But for Narsai the ultimate mandate for mission comes from neither Peter nor Paul, but from Jesus himself, who, as Narsai paraphrases him, told his disciples:

> Your (task) is this: to complete the mystery of preaching! And you shall be witnesses of the new way which I have opened up in my person. . . . You I send as messengers to the four quarters (of the earth), to convert the Gentiles to kinship with the House of Abraham . . . By you as the light I will banish the darkness of error, and by your flames I will enlighten the blind world . . . Go forth! Give gratis the freedom of life to immortality.[55]

Narsai died about 503 and was succeeded as director of the school by a biblical scholar, Elisa (d. ca. 510), and then by his nephew, Abraham of Beit Rabban (d. ca. 569).[56] In Abraham the school found the effective administrator it needed and under him the school reached its peak. Enrollment climbed to more than a thousand students. They overflowed the crowded old camel yard of a campus and, to the distress of the teachers, had to be lodged in town, where they were exposed to thievery, rapacious landlords, and, which troubled their teachers even more, all the temptations of a pagan Persian city.

Abraham solved that problem quickly by building a new classroom building and then, thanks to a gift from a wealthy Nestorian physician in the service of the shah, he added as many as eighty small student dormitories. He further improved the financial resources of the school by the purchase of a large farm, the income from which provided endowment for two chairs of theology and the expenses of a medical clinic.[57] One of Abraham's pupils was perhaps the historian Msiha-zkha, who about 560 wrote a chronicle of the church in Adiabene from its earliest times up to the patriarchate of Mar Aba.[58]

The School of Nisibis became the center for the Nestorianizing of the Persian church. Narsai, the first director, was no less fervently Nestorian than the bishop of Nisibis, Barsauma. One of his works that survives is a forensic homily on "the Three [Nestorian] Doctors," Theodore of Mopsuestia (350–428), Diodore of Tarsus (d. 394), and Nestorius, who followed them. The sermon throws salvos of Scripture quotations in their defense against the attacks of Cyril of Alexandria, "the Egyptian, the devastating wolf" and his Monophysite hordes of "demons and heretics."[59] Later Nestorians called Narsai "the Harp of the Spirit." He wrote beautiful hymns, some of which have become part of the Catholic liturgy as well as the Nestorian. But the Monophysites had a different name for him. They called him "Narsai the Leper." The name calling was a sign that the emotions and tensions of the great Western theological debate were spreading rapidly across Asia into Persia.

But unlike the situation in the West, where Monophysitism dominated the Eastern Roman Empire until the reforms of the emperors Justin and Justinian beginning about 518, farther east in Persia the presence of the School of Nisibis gave the advantage to the Dyophysites, the Nestorians.

When the Nestorian patriarch Acacius died, he was succeeded by Babai, an undistinguished man who ruled from 497 to 502. A curious account in the *Chronicle of Seert*, a Nestorian history by an unknown ninth- or tenth-century author, reports that permission for the election of Babai was given by the shah at the request of his "Christian astrologer" and that the bishops chose as the new patriarch the astrologer's father, Babai.[60] However questionable his background may have been, the new head of the church lost no time in calling a council of bishops, the Fifth General Synod of the Church of the East, in 497.[61]

This Fifth Synod was emphatically Nestorian, not so much in how it phrased its theology as in how it acted. Babai had been ridiculed by Monophysites as being practically illiterate and married besides,[62] but though he was no scholar he had the gift of acting decisively and moved quickly to settle divisions in the church and restore discipline. Acacius and Barsauma, rivals for the patriarchate in 485 and quarreling again in 491, were now dead, but animosities still smoldered among their followers. Babai wisely refused to take sides. Instead he simply abrogated the anathemas each had hurled at the other and declared peace.

But he did take sides in another far more threatening dispute that was tearing the church apart on both sides of the Persian border. This was the Monophysite controversy, almost a hundred years old now in the West, but only recently troubling Persia. The Fourth Synod, of Acacius, in 486 had condemned Monophysite doctrine,[63] but had named no names of Persian bishops and excluded no one. In 497 at the Fifth Synod divisions were sharper, and Papa, bishop of Beit Lapat, refused to attend the council. He was second only to the patriarch in rank and was the leader of the Monophysite faction in the Persian church. Angry, the council summoned him to appear before the bishops within a year and prove his orthodoxy or be excommunicated.

Thus by the close of the fifth century the widening ecclesiastic separation of Asia and the West was rapidly approaching the point of no return. The Third Synod in 424 had declared the Church of the East independent and equal in patriarchal jurisdiction. The Fourth Synod in 486 had broken with the West on church order in the matter of marriage of the clergy. It had also gradually moved away from the Byzantine West theologically. Now the Fifth Synod in 497 made that theological cleavage yet more open and abrasive by officially reprimanding a Monophysite-leaning bishop. The terms of the reprimand, which specifically repudiated the careful omissions of the emperor Zeno's *Henoticon* concerning whether Christ had one or two natures, were a direct denial of what Constantinople was defining as orthodoxy at the time.[64]

CONTROVERSY AND DECLINE

Such were the disputations that ushered in the sixth century with four decades of division and decline in the Persian church. It was now recognizably separated from the West both by its national context, which was Persian, and by its theology, which was Nestorian. From this time on, therefore, the Church of the East, as it still called itself, can with justification be called the Nestorian church, though it would be centuries before its members would commonly use that name. The separation, however, did not sharpen the church's own strength of identity nor did it improve its internal unity. Instead, once again it began to fall apart in dissension, and once again the threat to the peace of the church was not from outside, but from within.

There was no persecution. Shah Kavad (488–531) was benevolently disposed toward the church as a result of some surprising contacts with Christians among the Huns in central Asia, which we will describe later. The Zoroastrian hierarchy, although natural enemies of Christian growth, were too busy with an internal religious revolt in their own ranks, the rise of a heretical sect called the Mazdaks, to spend time attacking Christians.

Even the Christological controversy with the Monophysites was not yet as critical as it was soon to become. Across the border, as we have seen, the Western church had been cut to pieces by theological contention, but this was still a much smaller threat in Persia. The Monophysites, natural theological antagonists of the Dyophysite Nestorians, were busier with Byzantine church politics than with theology, and their strategy concentrated on the attempt to seize and control the patriarchate of Antioch. Peter the Fuller twice seized the patriarchal throne in that city and twice was driven out (in 468–471 and 475–477). But yet a third time he came back, this time to rule successfully as head of the Syrian church until his death (485–488).[65]

One of his first acts, in 485, was to appoint as bishop of Mabbogh, Philoxenus, who, next to Severus of Antioch, was the ablest theologian among the Syrian controversialists of the period. Philoxenus had been a fellow student in Edessa of many of the Persian Nestorians when Bishop Hiba was translating the Nestorian "fathers," Diodore and Theodore, into Syriac. Philoxenus, however, moved in the opposite direction theologically. Returning to the Antioch area he sided with the Monophysites and was banished with others of his persuasion in one of the periods of Chalcedonian orthodox ascendancy there. Brought back out of exile by Peter the Fuller and given the bishopric of Mabbogh (ancient Hierapolis), only a few miles across the Euphrates west of Edessa, Philoxenus took the offensive against the Nestorians. An early Monophysite biographer wrote of him admiringly, "(He) filled the Church with divine doctrines, and expounded the Scriptures, and laid open to disgrace the faith of the Nestorians."[66]

His arguments illustrate how the two sides misunderstood each other. The Trinity, he taught, "can neither be reduced nor diminished to Two [Persons]" (which is how he interpreted Nestorian emphasis on the humanity of the divine Christ in the incarnation), "nor added unto so that it becomes Four [Persons]" (which is how he read the Nestorian insistence that the incarnate Christ existed as two natures). He was a graceful writer as well as able scholar, his most enduring contribution was the production, with the help of his chorepiscopos Polycarp in 508, of a literal, revised translation of the whole New Testament, including the book of Revelation, into Syriac.[67] But when the high tide of Monophysitism receded in the Byzantine Empire and the emperor Justin came to the throne in 518 determined to restore Chalcedonian orthodoxy as the true faith of the whole Roman Empire, east and west, Philoxenus was again banished, first to Thrace, then to Paphlagonia where his enemies turned on him, shut him up in a high chamber, and suffocated him to death with smoke from fires in the rooms beneath.[68]

The activities of most Monophysites like Philoxenus were at that time confined to the Byzantine side of the Persian border. But as the fifth century ended, a fiery champion of the "Alexandrian heresy" took the fight into the heart of the Nestorian homeland, Persia. He was Simeon of Beit Arsham, "the Persian disputant," who began to travel widely through Mesopotamia challenging all who differed with him to public debate—Manichees, Bardaisanites, Eutychians, and Nestorians. At one such public confrontation he refused to be silenced even by the presence of the Nestorian patriarch, Babai. His tract "On Barsauma and the Sect of the Nestorians" is a vivid, bitter, contemporary picture of the Persian church as its Syrian Monophysite rivals saw it.[69] Simeon's zeal to spread his version of the faith is further evidenced by a letter he wrote to fellow Monophysites in Arabia. Nevertheless, when he died about 534 only one Monophysite bishop was left in all Persia.[70]

Much of the cutting critique in Simeon's broadside attack on Nestorian weaknesses was all too true. When the patriarch Babai died in 503 he passed the leadership of the Persian church to his archdeacon Silas (503–523), a mild and henpecked man who seemed to be more interested in his own family's ambitions than in the good of the church. Pushed perhaps by his wife, he named his own son-in-law as his successor. This man, Elisaeus, was a medical doctor whose only qualification for the highest post in the church was his membership in the patriarch's family. This was too blatant a case of nepotism to be tolerated. The bishops revolted and elected instead a man named Narses, not to be confused with the former director of the School of Nisibis. The supporters of Elisaeus refused to yield. Both sides hastened to enlist the backing of the Persian court which, behind the scenes, kept a controlling eye on church elections. The lobbying was intense, and Shah Kavad, not unhappy to see the church divided, simply postponed decision. For the next fifteen or sixteen years (524–539) the church was hopelessly and disgracefully split, with an elected but unconfirmed patriarch and a rival antipatriarch hurling anathemas at each other, and each racing to consecrate bishops and ordain priests in order to control for his side as many of the church's dioceses and congregations as possible.[71] It was a melancholy beginning to the sixth century for the Nestorians.

Mission into Central Asia

These unhappy years did, however, see the fruition of one outstanding achievement of the Persian church during the four decades of decline after the Synod of Babai. This was its missionary expansion eastward into the camps of the nomads of central Asia.

As early as A.D. 196 Bardaisan of Edessa had mentioned the presence of "[Christian] sisters" among the Gilanians on the shores of the Caspian Sea and among the Kushan in far-off Bactria.[72] Who they were, however, and what nameless missionaries had brought them the gospel is unknown. Perhaps they were captives from barbarian raids into Roman territory, though the reference does not seem to suggest this. Not until the end of the fifth century does evidence for the spread of Christianity to inner Asia become clear and unmistakable, and then it is dramatically connected with the romantic figure of Shah Kavad (488–497, 501–531), father of Chosroes the Great.

When Barsauma's friend and protector, Shah Peroz, died in 484 he left his throne not to his son Kavad but to his brother, Kavad's uncle, Vologases (Balash). Kavad revolted and claimed the throne as rightfully his but was defeated and fled for safety across the Oxus River to the domains of his father's old enemies, the White Huns (Hephthalites). Vologases died three years later and Kavad returned with the help of the Huns and was made shah.

He came to the throne in a time of national shame, social unrest, and religious ferment. The succession of military defeats suffered by his father, Peroz, at the hands of the Huns and the humiliation of Persians paying tribute to barbarians had weakened the people's pride in their empire and their confidence in its national religion,

Zoroastrianism. The time was ripe for the rise of a prophet and a prophet appeared, Mazdak. He preached a strange mixture of religious reform and a radical communism that sounds curiously modern.[73] All men are equal, he proclaimed. All things—money, food, women—are to be held in common and shared and shared alike. Property rights and marriage contracts are infringements on human liberty and equality. Love is free and not to be limited to one man for one woman. Shah Kavad himself became a convert to the new doctrine, perhaps as a populist gesture to win the masses and to weaken the power of the rich nobles who were beginning to turn against him. He underestimated, however, the power of the groups he was antagonizing, the aristocracy, who were understandably not attracted to Mazdak's communism, and the Zoroastrian hierarchy, which naturally opposed reforms so radical that in effect they constituted a new religion. Priests and nobles combined to depose him abruptly in 497 and set his brother, Zamasp, on the throne. Once again Kavad fled to refuge with the White Huns.

Among the followers of the shah who fled with him into exile were two Nestorian Christians, John of Resh-aina and Thomas the Tanner, both laymen. They were soon joined by ordained missionaries, Karaduset, the Nestorian bishop of Arran, west of the Caspian Sea, and four priests. The bishop felt he had been called by a vision to minister to Byzantine Christian captives among the Huns and to evangelize their captors. If possible, he hoped to ordain priests from among the nomads.

The ordained missionaries stayed only seven years, but the two laymen remained with the Huns for thirty. Life was difficult. The only food for all seven men, if the record is not exaggerated, was seven loaves of bread and one jar of water a day. But the mission proved to be an unqualified success. They preached and baptized. They reduced the oral language of the Huns to a written form for the first time and taught them to read and to write. Later, an Armenian bishop joined the group and added a knowledge of agriculture to the mission, teaching the restless horsemen of the steppes how to plant vegetables and sow corn.[74] The exiled shah, Kavad, noticed this and was impressed. About three years later, when he returned from exile and regained his throne, he remembered that Zoroastrians had organized his fall but Christians had helped him in his time of banishment. A Nestorian chronicler described his return thus:

> He asked the Turkic [Hun] king for help and the latter despatched an army with him to his country, and he dethroned Zamasp. . . . He killed some Magians and incarcerated many others. He was benevolent to-

ward the Christians because some of them had helped him on his flight to the king of the Turks [Huns].[75]

This earliest contemporary account of a Nestorian mission, with its note of glad acceptance of hardships for the cause of Christ, its full-rounded blend of spiritual and practical missionary methods—evangelism, education, and agriculture—and its compassion for captives combined with evangelistic concern for the captors does much to explain the almost unbelievable successes of Nestorian expansion across Asia in the next two centuries. It also suggests that unlike the unseemly quarrels in the church at the home base, those early Christian missionaries to central Asia learned how to set aside their differences and begin to work together, united in Christian mission, for the Armenian bishop who came to join the Nestorians among the Huns was a Monophysite.

NOTES

1. These guidelines were contained in his letter to Flavian, patriarch of Constantinople, which is called *The Tome of Leo*. Sent in 449 but ignored at the "Robber Council," its clear, articulate exposition of the Christology of the Latin church became the principal basis of the Creed of Chalcedon.

2. On Rabbula, see G. G. Blum, "Rabbula von Edessa, der Christ, der Bischof, der Theolog," in *CSCO*, vol. 300, Subsidia 34, esp. 42ff. The quotation is from J. B. Segal, *Edessa, The Blessed City* (Oxford: Clarendon, 1970), 135f.

3. Segal, *Edessa*, 91f.

4. See A. Voobus, "Investigations into the Text of the New Testament Used by Rabbula of Edessa," in *Contributions of the Baltic University* (Hamburg/Pinneberg, 1947), vol. 59, 37; B. Metzger, *Early Versions of the New Testament* (Oxford: Clarendon, 1977), 56–63; and F. C. Burkitt, *Evangelion da-Mepharreshe* 2 (Cambridge: Cambridge Univ. Press, 1904). Burkitt and most early scholars credited Rabbula with producing the Peshitta, but Voobus has shown that his was only one part of the process.

5. See Blum, "Rabbula von Edessa," esp. 160–65 on "Hat Rabbula am Konzil von Ephesus teilgenommen?"; and Segal, *Edessa*, 93.

6. Segal, *Edessa*, 150.

7. Segal, *Edessa*, 130.

8. The first, in 359–361, ended with the defeat of the Roman emperor Julian; the second was an indecisive war over Iberia, 371–376; the third, 420–422, was a Roman victory over the Persian shah Varahran V; and the fourth, in 440, at last brought a period of peace between Rome under Theodosius II,

who "reigned but never ruled" as we have seen above, and Persia under Yazdegerd II.

9. See A. Voobus, *History of the School of Nisibis,* in *CSCO,* vol. 266, Subsidia 26 (Louvain, 1965), 7–11, 46. W. A. Wigram, *History of the Assyrian Church A.D. 100–640* (London: SPCK, 1910), 149, states that Marun was head of the school, but he is clearly called only "a scribe of the School of the Persians," probably a teacher of writing (Voobus, p. 12).

10. See. J. Bois, "II Concile de Constantinople," in *Dictionnaire de Theologie Catholique,* 3 (Paris, 1908), col. 1258–59. The Council of Chalcedon in 451 refused to condemn Hiba's letter, but the Second Council of Constantinople in 553 declared the same letter heretical. At Chalcedon, only the imperial legates defended the letter as orthodox; the others chose merely not to condemn it and to require Hiba to accept Leo's *Tome* and assent to the anathema against Nestorius. On the difficulty of identifying the Persian bishop Mari, see J. Labourt, *Le Christianisme dans l'Empire Perse sous le dynastie Sassanide, 224–632* (Paris: Lecoffre, 1904), 133 n. 6, and B. J. Kidd, *Churches of Eastern Christendom from A.D. 451 to the Present* (London: Faith Press, 1927), 43, who suggests that since "Mari" means "My Lord" and Ardashir is the Persian name of Seleucia-Ctesiphon, the letter may well have been written to the Nestorian catholicos, or patriarch, Dadyeshu (421–456).

11. Labourt, *Le Christianisme,* 133.

12. It is sometimes forgotten that though the eastern Roman Empire survived as Byzantium after the western Empire fell, the "demoralizing effects of the barbarian immigrations . . . in the fifth century were almost as decisive a factor in the Byzantine East as in the West," G. Ostrogorsky, *History of the Byzantine State,* trans. J. M. Hussey (New Brunswick, NJ: Rutgers Univ. Press, 1957), 56. See also E. L. Woodward, *Christianity and Nationalism in the Later Roman Empire* (London: Longmans, Green, 1916).

13. An excellent introductory history of the Coptic church is in A. S. Atiya, *A History of Eastern Christianity* (London: Methuen, 1968), 1–166. For a Coptic perspective on the Christological controversy and a defense of Monophysitism from the Western accusation of heresy, see W. A. Girgis, *The Christological Teaching of the Non-Chalcedonian Churches* (Cairo, 1962).

14. See E. W. Brooks, "The Emperor Zeno and the Isaurians," *English Historical Review* 8 (London, 1893): 209–38.

15. Atiya, *Eastern Christianity,* 178.

16. See the English translation in J. C. Ayer, *Source-book for Ancient Church History* (New York: Scribner, 1913), 523–26.

17. Kidd, *Churches of Eastern Christendom,* 14.

18. For an English translation of the *Henoticon,* see Ayer, *Source-book,* 526–29.

19. Called "White Huns" by some and "Hephthalites" by others, they were part of the vast nomadic tribal mixture of central Asia, different from but probably related to Attila's Huns who had moved west into Europe. Some

call them "Iranian Huns." A common link to the earlier Hsiung-nu tribes on China's western borders is widely but not universally accepted. H. W. Bailey, "Harahuna" in *Asiatica: Festschrift Friedrich Weller* (Leipzig, 1954), ed. J. Schubert, 12–21. O. J. Maenchen-Helfen distinguishes the Hephthalites sharply from the Huns, stating that their only similarity was their ethnic name. *The World of the Huns* (Berkeley: Univ. of California Press, 1973), 378 n. 20.

20. See chap. 2, n. 8.

21. See G. Rawlinson, *The Seventh Great Oriental Monarchy*, vol. 1 (New York: Dodd, Mead, 1882), 305–27. The Armenians were granted toleration for their Christian faith by Peroz's successor, Balas (Rawlinson, 333f.).

22. This is especially true of the thirteenth-century Syrian historian Bar Hebraeus (Gregory Abul Faraj) in his *Chronography*, ed. and English trans. by E. A. W. Budge (Oxford: Oxford Univ. Press, 1932), and *Chronicon Ecclesiasticum*, ed. and Latin trans. J. B. Abbeloos and T. J. Lamy (Paris and Louvain: Maisonneuve, Peeters, 1872–77). The best source of early information on Barsauma is Simeon of Beit Arsham, a sixth-century writer whose letter "On Barsauma and the Sect of the Nestorians" is edited in J. S. Assemani, *Bibliotheca Orientalis* (1719–28), 1:346ff. It too betrays a Monophysite bias.

23. See p. 190.

24. According to the records of the Synod of Isaac in 410, J. B. Chabot, *Synodicon Orientale ou Recueil de Synodes Nestoriens* (Paris: Klincksieck, 1902), 272. Kidd, *Churches of Eastern Christendom*, 418, mistakenly places Kaskar as second in rank but its bishop was auxiliary in the metropolitanate of the catholicos.

25. *Letters*, 2, 4, from Barsoma (Barsauma) to Acacius, in Chabot, *Synodicon Orientale*, 532f., 536f.

26. Shimun of Beit Arsham, "On Barsauma," in Assemani, *Bibliotheca Orientientalis*, 1:346. See also Labourt, *Le Christianisme*, 136 n. 1; and J. B. Chabot, ed., *Chronique de Michel le Syrien . . .*, 2 vols. (Paris, 1901; reprint, Brussels, 1963), 2:123f.

27. See Labourt, *Le Christianisme*, 198f., and Budge, "The Monastery of Mar Mattai," in his introduction to Bar Hebraeus, *The Chronography*, liii–lxiii.

28. So reports the monophysite historian, Bar Hebraeus, *Chronography*, but the Nestorian 'Amr ibn Matte (*History of the Nestorian Patriarchs*, ed. H. Gismondi, 1896), in the next century, the fourteenth, implies that some of his imprisonment may have been before he was catholicos. 'Amr, in contrast to Bar Hebraeus, tends to favor Barsauma. See Wigram, *Assyrian Church*, 143.

29. It should be remembered that it was anti-Nestorian historians who emphasized Barsauma's role in betraying the patriarch, but it is true that he could not have been too unhappy at the downfall of his rival. See Labourt, *Le Christianisme*, 142 n. 6; and Wigram, *Assyrian Church*, 151f. The *Chronicle of Seert*, a thirteenth-century Nestorian history, blames the betrayal not on

Barsauma but on his partisans (*Histoire Nestorienne*, ed. A. Scher in *PO* [Paris, 1909], tome 7, fasc. 2, p. 101).

30. The major account of this rump council is in Bar Hebraeus, *Chronography*, but fragments of its actions have survived. See Chabot, *Synodicon Orientale*, 621ff. Its tribute to Theodore of Mopsuestia is quoted in a later council of the seventh century (Chabot, 211, 475). It is uncertain whether Babowai died before or after the council. The chronology of the period, including the date of Peroz's death, is disputed. If the patriarch did not die until after Barsauma's council, then the archbishop was in schism against him, and it is frequently called a schismatic council.

31. Here again there is uncertainty about the date. Barsauma's second letter mentions such a mission in 485, perhaps early 486 (Chabot, *Synodicon Orientale*, 533 n. 6, and 300 n. 3). But Bar Hebraeus dates the embassy as of about 491. Perhaps there were two missions. See Wigram, *Assyrian Church*, 169 n. 2; and Labourt, *Le Christianisme*, 151 n. 1.

32. On the Nestorianism of Acacius, see J. B. Chabot, *Littérature Syriaque* (Paris: Blond et Gay, 1934), 51f. Chabot disputes Assemani's assertion that Acacius was orthodox in the Chalcedonian sense. See also *Chronique de Seert*, tome 7, 112f.

33. Chabot, *Synodicon Orientale*, 300, 308, esp. the first letter of Barsauma, 531f.

34. The text of the letter is in Chabot's *Synodicon Orientale*, 526f. (in Syriac) and 532–34 (in French). Wigram's free paraphrase is in his *Assyrian Church*, 162f.

35. The acts of the synod are given in Chabot, *Synodicon Orientale*, 53–60 (Syriac) and 299–307 (French).

36. Chabot, *Synodicon Orientale*, 302.

37. Chabot, *Synodicon Orientale*, 302–306, 312.

38. Voobus, *History of the School of Nisibis*, 2 n. 8.

39. F. Nau cites this reference from Zachary's *Life of Severus*, in his article on "Barsumas" in *Dictionnaire de Theologie Catholique* 2 (Paris, 1905): 430–33.

40. See Labourt, *Le Christianisme*, 149f.

41. For example, R. E. Waterfield, *Christians in Persia* (London: Allen and Unwin, 1973), 27.

42. See Labourt, *Le Christianisme*, 132; and Wigram, *Assyrian Church*, 160.

43. The exact date of Narsai's departure is relatively unimportant. Scholars have generally favored either 489 (Noldeke, Sachau, Labourt, E. Honigmann, E. Nasibin, and early Chabot) or 457 (Duval, Mingana, Scher, Baumstark, Bardenhewer, Tisserant, later Chabot, and more recently, O. de Urbana and B. Spuler), with a scattered few suggesting either 431 or 449. For the arguments and references, see Voobus, *History of the School of Nisibis* 32–47. Voobus argues for "after 471 . . . but years before the liquidation of the school in 489" (p. 46), though, as he earlier admits, the only "historically

reliable" date in the chronology of Narsai's life is 496 when the School of Nisibis under his leadership issued its rules of governance.

44. W. Wright, *A Short History of Syriac Literature* (London: Black, 1894), 831.

45. On relations between Narsai and Barsauma, Voobus in his *History of the School of Nisibis,* contrasts two sources. The first he identifies as that of Barhadbesabba of Holwan (*Cause de la fondation des ecoles,* ed. A. Scher, in *PO,* vol. 4, 4 [Paris, 1902]), who was a disciple of Henana, director of the school from 571 to 596 (?). The second is another document attributed to Barhadbesabba, identified as Barhadbesabba 'Arbaia (*La seconde partie de l'histoire ecclesiastique,* ed. F. Nau, in *PO,* vol. 9, 5, (1913). The former exalts the role of Narsai, the latter of Barsauma in the school. Voobus rejects the theory that Narsai began teaching in Edessa under Barsauma as director. Who the earlier directors were is unknown. Voobus begins the list with Qiiore, who died about 437, followed by Narsai (See Voobus, *History of the School of Nisibis*), 10f., 34 n. 8, 37f., 49–53.

46. On the School of Nisibis I follow mainly A. Voobus, *History of the School of Nisibis.* See also J. B. Chabot, "L'Ecole de Nisibe, Son Histoire, Ses Statuts," in *Varia Syriaca,* vol. 1 (Paris, 1897), 55 pp.

47. *Msiha-zkha,* ed. A. Mingana, in *Sources Syriaques* (Leipzig: Harrasowitz, 1907), 150.

48. *Narsai doctorii syri homiliae et carmina,* 2 vols., ed. A. Mingana (Mausilii: Typis Fratrum Praedicatorum, 1905), 68ff., 90.

49. Narsai, *On the Three Doctors,* cited by Voobus, *History of the School of Nisibis,* 106.

50. C. van den Eynde, "Isho'dad of Merv, Commentary on the Old Testament," in *CSCO,* vol. 230, *Scriptores Syri,* t. 97 (Louvain, 1963), vif.; and B. Metzger, *The Text of the New Testament, Its Transmission, Corruption and Restoration* (New York: Oxford Univ. Press, 1968), 69f.

51. *The Statutes of the School of Nisibis,* ed. and trans. A. Voobus, in Papers of the Estonian Theological Society in Exile, vol. 12 (Stockholm, 1962).

52. A. Voobus, *History of the School of Nisibis,* 109–15.

53. Voobus, *History of the School of Nisibis,* 99, 117, citing Barhadbesabba 'Arbaia, *History,* 613.

54. See P. Kruger, "Ein Missionsdokument aus Fruh Christlicher Zeit," in *Zeitschrift fur Missionswissenschaft und religionswissenschaft,*" vol. 42: 271–291, esp. 272. I owe to S. Sunquist's doctoral diss., "Persia and the Persians," Princeton Theological Seminary, 1990, this reference to Kruger's translation and discussion of Narsai's homily on "The Memory of Peter and Paul" as a text on Christian mission.

55. F. G. McLeod, *Narsai's Metrical Homilies on the Nativity, Epiphany and Ascension: English Translation.* P.O., vol. 40, 1, no. 182 (Turnhout, Belgium: Brepols, 1979), 165. I owe this reference also to Sunquist.

56. For a discussion of questions concerning the line of succession, see Voobus, *History of the School of Nisibis,* 129–33. Many scholars, including Baumstark and Bardenhewer, follow Barhadbesabba of Holwan in naming Elisa' Bar Quzbai as second director. But more recent scholars, such as Labourt, Chabot, Kruger, and others, name Abraham as Narsai's successor, following the other Barhadbesabba ('Arbaia). Voobus prefers the older view. His listing is: Narsai (d. ca. 503); Elisa' (d. ca. 510); Abraham of Beit Rabban (d. ca. 569); Iso'iahb, who "became tired" and resigned after two years; Abraham, who served only one year; Henana, director from about 571 to 596. See 122f., 134ff., 230ff., and 234ff. Chabot in 1897 listed them in different order: Narsai, Abraham, Jean, Joseph Houzaya (d. 580), and Henana ("L'Ecole de Nisibe").

57. Voobus, *History of the School of Nisibis,* 146ff.

58. W. G. Young, *Patriarch, Shah and Caliph* (Rawalpind, India: Christian Study Center, 1974), 8. Young dates the writing of Msiha-zkha's (Mashiha-zkha) *History of the Church in Adiabene* (often called the *Chronicle of Arbela*) between 541 and 569. Its authenticity is much debated, on which see above chap. 3, n. 90.

59. Narsai, *Homily on the Three Doctors,* trans. F. Martin as "Homélie de Narses sur les trois docteurs Nestoriens," (extract from *Journal Asiatique* [Paris, 1900] in *Varia Syriaca,* vol. 1), text in Syriac, 9–51; in French, 52–106. See also Kathleen McVey, "The Memra of Narsai on the Three Nestorian Doctors" (extract from *Orientalia Christiana Analecta,* 221, [Rome, 1983]).

60. *Histoire Nestorienne; Chronicle of Seert,* in *PO,* t. 7, fasc. 2, 128f.

61. The acts of the Synod of Babai are contained in Chabot, *Synodicon Orientale,* 62–68 in Syriac, and 310–317, French trans.

62. By Bar Hebraeus, for example.

63. See pp. 197ff.

64. See pp. 192f.

65. The dates of Peter's periods of rule are somewhat uncertain, but estimates differ by only about one year.

66. E. A. W. Budge has edited the writings of Philoxenus and includes a brief biographical sketch: *The Discourses of Philoxenus, Bishop of Mabbogh,* A.D. 485–519, 2 vols. (London: Asher, 1894), vol. 2:xvii–xxiii.

67. See J. Gwynn, *The Apocalypse of St. John in a Syriac Version Hitherto Unknown* (Dublin and London: Hodges, Figgis, 1897).

68. Wright, *Syriac Literature,* 832.

69. Simeon of Beit Arsham (the name is also romanized as Sem'on of Bet Arsam), "On Barsauma and the Sect of the Nestorians," in J. S. Assemani, ed., *Bibliotheca Orientalis,* 3 vols. (Rome, 1719–28), 1:346. See also Wright, *Syriac Literature,* 832; Bar Hebraeus, *Chronicon Ecclesiasticum,* 2.85; 1.189.

70. At Singar, near Nisibis. Wigram, *Assyrian Church,* 181, citing Bar Hebraeus, 88.

71. Chabot, *Synodicon Orientale*, 339 n. 3, quoting extensively from 'Amr (ed. Gismondi, 22f.). See also Labourt, *Le Christianisme*, 160ff.; and Wigram, *Assyrian Church*, 179–81. The bishops' candidate, Narses, may have been the bishop of Hirta of that name, but the identification is uncertain.

72. Bardaisan, *Book of the Laws*, ed. H. J. W. Drijvers (Assen: Van Gorcum, 1965), 61. See chap. 3, p. 79.

73. See O. Klima, *Mazdak* (Prague: Nakladatelstvi, 1957); and M. Boyce, *Zoroastrians: Their Religious Beliefs and Practices* (London: Routledge and Kegan Paul, 1979).

74. This account of the Nestorian mission is by a Monophysite writing about 555, quoted in part and summarized by A. Mingana, "Early Spread of Christianity in Central Asia and the Far East," *Bulletin of the John Rylands Library* vol. 9, no. 2 (July 1925): 303f., citing *CSCO*, 3rd series, vol. 6, 215–18.

75. *Chronicle of Seert, PO*, t. 7, fasc. 2, p. 128.

Chapter *11*
Patriarch and Shah

"I am a Christian. I preach my own faith, and I want every man to join it. But I want every man to join it of his own free will and not of compulsion. I use force on no man."

—Patriach Mar Aba to Chosroes I
about A.D. 546

W HEN the bishops rebelled against the ecclesiastical nepotism of the misguided patriarch Silas and pulled themselves together to end the embarrassing schism of 524–539, they chose as patriarch a man not only respected on both sides of the conflict but a friend of the shah as well, which was not an inconsiderable advantage in troubled times. He was Paul, bishop-elect of Beit Lapat (Gundeshapur). Hopes of better days, however, were dashed by the death of the new leader within two months of his taking office. Yet out of that tragic disappointment came what was probably the greatest single period of church administration in the whole history of the Nestorian church, for they chose as Paul's successor Mar Aba, who, had he served as a pope in the West, would be styled Mar Aba the Great.

The Synod of Mar Aba (544) and His Reforms

Few men have faced greater handicaps as leader of a national church and overcome them so successfully as Mar Aba, patriarch of the Persian church from 540 to 552.[1] As head of a minority religion he was forced throughout his reign to cope with the bitter opposition of a powerful state religion. Moreover he was a convert from that religion, Zoroastrianism, and the penalty for that in Persia was death. The last patriarch who had been a convert, Babowai, had been killed.[2] Even the timing of his sudden call to leadership was most inopportune politically. After almost a decade of peace, in the very year of Mar Aba's accession, Persia launched a war against Constantinople that was to last for twenty-two years, and as always when Persia warred with the Christian West it looked with great suspicion on Christian Persians. This was all the more true after Constantinople had repudiated the *Henoticon* in 519 and ended its schism with Rome. No longer Monophysite, the enemy in Byzantium seemed in Persian eyes once again to be moving toward theological reconciliation with Persia's own troublesome minority, the Nestorians.

To the new patriarch the internal problems of the church were another burden as difficult to handle as his delicate relations with the government. The Eastern church was still scarred by the angers of eighteen years of division under the antipatriarchates. To top it all, for at least seven of his twelve short years in office, Mar Aba was forced to govern the church either from jail or from exile. But undaunted, he accepted the challenge and turned the ecclesiastical demoralization of his times into one of the few brief golden ages of the Church of the East.

He is remembered for four remarkable achievements. The first was a thoroughgoing reorganization of the church. No sooner had he been properly installed than he set out with great energy on a patriarchal tour of his troubled ecclesiastical provinces to restore order and decency where "the duality" (as he called the past schism) had made the church a monster and a scandal, like "a body with two heads" and "a woman with two husbands."[3]

The tour was in effect a traveling synod, for the patriarch held court wherever he found that as a result of the schism more than one bishop claimed the same diocese. After hearing both sides he would summarily confirm one man as bishop and dismiss all others with fairness, authority, and complete disregard of the candidates' partisan antecedents. With discipline thus reestablished, the judgments of this unusual itinerant church court were officially confirmed by a general council, the church's sixth, which he summoned about 544 and which is known as the Synod of Mar Aba.[4]

Mar Aba's second accomplishment was the reinvigoration and extension of theological education. During his first winter tour of the provinces he had found to his distress that many village Christians possessed all too inadequate an understanding of their faith. On the spot he began to draw up a confession of faith for them to learn, and it is greatly to the credit of this former teacher of the School of Nisibis that he endeavored to write it in simple, untechnical language so that even the unlearned could grasp its meaning.[5]

When he returned to the capital, Seleucia-Ctesiphon, he proceeded to found a new theological school (or perhaps reorganize an older, smaller one). He modeled it after his own more famous school in Nisibis. The capital, he felt, should be not only the seat of government in the church, but a center for its theological enlightenment as well.

A third major concern of the patriarch was how to revive the church spiritually and morally. During the years of division, he observed, Christians had grown selfish, arrogant, corrupt, immoral, and inordinately covetous of luxury. They were more like the pagan Zoroastrians from whose impurities he had himself been converted by the Spirit, he said, than like followers of Christ, whose disciple he strove to be.

Tradition tells the story of Mar Aba's conversion in this way. One day, traveling in his official capacity as secretary to the governor of a Persian province, he imperiously ordered a lesser wayfarer off a ferry to make room for his party. The stranger gave up his place with surprising grace. But sudden winds twice drove the boat back to shore and not until the courteous young man was invited back on board was the ferry able to make its way across the Tigris. Aba inquired about the surprising stranger and discovered that he was a Christian Jew.[6] Tradition has elaborated the miracle, but it may well have been the gentle example of an unassuming Christian that impressed Mar Aba more than any mysterious powers. At any rate, as patriarch he called the church to return to the self-denying simplicities of Christian life as practiced by the ascetics. He encouraged a revival of monasticism and thereby brought new vigor and new centers of strength into the church's politics-ridden structures.

Above all, Mar Aba gave himself to the work of reunion. Not only did he heal the wounds in his own church, he also reached out to restore broken relationships between the Christians east and west. Not long after his conversion Aba had made a pilgrimage to Christian centers in the West, Jerusalem, Egypt, Greece, and Constantinople. At the Byzantine capital he is said to have been received to communion as a matter of course and in no way treated as a heretic.[7]

Whether or not he was actually so well received in Constantinople as that report implies, in his general council of 544 he saw to it that the Church of the East brought itself more into official theological harmony with the non-Monophysite, orthodox West by adopting the creed and decrees of the Council of Chalcedon.[8] At the same time the council reiterated that the basic doctrinal position of the Persian church was the Creed of Nicaea as interpreted by Theodore of Mopsuestia:

> Our opinion—the opinion of all the bishops of the East—on the subject of the faith established by the 318 bishops [i.e., the Nicene Creed] which we defend with all our power, is that which was set forth by the holy friend of God, the blessed Mar Theodore, bishop and Interpreter of the holy Books.[9]

A few years later such recognition of Theodore's authority would be labeled heretical in the West. But in 544 it was no act of schism, though the emperor Justinian did, it is true, issue a personal edict that very year condemning the "Nestorianism" of Theodore. It is ironic that as the Church of the East was reaching out for reunion with the West, the West was making that reunion impossible. After much dispute and over the objections of Pope Vigilius, the Council of Constantinople in 553 officially condemned Theodore of Mopsuestia, the pioneer of Nestorian orthodoxy, as a heretic.

This was the sorry affair of the "Three Chapters" in which, along with Theodore of Mopsuestia, two other champions of Nestorianism were also condemned, Theodoret of Cyrus (423–458), and Hiba, bishop of Edessa, who had translated Theodore into Syriac.[10] All three were summarily anathematized, though Theodore had died in communion with the church and though Theodoret and Hiba had officially been cleared of taint by the Council of Chalcedon. Pope Vigilius rightly interpreted the move as an attack on the authority of the council, and only intense imperial pressure forced his assent. "Put the Pope on shipboard," ordered Justinian's strong-minded wife, Empress Theodora, "and bring him to [the Council]." So he was brought to the council and watched in dismay as it widened instead of healing the separation of East and West.[11]

Chosroes I and Mar Aba

The patriarchate of Mar Aba coincided with the greatest years of the Sassanian monarchy. Chosroes I (reigned 531–579) was at the height of his power, the mightiest Persian monarch in a thousand years. Not since the golden age of Cyrus the Great and Darius had Persia so dominated western Asia. In the first year of Mar Aba's patriarchate, 540, Chosroes fought Rome back to the shores of the Mediterranean and sacked Antioch, forcing Justinian, greatest of all the Byzantine emperors, to sue for peace. Antioch was stripped and burned.

Only two churches were spared. At Apamaea the Persians captured a famous fragment of the "true cross" encrusted with jewels. They sliced off the precious stones but Chosroes politely returned the old wood to the bishop. Later, between 561 and 571, Chosroes sent his armies the length of his empire to the east and hurled the Hephthalite Huns back into central Asia, slaying their king, it is said, with his own hand. On the south he sent a fleet down the Persian Gulf around Arabia and drove the Ethiopians out of Yemen back to Africa.

In his capital where the twin cities of Seleucia-Ctesiphon straddled the Tigris River the victorious shah began to build a huge new palace, the Taq-e-Kesra. Its broad, windowless facade dominated the skyline of Ctesiphon on the east bank, dwarfing the modest cathedral of Mar Aba just across the river on the west bank. Chosroes held court on a jewel-encrusted golden throne under a turbaned crown so heavy with precious stones that it could not be worn but had to be suspended above the throne by a cable to the 95-foot ceiling. Around and behind the shah were three lesser golden thrones, always empty but reserved, it is said, one for the emperor of China, one for the emperor of Byzantine Rome, and one for the king of the tribes (Khazar, Hephthalite Huns, or Turks).

Thus, symbolically, Iran ruled the world. But there were signs that spoke of fear behind the shah's fierce pride. Every night forty beds were prepared for Chosroes in different parts of the palace and kept waiting for him so that no lurking assassin might know for sure in which room he would sleep.[12] This undercurrent of insecurity, which no absolute monarch can ever escape, accounts perhaps for the exhibitions of cruelty and periods of persecution that occasionally marred his long and famous reign.

He began his rule, for example, by systematically hunting down and killing all his brothers—all the male offspring of the royal line— to ensure that there would be no ambitious rivals for the throne. Only one escaped. He also moved at once to eliminate in cold blood a religious minority that to him represented a threat to the empire. A hundred thousand Mazdaks were ordered executed and hung up on gibbets as an object lesson to all who would defy the power of the aristocracy and the sanctity of the national religion.[13]

But in general once his power was established Chosroes ruled as one of the fairest, best disciplined, and most effective of all the Sassanids. His tax reform spread the burden of the finances of the empire more equitably. He restored the might of Persia's armies, treated the bureaucracy autocratically but generously, and often championed the rights of the poor. An anecdote relates that a visiting Byzantine envoy noticed an irregularity in the great plaza before the palace. Immediately in front of the palace stood an unsightly shack. Upon inquiry he was amazed to discover that it belonged to a poor woman who refused to leave her only home, and the king, instead of crushing her, had ordered that she be left alone.[14]

Something of the same fairness governed the way Chosroes treated the Christians. For one thing, his own favorite wife was a Christian, though not much is known about her. She may have been Euphemia, a captive carried away from a Roman town on the Euphrates during the Persian invasion of Syria in 540.[15] The shah's personal physician was also a Christian, as were many others employed in the court as interpreters and secretaries for affairs of state. The wider learning, the industry, and the international contacts of the Christians earned them a rising reputation in the service of the empire.

But it is important to remember that however numerous Christians may have been at the court, their political power was minimal. The rules of the *melet* system,[16] by which Persia controlled its mi-

norities, left them politically neutralized as an isolated, circum-
scribed group set apart from normal subjects of the empire.
Christians could wield political power only within the Christian *melet*. Outside that narrow circle they might have influence, but not
authority. They were not the equals of their Zoroastrian counterparts; officially they were inferior. Some references suggest that they
may even have been required at times to wear a distinctive form of
dress, "the humble dress of a Christian," as alluded to in the life of
one of the saints, Mar Giwergis.[17]

In the sixth century the Persian church was growing in wealth
and influence, but socially it was middle class or below. This is how
W. A. Wigram describes it:

> The mercantile and artisan classes were largely of the (Christian) faith;
> the villagers, the agricultural class, were so to a very considerable ex-
> tent; the squire class, the feudal seigneur and his family, very seldom;
> and soldiers, hardly ever. Men of the civil service were Christians
> pretty frequently; while law was an ecclesiastical matter for all faiths,
> and its votaries were divided accordingly. Christians had almost a mo-
> nopoly of the medical profession.[18]

Among Christians mentioned in contemporary documents at Beit
Lapat, for example, appear the chief of the artisans, the head of the
guild of silversmiths, the president of the merchants, and elsewhere
a "keeper of all the Queen's camels," and the chief financial officer
of the empire under Chosroes.[19]

Chosroes is said to have had great respect for the patriarch,
Mar Aba, whose energy and ability in reorganizing and governing
the Persian Christian community (*melet*) could not have escaped the
shah's notice. But not even the tolerance and esteem of Chosroes
could prevent the outbreak of a limited persecution of Christians that
began about 544.

It may have been Mar Aba's popularity that aroused the jeal-
ousy of the Magian hierarchy, and envy of the spreading wealth and
influence of the church, or Christian criticism of Zoroastrian morals.
At any rate, shortly after the Sixth Nestorian General Synod, Persia's
Christians came under direct attack for the first time in sixty years,
since the execution of the patriarch Babowai by Shah Vologases.[20]
This time, too, the offensive centered on the person of the patriarch.
Mar Aba was vulnerable on three counts. In the first place, like
Babowai, he was a convert from Zoroastrianism, and such conver-
sion was illegal. Second, he admittedly sought to convert others.
Proselytizing was also illegal. And finally, his general council had

just condemned the Persian practice of marriage between close relatives as being incestuous by Christian standards.[21]

The Great Mobed himself brought charges against Mar Aba before the king, and when the king temporized and went off to war without trying the case, the Zoroastrian inquisition on its own authority arrested him as an apostate and proselytizer. Upon the king's return from his sortie against the Christian Lazi (allies of Byzantium in what is now part of Russian Georgia), Mar Aba appealed from the judgment of the Magians to the court of the shah.

Tradition records his defense. "I am a Christian," he proudly admitted. "I preach my own faith, and I want every man to join it." He did not deny the evangelistic obligations of his faith. "But," he added, "I want every man to join it of his own free will and not of compulsion. I use force on no man." As for the charge of contempt for Persian marriage customs, he denied forcing Christian customs on non-Christians but upheld his right as leader of the Christian *melet* to "warn those who are Christians to keep the laws of their religion."

The king, willing to save a man whose integrity he respected, asked Mar Aba to bend a little. "Stop receiving converts; admit to communion those married by Magian law (that is, those married to close relatives): and allow your people to eat Magian sacrifices," he urged. Such compromise was impossible for the patriarch, and at that the shah could do nothing but pronounce him guilty. He did, however, manage to save him from the death penalty. He ordered the patriarch to prison and, when emotions had cooled, commuted the sentence to exile.[22]

For the next seven years or more Mar Aba was forced to govern the church by correspondence from exile in remote Azerbaijan or from prison. This was no small task in a church as unruly as the Persian, but his control remained unchallenged. If anything, his administration grew stronger under adversity. The Zoroastrians tried to assassinate him, whereupon the strong-minded prelate, without waiting for permission from the shah, abruptly broke his exile and appeared suddenly at court to protest the outrage in person before the astonished ruler. The capital broke into an uproar. Zoroastrian zealots tried again to kill him on the spot, and multitudes of Christians poured out into the streets to surround him with an impassioned bodyguard wherever he went.

The shah wavered between the demands of justice and politics—he wished to treat justly an endangered minority leader whom he liked, yet he had to keep in mind the nationalistically powerful Zoroastrians whom he feared. Mar Aba was first imprisoned—as much to save his life as to pacify the Magians—then released, then imprisoned and released once again.[23]

The gravest crisis of Mar Aba's life, however, came toward the end of it. The shah's chief wife, but not his favorite, was the daughter of the Great Khan of the Turks, tribal nomads who were beginning to displace the Hephthalite Huns as the major power along the Oxus River on Persia's northeastern frontier. Chosroes had long tried in vain to convert his favorite wife, a Christian, to the national faith yet loved her all the more for her tenacity to her own faith. Their son, Anoshaghzad (or Nushizad), chose to be a Christian like his mother,[24] a fact that points to the increasing influence of the Christian movement in higher Iranian circles and of an unusually tolerant attitude toward its presence there.

The shah was irritated, but his reaction was mild. Instead of cutting off the young prince's Christian head he merely ordered him restricted to the palace grounds. Unfortunately, the young man did not limit his intransigence to his religion but carried it over into politics. Misled by a rumor that his father the shah, who was then warring in the north against the Byzantines, had been laid low by a fatal illness, the prince prematurely anticipated the royal death and in 551 seized the treasury, gathered an army, and proclaimed himself shah. He is said to have made a special point of calling upon his fellow Christians to rally to him.

But the shah was not dead. The upstart prince was quickly defeated by the emperor's veterans. And now the Christians, always suspect anyway, were never more vulnerable to retaliation. The jubilant Zoroastrians accused Mar Aba once more, this time of the most serious of all crimes, treason against the shah. And this time the king was in no merciful mood. He ordered Mar Aba blinded, thrown into a sand pit, and left to die. Before the sentence could be carried out, though, it became apparent that the accusers had lied in linking the patriarch with the rebellion, and once again Mar Aba was freed.

Although he did not long survive the cruel trial, this last ordeal was perhaps as great a service to the church he loved as any he had rendered in his life. His vindication by the court, his fearless innocence, obvious integrity, and unassailable loyalty to the empire probably saved the Persian church from what could easily have become the most devastating persecution in all its history. When he was released, the shah had asked him to undertake a mission to the center of the collapsing rebellion, Khuzistan, to warn Christians there not to become entangled in the conspiracy. Knowing very well what the shah could do to a religious minority once his anger was aroused against it, as in the massacre of the Mazdaks, Mar Aba agreed. His mission was successful and the church was saved from the deadly peril of official implication in an aborted revolution against an absolute monarch.

But, worn out by his sufferings and labors, Mar Aba died soon after his return from Khuzistan in February 552. Then came another demonstration of the popular appeal of Persian Christianity in the empire. Not even the intense hatred of the Zoroastrian power structure, which demanded that the patriarch's body be cast to the dogs, could prevent crowds of Christians from carrying the casket in triumphal procession through the streets of the capital from the smaller church of Beit Narkos, where Mar Aba had chosen to live in simple fashion rather than at the larger cathedral.[25] Bearing the body of their patriarch the long line of mourners moved across the great pontoon bridge over the Tigris, past the great palace of the shah, and on out to the monastery of the missionary-saint Pethion, where they buried him.[26]

Abraham of Kaskar and Monastic Revival

It was not only the reforms of Mar Aba that brought new life to Nestorian Christianity in this period. The sixth century also brought a revival of Christian monasticism that spread throughout the Persian Empire. The outstanding name in the revitalization of the monastic movement was Abraham of Kaskar (ca. 491–586).

From the time of the Sons and Daughters of the Covenant in the third century and Aphrahat in the first half of the fourth, Persian monks and ascetics had been the models for the spiritual Christian life, models more often admired than followed. But the latter part of the fifth century saw a weakening of traditional disciplines in the Christian community that reached into the monasteries. Attitudes toward priestly celibacy relaxed. Monks began to live openly with wives. Even a bishop, the powerful Barsauma of Nisibis, broke with tradition and took to wife a nun from a monastery who was sworn to vows of chastity. As we have seen, his rump council in 484 gave church sanction to the marriage of bishops, a break with tradition that was not repudiated by subsequent councils.[27] When Babai, a married man, succeeded Acacius as patriarch in 479, the more orthodox Christians were scandalized, to the delight of pagan Persians who had never understood the virtue of chastity, much less of celibacy.

It was in this period between the patriarchate of Acacius and the reforms of Mar Aba, from 497 to 540, which some historians have characterized as decades of decadence,[28] that Abraham of Kaskar grew to manhood. Tradition says he was baptized in the patriarchate of the much criticized Babai in 502. He studied at the School of Nisibis under Abraham of Beit Rabban. For a time he became a missionary to the Arabs of the semiautonomous Lakhmid kingdom of Hirta (or Hira) on Persia's southwestern frontier with Arabia. From there he traveled on to Egypt and was greatly impressed by the ascetic disciplines and stern life-style of the monks in the great desert monasteries around Scete. He returned to Mesopotamia zealous to recapture something of their self-control and strength for the Persian church. He withdrew into the mountains near Nisibis and founded what quickly became the greatest of all Persian monasteries, known simply as "the Great Monastery," on Mt. Izla.[29]

His stern example and flaming challenge to give up all for Christ drew crowds of disciples. Thomas of Marga wrote in the ninth century, "As formerly everyone who wished to learn and to become master of the heathen philosophy of the Greeks went to Athens . . . so now everyone who desired to be instructed in spiritual philosophy went to the holy Monastery of Rabban Mar Abraham."[30]

A copy of the rules "which were laid down by Mar Abraham the Great, the head of the ascetics in all Persia" has survived the years and a few excerpts suffice to capture the spirit of the movement. They show a dependence on the authority of Scripture and the traditions of the fathers and an insistence on disciplined prayer and worship, hard work, and gentleness and unity in love:

> Canon I. First of all a life of tranquility according to the command of the Fathers, and according to the word of the Apostle (Paul) which he spoke to the Thessalonians, "I ask from you . . . that you study to be quiet. . . ." And again the holy Mark, the solitary, said, "Therefore let us be content in our cells in quietness, and let us flee from idleness . . ."
>
> Canon III. Concerning prayer and reading and recital of the offices for the day and night . . . the Psalmist saith "Seven times in the day have I praised thee . . ."
>
> Canon IV. Of silence and of meekness . . . and of how a man should not intrude speech when his brethren are talking and of how he should speak with a gentle voice . . .
>
> Canon VIII. On the first day of the week when the brethren are gathered together, whosoever shall come first to the church shall take the Holy Book and shall . . . meditate upon it until all his brethren arrive, so that when each of them cometh his mind may be laid hold of

by the hearing of the reading, and they turn not aside to matters which are alien, or to narratives and rumors of battles and wars, or to conversation upon worldly matters, or to vain stories which do harm to the soul, or to that which is foreign to this life of excellence.

Canon IX. Fasting shall not be abrogated except for . . . sickness . . . , the arrival of strangers, a long journey, or hard manual labour which lasteth a whole day.

Canon X. When brethren come and they are accepted, let them be tried three years in the monastery, and then, if they have borne themselves in a befitting manner, the brethren shall give them permission to build cells for themselves. . . . If there be empty cells let them be given to them . . .

Canon XI. If any man preceiveth that his brother despiseth (any) one of these (admonitions) let him not report the matter among the brethren and trouble them, or to the head of the monastery to vex him, for a troublesome word troubleth the heart of a man, but let him call him, and speak to him privately according to the word of our Redeemer, "Rebuke him between thee and him only" (Matthew 18:15). And if he mendeth not, rebuke him before two or three, and if he mendeth not then, let him be admonished before the whole community, let him know that he is an alien to our congregation.[31]

Abraham is also credited with the invention of the Nestorian tonsure to distinguish priests of the Church of the East from the Monophysite (Jacobite) missionaries intruding from the West. Nestorians began to shave the top of the head leaving a bare circle like a wheel or a crown. The Jacobites from Antioch cut the hair from the front and back and sides of the head in the form of a cross. Tradition associated the Nestorian tonsure with St. Peter and Rome; in the "Greek tonsure" of Constantinople the whole head was shaved and this was associated with St. Paul.[32]

Abraham was succeeded as head of the Great Monastery at Mt. Izla first by Dadyeshu (Dadh'Isho), and then by Babhai (d. 630). It was under Babhai that the discipline at the monastery became less gentle and more severe, recalling the saying of an earlier monk, Arsenius, who like Abraham the Great had visited the monks of Scete in the Egyptian desert, "One hour's sleep is enough for a healthy monk."[33]

By that time, the Great Monastery has superseded the School of Nisibis as the center of Nestorian theological orthodoxy, for the latter, under its sixth head, Henana, had become the target of charges of grievous heresy, while the more strenuously orthodox disciples of Abraham, Dadyeshu, and Babhai were founding or earning control of at least sixty monasteries throughout the empire. It is probably true, as J. Labourt observes, that the Nestorian church would not have survived the invasion of Monophysitism, the wounds of the controversy over Henana's heresy, and, we might add, the Islamic conquest, without the contribution of the reforms of Abraham of Kaskar and his successors.[34]

NOTES

1. The *Life of Mar Aba,* the ancient, traditional biography of Mar Aba, is in the collection edited by P. Bedjan as *Histoire de Mar Jabalaha et de trois autres patriarches* . . . (Paris, 1895), 206–74.

2. See chap. 10, p. 196.

3. "Synod of Mar Aba," in J. B. Chabot, *Synodicon Orientale ou Recueil des Synodes Nestoriens* (Paris: Klincksieck, 1902), 340.

4. Chabot, *Synodicon Orientale,* 68–80 in Syriac, 318–32 in French translation. The records of the synod are not precise minutes, but rather a collection of documents prepared by or under the direction of Mar Aba and affirmed by the bishops in council.

5. Chabot, *Synodicon Orientale,* 540, 550

6. Labourt, *Le Christianisme dans l'Empire Perse sous le dynastie Sassanide, 224– 632* (Paris: Lecoffre, 1904), 163f., citing Bedjan, 211f.

7. Wigram, *History of the Assyrian Church A.D. 100–640* (London: SPCK, 1910), 185. But Labourt, *Le Christianisme.,* 167f., notes a tradition reported by Mari that the Byzantine court pressed Aba and a disciple, Thomas of Edessa, to anathematize Theodore of Mopsuestia, which they refused to do and barely escaped with their lives.

8. "Canons of Mar Aba," in Chabot, *Synodicon Orientale,* 556.

9. "Canons of Mar Aba," canon 40, Chabot, *Syndicon Orientale,* 561.

10. See chap. 10, p. 188.

11. B. J. Kidd, *The Churches of Eastern Christendom from A.D. 451 to the Present* (London: Faith Press, 1927), 42ff.

12. See A. Christensen, *L'Iran sous les Sassanides* (Copenhagen: Levin and Munksgaard, 1936), 380, 385ff., 400, 407, on the grandeur and insecurity of Chosroes.

13. G. Rawlinson, *The Seventh Great Oriental Monarchy* (London: Longmans, Green, 1876), 381.

14. Christensen, *L'Iran,* 371f., citing Mas-udi.

15. According to Procopius, as cited by Rawlinson, *Seventh Monarchy,* 450.

16. At different times these minority communities in the empire were called by different names, e.g., *melet* (or *millah*), *dhimmi* (*dzimmi*), and *rayah*. See A. R. Vine, *The Nestorian Churches* (London: Independent, 1947), 47.

17. Cited by Wigram, *Assyrian Church,* 231.

18. Wigram, *Assyrian Church,* 230.

19. Wigram, *Assyrian Church,* 230.

20. The execution of Babowai in 484, however, had been more for political than religious reasons, and the reported persecution which followed was directed only against Monophysites. Monophysite historians, in fact, blamed it more on Nestorian opposition than on pagan hate. See Labourt, *Le Christianisme,* 136, citing the seventh-century historian Michael the Syrian and the later Bar Hebraeus.

21. "Canons of Mar Aba," canon 38, Chabot, *Synodicon Orientale,* 561.

22. Wigram, *Assyrian churches,* 200–207, citing Bedjan, "Life of Mar Aba," 226ff. The Persian war against Lazica began in earnest sometime after 545 and dragged on intermittently for years. Rawlinson dates the war 549–557, but Mar Aba's exile was probably earlier, perhaps following a previous exploratory campaign.

23. Wigram, *Assyrian Church,* 200–207, citing Bedjan.

24. One tradition says he was baptized by a Monophysite bishop. See G. D. Malech, *History of the Syrian Nation and the Old Evangelical-Apostolic Church of the East* (Minneapolis, 1910), 187f.

25. On the Christian churches and monastery of Seleucia-Ctesiphon, see Christensen, *L'Iran,* 383, and map, 380.

26. Labourt, *Le Christianisme,* 189ff.; Rawlinson, *Seventh Monarchy,* 451ff.; Wigram, *Assyrian Church,* 207ff. But there are other conflicting accounts of his burial place. R. Duval, *Histoire politque, religeuse, et littéraire d'Edessa* (Paris, 1892), 138, 149f., 168, 176–79, thinks he was buried in Hirta by a Cyrus of Edessa (not the director of the school or the bishop of the same name), citing Mari and 'Amr. The *Life of Mar Aba* (Bedjan, *Histoire,* 271) says that he was buried in Seleucia.

27. See chap. 10, pp. 196, 198ff.

28. For example, Labourt, *Le Christianisme,* 154–62.

29. Thomas of Marga, *The Book of Governors,* 2 vols., ed. E. A. W. Budge (London: Kegan Paul, Trench and Trubner, 1893), 2:37n.

30. Thomas of Marga, *Book of Governors,* 2:41f.

31. Translated from the Syriac text in Mai, *Scriptorum Veterum. Nova Collectio* tom. x, 209ff., and quoted by Budge, in his introduction to *The Book of Governors,* 1:cxxxiv–cxl.

32. Budge, *Book of Governors,* 1:cxxxii; 2:40, 41 nn. 2 and 4.

33. Budge, *Book of Governors,* 1:clii.

34. Labourt, *Le Christianisme,* 324.

Chapter 12
The Decline of the Persians (622–651)

"My throne stands on four feet, not two. On Jews and Christians as well as Magians and Zoroastians."

—Attributed to Shah Hormizd
(579–590)

MAR Aba was the last noteworthy Eastern patriarch for a hundred years. This may have been because at last the Persian rulers began to realize how politically important the position of leader of the Christians had become. During the last years of Mar Aba's patriarchate a delegation from the chief of the Hephthalite Huns had arrived at the Persian capital after a long journey from beyond the Oxus River in the steppes of central Asia to ask the patriarch to consecrate their Christian leader as bishop for their nation.[1] Such a demonstration of the surprising expansion of Christian influence across the continent could not have gone unnoticed in the palace and may well account for the purposeful steps taken by the government in the decades that followed to control the church's power.

Shah over Patriarch

Ever since the edict of toleration of Yazdegerd I in 409 and the church's Synod of Isaac in 410,[2] Christians had enjoyed the status of membership in a recognized minority organization called in Persian a *melet*. The significance of this was largely unrecognized as long as the number of Christians remained small. But in the hundred and fifty years since Yazdegerd, Christianity had become, next to Zoroastrianism, the second most powerful religious force in the empire, and it was still spreading.

Religious minorities are troublesome irritants in the social fabric. Whether aroused by injustice, as Chosroes I had observed in the tumult surrounding the trials of Mar Aba, or spurred on by ambition, as he thought he detected in the revolt of his son, the Christian prince Anoshaghzad, minorities contain the seeds of revolution. The choices open to a political leader facing the growth of a potentially dangerous movement were three. He could join the movement, as the shah Kavadh had for a time done with the Mazdakians, he could eliminate it, as Chosroes himself had done with the same Mazdakians later, or, better yet, he could control it.

Chosroes rejected the first two alternatives. He did not choose to be a Roman Constantine and turn Christian. Nor did he want to be a persecutor. During one of the trials of Mar Aba, when the patriarch in the presence of the king said in his defense, "I preach my own faith, and I want every man to join it; but of his own free will," one of the king's servants, a Christian, cried out, "And if you would but hear him, sire, you would join us, and we would welcome you." The court fell silent at the interruption, expecting immediate punishment. Once when a councillor in a much less direct challenge had dared to interpose a question as the shah was announcing a tax reform, the king stopped him. "To what class do you belong?" he asked. "A secretary," he replied. "Then beat him to death with a writing case," the monarch coolly ordered. But in this case Chosroes was surprisingly gentle with the interrupting Christian. The Zoroastrian high *mobeds* demanded the man's death for his insolence but the king refused to condemn him.[3] He did not accept the evangelistic invitation, however. His favorite wife was a Christian, but conversion for himself would have been political suicide, as he well knew. Sixth-century Zoroastrianism held a far stronger patriotic and religious hold on the Iranian population than paganism had ever exerted in Constantine's Rome two hundred years earlier.

The safest and always the preferred method of dealing with minorities in absolute Asian monarchies was neither to join them nor to massacre them, but to dominate and control them. So in the election of Mar Aba's successor Chosroes directly intervened. It was no secret that the voice of the shah was by now as loud in patriarchal elections as that of all the bishops combined. He not only had the right of nomination, but also unlimited powers of pressure, and he exercised both.

The man he nominated was his own personal physician, Joseph, a Christian who had studied at the School of Nisibis. The shah's choice was quickly accepted by the bishops and just as quickly regretted. The new patriarch proved to be an unscrupulous and autocratic tyrant. It had become the custom for each succeeding patriarch, when possible, to regularize his reign by calling a general council or synod to signify the approval of the church and its acceptance of his authority. But Joseph, with the power of the shah already supporting him, felt no need of the formal consent of the bishops and refused to call a synod, thereby in effect rooting the authority of patriarchal succession in the will of a pagan ruler rather than in the consent of Christian bishops.

Joseph threw two bishops into prison for questioning his decisions. Not until after two years of pressure did he finally, in 554, call a council, the church's seventh,[4] and give the bishops the opportunity they sought to curb his dictatorial ways. They passed a new canon law that frankly noted the mounting criticisms of Joseph's one-man rule and decreed that even in cases requiring urgent action the judgments of the patriarch must have the concurrence of at least three bishops.[5] In more veiled language the council also warned against governmental interference in church affairs. It condemned secular influence in the election of bishops and lay patronage of unworthy priests, presumably by wealthy landowners and officials.[6]

This was as far as the bishops could then go in defying the patriarch, for the third council, the Synod of Dadyeshu, had ruled that a patriarch could not be deposed.[7]

Finally, in 566 or 567 the bishops called another council, pointedly without inviting Joseph, and formally deposed him, electing the little-known Ezekiel to take his place. But it was an empty gesture so long as canon law and the favor of the shah were on the patriarch's side. It took an adroit Christian with a sense of humor to present the church's case against the king's favorite without rousing the royal anger. Moses of Nisibis, another physician of the king, caught the attention of Chosroes with a story about an unusual gift the king had made to a poor but worthy man, the gift of an elephant. It was a magnificent gift, he said, and wonderfully generous of the shah, but when the man took the beast home he found he had problems. When the elephant was in the house there was no room for the family, and when the elephant ate the family had to go hungry. At last the man begged the king to take back his elephant. The shah laughed, and Moses drove home his point. "You gave us the Patriarch Joseph," he said, "and you were most generous. But now take back your elephant." And the king, amused, consented.[8]

But the interlocking pattern of ineffective church leadership and royal interference was not easily broken. The table of succession of Nestorian patriarchs from this time to the Muslim conquest is, with one exception, a most forgettable list:[9]

Joseph (552–567), the king's unpopular physician, was deposed by the bishops but not removed by the shah until 570.

Ezekiel (570–581), the patriarch Mar Aba's former baker, was elected in 566/7 but not consecrated until the shah permitted it in 570.[10]

Yeshuyab I (582–595), was a bishop greatly favored by Chosroes's successor Hormizd IV. But under the next shah, Chosroes II, Yeshuyab lost favor and died in exile at the court of the Christian Arab king of Hirta (or Hira) on the Persian border.

Sabaryeshu I (596–604), a saintly man, was more effective as hermit and missionary than as bishop, though he was greatly admired by the shah's favorite wife, Sirin.[11] In this election also the shah interfered, rejecting a list of five names presented by the bishops and naming one more to his and the queen's liking.

Gregory I (605–608), was appointed by a trick. The shah nominated the bishop of Nisibis, also named Gregory, but the bishops, knowing him to be a strict disciplinarian, elected another Gregory, a teacher in the school of Seleucia-Ctesiphon, pretending they believed he was the Gregory named by the shah. The angry ruler vowed, "As long as I live I will never have another patriarch . . . of the East."[12] We shall refer again to this later.

Vacancy (608–628). The shah refused to appoint a successor to Gregory. Nestorians and Monophysites fought each other to persuade the shah to fill the vacancy with one of their own.

Yeshuyab II (628–643). Statesmanlike and able, this patriarch was the one strong exception to the rule of mediocrity or worse that preceded the triumph of Islam.

The Controversy over the Teachings of Henana

The indecisiveness of Nestorian leadership in this period was aggravated by a controversy that erupted in the 570s at the School of Nisibis, the theological center of the church. It swirled around the stormy figure of Henana, sixth director of the school, who was accused of deserting the traditions of the father of Nestorian theology, Theodore of Mopsuestia. Henana's disloyalty to Theodore, "the Interpreter" of the Scriptures, held overtones of political as well as theological heresy, for in deserting Theodore, if the charge was true, he would be following the Roman and Byzantine line, not the Asian. At the Council of Constantinople in 553, the Byzantine emperor Justinian had pushed through an official condemnation of the three "Nestorians," Theodore, Theodoret of Cyrus, and Hiba of Edessa, in the hope that by denouncing Nestorians, who were already lost by the West to Persia anyway, he might win back the Monophysites of Africa and Syria and restore unity to his empire.[13]

Henana, a presbyter of Adiabene, became director of the School of Nisibis about 571. The school was then at the height of its renown. Enrollment, which had fallen for a while, climbed again to perhaps as many as eight hundred students.[14] As director, Henana also carried the title of "Interpreter," for central to all studies in the school was the interpretation of Scripture. The standard of interpretation in the Nestorian church had always been the commentaries of Theodore of Mopsuestia, the "Interpreter" par excellence. But Henana, enthusiastic, persuasive, and with an insatiable passion for study was carried beyond the great Theodore to read the works of other commentators. He was especially attracted by the writings of the famous preacher and patriarch of Constantinople, John Chrysostom.

Chrysostom's exegetical methods were not as loose and allegorical as those of another famous commentator, Origen of Alexandria, but he did allow himself more philosophical and homiletical freedom in interpreting the Bible than the strict literal and historical method of Theodore might have permitted, and this appealed to Henana, particularly in the interpretation of the book of Job. Theodore's commentary on Job had described it as little more than Greek fiction written by a non-Jewish author, though conveying important spiritual truth. Henana broke with Theodore, sided with Western orthodoxy, and shocked Nisibis by defending not only the canonicity of Job but also its historicity, contending that the book's author was none other than Moses himself.[15]

A graver theological divergence than that, in Nestorian eyes, was Henana's deviation from Persian orthodoxy in his theology of the nature of Christ's person. At one time or another his opponents branded him as guilty of five grave errors. The most serious was the accusation that he had surrendered to the Monophysites on the crucial point at issue between Nestorians and Jacobite Monophysites, namely, the doctrine of the relationship between the deity and humanity of Christ. Nestorian historians all agree that Henana dared to differ with Theodore of Mopsuestia's teaching that the union of the divine and human in Jesus, was a voluntary union (*synapheia*), like that between husband and wife, or soul and body. Henana seemed to prefer the tighter definition of the Western church's Creed of Chalcedon, which asserted that the unity of Christ's nature was not merely voluntary but basic and substantial ("hypostatic"). To heresy-hunting Nestorians, faced with a rising tide of Monophysite missionary activity in the Persian Empire, this was theological treason. But in fact, his theology may have veered not so much in the direction of Syrian Monophysitism, as toward Byzantine, orthodoxy.

Given the various forms Henana's departure from Nestorian tradition had taken, it is not surprising that the opposition soon gathered against him, but what does surprise is that he remained unchecked so long in his position as director of the church's most famous theological school. Just how early the controversy began is not clear, but he was still in control sixteen years after he first took office. There are signs that the attack began early, perhaps even before he became director.[16]

At any rate, not long after his directorate began there was enough discontent to persuade a later metropolitan of Nisibis, a bishop named Elias, to allow the formation of a rival and presumably more orthodox school in the city, "the School of Bet Sahde . . . at the gate by the mountain." This move was backed by that citadel of Nestorian orthodoxy, the Great Monastery on Mt. Izla. The first two directors of the new school were monks from that monastery, disciples of the famous Abraham of Kaskar.[17]

Henana soon came under condemnation by a full council of the church, the Ninth General Synod, called by Patriarch Yeshuyab I (Ishu'-yab I) in 585. He was not mentioned by name but there is no question about the identity of the enemy under attack, as recorded in the synod's records:

> Satan, the enemy of truth . . . has seduced many people whom he perversely leads to slander the divine teachings of the doctor of the church [Theodore of Mopsuestia]. . . . We therefore declare . . . that no man, whatever his ecclesiastical position may be, is permitted to defame [Theodore] . . . or to reject his holy writings, or to accept this other commentary. . . . Whoso dares to do so . . . let him be anathema.[18]

The "other commentary" so roundly condemned was obviously Henana's, and the intemperate language of the condemnation reveals something of the heat of the controversy. The council went on to excoriate Henana as a "lover of lies" whose studied elegance of language distorts the truth as wickedly as the provocative adornments of a prostitute perverts beauty.[19]

Nevertheless, whether because Henana's popularity at the School of Nisibis was too great or because discipline in the church had become too weak, little came of this wordy attack by the bishops. Five years later, in 590, the metropolitan of Nisibis, Bishop Semon, in giving his official approval to a new set of regulations for the school praised lavishly the same man the council had called a "lover of lies." Not only is he "skillful in his knowledge" the bishop said, which was true, but also "glorious in his humility," which was patently false.[20]

In that same year, 590, a new shah came to the throne, Chosroes (Khusro) II, grandson of the great Chosroes I and son of Hormizd IV. His father, the unfortunate Hormizd IV, has been called by at least one historian "one of the worst princes that ever ruled Persia,"[21] but others are not so harsh, and most Christian writers credit him with a remarkable tolerance in religious affairs.[22] In some ways, the decade of his reign, from 579 to 590, was a golden age of religious freedom in Zoroastrian Persia. When the Magian priests pressed him to persecute Jews and Christians, he gently refused, remarking that just as a great empire like Persia is bound to have differences of soil from desert to mountain, so also it should be able to contain within it without fear men of differing religious opinions. So favorably was Hormizd inclined toward Christians that he is said to have declared: "My throne stands on four feet, not two. On Jews and Christians as well as on Magians and Zoroastrians."[23]

But the latter years of Hormizd's reign were not happy. Beset by attacks from the Turks in the east and by grievous defeats at the hands of the Byzantine Romans in the west, his empire broke apart in civil war. Hormizd was deposed in a palace revolt, blinded, and cruelly put to death.

His son, Chosroes II, by contrast was "the last great king of Persia," though his beginnings were not auspicious. Officially he reigned for almost forty years (589–628), but he began by losing his throne in the civil war and fled across the Euphrates to humiliating refuge in the territory of the enemy, Constantinople. There the Byzantine emperor Maurice offered him protection in the home of a wealthy Christian family.[24] With Roman and Armenian help he returned the next year to reclaim his throne but for some time was forced to surround himself with a Roman bodyguard against assassination by his own Persian subjects. For the next eleven years, until 602, he was in effect a dependent of his friend the Roman emperor.

It is not surprising therefore that despite later victorious campaigns against the Byzantines, his early friendship with Rome was held against him as much as his tax increases, and he was criticized by his opponents and conversely praised by Christians for deserting the Persian religion, Zoroastrianism, and allegedly converting to the faith of Rome.[25] There is no evidence that he actually did so. He made no secret, however, of his attraction to the Christian religion, remembering with gratitude the warm hospitality with which he had been treated in exile. Not until his protector, Emperor Maurice, died did he resume the Persian wars against the West.

The most beautiful and best beloved of his many wives and three thousand concubines (some say he had twelve thousand, "the largest harem in history") was the Christian queen Sirin, an Aramaean. Another of his wives or concubines was also a Christian, Maria, who is variously described as a gift from the Roman governor of Egypt or as a daughter of the emperor Maurice in Constantinople.[26] Probably through Queen Sirin, Chosroes built a number of Nestorian churches for the Christians and brought Bibles from across the Persian border in Edessa for them. He also gave gifts to their theological opponents, the Monophysites.[27] A letter of Chosroes II, sent with a gift to the shrine of a Monophysite saint and martyr in Syria, has been preserved by the late sixth-century Christian historian Evagrius:

> Chosroes, king of kings, to the great martyr Sergius. I, Chosroes, king of kings, son of Hormisdas, have sent this alms-dish (?) and other gifts, not for men to admire them . . . but that the truth of that which has

been done should be proclaimed, and the many mercies and favours which I have received of thee. For I hold it as a piece of good fortune that my name should be inscribed upon thy vessels, O saint, that thou wouldest come to my aid, and Sira [Sirin] to conceive in her womb.[28]

In such a period of Persian-Roman detente the palace of the shah might easily have looked with approval on Henana's attempt to nudge strict Nestorian tradition in the direction of Western, Catholic orthodoxy. This may have been another reason why, when the storm broke upon Henana once more in 596, the controversial theologian was able again to escape punishment and retain for a while longer his position of power at the seminary of Nisibis. Though the ecclesiastical odds were all against him, Chosroes II might well have been disposed to protect him.

Henana's nearest enemy at the close of the sixth century was the new metropolitan installed that year as bishop of Nisibis. Gregory (Grigor) of Nisibis was a crusader. He is described by an eleventh-century chronicler as "a John the Baptist in his asceticism . . . , a Paul in evangelism, and an Elijah in his zeal for orthodoxy,"[29] and like an Elijah against the priests of Baal he fell upon Henana. But Henana had other still more dangerous and more unrelenting enemies, the monks of the Great Monastery. One of them, Giwergis (George), who had been a disciple of Abraham at Mt. Izla and who later became a famous saint and martyr, had opposed Henana from the beginning, accusing him of astrology and fatalism and of teaching that man and God were one but that Christ was neither, since he was only half God and half man. This was an obvious distortion of what Henana had actually taught.[30]

But a far more powerful voice from the monasteries soon joined in the attack, that of Babai the Great, who was fast becoming the most active and influential figure in the Nestorian ecclesiastical hierarchy. Born to great wealth he came originally to the School of Nisibis to study in its much admired department of medicine. There, he found himself also attracted to its equally famous department of biblical studies. After fifteen years of study and teaching at the hospital in the school he felt a call to give up all his possessions and enter the Great Monastery on Mt. Izla. On the mount he would shut himself away from all outside contacts to meditate for months at a time in a lonely grotto. After this period of spiritual exercises, he returned to his home country in the north (Beit Zabdai), where he opened a new monastery on his family estates and an attached school. It was from there that he began to strike at the director of his old school, Nisibis.[31]

The assault against Henana came to a head at the tenth general synod called in 596 by the new patriarch of the church, Sabaryeshu (d. 604). Sabaryeshu was the saintly bishop of Lashom, east of the Tigris, halfway between Seleucia-Ctesiphon and Arbela. Raised as a shepherd boy, he had left his sheep for a life of extreme asceticism. It is said that he limited himself strictly to only one meal a week.[32]

On a mission to the Arab kingdom of Hirta he so impressed their king, Naaman, that he reportedly forthwith became a Christian. Sabaryeshu's reputation as a holy man and faith healer spread beyond Persia. From as far away as Constantinople, the emperor Maurice sent to ask for the hood of his monastic robe as a sacred relic, giving him in return a piece of the "true cross." Sabaryeshu was a particular favorite of Queen Sirin and it was on her advice that Chosroes II brushed aside all other nominations from the bishops and insisted that the bishops elect this living saint to succeed the patriarch Yeshuyab who had died at the Christian court of the king of Hirta.[33]

The new patriarch acted early to settle the vexing problem of Henana. He called a synod, the tenth, to pass judgment on the charge that the church's leading theologian, head of its most famous theological school, was no defender of the faith but a heretic. As at the Ninth General Synod, eleven years before, the council upheld "the blessed Theodore" and condemned Henana's teachings as "insanities" in language even sharper than before. But still it did not anathematize him by name.[34] In a bewildering reversal it was not Henana but his orthodox opponent Gregory of Nisibis who soon found himself deposed.

The reasons for this abrupt turn of affairs are not altogether clear. It was probably partly due to Henana's great popularity in Nisibis and perhaps even more to Gregory's extreme unpopularity there. His high-handed ways made enemies of the town's populace and he had even alienated his natural allies, the monks of the area, by his demand for sweeping monastic reforms against the overly ascetic Messalians. To the townspeople he was too strict; to the ascetics not strict enough. There is also some evidence that he had quarreled with his superior, the patriarch Sabaryeshu.[35]

But far more likely is the probablility that the deciding factor against Gregory was the disfavor of the royal court. Strange currents were swirling in the murky waters of Persian palace politics. The most powerful Christian in Persia at the beginning of the seventh century was not the patriarch Sabaryeshu but Gabriel of Siggar (Singar),[36] the personal physician of Chosroes II. This man had gained immense influence over the king and seemed to have cast a spell over the queen through the happy coincidence that not long after he prescribed a bloodletting for the hitherto barren Sirin she gave birth to a healthy baby boy, the prince Merdansah.[37]

If the Nestorians of Zoroastrian Persia rejoiced that providence had given the Christian queen a son, ensuring high favor for them at court, their joy was short-lived. All too quickly it became evident that their Christian friend, the palace physician Gabriel, was finding it too easy to adapt his Christian conscience to the glittering ways of the richest aristocracy in the world of his time. Gabriel divorced his Christian wife and according to Nestorian histories openly replaced her with two pagan women. It was a common custom among Persians, but not among Christians, and the stern Bishop Gregory of Nisibis vehemently refused to bless the illicit union and excommunicated his most highly placed but straying adherent.[38]

The angry Gabriel shrugged off the censure by the Nestorians and to their dismay simply switched his allegiance to their bitter rivals, the Monophysites. That branch of the church, eager to add Persia to its strong bases in Egypt and Syria and with more of an eye on politics than on canon law, received him quickly into its communion. The political reward was immediate. Queen Sirin followed her physician into the Monophysite fold, and the court now added its own immense weight to the pleas from Nisibis that their scourge of a bishop be replaced with a gentler and more pliable man than Gregory. The patriarch, not unwilling to be rid of a troublemaker, acceded to the request and packed Gregory off to a monastery. It is to Sabaryeshu's credit, however, that despite threats from the throne he did not reverse the excommunication of the philandering physician.[39]

In the midst of these startling events Henana once more emerged from a church council's anathema still in command at the School of Nisibis. It is futile but tempting to speculate on what might have been. How easily the course of Christian history in Asia might have been changed at the end of the sixth century and the beginning of the seventh century had Henana's support at the Persian court, for example, been Nestorian rather than Jacobite (Monophysite). He would probably have become the next patriarch. Even with the stigma of collusion with the Monophysites working against him, his name figured prominently in the list of candidates when the patriarch Gregory died in 608.[40] And had the Persian-Roman detente not collapsed in 602 with new war between the empires, Henana's mediating position might well have provided the point for theological reconciliation between the Nestorian East and the Chalcedonian West. And had Constantinople and Persia not fought each other to exhaustion in those critical first decades of the seventh century, there might have been no Arab Armageddon in the desert, no victory for Islam. In which case, the Christian mission just beginning to spread across Asia to the Pacific might have been no isolated Nestorian beachhead but a united Christian adavance.

Of course none of that happened. Henana survived the conciliar condemnation of 596 and remained as director of the School of Nisibis, but his hold on the church was broken. Whether or not the favor of the Monophysites at court was of his own choosing,[41] it was the kiss of death. Even in his own school, students and teachers began to desert him. A passage in the *Chronicle of Seert* gives a moving description of the breakup of the once proud School of Nisibis. Gregory, bishop of Nisibis, had left for exile, shaking off the dust of the unbelieving city from his sandals at the gate. The school was shaken and divided at the spectacle of an orthodox bishop deposed and a compromised director retained. The tide turned against Henana, and the schism in the school became final sometime probably in the last years of the century. The *Chronicle* describes it thus:

> The students strongly affected by the decision of Sabryeshu [the patriarch] to reject the word of the bishop and accept Henana's . . . marched out of the school giving away all they had. They took with them [only] the gospels and the crosses wrapped in black veils, and the censers. They left the town praying and chanting the litany of the saints. There were about three hundred of them. The people of the city wept and sighed at their departure, but the wicked leaders were filled with joy at getting rid of [Bishop] Grigor [Gregory]. They did not know the misfortunes and calamities that were to fall upon them. . . . There remained in the school only twenty people, and about as many children . . .[42]

The exodus from the School of Nisibis dispersed the intellectual center of Persian Christianity into a number of new schools that were founded at that time, but mainly into two important centers. One was the Great Monastery on Mt. Izla, not far from Nisibis, the center of reform monasticism. The other, even more influential for a time due to the presence of the patriarch, was the School of Seleucia-Ctesiphon, which had been founded by Mar Aba.[43] Still a third intellectual and strongly Christian center was Gundeshapur, the new city built by the first Chosroes for the vast number of prisoners, many of them Christians, captured in his victories over Byzantine Rome. The school at Gundeshapur was famous for its medical department, like Nisibis, but it was also a center for biblical and philosophical studies, specializing in the translation of the works of the

Greek philosophers. The two adventuresome Persian monks who are credited in some accounts with the cross-cultural breakthrough that first brought silk cocoons out of China to the West in 551, smuggled inside hollow lengths of bamboo, may have been from Gundeshapur.[44]

The Breakdown of the Patriarchate

As if the collapse of the church's intellectual center, the School of Nisibis, was not enough, it was soon followed by another disaster, the disintegration of its ecclesiastical center, the patriarchate. Upon the death of Sabaryeshu in 604 a new patriarch was installed, but under rather shabby circumstances. The shah's surprising choice for the post was the orthodox but quarrelsome Gregory, not long since deposed as bishop of Nisibis. The council of bishops, however, remembering his unpopularity at Nisibis, were reluctant to have so opinionated and domineering a master. They threw their support instead to another Gregory who had the somewhat suspicious backing of the queen—suspicious because the queen had left the Nestorian church to turn Monophysite. This Gregory of Prat had been a favorite steward of the queen but was not himself a heretic. He had, in fact, become a teacher in the Nestorian theological school in Seleucia-Ctesiphon.

So the bishops sent word to the shah that they had indeed elected "Gregory" as patriarch but they craftily neglected to inform him that it was not *his* Gregory. Thus Gregory of Prat, not Gregory of Nisibis, became Patriarch Gregory I. With very bad grace, says W. A. Wigram, the shah accepted the *fait accompli*, but took his revenge by levying a heavy fine on the new patriarch and warning the church, "Patriarch he is and patriarch he shall be—but never again will I allow another election."[45]

The shah kept his word. The bishops' choice as patriarch, Gregory I (604–608), died after a rule so inglorious that upon his death the government arrested his closest followers and put them to torture to reveal where Gregory had hidden the treasures everyone knew he had stolen from the church.[46] The election of a new patriarch was not permitted. For twenty years, from 608 to 628, when the shah himself died, the church was officially leaderless and no bishops and no metropolitans (archbishops) were consecrated.

Of course a leadership of sorts did emerge. Three of the most powerful metropolitans of Persia, the northern bishops of Nisibis, Beit Garmai, and Adiabene, appointed Henana's bitter adversary, Babai the Great, abbot of the Great Monastery on Mt. Izla, to the post of inspector of monasteries. This enabled him to itinerate throughout the country and supervise church affairs without attracting government suspicion. His prestige and presence soon made him, in effect, the national administrator and liaison officer for the whole church.

Babai's authority in the north was partially matched in the south by that of Mar Aba, bishop of Kaskar and archdeacon of Seleucia-Ctesiphon. The Synod of Isaac had given the right of interim rule after the death of a patriarch to the bishop of Kaskar as auxiliary to the patriarch, but that rule, two centuries old by then, may have fallen into disuse. Mar Aba of Kaskar, not to be confused with the earlier, more famous Patriarch Mar Aba, was a distinguished scholar, philosopher, and linguist who introduced Aristotle's *Logic* into Persia and was sent by Chosroes II as an envoy to Maurice, the Byzantine emperor.[47]

The Spread of Monophysitism in Persia

This low point in the fortunes of the Nestorians, marked by the fall of the School of Nisibis and by the vacancy in the patriarchate, had been foreshadowed and alarmingly accentuated by a steady advance into Persian Asia of the Nestorians' most implacable rivals, the "one nature of Christ" Monophysites. The conversion of the Persian queen and the royal physician was only a late by-product of a Monophysite revival that had begun sixty years earlier under the remarkable leadership of a Syrian monk named Jacob Barada'i (Jacob Baradaeus). His missionary triumphs gave to the Monophysites the name Jacobite, by which they have ever since been known in Asia.[48]

The revival, however, came only after some very lean years. For most of the first half of the sixth century it was all the Monophysites could do to stay alive. Under two Byzantine emperors, Zeno and Anastasius, their fortunes soared. But in 518 a political revolution in Constantinople abruptly changed the ecclesiastical situation. Justin I (reigned 518–527), who seized power after a rebellion in Thrace, and his nephew, the great Justinian (reigned 527–565), were orthodox and Chalcedonian.[49] Just as the emperor Zeno had chosen to force the modified Monophysitism of his *Henoticon* on Christians to ensure that the church would be a unified and not a divisive influence in support of the Eastern empire, so the Justinians with their greater dreams of uniting East and West, Rome and Constantinople, in a revived Imperial Rome needed the support both of the pope in Rome and the patriarch in Constantinople, and they knew that the pope would never accept the *Henoticon*. That was what had caused the schism of 484.

So in the interests of a Greater Rome the emperors were willing to sacrifice the Monophysites and return to the Creed of Chalcedon. The first step was the deposition and exile of the greatest of the Monophysite leaders, Severus, patriarch of Antioch. Early in the year 519, under imperial pressure, the thirty-five year schism between Rome and Constantinople was brought to an end. The *Henoticon*, cornerstone of the Monophysite claim to be the orthodoxy of the empire, was condemned. Persecution quickly spread through the East.

Monophysite monks who refused to sign the condemnation were driven into the desert. Some crossed over into Persia. At least fifty-five Monophysite bishops were expelled from their dioceses during Justin's reign, and by the time of his death in 527 the exiled Severus gloomily observed that there were only three places left in all the world where "believing bishops" could be ordained, Alexandria in Egypt, Mardin in northeast Syria, and across the border in Persia.[50]

Four things saved the Monophysites from extinction. The first was a reluctant decision of Severus to allow the ordination of a separate, and therefore schismatic, line of Monophysite clergy in orthodox dioceses. Beginning about 530, John (b. 483), bishop of Tella, northeast of Edessa, began to ordain deacons, then priests, then bishops, including some "for the Christians of Persia." They came by the hundreds for ordination, "like a river," says the "Life of John of Tella" by John of Ephesus. They came from the coasts of Asia Minor and Armenia to Arzun, which was across the border in Persia. John is said to have ordained 840 members of his own monastery alone.[51]

The second factor that saved the Monophysites was the active patronage of Empress Theodora in Constantinople. Her husband, Justinian, might favor the orthodox church, but not his stormy and strong-minded wife. With the help of Severus she managed to convert even the orthodox patriarch of Constantinople, a weak man named Anthimus, to the Monophysite "heresy," and Anthimus was promptly deposed. But the empress, never inclined to admit defeat, brought in another patriarch to Constantinople, Athanasius of Alexandria, though he too had been deposed for the same heresy. Skillfully protecting him, the empress built up a "safe house" and power center around him for the whole Monophysite movement, pitting her refugee patriarch as a rival ecumenical patriarch against the orthodox bishop of Constantinople.[52]

Still a third reason for the renewal of the Monophysites was a deep and apparently irreversible groundswell of popular religious support for the persecuted sect. This had cultural and nationalistic overtones, for it was largely localized in Egypt, where it was omnipresent, and in the mountain monasteries of Syria.[53]

The fourth and probably decisive factor in the Monophysite revival was the organizing, missionary genius of Jacob Baradaeus who planted a trail of churches across Asia, which were to spread from Syria to India and which survive to this day and take his name as "Jacobite" Syrian orthodox.

Jacob Baradaeus (Yaqub al-Barada'i) was born in the city of Tella in eastern Syria about forty miles from Edessa, near the Persian border. He entered his ministry as an ascetic and lived in a monastery near Nisibis, not the Great Monastery, but the monastery of Phesilta. About 527 he came with a fellow monk, Sergius, to Constantinople where the two were received with honor by the empress Theodora and offered handsome accommodation. But Jacob chose to seal himself off from the world "in great retirement, and arduous labours and asceticism beyond measure."[54]

About 542 the king of the Ghassanid Arabs, al Harith ibn Jabadah, who served Byzantine Rome as military governor of the provinces of eastern Syria, sent an embassy to Empress Theodora asking among other things for two Monophysite missionary bishops. The Monophysite episcopate, as we have seen, had become almost extinct. Theodora arranged for the exiled patriarch, Theodosius, to consecrate two metropolitans for the Arab prince. She chose Jacob Baradaeus, who was titled bishop of Edessa, and Theodore, who was made bishop of Bostra in Roman Arabia. The latter ably served the Ghassanid Arabs, but it was Jacob who became the Monophysite apostle to Asia.

Jacob never really lived in Edessa, his episcopal seat. The police were too hot on his trail. Justinian, not happy with his wife's religious intrigues, gave orders for his arrest. But for over thirty-five years, from 542 to 578, Jacob eluded the spies and soldiers of the empire. He kept constantly on the move, hastily finishing his work in any town in a day or a night and quickly moving on before he was discovered. He traveled thirty or forty miles a day, all on foot. Riding a donkey or a horse, he thought, was too much of a luxury for a missionary. Most people took him for a beggar because his clothes were so tattered and pieced together that he was called Barada'i, "the patchwork man," which is said to be how he got his nickname, Barada'i. Sometimes his pursuers would meet him face to face but not recognize him. Thinking him a beggar, they would ask, "Have you heard any secret word about that deceiver, Jacob?" and he would say, "Yes, a long way back of here I heard some men say that he was about, and if you hurry perhaps you will catch him." So they would rush off, discover nothing, and be left "beating the air . . . biting their fingers . . . and gnashing their molars against the man mighty in the Lord," as his biographer tells the tale.[55]

From Constantinople to the Persian frontier Jacob Barda'i preached, encouraged, and above all ordained, making sure that his evangelistic efforts were not left to wither for lack of structural sinews. He is credited by admiring Monophysite historians with ordaining an unbelievable 100,000 clergy, 27 bishops, and 2 patriarchs.[56] The Jacobite missionary advance was not limited to the work of its apostle, Jacob, or even to that of the clergy he ordained. According to the ecclesiastical history of Zachariah of Mitylene, a man named Q'uiros (or Cyrus), "a believing bishop" (i.e., a Monophysite) ordained priests in Persia from about 537 to 544, after the death of John of Tella, "on account of the death and scant numbers of the pastors among the Persians." Since this was before the consecration of Jacob Barda'i, Cyrus and Theodosius of Constantinople must have been about the only Monophysite bishops then surviving and active.[57]

There is evidence, also, of the important role of lay evangelists in the expansion of the Jacobites. In his sixth-century *Lives of the Eastern Saints,* John of Ephesus tells the story of Elijah and Theodore, two traders "who besides wordly trade engaged moreover in divine [trade] also." They were natives of Amida in east Syria on the Roman side of the Persian frontier, but for twenty years they carried on their business in Persia, adding the witness of their lives to their testimony to the faith, for they "abstained entirely from the evil practices which traders of the world are want to follow, that is from oaths of all kinds, and from lying, and from extortion, and from diverse weights and measures."[58]

Another immensely important infusion of Monophysite strength into the Persian Empire was quite involuntary. It was the coming of the captives. In the fierce wars with Byzantine Rome in the fifth and early sixth centuries the triumphant Persian armies of Chosroes I (531–579) and Chosroes II (589–628) brought hundreds of thousands of Christian prisoners of war back east with them, including priests and even bishops. Many, of course, were Chalcedonian orthodox, but almost all were non-Nestorian. Twice Antioch itself was taken and sacked, in 540 and again in 611, and each time the lines of Christian slaves extended for miles. So great was the number of prisoners that whole new cities were built for them, the best known of which was a second Gundeshapur near Seleucia-Ctesiphon, the "better Antioch of Chosroes." This was so exact a model of the Syrian Antioch, which the shah had utterly destroyed, that an Arab historian declared that captives from Antioch found their way to their new homes in the reconstructed city without any need for directions.[59] It was only natural that among the unhappy ranks of these thousands of captured and displaced Christians in a pagan land the mission-minded Jacobite clergy, newly revitalized by Jacob Bar'Adai, should find some of their most receptive hearers.

Nevertheless, in Persia the Monophysites remained a small and uncomfortably stateless minority within a minority in the state-recognized Christian *melet*, which was headed by the Nestorian patriarch. The Monophysites made some attempts to organize a hierarchy for their missionary priests. Jacob Bar'Adai himself consecrated a bishop of Tagrit in 559, and when that bishop was martyred in 575 another was named to succeed him.[60]

The movement's center of greatest strength was among the monks of the clifflike Monastery of Mar Mattai in the Assyrian mountains north of Mosul, which according to tradition had been founded in the days of the Roman emperor Julian the Apostate.[61] But it was not until Gabriel, physician to Queen Sirin, turned Monophysite, and the queen with him, that the old quarrel between Alexandria and Antioch came to a head in Persia. Then for the first time "one-nature" Monophysites seriously challenged "two-nature" Nestorians for the leadership of the Christian *melet* in the empire. We do not know when the practice began, but a distinguishing outward sign of the Jacobites became their habit of making the sign of the cross with only one finger, to denote the one nature of Christ.

The Nestorian Counterattack

In the eyes of the Persians, the special, self-governing community within the state, the *melet*, included all Christians as being under the jurisdiction of the Nestorian patriarch whether they acknowledged his authority or not, and the Nestorians feared, not without cause, that Gabriel and the queen were maneuvering the shah to appoint a Monophysite as patriarch. Such a coup would amount to a legal seizure of the whole Nestorian church by the Jacobites.

Alarmed, the Nestorian bishops took counsel together to plan a desperate appeal to Chosroes warning him of the consequences should he try to force an alien bishop on their church and begging permission to end the vacancy in the patriarchate with the election of a bishop of their own. They chose the fearless old war-horse,

George (Giwergis) the Monk, to lead the assault against the Monophysite curtain around the shah in the palace. It was an anxious
moment for the Nestorians of Persia. Babai's "Life of Giwergis" describes how the delegation left for the capital singing Psalms 68 and
69, "Let God arise, let his enemies be scattered," and "Save me, O
God, for the waters are come in unto my soul." They received the
sign of the cross from the whole congregation as they processed
from the church and in turn blessed all those who remained to pray.

At Seleucia-Ctesiphon they sought out Nestorian nobles who
might have the shah's ear and found them almost in panic. "Go
back," they were told. "Don't ask us to speak to the king about this.
The heretics have become too strong." But George was inflexible. He
rallied the faithful to deliver the petition. The shah shrugged them
off. "How can we give you a head (patriarch) without first knowing
whether or not yours is the true Christian faith?" George accepted the challenge and prodded the shah into staging a religious debate where Nestorians and Monophysites could publicly press their
claims against each other.[62] What followed was the shameful spectacle of "a theological prize-fight," as Wigram calls it, between two
quarreling Christian groups in a pagan land with the power of deciding the winner incredibly resting in the hands of a Zoroastrian
umpire, the shah.[63]

The confession of faith drawn by the Nestorian side for the contest still survives.[64] This creed of the bishops and Babai the Great's
Book of the Union,[65] which was written about the same time, give us
the most systematic and detailed exposition of official Nestorian orthodoxy remaining from the Persian period. Here at last Nestorian
theology clearly and self-consciously separated itself from the orthodox (and Catholic) position, on the one hand, and what it considered
to be the Monophysite heresy, on the other.

It may help to review briefly the development of the controversy
that had split apart Monophysites (called Jacobites in Syria and
Copts in Egypt)[66] from the Nestorians (Dyophysites), and both of
them from the orthodox and Catholic West. Nestorius, at Antioch,
had in effect described the unity of Christ as "one person (prosopon)
in two natures (physis), human and divine."[67] The Monophysites,
however, defined it as "one person (hypostasis) and one nature (physis) both God and man."[68]

This was the impasse the orthodox Council of Chalcedon tried
to resolve in 451 by the compromise formula: "one person (hypostasis)
in two natures (physis)," taking the Monophysite word for "person"
but accepting the Nestorian insistence on two natures.

As if that were not complicated enough, when the Church of the East wrestled with these nonbiblical terms borrowed from Greek philosophy and tried to translate them into its own Syriac language, the confusion was compounded, particularly since the usage of some of the terms in the West was already changing. In the time of the Council of Nicaea (325), for example, two Greek words, *hypostasis* and *ousia*, were commonly used interchangeably to mean "person," and so the Eastern church understood them. But by the next century the latinizing West had already begun to make a critical distinction, translating *ousia* as "substance" or "basic being," and *hypostasis* as "person" (as in the "three persons," *hypostases*, of the Trinity, and the "one substance," *ousia*, of the Godhead).[69] At the same time, in the West, a weaker Greek word for "person," *prosopon*, which could mean mere "appearance" or "face" rather than permanent personality, was sometimes used for "person." But in the East the Persian church began to use this same word, *prosopon* (translated into the Syriac as *parsopa*), in the stronger sense of "permanent personality."[70]

The result was creedal confusion and misunderstanding as different people at different times used the various terms in Syriac or Greek with meanings not always easy to determine. In simplified form this is how, over the years, various protagonists of the Nestorian Church of the East expressed the controversial Christological formula when they tried to describe the nature of Jesus Christ:

Theodore of Mopsuestia (d. 428): two persons (*hypostasis*) and two natures (*physis*) in voluntary union.[71]

Synod of Acacius (486): one person (*parsopa*) and two natures (*keyane*, Syriac for the Greek *physis*) in voluntary union.[72]

Narsai (d. ca. 503): one person (*parsopa*) and two natures (*keyane*).[73]

Henana (d. ca. 609): one person (*qenuma*, for the Greek *hypostasis*), and two natures (*keyane*, for *physis*).[74]

Synod of Yeshuyab I (585): one person (*parsopa*, translating *prosopon*) and two natures (*keyane*).[75]

Babai the Great (d. 628): two persons (*qenuma*, translating *hypostasis*) and two natures (*keyane*, for *physis*).[76]

Synod of Bishops (612): two natures (*keyane,*) and two persons or substances (*qenuma*, translating *hypostasis*) in one union or lordship (*parsopa*, translating *prosopon*).[77]

Against the Monophysites, Nestorian theology now insisted that Christ had two natures, divine and human, not one. From Western orthodoxy it differed less explicitly. But it added the ambiguous phrase "two persons or substances" (*qenuma*) to the Chalcedonian orthodox formula "two natures in one person." What they meant by "two substances" is not altogether clear. Some translators of the Syriac render it as "two selves" or "two sets of natural characteristics" and therefore "two individuals." Others translate it in a less separating sense as "two modes of being" or "two consistencies." But to the Western church the reference seemed clearly heretical, for by *qenuma* the West understood *hypostasis* in the sense of essential personhood. The full Nestorian creed on this point, the personality of Christ, was: "Two natures (*keyane*) and two subsistencies (*qenuma*) in one Person (*parsopa*)." In the eyes of its opponents this divided Christ into two persons, united only in outward appearance.[78]

The Nestorians indignantly rejected the charge. It was not in Persia that heresies have abounded, they thundered. "In the land of the Persians ever since the days of the apostles down to our own times no heresy has raised its head to stir up schism and division," they declared to the shah, not altogether accurately. "How different from the land of the Romans," they exclaimed, where Manichaeans and Marcionites have flourished and where the "pernicious doctrines" of the Monophysites spread their poison.[79]

On the disputed doctrine of the nature of Jesus Christ the Nestorians declared themselves as orthodox as any. They accepted the creeds of Nicaea and Chalcedon as they interpreted the latter. They did *not* divide Christ into two persons, as their full statement clearly showed:

> There is a wonderful connection and indissoluble union between [Christ's] human nature, which was assumed, and God the Word who assumed it, a union existing from the first movement of conception. This teaches us to recognize only one Person (*parsopa*), our Saviour Jesus Christ, Son of God, begotten in the nature of his Godhead by the Father before all ages, without beginning, and born finally in the nature of his Manhood of the holy Virgin, the daughter of David . . .[80]

The debate was inconclusive, at least in the eyes of the royal referee. Chosroes probably intended to keep it that way. Better to have the Christians as a religious minority divided against themselves in the empire than united in making common cause against the national religion and upsetting the stability of the realm.

The Monophysites, counting on their unique position of influence in the palace, were the most disappointed, and their reaction was more extreme. Robbed of victory in the theological debate, the physician Gabriel moved on other fronts against the Nestorians. At Beit Lapat the shah had built a monastery in honor of St. Sergius to please his Christian queen. At that time she was still Nestorian, and the retreat remained in Nestorian hands. Now that she was a Monophysite, Gabriel demanded that it be placed in Monophysite hands. When he came to take it, however, an angry crowd of Nestorians drove him away. Frustrated, he went to the shah and accused the Nestorians of trying to kill him. In his anger he went even further. He denounced the Nestorian champion, George the Monk, as an apostate from the national religion. The accusation was true, but it was rarely used except in times of persecution, since the penalty was death. For a Christian to use it against another Christian was an indication of how deadly the bitterness that poisoned relations between the two Christian parties had become.

George proudly admitted his conversion from "the Magian error," Zoroastrianism, and was thrown into prison. Eight months later, in 615, he was taken by the shah's orders and crucified in the Persian manner, which was more humane than the Roman. His hands were tied to the crossed wood and archers pierced his body with flights of arrows.[81] Fittingly, his adversary Gabriel died a short time later and with the death of these two most contentious of Christians a measure of peace came for a time to Nestorian and Monophysites alike.

But for the Persian Empire there was to be no more peace.

The Fall of the Sassanid Dynasty

The last years of the Persian Empire under the Sassanid dynasty contained one short, fading sunburst of glory midway through the reign of Chosroes II. In the year 602 an army revolt in Constantinople forced Chosroes's friend, the emperor Maurice, off the Byzantine throne and elevated to the purple the usurper Phocas, "a common old man" as Eastern historians described him.[82] His soldiers took the deposed emperor's five sons and murdered them before his eyes, then put Maurice to death. Chosroes, whom Maurice had befriended in his days of exile, was outraged. He ordered his court into mourning. Then he declared war. The years of peace were over, but for all too short a time the Persians at least enjoyed a taste of victory.

In a series of crunching campaigns the Persians threw the Byzantine Romans back to the Mediterranean. They took Edessa in 607 and sacked Antioch in 611. Even when Phocas the Usurper was deposed that same year, and the new emperor, Heraclius, suggested peace now that the murder of Maurice was avenged, the Persians refused and the war went on. In 615 Persian armies poured into Jerusalem with the help of Jewish volunteers eager to recapture their sacred city from the Christians. They massacred thousands—ninety thousand men, wrote Bar Hebraeus[83]—and burned the churches and carried off "the true cross" found in the days of Constantine the Great by the empress Helena. This the Persians presented with fitting ceremony to their Christian queen, Sirin, the wife of Chosroes. In the next two years the all-victorious Persian armies overran Egypt, Libya, and Asia Minor as far as Chalcedon, coming within sight of Constantinople only a mile away across the Bosphorus. The beleaguered Heraclius prepared to flee and move his capital to Carthage in Africa but was dissuaded by the orthodox patriarch Sergius I. From the Black Sea to the African desert and from the island fortress of Rhodes to India the shah of Iran was supreme.

But as suddenly as its sun had risen, the glory faded and the night came. Eastern Rome still ruled the seas, and the emperor Heraclius in Constantinople was neither a coward nor a weakling. While the narrow waters of the Hellespont held back the Persians from his capital he reorganized his empire. Then in 622 he took to the seas for a series of darting counterattacks along the Asian coast that rolled the Persians back into the mountains and opened up the interior to four years of ravaging warfare.

The Byzantine victories so angered Chosroes, according to the Greek historian Theophanes, that he turned violently against the Christians in his realm and confiscated the church treasures of any congregations loyal to the patriarch in Constantinople. Theophanes adds that the shah ordered them all to turn Nestorian, but it appears that Nestorians too were not spared in these persecutions.[84]

By 627 the advancing Romans had reached the gates of Persia's secondary capital, Dastegherd, and Persia's famous heavy cavalry seemed unable to stop them. Then at last the shah's nerve broke and he fled without a fight, abandoning his palace with its forty thousand pillars of silver and its golden throne resting on four giant rubies. With only his Christian wife, Sirin, and her two sons Merdansah and Saliarus, he raced to seek safety in Seleucia-Ctesiphon, seventy miles to the south. That capital, too, might have fallen to the Byzantines had Heraclius chosen to press his advantage, but he decided to withdraw with his immense plunder, leaving Chosroes free but in disgrace. The shah's empire rebelled, and in 628 the monarch who had ruled more of the world for Persia than any Iranian in a thousand years was thrown into his own treasure house and deposed. When he complained of hunger, his son, the new shah, Kavad II, coldly told him to eat his treasures. Four days later he was dead.[85]

It is said that not long before his fall Chosroes II tried to transfer the succession from Crown Prince Siroes to Prince Merdansah, his son by his favorite wife, Queen Sirin, the Christian.[86] If true, this would suggest a Monophysite involvement in the tangled power politics of the palace and may account for what seem to be references to Christian opposition to the shah on the Nestorian side. The *Book of Governors* records that when Chosroes "had grown gray in all wickedness and become old . . . the blessed Shamta saw that the wickedness of Khusrau (Chosroes) the foolish king increased . . . [and] he rose up secretly . . . and slew with the sword the twenty-four sons of Khusrau. . . . And he took Sheroe (Siroes) . . . and he made Sheroe king without the wish and command of his father . . . and went in to the palace of Khusrau with his servants and slew him with the sword; and there was rest for the church in all quarters."[87]

Shamta (or Shamti) was the son of Yazdin, one of the wealthiest men in all Persia and head of a powerful Christian family, famous as pillars of the Nestorian church since the fifth century when Barsauma's council of Beit Lapat met in 484 on the family's estates near Dastegherd. For a while under Chosroes II, Shamta's father, Yazdin, was director of taxes for the whole empire. He was for the Nestorians what Gabriel, the chief physician, had been for the Monophysites, that is, their highest ranking official with direct access to the ear of the shah. But Yazdin fell from favor and died, perhaps murdered on the shah's orders, and his fortune and estates were confiscated, his sons impoverished. It is not surprising, therefore, to find one of the sons taking an active part in the rebellion against Chosroes.

But if Shamta expected Siroes, crowned as Kavad II, to reward him, he was cruelly disappointed. Successful revolutionaries have short memories. For the murder of his father, Kavad II ordered that the right hand of Shamta be cut off and that he be crucified in front of the Nestorian church of Beth Narkos in Seleucia-Ctesiphon.[88]

Chosroes II was the last of the great Sassanids, but by no means the last of the Sassanids. After him came the deluge, a bewildering flood of kings and kinglets who ruled for a day and vanished in the night. His son Siroes, Kavad II, lasted for only nine months, just long enough to make peace with Byzantine Rome and kill all his brothers before he died without an heir. This brought the immediate royal line to an end and the succession was in chaos. In the four or five brief years after the murder of Chosroes II no less than nine or ten claimants to the throne managed to seize power, including two royal princesses and one general who was not even of the royal family.

In the midst of this chaos, one small island of national stability seemed to some to be the Christian patriarchate. The royal family asked Yeshuyab II to lead an international embassy to sue for peace with Constantinople while they sought to restore order within their own nation.[89] By 632 when a forgotten grandson of Chosroes was found and enthroned as Yazdegerd III (632–651), though legitimacy was restored to the crown, the empire of the Sassanids was beyond all saving.[90] There was peace with Rome and order in the court, but Rome was no longer the enemy to be feared, and Persia needed more than order. It needed power, military power, for up from the southern desert like a sandstorm came a deadlier peril than either Constantinople or Persia had faced in centuries. The armies of the Arabs in a dazzling burst of conquest brought Eastern Rome to its knees and simply absorbed Persia as the desert sucks up water.

The Late Flowering of the Persian Church

Before the end, however, the Persian church, unlike the nation, enjoyed a time of peace and revival. The patriarchate was restored. Churches flourished. And Persian missionaries won converts in Arabia, established a Christian hierarchy in India, and successfully carried the gospel to the edge of Asia in the east.

In the brief rule of Shah Kovad II, after the death of Chosroes II who had so long blocked the Nestorians from electing a head of the church, permission was granted to end the vacancy. Joyfully the bishops turned to Mar Babai (the Great), the man who had knit them together during the interim, acting almost as patriarch but without title. The aging bishop thanked them but declined, asking permission to return to the solitary life of a monk at the Great Monastery on Mt. Izla. That is where he died a few years later, remembered no more as a man "hasty in speech and harsh in command" as when he had once crusaded against married monks, overly ascetic Messalians, Monophysites, and the "heretic" Henana, but justly eulogized by the whole church for unrewarded service as its leader in the days of tribulation and for unselfishly refusing its highest honor when better days had come.[91]

While Nestorians were choosing a patriarch, the Monophysites also, for the first time in Persia, were granted the privilege of electing a national head for their community. Their numbers had grown in the days of Gabriel the physician, and by his influence a bishop, Samuel, was consecrated at the capital, Seleucia-Ctesiphon. Up to then the bishop of Tagrit, Qam Ishu, had been acting head of the Monophysite priesthood in Persia. He ordained other bishops, notably one named Tubana, whose seat was at the monastery of Mar Mattai.

But the real spearhead of Monophysite advance seems to have been a missionary movement under the direction of a monk of Mar Mattai named Maruta from the mountains of Kurdistan, who had been educated at Edessa and returned to Persia about 605. Maruta was a friend of Gabriel and Samuel. He wrote tracts against the Nestorians, organized schools, and sent missionaries proselyting throughout the empire. In 628/9 Maruta was elected first maphrian of the Jacobite church in Persia.[92] He was not a patriarch, for he acknowledged the supremacy of the Monophysite (Jacobite) patriarch of Antioch, but like the patriarch of the Nestorians he was head of a *melet*, a self-governing community in the Persian society. It had become obvious to the Persian court after the great debate before Chosroes II that Persia's Christians were no longer one unified *melet*, but two.

The Nestorians were still by far the stronger of the two Christian communities in Persia. From various sources W. G. Young has carefully summarized the record of their growth after the Great Persecution and the reorganization of the church that followed. At the First General Synod in 410 the patriarch could count under his authority 5 metropolitans and 38 bishops, a total of 44. Fourteen years later at the Third General Synod in 424 there were 6 metropolitans and 54 bishops. Growth through most of the fifth century was slower, but by 650 and the Islamic conquest, the Nestorian hierarchy numbered 1 patriarch, 9 metropolitans, and 96 bishops, a total of 106.[93]

When Babai declined the patriarchate the choice of the bishops in 628 wisely fell upon a man who became their greatest leader since Mar Aba I, Yeshuyab of Gedala, bishop of Balad, a devout cleric whose gifts of administration and statesmanship came to be as much valued by the Zoroastrian Persian state as by the Christian church in this period of unparalleled turmoil. The royal court asked the new patriarch, known as Yeshuyab II (628–643), to lead a peace delegation with some of his principal bishops to Constantinople to ask for an end to the disastrous war.[94] Yeshuyab took with him in his delegation the three metropolitans of Nisibis, Adiabene, and Karka (Beit Selokh). They found the Byzantine conqueror at Aleppo, and Heraclius, who had a flair for theology,[95] took the opportunity to grill the Eastern prelates on their dogmas. Despite clear differences between East and West, which the Nestorian Council of Bishops in 612 had unhesitatingly declared, Yeshuyab managed to satisfy the Eastern Roman emperor of the orthodoxy of the Persian church and was received into communion. The envoys were equally successful in concluding a peace between Persia and Constantinople, as was their mandate from the shaky Persian throne.[96]

Not so happy was their homecoming. Along the way the delegation of Nestorian bishops found itself involved in a running series of encounters with argumentative Monophysite and orthodox clergy on the Byzantine side of the border. One member of the team, Bishop Sahdona, proud of his theological training at the School of Nisibis, accepted a challenge to debate with a Jacobite monk and to the scandal of the Persian church was converted to Monophysitism. When this became known later—for his defection developed only gradually—the Nestorians lamely attributed it to sorcery and excommunicated him.[97]

The patriarch Yeshuyab II, as leader of the delegation, also came under attack for heresy upon his return. Heresy was a startling charge to bring against one so unassailably orthodox that in his younger days at the School of Nisibis he had joined the long procession of teachers and students who left the school rather than accept the teachings of the compromised Henana and went off into exile with the champion of the faith, Bishop Gregory.[98] But in the eyes of the more militant Nestorians, their patriarch was now committing the sin of Henana.

His chief accuser was the bishop of Susa, Barsauma, who charged that when Yeshuyab took communion with the orthodox at the court of Heraclius in Constantinople he was in effect denying the true faith and accepting the accursed formula, "Mary, Mother of God (*theotokos*)," which the blessed Nestorius had denounced. But Barsauma's accusation did not stick. Yeshuyab simply affirmed his faithfulness to the Nestorian doctrine of the two natures of Christ and answered all charges of compromise by producing a transcript of his discussions with the orthodox patriarch in Constantinople. His courteous conduct in this controversy was a refreshing contrast to the bitter anger that had all too often been characteristic of such disputes in the past. He did not impugn the motives of Barsauma. Instead, praising him for his zeal against heresy, Yeshuyab quoted the proverb, "A blow from a friend is worth more than a kiss from an enemy," and by a gentle response to great provocation he restored peace in the church.[99]

But the greatest contribution of this able patriarch was not that he brought peace for a while to the church, or that he ended the long war between Persia and Constantinople, or that he later became the first to negotiate for his Christians a peaceful settlement of relationship with the invading Muslims. His more enduring claim to fame should probably be that he created the first metropolitanate of India and authorized Christianity's first mission to China. It was in the patriarchate of Yeshuyab II that the Nestorian hierarchy of India became independent of a Persian bishopric, answerable only to the patriarch, and it was in his rule, in 635, that Persian missionaries reached the capital of T'ang-dynasty China and before long were converting the migrating Turkish tribes of central Asia, making the Nestorian church for much of the next seven hundred years in truth as well as in name the Church of the East, the church of Asia. These were not the beginnings of Nestorian missions, but they were among its most glorious achievements.

So we must now move beyond the falling Persian Empire to discover how Christianity survived the Arab conquest in the Middle East, remained alive in India, and spread to the Far East across Asia to China.

NOTES

1. J. Labourt, *Le Christianisme dans l'Empire Perse sous le dynastie Sassanide 244–632* (Paris: Lecoffre, 1904), 189. Christianity had been introduced among the Huns by missionaries in the fifth century; see above chap. 10, pp. 207ff.

2. See chap. 8, p. 151ff.

3. A. Christensen, *L'Iran sous les Sassanides* (Copenhagen: Levin and Monksgaard, 1936), 376, citing the tenth-century Arab historian Tabari. See also W. A. Wigram, *History of the Assyrian Church A.D. 100–640* (London: SPCK, 1910), 201.

4. The records of the synod are in J. B. Chabot, *Synodicon Orientale ou Recueil des Synodes Nestoriens* (Paris: Klincksieck, 1902), 352–67.

5. Chabot, *Synodicon Orientale*, 358f., canon 7.

6. Chabot, *Synodicon Orientale*, 357, 359, canons 4 and 9.

7. Chabot, *Synodicon Orientale*, 287ff.

8. Chabot, *Synodicon Orientale*, 352 n. 1, citing Mari and 'Amr, *Vita Josephi*.

9. The classic record of Nestorian patriarchs is that of J. A. Assemani, *De Catholicis seu Patriarchis Chaldaeorum et Nestorianorum, Commentarius Historico-Chronologicus* (Rome, 1775), which lists the patriarchs for this period on pp. 29–44. A more recent listing is that of W. G. Young, *Patriarch, Shah and Caliph* (Rawalpindi, India: Christian Study Center, 1974), 73f., though in the spell-

ing I follow A. R. Vine, *The Nestorian Churches* (London: Independent, 1937), 80f., whose list is based on Assemani, Labourt, and J. B. Kidd.

10. Nestorian historians identify Ezekiel as Mar Aba's servant, but the Monophysite historian, Bar Hebraeus, calls him a son of the former short-lived patriarch Paul. See Labourt, *Le Christianisme,* 197f.

11. A life of Sabaryeshu (Sabr-Ishu', Sabriso), written by one of his con-temporaries, the hermit Peter, survives. The text (Syriac) is in P. Bedjan, ed., *Histoire de Mar Jabalaha et de trois autres patriarches . . .* (Paris, 1895), 288ff.

12. Young, *Patriarch, Shah and Caliph,* 74. See also Assemani, *De Catholicis,* 38ff.; Wigram, *Assyrian Church,* 246–49; Labourt, *Le Christianisme,* 222. Wigram and Labourt differ as to which of the two Gregorys was the shah's choice.

13. See B. J. Kidd, *The Churches of Eastern Christendom* (London, Faith Press, 1927), 42ff.

14. According to Mari there were eight hundred students; but the *Chronicle of Seert* (ed. A. Scher, *PO,* t. 7, p. 8n) says five hundred. See A. Voobus, *History of the School of Nisibis, CSCO,* vol. 266, subsidia t. 26 (Louvain, 1965), 238.

15. Voobus, *History of the School of Nisibis,* 46. Voobus cites Leontius, *Contra Nestorium,* III, col. 1365. See also Chabot, *Synodicon Orientale,* 399 in his translation of the acts of the synod of Yeshuyab I, 585, defending Theodore's interpretation against Henana. Henana's own commentary on Job, like all his other works, has not survived.

16. The *Chronicle of Seert* states that it began while Henana was still a teacher under a predecessor, Abraham of Beit Rabban, and that he was expelled for a time by the then metropolitan of Nisibis, Paul. *Chronicle of Seert,* t. 13, fasc. 4, no. 65, p. 530. But the chronological sequence of the passage is confused.

17. Voobus, *History of the School of Nisibis,* 265f. Iso'dena's *Book of Chastity,* written in the ninth century, gives the account of its founding by a Deacon Elisa and the appointment of its early directors. Later, the historians 'Amr and Mari put the date of its founding at between 570 and 580.

18. Chabot, *Synodicon Orientale,* 399.

19. Chabot, *Synodicon Orientale,* 400.

20. Voobus, *History of the School of Nisibis,* 303. The school enjoyed a some-what independent status, but was formally under the authority of the bishop of Nisibis. See J. B. Chabot, "L'Ecole de Nisibe, Son Histoire, Ses Statuts," in *Varia Syriaca,* vol 1 (Paris, 1897), 76. Its relations to the bishops, however, varied from outright hostility under the metropolitans Paul and Gregory to benevolent cooperation under metropolitan Semon whose epis-copate came between those two.

21. G. Rawlinson, *The Seventh Great Oriental Monarchy* (London: Longmans, Green, 1876), 473.

22. See Voobus, *History of the School of Nisibis,* 269n.

23. Quoted by Young, *Patriarch, Shah and Caliph,* 73, citing *CSCO* 3:6, p. 218. See also Rawlinson, *Seventh Monarchy,* 473.

24. Bar Hebraeus, *Chronography,* ed. and trans. E. A. W. Budge (Oxford: Oxford Univ. Press, 1932), 85f.

25. The report of his conversion was repeated by Eutychius, a tenth-century patriarch of Alexandria. See Christensen, *L'Iran,* 481.

26. Labourt, *Le Christianisme,* 209; Bar Hebraeus, *Chronography,* 85. Bar Hebraeus, a Monophysite writing many centuries later, reports as fact that Chosroes married Maria, the Christian emperor's daughter. Rawlinson, *Seventh Monarchy,* 504n, regards this as a fable.

27. Labourt, *Le Christianisme,* 209; Thomas of Marga, *Book of Governors,* 2 vols., ed. E. A. W. Budge (London: Kegan Paul, Trench and Trubner, 1893), 2:80 n. 5, and ff.

28. Evagrius, *Church History,* 6.21, quoted in Rawlinson, *Seventh Monarchy,* 497f., n. 4.

29. "Histoire de Gregoire," in the *Chronicle of Seert,* Part 2, t. 13, fasc. 4, no. 65, 507ff.

30. Wigram points out that Mar Giwergis twisted Henana's doctrine of the one *qenuma* by interpreting it with a statement Justinian would never have made: "One *qenuma* means necessarily one nature, and if, as Justinian asserts, half a nature and half a nature make one *qenuma,* then you have something that is neither God nor Man, a thing apart." Quoted from the "Life of Giwergis," in P. Bedjan, ed., *Histoire de Mar Jabalaha et de trois autres patriarches . . .* (Paris, 1895), 483, by Wigram, *Assyrian Church,* 244.

31. "Histoire de Mar Babai le Grand," in the *Chronicle of Seert,* 530ff. Voobus conjectures that it was because he early came to differ with Henana that Babai chose to teach at the hospital, not the seminary, in the School of Nisibis. Voobus, *History of the School of Nisibis,* 267.

32. Wigram, *Assyrian Church,* 240.

33. A "Life of Sabaryeshu" by a contemporary, the hermit Peter, has been preserved, ed. by P. Bedjan. See Labourt, *Le Christianisme,* 209–17; Wigram, *Assyrian Church,* 215–24.

34. Chabot, *Synodicon Orientale,* 456ff.

35. But Nestorian tradition, naturally, treats the prickly bishop Gregory more kindly as a stout defender of the faith against the Monophysites. See "Histoire de Gregoire," in the *Chronicle of Seert;* and Iso'dena, *Book of Chastity,* ed. J. B. Chabot, in *Mélanges d'archeologie et d'histoire,* no. 16 (Paris, 1896).

36. Labourt, *Le Christianisme,* 215ff.

37. Labourt, *Le Christianisme,* 219.

38. The *Chronicle of Seert,* 498, 510; and the *Chronicon anonymum,* ed. I. Guidi, in *Chronica minora* I, *CSCO* 1, Syr. 1 (Louvain, 1903), 18f.

39. *Chronicle of Seert.*

40. See the *Chronicle of Seert,* t. 13, no. 65, p. 537n.

41. Nestorian historians charge that Henana actively sought the aid of the physician Gabriel at court. *Chronicle of Seert,* 510.

42. *Chronicle of Seert,* 510f.

43. See chap 11, p. 218.

44. The story is in Gibbon's *Decline and Fall* (Bury, ed., 1909), 4:233f.

45. Wigram, *Assyrian Church,* 247. The *Chronicle of Seert,* t. 13, no. 65, 521ff.; Thomas of Marga, in Budge, *Book of Governors,* all give details of the deception. Labourt, *Le Christianisme,* 222, cites the annalists as stating that the bishops, too, favored Gregory of Nisibis, and that it was the Monophysites and followers of Henana who maneuvered the substitution of the other Gregory, but this would seem to be an attempt of later Nestorian historians to shift to others the blame for the election of a bad patriarch.

46. Thomas of Marga, *Book of Governors,* 88n. The *Chronicle of Seert* adds that Gregory was publicly lampooned in posters for his avarice and love of luxury. One satire pictured him examining a piece of gold in his hand with a young girl on his lap (p. 523.)

47. See Chabot, *Synodicon Orientale,* 272; *Chronicle of Seert,* 524; and Wigram, *Assyrian Church,* 252.

48. Bar'Adai was originally a nickname given to Jacob by his opponents. The Monophysites adopted it for themselves, tracing it, however, to the apostle James, rather than to Jacob Baradaeus. See J. B. Kidd, *Churches of Eastern Christendom,* 90.

49. In actual fact Justinian cherished some unorthodox tendencies, such as theopaschism, the doctrine that the deity of the Father and Son in the Trinity is so inseparable that it was not just the Son but the Father who suffered on the cross. See W. H. C. Frend, *Martyrdom and Persecution in the Early Church* (New York: New York Univ. Press, 1963), 245, 266f.

50. Frend, *Martyrdom and Persecution,* 234–54, esp. 253. See also "Life of John of Tella" in John of Ephesus, 519. *Lives of the Eastern Saints,* English translation by E. W. Brooks in *PO* vol. 18 (1924), and Susan Ashbrook Harvey, *Asceticism and Society in Crisis: John of Ephesus* and the "Lives of the Eastern Saints" (Berkeley: Univ. of California Press, 1990), 100–105.

51. "Life of John of Tella," 515–19; and Frend, *Martyrdom and Persecution,* 260ff.

52. Theodora gathered more than five hundred Monophysite monks and clergy into her community in the palace of Hormisdas as they fled the persecutions. See "The Holy Communities Which Theodora the Queen Gathered Together in Constantinople . . ." and "History of the Five Blessed Patriarchs," in John of Ephesus, 676–690; and Frend, *Martyrdom and Persecution,* 270ff., 274, 288f.

53. See E. Honigmann, "La Hiérarchie monophysite au temps de Jacques

Baradée (542–578)" in *CSCO*, subsidia, vol. 2 (Louvain, 1951), 156–286, especially his maps of the distribution of Monophysitism in the Byzantine Empire.

54. The classic biography is "Vita Baradaea" ("Life of James") by the early Jacobite Syrian historian, John of Ephesus, in his biographies of *Eastern Saints*, 690–97. There is also an "Apocryphal Life of James," *ibid.*, vol. 19. See also Honigmann, "La Hiérarchie monophysite."

55. John of Ephesus, "Life of James," 694f. See also Frend, *Martyrdom and Persecution*, 285f.; and Atiya, *History of Eastern Christianity*, 180ff.

56. See E. Honigmann, "La Hiérarchie monophysite."

57. Zachariah of Mitylene, *The Syriac Chronicle*, vol. 10, no. 12, trans. and ed. F. J. Hamilton and E. W. Brooks (London: Methuen, 1899), 314. See also Honigmann, "La Hiérarchie monophysite," citing Bar Hebraeus, *Chronicon ecclesiasticum*, ed. Abbeloos and Lamy, 3 vols (Paris: Maisonneuve), vol. 1, col. 213 f; and Frend, *Martyrdom and Persecution*, 284, citing Michael the Syrian, *Chronique*, 9, 29.

58. John of Ephesus, "Life of James," in *PO.*, vol. 18, 576–85, esp. 577.

59. P. M. Sykes, *History of Persia*, 3d ed., 2 vols. (London: Macmillan, 1951), 1:489, citing Tabari, *Annals*.

60. The martyred bishop was Ahudemmah (or Akha d'Imeh); his successor, Qam Ishu. See Labourt, *Le Christianisme*, 198f.; Wigram, *Assyrian Church*, 242.

61. See "The Monastery of Mar Mattai on Jabal Maklub," in E. A. W. Budge's introduction to *The Chronography of Gregory Abul Faraj . . . Commonly Known as Bar Hebraeus . . .* (Oxford: Oxford Univ. Press, 1932), liii–lxiii.

62. Chabot, *Synodicon Orientale*, 629–32, where the author translates into French a considerable section of Babai's "Life of Giwergis" from the Syriac of P. Bedjan, ed., *Histoire de Mar Jabalaha . . .*

63. Wigram, *Assyrian Church*, 259.

64. Chabot, *Synodicon Orientale*, 562–98, in Syriac with French translation.

65. Babai, *Liber de unione*, ed. A. Vaschalde, in *CSCO*, scr. syri, 61 (Paris, 1915).

66. The Armenian church was also Monophysite.

67. In the *Bazaar of Heracleides* the word Nestorius used for "person" is the Syriac *parsopa*, a translation of the Greek *prosopon*. Whether or not he intentionally translated the weaker Greek word for "person" instead of the stronger *hypostasis*, it was in the weaker sense that his opponents interpreted his position. See above, chap. 9, p. 176f.; and J. F. Bethune-Baker, *An Introduction to the Early History of Christian Doctrine to the Time of Chalcedon*, 3d. ed. (London: Methuen, 1933), 263ff.

68. Bethune-Baker, *Christian Doctrine*, 263ff.

69. Bethune-Baker, *Christian Doctrine*, 263ff.

70. Bethune-Baker, *Christian Doctrine*, 263f. This was the word used by the Sabellian heretics of the third century and was therefore viewed with some suspicion by the orthodox. See W. A. Wigram, *Assyrian Church*, 279ff.; Voobus, *History of the School of Nisibis*, 251ff. For a recent Nestorian perspective, see also Mar Aprem, *The Council of Ephesus of 431*, (Trichur, India: Mar Narsai Press, 1978), 104-22.

71. Bethune-Baker, *Christian Doctrine*, 259f.; but Voobus, *History of the School of Nisibis*, 253f., points out that Theodore, according to Babai, spoke of the "one *parsupa* of Christ."

72. Chabot, *Synodicon Orientale*, 302; Wigram, *Assyrian Church*, 270. "Perfect God and perfect Man in the unity of the *parsupa* (person) of our Redeemer."

73. See Narsai, *Narsai's Metrical Homilies*, English translation by F. McLeod, in *PO* vol. 40.1 (Turnhout, Belgium: Brepols, 1979), 25ff.; Voobus, *History of the School of Nisibis*, 252f.

74. Voobus, *History of the School of Nisibis*, 249ff.

75. Chabot, *Synodicon Orientale*, 397, 455.

76. Voobus, *History of the School of Nisibis*, 249ff.

77. Chabot, *Synodicon Orientale*, 592; Voobus, *History of the School of Nisibis*, 253.

78. See A. Grillmeier, *Christ in the Christian Tradition*, vol 1., *From the Apostolic Age to Chalcedon*, 2d ed. rev. (London: and Oxford: Mowbray's 1975), 559–68; Bethune-Baker, *Christian Doctrine*, 82ff.; Voobus, *History of the School of Nisibis*, 250ff.

79. Chabot, *Synodicon Orientale*, 585.

80. Chabot, *Synodicon Orientale*, 582f. Chabot (p. 611) implies recognition of Chalcedon. CF. Mar Aprem, *Council of Ephesus*, 105–24, 144f.

81. *Chronicle of Seert*, t. 13, no. 65, 538f.

82. Bar Hebraeus, *Chronography* (Budge), 86.

83. Bar Hebraeus, *Chronography* (Budge), 87.

84. Rawlinson, *Seventh Monarchy*, 516, citing Theophanes, *Chronographia*, 263A. Cf. Christensen, *L'Iran*, 486. The *Chronicon anonymum* speaks of the persecution as including Nestorians and Monophysites as well as the orthodox Chalcedonians loyal to the Greek patriarch.

85. Thomas of Marga, *Book of Governors* (Budge), 2:112ff.; Rawlinson, *Seventh Monarchy*, 527f.

86. Rawlinson, *Seventh Monarchy*, 526, citing Theophanes, *Chronographia*, 270C.

87. Thomas of Marga, *Book of Governors*, 2:112ff.

88. Thomas of Marga, *Book of Governors*, 2:81n, 115n. See also *Chronicon anonymum*, ed. Guidi, 1041f. (trans. Noeldeke, p. 353).

89. See below, pp. 255f.

90. See *Chronicle of Seert*, Part II, 579ff.; Rawlinson, *Seventh Monarchy* (one vol. ed., 1876), 542ff.

91. Thomas of Marga, *Book of Governors*, 2:46ff., 115f. He is said to have written more than eighty books. A list of the most important ones is preserved in the *Chronicle of Seert*, 532ff.

92. A "Life of Maruta" was written by his successor Denha, the second maphrian. Edited by F. Nau as, *Histoires d'Ahoudemmeh et de Marouta . . .*, it is in *PO*, 3 (1905). Under the maphrian, the Monophysite hierarchy in Persia was organized with two other metropolitanates, Mar Mattai and Tagrit, and twelve bishoprics. It is doubtful that either the title of "maphrian" or the full quota of bishoprics was recognized until later. See Labourt, *Le Christianisme*, 240f., and Wigram, *Assyrian Church*, 264.

93. Young, *Patriarch, Shah and Caliph*, 37–47.

94. The overtures for peace were initiated in the short reign of Kavad II, but the peace party was sent by his sister and successor Queen Boran. See the *Chronicle of Seert*, *PO*, t. 13, no. 65, p. 558ff., and the *Book of Governors*, 1:lxxxiv–xsvii. See also P. Scott-Moncrieff, *The Book of Consolation, or the Pastoral Epistles of Mar Isho-yabh of Kuphlana in Adiabene*, part 1 (London: Luzac, 1904), xff.

95. Heraclius (610–641), like other Byzantine emperors before him, worked hard to find a compromise formula that might bring together the orthodox and the Monophysites and thereby strengthen the unity of his empire. His formula, the *Ecthesis* of 638, led to the Monothelite controversy as to whether there were one or two "wills" ("center of operations") in the divine-human Christ.

96. The charge to the ambassadors was, "Let them make to pass away and to be blotted out all the discord and enmity which have existed between the Persians and the Greeks, and by their wisdom let them sow peace in the two countries," *Book of Governors*, 2:125.

97. *Book of Governors*, 1:lxxix–xcv. Budge, in editing Thomas of Marga, here includes the Syriac text of five letters of Yeshuyab III, written in 647 before he became patriarch, on the subject of Sahdona's heresy. It was this patriarch, Yeshuyab III, not Yeshuyab II, who finally expelled Sahdona. There is considerable variation to the dates ascribed to the two patriarchs, however. Vine (*Nestorian Churches*, 81) gives 628–643 for Yeshuyab II and 650–660 for Yeshuyab III.

98. *Chronicle of Seert*, *PO*, 13, no. 65, 554.

99. *Chronicle of Seert*, 562–76. The *Chronicle* records two letters of Barsauma, one a public letter accusing Yeshuyab of heresy and the other a private and more vitriolic accusation of taking bribes.

Chapter *13*
Indian Christianity and Its Relation to Persia

"Even in the Island of Taprobane [Ceylon] in inner India, where also the Indian sea is, there is a church of Christians, clergy and believers. I do not know whether there are Christians even beyond Taprobane. The same is true in the place called Male, where the pepper grows . . ."

—Cosmas Indicopleustes, about 547

T URNING now from developments at the church's center in Persia to its relationships and missionary outreach across the world's largest continent in India and Arabia in the south and farther to the Asian east in China, we begin by picking up again the ancient story of the church in India.[1]

The oldest missionary relationships of the Persian church may well have been with the Thomas Christians of India, but it must be remembered that little is known with complete certainty about the first few centuries of the Indian church. Strong traditions affirm the mission of Thomas in the first century, as we have seen. And Egyptian reports of a mission of Pantaenus attest to the probable continuing presence of Christians in India at the end of the second century. But it is only in the fourth century, from about 300, as the Persian church was first organizing itself into a national body under central patriarchal authority, that a series of fragmentary but sustained historical allusions provide fairly satisfying evidence of at least intermittent communication between the Church of the East in Persia and Christians in India.

The first such references are to a mission of Bishop David of Basra about 300, and an enigmatic notice of a "John . . . of Persia and in the great India" who is said to have attended the Council of Nicaea in 325. These both date to before the Great Persecution in Persia of 340 to 380 and have already been described.[2] In connection with that persecution, a persistent tradition from India relates that in 345 a Nestorian merchant, Thomas of Cana, reached Cranganore on the Malabar Coast in southwest India, bringing with him a group of Christian families, perhaps as many as four hundred people, including deacons, priests, and a bishop. They were welcomed by the Christian community they found there but were dismayed to find that these Indian Christians, who traced their origins back to the apostle Thomas, were without local leadership, had become badly divided by false teachings, and were dwindling in numbers. The new arrivals reinvigorated the church and secured for it recognition and high caste status from the the local Indian "king" in Malabar. The most often quoted version of this late and unclear tradition is that of a Jacobite priest of Malabar named Matthew, written in 1730.[3]

By that late date the oral tradition had become so clouded with inconsistencies and confusion that S. Neill wisely categorizes it as lying somewhere "in the uncertain land between history and fiction."[4] In its favor is the fact that the traditional date, 345, of the reported arrival of this Thomas (Thomas of Cana) falls in the early years of the great Persian persecution, a period when it can be assumed with a high degree of probability that groups of Christian refugees would seek safety in emigration, some of them perhaps to India. And however uncertain may be its date and its details, it has been celebrated with many elaborations in songs and plays by Indian Christian communities since at least the sixteenth and seventeenth centuries. Some say there were copper plates, records of royal deeds made out to Thomas of Cana, that were known to the Portuguese in the sixteenth century, but if so they have been long lost though the reported text survives.[5]

The arrival of a less orthodox Christian visitor to India a few years later, about 354, is better known in Western church histories. He was Theophilus "the Indian," a native of islands in the Arabian or Indian Ocean, who was held in Rome as a hostage, converted to Christianity, and sent by Emperor Constantius on an embassy that included visits to Arabia, to his homeland in the islands, and to "other parts of India" (which may or may not have been India proper). There he found Christians whose liturgical practices grated on his sensibilities. The Indians, he said, "listened to the reading of the Gospel in a sitting posture, and did other things which were repugnant to the divine law." He did approve of their doctrine, however, though that is somewhat hard to believe, for Theophilus was an Arian heretic, as was the historian who recorded the visit, his contemporary Philostorgius (ca. 368–439). No other accounts speak of Arians in India.[6]

As A. E. Medlycott points out, the value of the report of Theophilus is its evidence that by the middle of the fourth century India or its adjacent territories had indigenous, worshiping congregations ministered to by local clergy, with customs, such as sitting for the Gospel, that were well adapted to the Indian culture though divergent from accepted Western church practice.[7] The Indian Christians as Theophilus described them did not know that they were disobeying the *Apostolic Constitutions* of fourth-century Syria, which prescribed that "When the Gospel is being read, let all the presbyters, the deacons, and all people stand in perfect stillness,"[8] and though the intruding visitor wrote that he had taught them better before he left, one suspects that custom soon again prevailed.

There was, as yet in the fourth century, no evidence of an independent Indian ecclesiastical structure above the congregational level, though at least one version of the uncertain Thomas of Cana story mentions a bishop among the new arrivals. But early in the fifth century, the ecclesiastical ties between Persia and the Christians of India were regularized and strengthened, and at least from that time on India's Christian communities were hierarchically dependent on the Persian church. The channel of Persian ecclesiastical authority in India was through the bishopric of Rewardashir, which was strategically located on the direct sea route to India near the head of the Persian Gulf on its eastern side. About 410 or 420 this bishopric was elevated to a metropolitanate (archbishopric) and was given jurisdiction over relations with the churches of the Indian subcontinent.[9]

Their ecclesiastical language became Syriac, though even before that they may have ceased to use local dialects in their services. They sent their priests to Persia for study. The name of one of them about 425 is known from a reference in a commentary on Romans by Isho'dad of Merv: "This Epistle has been translated from Greek into Syriac, by Mar Komai, with the help of Daniel the priest, the Indian."[10] About 470, mindful of his responsibility for correct Nestorian theological education of the Indian clergy, the metropolitan Ma'na of Rewardashir sent "to the islands of the Sea, and to India, all the books he had translated" from Greek into Syriac. These were the writings of the two great Nestorian fathers, Diodore of Tarsus and Theodore of Mopsuestia,[11] and perhaps he included some of his own writings in Pahlavi (i.e., Sassanian Persian).

But it is from the early sixth century, in the famous *Christian Topography* of Cosmas Indicopleustes (Cosmas, the Indian Voyager) that historians find the first completely satisfying documentary evidence of an early church in Indian South Asia.[12] Cosmas was a Nestorian from Monophysite Alexandria, a merchant and an explorer with a thirst for knowledge about the shape of the world. His book about his travels (though apparently he never actually reached India) almost incidentally mentions some extremely interesting bits of information about Christians on the Indian subcontinent. This is what he says in noting that as Christian prophecy had foretold, the church cannot be destroyed, and is filling "the whole world":

> Even in the Island of Taprobane [usually taken to refer to Ceylon] in inner India, where also the Indian sea is, there is a church of Christians, clergy and believers. I do not know whether there are Christians even beyond Taprobane. The same is true in the place called Male, where the pepper grows, and in the place called Kaliana, and there is a bishop appointed from Persia. The same is true of the island called Dioscorides [Socotra] in the same Indian sea. (Book III, 64)

And again, commenting on the island of Taprobane:

> This is the great island in the ocean situated in the Indian sea. By the Indians it is called Sielendipa, among the Greeks Taprobane. There the jacinth stone is found. It lies beyond the country where the pepper grows . . .

This same island has a church of Persian Christians who are resident in that country, and a priest sent from Persia, and a deacon, and all that is requisite for the conduct of the worship of the Church. But the natives and their kings are heathens. (Book XI, 13)[13]

Here at last is brief but specific historical confirmation of three important facts partially suggested by the train of traditions and fragments we have been piecing together in search of the foundations of the Indian church. First, by the middle of the sixth century the Indian church was organized and well established with bishops, clergy, and believers. Second, it was strongly related to and dependent on the Persian church, which by then was Nestorian. Third, it was only a tiny minority community, a separated, distinctive cultural island in a vast non-Christian sea.

But two other important facts must be recognized as modifying that general picture. For one thing, it was not a daughter church of the Persian hierarchy. It already had a long history of its own. Ever since the ancient, third-century *Acts of Thomas,* Persians and Syrians had been unanimous in recognizing the apostolic, independent origins of Indian Christianity. Moreover, however dependent the Indian church structure later became on Syrian Persia, the fourth-century report of Theodosius the Indian is evidence that at least two hundred years before Cosmas it had already begun the indispensable process of accommodating Christian practice to Indian ways. In its threefold balance of adaptation to national culture, of persistent identification with its own traditional Christian roots, and of connectional relations with a wider, international Christian network of authority may well lie the secret of the survival of so small a Christian family against such great odds for so many silent centuries.

The last glimpse history gives us of Persian-Indian relations before the Islamic tidal wave engulfed Persia does not change the picture but gives ground for hope of precisely such a survival. Apparently the churches in India were increasing in such numbers in the early seventh century that sometime in the patriarchate of Yeshuyab II (628–643), or Yeshuyab III (650–660) jurisdiction over Indian affairs was taken from the metropolitan of Rewardashir and given to a metropolitanate newly created for India itself. Where it was located and how many Indian bishoprics were created under it are not known. Mingana quotes a later canonist of the Arab period as saying that between six and twelve suffragan bishops were consecrated for India, that the metropolitan of India outranked that of China, and that China outranked central Asia (Samarkand).[14]

Seleucia-Ctesiphon, the Persian capital and seat of the patriarch, fell to the invaders in 637, and a letter of the patriarch Yeshuyab III (650–ca.660) written in the first years of the occupation confirms that the Nestorian connection with India had barely survived the Muslim conquest and was in danger of disappearing altogether. Mingana quotes from his letter to the rebellious metropolitan of Rewardashir:

> "Remember . . . that as you closed the door of the episcopal ordination in the face of many people of India . . . so also did our predecessors close in the face of your spiritual necessities the door of the gift of God [i.e., episcopal ordination]. . . . [T]he episcopal succession has been interrupted in India, and the country has since sat in darkness, far from the light of the divine teaching by means of rightful bishops . . ."[15]

This seems to blame a failure of communication between the patriarchate and India on the jealousy of the metropolitan of Rewardashir over the creation of an independent metropolitanate of India.

NOTES

1. For the early history see chap. 2.

2. See chap. 7.

3. Published in Syriac original with Latin translation in S. Giamil, *Genuinae Relationes inter Sedem Apostolicam et Assyrorum seu Chaldaeorum Ecclesiam . . .*, (Rome, 1902), 552–64. See A. M. Mundadan, "Indian Church and the East Syrian Church," Part 2, "Relations Before the Sixteenth Century," in *Indian Church History Review* 6, no. 1 (June 1972); and G. M. Moraes, *A History of Christianity in India*, vol. 1 (Bombay: Manaktalas, 1964), 61–70. Another version is in W. J. Richards, *The Indian Churches of St. Thomas* (London, 1908), 72–77. Also A. Mingana, *The Early Spread of Christianity in India*, reprint from the *Bulletin of the John Rylands Library* 10, no. 2 (July 1926): 42–45.

4. S. Neill, *A History of Christianity in India*, vol. 1, *The Beginnings to A.D. 1707* (Cambridge: Cambridge Univ. Press, 1984), 42f. Many historians, while accepting the possibility of a fourth-century emigration, note the alternative possibility that this has been confused with a later ninth-century arrival of Syrian Christians from Persia. Mingana, for example (*Christianity in India*, 44n) dismisses the whole Thomas of Cana story as a "stupid chronological mistake of about four centuries and a half."

5. A. M. Mundadan, *Sixteenth-Century Traditions of St. Thomas Christians* (Bangalore: Dharmaram College, 1970), 115, 132–35; S. G. Pothan, *The Syrian Christians of Kerala* (Bombay and London: Leaders Press, 1963), 22–24; and L. W. Brown, *The Indian Christians of St. Thomas* (Cambridge: Cambridge Univ. Press, 1956), 74f., 85–90.

6. K. S. Latourette, *A History of the Expansion of Christianity*, vol. 1, *The First Five Centuries* (New York: Harper, 1937), 232, 234, citing the epitome by

Photius of Philostorgius, *Ecclesiastical History,* bk. 3, chaps. 4, 5. See also Mingana, *Christianity in India,* 26–28; and G. M. Rae, *The Syrian Church in India* (Edinburgh, London: Blackwood, 1892), 97; both argue that Theophilus visited what we now know as India, as well as "Felix Arabia," which was often confused with India in writings of that period.

7. See A. E. Medlycott, *India and the Apostle Thomas* (London: Nutt, 1905), 188–202. Medlycott names the Maldives as the birthplace of Theophilus. Others speculate that it was Socotra.

8. *Apostolic Constitutions,* bk. 2, chap. 57, cited by Mingana, *Christianity in India,* 27.

9. Mingana, *Christianity in India,* 64. On the dependence of the Indian church on Persia, see below, chap. 22, p. 501.

10. Quoted by Mingana, *Christianity in India,* 27, citing M. D. Gibson, ed., in *Horae Semiticae. The Commentaries of Isho'dad of Merv,* 5, 34.

11. *Chronicle of Seert,* ed. A. Scher, *PO,* t. 7, f.2, 116f.

12. The best edition is by W. Wolska-Conus, in *Sources Chrétiennes,* nos. 141, 159, 197 (Paris, 1968, 1970, 1973). See also J. W. McCrindle, *Christian Topography of Cosmas, an Egyptian Monk* (London, Hakluyt Society, 1897). Cosmas, differing with St. Basil who wasted no time debating theologically on the shape of the earth, argued literally from Scripture that the world was flat, since, for example, we could not "tread on serpents and scorpions" (Luke 10:19) while walking upside down! (bk. 2, 23ff.).

13. I take the translation from Neill, *A History of Christianity in India,* 1:36, 37, but I am not convinced by his rejection of Ceylon as the equivalent of Cosmas's Taprobane. He argues for its location in the estuary of the Tamraparni River in South India. C. B. Firth, *An Introduction to Indian Church History* (Madras: Christian Literature Society, 1961), 23, identifies Kaliana as probably either Quilon in Travancore or Kalyan, northeast of Bombay.

14. Mingana, *Christian in India,* 64. The canonist he refers to was Ibn at-Tayib, whose full text on this point can be found in another of Mingana's works, "Early Spread of Christianity in Central Asia, and the Far East," *Bulletin of the John Rylands Library* 10, no. 2 (July 1925): 297–371; reprint (1925), 75f.

15. Mingana, "Christianity in Central Asia," 31ff. See also E. Tisserant, "L'Eglise Nestorienne," *Dictionnaire de Theologie Catholique,* 11:197.

Chapter *14*
The Christian Kingdoms of the Arabs

"The gospel remained marginal to Arab [nomad] society . . . The community loved the holy one [monk or priest] provided he served it in conformity with its own rules and left it undisturbed by any challenge to change. . . . In this respect, the Christianity of the nomads contrasts with the quality in depth of the Christianity of settled Arabs in Syria and the fertile crescent . . ."

—J. S. Trimingham, *Christianity Among the Arabs in Pre-Islamic Times* (1979) 309, 311

SOUTH and west of Persia and separating the Iranian Empire from Africa lay the huge peninsula of Arabia, in size a third as large as the continental United States but in population only sparsely inhabited by fiercely independent Bedouin tribes. The Roman world in general ignored it as containing nothing but sand and a few palms. The very word, "Arab," means desert. One thing alone made southern Arabia important to Rome. It flanked the West's only reliable trade route to Asia, down the Red Sea and across the Indian Ocean. The northern stretches of the peninsula also possessed a strategic importance but for another reason. Arab tribes there along the desert side of the Fertile Crescent developed into semi-independent kingdoms useful as buffer states to both Rome and Persia on their desert borders, first the Nabataeans and Palmyrenes in the west, then the Lakhmid of Hirta on the Persian border west of the Euphrates, and finally the Ghassan on the Roman border south and east of the Jordan. Far to the south, separated from Africa by the narrow waters of the Red Sea, was ancient Yemen of the Himyarites. Both Ghassans and Lakhmids traced their ancestry to a common origin in the older Himyarite Yemen, as did some of the smaller clan principalities like the western Tanukhs.[1]

Though now the peninsula is one of the least Christian areas on the surface of the globe, for a time before the Islamic conquest three of the largest Arab kingdoms were Christian. Little is known of any Christian communities in Arabia before the fourth century, but it must be remembered that the apostle Paul was converted in Arab territory and wrestled his way through the spiritual and religious consequences of his conversion not by seeking out the apostles in Jerusalem, but by going "into Arabia" (probably Nabataea) and presumably staying with Christians there (Gal. 1:15–17).

Christianity naturally spread earliest and fastest among the Arab tribes in contact with Rome. The first specific report of a Christian community in Arab territory beyond the area of Roman influence comes from the history of the Persian church in Adiabene, which mentions a bishopric, Persian not Arab, at Beit Katraye on the Persian Gulf in what is now Qatar, near Bahrain.[2] Nomads, however, pay little attention to political borders, and it probably made little difference, except to their leaders, whether the Bedouin encampments were in Persia or in Rome.

It was in the unmarked desert that nomad Arabs met Christian ascetics and were impressed. On or near the Persian side of the shifting border "the first known bishop of nomad Arabs," Pamphilos of the Tannaye, was an ascetic from the Syrian desert in Mesopotamia and as such attended the Council of Nicaea. Mawiyya, whom J. S. Trimingham calls "the first Christian Arab queen," became the leader of the western Tanukh tribe when her husband, the sheik, died about 373. The whole tribe, along with a neighboring tribe from the same desert area between the Euphrates and the Hellenistic Roman towns north of Damascus, had become Christian, according to Sozomen, about ten years earlier through contact with priests and "with monks who dwelt in the neighboring deserts and who were distinguished by their purity of life and by their miraculous gifts."[3] These western Tanukhs were considered Roman tributaries, but their independent-minded queen, Mawiyya, broke the relationship and rebelled. She fought so successfully against Valens, Roman emperor of the East, that when Valens, who favored the Arian heresy, tried to make peace, she refused until he agreed to send her an orthodox, ascetic man of the desert as bishop for her people. The man she chose, Moses, was probably from the Sinai peninsula.[4]

The first documented Christian mission to southern Arabia must be credited to a date earlier in that same period of Arian heresy in Constantinople. About 354 the Roman emperor Constantius, son of Constantine the Great, sent Theophilus "the Indian," an Arian deacon, to lead an embassy into southern Asia, as we have noted.[5] On its way to India, the embassy visited the southwest corner of Arabia in what is now Yemen. In the time of Christ this area was ruled by the kings of the Himyarites, whose power lasted until about 525. These "Phoenicians of the southern sea," as the Himyarites have been described, had grown rich on their monopoly of the trade route by sea to India. But when, in the first century, the Romans discovered the secret of the monsoon winds across the Indian Ocean, Rome broke the monopoly of the Arabs, and Roman power began to spread down the peninsula.

The Roman mission of 356 was primarily political, designed to forestall any intrusion of Persian forces that might threaten the thin, rich line of Roman trade with India. But Theophilus the deacon, mindful of more than politics, is reported to have witnessed to his Christian faith so zealously before the king that the ruler of the Himyarites was converted and three or four churches were built. One was in the Roman colony at Aden, and two in Himyarite territory, one at Zafar, their capital, and another at San'a,' which was already famous for "the first skyscraper in recorded history," a twenty-story castle of the king. Another church was built at Hormuz on the Persian Gulf.[6] But Theophilus left no permanent mark in Arabia, for Byzantine Christian influence that far south was only sporadic.

Nestorians from Persia and Monophysites from Syria laid the more abiding foundations of pre-Islamic Christianity in Arabia.

Beginning about 339 or 340 the great Persian persecutions of Shapur II sent waves of Christian refugees out of Persia. Many of them undoubtedly found haven in Arabia and bore a Christian witness there, but with what results we do not know. These were the same persecutions that may have driven Thomas of Cana to India. About that time also missionaries moved down the Arab side of the Persian Gulf preaching the faith and establishing missionary monasteries. The earliest known by name is Abdisho, who, perhaps about 390, built a monastery on the island of Bahrain.[7] The first documented Nestorian synod, in 410, included bishop delegates from Qatar and Bahrain.[8]

It was at about the same time that the faith was first systematically propagated in lower Arabia, not by a foreign Persian missionary but through the efforts of a native Arab. In the reign of the Persian shah Yazdegerd I (399–420), according to the *Chronicle of Seert*, a Yemeni merchant named Hayyan left the kingdom of the Himyarites in Arabia's southwest corner to travel to Constantinople on a business trip. He chose to return by way of Persia, stopping for a time in the Arab tributary kingdom of al-Hirta (Hira) on the Persian border east of the Euphrates. There he met a group of Nestorians and was converted. With all the enthusiasm of a new convert he went on home to evangelize the Arabs in his native Yemen, according to the *Chronicle of Seert*, beginning with members of his own family but carrying the gospel also across the border into other Arab regions.[9]

Hirta (or Hira), where Hayyan is said to have been converted, was a natural stopping place for him. It had been settled by Tanukh Arabs migrating north from his homeland in Yemen in the third century. In the confused period following the fall of the Parthian Persian dynasty in 225 they found unoccupied fertile land west of the Euphrates not far from ancient Babylon and there one group of them settled among what appears to have been a largely Christian native population belonging to the Church of the East (east Syrian, later called Nestorian). Another section of the clan, the western Tanukhs, who were later to be ruled by Queen Mawwiya, continued north and east to the fringes of Roman Syria. By 328 the Tanukhs who remained east of the desert had made of Hirta a semiautonomous border kingdom, sometimes called the Lakhmid kingdom after its tribal founder. It was so closely allied to Persia that Shah Yazdegerd I sent his son there, perhaps at the very time of Hayyan's visit, to benefit from the dry and healthy desert air. As early as 410 it became the seat of a Nestorian bishop, Hosea, and remained the head of a Christian diocese, perhaps intermittently for seven hundred years.[10]

G. E. von Grunebaum makes the important point that unlike the Jacobite Monophysites of Arabia, who remained nomads, the Nestorian Christians of Hirta formed a close community calling themselves "servants of God" whose inner unity transcended traditional Arab tribal differences. He goes further to suggest that this was not only the "first known example of Arabic speakers grouped by a common ideology," but may well have been a model for the later politico-religious "community" of the Muslims, the *umma*.[11]

The Arab king al-Numan (ca. 400–418) was a pagan and sometimes persecuted his Christian subjects but the faith spread and eventually reached even into the palace. The most famous of all the Lakhmid kings was al-Mundir III (ca. 505–554), whose mother, Mariyah (or Mawiyah—the name recalls the relationship with the western Tanukh)[12] became a Christian toward the end of the fifth century. Al-Mundir's wife, Queen Hind, was also a Christian, a princess from a neighboring Arab kingdom (perhaps Ghassan). She was so devoted to the Christian faith that after the death of the king, her husband, and the enthronement of her son 'Amr (554–569), she built a Christian convent in the capital and perhaps entered it herself as a nun, for she described herself in an inscription on its walls as "the maid of Christ and the mother of His slave ['Amr]."[13]

It is not likely, however, that 'Amr was ever baptized. Though some of the Lakhmid queens and many of their subjects embraced the faith, the kings of Hirta were reluctant to follow them into the church. The reason is fairly obvious. They were politically tied to non-Christian, Zoroastrian Persia. Their rivals, the Ghassanid kings across the desert to the west, could be openly Christian with advantage, for they were vassals of Byzantium, but in Persia Christianity was a political liability. It is therefore probably no coincidence that in Hirta their "first Christian king," as some have called him, was also the last. He was al-Numan III (ca. 580–602). When he died Persia abruptly reduced the power of the Lakhmid rulers to that of chieftains subordinate to a Persian governor.[14]

Persia might tolerate religious minorities like the Christians but it gave short shrift to the faintest suggestion of political ambitions among such minorities. Even so the Christian community, which had had a Nestorian bishop since 410, remained one of the strongest in the empire, surviving long into Muslim times as "the Ibadi."[15] It was through the Arab Christians of Hirta that desert Arabs were taught Syriac and learned to read and write, giving them a cultural advantage over most of the rest of the people of the northern Arabian peninsula.[16]

Meanwhile, far southwest across Arabia in Yemen where Hayyan had begun the work of evangelizing his Himyarite countrymen, Judaism also began to make converts, among them a Himyarite king. King Abu-Karib As'ad, who unified and ruled Yemen from about 385 to 420, is said by Arab tradition to have accepted the Jewish religion. Some support for the tradition is found in the fact that from about the middle of the fifth century onward, monotheistic inscriptions "probably of Jewish origin" begin to appear in the region.[17] At the beginning of the sixth century, about 500, the missionary situation was made even more complex by the arrival of Monophysite evangelists, notably the famous ascetic Phemion, who was captured by an Arab caravan passing through Syria and brought to Najran, northwest of the Himyarites, where his life and teaching made a great impression.[18]

By this time the kings of the Himyarites were clearly Jewish by faith, not Christian. A long-lost Syriac work, discovered in this century, *The Book of the Himyarites*, gives what may be an almost contemporary account of the stormy confrontation of these two monotheistic faiths, Christianity and Judaism, in polytheistic, animistic Arabia before the rise of Islam.[19] The author, a Monophysite, pictures it as a direct clash between the Jewish Arab king of the Himyarites, dhu-Nawas, and the Monophysite Christians of Najran together with their Christian allies from Ethiopia. Najran had become Christian about 500 through the witness of the Syrian Jacobite ascetic, Phemion (Faymiyun).[20]

The persecution began about 522, though there is great uncertainty about the dates.[21] Perhaps it started with extortion disguised as taxation levied against the Christians by the king. Hostility intensified, with Christians burning Jewish synagogues in Najran and the Arabs of Jewish faith tearing down Christian churches in the south. The Christians appealed for help to the nearest Christian power, Ethiopia, only fifteen miles across the Straits of Bab-al-Mandab from the Yemenite southwest corner of Arabia. The ruler of the Axumite Ethiopian empire ('Ella 'Asbeha, or Elesbaan, who is called Kaleb of Abyssinia in the *Book of the Himyarites*) had long claimed sovereignty, real or imagined, over Arabia and responded to the appeal of the Arab Christians with a massive invasion in 523 that drove the Himyarite king, dhu-Nawas (called Masruq in the book) from his capital of Zafar. There the African invaders installed an Ethiopian garrison, of occupation and returned to Ethiopia. But the Himyarites, pagan and Jewish together, regrouped against the Christians and their foreign allies, recaptured Zafar, slaughtered the Ethiopian garrison and massacred the Christians. Then King dhu-Nawas (whose name means "long-hair") marched north against the main center of Christian opposition, Najran. He took the town by treachery and cruelly killed its Christians in a bloodbath that lasted for days.[22]

Stories of martyrs are not often completely trustworthy but one from the *Book of the Himyarites* is worth repeating. A man of Najran was stopped on the road by the invaders. "Are you a Christian?" they asked. "Yes," he said. "Then hold up your right hand." He held it up and they cut it off. They asked him again, "Are you a Christian?" "Yes." "Then hold up your other hand." And "immediately, with joy," the account says, he held up his left hand and it too was cut off. "Now, are you still a Christian?" they asked him. And he said very firmly, "Yes, in life and death I am a Christian." Whereupon they cut off his feet and left him there to die. But still a Christian.[23]

The shocking massacre at Najran horrified the Christian world and widened the conflict by drawing in both Roman Byzantium and Sassanid Persia. It was reported that the Jewish-Arab prince dhu-Nawas burned alive "427 ecclesiastics, monks and nuns, killed 4,252 Christians and enslaved 1,297 children and young people below the age of 15."[24]

One line of tradition relates that the Himyarite Christians appealed for help to the Byzantine emperor Justin, who asked his Christian ally the negus (king) of Abyssinia, as being nearer the scene of action, to go to the aid of the persecuted Arab Christians. This is not likely. The Ethiopians were already directly involved in Arabia and would need no Romans from Constantinople to tell them to avenge the massacre of their garrison at Zafar. It is more probable that politics and commerce as much as religion brought Constantinople into the conflict. Procopius the Greek historian indicates as much. The emperor intervened "to injure the Persians," he wrote, and to protect the Roman trade route to India.[25] This intervention by Constantinople did not include Byzantine military action but took the form of active encouragment of an Ethiopian invasion.

On the other side, another tradition reports that dhu-Nawas, the persecutor of the Himyarite and Najran Christians wrote to the Arab king of Hirta, al-Mundir III, and to the Persian shah calling on them for help in wiping out the Christians.[26] This appeal must have fallen oddly on the ear of the Hirta prince, for both his wife and mother were Christian. Perhaps dhu-Nawas was counting on the theological enmity between Nestorians (in Hirta) and Monophysites (in Yemen and Ethiopia), and he may have been at least partly successful in a policy of dividing and conquering the rival Arab Christian or partly Christian communities, for the *Book of the Himyarites* speaks of "Christians in name" only who were persuaded to carry deceiving messages to the Christian garrison at Zafar. At least one of these couriers or spies was from Hirta.[27]

At any rate, whether in response to these political maneuverings of the great powers or not, the negus of Ethiopia poured an army reportedly of seventy thousand men across the Straits of Bab-al-Mandab. They utterly routed the royal Himyarite army, killed "the tyrant Masruq" (dhu-Nawas), and proceeded to massacre such numbers of pagans and Jews that even non-Christian Arabs began to tattoo a cross on their hands to escape death. The concluding paragraphs of the *Book of the Himyarites* are a disquieting paean of praise for the speedy vengeance meted out to "the crucifiers" (Arabs of Jewish faith), citing Old Testament parallels from the flood to the slaughter of the Amalekites.[28]

A prince of the royal line was found who proclaimed himself a Christian. This man the Ethiopians installed as the Himyarite king, but, Christian or not, the Arab dynasty did not long survive the invasion. The commander of the African forces occupying Yemen, a man named Abraha, deposed the puppet prince and declared himself an independent king, subject not even to the Ethiopian negus. Ethiopia launched two attempts to reassert control but failed and finally contented itself with a grant of recognition to the usurper on condition that he pay tribute.[29]

Christianity flourished under the new African ruler, Abraha. He built "one of the most magnificent cathedrals of the age"[30] in his capital, San'a', and proceeded to make it a center for Arabian religious pilgrimage rivaling even pre-Islamic Mecca, where the 360 idols of the Kaaba, one for each day of the year, drew multitudes of Bedouins to primitive pagan worship long before Mecca became the holy place of Islam.

A tradition as old as the Koran relates that this competition for the pilgrim traffic flared quickly into open war. Pagan Bedouins stole into the new church in San'a' on the eve of its consecration and defiled its altar with dung and smeared filth on the cross. In revenge Abraha swore to destroy the Kaaba and marched against Mecca, which was about four hundred miles north up the west coast of the peninsula. He rode a white elephant across the sands to the vast astonishment of the camel-riding Arabs, and the year of the invasion, 570 or 571, has ever since been known in Arab annals as the "Year of the Elephant."

A series of skirmishes in which the Himyarites were easily victorious left Mecca virtually defenseless and induced its leading sheikh, the aged Abd al-Muttalib, to try to negotiate a ransom for the city. The attacking ruler, Abraha, offered what seemed to him to be generous terms. He wished to take no man's life, he said, but only to destroy the nest of idols, and then he would retire. But to the Bedouins the idols were as sacred as the cathedral cross to the Christians, and to the old pagan sheikh more precious than human life. He could not compromise and rode sadly back to Mecca to rally his men for a fight to the death for their Holy Place. Unexpectedly, it was the Christians who were routed in the battle that ensued, perhaps ambushed in a narrow *wadi*, perhaps stricken by a plague, or perhaps, as the Koran declares, they were destroyed by a miracle.[31]

It was a minor battle in a lost desert world, only imperfectly remembered even by tradition. But it may well have set in motion forces and influences that were drastically to affect the future of Christianity across all western Asia and northern Africa. Fifty-five days after the Battle of the Elephant, according to tradition, a baby was born in Mecca. His grandfather was the hero of that battle, the old Bedouin sheikh Abd al-Muttalib. The baby's name was Muhammad, and it was his family that held a proprietary interest in Mecca's pre-Islamic, animistic pilgrim trade. His great-grandfather, Hashim, had won for his clan of the Quraysh (Koreish) tribe the right to provide food and water for the pilgrims. His grandfather, Abd al-Muttalib, had fought to protect that right and the faith that inspired it against a Christian attack.[32]

Recent scholarship tells us that tradition was wrong about the date of the invasion, and that Muhammad was born probably about twenty-five years after the Year of the Elephant.[33] But it may have been at least in part the family's memory of the enmity of the Christians, and pride in his grandfather's victory over them, that moved Muhammad, when the time came to lead his people out of their pagan superstitions, to root his new faith not in the monotheism of Jerusalem or Bethlehem but in the chief god of the Kaaba, Allah.

As for the Christian Himyarites and their Ethiopian allies, they returned defeated and disgraced to find themselves unable to maintain power even in their homeland, Yemen. It was a time of truce between Constantinople and Persia and Shah Chosroes II took advantage of the peace on Persia's northern borders to attack south against Byzantium's allies, the Ethiopians. He aimed his attack against the Ethiopian tributary state of Himyarite Yemen. The report may be true that he was encouraged in this by a refugee in his court, a son of the last native Himyarite king who had escaped when his father, dhu-Nawas "the tyrant," was killed in the Ethiopian invasion. Using the refugee prince Sayf ibn-dhi-Yazen to rally nationalist Himyarite emotions to their side, the Persians landed at Aden in 575 and easily defeated the African-led garrisons of Yemen. But if the Himyarite Jewish dynasty dreamed of recovering the power it had lost to the Arab and Ethiopian Christians who had deposed them, it was disappointed. Prince Sayf was murdered and replaced by a Persian satrap and the Himyarites, as G. Rawlinson has observed, "gained nothing but a change of masters."[34] Persia had added Yemen on the Red Sea to Herat on the Persian Gulf, thus lengthening its string of border principalities to control almost the entire length of the strategic sea route to India.

It is worth noting as a significant weakness in the early Christian missions in Arabia that the major areas of Christian strength on the eve of the rise of Islam were all foreign dominated. The Ghassanid kingdom in the northwest of the peninsula had for four centuries been tributary to Rome. The Lakhmid kingdom on the northeast was absorbed by Persia. And in the southwest, the Himyarites, independent for centuries, came first under the sway of Christian Ethiopia and then fell to Persia. The Christian faith retained a foreign tinge in the Arabian peninsula. Nowhere was it able to establish an authentic Arabic base. It had not yet even translated the Scriptures into Arabic.

NOTES

1. On the early Arab states and kingdoms, see P. Hitti, *History of the Arabs from the Earliest Times to the Present*, 5th ed. (New York: Macmillan, 1951), chaps. 5 and 6, pp. 49–86.

2. A. Mingana, ed., *Sources Syriaques*, vol. 1, *Msiha-zkha* (Leipzig: Harrasowitz, 1907), 106.

3. J. S. Trimingham, "Mawiyya: The First Christian Arab Queen," in *The Near East School of Theology Theological Review*, vol. I, no. 1 (Beirut, 1978): 3–10. The quotation is from his citation of a longer section of Sozomen's *Ecclesiastical History* 6. 38. Trimingham identifies the two tribes through a reference from Tabari's *Ta'rikh* (p. 10 nn. 7, 8).

4. Trimingham, "Mawiyya," 8.

5. See chap. 13, p. 267.

6. Philostorgius, *Ecclesiastical History* 3. 4–5; Hitti, *History of the Arabs*, 56–61; J. Stewart, *Nestorian Missionary Enterprise: The Story of a Church on Fire* (Edinburgh: Clark, 1928), 52ff.

7. *Chronicle of Seert*, ed. A. Scher, *PO*, t. 5, p. 311.

8. J. B. Chabot, *Synodicon Orientale ou Recueil de Synodes Nestoriens* (Paris: Klincksieck, 1902), 273. A. Mingana identifies "the Isles" in the records as the district of the Qatars, and "Ardu and Todoru" as bishoprics of Bahrain, "Early Spread of Christianity in India," *Bulletin of the John Rylands Library*, 10, no. 2 (July 1926): 435–510; reprint, 7.

9. *Chronicle of Seert*, 5, 330f., spelling his name Hannan. The *Chronicle* dates from about four to six hundred years later.

10. J. S. Trimingham, *Christianity Among the Arabs in Pre-Islamic Times* (London: Longman, 1979), 156–58.

11. G. E. von Grunebaum, *Classical Islam: A History 600–1258* (London: Allen & Unwin, 1970), 23.

12. Another similarity is that the Lakhmid Mariya, like the western Arab queen, is said to have invited a bishop named Moses to come to minister to her people. The parallels suggest the possibility that later eastern tradition about the origins of Christianity in Hirta confused stories of the fifth-century Mariya (Mawiya) of Hirta with those of the earlier fourth-century Arab queen of the same or similar name on the western side of the desert.

13. Hitti, *History of the Arabs*, 83, citing Yaqut, the Arab geographer (1179–1229), author of *Mu'jam al-Buldan*, a geographical dictionary (ed. F. Wustenfeld, 6 vols. [Leipzig, 1866–73]).

14. Hitti, *History of the Arabs*, 84.

15. On the Lakhmids, see also Trimingham, *Christianity Among the Arabs*, 188–202, and G. Rothstein, *Die Dynastie der Lahmiden in al-Hira* (Berlin, 1899). The medieval Nestorian historian 'Amr gives a somewhat different account of Christianity in Hirta. According to him, King al-Mundir was baptized in 512 by Simon, bishop of Hirta, and it was al-Mundir's sister, Henda, who founded the convent. (See A. R. Vine, *The Nestorian Churches* [London: Independent, 1948]), 76.

16. M. M. Siddiqi, *Development of Islamic State and Society* (Lahore, Pakistan: Institute of Islamic Culture, 1956), 3–4, 19.

17. M. Rodinson, *Mohammed*, trans. A. Carter (Harmondsworth, Eng.: Penguin Press, 1971), 30; Hitti, *History of the Arabs*, 60. The king's name is also given as Abkarib As'ad.

18. Robinson, 61; and W. Wright, "Syriac Literature," *Encyclopedia Britannica*, 9th. ed.

19. A. Moberg, ed., *The Book of the Himyarites* (London and Oxford, 1924). Moberg dates the manuscript fragments, which were found used as stuffing in the board covers of a Jacobite liturgical collection, at 932, but fixes the date of the original at 525.

20. According to the tradition reported both by ibn Hisham (*Sirah*, ed. Winsterfeld [Gottingen, 1858], 20–22); and by al-Tabari (*Tarikh al-Rusul*, vol. 1, ed. de Goeje [Leiden, 1879–1901]).

21. Some date the beginning of persecution to the first year of the reign of

dhu-Nawas in 510 and assign the first invasion from Ethiopia to the year 512 (Rodinson, *Mohammed*, 31).

22. See the bibliography in Moberg, *Book of the Himyarites*, xxivf. The most important ecclesiastical sources are "The Martyrology of Harith," which is based, according to Moberg, on *The Book of the Himyarites*, and the *Letter of Simeon of Beth Arsham*, which may have been written even earlier than *The Book of the Himyarites* but is more fragmentary and diffuse. Secular Western sources include Procopius *De bello Persico* 1.19–20, and Cosmas Indicopleustes, ed. W. Wolska-Conus in *Sources Chrétiennes* (Paris, 1968, 1970, 1973). The important early Arab sources are Ibn Hisham and al-Tabari. This traditional material is both corroborated and corrected by recent archaeological discoveries analyzed by J. Ryckmans, *La Persécution des Chrétiens Himyarites au Sixième Siècle* (Istanbul: Nederlands Hist.-Arch. Inst. in het Nabije Oosten, 1956), and "Le Christianisme en Arabie de Sud preislamique" in *L'Orient cristiano nella storia della Civilta* (Rome: Academia nazionale dei Lincei, 1964), 413–53. The traditional date for the infamous massacre in Najran is 523, but the evidence of sixth-century Arabic inscriptions leads Ryckmans (*La Persécution*, 18–21) to prefer a date in the fall of 524.

23. *Book of the Himyarites*, 9a (Moberg, cvi).

24. Rodinson, *Mohammed*, 31.

25. See *Letter of Simeon of Beth Arsham*, cf. n. 21 above. Like later Arab sources this tradition makes no mention of the earlier Ethiopian invasion, as Ryckmans points out, *La Persécution*, 19f. See also Procopius *De bello Persico* 1. 19. 1; 1:20. 9–11.

26. "The Martyrology of Harith," cf. n. 21 above. Moberg, *Book of the Himyarites*, xxxiv.

27. *Book of the Himyarites*, 7a (Moberg, cv).

28. *Book of the Himyarites*, 49a–51b (Moberg, cxxxviiff.).

29. J. Ryckmans, *La Persécution*, 7f., 21f. He dates Abraha's seizure of power at 530. Procopius gives the name of the puppet Arab Christian prince as Simiphaios (*De bello Persico* 1. 20. 3, 4); and G. Ryckmans reports the name as appearing on a sixth-century Arab inscription as Sumyafa' 'Aswa, king and "governor for the Count of the Negus." See G. Ryckmans, "Une inscription chrétienne sabéenne aux Musees d'Antiquites d'Istanbul," *Le Muséon*, 59 (1946): 165–72.

30. Hitti, *History of the Arabs*, 62.

31. The Koran (Quran) celebrates the victory in the *Sura* of "The Elephant," no. 105 (Eng. trans. A. J. Arberry):

Hast thou not seen how thy Lord did with the Men of the Elephant?
Did He not make their guile to go astray?
And he loosed upon them birds in flight,
Hurling against them stones of baked clay,
And He made them like green blades devoured.

See also the vivid account of the campaign in S. M. Zwemer, *Arabia: The Cradle of Islam* (New York: Revell, 1900), 308–13; and in W. Muir, *The Life of Mohammed* (Edinburgh: Grant, 1923), cxvif.

32. On Hashim and Abd al-Muttalib, see W. Muir, *Life of Mohammed*, cviii–cxvi. The Quraysh (Koreish) were legendarily descended from Abraham through Ishmael. It is from Muhammad's great-grandfather, Hashim, that the modern Hashimite kings of Jordan and Saudi Arabia trace their descent and take their dynastic name.

33. J. S. Trimingham, *Christianity Among the Arabs*, 305n. 48.

34. G. Rawlinson, *The Seventh Great Oriental Monarchy* (London: Longmans, Green, 1876), 426. See also Hitti, *History of the Arabs*, 65f.

PART II

Outreach: The Ends of the Earth (From Alopen to the Crusades)

Chapter *15*
The First Christian
Mission to China

"When the accomplished Emperor T'ai-tsung began
his magnificent career in glory and splendour . . .
there was a highly virtuous man named Alopen in
the Kingdom of Ta-chin. Auguring from the azure
sky he decided to carry the true Scriptures (Sutras)
with him, and observing the course of the winds, he
made his way through difficulties and perils. Thus in
the ninth year of Chen-Kuan [A.D. 635] he arrived at
Chang'an. The Emperor despatched his Minister,
Duke Fang Hsuan-ling to meet the visitor and
conduct him to the Palace. The Scriptures were
translated in the Imperial Library."

—The Nestorian Monument, 781
(Saeki translation)

FAR across the eastern edges of Persia and beyond the lands of the Turkish and Mongol nomads of central Asia lay the great empire of China. From early times Western Christians have handed down tales and traditions of how the gospel had been preached even to the Chinese who live at the end of the world where the sun rises from the sea. Some went so far as to claim that before his martyrdom St. Thomas left India and "set sail into China on board of Chinese ships . . . and landed at a town named Camballe, which is . . . unknown to us."[1] But were the old tales true? Had Christian missionaries ever actually broken through the barrier seas or the ring of fierce warrior tribes that separated China proper from the West? Had they ever crossed the deserts and high mountains that isolated central Asia from the world?

How Old Is Chinese Christianity?

When the Jesuits reached China in the sixteenth century they found a colony of Jews in Kaifeng, but no Christians.[2] Perhaps the reports of ancient missions to China were nothing but wishful thinking, though some remembered the vanished Franciscan missions to the Mongols in the thirteenth century, others believed Marco Polo's reports of Christians in Kublai Khan's China, and a few even accepted the unlikely references to a mission of St. Thomas from India to China. But if Christians had indeed been in China before the Jesuits, there was nothing left to show for it.

Then came a dramatic discovery. In 1623,[3] workmen digging not far from what is now Hsian (Xian), the ancient T'ang-dynasty capital Chang'an, uncovered a great stone more than nine feet high and three and a third feet wide of black granular limestone, beautifully inscribed in Chinese characters beneath a design at the top centering around a cross rising from a lotus blossom. Large characters under the cross proclaimed it to be "A Monument Commemorating the Propagation of the Ta-ch'in (Syrian) Luminous Religion in China" (*ta ch'in ching jyan liao tung jung guo bei*). It was a monument erected in 781 telling of the arrival of a Nestorian missionary in the Chinese capital in 635.

With the discovery of this stone, Western knowledge of the history of Christianity in China, as distinct from Mongolia outside the wall, was expanded by almost seven hundred years. It described how a Persian reached the capital of T'ang China with the gospel as early as Aidan's mission from Iona into England, fifty-five years before Willibrord's pioneering mission to the Frisian tribes of northern

Europe, and a hundred and fifty years before Charlemagne's militant conversion of the Saxons.]

We shall discuss the monument again later, but first let us trace something of the background history of Christianity in central Asia as it relates to this first known opening of China to Christian missionary outreach. We have noted the progress of Christianity from Persia among the Turkic nomads in Bactria. Let us now observe from the Chinese side how the faith moved across Asia.]

During the three and a half centuries of wars and disorder that began with the decline of the Later Han dynasty, the empire's northwest frontier shattered into tribal fiefdoms and the empire itself became a patchwork land of "the sixteen kingdoms." Outside the Great Wall Asia belonged to the nomads, not to the Chinese, and it was through these tribes of wild horsemen that, beginning about the end of the sixth century, Christianity came irregularly and with varying effect into contact with the Chinese.[The pattern of expansion was a complete reversal of that of the missionary conquest of Europe. There the gospel moved centrifugally out from a fading Roman center to win the barbarians on the fringes of the empire. In east Asia the faith came centripetally from the barbarian outerland to reach the heart of civilization, China.]

A word must be said about the tangled history of the northern Chinese frontier. Periods of stability and relatively normal trade between China and the West along the land routes of the Old Silk Road were rare in the Christian era. One such, as we have seen,[4] occurred in the Later Han dynasty about 74–102, but when the dynasty weakened after 180, China lost control of central Asia to a bewildering succession of dominant tribes. By the third century A.D. power had shifted to a coalition or "kingdom" of Mongol Hsien-pei tribes. Two hundred years later in the fifth century the Juan-juan, also largely Mongol, dominated north of the wall, and to their south, moving from Manchuria into China proper, the Turko-Mongolian[5] tribes of the Toba Turks formed a powerful Buddhist dynasty (the Northern Wei, 386–534). In the sixth century, the north outside the wall was dominated by T'u-chueh Turks who had revolted and destroyed their former masters, the Juan-juan, but inside the wall the Toba Turks and their successors, now thoroughly sinicized but still strongly Buddhist, controlled northern China as far south as the old capital Chang'an.[6]

Two contemporary Western historians of that time in Byzantium, Procopius and Theophanes, relate a report that in 551 Nestorian monks appeared before the emperor Justinian in Constantinople with a hidden treasure, silkworms concealed in a bamboo tube. The

Chinese had long exported silk to the West but closely guarded the secret of its culture. It is probable, therefore, that the monks came not from China, for it is not known that missionaries had yet penetrated that far, but from the territory of the western T'u-chueh Turks, who by then controlled the Old Silk Road outside the Wall and were conquering their way west into Bactria, where they had joined the Persian shah Chosroes I in a two-sided attack on the Hephthalite Huns.[7] However, as early as 455 a Persian embassy had reached the Wei dynasty capital in north China just outside the Great Wall at Ta'tung,[8] and Persian Nestorians might therefore conceivably have been in China before the end of the fifth century. But that is speculation.

Nevertheless Nestorian missionaries had already successfully worked among the Hephthalites in Bactria for almost a hundred years[9] and now began to turn their attention to the victorious Turkic T'u-chueh. About 591, among Turkish prisoners captured and sent to Constantinople when Byzantium in a rare period of Roman-Persian amity was helping Shah Chosroes II quell a rebellion, some of the Turks who had been fighting with the Persian rebels were found with crosses tattooed on their foreheads. When asked what the crosses meant, they replied that Christians among them had said it would ward off the pestilence.[10] It is an irony of history that the Turks, who in the Middle Ages were a symbol of enmity to the cross, had once long before been identified by that same Christian symbol.

By then, however, the days were drawing to a close when the tribal horsemen of the Turks and Mongols could dominate the central Asiatic steppes and keep a fragmented China from direct contact with the West. In 581 a young general of mixed Chinese-Turkish blood in one of the northern kingdoms that had been part of the Toba Turk realm overthrew his feudal overlord and in 589 declared himself emperor of a new dynasty, the Sui, which would rule all China from the old capital, Chang'an (modern Xian). Short-lived though the Sui dynasty proved to be (581–618),[11] its great accomplishment was the unification of China after the "centuries of discord." It prepared the way for the rise of the greatest of all China's long line of imperial houses, the mighty T'ang dynasty (618–907), which ruled in what is not without reason often referred to as the golden age of China.

The founder and first emperor of the T'ang dynasty, Li Yuan, was given the dynastic name Kao-tsung. He was half Turk and it was with the help of three thousand Turkic cavalry that he captured the Chinese capital, Chang'an, from the last Sui emperor. His mother, who came from the politically powerful Turkic-Mongolian (Hsien-pei) Tu-ku family, has been described, without convincing evidence, as a Nestorian Christian.[12] But however Turkish the roots of the dynasty may have been and whether that in any way contributed to its favorable reception of the first known Christian mission to China, the rule of the T'ang was thoroughly Chinese and began with the subjugation and incorporation into the empire of the Turkish confederations along the Old Silk Road.[13]

Alopen and the First Christian Mission
(635–649)

It was precisely along that Old Silk Road in the "golden age" of the T'ang that history produced the first recorded notice of the missionary entry of the Christian faith into the Chinese empire. It is inscribed in stone on the broad face of the famous Nestorian monument thus:

> When the accomplished Emperor T'ai-tsung [627–649] began his magnificent career in glory and splendour . . . behold there was a highly virtuous man named Alopen[14] in the Kingdom of Ta-ch'in. Auguring from the azure sky he decided to carry the true Sutras with him, and observing the course of the winds, he made his way through difficulties and perils. Thus in the ninth year of the period named Chen-Kuan [635] he arrived at Chang'an. The Emperor despatched his Minister, Duke Fang Hsuan-ling, with a guard of honour, to the western suburb to meet the visitor and conduct him to the Palace. The Sutras were translated in the Imperial Library. [His Majesty] investigated "the Way" in his own forbidden apartments, and being deeply convinced of its correctness and truth, he gave special orders for its propagation . . .[15]

The long inscription on the monument, which contains more than 1,756 Chinese characters and about 70 Syriac words together with a long list of names of Persian or Syrian missionaries, is dated 781 ("the second year of the Chien-chung period" in Chinese, "the year 1092 of the Greeks"[16] in Syriac), but it pinpoints the arrival of Alopen's mission at the year 635 ("the ninth year of the Chen-kuan period," i.e., the ninth year of the emperor T'ai-tsung). Alopen was probably not the first Christian in China. Sassanid Persia had opened trade connections with China in the fifth century,[17] and Nestorians were numerous in the merchant class of those times, but the earliest recorded (though somewhat ambiguous) reference to a Nestorian Christian in China proper is the mention of a Mar Sergis as head of an important immigrant family from the "western lands" who settled in 578 in Lint'ao about three hundred miles west of Chang'an in Kansu along the Old Silk Road.[18]

The warm welcome by a T'ang emperor was an unanticipated providence. Had Alopen arrived ten years earlier, in the reign of the first T'ang emperor, Kao-tsu, he might well have been expelled. Though the religion of northern China was basically Buddhist and though his family had been strongly Buddhist, the first T'ang emperor, Kao-tsu, had turned anti-Buddhist, accepting the usual Confucian argument that Buddhism was alien and un-Chinese. An imperial edict of 626 ordered the secularization of large numbers of Buddhist priests, and the reduction of Buddhist and Taoist temples in the capital from some 130 to "three Buddhist and one Taoist."[19]

Buddhism he rejected as Western. "The Buddha was of the West. His words were mischievous and he was far from us," argued his chief adviser.[20] The same xenophobic argument would have applied to Christianity.

But in that same year, 626, Kao-tsu's second son, T'ai-tsung, seized power, assassinating his elder brother the crown prince and forcing his father to abdicate. [He was greatly helped in his palace coup by militant Buddhist priests.] In [return for their support he reversed the antiforeign, anti-Buddhist policies of his father, built Buddhist temples, and ordered the ordination of three thousand priests.[21] The twenty-two years of his reign were a period of wide religious toleration as, for the sake of political stability, he tried to balance the competing claims of China's three major faiths, Buddhism, Taoism, and Confucianism. An unplanned by-product of this toleration was the opening of the door to the introduction of other faiths, especially from Persia by way of central Asia. In 631 he admitted the "Hsien" ("Heaven-Spirit") religion into the capital. This was probably Zoroastrianism or Manichaeism.[22] In 635 he welcomed Christianity.

[Three years later, according to the monument, he issued an [edict of universal toleration,] carefully neutral but specifically granting approval to the propagation of Christianity throughout the empire:

> The Way had not, at all times and in all places, the selfsame name; the Sage had not, at all times and in all places, the selfsame human body. [Heaven] caused a suitable religion to be instituted for every region and clime so that each one of the races of mankind might be saved. Bishop Alopen of the Kingdom of Ta-chin, bringing with him the Sutras and Images, has come from afar and presented them at our Capital. Having carefully examined the scope of his teaching, we find it to be mysteriously spiritual, and of silent operation. Having observed its principal

and most essential points, we reached the conclusion that they cover all that is most important in life. Their language is free from perplexing expressions; their principles are so simple that they "remain as the fish would remain [if] the net [of language] were forgotten." This Teaching is helpful to all creatures and beneficial to all men. So let it have free course throughout the Empire.[23]]

One [reason for this tolerant attitude, apart from its political uses, may well have been the emperor's intense interest in a revival of learning] [He was not only a warrior but also a patron of the arts.] The library he built in his capital next to his palace is said to have contained two hundred thousand volumes and must have been as impressive as any library in the world of that time, including the great library of Alexandria. He kept eighteen distinguished scholars in the library working on a standard edition of the Confucian texts and commentaries.[24] [When he discovered that the new faith the Persian missionaries had brought was the religion of a book, he was immediately interested.] He [received Alopen as an honored guest, brought him into the library, and ordered him to begin translating his Scriptures. It was an auspicious beginning for the Christian mission to China.]

In the [year of the edict of toleration, 638,] the [first Christian church was built in China at the capital Chang'an, the largest city in the world.] The [emperor himself gave orders for its construction with funds from his own treasury. In his calculatedly tolerant way he had done the same for the construction of Buddhist and Taoist temples.] As a [mark of special honor he sent his portrait to be hung on the church wall. By that time, as the edict noted, there were twenty-one monks in China, probably all Persian.]

Beginnings of Persecution (656–712)

When T'ai-tsung died in 649, he was succeeded by his son Kao-tsung (649–683) who, following in his father's footsteps continued to favor the Nestorians and "added the final embellishment to the true sect" as the monument tablet states. In every prefecture, it claims, he established "illustrious monasteries." The number is probably a pious exaggeration, for that would mean 358 Nestorian monasteries or churches in China in the last half of the seventh century. There are, however, records of at least eleven such churches in that period, and there may well have been more. There were two in Chang'an, and one each in Loyang, Chou-chin (where the tablet was probably found), Chengtu and Mt. Omei (both in Szechwan), Lingwu, and four other places.[25]

Sometime during his reign the tablet states that Kao-tsung gave Alopen the title "great patron and spiritual lord of the empire," which suggests either honorific but nominal recognition by the Chinese court or that with the consent of the Persian patriarch in Seleucia-Ctesiphon he was elevated to the rank of archbishop (metropolitan) of China. There is no corroborating evidence in Persian sources, however, to confirm such an appointment so early.[26]

Despite these signs of progress, omens of difficulties to come began to appear in the long reign of Kao-tsung. Though like his father he was tolerant toward Christians, he became increasingly inclined to favor Buddhism, not so much from personal preference as through intense pressures from his second wife, the empress Wu and her family.[27]

For all his kindnesses to the Christians, this emperor did them one almost fatal disservice. He took one of his deceased father's concubines into his own palace ménage. This was a sin by all standards—Confucian and Buddhist as well as Christian—and he paid dearly for his sin. The concubine and later empress Wu Hou (sometimes written as Wu Chao) is the "wicked witch" of traditional Chinese history. Taken into the harem of the great T'ai-tsung at the age of twelve in 638 and forced into a Buddhist monastery when he died, the widow, as tradition has it, longed to return to the corridors of power, took advantage of a visit to her nunnery by the new emperor and so beguiled him by her beauty, which not even a shaved head could dim, that against all advice he took her out of the monastery and made her his concubine. The cruelly ambitious girl soon bore the emperor a son and callously murdered her own baby in order to throw the blame on her great rival, the queen. The queen was degraded and Wu Hou took her place, chopping off the hands and feet of her rival and leaving her to die. Kao-tsung was never able to shake himself free from her spell. The new queen completely dominated the government for the remaining twenty-seven years of his reign.[28] When he died in 683, the first days of growth for the Christian church in China ended, and under the Buddhist empress dowager, the ruthless Wu Hou, the days of persecution began.

Wu Hou deposed her two sons from the throne in quick succession and took power herself, setting up a new dynasty (690–705) in her own name. Powerful, single-minded, and selfish, she took a Buddhist monk as a lover, but despite this flouting of Buddhist conventions she remained fanatically pro-Buddhist, and in return the Buddhists hailed her as an incarnation of their messiah, the Maitreya

Buddha.[29] She officially declared Buddhism the state religion in 691 and about the same time apparently began privately to encourage opposition to the Christians. Persecution began in 698 when mobs sacked the Christian church or monastery in the eastern capital, Lo-yang, which had been a Buddhist stronghold for six hundred years. Outright persecution was never official but within fourteen years it had reached the western capital at Chang'an where hostile crowds were allowed to invade and violate the historic Nestorian church in the west ward of the city, the first Christian church in China.[30]

Recovery of the Church (712–781)

The violation of the great Chang'an church was the last, dying spasm of the anti-Christian opposition, for by that time the power behind the persecutions was dead. The usurping Empress Wu, eighty years old, had retired in 705. Wicked she may have been, but without her strong presence the empire fell into disorder until a capable grandson, the emperor Hsuan-tsung ascended the throne for the longest reign of the T'ang dynasty (712–756). For the church this was a period of recovery, but for China it proved to be the beginning of gradual decline of its empire, which now was forced to confront on its western borders the rise of a new rapidly expanding world power, the Arabs.

As we will see in the next chapter, the Arabs swept into Persia in 636, soon captured the capital, Seleucia-Ctesiphon, and forced the Persian shah to flee east into central Asia. From Balkh òn the Silk Road he appealed in vain for Chinese help. He was killed by his own retainers, but his son, the Persian crown prince, escaped and finally found refuge, in 677, in the T'ang-dynasty capital, Chang'an. When he died the Chinese gave his son, the last of the great Sassanid royal line, the title "King of Persia," but he died in exile at the T'ang court in 707, only a short walk away from the church of the Persian missionaries.

Whether he ever met the missionaries or not is unknown. Perhaps the report of a "great Persian chieftain," thought by some to have been a Nestorian, who was appointed "imperial envoy" to the tribes of Tibet by the emperor Kao-tsung (649–683), son of the emperor who had treated Alopen with such kindness, is somehow related to this high-ranking community of Persian refugees in the Chinese capital.[31] Better attested is the fact that not much more than one hundred years later the great Timothy I, Nestorian patriarch in Baghdad (778–820), referred to Christians in Tibet, in one of his let-

ters and indicated that he intended to consecrate a missionary metropolitan for them.[32]

It was not a homogeneous community, that gathering of expa-
triate Persians in the Chinese capital—a Zoroastrian court in exile, a
mixture of Manichee, Christian, and Zoroastrian traders, and a small
missionary outpost of a Persian minority religion, the Nestorians—
all of them cut off by Arab conquest from their own vanished imperial homeland far away. Fortunately for the Nestorians in China,
the T'ang dynasty did not yet regard the Arabs as a threat to China,
for its enemies at the moment were not in the far west but in the
north, the Turko-Mongols and the Koreans. So though China
granted asylum to the last of the Sassanids, it refused to go to war
for Persia against Islam. Such a war would have completely broken
the last link between the Nestorian mission and its home base in
Persia.

That link had always been tenuous at best. More than forty-five
hundred miles of incredibly difficult land travel and an even greater
distance by sea separated Seleucia-Ctesiphon and Baghdad from
Chang'an. When the Nestorian monument was erected in 781, the
inscription was dated "in the days of the Father of Fathers, my Lord
Hanan-Ishu [Hananyeshu II], Catholicos, Patriarch," but Hananyeshu had been dead for a year or more. News traveled very slowly
between Persia and China.[33] In the records of the Nestorian synods
there is not even a mention of China, and the earliest reference
among Persian Nestorians to an organized church there is a passing
mention in a letter of the patriarch Timothy I after 781.[34] From the
same patriarch's letters we learn the name of a metropolitan bishop
in Chang'an, David, who might possibly have been the "priest
David" mentioned in Syriac on the monument.[35] It is safe to say that
the metropolitanate in China was probably not created until after
650, perhaps by the Patriarch Saliba-Zakha between 712 and 728.[36]
The seat of the metropolitan must have been Chang'an, and the
official word of the announcement might have been brought by the
Nestorian bishop Chi-lieh, who accompanied an Arab embassy to
China in 713 and reached the capital in 732. However there is no
record in any Persian church sources of the actual appointment of
the first metropolitan of China.

As this mention of an eighth-century Christian bishop traveling
to China with an Arab embassy confirms, the Arab conquest of Persia did not prove as disastrous to the Nestorian home church as had
been feared. Up until the reign of Harun al-Rashid, of *Arabian Nights*
fame (786–809), the Muslim Arabs were on the whole unexpectedly tolerant of the Nestorian minority in conquered Persia. They

destroyed Zoroastrianism, for that was the state religion of the conquered Sassanids. But toward the Christian minority they were rather lenient. The Umayyad caliphs (661–750) granted a considerable measure of religious freedom to the Nestorians and employed them widely in high administrative positions. It was from the Nestorians that the Arabs learned much of the Greek science and learning they were later to pass on to a Europe, which, overrun by barbarian invasions, was losing much of its ancient Greek heritage.

The Arab conquest, therefore, did not immediately interrupt the mission to China. In fact, some say that the spread of Arab empire across Asia actually stimulated Nestorian missions.[37] Nestorian missionaries accompanied Arab embassies to China, taking advantage of Arab sea and trade routes to the Far East that were far superior to the long and arduous hardships of the Old Silk Road. The first Arab embassy to China was sent by the third caliph, 'Uthman, who was Muhammad's father-in-law. It reached the T'ang court in the early years of Kao-tsung, about 651. A second followed much later in 713, and it was probably with this embassy that the Nestorian bishop arrived, named both on the Nestorian tablet and in T'ang dynasty documents as Chi-lieh. He probably ministered mainly to the large foreign community in the expanding port city of Canton and established important contacts with government officials. In 732 he accompanied a third Arab envoy to Chang'an where he was honored at court by the gift of "a purple-coloured vestment besides fifty pieces of silk."[38] It is clear that Muslim Arabs were not averse to making use of a hundred years of Nestorian experience in China by employing the Persian missionaries as interpreters and advisers.

That same year, 732, Charlemagne's grandfather, Charles Martel, first checked the advance of Islam westward, a seemingly irresistible advance that until then stretched virtually unchallenged from southern France and Spain across North Africa and on through Persia into the grasslands and deserts of central Asia as far as the borders of China itself. Rome was still shrinking in power and size. The imperial giants of the world were the Arabs and the Chinese, and as the Arabs moved east and the Chinese west, the two empires were on a collision course. By 741 Arab armies threatened Tibet. Alarmed at the prospect that Arab and Tibetan armies might unite in a fearsome alliance against him, the Chinese emperor Hsuan-tsung sent his trusted general, a Korean named Kao Hsien-chih, racing east to forestall the union. Marching his troops across the high heart of central Asia in one of the most extraordinary campaigns of Asiatic history, General Kao drove his men north and west of the Pamirs across the mountainous heart of the continent. There, in 747, he successfully broke up the Arab-Tibetan coalition. But Arab power was at its height, and four years later in 751, at Talas in what is now the isolated central Asiatic Republic of Kirghistan, his Chinese army was defeated. "This encounter," writes E. O. Reischauer, "although fought in an area remote from the centers of Chinese and Arab power, was one of the most fateful battles of history. It marked the end of Chinese control over Central Asia and the beginning of five centuries of steady military decline for the Chinese Empire. It also marked the beginning of the Arab conquest of Central Asia. Soon the area was permanently converted to Islam."[39]

As for the church in China, these years between 712 and 781 were years of greater progress than in any other period of the two and a half centuries of the life of this first community of Christians in China. The tablet proudly reports the restoration of church buildings, and the granting of imperial portraits to be hung in them, and its authors express their exultation at these signs of a return to court favor in extravagant prose:

> Although the [countenances] shine forth with such dazzling brilliance, yet the gracious Imperial faces are so gentle that they may be gazed upon at a distance of less than a foot.[40]

Perhaps they may be excused for the fulsome language. The persecution was over. Five royal brothers of the emperor had come in procession to inspect the rebuilding of the ravaged church, an unprecedented sign of favor.[41]

New missionaries arrived from Persia by sea in 744 with a bishop named Chi-ho and were invited to say mass at the palace. In October 745 the official Chinese name for the Christian religion was changed from "the Persian religion" to "the Syrian (Ta-ch'in) religion," perhaps in belated recognition that the capital of the Arab empire had moved in 661 under the Umayyad caliphate to Syrian Damascus from its earlier Arab power bases Medina and Kufa. This was a help to the Christian missionaries who were often confused with the adherents of the Persian religions, Zoroastrianism and Manichaeism. The imperial edict of Emperor Hsuan-tsung reads:

> The Persian religion of the scriptures, starting from Ta-ch'in and coming to preach and practise, has long existed in the Middle Kingdom. When they first built monasteries, ["Persian"] was consequently taken for the name. Wishing to show men the necessity of correct knowledge of the original [we decree that] the Persian Monasteries at the two capitals must be changed to Ta-ch'in [Syrian] Monasteries. Those which are founded in [other] departments and districts of the empire will also observe this.[42]

But while the church was basking in royal favor, the dynasty was weakening politically despite its apparent recovery from the usurpation of Empress Wu. Her grandson Hsuan-tsung's long reign, which started so auspiciously, ended in disaster. His abdication is often cited as the beginning of the decline of the T'ang dynasty but was only a grim revelation of corruptions, loss of central control, and weakening loyalties that had been building up for years. In 755 a Turkish general of the emperor revolted and seized and sacked the capital, destroying the great library. The seventy-year-old emperor, mourning more over the death of his favorite concubine, Yang Kwei-fei, in the flight from Chang'an than in the loss of his capital, had no will left to fight. He abdicated in favor of his son, Su-tsung (756–762), who with the help of the famous general Duke Kuo Tzu-i, the friend of the Christians, was able to rally three armies and defeat the leader of the insurrection, An Lu-shan.

With these three armies, three foreign religions visibly flourished in the last half of the eighth century. The first, always the strongest and no newcomer, was Buddhism, which was regulated but supported by the emperor and was popular in his royal army. The second, the latest arrival, was Islam, which was the religion of an Arab army sent by the caliph in Baghdad as a gesture of friendship when internal divisions in the Islamic homeland had ended a century of almost unbroken Arab military expansion. The third was Nestorian Christianity, which, along with its sometime look-alike Manichaeism, was becoming the religion of many of the emperor's Uighur allies. Through the persistent labors of Nestorian missionaries—both priests and traders—on the Old Silk Road the Christian faith had spread widely among this warlike tribe, which was now the dominant Mongol power on the northwest frontier.

The Uighurs formed a semiautonomous empire in 744 that controlled the Silk Road and adopted Manichaeism as its state religion about 762, finding that faith more pliable and religiously flexible than Christianity. It was through the Uighurs that the Mongols received their alphabet, which had been brought to them through Persian Sogdia by Nestorians and Manichaeans.[43]

Three men stand out in this period as influential in the Nestorian church in China: a non-Christian protector, Duke Kuo Tzu-i; a powerful Christian benefactor, Issu (or Yazdbozid); and his son Ching-ching (or Adam),[44] who was the priest to whom most credit is given for the translation and composition of the inscription on the Nestorian monument.[45]

Duke Kuo Tzu-i, the greatest general of this period, has been called by historians "one of the finest characters in all Chinese history."[46] Under Emperor Su-tsung he ended the An Lu-shan rebellion. Under the next emperor, T'ai-tsung (762–779), he saved the country from a Tibetan invasion and quelled a mutiny of the Uighurs. It was said that his very name was enough to frighten enemies away. Much of the favor the Nestorian church enjoyed at court during these years may well have been due to the patronage of this powerful leader and his impressive family. He had eight sons and seven sons-in-law, all in high position in government, and by the time he died in honor at the age of eighty-five early in the reign of Te-tsung (called Chien-chung on the tablet), his extended family is said to have numbered three thousand. It is not likely that he was himself a Christian, but he was at least a great friend of the church.[47] He is a symbol of the military protection the church enjoyed.

Issu was both a Nestorian priest and a high-ranking general in the Chinese army. The tablet has a great deal to say about him, which is not surprising since he was responsible for its erection. He is called "Warden of the Palace Gate, Vice-General of the Northern Marches, Joint Probationary Imperial Chamberlain,"[48] "claw and tusk" to the duke, and "ear and eye" to the army. It was not at all unknown for priests, whether Buddhist or Christian, to serve in the army. Issu, whose Persian name was Yazdbozid, was the son of a priest-missionary who had come from Balkh (now in northern Afghanistan), and though described as a married monk, he wore the white robes of a secular priest in worship. The monastic clergy wore black. In Chang'an, Issu's position as assistant to the Nestorian bishop and his reputation for clothing the poor, healing the sick, and serving the poor was as notable a benefit to the church's mission as his fame in war. This unusual combination of social, ecclesiastical, and military prominence makes him a symbol of the political connections that gave considerable influence to Christianity under the rule of the T'ang in this period.

A third Christian leader of the eighth-century church in China was Adam, a bishop and missionary-scholar so famed for his knowledge of Chinese language and literature that even Buddhist missionaries came to him for help in translating their own sacred books. His Chinese name was Ching-ching, and it was he who composed the elegant inscription on the tablet. He is mentioned as a prolific translator in a later document from the tenth century, *The Book of the Honored Ones*, which contains a bibliography of thirty-five Chinese works of which thirty, it claims, were translated by Adam ("Priest Ching-ching, Bishop of this Religion"). The titles listed are ambiguous, but those that seem to be Bible translations or paraphrases suggest that whatever parts of the Christian Bible were

submit or present

rendered into Chinese in the three hundred years of T'ang Christianity (or at least the only parts translated by Adam) were perhaps, the Gospels and portions of the book of Acts, Paul's Epistles, the Psalter, and, less certainly, parts of the Pentateuch and Isaiah. At least four of the works on the list survive, and if not directly the work of Adam are probably from his century, the eighth.[49]

One in particular is worth quoting, a beautiful translation into Chinese of the Syriac *Gloria in Excelsis Deo*, which is still sung in Syriac by Nestorian Christians. I borrow below the free translation by J. Foster, who points out, "we of the West had to wait till the Reformation to sing this noble praise in our own tongue. Chinese Christians beat us by more than seven centuries!"[50]

> The angels of the highest heavens in deepest reverence praise.
> Great earth its universal peace doth call again to mind.
> And man's own spirit-nature knows his refuge and repose.
> The Powers Three in Alaha their gracious Father find. . . .
>
> Great Holy-One Who art adored by all, Messiah Thou,
> We praise Thy gracious Father for His ocean-store of love.
> Great Holy-One Who dost proceed from Him, the Holy Ghost,
> We know Thy will shall here be done, all human thought above.[51]

If the four Tun-huang documents discovered in the twentieth century in caves along the Old Silk Road and attributed to the eighth-century Chinese church[52] are dated correctly, some weight must be given to the charges of syncretism leveled against T'ang Christianity. At least two of them, "On Mysterious Rest and Joy" and "On the Origin of Origins," though credited to Adam, are more Taoist than Christian, containing only a few Christian words here and there, such as "Nazareth," "Messiah," "the true Luminous Teaching," and the Syriac word for "Spirit" (phoneticized *lo-ha*).[53] But whether Adam is to be charged with the sub-Christian flavor of these writings or not, there is no question that he was well known and active in non-Christian circles. A Japanese scholar, J. Takakusu, discovered a revealing reference to him in a catalogue of late eighth- and early ninth-century Buddhist translations. This Buddhist work written by a priest in a Buddhist temple only a few blocks from the old Nestorian church in Chang'an relates that the famous Buddhist missionary, Prajna, reached the Chinese capital in 782 from northern India and and was asked to translate the Buddhist sutras he had brought with him. "But because at that time Prajna was not familiar with the Hu [Uighur] language nor understood the Chinese language," he asked "Ching-ching (Adam), a Persian priest of the mon-

astery of Ta-ts'in" to help with the translation, and the two
missionaries, one Buddhist and the other Nestorian, translated
seven volumes.[54]

⎡This incident of interfaith collaboration has further ramifications, *developments or consequences, from one to complicated problem* both missionary and theological.⎦ In the same Buddhist monastery
with the Indian missionary there were living and studying at the
time (804) two equally famous figures in the history of Japanese Buddhism. One was the great Kobo Daishi (Kukai), founder of Japan's
Shingon ("true word") sect of Tantric Buddhism, who carried back
with him to Japan as one of his treasures the sutra on which Prajna
and Adam might have been working together.[55] The other scholar
from Japan in Chang'an at the time was Dengyo Daishi (Saicho),
founder of the Tendai (or Lotus) school of Japanese Buddhism, out
of which grew such later popular reform movements as Pure Land,
Zen, and Nichiren Buddhism. Few have so powerfully influenced
the whole course of Buddhism in Japan. Who can resist the temptation, therefore, to speculate on⎡how much a chance association of
these men, through Prajna, with the cooperative Nestorian scholar
Adam, might possibly have seeded Christian ideas into the variations of northern Buddhist belief as it developed in Japan?⎦

Our more immediate concern, however, is the reverse of that
question. ⎡How far did the flow of Buddhist ideas in the opposite
direction, into Christian thought, change the theology of T'ang-
dynasty Christianity? And how far did theological compromise, if
such there was, contribute to the disappearance of this earliest Chinese Christianity?⎦

Disappearance of the Nestorians from China
(781–980)

Sometime in the two hundred years between the erection of the
Nestorian tablet in 781 and the decades of chaos and civil strife that
followed the shattering fall of the T'ang dynasty in 907, the Nestorian church completely vanished from its beachhead in China. An
Arab record written at the end of the tenth century reads: *a first achievement that opens the way for further developments; a foothold*

> In the year 377 (A.D. 987), in the Christian quarter [of Baghdad] behind
> the Church, I met a monk from Najran who seven years before had
> been sent by the Catholicos to China with five other clergy to set in
> order the affairs of the Christian church. . . . I asked him for some
> information about his journey and he told me that Christianity was just
> extinct in China; the native Christians had perished in one way or

another; the church which they had used had been destroyed, and there was only one Christian left in the land . . .[56]

This report of the disappearance of Nestorianism from China is cor-roborated by the fact that from the eleventh century to the rise of the Yuan dynasty in the thirteenth century Nestorians cease to be men-tioned in Chinese historical records except in the past tense.

What happened to wipe out a church that had seemed on the verge of such great missionary success in China? No one has yet given a completely satisfactory answer though many theories have been advanced.[57] All are reasonable but no single one can be con-sidered definitive. The source materials are too scant to allow any-thing but tentative conjectures. The most plausible suggestions can be grouped in four categories: religious, theological, missiological, and political.

In the first category of reasons for the disappearance of the church belong the religious persecutions that fell upon Christians in the ninth century. For the most part they were not specifically anti-Christian but were part of a rising tide of xenophobia and sectarian religious strife that grew in direct proportion to the weakening of national unity under a succession of ineffectual emperors. The most severe religious persecutions in the entire history of the usually tol-erant T'ang dynasty occurred between 840 and 846 in the reign of the moody and superstitious emperor Wu-tsung. They were directed against what Confucianists branded as the followers of "foreign re-ligions," primarily Buddhists, but also Manichaeans and Christians.

First to feel the edge of attack were the Manichaeans in 843. They had come to China from Persia under the protection of the Uighur "empire," whose central Asiatic cavalry had helped the T'ang dynasty's rise to imperial power. For two hundred years Uighur khans were the loyal allies and principal military support of the Chi-nese against the restless, encroaching tribes of the northwest. Mis-sions from Persia, both Nestorian and Manichaean, had worked among them with considerable success, the Manichaeans apparently somewhat more successfully than the Christians, at least in the Ui-ghur capital.[58]

But in the early 830s a rival tribe, the Kirghiz Turks clashed with the Uighurs for control of central Asia and defeated them, driving some as refugees into China proper, while others survived in scat-tered groups around the Tarim River basin where they are numerous and racially distinct to this day. No longer protected by Uighur mil-itary and political power, their dominant religion, Manichaeism, was ordered destroyed. A decree of Wu-tsung in 843 directed the confiscation of Manichaean books, the public burning of their images, and appropriation of their property by the government. In Chang'an seventy Manichaean women, probably nuns, were put to death.[59] It is not at all improbable that some of the hatred spilled over onto the Nestorians, who were also Persian in origin and often confused with the Manichaeans.

It was the Buddhists, however, who suffered most severely under the main thrust of the attack on foreign religions. In 845, the Taoist Wu-tsung issued a second decree against non-Chinese religions. The text survives in the *Old T'ang Records:*

> It was commanded that the Board of Worship inspect all monasteries throughout the Empire. . . . The grand total of monasteries amounted to 4600, of hermitages 40,000, of monks and nuns 265,500. . . . [Only] one monastery will be left in each (Prefecture). . . . In the subsidiary prefectures, monasteries would be altogether abolished. In . . . (Chang'an) and (Loyang) it is requested that ten monasteries be left, with ten monks for each. . . . On days of pilgrimage it is fitting that officials should go to Taoist temples. . . . Bronze images, bells and clappers should . . . be turned into coinage. . . . As for the Ta Ch'in (Syrian) (and) Muh-hu-fu (Zoroastrian) forms of worship, since Buddhism has already been cast out, these heresies must not be allowed to survive. People belonging to these also are to be compelled to return to the world . . . and become taxpayers. As for foreigners, let them be returned to their own countries, there to suffer restraint . . .[60]

The decree goes on to state that more than three thousand Nestorian and Zoroastrian priests or monks were compelled to "return to the world."[61]

If Buddhism, powerful as it was under the T'ang dynasty, which has been called "the Buddhist age of China,"[62] never completely recovered from that nationwide persecution, how much more crippling must have been its effect on the small, scattered groups of Christians in the empire? It took more than four hundred years for Buddhism to regain under the Mongol dynasty something of the numerical strength it had enjoyed in the reign of the T'ang.[63] Even a belated edict of toleration issued by the new emperor, Hsiuan-tsung (847–859), was probably not enough to save the Nestorians from virtual extinction. It read:

> Whereas in the last year of Hui Ch'eng there was an inspection of monastic buildings, although these religions are called foreign they are fundamentally of no detriment to the truth. . . . Too extreme a reformation does not appear to be a happy augury. . . . If there are former

famous monks surviving, they may again repair and erect [the temples] and live there, the local officials having no power to forbid them.[64]

A second factor often adduced as a primary reason for the failure of the Nestorians in T'ang China is theological. They are accused of watering down the faith. Years ago J. Legge of Oxford dismissed the theology of the Nestorian monument as "swamped by Confucian, Taoist and Buddhist ideas, a certain degenerate, nominal Christianity."[65] But does the evidence of the surviving texts support such excessive condemnation?

Much depends on a cautious use of all the few source materials available. In 1888 Legge had only the Nestorian monument on which to base his sweeping judgment. A few years later he might not have been so dogmatic. He had no way of knowing that beginning in the 1890s a treasure trove of priceless T'ang and pre-T'ang historical, religious, and genealogical records would be uncovered and would dramatically expand our knowledge of China and of Christianity in China in the days of the T'ang. At the Tun-huang oasis, sealed away for almost a thousand years behind a wall in a Buddhist cave-temple where the southern branch of the Old Silk Road skirts the waterless wastes and sand dunes of the Takla Makan desert, startled scholars began to find among hundreds of ancient manuscripts and written fragments some unmistakably Christian documents. More were soon found around Turfan on the northern branch of the Silk Road trade route.[66] To the study of religion in China in the T'ang dynasty they are as important as the Dead Sea Scrolls to first-century Judaism or the Nag Hammadi trove to the understanding of Gnosticism.[67]

At least nine such Christian manuscripts in Chinese have been identified. Four of them may well date back to the very beginnings of the Nestorian mission to China in the seventh century and have been called "the Bishop Alopen documents."[68] Four more have been attributed to the period of the Nestorian monument, the eighth century, and are called by Saeki "the Bishop Cyriacus (Bishop *Chi-lieh*) documents."[69] A ninth document, the *Book of Praise* (or *Book of the Honored Ones*), is much later, probably from the tenth or early eleventh century.[70] To these Chinese sources should be added two groups of later Syriac documents that were also discovered.[71]

The dating, of course, must be considered tentative, and the evidence is still too scant for dogmatic conclusions, but there is enough to suggest that the theology of the Nestorians in China may have been more orthodox, especially in its earlier years, than the monument taken by itself has led some to believe. Comparing the earlier with the later writings, though the Chinese style improves, the theology does in fact seem to weaken. However, even the later documents, including the monument inscription, do not quite justify the wholesale charges of heresy leveled against those early missionaries. Only in two of the works, the "Sutra of Mysterious Rest and Joy" and the "Sutra on the Origin of Origins," are the touches of Christian language so few and so vague and the Taoist imagery so vivid that the mixture is closer to syncretism than to missionary contextualization.

[Three questions must be asked and answered][First] how much of what the Western opponents of Nestorianism have long branded as "Nestorian heresy" is found in the early Chinese evidence? A brief answer would be: scarcely any at all. The second question is, how much of historic Christian orthodoxy do these surviving materials transmit into the Chinese language? The brief answer to this would be: a great deal. The third question, the one that arouses the most debate is, how much has the translation process been distorted by a syncretized theology?

Taking the first question first, there is virtually nothing in the documents that can be conclusively labeled "Nestorianism" even by the standards of the Chalcedonian orthodoxy of Constantinople and Rome. The major charges leveled against the Nestorians in the great controversy of the fifth century had revolved around their Christology, which, it was claimed, weakened the deity of Christ, focused too much on his humanity, and destroyed the integrity of his person by dividing the deity from the humanity, thereby producing the heresy of "two persons" in the Messiah. As proof of orthodoxy they demanded that the Nestorians repudiate their condemnation of the title "God-bearer" (*theotokos*) for the Virgin Mary. Nestorius had said, "Mary did not bear the Godhead," and preferred the phrase "Christ-bearer."[72] But there is no Nestorian diatribe in China against the use of the title *theotokos* ("God-bearer," or Mother of God) for Mary. It is true that the Syriac documents from the Tun-huang–Turfan area do frequently use "Mother of Christ" rather than "Mother of God" in praise of the Virgin,[73] but they do not revive the old debate. The missionaries apparently simply left their foreign ecclesiastical quarrels at home for the sake of their mission in the Far East.

Furthermore, the Christology of the documents is essentially orthodox. There is one possible exception. A phrase in the inscription on the monument can be translated either "divided by nature," or "divided Person."[74] If the former is correct, it would be orthodox. "Divided by nature" does not contradict the Chalcedonian formula "two natures in one person." But "divided Person" favors the Antiochene Nestorian emphasis on separation of the two natures, which their opponents interpreted as heretical denial of the unity of the "person." In Chinese, however, the distinction between "person" and "nature," so crucial to the controversialists at Chalcedon, is virtually impossible to translate. The best solution may well be simply to let the translation bypass the problem, as does J. Foster[75] when he renders it in English, "Whereupon (one person of) our Trinity became incarnate," thereby transferring the suggestion of division from the nature of the Son to the action of the Trinity in sending him forth in mission. The Chinese ideographs (san i fen shen, literally, "three one divide body") can be interpreted as more of an affirmation that Christ was still divine and part of the Trinity, though in becoming human he entered the realm of the finite, than that he became two persons, which was what the Nestorians were accused of teaching.

A reference in a later document, the Book of Praise (literally, Honor Discourse, or in Chinese Tsun-ching), which is dated perhaps 150 years later than the monument,[76] makes the orthodoxy of the early Nestorians in China, on this point at least, more clear. In its opening ascription of praise to the Trinity is the phrase, the "above Three Persons [san shen, i.e., Father, Son, and Holy Spirit] uniting together into One and the Same Body [i t'i]." It would be difficult to get much closer to today's orthodox Chinese terminology for the Trinity, "three persons in one substance," san wei, i t'i.[77]

The second question that must be asked is this. If the documents are not heretical, how much of basic orthodoxy do they contain? This is easy to answer. They hold to all the essentials. Of course it is obvious in the older materials, the "Alopen documents," that the first missionaries quite understandably were struggling with the Chinese language.[78] Nevertheless they managed remarkably well to transmit the core of the biblical Christian message with considerable strength and detail into a difficult foreign tongue. The earliest manuscript of all, the "Jesus-Messiah Sutra," which, if Saeki's dating is correct, may have been written by Alopen himself, is a brief summary of the good news of the gospel, which the Persian missionaries had brought to China.[79] It begins boldly with the name of Jesus (two Chinese characters, Hsu-t'ing, which we are told in seventh-century T'ang China could be pronounced "Ye-su").[80] Then there follows a poetic theological introduction of two basic doctrines: of God as Lord of all life and of human nature as wayward and sinful.[81]

The "Jesus-Messiah Sutra" proclaims that God, the Lord of Heaven, is omnipresent and all-knowing but invisible "like the wind." He is the only source and support of human life. Yet many ignore him and make their own gods, "saying, we have each our own special Lord of Heaven." So sin came into the world, "because our original ancestor committed the sin of disobedience in 'the Garden of seed-and-fruit bearing (trees).'" People make for themselves "images of gold, silver and copper, . . . of clay or wood." They should rather "fear the Lord of Heaven and should correct themselves by repenting of the sins they have committed."

A second section[82] seems to be an attempt to interpret and adapt the Ten Commandments as rules for Christian life in a Chinese culture. First are the three great "precepts": "obey the Lord of Heaven; obey the Sacred Superior [the Emperor]; and obey father and mother." Seven other commandments follow: be kind and good to all living beings; do not kill; do not commit adultery; do not steal; do not covet; do not "forge a false document," and do not "serve the Lord of Heaven . . . at another's expense."

Added to these "ten commandments" are other important rules of life. Do not take advantage of the defenseless; do not turn away from the poor; feed the hungry even though they be your enemies; help those who work hard; clothe the naked; do not deride the disabled; care for widows and orphans; and do not quarrel among yourselves or take each other to court before the magistrates. But above all, "obey . . . the Lord of Heaven."

The final section is a succint and faithful condensation of gospel history.[83] Since all have sinned, God "made the Cool Wind (i.e., the Holy Spirit) to enter a virgin named Mo-yen (Mary)." He thus made clear his power so that all might believe and "return to 'good relation.'" Mary bore "a son named Ishu (Jesus)" . . . the Messiah. He was baptized by John, and "a voice sounded, 'The Messiah is my son.'" His will is to lead all to give up their false gods. He gathered twelve disciples, raised the dead to life, gave sight to the blind, healed the sick, and cast out devils. But those who did not believe accused him falsely and brought him before *P'i-lo-tu-ssu* (Pilate), who said "I cannot see any crime deserving of death. I cannot kill this (man)." But the wicked ones forced him to sentence Jesus to death. So the Messiah,

> gave up His body . . . to be sacrificed for the sake of all mankind . . . , suffering death for them. [They] bound Him upon the tree between two highwaymen . . . and the earth quaked and the mountains were rent and all the gates of graves in the world were opened. . . . Seeing these things, how can anyone [say] that he does not believe what is taught in the Sutras. Those who live or die . . . for the sake of the Messiah are faithful believers, and so . . .[84]

Here the manuscript, torn and falling apart, abruptly ends. We do not know how much of it has been lost.

[This earliest summary of the Christian faith in Chinese scarcely supports the remark of a missionary friend quoted with approval by J. Legge.]When asked why Nestorianism failed, his reply was, "How could it succeed? There was no gospel in it."[85] On the contrary, however much its labored translation into the Chinese may have rendered the wording unfamiliar, the "Jesus-Messiah Sutra" is full gospel. The essentials are there from original sin to the substitution-ary atonement,[86] from the virgin birth to the cross,[87] from the Ten Commandments to repentance and correction,[88] from eternal pun-ishment for unbelief to salvation by faith not works,[89] from condem-nation of idols to love of enemies,[90] from the equivalent of the Pauline injunction to "be subject to the governing authorities" (Rom. 13:1) to "feed the hungry, clothe the naked and care for widows and orphans."[91]

Even more detailed are some of the summaries of biblical history in other documents found at Tun-huang and Turfan. The fourth of the "Alopen documents," for example, the "Discourse on Almsgiv-ing," which dates itself at "641 years since the time of the birth of the Messiah,"[92] contains a lengthy condensation of the Sermon on the Mount, a vivid description of the crucifixion, and a full account of the Gospel record of the Resurrection.

[On two pivotal theological points, Christology and evangelism,] it takes a clear, strong stand with the historical Christian tradition. It states that salvation is through Christ alone: "Only by . . . the suc-cour [help] of the Holy Mystery through the Messiah can all people be saved."[93] And on that foundation, it adds this significant re-minder of the Great Commission:

> The disciples of the Messiah understood clearly . . . and went forth into all parts of the world, (doing what was commanded . . .): "Preach . . . my words to all the races of mankind, mark them in the name of the Father and the Son and the Holy Wind, and make them decide to observe completely what was taught by me . . . for I shall be with you even to the end of the world."[94]

But debate still rages over the thesis that it was the willingness of the Nestorian missionaries to accept theological compromises in order to make Christianity comprehensible in the alien religious thought-world of seventh- and eighth-century China that led in the end to their shockingly complete disappearance in the ninth and tenth centuries. So the third question must still be addressed. How syncretistic did it really become?

Over against the many signs of orthodoxy described above, there are more passages than some would like to admit that clearly suggest compromise and accommodation beyond the usually acceptable limits of missionary adaptation. Why is the name Buddha used so frequently for "God" in the earliest document, the "Jesus-Messiah Sutra"?[95] What are we to make of such statements as these in the same Christian work:

> All the Buddhas as well as the Kinnaras and the Superintending Devas and Arhans can see the Lord of Heaven.

> Man . . . in extremity will always do honour to the name of Buddha.

> Those who have received the Lord of Heaven and His teaching must first teach other people to worship all Devas. Then the Buddha will be worthy to receive the suffering and to set up the Heaven and the Earth and make this world exist only for perfecting the concatenation of the causes of existence in purity and dignity.[96]

Could these be merely lapses of communication between Persian missionaries who did not yet read Chinese and their Chinese helpers who knew no Persian? To the Chinese, the best translation of "angels and archangels and hosts of heaven" may well have been "Buddhas, Kinnaras, and Superintending Devas." And as for the missionaries in those first few months in China while they were still suffering from the initial shock of exposure to the mysteries of Chinese ideographs, when the emperor suddenly ordered them to translate their sacred books it would be no surprise if "the name of the Lord" could become "the name of Buddha" without their even noticing the difference.

But can they be excused so easily? By 638, three years after Alopen's arrival, which is the earliest proposed dating of the "Jesus-Messiah Sutra," the Persians should have been familiar with the name of the Buddha. Moreover, even in the eighth century, a hundred and more years later, both in the second group of Tunhuang–Turfan documents and on the monument itself, the same kind of confusion in the use of religious language persists. Buddhist, Taoist, and Confucian imagery is still pervasively present and potentially misleading although, particularly on the monument, it is used with more restraint and sophistication.

Because the monument's inscription is the most certainly authentic of all the sources of our knowledge of T'ang-dynasty Christianity and because it contains the most systematic condensation of the theology of the period, it may be worthwhile simply to quote its fairly brief theological introduction in an appendix (see appendix) and let readers decide whether the gospel is critically diluted or better communicated to Chinese minds by the missionary attempt to accommodate Christian truth to Chinese language and imagery. Criticisms, however harsh, cannot lightly be dismissed. "We cannot but deplore the absence from the inscription of all mention of some of the most important and even fundamental truths of the Christian system," wrote J. Legge long ago.[97]

But[to give the monument its due, there is little evidence of a serious deterioration of orthodoxy since the founding of the mission.] On examination,[what was written on the stone is as orthodox as what was written by the first missionaries a century and more earlier.]The long inscription begins with an unmistakably trinitarian statement: "There is one . . . , the Origin of the Origins . . . our Aloha ["God"], the Triune mysterious person." This can be taken as a reference to the first person of the Trinity, since the next two mentions of the Trinity focus in order on the Son ("one Person of our Trinity, the Messiah") and on the Holy Spirit ("the Holy Spirit, another Person of the Trinity").[98]

Then follows in orthdox order the doctrines of creation, of human nature as created originally good, of sin and the Fall, and of salvation through the Messiah, "the Lord of the Universe," who was born of a virgin and "appeared upon earth as a man."

[The paragraphs on Christian life are a satisfying balance of piety and social responsibility, of worship and witness. There is a call to evangelize and a repudiation of slavery, a summons to prayer and a challenge to give up personal wealth for the sake of the poor, a declaration that all people are equal and a reminder to the faithful that seven times a day they should pause for worship and for praise.]

[It is in the section on salvation that the borrowings from non-Christian religious concepts are most prominent and troubling.] Phrases like "the eight cardinal virtues," "hanging up the . . . sun," and "He took an oar in the vessel of mercy" are Buddhist, the last named clearly speaking either of the Amitabha Buddha's boat, which carries the faithful to the Western Paradise, or to the Buddhist goddess of Mercy, Kuan-yin, who is herself the "boat of mercy." The "new teaching of non-assertion" is Taoist. "How to rule both families and kingdoms" is Confucian. The "two principles of nature" (*yin* and *yang*) is basic Taoist and Confucian theory of the structure of the universe.[99]

But the[line between distortion and adaptation or contextualization is difficult to define, and a baptized use of alien terminology and customs has long and honorable precedents in the history of the expansion of Christianity stretching back through Gregory the Great's counsel of adaptation to pagan English ways to the hellenizing of the gospel sometimes attributed to the apostles Paul and John.

Far more troubling than its adaptations are its omissions. There is no mention of Christ's crucifixion,[100] death, and resurrection on the tablet. There is little emphasis on the centrality of Scripture, which was so basic a premise of Nestorian theological studies in Persia.[101] But it is hardly fair to expect a complete systematic theology to be written on the face of even a reasonably large stone slab, and the crucifixion, death, and resurrection of the Lord are all amply emphasized in the other Nestorian documents of the time, as we have already noted. Indeed, the first of the documents, the "Jesus-Messiah Sutra," contains clear warning against the syncretistic pluralism of those who say "we each have our own special Lord of Heaven. Each faith has its abiding (merit)."[102]

From very different theological perspectives a consensus has emerged that from the limited evidence available T'ang-dynasty Christianity was neither heretically Nestorian nor fatally syncretistic. Its heresy from the Protestant viewpoint, if its last surviving Chinese text, the tenth-century *Book of Praise,* is any indication, "was not its Christology but [its] necrolatry. . . . Strange is it indeed," observes J. Young, "that the mission which set out with such vision, zeal and sacrifice and promise to bring life to lost men, should end its days engrossed in prayers for the dead."[103]

Nor was it syncretistic enough to satisfy the Buddhists who persecuted it. Adam, who wrote the inscription, may sometimes have carried tolerance too far, as when he collaborated with the newly arrived Buddhist missionary from India, Prajna, who needed help in translating his sacred books into Chinese, but J. Foster concludes that as far as the Buddhists were concerned, Adam "was dangerous not because he was making Christianity too Buddhist, but because he was trying to make Buddhism too Christian."[104]

Still another explanation sometimes given for the disappearance of the church in tenth-century China was that it never became Chinese; it remained a church of foreigners. The missionaries were Persian. Their names on the monument are almost entirely Syriac or the Chinese equivalents for Syriac names. Adam (Ching-ching), who composed its inscription, was from central Asia. The last glimpses of the church, from the Tun-huang and Turfan discoveries, come not from the Chinese center but from tribal territory in central Asia far out toward the northwest border. And yet, the very fact that almost all the information we have about that church comes from documents in the Chinese language points to a degree of successful rootage in the national culture that may well have had more far-reaching fruit than the rare glimpses of it that survive can convey. Had it been a religion of foreigners and for foreigners, why are there not more Syriac traces and less Chinese?

If any conclusion at all can be drawn from these various attempts to explain the cause of the collapse of the Chinese church in T'ang dynasty China, it should probably be that the decisive factor was neither religious persecution, nor theological compromise, nor even its foreignness, but rather the fall of an imperial house on which the church had too long relied for its patronage and protection. Dependence on government is a dangerous and uncertain foundation for Christian survival. When a church writes "Obey the Emperor" into its version of the Ten Commandments it is writing a recipe for its own destruction.

The critical turning point in the fortunes of the T'ang empire was the An Lu-shan rebellion of 756. The inscription on the monument was written twenty-five years later and in some ways marks the peak of Nestorian influence in China. Imperial dynasty and missionary church both began their decline in the last half of the eighth century. It would be a hundred years before the great persecution of religions, including the Christian church, began, and the dynasty recovered and survived for another one hundred and fifty years with intermittent moments of glory. But the basic weakening of the central imperial power can be traced to the uprising that almost ended the dynasty in the middle of the eighth century. It no longer had the power that had once opened up China to foreign religions and had largely protected them for a century and a half. It never again quite so completely controlled the restless tribes on the central Asiatic border or the powerful warlords that kept order in the outer provinces at the price of social regionalism.

In the last quarter of the eighth century the center itself began to slip into decline. Palace eunuchs usurped more and more of the powers of the weakening throne. Of the last twelve T'ang emperors who ruled China in the ninth century and the first decade of the tenth, only four can be described as effective.[105] The whole country was in turmoil. Towns and whole provinces fell to rebels who were particularly cruel to foreign religionists. In the fall of Canton, for example, in 878, an Arab traveler reported that a hundred and twenty thousand Muslims, Jews, Christians, and Zoroastrians were slaughtered.[106]

The last T'ang emperor, a fourteen-year-old boy, saw all his nine brothers put to death by the commander of his army, and shortly thereafter, fearing for his own life, he abdicated in 907. Thus ended the greatest dynasty China has ever known, [protector of religious liberties and for the most part the friend of Christians] As it disappeared, [the church, which had relied too much upon its favor, disappeared with it in the violence and civil wars of the age of "the ten kingdoms" and "the five dynasties" and their most significant successor, the Sung dynasty (960–1279), which split China up within itself for the next three hundred and seventy years.[107] The discouraged Nestorian monk in the Christian quarter of Baghdad was probably right in 987 when he said, "There is not a single Christian left in China."[108]

Thus the first wave of Christian advance to the Far East came in with one change of the political tide and was washed away by the next. But it was not to be the last of Christianity in China.

NOTES

1. A. de Gouvea, *Joznado do Ancebispo Dom., Meneses . . .*, French translation by J. B. Glen, *Histoire orientale, des grans progrès de l'eglise Catholique, Apostolique et Romaine* (Anvers: Verdussen, 1609), 3, 4, 6–9, as cited by A. C. Moule. For a critical analysis of such China traditions about St. Thomas, see Moule's *Christians in China Before the Year 1550* (London: Society for Promoting Christian Knowledge, 1930), 10–26. He believes (p. 22) that the earliest mention of Christianity in China is by Arnobius, writing about A.D. 300 and reporting without any supporting evidence Christian success "among the Seres" (*Arnobii Disputationum adversus Gentes Libri Octo* [Rome, 1542], fol. xviiv). A few phrases in the Syriac breviary are also often quoted such as "By St. Thomas the Chinese also with the Ethiopians have turned to the truth," but these cannot be proved to trace back further than a seventh-century revision of the Nestorian liturgy, by which time Nestorian missions had already reached China (Moule, 11f.).

2. M. Ricci, *Opera storiche del P. Matteo Ricci, S.I.*, vol. 2, pp. 289–93, cited by Moule, *Christians in China*, 1-g. See D. Leslie, *The Survival of the Chinese Jews* (Leiden: Brill, 1972); also T. Torrance, *China's First Missionaries: Ancient "Israelites,"* 2d ed. (Chicago: D. Shaw, 1988).

3. Many authorities (Moule, *Christians in China*, 27; J. Foster, *The Church of the T'ang Dynasty* [London: SPCK, 1939], 35; J. Legge, *The Nestorian Monument of Hsi-an Fu in Shen-Hsi, China* [London: Trubner, 1888]; A. Wylie, "Nestorian Monument at Si-ngan Fu, China," *Missionary Review* 8, no. 3 [May–June 1885]: 184–92; and others) date the finding at 1625, but Saeki argues convincingly for 1623 (P. Y. Saeki, *The Nestorian Documents and Relics in China*, 2d ed. [Tokyo: Maruzen, 1951], 28–35). J. Dauvillier concludes either date is reasonable, in his introduction to Paul Pelliot, *Recherches sur*

les Chretiens d'Asie Central et d'Extrême-Orient, 2.1. *La Stèle de Si-ngan-fou* (Paris: G. Mandel, 1983).

4. See chap. 1, p. 14.

5. The distinction made by modern writers between "Mongols" and "Turkic" in that period is more linguistic than racial, as noted before.

6. In later periods, if we may anticipate, the same patterns of shifting tribal dominance continued outside the Wall. In the eighth century power moved to the Uighur Turks; in the tenth to the Mongol Khitan (from whom the West took the name "China"); and finally in the thirteenth century, as the whole world was to discover when the Mongols of Genghis Khan seized control, Mongolia became the power center not only of central Asia but of the whole continent. (See the chronology in Rene Grousset, *The Empire of the Steppes: A History of Central Asia,* trans. N. Walford [New Brunswick, NJ: Rutgers Univ. Press, 1970], xxiv.)

7. See extracts from Procopius, *De bello Gothico,* and Theophanes in H. Yule, rev. H. Cordier, *Cathay and the Way Thither* (London: Hakluyt Society, 1913–16), 1:23f., 203ff. Procopius mentions "monks" coming from India; but Theophanes writes of only one "from the country of the Seres." On the same subject and its historical context see Grousset, *Empire of the Steppes,* 82f.

8. J. Asmussen, *Xuastvanift: Studies in Manichaeism* (Copenhagen: Munksgaard, 1965), 149.

9. See chap. 10, pp. 207ff.

10. Yule, Cathay, 1:115, citing Theophylactus Simocatta, v. 10, and Theophanes, *Chronographia,* A.M. 6081.

11. Though not declared until 589, the Sui dynasty's beginning is usually antedated to the year of the overthrow of the ruler of Northern Chou in 581.

12. E. H. Parker, *A Thousand Years of the Tartars* (London: Kegan Paul, Trench and Trubner, 1895; reprint by Dawsons of Pall Mall, 1969), 129. Parker bases his history on extensive Chinese sources, but for this unlikely statement he cites only an unnamed and unsupported European source. All the available evidence indicates that the royal women of the Tu-ku family were devout Buddhists. One such, the wife of the Sui emperor Wen-ti, would not allow her husband to take a concubine, but that hardly indicates she was a Christian. More probably she was simply a strong-minded, jealous wife. See A. F. Wright, "T'ang Tai-Tsung and Buddhism," in *Perspectives on the T'ang,* ed. A. F. Wright and D. Twitchett (Taiwan: Rainbow Bridge, 1973), 240.

13. Rulers of the T'ang dynasty (618–907) of most significance in the history of the church were:

1. Kao-tsu, 618–626	7. Hsuan-tsung, 712–756
2. T'ai-tsung, 626–649	[An Lu-shan rebellion,
3. Kao-tsung, 649–683	755–757]
6. Empress Wu (Wu Hou), 690–705	8. Su-tsung, 756–762

9. T'ai-tsung, 762–769	16. Wu-tsung, 840–846
10. Te-tsung, 779–805	17. Hsiuan-tsung, 846–859
12. Hsien-tsung, 805–820	

The best overall history of the period, though it makes little mention of Christianity, is *The Cambridge History of China*, vol. 3, *Sui and T'ang China, Part I*, ed. D. Twitchett and J. K. Fairbank (Cambridge: Cambridge Univ. Press, 1979). For a critical analysis of Chinese source materials for the period, see especially pp. 589–906.

14. A-lo-pen. He is known to history only by his Chinese name, whose three ideographs (lit., "ah-silk-origin") make no more sense literally translated than my own name in Chinese, Ma-pu san-le (lit., "thrice-joyful horse-blanket"). They merely represent the transliteration of the sound of his unknown Syriac name into Chinese characters. The usual conjecture is that the three syllables (the common structure of Chinese names) represent the Nestorian name "Yabh-allaha," though Saeki argues for "Abraham" (*Nestorian Documents*, 84f.

15. The translations of this and other Chinese Nestorian documents by the Japanese scholar P. Y. Saeki, which I use extensively, are in some instances more a conjectural paraphrase than a critical translation and are admittedly no more free from errors than other translations, but they are a more complete collection and they do preserve better than some the flavor of the Chinese, particularly as they note the use of Taoist, Buddhist, and Confucian terminology. The full inscription, with notes, is in Saeki, *Nestorian Documents*, 57–112, a revised and enlarged edition (1951) of his earlier 1937 work. References will be made below to a number of other translations, the best of which are: Wylie, "Nestorian Monument"; Legge, *Nestorian Monument*, 3–31, with Chinese text and translation; Moule, *Christians in China*, 34–52; and Foster, *The Church of the T'ang Dynasty*, 134–151. The earliest translation, into Latin, was made by an anonymous Jesuit in 1625, perhaps Nicholas Trigault, the first European to see the newly discovered stone slab.

16. The first year of the Greeks is usually set at 311 B.C. by our calendar. There are some differences of computation in the Syrian churches on this varying between 309–313 B.C. (see Mingana, "Early Spread of Christianity in Central Asia," 331). The date 751 given in the article on "Nestorianism" in the *Encyclopedia of Asian History* (New York: Scribner, 1988), vol. 3 is a typographical error.

17. See p. 290 n. 8.

18. Saeki, *Nestorian Documents*, 86, gives the Chinese reference.

19. Wright, "T'ang Tai-Tsung," 245f. The motive may have been as much financial as anti-foreign, for the royal treasury confiscated much of the wealth of the closed temples.

20. The adviser was the strong Confucianist, Fu I. See Wright, "T'ang Tai-

Tsung," 245; and, for the quotation from the rescript, Foster, *Church of the T'ang Dynasty*, 40.

21. Wright, "T'ang Tai-Tsung," 247. See his careful analysis (pp. 256–63) of the complexities of T'ai-tsung's policy of balancing favors sometimes toward Buddhism, sometimes toward Taoism (from whose founder the T'ang emperors claimed descent).

22. Zoroastrianism was sometimes called the "Hsien" religion in T'ang records, sometimes "mu-hu-fu"; Manichaeism was also sometimes named "Hsien," sometimes "Mo-ni." Moule, *Christians in China*, 69f.

23. There is independent witness to this edict in a shorter version first found by A. Wylie in the tenth-century encyclopedia of T'ang-dynasty administration, the *T'ang hui yao*, vol. 49. The translation above is from Saeki, *Nestorian Documents*, 57f., 456. The strong syncretistic tinge in the religious philosophy of the rescript is not necessarily the theology of the Nestorian authors of the inscription, though it does imply some measure of approval of pluralism. Their inclusion of the full text of the edict may simply have been due to the missionaries' eagerness to establish their own right to evangelize, along with the similar rights of other religions in China.

24. Twitchett and Wright, *Perspectives on the T'ang*, 16; Foster, *Church of the T'ang Dynasty*, 39.

25. Foster, *Church of the T'ang Dynasty*, 61.

26. If Alopen was made metropolitan, it must have been after 650 (for before the accession of Kao-tsung there is not even the suggestion of a metropolitan appointment in China). See below, nn. 32, 34, and Foster's more positive discussion of the possibility of Alopen's promotion (*Church of the T'ang Dynasty*, 62ff.).

27. See S. Weinstein, "Imperial Patronage in the Formation of T'ang Buddhism," in Wright and Twitchett, eds., *Perspectives on the T'ang*, 266f.

28. For traditional Chinese historiography concerning this period, see J. MacGowan, *The Imperial History of China*, 2d ed. (Shangai: American Presbyterian Mission Press, 1906), 302ff. Cf. the more balanced treatment of Empress Wu's reign in Twitchett and Fairbank, *Sui and T'ang China*, vol. 3 in *Cambridge History of China*, 245ff.

29. Wright and Twitchett, *Perspectives on the T'ang*, 5. In the same volume (302ff.) see Weinstein's well-documented account of the empress's patronage of Buddhism, "Imperial Patronage."

30. See Foster, *Church of the T'ang Dynasty*, 67ff.

31. A stone tablet now in Japan, which is neither as specifically Christian nor as well authenticated as the Nestorian tablet, identifies this Persian governor of Tibet as Alohan and states that he set up a monument proclaiming "the Holy Way to the wild tribes." But nowhere does it indicate that he was Nestorian, and the reference to "Holy teaching" could as well be Buddhist as Christian. Saeki, *Nestorian Documents*, 453–55.

32. On the subject of a metropolitanate in Tibet, see J. Dauvillier, "Temoignages nouveaux sur le Christianisme nestorien chez les Tibetans," in *Histoire et institutions des Eglise orientales au Moyen Age* (London: Variorum Reprints, 1983), 2:165. His sources are indicated there and in the preceding article (1:293–96). On Buddhism, see also G. Tucci, *The Religions of Tibet* (Berkeley, CA: Univ. of California Press, 1980).

33. See the lengthy discussion of the date by Saeki, *Nestorian Documents*, 101ff.

34. See J. Dauvillier, "Temoignages nouveaux."

35. As Saeki in his first edition (1916) noted, p. 187. Thomas of Marga, secretary of the Nestorian patriarch in Baghdad (832–840), cites the "letters of Mar Timothy" as the source of information about "David, Metropolitan of Beth Sinaye [China]," *Book of Governors*, trans. E. A. W. Budge (1893), 2:448.

36. Following the suggested listings of W. G. Young, *Patriarch, Shah and Caliph* (Rawalpindi, India: Christian Study Center, 1974), 192.

37. See H. C. Luke, *Mosul and Its Minorities* (London: M. Hopkinson, 1925).

38. Bishop Chi-lieh's Syriac name is sometimes given as Bishop Gabriel, and sometimes as Cyriacus, both of which names appear on the monument but are not necessarily to be identified with Chi-lieh. J. E. Heller, in *Das Nestorianische Denkmal in Singan* (1897, p. 48) argues for Gabriel, but Saeki prefers Cyriacus (*Nestorian Documents*, 93). The notice of Chi-lieh's 713 visit is in a tenth-century document, *Ts'e-fu yuan-kwei* ([Peking: 1960], 546); the notice of the second visit, in 732, is in the same work (p. 971). The documents are translated by Saeki, *Nestorian Documents*, 92–94. For Chi-lieh's mixed reception in Canton by government officials see Shiu-Keung Lee, *The Cross and the Lotus* (Hong Kong: Christian Study Centre on Chinese Religion and Culture, 1971), 7f.

39. E. O. Reischauer and J. K. Fairbank, *East Asia: The Great Tradition* (Boston: Houghton Mifflin, 1958), 190f.

40. Saeki, *Nestorian Documents*, 60.

41. "The Prince of Ning-kuo and four other royal princes" says the inscription.

42. *T'ang hui yao*, vol. 49, fol. 10v. Trans. Moule, *Christians in China*, 67. The Arabs moved their capital again in 762 to Baghdad.

43. See C. Mackerras, *The Uighur Empire* (Canberra: Australian National University, 1988).

44. The tablet seems to contain the name of two Adams, one a priest and composer of the inscription, the other a deacon. It designates the deacon as the son of Issu. But an argument can be made that the two are the same. See Foster, *Church of T'ang Dynasty*, 108n. Saeki (*Nestorian Documents*, 81) distinguishes one from the other.

45. Asmussen, *Xuastvanift*, 140–50; and see also C. Mackerras, *The Uighur*

Empire, and H. Howorth, *History of the Mongols,* 5 vols. (1876; reprint, Taiwan: Ch'eng Wen, 1970), 1:182f.

46. MacGowan, *Imperial History,* 325.

47. See Foster, *Church of the T'ang Dynasty,* 80, 97.

48. The translation of the titles is Foster's, *Church of the T'ang Dynasty,* 144. Cf. Saeki, *Nestorian Documents,* 63.

49. See Saeki, *Nestorian Documents,* 34–37, 273–76, 469f.; Foster, *Church of the T'ang Dynasty,* 107–14. The Chinese title of the document containing the bibliographical list is *Tsun-ching* (lit., "Honour Sutra"). Saeki calls it *Book of Praise* and gives reasons for dating it in the tenth century (pp. 249–53); Foster names it *Book of the Honoured Ones.* The identification of biblical books is partly guesswork, e.g., the Psalter (lit., "David Sacred King Book"); Pauline portions (lit., "St. Paul Book); and Gospels (*a-ssu-ch'u-li-yung sutra,* which has been tentatively translated *evangelium*).

50. Foster, *Church of the T'ang Dynasty,* 154. Saeki titles this *Gloria* "The Nestorian Motwa Hymn in Adoration of the Holy Trinity" (*San-wei-tsan-sutra*), *Nestorian Documents,* 266ff. The other three eighth-century documents sometimes attributed to Adam (Bishop Ching-ching) are "Hymn in Adoration of the Transfiguration of Our Lord" (*T'ung-chen sutra*), "The Sutra of Mysterious Rest and Joy" (*Chih-hsuan-an-lo-sutra*), and "The Sutra on the Origin of Origins" (*Hsuan-yuan-chih-pen-sutra*). All four come from the Tun-huang cave discoveries of the early twentieth century.

51. Foster, *Church of the T'ang Dynasty,* 135–37.

52. The "Gloria," the "Hymn in Adoration of the Transfiguration," the "Sutra of Mysterious Rest and Joy," and the "Sutra on the Origin of Origins." See the complete list below (n. 68, 69, 70) of Chinese documents attributed to the T'ang period.

53. Saeki, *Nestorian Documents,* 262ff., 303.

54. J. Takakusu cites as his source the *Chen-yuan Hsin-ting Shih-chao Mu-lu* (which Saeki calls "The Catalogue of [the Books of] Teaching of Shakya [Buddha], A.D. 785–804") in the "Bodleian Library, Japanese, 6500, vol. 8 fol. 5vo." (Saeki, *Nestorian Documents,* 462ff.). See Takakusu's own English translation of part of the text in *T'oung-pao* (Shanghai, 1896), 589–91. Saeki, *Nestorian Documents,* 113ff.

55. Saeki, *Nestorian Documents,* 84, 462ff. The *Satparamitta* sutra. There are more than ten thousand Shingon temples in modern Japan. The connection with a Nestorian missionary is purely speculative.

56. Abu'l Faraj, *Kitab al Fihrist,* cited by Moule, *Christians in China,* 75f. The last phrase may be read also as "not one Christian left." P. Hitti attributes the encounter to al-Nadim, a Baghdad librarian and book dealer (d. 995), "to whose catalogue we possibly owe that scholarly and remarkable work *al-Fihrist,*" Hitti, *History of the Arabs from the Earliest Times to the Present,* 5th ed. (New York: Macmillan, 1951), 356, 414.

57. Some list three reasons, some five, and Saeki has ten. See K. S. Latourette, for example, in his *A History of Christian Missions in China* (New York: Macmillan, 1929), 58f.; and Foster, *Church of the T'ang Dynasty*, 116ff.; and P. Y. Saeki, "The Christian Mission Beyond the Roman Empire in China and Japan," *The Mainichi Newspaper* (Tokyo, 30/31 July 1959). I owe this reference to J. M. L. Young, "The Theology and Influence of the Nestorian Mission to China, 635–1036," *Reformed Bulletin of Missions* (Philadelphia), in two parts, vol. 5, no. 1 (November 1969) and no. 2 (April 1970).

58. See Mackerras, *Uighur Empire*, 8ff., 168n. 232.

59. Foster, *Church of the T'ang Dynasty*, 128f., citing the *New T'ang Records* (*Hsin-T'ang-yao*) and "a book called *Collected Memoirs of the Founder of Buddhism*."

60. Foster, *Church of the T'ang Dynasty*, 121f., quoting the *Chiu-T'ang-shu* (Old T'ang Records), written about 941, which with its eleventh-century revision (*Hsin-T'ang-shu*) comprise the full dynastic history of the T'ang compiled by the dynasty that succeeded it, as was customary. Peking, 16 vols., and 20 vols. (1975).

61. Literally "Ta-ch'in" (Syrian) and "Mu-hu-fu" (which may refer to both Manichaeans and Zoroastrians).

62. K. S. Latourette, *The Chinese: Their History and Culture*, 2d ed., rev. (New York: Macmillan, 1941), 211.

63. Foster, *Church of the T'ang Dynasty*, 126.

64. Foster, *Church of the T'ang Dynasty*, 127.

65. Quoted by Foster, *Church of the T'ang Dynasty*, 112, but I have not been able to find this statement in any of Legge's works available to me.

66. On the Tun-huang and Turfan discoveries see Twitchett and Fairbank, *Sui and T'ang China*, vol. 3 in *Cambridge History of China*, 46–47. The documents date from the fifth to the tenth centuries (406–995). They provide "primary documentation which has survived intact . . . and which is totally independent of the historian or of the processes of official historiography."

67. The documents had been preserved because paper was scarce and the back of the pages was used for copying Buddhist literature. Other finds were made near Turfan, north and west of Tun-huang on the trade route. Only from about 1907 did the materials begin to be translated.

68. The four that Saeki describes as the "Bishop Alopen Documents" and dates to the seventh century, are as follows:

1. "The Jesus-Messiah Sutra" (*Hsu-t'ing Mi-shih-so-ching*), acquired by J. Takakusu in 1922 and dated by Saeki to 635–638; and three "Discourses on Monotheism" acquired by K. Tomeoka in 1916 and dated by Saeki to 641. But Foster (46f.) notes that Saeki ignores a sixth-century calendar change by Dionysius Exiguus that might change this dating to 638.

2. "Parable, Part II: A Discourse on Monotheism" (*Yu-ti-erh*).

3. "On the Oneness of the Lord of the Universe" (*I-tien-lun-ti-i*).

4. "Discourse on Almsgiving" (*Shih-tsun-pu-shih-lun-ti-san*).

For notes and text, see Saeki, *Nestorian Documents*, 113–247.

69.Saeki rejects the attribution of these eighth-century works to Bishop Ching-ching (Adam) who composed the Nestorian inscription in 781 (*Nestorian Documents*, 248ff.). For easier reference I will continue to number consecutively the Tun-huang and Turfan documents that may be Nestorian:

5. "Hymn in Adoration of the Holy Trinity" (*Ta-chin-san-wei-meng-to-san*) discovered by Prof. Pelliot in 1908 and often referred to as the Tunhuang "Gloria in Excelsis."

6. "The Sutra on the Origin of Origins" (*Hsuan-yuan-chih-pen-sutra*), which bears the date 717.

7. "Hymn in Adoration of the Transfiguration" (*Ta-sheng-t'ung-chen-kwei-fa-tsan*), a short fragment dated 720.

8. "The Sutra of Mysterious Rest and Joy" (*Chih-hsuan-an-lo-sutra*), which is strongly Taoist.

9. "The Book of Praise" (lit., "Honor Discourse," *Tsun-ching*), discovered by Prof. Pelliot in 1908 at Tun-huang.

70. Saeki also calls this "the Nestorian Diptychs" (pp. 5, 8). For notes and translation see Saeki, *Nestorian Documents*, 248ff., 273ff. See above, n. 49.

71. One group is from a collection in Peking, and another was discovered at Turfan. See notes and translation in Saeki, *Nestorian Documents*, 315–33, 334–47.

72. See the discussion in chap. 9, p. 173.

73. Saeki, *Nestorian Documents*, 338, 339.

74. Wylie, "*Nestorian Monument*," 187; Moule, *Christians in China*, 36.

75. Foster, *Church of the T'ang Dynasty*, 136.

76. See Saeki, *Nestorian Documents*, 253 for the date, 276 for the text. He thus disagrees on good grounds with Moule's date of ca. 800 for the document (Moule, *Christians in China*, 52).

77. As Young points out, "Theology and Influence," 9f. See Saeki, *Nestorian Documents*, 273. But see the counterargument of R. Suter that the phrase is more Nestorian ("The words *san-i-fan-shen* in the inscription on the Nestorian Monument," *Journal of the American Oriental Society* 58 [1938]: 384–93).

78. Moule sympathetically remarks about the "Jesus-Messiah Sutra": "The extraordinary style, which in very many places quite baffles the translator, and the large number of wrongly written words justify Prof. Haneda in guessing that it is the work of a foreigner who had not progressed very far in the study of the Chinese language" (*Christians in China*, 58). It has been asserted that Chinese offers only two alternatives to the translator: translation by transcription, which is essentially confusing, or translation by interpretation, which lends itself to misinterpretation.

79. Saeki (*Nestorian Documents*, 125-46); references follow his sentence num-

bering. On the possibility of authorship by Alopen, see Saeki, 115ff. Foster agrees with the early dating, but takes issue with Saeki'l translation of the title, which he calls "The Book, An Introduction to the Messiah" (Foster, *Church of the T'ang Dynasty*, 45ff.). See also Lee Chang-Sik, "A Study of a Chinese Nestorian Sutra," *N. E. Asia Journal of Theology*, No. 13 (Sept. 1974).

80. Saeki, *Nestorian Documents*, 145.

81. "Jesus-Messiah Sutra," sentences 1–79 of the Saeki translation, pp. 126–32.

82. "Jesus-Messiah Sutra," sentences 79–149, Saeki, pp. 132–40.

83. "Jesus-Messiah Sutra," sentences 149–206, Saeki, pp. 140–46. The last page or pages are missing.

84. "Jesus-Messiah Sutra," sentences 198–206, Saeki, p. 145f.

85. Legge, *Nestorian Documents*, 54.

86. "Jesus-Messiah Sutra," sentences 54 and 199 (Saeki, pp. 130, 199). Document no. 4, "On Almsgiving" is even more specific about the atonement: "He came to suffer the punishment on His body in accordance with the law. Thus He suffered the punishment in love for you in order that the seed and nature of Adam in you may be won and transformed by Him" (sentence 98f., Saeki, p. 214).

87. "Jesus-Messiah Sutra," sentences 150f. and 201ff.

88. "Jesus-Messiah Sutra," sentences 90–111 and 78.

89. "They shall be cast out into Hell forever" ("On Almsgiving," sentence 262; Saeki, p. 230); "All the human beings who have faith will come to the Lord of the universe . . ." (sentence 157, Saeki, p. 220); and "He . . . bore all the sins of mankind, and for them He suffered the punishment Himself. No meritorious deed is necessary . . ." ("On the Oneness of the Ruler of the Universe," sentences 136, 137, Saeki, p. 185).

90. "Jesus-Messiah Sutra," sentences 63ff., 105, 115.

91. "Jesus-Messiah Sutra," sentences 91, 113–27 (Saeki, pp. 134, 136ff.).

92. "On Almsgiving," Saeki, p. 226. See his note on p. 246.

93. "On Almsgiving," sentence 103, Saeki, p. 214.

94. "On Almsgiving," Saeki, pp. 206–19; The Great Commission translated in sentences 145, 146, p. 218f., and a shorter version in sentences 228, 229, p. 227.

95. Saeki marks the instances (pp. 119, 126–29, 134–37, etc.).

96. "Jesus-Messiah Sutra," sentences 4, 20, 96–97; Saeki, pp. 125, 127, 134f.

97. Legge, *Nestorian Monument*, 34.

98. See the more complete text in the appendix to this chapter, and compare that with Young's analysis of the literal word-order of the Chinese in his "Theology and Influence," part 2, p. 9.

99. The phrases are found in the appendix to this volume.

100. Though Moule tentatively suggests that "hanging up the bright sun" may be "a veiled allusion to the crucifixion" (*Christians in China*, 37n. 20).

101. Though both Wylie's and Moule's translations are stronger on this point than Saeki's. See Wylie, "Nestorian Monument," 187; Moule, *Christians in China*, 37.

102. "Jesus-Messiah Sutra," sentence 23, Saeki, p. 127.

103. Young, "Theology and Influence," pt. 2, p. 20.

104. Foster, *Church of the T'ang Dynasty*, 113f.; and Saeki, *Nestorian Documents*, 34.

105. Te-tsung (779–805), Hsien-tsung (805–820), Wu-tsung (840–846) and Hsiuan-tsung (846–859).

106. Foster, *Church of the T'ang Dynasty*, 130, citing Abu Zeid who reached China in 878 and wrote *Achbar ul Sin wal Hind* (*Observations upon China and India*).

107. There is a fleeting reference to Christians still surviving in China in 942 in the report of an Arab poet, Abu Dulaf, who had been sent from the court of the Samanid ruler of Bokhara with an embassy to China. He reported seeing Christians and churches in several unidentified Chinese cities. A. S. Atiya, *A History of Eastern Christianity* (London: Methuen, 1968), 262. However, it is not clear whether these were in China proper or to the east of the Chinese border in central Asia.

108. See above, p. 302.

Chapter *16*
Christianity and
Early Islam (622–1000)

"When 'Umar b.'Abd al-Aziz came into power [A.D. 717] they [the Christians of Najran] complained to him that they were in danger of extinction . . . , that the continual raids of the Arabs overburdened them with heavy taxes for revictualing them, and that they suffered from the unjust treatment of [the governor]. By 'Umar's orders their census was taken, and it was found that they were reduced to one-tenth of their original number . . ."

—Baladhuri (d. 892)
Translated by Hitti

TWO men, Muhammad in Asia and Charlemagne in the West, may well have changed the history of the world more decisively and dramatically than anyone else in the second five hundred years of the Christian age (500 to 1000). Muhammad (Mohammed) is a symbol of Christianity's near defeat in Asia, Charlemagne of its near triumph in the West. In the history of the church, defeat is never final and triumph is never quite complete, but for Asian Christianity, the loss of the Middle East to Islam was more than the loss of its home and birthplace; it marked the first permanent check to Christian expansion in all the previous six hundred years of the history of the church.

The Muslim conquest of the mid-seventh century, which so abruptly terminated the Persian era of Asian church history, was not the end of Persian Christianity. It was a time of upheaval of empires but it did not bring down upon the church the immediate havoc of religious persecution and massacre with which it is popularly associated. On the contrary, there is considerable evidence that the Nestorians in Persia welcomed the Arabs as liberators from Zoroastrian oppression and that the Arab conquerors in turn found it more to their advantage to segregate and use the Christians than to exterminate them. Gibbon's unforgettable metaphor of Christians facing a "a Mohammed with the sword in one hand and the Koran in the other" is doubly misleading. To Muhammad the "holy book" was the Bible; the Koran (al-Qur'an) appeared only after his death. And a better metaphor than the "sword," as far as Muslim-Christian relationships were concerned, would be a net, for after the conquest Christians found themselves caught in the web of Islam but not usually under its sword. The net, if not always comfortable, was at least safer than the sword.

The unknown author of the *Chronicle of Seert*, a history of the Nestorians written perhaps as early as the ninth century,[1] describes the Persian Christian reaction to the victors in very positive terms. Neither Christians nor Jews were required to give up their religion, and although they were heavily taxed, on the whole they were not violently abused. The Christian chronicler says:

> The Arabs treated them with generosity and by the grace of God (may He be exalted) prosperity reigned and the hearts of Christians rejoiced at the ascendancy of the Arabs. May God affirm and make it triumphant!

Muhammad and the Christians

As the Arab tide rolled in, Christians very early claimed the authority of Muhammad himself in defense of their religious rights. Christian and Arab sources alike preserved copies or excerpts of a treaty said to have been concluded by the Prophet with the Christians of Najran (northern Yemen) and "all other Christian sects."[2] It is possible that he did indeed reach a special agreement with the church in Najran, which was well known to the Arabs as the chief Christian center of southern Arabia,[3] and this may have served as a rough model for later arrangements. But details of Muhammad's life are far too uncertain[4] to allow authenticity to any of the formal legal commitments with Christian communities that have been attributed to him. The first comprehensive attempt to outline the status of Christians under Islam is probably the Covenant of 'Umar (or Omar), father-in-law of Muhammad, who ruled as the Prophet's second successor from two years after Muhammad's death (634), to ten years after the Arabs took Seleucia-Ctesiphon, capital of the Persian Empire (644).

But Muhammad did have personal contacts with Christians and had formed a generally favorable opinion of them years before his successors so completely conquered them. The story of his first meeting with a Christian is as unreliable as most of the anecdotes of his early life, but both Arab and Christian historians often repeated it. The earliest and most trustworthy of the Muslim biographers of the Prophet, the eighth-century writer ibn-Ishaq, relates that at the age of twelve, on a caravan trip to Syria with his uncle, the young Muhammad met a Christian monk named Bahira at Bostra, which was the seat of the Monophysite bishop of the desert Arabs. The old monk recognized signs of greatness in the boy and protected him from some who would have harmed him.[5] The same biographer names another Christian, Jabr, who was perhaps an Ethiopian, as exerting great influence on the Prophet:

> According to my information the apostle used often to sit at al-Marwa [a hill overlooking Mecca] at the booth of a young Christian called Jabr, a slave of the B. al-Hadrami [tribe], and they used to say, "The one who teaches Muhammed most of what he brings is Jabr the Christian."[6]

Another tradition suggests that a cousin of the Prophet's first wife was a Christian. His name was Waraqah ibn Naufal, and it is true that of all Muhammad's acquaintances he was the most informed about Christianity. He is described as a *hanif*, a term denoting one who has become dissatisfied with paganism and is attracted to vaguely monotheistic ideas.[7] Some say that he did become a Christian before his death.[8] But Muhammad's family, the Hashim, who belonged to the Quraysh tribe, had a vested interest in paganism. His great-grandfather, Hashim, had won for the Quraysh the right to provide food and water for pilgrims to the Kaaba, the "Holy House" in Mecca, which Muslim tradition would later identify as the place where the angel appeared to Hagar in the desert and saved the father of the Arabs, the infant Ishmael (Isma'il; cf. Gen. 21:15–20). At the time Muhammad was born, however, the Holy House was still full of idols, the holiest of which were the "black stone," which according to some traditions had come down out of paradise, and the Moabite statue of Hubal, chief of the many gods of Mecca.

Muhammad was an unlikely leader. His family was poor and declining in power. His father had died before he was born, so by Arab custom he could not even inherit his father's property, and he was brought up by an uncle, the Hashim family chief. But when he was twenty-five his fortunes began to change. He married a wealthy widow fifteen years older than he was, and in the more leisurely life that this brought him he entered into a period of mystic experiences and meditation. About the year 610, while a triumphant Persia was pushing back the armies of Constantinople through Edessa to Antioch and the Mediterranean, the forty-year-old Muhammad's meditations began to be interrupted by visions and voices he felt were calling him to be "the messenger of God."[9]

It was a time of social unrest in the Arabian peninsula. Rome and Persia had been slowly but effectively destroying each other in a hundred years of almost incessant war (540–629). As the war continued into the seventh century the exhausted empires were less and less able to protect their Arab client-states on the desert borders, the Ghassanid kings in the northwest who owed allegiance to Rome, and Lakhmid and Yemen in the east and south who looked to Persia. In those kingdoms Christian Arab communities had been planted by Monophysites on Rome's southern border and by Nestorians nearer Persia. New wealth was accumulating in the politically neutral center along the strategic north-south caravan route from Africa to Roman Syria outside the Arab kingdoms where Christian Arab communities had begun to flourish. But now economic and political power was draining away from the evangelized borders of empire into the unreached center along the caravan route from Africa to Syria and its pagan trade cities of the desert, Medina and Mecca.[10]

Into this ferment of change, Muhammad's revelations brought two most troubling and divisive pronouncements, one religious, the other social. To the pagans he began to preach against idols and proclaimed that there is only one good and all-powerful God. This threatened Mecca's chief source of pride, the Holy House, the shrine of the gods. And to the rich, who were profiting most from both caravans and pilgrims, he preached that wealth must be shared with the poor. This was quite understandably less popular with the rich than with the poor. It weakened clan loyalties, dividing the people not by families but by possessions. It upset the whole city, and in an unforgettable incident the richer and more powerful members of his own clan, the Quraysh, drove Muhammad out of Mecca as a troublemaker.[11]

With some seventy followers, he found refuge in Yathrib, which was renamed in his honor Medina,[12] about two hundred miles north of Mecca. All Muslim history is dated from this momentous pilgrimage in the year A.D. 622, known as the *hegira* (or *hijrah*, which denotes a change of direction, hence "the emigration," or less accurately "the flight").[13]

In Medina he continued his crusade against polytheism. His most significant religious contacts there were with Jews, of whom there was a large community in Medina, and he concluded a covenant of mutual toleration with them, for it seemed logical to him to try to draw those two monotheistic groups, Jews and Muslims, together.[14] He began to draw up rules of worship for his own followers and even thought of using a trumpet as the Jews did to call them to prayer. But the Muslim-Jewish alliance all too soon broke down. Muslim tradition implies that it was because too many Jews in Medina began to identify Muhammad with the coming of their messiah and began to join the pilgrims from Mecca.[15]

At any rate, it was not in alliance with the Jews but with the pagan communities of Arabic Medina that Muhammad eventually found his place of leadership.[16] Here at last he won acceptance as a prophet of religion, here he learned to rouse his followers to war, and here he honed his political skills as a strategic, politically neutral referee in the tribal rivalries that were tearing the town apart. He began by uniting the quarreling people of Medina against their Arabic commercial rivals (and his own opponents) in Mecca and led them in devastating raids on Meccan caravans. Then he took advantage of his estrangement from the Jewish community to unite the Arabs religiously against the Jews. He urged them to reject the exclusivist claim of the Jews to be the "children of God" and further aroused them to jealousy of Jewish prosperity. In a tragic series of episodes for which the Prophet has been greatly criticized, the Jews of Medina were driven from the city by exile, assassination, and execution.[17] Where once he had worshiped toward Jerusalem, he turned his people instead toward Mecca as the holy city and its holy place, the Kaaba. The Fast of Ramadan replaced the Day of Atonement. By then, in 630, the armies of a united Medina had occupied Mecca, led in triumph by the religious leader the Meccans had ridiculed and rejected, Muhammad. Islam had become more than the first step toward the unification of the Arabian peninsula, more than a variation on Judaic religion. It was the beginning of a new and universal vision that would embrace a far greater goal, the conquest of the world.

Late that same year, Muhammad led an army of thirty thousand men north against Persia's southern borders, with what might later have become highly significant help from two largely Christian (Monophysite) Arab tribes, the Bakr banu-Wail and the Taghlib. But two years later Muhammad was dead.

Christianity and the Koran

For the most authentic indication of early Muslim attitudes we must turn first of all to the Koran.[18] The 114 *surahs* (chapters) of the Koran did not appear in writing in collected form until after Muhammad's death, but were gathered and edited by his secretary during the reign of the Prophet's successors. An initial collection was attempted under the caliph 'Umar, and the accepted canonical version under the caliph 'Uthman (644–656). The dating of the various visions and prophecies is highly debatable, and scholars often disagree on which *surahs* can be traced to Muhammad's early period in Mecca and which come from the later Medina period. But accepting some degree of gradual change in Muhammad's understanding of the Christian faith and judging from the Koran as a whole, it can be said that he was both surprisingly tolerant of Christianity and surprisingly uninformed about it.

Muhammad's general principle concerning the Christian revelation in both the Old Testament and the New Testament was that there is no conflict between the word of God as it came to the Jewish prophets and to Jesus and the apostles, and the word of God as it was revealed directly to him.[19] In the Koran the influence of the Old Testament is predominant. What references there are to New Testament teachings, though significant, are rather scattered and uneven. The fault was not Muhammad's. As L. E. Browne has remarked, if Christians had seized the opportunity in that age when

Arabia was barely becoming literate and had "made the first Arabic book the Bible, instead of the Quran, the whole course of the religious history of the East might have been different."[20] But after at least three hundred years in Arabia, Christians, whether Chalcedonian, Nestorian, or Monophysite, had made no translation of the New Testament into Arabic.[21] So when the Prophet sought for a name for the One, True God, the same God whom he thought Christians and Jews also worshiped, he did not use the Hebrew or the Greek name for God but "rather hesitantly" chose the name Arabs used for the pagan Supreme Being, *Allah.*[22] Keeping his religion strictly monotheistic by purging it of the clutter of Arabic gods and superstitions, but at the same time keeping it firmly embedded in Arabic tradition, proved to be a master stroke of cultural adaptation.

As for Jesus Christ, Muhammad speaks of him with the highest respect, but only as one of the greatest of the prophets. His earliest mention of Jesus in the Koran (according to traditional dating)[23] is in Surah 19, where Jesus is described as a prophet of the Book, like Moses. Though Moses is mentioned more often, Muhammad ascribes more titles of honor to Jesus than to any other figure in the history of his "true religion," Islam. Jesus is never criticized. He is "Messenger," "Prophet," "Servant," "Word of truth," and "Spirit of God," "Son of Mary," "the Messiah." He was born of a virgin, he worked miracles, and he was taken up alive into heaven.[24] His main mission on earth, however, was to confirm the law that prophets before him had given to the seed of Abraham and to bring "glad tidings of an Apostle" who would come after him and "whose name shall be Ahmad [Muhammad]" (61:6).

Many of the details the Koran adds to the story of the life and work of Jesus turn into fantasy, with echoes of third-century apocryphal Christian documents. The birth of Christ, for example, takes place under a palm tree in the desert, and an angel instructs Mary to shake the tree and eat its dates. He calls down a feast from heaven, and a table is lowered from the skies. More serious in its theological implications is the manner in which the account of the crucifixion in the Koran deviates from that in the New Testament. The Koran states that Jesus did not die but was rescued from the cross by a ruse and a substitute was provided to take his place (19:22–26; 3:49; 5:112–118; 4:157).[25]

It is impossible to pinpoint chronologically just when and how the differences between Muhammad and the Christians became increasingly obvious to him, for the dating of the chapters of the Koran is too uncertain. But the major points of contention are quite clear by the time the Koran began to take written shape, perhaps not long before his death in 632. The first collection, as we have noted, was not assembled until the caliphate of 'Umar (634–644), "from date leaves and tablets of white stone, and from the breasts of men" according to tradition. The final canonical editing was completed under the next caliph, 'Uthman (644–656).[26]

By that time the Prophet is represented as explicitly repudiating such central Christian doctrines as the Trinity and the deity of Jesus Christ. He accepts the ascension but bypasses the cross. His differences from those he still calls "People of the Book" he now explains by rejecting the integrity of the Christian Scriptures and accuses Christians of altering their own written records of God's revelation, for since God does not change, his word to them must originally have been in complete accord with his revelations to the last and greatest of the prophets, Muhammad:

> Believe in God and in the Apostles, and say not "There are three." . . . The Lord is one God. Far be it from Him that there should be to Him a Son. . . . O Jesus, son of Mary! Didst thou say unto men, "Worship me and my mother as gods . . ."? He will say . . . "Never could I say what I had no right (to say)." . . . The transgressors [Christians] . . . changed the word from that which had been given them. . . . Ye people of the Book! Why do you clothe truth with falsehood and conceal the truth? (4:171; 5:119; 7:162; 3:71)[27]

Nevertheless, for the most part the Prophet remained friendly toward the Christian communities he encountered in Arabia. This is in marked contrast to his attitude toward the Jews:

> Strongest among men in enmity to the Believers wilt thou find the Jews and Pagans [polytheists]; and nearest among them in love to the Believers wilt thou find those who say, 'We are Christians' [Nazarenes]." . . . These are men devoted to learning [priests] and men who have renounced the world [monks], and they are not arrogant. (5:85)

But scattered progressively through the Koran are hints of a hardening of the Islamic mind-set as differences of belief and teaching became more and more obvious. Then Christians and Jews are berated equally:

> O ye who believe, take not the Jews and the Christians for friends and protectors; they are but friends and protectors to each other. And he amongst you that turns to them (for friendship) is of them. Verily, God guideth not a people unjust. (5:54)

It is apparent that by the time of his death, the Prophet saw very clearly that his first hopes of attracting the earlier monotheists, Jews and Christians, to his newer revelation had been an illusion. But by that time also, any substantial Christian hope of converting Islam to Christian monotheism was gone.

Why did Muhammad, who was at first so open to the witness of the Old and New Testaments, not become a Christian? One reason has already been suggested. There was no Bible in Arabic. He was never given the chance to know the Scriptures of the Christian canon in their true, fully accepted form, and what fragments he had heard about its contents were insufficiently persuasive. It is quite possible that underlying and related to this was an element of cultural insensitivity toward Arabs on the part of Christians in imperial Persia and Byzantine Syria. Why had Asian missionaries translated the Scriptures into the tongues of better known cultures—into Syriac and in part into Chinese—but not into Arabic? Did they consider Arabic not worth the effort? They had even at times begun to put portions into some tribal languages of central Asia, but not into Arabic. If this hinted at a cultural, racial prejudice, the Arabs who were fiercely proud of their identity, could not have failed to resent it.

A second reason may have been the sad spectacle of Christian disunity. As he became aware of the angry divisions in the Christianity of the Middle East, Nestorian, Monophysite, and Chalcedonian, to say nothing of the schisms of the heretical sects, Muhammad may well have concluded that his quest for Arab unity and religious reform could never be accomplished within a Christian framework. A third reason, probably, was the negative effect of Christianity's political connections to Arabia's imperialist neighbors. Byzantium was Chalcedonian orthodox; Persia's largest religious minority was Nestorian, and Ethiopia was Monophysite. Byzantine Syria also had a considerable Monophysite population. "The Quran," as W. M. Watt has written, "offered the Arabs a monotheism comparable to Judaism and Christianity but without their political ties."[28]

However, overriding all such rationalizations and conjectures as to why Muhammad never became a Christian is surely the burning certainty in his soul that the one true God, "the Merciful, the Compassionate," had chosen him above all the prophets and had spoken to him directly in a way he had never spoken to any man before or since. Muhammad's power came not in the context of his reaction to other faiths, other social patterns, or other governments; his power was in the transparent sincerity of his own religious convictions. He was a prophet self-authenticated. That was his strength; and to those who did not follow him that was his weakness.

Christianity Under the Patriarchal Caliphs
(632–661)

Muhammad's public mission lasted only ten years, from the *hegira* in 622 to his death in 632, which was almost four times as long as the brief public life of Jesus Christ. In those ten years he created a far more visible community than any achieved by the early Christians in their first 280 years. But at his death it was still a religious community held together only by the presence and authority of a single individual, the Prophet. It was left to his family, his closest relatives by marriage, to transform that religious center in less than thirty more years into a political and military empire that shook the world. This period has been called the patriarchal caliphate (632–661).[29]

The transformation was far from peaceful. It can best be described, perhaps, by borrowing a metaphor from nuclear physics and calling it power by fission. Its religious convictions were not diluted. But fueled by the passions of family divisions and shaped by rivalries for personal power, what had been a religious reformation emerged as an explosively expanding world-class empire. When Muhammad died, his power did not even reach all of the Arabian peninsula. By the end of the patriarchal caliphate, the rule of Arabic Islam, though still uneven, stretched west through the richest provinces of North Africa halfway to the Atlantic Ocean, north to the eastern shores of the Black Sea, and east into Asia to within striking distance of India and China. Except for Asia Minor, all of ancient Christian Roman Asia was under Islamic rule.

At the time of his death, however, it must have appeared to most of the world that Muhammad's hopes of uniting the Arabs into his community were as illusory as his dream of convincing Christians and Jews of the authenticity of his new revelations.[30] He died without a male heir and the problem of choosing a successor almost broke up the Muslim unity the Prophet had carefully forged. He had sixteen wives,[31] many of them taken to smooth over tribal rivalries. His two favorites were Aisha, whom he married when she was nine, and the beautiful Mariya, a Coptic Christian. Two of his other wives were Jews. Had either the Christian or the Jews borne him a surviving son, the question of succession might have become complicated religiously. History however records only one son to survive infancy, Ibrahim, born of the Christian Mariya, but the little boy whom the Prophet might have expected to appoint as his successor died before he was two.

Without a son to inherit his mantle, and no prearrangement for the succession, some suggested that the leadership be divided between Mecca and Medina, but better counsel prevailed and the Prophet's close companion, Abu Bakr, was chosen as first caliph.[32] All four of the first caliphs were directly related to Muhammad. Abu Bakr was his father-in-law; so also was 'Umar I, while 'Uthman and 'Ali were sons-in-law. Rule by family connection had succeeded rule by the Prophet.

But family feuds almost destroyed the community. "External Power and Internal Division" is how one historian describes this period.[33] Some measure of its inner discord is the fact that despite the enormous victories of the faith and the political consolidation of central power in a single recognized ruler, only one of the first four caliphs died a peaceful death. Two, 'Uthman and 'Ali, were murdered by fellow Muslims, and another, 'Umar, by his Persian slave. Before the period closed, Islamic unity had been irrevocably destroyed, cut in two by all-out civil war between the followers of Muhammad's two sons-in-law.

The schism has never been healed. 'Uthman, the third caliph, though married to Muhammad's daughter Ruqayya, favored his own family, the Umayyads of Mecca, above the blood relations of Muhammad. He placed the authority for succession to the caliphate not in blood descent from the Prophet, but in the will of the Prophet's community, which alone could guarantee the purity of his religious heritage as revealed in the Koran and interpreted by the Traditions. To the dismay of the other son-in-law, 'Ali, whose marriage to Muhammad's daughter Fatima brought his sons into the bloodline of succession, 'Uthman further weakened the claims of blood succession and strengthened the authority of the community and the Koran, by ordering the editing of an authorized version of the Scripture. The point was obvious. The government of the community must authenticate the edition, not the descendants of the prophet. He commanded all private copies that differed from it to be destroyed.[34]

When 'Uthman was murdered and 'Ali was made fourth caliph despite his implication, rightly or wrongly, in the murder, the family feud became a war, Umayyads against 'Alids. 'Ali's rule was short-lived and bloody. He too was murdered during the unresolved civil strife and was succeeded by the family of 'Uthman, the Umayyads, whose caliphate lasted for almost a hundred years.

But the death of the two rivals, 'Uthman and 'Ali, neither ended the schism nor decided the issue of where the center of temporal and religious authority in Islam should reside. To this day 'Ali still has his followers. They are called Shi'ites (from shi'at 'Ali, party of 'Ali). They place authority not in a caliph, an elected civil leader, but in a religious leader, an *imam* who must be a descendant of Muhammad through 'Ali's wife Fatima and who in his own person combines spiritual and political power. The Shi'ites are the most powerful minority branch of Islam and their center is more Iranian than Arabic. By contrast, the Islamic Arab majority, now called Sunnites, place authority as did their prototype 'Uthman in the religious community that perpetuates the life and practice (*sunnah*) of the Prophet, chooses its own rulers, and authenticates the interpretation of the Koran. But the two branches of Islam are alike in this: both the community of the Sunnites and the imam of the Shi'ites base the truth of their teaching on the ultimate authority of the Koran and the Traditions.[35]

Through all the tragic family fissions of those years, the driving expansion of the faith never slackened. The first caliph, Abu Bakr, ruled for only two years but quickly proved his worth, first quelling the rebellions of the restless tribes of the Arabian peninsula, then sending Arab armies north against mighty Persia and Byzantine Palestine. Under the attacks of the next caliph, 'Umar, the partly Christianized Arab buffer states of Yemen in the far south, of the Lakhmids on the Persian border and of the Ghassanids east of the Jordan, melted away,[36] and the lean and hungry warriors from the desert poured in upon the richest empires in the world outside China. As in Europe barbarians from the forests of the north had broken the power of imperial Rome, so now in Asia, but not from the north, the tribes sprang up out of the sands of the south and poured into the Fertile Crescent, into the heart of Greco-Persian Asia. The collapse of the civilization of the Middle East in the seventh century was every bit as shocking as the sack of Rome two hundred years before.

In two pitched battles within the space of one year, 636, the Bedouin Arabs defeated two of the most powerful dynasties in history, Sassanid Persia and Byzantine Rome. At Yarmuk east of the Jordan, they routed the forces of the emperor Heraclius of Constantinople and pushed Byzantium back into the mountains of Asia Minor. After Yarmuk, Heraclius is said to have mourned the loss of Asia with the lament, "Farewell, O Syria, and what an excellent country this is for the enemy."[37] Shortly thereafter, the second caliph, 'Umar, built the first Moslem mosque in Jerusalem.

In the same year, at Qaddisiyya, south of old Babylon on the other side of the desert, camel-riding Arabs routed the heavy cavalry of Shah Yazdegerd III of Persia. His capital, Seleucia-Ctesiphon, with all its riches fell to long-haired nomads who scarcely knew one precious stone from another, but who pursued the last shah of the Sassanids slowly but relentlessy eastward toward China where he hoped to find refuge. He never reached safety. In 651, near the present Afghan border he was murdered by one of his own subjects in Merv, a caravan stop on the Old Silk Road and the seat of the Nestorian bishop farthest east in Persia on the missionary route to China.[38]

The reign of 'Umar I (634–644), the second caliph, is as notable in the history of the church of the East for his edict concerning the treatment of Christians in conquered territory, as for his stunning victories over Christian Byzantium and Zoroastrian Persia. "The Covenant of Omar ('Umar)," as it is called, was a key part of his administrative reorganization of the Muslim state, which turned Islam from an army into an empire. In its traditional form it traces back probably no further than about 820, but its foundational outline is clearly rooted in a number of treaties made with Christian cities in the time of 'Umar I. An example is the agreement imposed by 'Umar when he took Jerusalem about 638. The terms are simple and unconditional but rather reassuring:

> He gave them security for their lives, property, churches, crosses, their sick and healthy, and the rest of their religion. Their churches shall not be used as dwellings nor destroyed. . . . They shall not be persecuted for religion's sake. No Jew shall dwell with them there. Whoso wishes to go to the Greeks and take his property with him shall leave his churches and crosses. There shall be no payment of tribute till the harvest is gathered in.[39]

In other cities and as time went on, the caliphate began to codify the rules governing captured people of other religions, and the covenants became more explicit and detailed. A number of factors complicated the problem of the status of minorities. Some of the basic divisions were not only religious but ethnic. There was the difference between Arab and non-Arab as vast numbers of the conquered turned Muslim. There was the difference between the two kinds of "people of the Book," Muslims, on the one hand, and Christians and Jews, on the other. And there was the gulf between "people of the Book" and pagans. In the latter category Zoroastrians came to be considered as on a higher plane than idolaters, though they were more repressed than Christians, because to the Arabs they represented the possibility of a revival of Persian nationalism.

The first distinction, that between Arabs and non-Arabs, was extremely important and strongly affected any religious factors that might be involved. For Arabs after the conquest there was no choice between idolatrous polytheism and Islam. Arabs must be Muslims or die. There was no middle ground, no way of evading the death penalty by payment of taxes. Loyalty to the Koran was essential to the unity of the Arabic ethnic center, whatever internal divisions might otherwise develop.

There are reasons to believe, however, that in the days of first contact with Arab Christians before Muhammad's death, the earliest formal conditions imposed on Arab Christians may not have been so severe. In two instances, at least, where large Christian communities were involved, Arab Christians were allowed to keep their faith. When later challenged by Muhammad's successors, they appealed to the word of the Prophet. Najran, in the south just north of Yemen proper, is said to have had a population of forty thousand Christian Arabs, largely Monophysite; it was granted immunity allegedly by Muhammad himself from forcible conversion upon payment of tribute. But when 'Umar I decreed that "there can be no two religions at the same time in the Arabian peninsula," they were expelled into Mesopotamia, yet allowed still to retain their faith.[40] Farther south the Arab Christians in Yemen proper were not even forced to emigrate.

Another exception was the treatment of the powerful Arab tribe of the Taghlib in the northeast who greatly aided Muhammad in his last campaigns against the southern edges of Syria and Mesopotamia. The Taghlib had been largely converted to Christianity by contact with Nestorian missionaries in the border kingdom of the Lakhmids. Later, after the conquest, it was demanded that as Arabs the Taghlib must convert to Islam or declare themselves non-Arab, but they refused. They were as proud of their Arab blood as of their Christian faith and were willing to give up neither. A compromise was reached. They were allowed to retain their status as Arabs without conversion if they would agree to pay double the Muslim poor tax and promise not to baptize their children. They agreed. However, in practice, they managed to persuade themselves and their overlords that the prohibition against baptism of children was neither reasonable nor necessary and continued to baptize them anyway.[41] Nevertheless, the basic rule for Arabs remained the classic choice, Islam or death.

For non-Arabs, however, the alternatives proposed by the conquerors were more lenient and therefore far more tempting. It was not Islam or death that faced the wavering Persian or Syrian Christian, but a choice between Islam or a withering decline in a religious ghetto, known as the *dhimmi*.[42] Since the shape of that Christian ghetto is only foreshadowed by the policies of 'Umar and does not find its final form as outlined by the "Covenant of Omar" until well into the following period of the Umayyad caliphs and beyond, we shall describe it later.

Under the patriarchal caliphs and all through the turbulent years of the civil wars, apart from the killings and horrors to be expected in any war, treatment of Christians in the conquered territories of Persia and Byzantine Syria proved to be remarkably generous.[43] The conquest of Syria in particular brought enormous numbers of Christians under Muslim rule and faced the caliphs with a religious problem greater than any faced by the Persian shahs before them. Christianity was only a minority religion in Persia, but in Syria it was the religion of the vast majority. An even more threatening problem to Muslim rule was the higher intellectual and social background of the Christians. In sophisticated Persia, Christianity and Zorastrianism had met as the religions of imperial equals, though the home ground advantage was with the Zoroastrians. But in the first rough years of Arab conquest, it was the conquered who represented civilization, and the conquerors were still nomad warriors from the desert. They shunned the cities and built army camps for themselves in centers like Basra and Kufa.

In such a situation, the Arab victors found that the most efficient system of pacifying and ruling non-Muslim believers in conquered territories—if they were not to massacre them—was to separate them from the fighting Arabs and, following the example of the shahs of fallen Persia, group them into religiously segregated enclaves, limit their political rights to the bounds of their own communities, and then put them to useful employment.

Service in the army was forbidden to them. Farming, as a lower and naturally isolated occupation, was left almost entirely to the defeated population regardless of religion. But some respected occupations were for years dominated by Christians and Jews. As late as several generations after Muhammad, Christian and Jewish communities of physicians, musicians, and merchants could be found even in Mecca.[44] The caliph 'Uthman is said to have been so impressed with the Christian poet Abu Zubaid that he asked him to come up and sit in honor next to him.[45] Their superior education made Christians much in demand as administrative secretaries and teachers, as philosophers, architects, scientists, and artists, and some rose to high but extremely vulnerable positions in national and provincial governments. Al-Ashari, the governor of Basrah under the Caliph 'Umar I, employed a Christian secretary,[46] and for the first half century of Muslim rule—since until that time official records were kept not in Arabic but in Greek, Persian, and Coptic,[47]—an enormous number of clerks and secretaries and administrative assistants found employment in the various offices of government. Most of them, in Syria at least, were either Christians or had been Christians before entering Muslim service.

At first the caliphs did not distinguish between the three major branches of the church in Asia: Nestorians in Mesopotamia and Persia; Monophysite Jacobites mostly in Syria; and Chalcedonian orthodox (called Melkites because of their allegiance to the emperor, *melek*, in Constantinople) throughout the conquered Byzantine provinces. Nestorians were the most favored, and their patriarch was permitted to keep his residence in the old Persian capital of Seleucia-Ctesiphon. The patriarch at the time of the conquest was Yeshuyab II (628–643). It was he who is claimed to have negotiated with Muhammad himself the first agreement on the favorable status of Nestorians under Islam, and it was in his patriarchate that Alopen reached the Far East with the first known Christian mission to China.

Yeshuyab's successor in the Nestorian patriarchate, Marama (647–650), has also been dubiously credited with winning a similar contract of protection for Christians from the caliph 'Ali.[48] The third Nestorian patriarch of the conquest, Yeshuyab III (650–660), seems to have adjusted easily to the change from non-Christian Persian rule to non-Christian Arab rule. In a letter to the bishop of Fars he praised his new overlords, "They have not attacked the Christian religion, but rather they have commended our faith, honoured our priests . . . and conferred benefits on churches and monasteries." He even felt secure enough in the new relationship to remind the bishop that his ecclesiastical authority and responsibility for the churches of India remained unchanged and that the bishop had been neglecting his missionary duties.[49] Later, in 762, when the Arabs moved their center of government from Damascus to Baghdad, only the Nestorians were allowed to move the patriarchate into the new capital.

The Monophysites were not permitted an episcopal see either in Seleucia-Ctesiphon or in Baghdad. Nevertheless, the Jacobites, as they were now called, found that at the very least their legal position as a religious body had been improved rather than impaired by the Arab conquest. Under the orthodox Byzantine rule of Constantinople they had been outlawed as heretics ever since the persecutions of the emperor Justin in 521. Their priests, bishops, and patriarch were not recognized by the state. But since to the Muslims all Christians were heretics, Jacobites were no more severely discriminated against than Nestorians or orthodox, despite some favoritism displayed to the Nestorians in Persia.

The highest-ranking Jacobite prelate in Mesopotamia before the conquest had been Marutha, metropolitan of Tagrit (Tekrit) (629–

649), a smaller town on the Tigris about 150 miles upriver from Seleucia-Ctesiphon. He was the first bishop to receive from the patriarch in Antioch the title "maphrian of the East," which conferred upon him authority over all of Jacobite Asia east of the Euphrates.[50] The vital center of Jacobite learning under the Arab empire, however, was neither Antioch nor Tagrit, but the famous "Eagle's Nest," the Monastery of Kenneshre, on the Euphrates. There, Monophysite monks fleeing the persecutions by the orthodox had established a Jacobite parallel to the Nestorian School of Nisibis. Its two most influential graduates were the fellow schoolmates Jacob of Edessa (633–708) and George, bishop of the Arabs (686–724). Bishop Jacob produced a revision of the complete Syriac Old Testament and the Syriac liturgy, and Bishop George is famous for a highly regarded Syriac commentary on Aristotle's *Organon*.[51]

Christianity Under the Umayyad Caliphate (661–750)

The death of 'Ali and the defeat of his Shi'ite partisans ended the first Islamic civil war and marks the beginning of a royal Muslim dynasty, the Umayyads. In the patriarchal period caliphs had been elected by a form of republican consent, but the first of the Umayyad caliphs, Mu'awiya (661–680), named his own son as his successor and founded a hereditary caliphate.[52] He also moved the seat of government out of Persia, to Damascus in Syria, which, unlike Arabia and Persia, was Christian territory.

The Umayyad caliphate has been characterized as a period of the secularizing and Arabizing of Islam. This was true to some extent, as their more fundamentalist Shi'ite rivals did not fail to point out. War, law, and politics did in fact seem to occupy the attention of the hereditary caliphs more than religion. But for this very reason, the Umayyad period proved to be almost a hundred years of considerable tolerance of Christians. It could hardly have been otherwise when the Muslim conquerors were still suffering from never-ceasing internal Arabic rivalries, when the loyalty of their Syrian political and military base was absolutely essential for the preservation of the unity of the empire, and when their capital of Damascus was surrounded by a sea of Syrian Christians.

For the first few generations after the conquest, in many ways Syria's Christians seemed almost as content with the change to Arabic rule as were the Nestorians in Persia. It is true that the change had been sharper in Syria than in Persia. For the Persian Christians the conquest was only a transition from one non-Christian empire to another, whereas Syria, which ever since Constantine the Great had been ruled by Christians, now had to adjust to life in a Muslim empire. But historians have noted that in the period preceding the conquest a rising tide of grievance was stirring discontent in Syria against Byzantine Constantinople over high taxes, oppressive landlords, and wars that never stopped. There were other factors also that made the prospect of Arab rule at least tolerable as an alternative. For one thing, Syria already had a large Arabic and mixed Arabic population, infused for centuries with migrations of northern Arabic tribes. To many Syrians the Greco-Romans were still aliens and the Arabs were part relatives. In religion as well as race, to the large community of Syrian Jacobite Christians, Arabic Islam seemed no more hostile than Byzantine orthodoxy. They remembered that before the Muslim invasion, in the exhausting seesaw battles of the early seventh century between Greek emperors and the Persian shahs (from 603 to 627), the pagan Persians had been kind to Monophysites in captured Damascus, Antioch, and Jerusalem, whereas the triumphant return of the Christian emperor, Heraclius, meant persecution again as heretics.[53]

So in a surprisingly large measure, Syrians had welcomed the conquest, and when the Umayyad dynasty moved its capital to Syrian Damascus, Syria responded to the favor by becoming the center of support for the new regime. All three of the mainstream Christian bodies in Syria, Melkite (Byzantine orthodox), Monophysite (Antiochene Jacobite), and Persian Nestorian found something to their advantage in the situation despite all the cruelties of the Muslim onslaught. Orthodox clergy were freed from excessive interference by Byzantine emperors in church affairs; Monophysites were rescued from harassment by the orthodox; and Persian Nestorians found themselves better regarded by Arab Muslims than by their former overlords, Persian Zoroastrians.

In Syria, one of the principal figures in the comparatively bloodless surrender of Damascus to the Arab invaders had been Mansur ibn-Sarjun (Sergius), of a distinguished Byzantine orthodox family that may have been of Arabic origin.[54] When Mu'awiya, governor of the province, became the Umayyad caliph of all Islam he appointed Mansur to the highest position in his government outside the military, that of controller of finance. His son ibn-Mansur inherited much of the same official duties, and his grandson was the famous John of Damascus, administrator, monk, theologian, and apologist. There was little pressure on the Mansurs to abandon their Christian faith. In fact John of Damascus was bold enough to write a strong tract against Islam, which he none too tactfully called "the Ishmaelite heresy."

At the age of twelve John of Damascus (ca. 675–749)[55] had been given a captured Sicilian monk as his tutor in Greek. Christian clergy were still in high favor with the Arabs in Syria and had, in fact, been charged by the Umayyad caliphs to remain in control of most of the empire's schools of higher learning. The young John had already been enrolled as a student in an Arabic school where he presumably memorized the prescribed teachings of the Koran and the Traditions and where, it is said, he was a friend and fellow student of the caliph's son, the future Caliph Yazid I. But under the guidance of his new tutor a whole new world of knowledge was opened up to him, and he was entranced by Greek history, science, philosophy, theology, and music. When his father died (about 695), John was appointed secretary to the prince of Damascus, the Caliph 'Abd al-Malik in political power.

But for reasons unknown, about the year 726 he retired from public office and entered the great monastery of Mar Saba (St. Sabas) near Jerusalem. Perhaps it was his stormy involvement in defense of the veneration of icons against the iconoclastic Greek emperor Leo III that led to this change. Or perhaps it was simply because he wanted to write and study. Less likely is the legend that he was betrayed by a forged letter from the emperor in Constantinople identifying him as an accomplice of the caliph's Byzantine enemies.[56] At any rate he left the service of the Muslim state and devoted himself to "the study of the divine law." The legend may at least reflect the fact that it was about the time of John's retirement to Mar Saba that the treatment of Christians in the Arab empire began to worsen.[57]

The prominent part John of Damascus played in the iconoclastic controversy belongs more to Western than Asian church history, but there is an irony in the arguments of the antagonists—John in favor of images and the emperors Leo III and Constantine V against them—that illuminates the relationship between Christians East and West at the time. Each side accused the other of being "Saracen-minded," and not without at least some reason. Leo III condemned the veneration of icons in 726. Was he or was he not copying an edict against images issued five years earlier by the "Saracen" caliph, Yazid II, in 721?[58] But on the other hand, why did John, who denounced iconoclastic Christian emperors for interfering in church affairs, not also speak out against Muslim caliphs who were beginning to harden the limits of freedom permitted to Christians in the *dhimmis?* While John was still writing the *Fount of Knowledge,* a nearby bishop, Peter of Maimuma near Gaza, was executed for preaching against Islam.[59]

To his credit, in his writings at least, John of Damascus was as forthright as any martyr. The *Fount of Knowledge*,[60] his major work, is a massive synthesis of all Greek theology and learning up to his own time and has been called "the last work of any theological importance to appear in the East."[61] It was translated into Arabic in the tenth century and appeared in many Greek and Latin editions in Europe where it was a model for Thomas of Aquinas's *Summa Theologica*. Chapter 101 of Part II ("On Heresies") contains his judgment against Islam. It is not a dialogue, it is a polemic. It begins with the unequivocal statement:

> There is also the superstition of the Ishmaelites which to this day prevails and keeps people in error, being a forerunner of the Antichrist.[62]

But as the argument continues, though John does not soften his language, he does at least credit Muhammad with leading his people from idolatry to monotheism, to the "One God, creator of all, who has [not] been begotten . . ." Then the argument quickly resumes. John was no gentle compromiser. He was severely careful (and was usually successful) neither to distort Muslim teaching nor to paint it any more Christian than it actually was, and he finished the sentence with the complete Islamic formula: "who has neither been begotten *nor has begotten*" (italics mine),[63] thereby at the very beginning clearly relating all his criticisms to the basic theological difference between Islam and Christianity, namely Christology. He "transmits to the Christians a most accurate account of the Muslim point of view with regard, especially, to the most delicate topic in a Muslim-Christian dialogue."[64] His subsequent arguments are subsidiary: the lack of reference to Muhammad's prophethood in the Bible (which Muslims accept as revelation); the impossibility of separating God from his Word and his Spirit;[65] the defense of Christian veneration of the cross as no more an idolatry than the Muslim veneration of the black stone in the Kaaba; and criticisms of Muslim polygamy. All these are lesser differences. To John, the crucial difference is this: the God of the Muslims is not the Christian God. Allah had no son. John's God is the Father of Jesus Christ.

We will compare, in another section below, this Christian polemic against Islam in Umayyad Persia to an important, gentler debate between a Christian and a Muslim a generation later in the 'Abbasid dynasty between the Nestorian patriarch Timothy I and the caliph Mahdi, which was a genuine dialogue, not a polemic.[66]

All through the Umayyad dynasty Christians were far more prominent in society than their *dhimmi* status might lead us to believe. Their physicians had been famous in the Sassanid empire and were no less so under their Muslim successors. The first caliph in Damascus, Mu'awiya, brought into the court as his personal physician the Christian ibn-Uthal, and was so impressed with his trustworthiness that he promoted him, according to some Arab accounts, to the rank of financial administrator of the province of Hims. The "earliest scientific book in the language of Islam" was a treatise on medicine by a Syrian Christian priest in Alexandria, translated into Arabic by a Persian Jewish physician. Another conspicuous Christian who moved easily in high court circles was al-Akhtal (b. 640), who has been called "the Ummayad poet laureate." P. K. Hitti graphically describes how the Christian poet would "enter the caliphal palace with a cross dangling from his neck and recite his poems to the delight of the Moslem caliph and his entourage."[67]

Across the Euphrates in Persia Christians were fewer and mostly Nestorian. Under the Persian Sassanid emperors they had long been used to the ghettolike restrictions of the Persian *melet* system, which the Arabs now borrowed for ruling the same conquered religious minorities. What the Persians called the *melet*, in Arabic became the *dhimmi* (sometimes transliterated *jimmi*).[68] We have described it before as a system that separated religious groups who did not belong to the national religion from the social, political, and military mainstream of the empire's life. As the Arabs consolidated their control, its outlines and main features developed only gradually. To Christians the Arab *dhimmis* must have seemed an improvement over the Persian. As "people of the Book" they were freed from the military draft and from forced labor (the corvée), which had not been the case under Sassanid rule.[69]

The first and most obvious imposition was financial. Non-Muslims paid tribute or taxes, and as time went on the taxes grew heavier and the social discrimination more oppressive. Had not both tribute and humiliation of nonbelievers been commanded in the Koran?[70] Moreover, since non-Muslims were excluded from military service for reasons of national security, extra taxation seemed not unreasonable as a substitute.

But when such tax pressures made conversion to Islam very appealing and when conversions began to multiply as the newly converted non-Arabs (the *mawali*) were enlisted for army service and therefore presumably became eligible for government pension and support, the caliphate was alarmed at the financial consequences. It tried to make a distinction between original Arab Muslims and later non-Arab converts. The former were declared superior in status despite the testimony of pure Islamic doctrine to the contrary. Non-Arabs were to receive no pension and were not allowed in the cavalry but were allotted a share of the booty in the expanding conquest.

Another point of discrimination, the land tax, developed in diffent forms in different places. In some areas even Arab Muslims were expected to pay a form of land tax when they became land-owners, which occurred usually by state grant,[71] but sometimes this seems to have been levied only on non-Arabs. At any rate it seemed to many that the empire appeared to be moving toward a three-tiered society in which the gravest danger was the division of Islam into Arab against non-Arab, old Muslims against new converts. It placed Arab Muslims at the top. Non-Arab Muslims (the *mawali*, literally "clients," a term which included most Zoroastrians, and Christian converts to Islam) were in the middle protesting this kind of discrimination among fellow Muslims.[72] At the bottom with no right of protest at all were the non-Muslims (Christians, Jews, Zoroastrians, and Manichaeans), recognized and protected by the state and free to practice their religions but only at a heavy price.

How heavy that price had become is apparent in the severe phrases of "the Covenant of Omar." It describes how life is to be lived at the bottom of the social scale by those whose religious convictions squeezed them into the category of *dhimmis,* the people of the religious ghettos. The covenant has been mistakenly antedated to the seventh century and attributed to 'Umar I, but in fact and in practice it only gradually took shape under the Umayyad caliphs and did not reach its most definitive versions until the early ninth century. The best text is translated by A. S. Tritton, from which the following summary is abstracted.[73] It begins:

> I, and all Muslims, promise you and your fellow Christians security as long as you and they keep the conditions we impose upon you. Which are: you shall be under Muslim laws and no other, and shall not refuse to do anything we demand of you . . .

Then follows a long list of commands and prohibitions that fall into three categories: criticism of the Muslim religion, major crimes, and lesser misdemeanors. For the first two the penalty was forfeiture of life and property. Major crimes included adultery with or marrying a Muslim woman, robbing a Muslim, evangelizing a Muslim, or helping the enemies of Islam. For Christians, the most damaging stricture was the prohibition of "turning a Muslim from his religion."

Lesser trespasses brought lesser penalties. For accidentally killing a Muslim the punishment was the payment of blood money. For selling Muslims forbidden things such as wine, pigs, or blood, the penalty was forfeiture of the price received. For thievery the guilty man's hand was cut off. These punishments were no more severe for Christians than for Muslims.

There were also certain restrictions imposed on the practice of the Christian religion, but no prohibition of Christian faith and practice within the Christian community:

> You shall not display the cross in any Moslem town, nor parade your idolatry, nor build a church, nor beat the wooden clappers [used instead of bells by Nestorians], nor use your idolatrous language about Jesus the Son of Mary to any Moslem.[74]

In return for such restraint, the conquerors promised not to destroy or loot already existing churches and monasteries or hinder or forbid Christian worship in the churches in any way.

In addition to the religious restrictions, the covenant imposes a wide burden of social humliations upon Christians and other religious minorities. These rules were probably not imposed all at once but rather represent a gradual development of discriminatory practices that were collected and added to later editions of the text as accepted precedents. Christians, for example, were ordered to wear a distinctive girdle around their waists so that they might not be confused with Arabs. Later, a large yellow patch on their outer garments, front and back, marked the wearers as Christians.[75] Special haircuts were mandatory, cut short in front. They had to ride side-saddle, not astride the horse like a soldier or an Arab. They were forbidden to take the high center of the road but had to leave that free for Muslims they might meet; they also could not take the chief seats in assemblies.[76]

The final, and in some ways the most effective disability of all imposed on the Christian *dhimmis* was financial, as we have already observed. The price the Christian had to pay for the right to believe and worship was double taxation.

The sixth Umayyad caliphate, that of the pious and zealous 'Umar II (717–720), might with some justification be described as the first period of general persecution of Christians and other non-Muslims by the government. In his short reign 'Umar tightened the financial pressures on the vulnerable Christian communities and began to squeeze the weak of faith into the protective fold of Islam. He rewarded new converts (*mawali*) by releasing them from a large share of the tax burden imposed on non-Muslims, forbade the building of new churches, and even ordered any recently erected churches and synagogues to be demolished. Fortunately for the Christians who were expected to compensate by their increased taxes for the resultant sharp loss of revenue, the change was too drastic for effective implementation and was dropped when he died.[77] But the mass conversions to Islam were irreversible. The penalty for apostasy was death.

But it was division within Islam, not the suppression of minority religions, that finally brought an end to the Umayyad dynasty. Civil war had already broken out between northern Arabs (Kalbites) and southern Arabs (Qaysites) under the fourth caliph, Marwan I, and was never really ended despite a decisive northern victory in 684. The older split between Sunni (in Syria and elsewhere) and Shi'ites (in Iran) still simmered and spilled over into occasional violence and rebellion. Muslim pietists were incensed at the general political pragmatism of most Umayyad caliphs and never gave them complete loyalty. Moreover, the uncertainties of the process of selecting successors to the throne threw the government into turmoil after the death of each caliph. The choice was not limited to the eldest son but could vary widely and arbitrarily among members of the royal family. Of the fourteen Umayyad caliphs, only four managed to pass the power on directly to their sons.[78]

Upon the death of its tenth caliph, the wise and able Hisham (724–743), the dynasty virtually collapsed. Christians had praised his statesmanlike tolerance of religious minorities, a policy that ended the repressive edicts of 'Umar II. Hisham's viceroy in the east, Khalid, was particularly noted for kindness to minorities. As the son of a Christian mother he treated the Christians, Jews, and Zoroastrians across the Euphrates with unusual justice and courtesy. But the four caliphs who followed him proved unable to cope with the unending explosions of religious and political rebellion that flared throughout the empire. Fighting under the white banners of his dynasty, the last Umayyad in the east fell in 750[79] and was replaced by a line of rulers, the 'Abbasids, who traced their blood descent to al-'Abbas, a paternal uncle of Muhammad, in whose name and under whose black banner they promised to restore the true, original Islam of the Prophet.

An act of that last Umayyad caliph, Marwan II (745–750), is typical of his dynasty's pragmatic tolerance of Christians. In the first year of his reign, which opened with a vigorous reform that bore promise for a while of revitalizing the dynasty, he officially recognized John II as Jacobite patriarch of Antioch with authority over the

Monophysite churches of Asia.[80] The fact that Constantinople, Islam's enemy, considered Jacobites to be as heretical as Nestorians and oppressed both no doubt had much to do with this restoration of the Monophysites to favor by the Arabs. They remained the dominant Christian party in Syria, as the Nestorians were in former Persian territory. But Melkites remained under suspicion of collaboration with Constantinople and increasing numbers emigrated into Byzantine territory. For most of the next three centuries, all three of these religious minorities enjoyed equal legal standing and protection as *dhimmis* in Islamic territory, though eventually by the beginning of the eleventh century the Nestorian patriarch had become the acknowledged head of all Christians in Asia under Arab rule.[81]

The change in dynasty that followed the fall of the Ummayad caliphs in 750, however, brought no change for the better for any Christians.

Christianity Under the Early 'Abbasids (750–850)

The 'Abbasids ruled Islam in Asia for the next half a millennium, from 750 to 1258 as "the most celebrated and longest-lived dynasty in Islam." They claimed to be more strictly orthodox than their predecessors and proved to be more aggressively Muslim in the treatment of religious minorities than the practical-minded Umayyads. The first caliph of the dynasty called himself "the bloodshedder (al-Saffah)."[82] But in fact it was not until the time of the third caliph, Mahdi (775–785), after the dynasty had been firmly established in its new capital, that the restrictions of the so-called "Covenant of Omar," described previously, began to tighten and not until after 800 that the covenant received its final legal editing and made the ninth century a period of increasing social and religious discrimination. But after 900, as the caliphate slowly disintegrated under the pressures of Islam's angry internal religious conflicts and the political loss of North Africa and Egypt, the weakness of the dynasty brought for a while more freedom again for Christians and Jews.

The new dynasty moved the center of government out of Syria, which had been the power base of the Umayyads, eastward into Iraq (Mesopotamia) and in 762 its second caliph, Mansur (754–775), built a magnificent new capital at Baghdad some twenty miles upstream from the ancient Persian capital of Seleucia-Ctesiphon on the Tigris, which he plundered for its brick and marble. He chose the site not only for its military advantage but also, as he said, because it will "put us in touch with lands as far as China."[83] This was one of the first intimations of a shift in the orientation of the empire from a Mediterranean to an Asiatic base. As the result of military setbacks west and north by the Franks at the Pyrenees, by Byzantium in Asia Minor, and later by the Fatimids in Egypt, the future, as far as the 'Abbasids were concerned, was to be rooted in a continent in which Syria was only a western coastal sliver, and its eastern edge, though reachable, was as far away as T'ang-dynasty China.

Another basic change in the empire developed almost unnoticed at first and was not geographic but ethnic. To put it more precisely, it was the change in the ethnic composition of the governing Arabic community. The 'Abbasids, who came to power on a tide of Islamic orthodoxy, gave religion a recognized priority over race. True religion, not Arab birth, was to be the basis of Islamic rule. As a modern Arab historian has pointed out, "The Umayyad empire was Arab, the 'Abbasid was more international. The 'Abbasid was an empire of Neo-Moslems in which the Arabs formed only one of the many component races."[84] Yet it remained essentially Asian, for as time went on the Muslim regimes that sprang up outside Asia in Egypt, North Africa, and Spain granted the central caliphate in Baghdad a recognition that was more hostile than nominal, and one by one they asserted their independence.

The emphasis on true religion did not at first worsen the treatment of Christians in the empire or further exacerbate friction between Sunni and Shi'ite Muslims. The third caliph, Mahdi, opened his rule with a determined effort to appease the Iranian Shi'ite opponents of Baghdad orthodoxy, and in an unusually irenic gesture toward Christians staged a famous debate that brought him face to face with the Nestorian patriarch Timothy I (779–823).[85]

TIMOTHY I AND THE CALIPHS

Considering the times and the situation, it was a remarkable display of tolerance and courtesy. The caliph was all-powerful, but since he had invited the argument himself, he debated on equal terms with the Christian. He was gracious but candid.

As the patriarch later recorded the proceedings,[86] he had scarcely finished the customary complimentary address when the caliph "did something to me which he had never done before; he said to me, 'O Catholicos, [how can] a man like you who possesses all this knowledge and utters such sublime words concerning God, . . . [say that God] married a woman from whom He begat a Son.'" Thus, as bluntly as when John of Damascus forty years earlier wrote against Islam, the arguments began again on the subject of Christology. But Timothy was no polemicist, and times had changed. He coolly agreed that the statement was a blasphemy, "Who would say such a thing?" Nevertheless, he continued, "Christ is the Son of God—not, however, "in the carnal way."[87] And the debate went on for two days.

The arguments ranged from how God could have a son and how he could die, to the mathematical contradiction involved in the doctrine of the Trinity; and from Muslim claims of Muhammad's supreme prophethood to their charges that Christians had corrupted their own Scriptures.

Considering the nature of the audience, the patriarch made skillful use of metaphors. Of the birth of Jesus as God's Son, he said that Jesus was born from a virgin as man (a statement all Muslims accepted from the Koran), but from God he was born "as light is born of the sun and [as] word [is born] of the soul."[88] So also with the difficult matter of Trinity in unity. "If He is three, He is not one," said the caliph. No, it is not quite like that, Timothy replied, it is more like a three-denarii gold coin, "one in its gold, that is to say in its nature, and three in its persons, that is to say in the number of denarii." When the caliph began to challenge the metaphors, the patriarch disarmingly admitted the limitations of parallels between the physical and the spiritual, "In every comparison there is a time at which one must stop, because it does not resemble reality in everything."[89] So he is careful not to base his defense on metaphor alone, but again and again appeals to the testimony of "the Book" (the Torah, Prophets, Gospels, and Epistles), knowing that "the Book" is common authority for Muslim and Christians alike.[90] When the caliph murmured about Christians corrupting their scriptures to suit their purpose, he replied reasonably enough, "Even if we were able to corrupt the Books of the Torah and the Gospel that we have with us, how could we have tampered with those that are with the Jews?"[91]

On the second day the caliph asked, "Did you bring a Gospel with you, as I asked?" Yes, said the patriarch. "Who gave it to you?" said the caliph and Timothy answered,

> The Word of God gave us the Gospel, O God-loving King. . . . We Christians believe that although the Gospel was given to us by the Apostles, it was not given as from them but as from God, His Word, and His Spirit.

Then suddenly the caliph asked the most sensitive question of all. "What do you say about Muhammad?" One can almost sense the tense silence in the room as all wondered how the Christian from the *dhimmi* would answer his Muslim king. The answer is worth quoting at some length because of the striking difference it displays between the polemical, controversial manner of John of Damascus, who brusquely described Muhammad as "a false prophet," and the way Timothy managed to combine polite dialogue with Christian integrity. The patriarch said:

> Muhammad is worthy of all praise, by all reasonable people, O my Sovereign. He walked in the path of the prophets and trod in the track of the lovers of God. All the prophets taught the doctrine of one God, and since Muhammad taught the doctrine of the unity of God, he walked, therefore, in the path of the prophets. Further, all the prophets drove men away from bad works, and brought them nearer to good works, and since Muhammad drove his people away from bad works and brought them nearer to the good ones, he walked, therefore, in the path of the prophets. Again, all the prophets separated men from idolatry and polytheism, and attached them to God and to his cult, and since Muhammad separated his people from idolatry and polytheism, and attached them to the cult and the knowledge of one God, beside whom there is no other God, it is obvious that he walked in the path of the prophets. Finally Muhammed taught about God, His Word and His Spirit, and since all the prophets had prophesied about God, His Word and His Spirit, Muhammad walked, therefore, in the path of all the prophets.[92]

And the caliph said, "You should, therefore, accept the word of the Prophet." "Which words?" asked the patriarch. "That God is one and there is no other," said the caliph. Timothy agreed. "This belief in one God, I have learned from the Torah, from the Prophets and from the Gospel," he said. "I stand by it and shall die in it. . . . I believe in one God in three, and three in one, but not in three different Godheads, however, but in the persons of God's Word and His Spirit."[93]

There was no declared winner of the debate. In a sense both won, for the affair ended in what could be described as the high point in Muslim and Christian relationships in the whole history of the Muslim conquest. The caliph said, "If you [only] accepted Muhammad as a prophet, your words would be beautiful and your meanings fine." And the patriarch, equally courteous, compared the gospel to a precious pearl and closed with this prayer for the caliph, "May God grant to us that we may . . . share it [the precious pearl of the faith] with you. . . . We pray God who is King of Kings and Lord of Lords, to preserve the crown of the kingdom and the throne of the Commander of the Faithful [the caliph] for multitudinous days and numerous years."[94]

Timothy I (779–823, or 778–821),[95] who came from Adiabene, the ancient seat of the earliest Persian Christians, was the greatest of all the patriarchs who served under the caliphate.[96] The year of the debate, probably 781, was also the year that saw the erection of the Nestorian monument in China and so may well mark not only a peak in intercommunication between Islam and Christianity, but also the height of Nestorian influence in the second half of the first Christian millennium in Asia's two greatest empires, 'Abbasid Arabia and T'ang China.

Timothy was as skillful a diplomat in his dealings with ambitious bishops as with absolute monarchs. L. E. Browne relates a story about his election to the patriarchate illustrating the combination of wordly ingenuity and Christian integrity that was a characteristic of his administration. As the electors[97] gathered for the vote he allowed them sight of some heavy sacks, which, corrupted by the society of the time, they presumed to be money available for distribution if he were elected. After the election the sacks turned out to be filled with nothing but stones, and the unruffled new patriarch chided them, "The priesthood is not to be sold for money."[98] Conversely, though it credits the patriarch with personal integrity, the incident also implies that even after a generation under Muslim rule the church was still wealthy and was becoming distressingly vulnerable to the corruption that so often accompanies ecclesiastical affluence.

Timothy presided as patriarch for more than forty years (778–823), serving also under Mahdi's three successors. Once, in a time of severe pressure on Christians, the caliph Harun al-Rashid asked him, "Tell me briefly which religion is the true one in God's eyes." How could he answer? If he said "Christianity" he could be deposed or imprisoned, but to say "Islam" would be apostasy. Timothy never hesitated. "That religion," he replied, "of which the rules and precepts correspond with the works of God."[99]

As a theologian within the church he strongly defended Nestorian orthodoxy. Twice in general synods he argued against deviations, first in 790 and again in 804, insisting on "purity of faith and knowledge of the Scripures." As Baumstark observes, it was in his time that the heresies of Henana were finally put to rest.[100]

He was also a strongly missionary-minded patriarch, not content simply to teach and defend the faith but eager to expand it. He appointed a bishop for Yemen at its old capital, San'a, despite earlier Muslim precedents of stringent prohibition of Christianity among Arabs.[101] He prayed openly before a Muslim caliph, as we have seen, that Christians might share "the pearl" of the gospel with Muslims, adding with evangelistic directness, "God has placed the pearl of His face before all of us like the shining rays of the sun, and every one who wishes can enjoy the light of the sun." Nor was his zeal limited to the empire, for his position gave him authority over the Nestorians in T'ang-dynasty China and the Thomas Christians of India. It was Timothy who wisely granted to the churches of southern India independence from the Persian metropolitanate of Fars (Rewardashir), appointing what appears to have been the first known metropolitan in India.[102] Mingana also reports an assertion of Mari, the twelfth-century Nestorian historian, that "Timothy converted to the (Christian) faith the Khagan (king) of the Turks . . . and instructed many in Christian doctrine."[103]

Timothy was educated, it appears, at the great Adiabene monastery of Beit 'Abhe, "Mother of Patriarchs and Bishops."[104] And of missionaries, we might add. The power of Nestorian missionary outreach must never be attributed so much to the ecclesiastical center of the church, the patriarchate, as to its centers of spiritual renewal in the monasteries. Thomas, bishop of Marga about 840, writing a history of the monastics of Beit 'Abhe, which he had himself entered as a youth before rising to prominence as bishop and metropolitan, proudly records the names of four patriarchs who had been sons of the monastery. He is equally proud of its missionaries: of a martyred missionary bishop, Shubhhal-Isho', an Arab "crowned . . . with swords" by pagans in the mountains around the Caspian Sea,[105] and of David, elected to be missionary bishop of Beit Sinaye (China).[106] Thomas describes the missionary work of the monasteries thus: they sent out men not just to "established and princely thrones . . . in flourishing towns and civilized countries, but also [to] countries which were destitute of all knowledge of Divine things and holy doctrines, and which abounded in sorcery and idolatry . . . that they might uproot the evil and sow the good, and drive out the darkness of error and make to shine upon them the glorious light of their doctrine."[107]

Perhaps it was Timothy's commitment to monastic renewal at home as well as to the worldwide spread of the gospel that also led him, in a world that seemed to be turning Muslim, to work co-operatively with, instead of against, the Christians of the non-Nestorian *dhimmis*, the Jacobites and Melkites. Apparently, as appears from comments in his letters, he had been given a measure of authority over them through the influence of Harun al-Rashid's personal physician, the Nestorian Gabriel b. Buhtisu, and treated them with even-handed, ecumenical fairness while not wavering an inch from his own strongly held Nestorian theology.[108]

His patriarchate coincided with the great age of Muslim intellectual ferment and inquiry that P. K. Hitti calls "the epoch of translation" (ca. 750–850), a time when Islamic thinkers were first discovering the world of Greek science and philosophy and the church in the West was in the process of forgetting it. One of the greatest contributions of the Asian church to the history of human thought was its key role in transmitting to the Arab empire the heritage of the Greek classics and, through the Arabs, preserving them for rediscovery and transformation of the West in the Renaissance and Reformation.

Arabian education remained in debt to the scholars of the Christian *dhimmis* all through the first hundred years of the 'Abbasid dynasty. One of the reasons Caliph Mahdi welcomed Timothy to debate was undoubtedly because Timothy was a zealous patron of education, familiar with Aristotle and well versed in Greek and Syriac texts.[109] "Remember that the school is the mother and nurse of sons of the church," he once wrote.[110]

Thanks in large part to pioneering Christian translators, the Arabs, who hitherto had been little schooled but were possessed of quick and inquiring minds, were propelled into an intellectual revolution. As Hitti puts it, "In only a few decades Arab scholars assimilated what had taken the Greeks centuries to develop."[111] Some astronomical and mathematical works were brought to Baghdad by travelers from India but the earliest and by far the most important source was classical Greece communicated through Christian Greece to Christian Syrians and Persians and passed on by them to the Arabs.[112]

One of the earliest translators was Theophilus (Thawafil) ibn Tuma (d. 785), a Maronite Christian[113] and astrologer of Mahdi, the caliph who debated with Timothy I. He translated parts of Homer's *Iliad* into Arabic. Another was a Syrian Christian Yuhanna ibn-Masawayh (d. 857), who was as witty as he was learned and translated medical books for Harun al-Rashid. Hitti relates the story that when he was taunted by a court attendant, he turned on the man and said, "If the folly with which you are afflicted were turned into intelligence and divided among a hundred beetles, each would then become more intelligent than Aristotle."[114]

But the greatest of all was Yuhanna's student, Hunayn ibn-Ishaq (809–873), a Nestorian from Hirta, which once had been the capital of the old Lakhmid Arab kingdom on Persia's southern border. From the lowly post of physician's clerk he rose to become superintendent of the library and school of Caliph Ma'mun (813–833). This gave him responsibility over all the court's scientific translation projects, where texts were usually translated first from Greek into Syriac, which was the language of the Nestorian church, and then from Syriac into Arabic. Much of the translation into Arabic was done by Hunayn's son Ishaq who became the Arab empire's foremost translator of the works of Aristotle. Hunayn himself is credited with translations of Galen, Hippocrates, Plato's *Republic,* and many other works.[115]

The caliph is said to have paid Hunayn in gold the weight of the books he translated, so precious were they considered. Hitti further reports that this Christian scholar, translator of the most famous medical books of the world of his time and times long after, was so trusted at the Muslim court that the tenth caliph, Mutawakkil, made him his personal physician. However, when Hunayn refused to poison one of the caliph's enemies he was clapped into jail. The caliph asked what kept him from obeying the order. He told the caliph:

> Two things: my religion and my profession. My religion decrees that we should do good even to our enemies, how much more to our friends. And my profession is instituted for the benefit of humanity and limited to their relief and cure . . .[116]

The incident was an omen of things to come. Mutawakkil, grandson of Harun al-Rashid by a Turkish slave, took alarm at the explosion of new knowledge pouring into the empire from non-Muslim sources. His caliphate (847–861) hardened the empire into a pattern of rigid Sunnite orthodoxy that began to stifle independent research and scientific inquiry and increase the suppression of religious dissent by force when he thought necessary.

He turned first on educated, free-thinking Muslims called Mu-'tazilites, whose speculative theories about free will and advocacy of less literal interpretation of the Koran had been officially approved by his uncle, the caliph Ma'mun, but who now were branded as heretics. This drove many into secret reconversion to Christianity or Zoroastrianism or into the underground "cells" of the Manichaeans, who had found more tolerance in central Asia than at the Mesopotamian center of the caliphate.[117]

For his persecution of Christians Mutawakkil was labeled "hater of Christians" by the thirteenth-century Jacobite historian Bar Hebraeus (Abul Faraj, in Arabic), which may not be entirely fair. For one thing, he suppressed Shi'ite Muslims even more violently than Christians.[118] And in justice it must be pointed out that at no time under the 'Abbasids were Christians ever really free from pressures and discrimination. Mutawakkil's policies, while more sharply reactionary, were little more severe on Christians than what they had already experienced before. Violent persecution when it did occur was usually short and localized. Oppression and discrimination, on the other hand, were cumulative.

Even under the generous caliph Mahdi, a hundred years earlier, the empire was not always kind. At one point, angry at a defeat on the border at the hands of his Byzantine Christian enemies, Mahdi ordered the destruction of some churches and as added punishment forbade Christians to have slaves.[119] This was the same caliph who debated so politely with Timothy I. In his reign also, the rise of a disturbingly radical and ascetic Manichaean sect brought a spasm of ruthless oppression directed mostly against the radicals but broadening into harassment of Christian monasteries whose monks were sometimes confused with Manichaeans.[120] Against the Christians it took a short, cruel twist and focused especially on women. Manichaeans were more often summarily executed, but Christian women were strung up and whipped with bull's-hide lashes for as many as a thousand strokes to make them apostatize.[121]

Less severe but longer lasting were the pressures under Mahdi's second son, Harun al-Rashid, of *Arabian Nights* fame, whose celebrated reign (785–809) is remembered in Arab history as the pinnacle of 'Abbasid power and wealth. His siege of Constantinople forced the regent-empress Irene to sue for peace and pay a humiliatingly large tribute.[122] Poet, scholar, and master of the East, the caliph regally exchanged gifts with Charlemagne, whom he regarded as master of the West. But by the Christians of the East he is remembered with some bitterness as occasional destroyer of churches and persecutor of the faithful.

Perhaps because of his war with Christian Constantinople, toward the end of his rule, in 807, he ordered all churches in border lands torn down, as well as any that had been built since the conquest. How many were actually destroyed is not known. Some were immediately rebuilt by order of Harun himself, but the threat remained, and an incident that occurred about ten years later indicates how severe it was in various parts of the empire. An anonymous chronicle records that Arab Muslims from the old Osrhoene area of Edessa, Samosata, and Harran asked the governor (Abdulla ibn-Tahir) to destroy any Christian churches built in the last ten years, but he refused. "The poor Christians have not rebuilt one-tenth of the churches which have been ruined and burnt," he told them. On the whole, the report adds, Christians under that governor prospered in peace, but their activities continued to be limited.

By that time, about 820 according to A. S. Tritton's study of non-Muslims under the caliphs, the building of new churches and synagogues was prohibited in Muslim towns, and only elsewhere could "Christians build churches as they pleased and celebrate their festivals."[123] Harun al-Rashid also revived an earlier practice of forcing Christians, Jews, and other religious minorities to mark themselves publicly as non-Muslims by their dress.

Christians and Jews were further crippled in any defense of themselves before the law by a Muslim juridical ruling that their testimony could not be received in court against Muslims, since the Koran plainly charges that they had corrupted their Scriptures and were therefore untrustworthy (2:70; 5:16–18). But there were exceptions, and different schools of Muslim law interpreted this particular form of discrimination in differing ways. For example, could a Muslim sick unto death on a journey call on a Christian or Jew to witness to his last will and testament? Some said yes, others no. Muslims also argued over whether a non-Muslim could be accepted as a witness against another non-Muslim. But where the testimony of non-Muslims was accepted, they could swear only by God, not by "God who revealed the Gospel to Jesus" or if Jewish not by "God who revealed the Law."[124]

Christian family life was also adversely affected. The unbroken law was that a Muslim woman could never marry a non-Muslim. A Christian woman married to a Muslim had to compromise and obey some of the Muslim rituals of washing, or her husband lost all rights. If a Christian woman turned Muslim in the absence of her Christian husband she could marry again before his return. Moreover, if either Christian parent turned Muslim, their underage children were reckoned as Muslim.[125]

The Decline of the Church (850–1000)

It is not easy to point to any date as the beginning of the decline of the church in the 'Abbasid empire, but perhaps the repressive caliphate of Mutawakkil (847–861) in the middle of the ninth century is as accurate as any. If so, it suggests a hitherto unremarked parallel to the decline of the Nestorians in T'ang-dynasty China after the religious persecutions of the emperor Wu Tsung (840–846).[126] Mid-ninth century seems to be the point of no return for Christian growth and freedom in both eastern and western Asia in those first one thousand years.

In 849[127] Mutawakkil abruptly deposed Patriarch Theodosius and in 850 revived and intensified the offensive practice of marking

Christians by their yellow clothes and patches. Mari, the Nestorian historian, describes the persecution thus:

> [A jealous Christian] began out of hatred to accuse [the Patriarch The-
> odosius]. . . . And al-Mutawakkil was angry and commanded him
> [Theodosius] to be deposed, and a month after his appointment sent to
> Baghdad and put him in prison, and proceeded to destroy the churches
> and monasteries. . . . And he prevented the Christians from riding on
> horses, and he commanded them to wear dyed garments and to put a
> patch upon their shirts, and that none of them should be seen in the
> market on Friday, and that the graves of their dead should be de-
> stroyed, and that their children should not learn Arabic in the schools,
> and that their house-tax should be brought to the mosque, and that the
> wooden images of devils should be erected on their gates, and a sound
> summoning them to prayer should not be heard, and place should not
> be set apart for the liturgy . . .[128]

It was a mark of special shame in Asian eyes that they were forced to deface the graves of their ancestors by razing them level to the ground. Mob uprisings occurred against Christians in 923/924 near Jerusalem, in Hims and in Damascus, but not by order of the caliph and with no executions.

More disturbing than oppression by a non-Christian society as a factor in the church's decline are hints in the histories of the times that the church was decaying from within. The records of the patriarchs are unpleasantly laced with stories of ecclesiastical bribery and greed. Thomas of Marga relates how the patriarch Salibazacha tried to steal from the monks of Beit 'Abhe their precious copy of the Gospels that was splendidly adorned with gold and jewels.[129] The Nestorian patriarch Abraham III (905–937) used large sums in bribes to the caliph to discredit his rival, the Jacobite patriarch of Antioch, and strip from him the right to maintain a resident Jacobite bishop in Baghdad.[130]

Yet more distressing are evidences of corruption in the monasteries. For all his admiration of the great saints always found there, Thomas of Marga is too honest to hide the sins of others not so saintly. He tells of monks who had secretly taken wives,[131] and of schisms and insubordination,[132] and of the heresies of the overly ascetic Messalians,[133] and of the decline of worship and liturgy, when, as he described it, all was in confusion and "each country, town, and monastery and school had its own hymns and songs of praise and tunes, and sang them [each] in its own way."[134] Already in the eighth century his great monastery was in decline. Its land, which was its agricultural endowment, was poorly kept and its monks, said one observer, "are utterly destitute."[135] In 832 when

Thomas entered the monastery, marauding Kurds had recently looted it and its end was near.

But the recital of such examples of discrimination and decay must not allow us to paint in too dark colors the life of Christians under the 'Abbasids even in the period of their decline. The *dhimmi* system protected as well as deprived. There were few martyrs, and no underground church. Many fled, mostly into Roman territory, but there were few executions and no general massacres. The Christian patriarchs, Nestorian and Jacobite, still ruled in their seats of honor, and bishops and priests freely preached and administered the sacraments.

As the tenth century ended at the year 1000, organizationally, if not in numbers, the church was still growing. It had added eight new Nestorian metropolitanates (archbishoprics) while coping with all the handicaps of a restricted religious minority under Muslim rule. Five hundred years earlier, when Nestorians at the Fifth Synod (of Babai in 497) had finally and irrevocably asserted the complete independence of their Persian Church of the East from the church of the West, there had been only seven such provinces.[136] By the year 1000, after another century and a half under Zoroastrian Persia, followed by three and a half centuries under Islam, there were fifteen recognized Nestorian metropolitan provinces within the 'Abbasid empire.

The Nestorian patriarch was acknowledged to be the principal leader of all Christians. There were earlier suggestions of such Nestorian primacy, by Timothy I (778–820) for example, and an even clearer, though morally clouded, case in the time of Patriarch Abraham III (905–937), who by questionable means persuaded the caliph to prohibit the Jacobites from seating a bishop in Baghdad, as noted previously. But the first direct evidence of Muslim recognition of Nestorian primacy is a certificate granted by the caliph al-Kaim to the patriarch Ebedyeshu II ('Abdishu, 1074–1090) late in the eleventh century. As quoted by the historian Mari, writing about sixty years later in 1140, it reads:

It is you whom the Prince of Believers [the Caliph] has made catholicos of the Nestorian Christians living in Baghdad and the other regions and provinces, and and he declares you to be their bishop, and that of the Jacobites and of the Rum (Byzantines?) who inhabit the land of the Muslims or who come there, and he orders all to obey you.[137]

But his primacy hid the hard fact that as the tenth century ended, the appointment of patriarchs was in the caliph's, not the church's hands. He could override even the right of bishops to elect their own patriarch.[138]

By 1000 also, there was still great wealth in the church. Christian laymen could be found in high positions in education and government despite their second-class social status as *dhimmis*. They were sought after as teachers and personal secretaries but were no longer as necessary as in the golden age of translation two hundred years earlier. Arab Muslims and Syrian or Persian converts to Islam, now equally well trained, were taking their places in ever-increasing numbers. Christian merchants and landowners still had great wealth and aroused much envy, but heavy taxes were slowly squeezing Christians out of major financial influence, just as they had from the beginning been denied social equality and visible political influence.

Christians held their own longest perhaps in the field of medicine. For two hundred and fifty years, ever since the second caliph, Mansur, turned to the famous Nestorian medical school in Gundishapur (Beit Lapat) and in 765 brought its director, Georgius ibn-Buhtisu, of a noted Persian medical family, to be his personal physician in newly founded Baghdad,[139] most 'Abbasid caliphs had chosen Christians as their doctors. This continued even into the eleventh century. But many of them, like 'Ali al-Tabari (fl. ca. 854), were unable to stand the pressures and left the faith. This Tabari (not to be confused with his contemporary the great historian of Islam Abu-Ja'far al-Tabari) was personal physician to Caliph Mutawakkil and converted to Islam during the difficult years of that caliphate. By order of that "hater of Christians" he wrote the most effective and sustained defense of Islam against Christianity yet produced up to that time, *The Book of Religion and Empire (Kitab al-Din . . .).*[140]

> If we were to ask the Christians in particular why they disbelieve in the Prophet, they would say, Because of three reasons, first because we do not find that any of the prophets prohesied about him before his coming, secondly because we do not find in the Quran any mention of a miracle . . . , and thirdly because Christ prophesied that there would be no prophet after Him. These are their strongest argements, and I will refute them by the help of God.[141]

Thus at the end of the first Christian millennium, the church was wounded, perhaps fatally, and declining. Why? Comparisons with the West under pagan Rome are misleading. In three hundred years Western Christians were given a Constantine; Asia still had no Constantine after nine hundred years. But the question remains: why? Persecution, yes; but violence under the Persian Sassanids lasted longer and was more brutal, yet the church survived with vigor. Taxation? Social ostracism? Deprivation of political freedoms?

Yes, all these, and it is true that Asia's Christians by the year 1000 had known the weight of these burdens longer than any Christian community anywhere in the world of that first millennium.[142] But none of these quite answers the question. The Christian tradition is that no force in this world can destroy the church. In the words of St. Paul, "We are afflicted . . . but not crushed . . .; persecuted but not forsaken; struck down but not driven to despair" (2 Cor. 4:8–9). Why not in ninth-century Asia?

Perhaps the best answer lies almost hidden in a phrase of a famous dialogue between a Christian, 'Abd al-Masih al-Kindi, and a Muslim apologist, al-Hashimi. It was reportedly held before the caliph Ma'mun in the ninth century. Toward the end of the long debate, the Christian confessed, "But now the monks are no longer really missionaries."[143]

If Christians were no longer evangelizing and the monasteries no longer producing missionaries, the decline might well be fatal. And yet, after three hundred years under Islamic rule the church of the *dhimmis*, though separated, battered, limited, and self-wounded, was still surviving and still undefeated as part of what Christians call "the body of Christ on earth."

NOTES

1. *Histoire Nestorienne (Chronicle of Seert)*, ed. A. Scher, in *PO* t. 13, fasc. 4, no. 65, p. 581f. The date of the *Chronicle* is uncertain; internal evidence suggests either after 828 or after 1228.

2. On the Christian side, the treaty is quoted at length by the *Chronicle of Seert* (*PO*, 601ff.), which extends its provisions to all Christian sects, as quoted. Mari ibn Suleiman, a Nestorian historian of the twelfth century, gives a different version that attributes the pact to a direct meeting between Muhammad before his death in 632 and the Nestorian patriarch Yeshuyab II (628–643), cited by L. E. Browne, *The Eclipse of Christianity in Asia from the Time of Muhammad till the Fourteenth Century* (Cambridge: Cambridge Univ. Press, 1933), 41. On the Arab side references to the treaty are found in Baladhuri, a ninth-century Persian historian (*Kitab al-farq bain al-firaq*, trans. P. K. Hitti [Cairo, 1924]). Six copies of the "Covenant of the Prophet" are still preserved in St. Catherine's Monastery at the foot of Mt. Sinai (A. S. Atiya, *A History of Eastern Christianity* (London: Methuen, 1968), 268.

3. There are numerous references to Christian Najran in the early biographies of Muhammad, especially in ibn-Ishaq's *Life of Muhammed*, trans. A. Guillaume (Oxford: Oxford Univ. Press, 1955), 14ff., and see Guillaume's comments on p. xviii. See also ibn-Ishaq's lengthy account of the Christian deputation from Najran to Muhammad in Medina, probably based on later memories, 270ff.

4. Not until at least 125 years after Muhammad's death do the first collections of the historical traditions of his life begin to appear.

5. ibn-Ishaq (707–773), *Sirat Rasul Allah* (as edited in the ninth century by ibn-Hisham), trans. Guillaume as *The Life of Muhammed*, 79–81. This is the first and best of the early biographies of the Prophet, well documented for the period after the *hegira (hijrah)* of 622 but uncritical about the years before. Muslim historians used the legend to indicate recognition of Muhammad's holiness by a Christian, while Christians referred to it as proof that Christian teaching was the source of the Prophet's inspiration.

6. ibn-Ishaq, *Life,* trans. Guillaume, 180. These early anecdotes are from the more uncritical section of the biography, the early period at Mecca.

7. R. Bell, *The Origin of Islam in Its Christian Environment* (London: Cass, 1926, reprint, 1968), 57f.

8. See K. Cragg, *Muhammad and the Christian* (Maryknoll, NY: Orbis, 1984), 18.

9. See the account of his visions in the Koran, 53:1–18.

10. "The extraordinary events of the seventh century completely reversed the role of the Arabs. From a peninsular people who had played a marginal and subordinate role in history, they develop into an imperial race, and succeed in terminating the Indo-European interregnum in the Near East, reasserting Semite political presence in the region, and carrying the Semitic political factor into the medieval world by the foundation of a universal state," Irfan Shahid, in P. M. Holt et al., eds., *The Cambridge History of Islam,* vols. 1 and 2 (Cambridge: Cambridge Univ. Press, 1970), 1:25f.

11. ibn-Ishaq, *Life,* trans. Guillaume, 112–231.

12. *Madinat al-nabi,* i.e., "city of the Prophet."

13. A.H. (*anno Hegirae*) 1, therefore, is A.D. 622. On the problem of correlating the Koranic and Western calendars and fixing the date, see *E. J. Brill's First Encyclopedia of Islam,* "Hidjra (Hegira)," (Leiden, 1987).

14. "The Jews have their religion and the Muslims have theirs. . . . Each must help the other against anyone who attacks the people of this document," ibn-Ishaq, *Life,* 233.

15. ibn-Ishaq, *Life,* 239–70.

16. The best critical analysis of this period is W. M. Watt's *Muhammad at Medina* (Oxford: Clarendon, 1956), whose interpretation I follow.

17. See the account and analysis in Watt, *Muhammad at Medina,* 204–20. Also ibn-Ishaq, *Life,* 239–47.

18. In the later development of Islam, however, it must be remembered that, as Goldziher noted long ago, "the *Sunna* [tradition] is the judge over the Koran, and not the Koran judge of the *Sunna*" (I. Goldziher, *Mohammedanische Studien,* vol. 2 [Halle: Niemeyer, 1889], 19).

19. See Bell's discussion of Christian and Jewish influences on Muhammad, *Origin of Islam,* 100ff.

20. Browne, *Eclipse of Christianity,* 14. Historians are uncertain about the degree of Muhammad's own literacy. He used secretaries. One of his wives (Hafsa) could read and write; two others could read but not write.

21. It is not known when the first translation of the Gospels into Arabic was made. A tradition, repeated by Bar Hebraeus (Abu'l Faraj) in the thirteenth century, relates that an Arab prince ordered "a Monophysite named John" to make a translation around the year 635, but the earliest surviving fragments cannot be dated earlier than the ninth century (see B. Spuler, *The Muslim World,* pt. I [Leiden: Brill, 1960], 26 n. 1. Whatever Muhammad may have learned directly of the Christian Scriptures must have come from oral communication. See *The Encyclopedia of Islam* (Leiden: Brill, 1913–1936ff.) on "injil" (or *indjil,* "gospel"). *Injil* in the Koran refers primarily to the revelation of God to Jesus and secondarily to the Christian Scriptures.

22. Spuler, 1:117.

23. References and quotations from the Koran are from the translation of A. Yusuf Ali, *The Meaning of the Glorious Quran: Text* [Arabic], *Translation* [English] *and Commentary* (Cairo, Beirut, and Lahore, 1938ff.), which is the work of a committed Muslim. For felicitous English phrasing compare A. J. Arberry in Oxford's The World's Classics series, *The Koran Interpreted* (Oxford, London, New York: Oxford University Press, 1964). Verse numbering varies slightly in other translations.

24. See especially Surahs 3, 5, and 19, which are named for events connected with Jesus. Other scattered references should be noted, particularly 2:87, 253; 4:157–159, 171; 9:30–31; 43:57–65; 57:26–27; and 61:6. For extended treatments of Jesus as portrayed in the Koran see G. Parrinder, *Jesus in the Qu'ran* (New York: Sheldon, 1965); and S. M. Zwemer, *The Moslem Christ, An Essay on the Life, Character, and Teachings of Jesus Christ According to the Koran and Orthodox Tradition* (New York: American Tract Society, 1912); and Cragg, *Muhammad and the Christian,* 100–120.

25. Muslim commentators have never quite been able to correlate the statement in Surah 4:157 that Jesus did not die, with that in Surah 3:55, where God says (in literal translation) "I will make thee die." Muslim translations soften this in English to "I will take thee."

26. W. Muir, *The Life of Mohammed* (Edinburgh: Grant, 1923), xxff.

27. Some, like T. P. Hughes, in *A Dictionary of Islam* (Lahore: Premier Book House, 1885; reprint 1964) argue that the Koran never disputes the genuine inspiration of the New Testament text, but only refers to its distortion by Christians in their reading of it (see article on "Injil").

28. Holt, *Cambridge History of Islam* 1:33–35. See also Bell, *Origin of Islam,* 12ff.

29. In this first period the caliphate, with its capital in Medina, had four rulers:

Abu Bakr, 632–634. Father-in-law of Muhammad through his daughter Aisha; united rebellious Arab tribes.

'Umar (Omar), 634–644. Father-in-law of Muhammad through his daughter Hafsa; defeated Byzantines and Persians from Alexandria, Jerusalem, Damascus, and Seleucia-Ctesiphon and the east; regulated relations with the Christian minority.

'Uthman, 644–656. Son-in-law of Muhammad through marriage to two of the Prophet's daughters, Ruqayya and Umm Kulthum; ordered compilation of the authorized edition of the Koran.

'Ali, 656–661. Son-in-law of Muhammad through Fatima; his civil war against the Umayyad family of 'Uthman divided Islam into what became Shi'ite against Sunni sections.

30. Surah 49:14 expresses Muhammad's disappointment at more than their tribal disunity; it chides the Bedouins for not even being believers, but only people who have outwardly submitted to Islam. "Not yet has faith entered your hearts."

31. Some say six or seven, others "about a dozen," but the distinction between wife and concubine is ambiguous. The two primary categories were dowered wives and undowered wives, slave or free. Mariyah the Copt and mother of his only son was a slave, not a captured slave but one received as a gift. See Watt, *Muhammad at Medina*, 395ff. Most of the marriages had supportive political motives, as was the Arab custom. See Watt, 395ff.; Muir, *Life of Muhammed*, 289ff., 298ff.; M. Rodinson, *Mohammed*, trans. A. Carter (Harmondsworth, England: Penguin, 1971), 279ff.

32. The term *caliph* is from the Arabic *khalifah*, "successor," not "prophet," for in Islam, Muhammad is the last and greatest of the prophets.

33. G. E. von Grunebaum, *Classical Islam: A History 600–1258*, trans. K. Watson (London: Allen & Unwin, 1970).

34. See H. A. R. Gibb and J. H. Kraemer, eds., *Shorter Encyclopedia of Islam* (Leiden: Brill, 1953), s.v. "Quran."

35. The Traditions (*hadith*) are the collected oral traditions about Muhammad. The standard and most authoritative edition, "the six books," is the work of al-Bukhari (810–970), whose *Al-Jami' as-Sahih*, is a selective and classified compilation made from 600,000 traditions. "An oath taken on it is valid, as if taken on the Koran," writes P. K. Hitti, *History of the Arabs from Earliest Times to the Present*, 5th ed. (New York: Macmillan, 1953), 395.

36. The last king of the Lakhmids (Persian Arabia), was al-Numan III, a Nestorian Christian who died in 602. The Druze of modern Lebanon trace their origins to him. West of the desert in the kingdom of the Ghassanids (Byzantine Arabia), the later kings became zealous Monophysite Christians, thereby losing the trust of Constantinople though their last king, Jabala

ibn-al-Ayham, fought for the Byzantine emperor Heraclius against the Arab advance. When Roman Syria fell to Islam in 636 he turned Muslim, only to renounce his conversion and turn Christian again against the caliph 'Umar. See Hitti, *History of the Arabs*, 78–86.

37. al-Baladhuri, *The Origins of the Islamic State (Kitab Futuh al-Buldan)*, trans. P. K. Hitti (New York: Columbia Univ. Press, 1916), 210. The Muslim historian Baladhuri died in 892.

38. Shi'ite Muslim tradition traces part of its authority in Iran to the alleged marriage of their martyred saint, Husain, son of 'Ali, to the daughter of the last Sassanid shah of Persia, Yazdegerd III. A. E. Belyaev, *Arabs, Islam and the Arab Caliphate in the Early Middle Ages* (London and New York: Pall Mall and Praeger, 1965), 181.

39. Quoted by A. S. Tritton, *The Caliphs and Their Non-Muslim Subjects* (London: F. Cass, 1970), 10, from Baladhuri, *Futuh al-Buldan;* but cf. Baladhuri, *Origins*, trans. Hitti, 187ff., 198, 201, 213f.

40. Baladhuri, *Origins*, 98–105.

41. Baladhuri, *Origins*, 284–86. See also Tritton, *Caliphs*, 89ff.; and Browne, *Eclipse of Christianity*, 32f.

42. Browne notes as "a solitary example of forced conversion of Christians to Islam" the Muslim attack on the servants of the Monastery of St. Catherine at Mt. Sinai, *Eclipse of Christianity*, 38. But it must be pointed out that this took place in the Arabian peninsula, not in conquered foreign territory.

43. See, for example, M. M. Siddiqi, *Development of Islamic State and Society* (Lahore, Pakistan: Institute of Islamic Culture, 1956). His pro-Muslim viewpoint is very obvious but should be listened to.

44. Hitti, *History of the Arabs*, 105.

45. Tritton, *Caliphs*, 141.

46. Tritton, *Caliphs*, 18f.

47. Tritton, *Caliphs*, 18f.

48. Both treaties are reported by the twelfth-century Nestorian historian Mari ibn Suleiman, whose *Book of the Tower* tends to use earlier sources uncritically. See Browne, *Eclipse of Christianity*, 41.

49. Browne, *Eclipse of Christianity*, 41, citing Assemani III, pt. II, xcvi.

50. Prefiguring the creation of the maphrianate was the elevation in 559 of the bishop of Beth Arabaye to the title of "metropolitan of the East." This first Jacobite metropolitan in Persia was martyred in 575 by Chosroes I. (See Atiya, *History of Eastern Christianity*, 183f.) The greatest of the maphrians was the thirteenth-century Bar Hebraeus, encyclopaedic historian and chronicler of the church in Asia up to the time of the Mongol invasions.

51. Atiya, *History of Eastern Christianity*, 195ff. For details of Bishop George's life, see Kathleen McVey "A Memra on the Life of Severus of Antioch by George, Bishop of the Arab Tribes," Ph.D. diss., Harvard, 1977.

52. The principal Umayyad caliphs were:

  1. Mu'awiya I (661–680), who made Syria the center of power.

  2. Yazid I (680–683), whose victory over a Shiite rebellion created a Shiite martyr-saint, Husain ibn-Ali, grandson of the Prophet.

  5. Abd al-Malik (685–705), who reformed and strengthened government finances and structures.

  6. Walid I (705–715), whose generals conquered central Asia and spread Islam eastward to the borders of China and India.

  8. 'Umar II (717–720), who freed converts to Islam from poll tax.

  10. Hisham (724–743), who restored a policy of tolerance to minorities.

  11. Walid II (743–744), who faced tribal rivalries and dynastic decline.

  14. Marwan II (745–750), last of the Umayyads.

53. Baladhuri, *Origins*, 210f. See also A. A. Vasiliev, *History of the Byzantine Empire*, 2 vols. (Madison: Univ. of Wisconsin Press, 1958), 1:194ff.

54. The family might have been of Kalb or Taghlib tribal origin, but that is only conjecture from the name. Baladhuri gives a vivid account of the surrender and the lenient terms granted the Christians in Damascus. Baladhuri, *Origins*, 186–93.

55. For the best critical summary of the biographical data available about this important figure, I rely principally on D. J. Sahas, *John of Damascus on Islam: The "Heresy of the Ishmaelites"* (Leiden: Brill, 1972), 32–48. Cf. J. Nasrallah, *Saint Jean de Damas, Son epoque, sa vie, son oeuvre* (Paris: Office des Editions Universitaires, 1950). John of Damascus belongs as much to Western church history as to Asian, but because of his unique position under Muslim rule he cannot be ignored in this survey. Sahas suggests 652 for John's birth, much earlier than the traditional 675. See Sahas, 38–48.

56. The legend is recorded in a hagiographic eleventh-century biography of John attributed to a patriarch of Jerusalem named John. The caliph ordered his hand cut off in punishment, says the *Life*, but when he prayed before an icon of the Holy Mother of God, it was miraculously restored.

57. Under Caliph 'Umar II (717–720). See below, p. 346.

58. A. A. Vasiliev, "The Iconoclastic Edict of Yazid II, A.D. 721", in *Dumbarton Oaks Papers*, 9–10 (1955–56): 25–47, cited by Sahas, *John*, 9ff.

59. Sahas, *John*, 54.

60. For the text in English of John of Damascus's chapter 101 on Islam in the *Fount of Knowledge*, pt. II (*De Haeresibus*), see John of Damascus, *Writings*, trans. F. H. Chase, Jr., vol. 37, *The Fathers of the Church* (New York: Fathers of the Church, Inc., 1958), 153–60. For critical comment, see Sahas, *John*, 67–95.

61. John of Damascus, *Writings* (Chase's introduction). For a short, perceptive analysis of John's theology as more philosophic and scholastic than

religious, see A. C. McGiffert, *A History of Christian Thought*, vol. 1 (New York: Scribner, 1932), 310–29.

62. John, *Writings*, 153. He was no less abrupt in his condemnation of Nestorians ("The Nestorians hold that God the Word exists by Himself and separately, and that His humanity exists by itself. . . . They do not attribute the both to the same Person"). At greater length he chastised Monophysites as "clumsy and stupid" in theological argument, "a godless and most abominable heresy," 138ff.

63. John, *Writings*. See the Koran, Surah 112.

64. Sahas, *John*, 79, whose complete critical commentary on the text (pp. 67–95) should be consulted.

65. John, *Writings*, 155ff. "As long as you say that Christ is the Word of God and Spirit . . ., if the Word of God is in God, then it is obvious that He is God. If however, He is outside of God, then, according to you, God is without word [reason] and without spirit . . . as if you were dealing with a stone or a piece of wood."

66. See pp. 349ff.

67. Hitti, *History of the Arabs*, 196, 254. See also H. Lammens, "Le Chantre des Omiades, Notes biographiques et litteraires sur le poete Arabe Chrétien Ahtal," *Journal Asiatique*, Neuvieme serie, 4 (Paris, 1894): 94–176, 193–241, 381–459.

68. The word is not quite equivalent to "ghetto," which has a spacial, localized connotation. *Dhimmi* is the one restricted but protected by the system, i.e., referring to the *people* in the ghetto; *dhimma* is the relationship between Muslim protector and the religious minorities (*dhimmis*) thus protected, i.e., the *system*, but not the place.

69. See 'A. al-H. Zarrinkub, in *Cambridge History of Iran*, vol. 4, *The Selected, Parthian and Sasanian Periods*, ed. E. Yarshatir, 1983, 50f. But many of the old penalties remained in force.

70. Surah 9 states, "Make war upon such of those to whom the Scriptures have been given as believe not in God . . . and who profess not the profession of the truth, until they pay tribute out of hand, and they be humbled." On taxation in this period, see D. C. Dennett, *Conversion and the Poll Tax in Early Islam* (Cambridge, MA: Harvard Univ. Press, 1950); and Tritton, *Caliphs*.

71. von Grunebaum, *Classical Islam*, 57, observes that in the Syrian provinces most Byzantine landowners abandoned their lands to the Arabs, but in Persia the owners "managed by and large to stay on."

72. These non-Arab, or "new" Muslims, were most numerous and active in Mesopotamia and Persia and were particularly resentful of the discriminatory taxes to which they were subjected. See Belyaev, *Arabs*, 178–84.

73. Tritton, *Caliphs*, 12ff., quoting from the *Kitab ul Umm*. This version dates

perhaps to around 810, but seems to combine features of a number of earlier texts.

74. Tritton, *Caliphs*, 13f.

75. Tritton, *Caliphs*, 118. This is uncomfortably reminiscent of Nazi impositions on Jews.

76. Tritton, *Caliphs*, 14.

77. This is in part an oversimplification. His tax policy is sometimes described as forgiveness of land tax (*kharaj*) for Muslim landowners and new converts and as double tax, that is land tax plus poll tax (*jizya*) for non-Muslims, but the two terms are used to interchangeably under the Umayyads, and taxes were collected so differently in various regions, that no such simplification is possible. All that can be said with certainty is that Umar lowered taxes drastically for Muslims and raised them for the people of the religious ghettos. See Tritton, *Caliphs*, 197-215, as amended by the research of F. Lokkegaard, *Islamic Taxation* (1930), and Dennett, *Conversion and the Poll Tax*.

78. Hitti, *History of the Arabs*, 222, 281f; see also Albert Hourani, *A History of the Arab Peoples* (Cambridge: Harvard U. Press, 1991), 30-33.

79. A collateral Umayyad dynasty survived in Spain until 1031. See Tritton, *Caliphs*, 22, 45, 79f.; Hitti, *History of the Arabs*, 234. The Khalid referred to is Khalid ul Kasri.

80. Browne, *Eclipse*, 51, citing Bar Hebraeus, *Chronicon Ecclesiasticum*.

81. Browne, *Eclipse*, citing Mari and Assemani (*Biblioteca Orientalis*).

82. The more noted Abbasid caliphs (whose names I give here with the nominal prefix "al-", which elsewhere will usually be omitted, and which are royal titles, not their personal names). See the list of Abbasids in Hourani, *History of the Arab Peoples*, 488. The names were:

1. al-Saffah (750-754), whose personal name, Abul Abbas, gave his dynasty the name Abbasid.

2. al-Mansur (754–775), turned against his Shi'ite allies, but adopted Persian ways and moved the capital to Damascus.

3. al-Mahdi (775–785), friend of the Nestorian patriarch Timothy I, but did not prevent sporadic persecution.

5. Harun al-Rashid (785–809), ruled at the height of 'Abbasid power, allowed further oppression of Christians.

6. al-Amin (809–813); decline of Arab influence.

7. al-Ma'mun (813–833); power flows to the provinces.

8. al-Mu'tasim (833–847), moved the court to Samarra but was unable to escape the rising power of the Turks in his empire.

10. al-Mutawakkil (847–861), revitalized Sunni orthodoxy and increased social and financial pressures on religious minorities.

15. al-Mu'tamid (870–892), encouraged the collection of "the Traditions" of the Muslim religion.

18. al-Muqtadir (908–932), lost western North Africa to the Fatimids, a sectarian Shi'ite dynasty.

22. al-Mustakfi (944–946), a puppet of Shi'ite Buyids (Buwayhids) from Iran who seized Baghdad, controlled the empire, and left to the caliph little but his religious authority.

23.   al-Muti' (946–974), lost Egypt to the Fatimids.

For an extensive survey of Arab sources in early 'Abbasid history, see F. Omar, *The 'Abbasid Caliphate, 750–786* (Baghdad: Univ. of Baghdad, 1969).

83. For the reference to China, see Hitti, p. 292, citing Tabari (ed. de Goeje [Leiden, 1881–82]), vol. 3, p. 272.

84. Hitti, *History of the Arabs,* 289f. Recent analyses interpret this also in terms of a replacement of Syrian influence with Iraqi-Iranian influence in administration (see *Cambridge History of Islam,* 1:108).

85. This was not the first open debate between a Christian apologist and a prominent Muslim. "The earliest and most important record," wrote Mingana in 1922, "seems to be the colloquy which took place in Syria between the Arab generals and the Monophysite Patriarch of Antioch, John I . . . in A.D. 639," the text of which was published by F. Nau in *Journal Asiatique* (1915) and summarized by Mingana in 1916. See A. Mingana, in his introduction to 'Ali al-Tabari's *Kitab al-Din* (Manchester: Manchester Univ. Press, 1922), vi.

86. Timothy I, *The Apology of Timothy the Patriarch before the Caliph Mahdi,* Syriac text and English translation ed. and trans. A. Mingana as "Woodbrooke Studies" no. 3, in *Bulletin of the John Rylands Library, Manchester* 12, no. 1 (January 1928): 137–298. See H. Putnam's critical analysis of the Arabic text with French translation, *L'Eglise et l'Islam sous Timothée I (780–823)* (Beirut: Dar el-Machreq, 1975), 169–327.

87. Timothy I, *Apology,* ed. Mingana, 152f.

88. Timothy I, *Apology,* 153ff.

89. Timothy I, *Apology,* 198ff., 205, 215.

90. Timothy I, *Apology,* 171f.; see pp. 153, 156, 159, 208, and *passim.*

91. Timothy I, *Apology,* 193. In his development of this argument Timothy reflects the anti-Judaic temper that increasingly marred Christian-Jewish relations from the late fourth century on, in Asia as well as in the West.

92. Timothy I, *Apology,* 197. Note that Timothy does not describe Muhammad as a prophet, but as "walking in the path of the prophets." He had already told the Caliph that "there is only one prophet who would come to the world after . . . Jesus Christ," and that is Elijah, quoting Malachi 4:4–6. (p. 190).

93. Timothy I, *Apology,* 197f.

94. Timothy I, *Apology,* 224–26.

95. On Timothy I and his patriarchate, see Putnam, *L'Eglise et l'Islam*; and R. J. Bidawid, *Les Lettres du Patriarche Nestorien Timothée I* (Vatican City: Bibliotheca Apostolica Vaticana, 1956), esp. 1–44, which summarizes his life, works, and fifty-nine of his surviving letters.

96. A. R. Vine (*The Nestorian Churches* [London: Independent, 1937]) lists the patriarchs of Seleucia-Ctesiphon for the first two hundred years of the 'Abbasid caliphate (750–1000) as follows:

Mar Aba II (742–752), Surinus (754), Jacob II (754–773), Hananyeshu II (774–778), Timothy I (778–820), Josue (820–824), Georgius II (825–829), VACANCY (829–832), Sabaryeshu II (832–836), Abraham II (836–849), VACANCY (849–852), Theodosius (852–858), Sergius (860–872), VACANCY (872–877), Enos (877–884), John II (884–892), John III (892–898), John IV (900–905), Abraham III (905–937), Emmanuel (938–960), Israel (962), Ebedyeshu I (936–986), Mares (987–1001).

97. Timothy was elected by a convocation of only four of the eight electoral metropolitans (Damascus, Holwan, Beth Seluk, and Merv). Even the prime metropolitan (of Beit Lapat) was not present. The election was disputed and Timothy accepted reconsecration by the metropolitan of Beit Lapat (J. B. Chabot, ed., *Synodicon Orientale ou Recueil de Synodes Nestoriens* (Paris: Klincksieck, 1902), 605–606.

98. Browne, *Eclipse of Christianity*, 57, citing Mari, fol. 185b, 'Amr, p. 64.

99. Vine, *Nestorian Churches*, 109f.

100. Chabot, *Synodicon Orientale*, 604–607; A. Baumstark, *Geschichte der syrischen Literatur* (Bonn: Markus and Weber, 1922), 217.

101. Cf. Vine, *Nestorian Churches*, 125; and see chap. 13, pp. 270, 271 n. 15.

102. Bar Hebraeus, *Eccl. Chronicle*, cited by Mingana, "Early Spread of Christianity in India," *Bulletin of the John Rylands Library* 10, no. 2 (July 1926): 467 (pp. 34–36 in reprint as pamphlet).

103. Mingana, "Early Spread of Christianity in Central Asia and the Far East," *Bulletin of the John Rylands Library* 9, no. 2 (July 1925): 308, citing Mari, the *Book of the Tower* (ca. 1140).

104. The phrase is from W. Budge in his introduction to Thomas of Marga's *Book of Governors* 2 vols. (London: Kegan, Paul, Trench, Trubner, 1893), 1:cxv n. 1, and cxvi.

105. Thomas of Marga, *The Book of Governors*, ed. Budge, 2:469–86.

106. Thomas of Marga, *Book of Governors*, 2:448.

107. Thomas of Marga, *Book of Governors*, 2:489.

108. See his letter to the bishop of Elam; and a letter against the doctrines of Cyril of Alexandria. Timothy I, *Letters*, ed. O. Braun as "Timothei Patriarchae I epistolae," letters 21 and 39, in *CSCO Script. Syri*, series 2a, t. 57 (Syrian text and Latin translation; 1914, 1915). On his relations with non-Nestorian Christians see Putnam, *L'Eglise et l'Islam*, 84–88.

109. Putnam, *L'Eglise et l'Islam*, 85.

110. A. Fortescue, *The Lesser Eastern Churches* (London: Catholic Truth Society, 1913), 95, citing G. D. Malech, *History of the Syrian Nation*, 269f.

111. Hitti, *History of the Arabs*, 307.

112. Second only to the Christians in the early translation work was a school of star-worshiping Sabians from the vicinity of Edessa who had always been interested in astronomy and mathematics. Hitti, *History of the Arabs*, 314f.

113. Until the fifteenth century the Maronites were a separatist sect in the mountains of Lebanon who were considered heretics because of their doctrine of the "one divine will" in Christ, a belief that would make his human nature incomplete. About 1445, no longer unorthodox, they joined the Roman communion as one of its Uniate branches.

114. Hitti, *History of the Arabs*, 311f.

115. Hitti, *History of the Arabs*, 312–14. Thanks to Hunayn, says Hitti, "seven books of Galen's anatomy, lost in the original Greek, have been preserved in Arabic. Hunayn's version of the Old Testament from the Greek Septuagint did not survive."

116. Hitti, *History of the Arabs*, citing Ibn al-'Ibri, pp. 251–52.

117. B. Spuler, *The Muslim World*, 3 vols. (Leiden: Brill, 1960, 1969), 1:64f.

118. See Hitti, *History of the Arabs*, 439f.

119. See Putnam, *L'Eglise et l'Islam*, 132f. Today we would applaud the action forbidding slavery; then it was considered economic harrassment.

120. See the polemic against Christians by Jahiz (d. 869), a Muslim philosoper of the Mu'tazilite school: "When you hear their [the Christians'] speech about pardon and forgiveness, and their talk of the wandering monastic life, and their grumbling against anyone who eats flesh . . . and their encouraging continence in marriage . . . and their praise of the Catholicus . . . you know that between their religion and that of the *Zindiqs* [Manichaeans] there is an affinity," Browne, *Eclipse of Christianity*, 69, citing Finkel, *Three Essays*.

121. Vine, *Nestorian Churches*, 93.

122. Between 70,000 and 90,000 dinars, about $2 million or more today. See Hitti, *History of the Arabs*, 171n, 299.

123. Tritton, *Caliphs*, 49, citing *Kitab ul Umm* and an "Anonymous Syriac Chronicle" in *CSCO*, ser. 3, vols. 14, 15. See also Tritton's comments on the irregularity both of the terms and enforcement of the orders against new church building, 37ff.

124. Tritton, *Caliphs*, 186f.

125. Tritton, *Caliphs*, 187ff.

126. See chap. 15, pp. 303f.

127. The exact date is debated, as is the date of Theodosius' death. See Vine, *Nestorian Churches*, 95, 138.

128. Browne, *Eclipse of Christianity*, 54, citing Mari, fol. 191a–191b, and Bar Hebraeus, *Chronicon Ecclesiasticum* 2, col. 192. There are differences in the accounts.

129. Thomas of Marga, *Book of Governors*, 2:228–30.

130. Browne, *Eclipse of Christianity*, 57f., citing a quotation from Bar Hebraeus in Assemani, *Bibliotheca Orientalis* 3, pt. 2.

131. Thomas of Marga, *Book of Governors*, 2:53ff.

132. Thomas of Marga, *Book of Governors*, 2:153ff. Here Budge inserts the Arabic text of the patriarch's letter to the rebellious metropolitan of Fars (Rewardashir).

133. Thomas of Marga, *Book of Governors*, 2:91ff.

134. Thomas of Marga, *Book of Governors*, 2:293.

135. Thomas of Marga, *Book of Governors*, 2:247f.

136. Vine, *Nestorian Churches*, 57, 112–24, gives the two lists as follows. In 500 seven metropolitan provinces in the Persian empire: Kaskar, Nisibis, Teredon (Basra), Adiabene (Erbil, i.e., Arbela), Garamaea (Karkha), Khurasan (Merv), Atropatene (Taurisium). But by 1000 he lists these additional metropolitanates in the 'Abbasid empire: Gundishapur (established 834), Mosul (est. 651), Holwan (est. 754, later including Hamadan), Fars (est. probably at Rewardashir before 650), Herat (est. eighth century), Arran (est. at Bardaa about 900), Rai, near modern Teheran (est. about 778), and Dailan on the Caspian shore (est. at Mukar about 780). Cf. the list of metropolitans and bishops in W. G. Young, *Patriarch, Shah and Caliph*, 189–196.

In addition he lists the following metropolitanates outside the old Persian empire: China (est. at Chang'an about 636), Damascus (est. before end of seventh century), Turkestan (est. at Samarkand about 781), India (est. about 800). A metropolitan of Jerusalem was named in 1065 to care for Nestorian pilgrims. See also below, chap. 20, p. 449f.

137. Maris, Amri and Slibae, *De Patriarchis nestorianorum commentaria*, in Arabic, ed. with Latin translation by R. Gismondi, first part (Rome, 1899), 135/117. For further documentation on the authority of the Nestorian patriarchs, see Putnam, *L'Eglise of l'Islam*, 85–88. Cf. Vine, *Nestorian Churches*, 106, who uses another text (perhaps following J. S. Assemani, *Bibliotheca Orientalis* 3(2): 100) and translates "Jacobites and Rum" as "Rum [Roman Catholics], Jacobites and Melkites."

138. Browne, *Eclipse of Christianity*, 51.

139. On the Buhtisu family and other Christian physicians, see Putnam, *L'Eglise et l'Islam*, 97–104.

140. The *Kitab al-Din w'al-dawlah* by 'Ali ibn Saul Tabari, trans. A. Mingana (Manchester: University of Manchester, 1922). It was Bar Hebraeus who used the epithet "hater of Christians" about Mutawakkil.

141. Quoted by Browne, *Eclipse of Christianity*, 117.

142. A possible exception is the St. Thomas community in India, but the available evidence there is insufficient for comparison.

143. "Or les moines ne sont pas actuellement des propagandistes," George Tartar, ed. and trans. into French, *Dialogue Islamo-Chretien sous le calife Al-Mamum (813–834)* (Paris: Etudes Coraniques, Nouvelles Editions Latines, 1985), 280, a translation of al-Kindi's *Risalat (Apology)*. Al-Kindi (not the Muslim historian ibn-Ishaq al-Kindi) spoke or wrote the sentence as he was trying to explain why the Christian message was no longer attested by accompanying miracles.

Chapter *17*
The Survival of Christianity Under Medieval Islam (1000–1258)

"The most noble order [of the caliph] went forth . . . to make you catholicus of the Nestorian Christians in Baghdad and the other lands of Islam, and head of them and the others, Greeks, Jacobites and Melkites in the whole land . . . to protect you and the people of your faith in their persons and their property . . . and to confirm established customs in the burying of your dead and the protection of your churches and monasteries . . ."

—Charter granted to Patriarch
Abdishu III (A.D. 1138).
Translated by A. S. Tritton, *The
Caliphs and their Non-Muslim
Subjects*, 87f.

The Beginning of a New Millennium

As the Christian calendar crept closer to the year A.D. 1000 some in the Christianized West murmured fearfully about the coming of the Day of Judgment and the end of the world. But Asia followed different calendars and took little notice of the ending of a Christian millennium. Yet Asians too, for other reasons, might well have been wondering if their world was not about to fall apart. It was a time of declining empires and collapsing civilizations on the great continent. Time was shaping Asia into new and uncomfortable configurations.

For centuries the most powerful empires of Asia had been the T'ang dynasty in China at one end of the continent and the Arab empire of Islam at the other. But now suddenly the T'ang were gone, and the Arab heirs of Muhammad were losing their western boundaries to Fatimid Egypt and Christian Constantinople, while their eastern provinces were falling in great blocs to resurgent Persians and rising Turks. The warriors of the Islamic conquest had become puppets in the hands of their own mercenaries, the Turks. At one point, about the year 950, the people of Baghdad might have looked with pity on the sight of three of their former rulers,[1] deposed, blinded, begging for food in the streets. By 1000 the decline of the 'Abbasid empire was irreversible.

At the same time India saw its entire northwest fall to nomadic Turkic invaders from central Asia. About 1000 a Turkish leader, Mahmud the "Idol-Breaker," Muslim sultan of Ghazni, stormed out of what is now Afghanistan into Kashmir. He cut a wide swath across the fertile plains of northern India, toppling thrones and dynasties and plundering the golden temples. This was the beginning of the forcible conversion to Islam of the rich and Hindu Punjab in what is now Pakistan.

In the Far East, the downfall of the once-glorious T'ang empire left China splintered into "the five dynasties and the ten kingdoms." Not even the reappearance of some semblance of imperial power under the early Sung emperors (960–1127) kept Manchu and Mongol tribes from pouring through the Great Wall to strip the empire of its northern territories and threaten its continuing existence. In the year 1002 an official Korean embassy congratulated the Khitan "emperor" of the Liao rulers of Manchuria for his victory over imperial Sung China.

All across Asia the centers of civilization were crumbling, and the church did not escape the shock of the earthquakes.

The church in Asia at the beginning of this second millennium of its history faced prospects as bleak and unpromising as the apparent disintegration of the political and social structures of the whole continent. In contrast to Europe, where the opening of the second millennium marked the period of the evangelizing of the last pagan northern fringes of the Christian West from Scotland and Scandinavia to Prussia, Poland, and the Balkans, Asia was only a scattered sprinkling of still unsecured Christian beachheads.

The Nestorians in T'ang China had disappeared. Central Asia and northeastern India were turning Muslim. The Thomas Christians of southern India were prospering and respectable but were socially isolated as a minority caste community.

Only in the Middle East (western Asia) was there a significantly large nationally recognized body of Christians, but even there its status was severely limited and its survival precarious. On the narrow Mediterranean fringes of what had once been Byzantine Christian Asia, the old Melkite (Byzantine orthodox) and Jacobite (Syrian orthodox) communities were still comparatively numerous but they were linked separately, the first to Constantinople and the second to Antioch, which made their relationships uncomfortable. The Nestorian patriarch in Baghdad counted the allegiance of some 250 bishops in Asia, 20 metropolitans, and, at a guess, perhaps as many as 12 million adherents out of a worldwide population of 270 million people and maybe 50 million Christians.[2] His ecclesiastical jurisdiction covered the whole continent to India and China. But outside the *dhimmis*, the Christian minority communities of the 'Abbasid empire, Christianity was almost invisible. In no part of Asia after the Muslim conquest and before the age of Western discovery did a Christian community emerge in any Asian nation with enough numbers to produce a base for contributing a distinctive Christian character to the national identity.

The miracle is that the church survived at all. It survived the downfall of its Muslim overlords, the 'Abbasids. That might have been expected in the context of Arab decline. But it also survived the nearly fatal embrace of the Crusaders from Christian Europe, who came pouring into Asia ostensibly to set its Christians free but left them instead more misunderstood and vulnerable than ever before. It even survived the thundering onslaught of the new barbarians, the Mongols of Genghis Khan.

For the church in Asia the five centuries after the first Christian millennium contained only intermittent periods of growth and expansion. The years 1000 to 1500 could more truthfully be named the period of Christian survival in Asia, not victory.

The Breakup of the 'Abbasid Caliphate (1000–1258)

By the year 1000 the great Islamic empire of the 'Abbasid caliphs was falling apart. They had wrested power from their kinsmen of the Umayyad dynastic line in 750 and for the first hundred years of their rule had raised Arab prestige and wealth to the greatest height Arabs were ever to achieve.

But in actual power the caliphate by 850 had already begun to deteriorate. From that point on for four more long centuries, despite some moments of brilliance, the empire shriveled away to a slow humiliating death. In 1258 Arab Baghdad fell to the Mongols. The last Arab caliph of the warrior tribes that had dominated western Asia from Jerusalem to the far eastern edges of Persia was rolled in a rug and executed by Mongol nomads storming out of the windy steppes of central Asia into the Middle East as once the caliph's Arab ancestors had poured up from the desert six hundred years before.

Unexpectedly, the queen of the new conqueror in Baghdad proved to be a devout Christian Mongol. How that came about takes the story back to the year 1000, where this part of the history of Christianity in Asia must begin. Unlike the Nestorian church in tenth-century China, which completely disappeared when the great T'ang dynasty fell, the Nestorians in Persia outlasted the rise and fall of their Arab rulers, the 'Abbasids, and not only survived in the Muslim west but remained as an intermittent but ineradicable missionary presence across Asia from the Mediterranean coast to the China Sea until the arrival of the first Europeans.

The reason for the decline of the 'Abbasids is primarily a complex interwoven mixture of religious, ethnic, and political factors within Islam itself.[3] It was not the unsettling presence of non-Muslim minorities in the empire, such as Christians and Jews, or even the bruising onslaught of the Crusades that brought down the caliphate. Far more fatal were Islam's own splintering tribal and national rivalries, its bloody battles over succession to temporal power, and unresolved disputes about the center of spiritual authority in Islamic law and theology. Had not Muhammad himself warned, according to one line of tradition, that "The Israelites have been divided into seventy-one or seventy-two sects, and so have the Christians, but my community shall be divided into seventy-three"?[4]

The first and longest lasting divisive factor was religious. Islam's civil wars from the beginning revolved around two rival orthodoxies, the Sunnites (or Sunnis) and the Shi'ites (or 'Alids),[5] whose clash of

Muslim loyalties produced innumerable variations and a procession of losers and winners in the caliphate. Sunnite Umayyads overcame Shi'ite 'Alids in 650 to establish the first Arab dynasty,[6] and a hundred years later the founders of the second dynasty, the 'Abbasids, suspended their Sunnite sympathies long enough to persuade radical Shi'ites to join them in toppling the last of the Umayyads. Then, like so many revolutionaries before and since, they turned ruthlessly on their Shi'ite allies to build up Sunnite orthodoxy as the religious center of Arabic Islam.[7] That war, Sunnite against Shi'ite, has never ended.

Religious controversies also fueled the political divisions that marked the second factor in the empire's decline, for church and state are never rightly separated in Islam. Bitter theological differences, Sunnite and Shi'ite, eroded Arab unity in the ninth and tenth centuries and were effectively exploited to split the 'Abbasid caliphate into three warring empires, Umayyad Spain (Sunnite), Fatimid Egypt (Shi'ite), and 'Abbasid Asia in which a Sunnite majority and a Shi'ite minority (for the most part Persian) maintained an uneasy, volatile mixture of both competing orthodoxies.

The third factor in the dividing of Islam was ethnicity. From this viewpoint, the history of the 'Abbasids in Asia, which is our primary area of concern, divides into what B. Lewis describes as three "overlapping periods."[8] The first period was of the Arabs, whose conquest and rule we have been describing in the preceding chapters, but who after two hundred years of dominion in western Asia began to falter about the middle of the ninth century. The second period was a "Persian renaissance," which peaked in the tenth century. The third was the rise of the Turks, who overtook the Persians and ruled oriental western Asia for the next thousand years, save for a rough, brief interruption by their distant eastern cousins, the Mongols, in the thirteenth century.

Through it all the Church of the East survived. The more severely its Muslim overlords were preoccupied with their own internal rivalries, the less troubled, usually, were the minorities that held to other religions.

Christians During the "Persian Renaissance" (945–1055)

The first successful challenge to the 'Abbasid center in Baghdad came from the east, from Persia. The Persians, once proud, rich, and

Zoroastrian before the fall of their empire, were still possessed of considerable wealth in land holdings and remained persistent in preserving their Persian language and literature even after the conquest. Zoroastrians had always converted more rapidly to Islam than the Christians. Now by the tenth century, as the Turks poured in from north and east, the Zoroastrians feared the newcomers even more than the Arabs to whose rule they had become accustomed.[9] Their Zoroastrian religious structure of high priests and *mobeds* all but disappeared in sharp contrast to the enduring powers of the Christian patriarchates.

Baghdad found it politically expedient to rule its provinces on the central Asiatic borders of old Persia through Persian converts to Islam. Left largely to their own devices so long as they regularly channeled revenues to the capital and protected the 'Abbasid heartland in Mesopotamia from eastern invasions, the independent-minded Persians began to operate as semiautonomous local Iranian dynasties. They were Muslim but inclined more to Shi'ite than Sunnite doctrine and were politically restless under Arab domination from faraway Baghdad. These Persian warlords of the border became the missionary agents in the Islamization of the central Asiatic frontier, drawing the migrating shamanist tribes of the Turks into their cities and impressing them with the superior civilization and glittering wealth of the Muslim world of west Asia. But west Asia was no longer in control of Islam, and Sunnite Muslim orthodoxy itself was in peril.

In 945 a Shi'ite leader of mountain warriors on the southwest coast of the Caspian Sea, claiming Persian descent from the last emperor of the Sassanid dynasty and asserting his religious authority as a Shi'ite Muslim, seized Baghdad and deposed and blinded the Sunnite Arab caliph. As an outsider he was politically shrewd enough not to take for himself the title of caliph. Instead he separated the religious and administrative functions of the caliphate and installed as caliph a suitably royal, properly orthodox Sunnite 'Abbasid to succeed to the office of spiritual leader. But he purposefully and effectively stripped the caliph of his military and political powers and transferred the control of all such temporal affairs to himself as *amir*. For the next hundred years the empire was left with a succession of Sunnite Arab Muslims as puppet caliphs in the hands of Shi'ite Persian *amirs* who ruled the state.[10] This was the "Persian renaissance," the Buyid (or Buwayhid) period (945–1055), named for the Persian conqueror, Ahmad ibn-Buwayh. Some describe it as a period when 'Abbasids reigned but Buyids ruled in Baghdad.

However tragic these years were for the caliphs, for Christians it was a time of peace and tolerance. The greatest of the Buyid *amirs,* 'Adud (949–983), "the most illustrious ruler of his time," appointed a Christian, Nasr ibn-Harun, as his administrative *vizier,* with authority to build and repair churches and monasteries for the Christians throughout Mesopotamia (Iraq) and Persia (Iran).[11]

But when the power of the Buyid masters over their Arab caliphs loosened after 1000, once again in Baghdad religious dissidents felt the pressures of persecution. The caliph al-Qadir (991–1031) boldly seized a city mosque from the Shi'ites and turned it over to Sunnite leadership. Around 1012 he compelled Christians to wear distinctive clothing. There were stonings, and mobs broke up Christian funeral processions. Christian chroniclers lamented that many who "were not religious became Muslims and there was great affliction."[12] The Nestorian patriarch in the capital, however, as head of the largest community of Christians in the empire, was still a figure of considerable political influence.[13] The much-quoted statement in J. M. Neale's *History of the Holy Eastern Church* that "it may be doubted whether Innocent III possessed more spiritual power than the Patriarch in the city of the Caliphs,"[14] is not altogether exaggeration. He was speaking of the end of the twelfth century, but the roots of Christian expansion were already spreading vigorously before the tenth century, particularly in central Asia.

A missionary of the ninth century, Shabhalishu, is described as able to speak in Turkish, Tartar, and Mongol dialects.[15] In the tenth and eleventh centuries once more Nestorian missionaries pushed tirelessly eastward toward China from Merv and Bokhara and Tashkent in 'Abbasid territory. They reported considerable success among the Mongol tribes of the Keraits, Uighurs, Naimans, and Merkits.

It was in this period that there occurred the encounter in the Christian quarter of Baghdad, referred to earlier, between a Muslim writer and a Nestorian priest returning from China after the fall of the T'ang dynasty.[16] Despite the Christian's melancholy report that he found no trace of the missionaries or converts he had hoped to find in imperial China and despite the apparent loss to Islam of the Turkish tribes drifting west from central Asia, there is convincing evidence of Nestorian successes among the Mongol tribes eastward between the Turks and the Chinese, as we shall see later.

Christianity in Asia Under the Fatimids of Egypt (969–1043)

The tenth century was also, as mentioned above, a time of disastrous dismemberment of the caliphate into three Muslim empires, each on a different continent. All were Muslim, but two were orthodox Sunni and one was Shi'ite. In Asia the 'Abbasid caliph reigned in the imperial capital Baghdad, at least in name. In Europe a surviving line of the older Umayyad dynasty of Sunni Muslim caliphs, who had narrowly escaped the wholesale execution of the royal house by the victorious 'Abbasids in the eighth century, ruled southern Spain from their capital, Cordova, until 1301. The Arab/Berber Moors in fact held footholds in Spain until as late as 1492. The third Muslim empire was in North Africa, where an Arab Shi'ite caliphate known as the Fatimid dynasty separated itself from Baghdad and ruled Egypt and much of the southern Mediterranean coast until it fell in 1171.

Spain was far away and it was Egypt Baghdad feared most, though always lurking in the background was the threat of a more enormous danger, the possibility that Shi'ite religious rule in Fatimid Egypt on one side of the 'Abbasid capital might unite with Shi'ite rebellion in Persia on the other side of the empire and overturn three centuries of Sunni Muslim dominance of the Islamic heartland.

Early in the tenth century a Shi'ite claiming descent as an *imam* through Fatima, Muhammad's daughter, by way of the seventh hereditary *imam*, Isma'il, seized control of what is now Tunisia and from there extended his rebel rule east and west across North Africa from Morocco to Egypt. Unlike their 'Abbasid rivals in Baghdad who were losing temporal power to their Persian Shi'ite generals, the Fatimid rulers kept in their own hands both the military and the spiritual power as *imam* or *caliph*.[17] In 969 they entered what is now Old Cairo and founded their rival Muslim dynasty, the Fatimid.

It was not long before the Fatimids began to move back into Asia. In the same year, 969, they captured Damascus, threatened Baghdad itself, and by about 1000 ruled the Mediterranean from the Atlantic seaboard of North Africa to Jerusalem and Lebanon north of Beirut.

But this was the high point of Fatimid expansion into Asia. While Shi'ite Fatimids were advancing from Egypt against the Islamic center in Mesopotamia, from the north came a resurgent Byzantine Constantinople sensing 'Abbasid weakness and pouring its Christian armies across northern Syria. The thirty-year crusade (969–1025) of two Byzantine emperors, Nicephorus Phocas and Basil II, and their Armenian general John Zimisces carried the cross once more as far east as Damascus, then on eastward to Edessa and Nisibis, and south to the gates of Jerusalem. This might well be called the first of the Crusades except that Byzantium had always been fighting against the caliphs, and it was no more successful in the end than the "Great Crusades" from farther west which were to devastate the same shattered cities a hundred years later. Christian Byzantium was soon pushed back from Jerusalem, and southern Syria after 997 remained in Fatimid Muslim hands. Briefly about 1057, when the dynasty forged a short-lived alliance with Turks in Iraq, even Baghdad recognized the Fatimid ruler in Cairo as caliph of Islam.

At the height of the Cairo dynasty's power during the first years of Fatimid rule Christians not only survived but prospered. Syria remained essentially Christian, and as late as the early tenth century Mesopotamia (northern Iraq) was "[Muslim] in name but Christian in character."[18] It is sometimes forgotten by those who imagine the early medieval Middle East stripped of Christians as it is today, that in fact up until the time of the Crusades, Asian Christians were still in the majority west of the Euphrates and that its extremely important middle class of doctors, lawyers, clergymen, merchants, and bankers was composed primarily of Nestorians, Jacobites, and Jews.[19]

Under al-'Aziz (975–996), the fifth Fatimid ruler, the Egyptian Arab dynasty stopped the crusading Byzantines as they pushed down the Syrian coast from Asia Minor. Its caliphs ruled from the Atlantic to southern Syria with far greater toleration and effectiveness than their rival 'Abbasid cousins governed Baghdad. Despite the border war raging in the north, Egypt and southern Syria enjoyed a time of peace, prosperity, and unprecedented religious toleration on the Mediterranean coast.

In those early years of the Fatimid regime, the Egyptian caliphate (or anticaliphate, as it was regarded by Sunnites) was tolerant not only by choice but by necessity, for it was heavily dependent on non-Muslims and non-Arabs for internal administrative stability. Al-'Aziz administered his empire through a Christian vizier (*wazir*), a Nestorian whose name, 'Isa ibn-Nastur, is literally "Jesus the son of Nestorius." The caliph's wife was Russian, a sister of two orthodox (Melkite) patriarchs, the patriarch of Antioch and the patriarch of Jerusalem. His deputy vizier was a Jewish convert to Islam, a brilliant and tolerant finance minister. Churches were built, sometimes with money given by the caliph himself and by workmen protected from angry Muslims by guards supplied by the Shi'ite government.[20]

But when al-'Aziz died in 996 and was succeeded by his son, the "mad caliph" al-Hakim (996–1021), twenty-one years of unprecedented toleration were followed by a short, equally unprecedented persecution of Christians in Syria and Egypt. The new caliph was only eleven years old. One of his early acts, in 1002 while still in his teens, was to execute his father's Christian vizier, 'Isa ibn-Nastur. Five years later he began to burn crosses and order small mosques to be placed on the flat tops of Christian churches. L. E. Browne quotes a passage from the twelfth-century Nestorian historian Mari that describes the major persecution that followed for about ten years, peaking between 1009 and 1016:

> And in his [al-Hakim's] days the Christians of Egypt and Syria were persecuted and the churches of Jerusalem were destroyed . . . and the Christians were made to wear a wooden cross of five pounds weight around their necks, and a large number became Muslim; and hearts were torn with pity . . .[21]

The days of persecution were mercifully short. The manic-depressive young caliph began to fall into what his opponents called madness and his supporters interpreted as divine ecstasy. He relaxed his attacks against Christians and Jews. To the horror of orthodox Islam he declared himself divine, an incarnation of God, and diverted his anger from Christians to Muslims who refused to recognize his deity. It is believed that probably in retaliation for this blasphemy he was secretly killed in 1021 but his body was never found and a sect of his followers, called Druze, still survives in Syria and Lebanon to this day. They claim he is not dead but only "in hiding" and at the appointed time will return as the messianic Mahdi.

After Hakim the dynasty deteriorated. His successor, al-Zahir, was only sixteen, cared little about politics, and was dominated by his older sister. But he made one wise move. When the sister died in 1027, he signed a treaty of peace with the emperor of Constantinople, Constantine VIII, that contained two significant provisions concerning religion. One allowed the restoration of the Church of the Holy Sepulchre in Jerusalem and, in return, the refurbishing of a Muslim mosque in the Byzantine capital. The other item was even more important for the Christians of Fatimid Egypt and Asia (Syria and Palestine), who had suffered sorely under Hakim. The treaty stipulated that Christians who had been forcibly converted to Islam by the persecutions could again publicly return to their former faith without retribution. How long this concession remained in effect we do not know.[22]

The Rise of the Turks (992–1095)

The Fatimids, though Arabs, ruled predominantly in Africa, not in Asia, and affected Asian history only along that continent's western coast. Farther east in Asia during the long decline of the Arabs, another storm was brewing that would blow away the last weakening remnants of Arab 'Abbasid power altogether at its political heart, Mesopotamia. The storm center came out of the east in a swirling cloud of tribal Turks moving west and south from central Asia.

On the eve of the old millennium in the closing half of the tenth century, a fierce group of Turkic people, the Karluk or Ilek Turks, ruled by a powerful family that called itself Karakhanid, began to move out of the desert oasis city of Kashgar and over the mountains that separated the Chinese from the Iranian side of central Asia, across the borders of the 'Abbasid empire into the green valleys of Bokhara and Samarkand where the "Persian renaissance" was flourishing. Transoxiana, as the region north of the Oxus (Amu Darya) River is known, was then governed with almost complete independence and great flair by a Persian family, the Samanids. It was a center of Persian literature and science combined with Muslim missionary zeal for the conversion of their Turkic, barbarian neighbors. The new neighbors, however, kept moving in. They took Bokhara in 999,[23] seizing its power and wealth but accepting the religion of the Samanids to which they had already been introduced by Muslim missionaries. The missionaries were of two kinds. There were the traders moving constantly east and west along the Old Silk Road and bearing practical witness to their faith by the regularity of their public prayers. And there were the Sufis, pietist Muslim mystics with an important center across the Oxus in Balkh and with roots in early Syrian Christian asceticism.[24]

The missionary effectiveness of the Sufis lay more in example than in evangelism. They impressed the shamanist Turks with the radical asceticism of a life-style that to the nomads was visible proof of holiness. It was also about this time that Sufi sects that emphasized a teaching ministry as well as personal piety began to be organized. In one commentary on a tenth-century Sufi text, the third stage of the mystic's spiritual journey is described in vivid missionary terms as that of a "Director of Souls," who "like a camel-driver speeds everyone to his home."[25]

This Karakhanid dynasty, which some call "the first Islamic Turkic dynasty," dominated the strategic section of the Old Silk

Road from Bokhara over the high passes to Kashgar and the desert from 999 to 1074. But the future was not to be shaped by Karluk Turks but by another Turkic tribe, the Seljuks (Ghuzz Turks, called Turkomans by Arabs), who came after them in waves rolling west.

The first Seljuks may have been Nestorian Christians. Their earliest known leader, Seljuk, is said by tradition to have had two sons bearing Christian names, Mika'il (Michael) and Musa (Moses), and a grandson, Dawud (David).[26] The tribe came out of central Asia apparently to assist its fellow Turks, the Karakhanids of Bokhara and Samarkand as mercenary warriors, but, discontented with that role, a grandson of Seljuk bearing the Turkish name Toghril Beg (or Tughril, d. 1063) moved south to help the Turkish dynasty of the Ghaznavids of Afghanistan invade India.

But still unsatisfied with a subordinate role, the Seljuks turned on their masters and in 1040 carved out the beginnings of an empire for themselves in far eastern Persia between the Karakhanids north of the Oxus and the Ghaznavid empire in Afghanistan and the Punjab. From there, gathering momentum like a wave they moved restlessly westward against the Arab-Persian empire of the 'Abbasids. Fifteen years later Toghril and his Turkoman troops entered Baghdad in triumph as believing Sunnite Muslims to free the Sunnite Arab caliph from his Persian Shi'ite lords, the Buyids. The Seljuks, however, were neither Arab nor Persian. They were Turks, and the Middle East had new Muslim masters. The year was 1055.

For the next thirty years the Turks continued their inexorable advance west. Toghril's nephew Alp Arslan (1063–1072) conquered Christian Armenia and crowned that victory with a far greater one in 1071 at the battle of Manzikert (Malazgirt), where once again the superiority of Asian archers against Western cavalry proved decisive. The utter rout of the Byzantine land armies that followed startled the world of two continents. The emperor Romanus Diogenes himself could not escape and was captured by the Turks. It was, as P. K. Hitti points out, the first time Muslims had ever gained a permanent footing in "the land of the Romans," and Asia Minor has been Muslim ever since.[27]

But what Turkic nomads from the east had accomplished for Sunnite orthodoxy in the name of Muhammad, the flower of the Christian chivalry of Europe was about to attempt to duplicate from the West. They came fighting under another banner, the cross, and in another Name, but they too sought to restore western Asia to "the faith."

The Crusades (1095–1291)

The first of the Great Crusades began in 1095 with a call by Pope Urban II to the Christian lords of western Europe to rescue the Holy Land from the Turks.

Western history tends either to romanticize the heroism or exaggerate the imperialist violence of the two centuries that brought East and West, Muslims and Christians, into eight or nine great series of battles that are popularly called "the Crusades." But from the perspective of Asia as a whole, the Crusades are not as uniquely significant as might be thought. From that larger continental viewpoint, there are three distinguishing features of the age: the fall of the Arabs, the triumph of the Turks pouring in from the east, and the brief, bitter, failing interlude of Atlantic Europe's intervention from the west.

Many choose to remember the Crusades only in terms of that third factor, West against East, as an unprecedented example of religious imperialism, but religious and imperialist wars were nothing new to western Asia. Its history had pitted Constantinian Rome against Zoroastrian Persia since the fourth century. It had seen Muslims carve a religious empire out of Christian western Asia, North Africa, and Spain and absorb Zoroastrian Persia. Christian Byzantium was still fighting Islam for Asia Minor and Syria, while Muslims fought Muslims, Shi'ites against Sunnites, for the 'Abbasid empire. Now finally in the eleventh century, two new imperial powers, Seljuk Muslim Turks and Christian western Europeans, rushed in from opposite ends of the compass to claim western Asia as their own. Neither succeeded, though the ultimate winners were at least cousins of the Seljuks, the Ottoman Turks. Least successful of all were the Crusaders.

The military details[28] of the Crusades are familiar and need not detain us, for they directly affected little of Asia beyond the narrow borders of old Roman Asia. But the hard fact remains that however much a larger perspective diminishes the singularity of the crusades in world history, in the long memory of race and religion those failed invasions, launched in the name of One who said, "Love your enemies," permanently tarnished the popular image of Christian expansion with stains of brutality and coercion that not even the gentler virtues of the Christian world mission have ever quite been able to erase. History forgives successful violence very quickly but compounds the condemnation of its failures for centuries.

The First Crusade, which is sometimes called "the French Crusade," landed in Asia in 1097 near Nicaea, where the history-making

First Ecumenical Council of Christendom had met in 325. But its roots had been growing for almost a century. In 1009 the mad caliph of Cairo, al-Hakim, tore down the Church of the Holy Sepulchre in Jerusalem, the most holy shrine in Christendom. Then he added insult to injury and repudiated a treaty reportedly agreed upon two hundred years earlier by two of the greatest figures in Christian and Islamic history, the Holy Roman Emperor Charlemagne and the 'Abbasid caliph Harun al-Rashid. It was this treaty that despite wars and revolutions had long allowed a steady stream of pilgrims safe passage from the West to worship at Christian shrines in Muslim Jerusalem.[29]

Then came the Turks, far fiercer than the Arabs. They took Jerusalem in 1070, and the next year destroyed the armies of Constantinople at Manzikert. Despite the fact that less than twenty years earlier the Great Schism of 1054 had permanently separated pope from patriarch and Roman Catholicism from Greek Orthodoxy, the frightening approach of the Turks, whose ferocity was already legendary, drove Michael VII, the Eastern Roman Emperor, to overcome his religious scruples and write the pope asking for help and reunion.

So in 1095 Pope Urban II issued his call, and the French landed across the Bosphorus in May 1097. The Anatolian Muslim capital of Nicaea surrendered in June. A year later they took Syrian Antioch. And before another year had passed Jerusalem was once more in Christian hands (July 1099). The secret of their success in contrast to Byzantine failure at the hands of the Turks was not so much their Christian faith, though crusading enthusiasm was an important factor, or their Christian conduct—they mercilessly massacred the people of Jerusalem[30]—or their Christian unity, for the leaders were notoriously jealous and unsupportive of each other. It was rather the greater disunity of the Muslim defenders of the Holy Land that opened the way to Christian victory in that First Crusade.

The Seljuks had conquered the 'Abbasid empire, but were unable to keep it united. Like their predecessors the Buyids, they preserved the outer facade of the Arab caliphate, taking the power to themselves as "sultans" but not the religious and ceremonial title of caliph. Yet the empire was too huge and too sophisticated to be held together by nomads so recently civilized. Even before the arrival of the Crusaders it had begun to crumble. Only three Seljuk sultans were able to rule the whole empire, which stretched, it must be remembered, from Kashgar in central Asia to Yemen on the Red Sea and to within sight of Constantinople on the Bosphorus.

When the third sultan, grandson of the conqueror Toghril Beg, died in 1092, only thirty-seven years after the Seljuk capture of Baghdad, the nomadic practice of dividing the inheritance and distributing it in pieces to the next generation reasserted itself. The Middle East became a cluster of Turkish principalities no longer ruled from Baghdad. Asia Minor (Anatolia) on the eve of the Crusades was the Seljuk sultanate of Rum. Its capital was Nicaea. Antioch was governed by an independent Seljuk *amir* nominally supported from northern, not southern, Mesopotamia. Jerusalem was in the hands of the Egyptian Fatimids, rivals both of Christian Byzantium and Seljuk Islam, who had not been sorry to watch the defeat of the Turks in the north but realized too late that all Islam was under attack. The Arab caliph of Egypt was a boy only ten years old at the time.

One by one, lacking mutual support, the independent Muslim units fell to the Crusaders: Asia Minor, so recently Byzantine Christian; Edessa, mother of Asian Christianity; Cilicia, where St. Paul was born; Antioch, where Christians were first called "Christians"; Tripoli; and finally the Holy City, Jerusalem. The story of the little Latin kingdoms on the Mediterranean coast that rival Crusaders took over from the divided Muslims and then divided among themselves belongs more to Western church history than to that of Asia, but a word should be said about what happened to the people, especially the Christians, of the lands the Crusaders sincerely thought they had liberated.

They were of three kinds, the Crusaders, the Christian immigrants, and the native Christians. The original Crusaders numbered probably not more than thirty thousand,[31] most of whom either returned home or died early in a climate and culture to which they were unaccustomed. In the years that followed they were joined by some numbers of immigrants from the Christian West, a mixture of pious people seeking holiness in a holy land, traders greedy to tap the legendary riches of the East, and a dangerous sprinkling of criminals deported as good riddance from Europe but considered useful as a population support for the Crusaders. These, with the possible exception of the last group, formed the ruling Frankish elite.

The native Syrian population, nominally Muslim but with a considerable portion still Christian after five hundred years of Muslim rule, was not greatly impressed with its new masters. Though in major cities like Edessa and Antioch Christians were actually in the majority, they had adapted more slowly to Islamic society than in Iran or Iraq[32] and had passively accepted Islamic governance and much of its way of life. They were shocked to find that in many ways, particularly in science and medicine, the eleventh-century European Christian culture of their liberators was inferior and somewhat barbaric in comparison to that of the Arab-Persian civilization of the 'Abbasids. A Christian doctor, a Syrian, was sent to minister to a wounded Frankish knight. He treated his leg with poultices and the abscess broke and began to heal. But a Frankish doctor roughly interrupted, told the Syrian he knew nothing, sent for a strong man and a sharp axe, struck two tremendous blows, and "the marrow spurted out of the leg, and the patient died instantaneously." Returning home the Syrian Christian ironically reported, "I came away having learnt things about medical methods that I never knew before."[33] As for the defeated Muslims, their personal impressions of the invaders are vividly compressed into one sentence from an early twelfth-century Arab chronicler:

> All those who were well-informed about the Franj (Franks) saw them as beasts superior in courage and fighting ardour but in nothing else, just as animals are superior in strength and aggression.[34]

Ecclesiastically, after the first flush of enthusiasm over the arrival of fellow Christians had passed, the large Monophysite communities of the Jacobites and Armenians took no more kindly to Latin Christian discrimination against their churches as heretical than to their mistreatment by their former masters, whether Byzantine or Muslim. To the victorious Frankish Crusaders, the native Christians, whether Jacobite, Armenian, Greek Orthodox, Maronite, or Nestorian, were "people who did not obey Rome" and were to be treated as such.

But what kind of treatment did such status require? The Greek Orthodox were schismatic, divided by the great separation of 1054 between Eastern Orthodoxy and Western Catholicism, and were political rivals as well. But they were also military allies and orthodox Christians. At first the Latin clergy recognized their hierarchies as coequal, but the ancient jealousies proved to be irrepressible and the Byzantine patriarchs of Jerusalem and Antioch were nudged out of Asia into exile to Constantinople.[35]

The Latin Crusaders placed the other communities of Asian Christians (Jacobite or Syrian Orthodox, Armenian Orthodox, Nestorian, and Maronite) in a different category. They were officially heretical, not schismatic, and curiously this made them easier to deal with and secured them somewhat favored treatment. Rome was eager to win them back into a restoration of Christian unity under the papacy. The Maronites were most successfully thus absorbed. In

1182, according to "the greatest of medieval historians," William of Tyre, forty thousand Maronites emerged from their mountain refuges and joined the Crusaders against the Turks. They also officially renounced their monothelite heresy (that Christ had two natures, divine and human, but only one will) and made their submission to the pope who, in turn, allowed them to retain their own Syriac liturgy.[36]

The Jacobites and Armenians welcomed the Crusaders as liberators but remained Orthodox, and as ecclesiastically independent of Latin Christianity as was possible under the circumstances. As native Syrian Christians and historic enemies of Constantinople, the Jacobites seem to have been more favored, and their bishops were rewarded with a somewhat patronizing recognition as "suffragans of the Latin hierarchy."[37] In reading the story of the Crusades through Asian Christian eyes, it is important to remember, as N. P. Zacour has observed, "that the only request for [Western European] aid did not come from Syrian Christians, but from Constantinople,"[38] and Constantinople was soon disenchanted with its arrogant Western European allies.

The age of the Crusades also saw the rebirth of a humbler form of Western Christian mission to the East more in the spirit of the Christ, in whose name it was practiced. It is best exemplified by the emergence of two new Roman Catholic missionary orders, the Franciscans in 1209 and the Dominicans in 1220/21. St. Francis of Assisi never reached Asia, but his personal mission to Egypt to preach Christ to the Fatimid sultan whose armies then held Jerusalem was a model of innocent faith, unarmed witness, and a complete willingness to die for his Lord that inspired members of his order in that same century and with the same utter disregard of their own safety to become the first Europeans to preach to the Mongols and the Chinese.

St. Dominic also sent his "preaching friars" into Asia, notably among the Turkic Cumans of what is now southwestern Russia. Both orders followed the Crusaders into Syria and Palestine, chiding unchristian behavior among the colonists, striving to heal the divisions of the various Christian churches, and faithfully reaching out in evangelistic witness to Muslims. The Catholic historian of missions, J. Schmidlin, has reported that the Dominican William of Tripolis baptized more than a thousand Muslims there.[39]

In summary, the age of the Crusades divides better into three periods than into eight crusades. The first is the attack of the Franks, which we have been describing (1097–1143/4). It ends with the accession of the first Asian-born Latin king of Jerusalem, Baldwin III, the fall of Edessa to the Muslims, the orientalizing of the Frankish colonialists, and the military decline of their Latin kingdoms. Curiously, in their period of decline the indigenizing Frankish Christians began to learn indispensable lessons in the government of populations from different cultures. B. Lewis quotes the remark of a Spanish Muslim traveler in the East that it was "common opinion" that the Franks there were far better overlords of their Muslim subjects in the countryside than contemporary Muslim rulers.[40] But it was too late.

The second period (1144–1187) is dominated by the Islamic counterattack (*jihad*) of the great Saladin (1138–1193). Few have more nearly accomplished the impossible than this remarkable man. He was neither Arab, Persian, nor Turk. He was a Kurd, a man of a race that has suffered more from the cruelties of history than even the Armenians or the Jews. Yet he managed to unite the intractably fractured forces of divided Islam and lead them to victory over the invading Christian colonizers. Moreover, though his work of reconciliation began in Shi'ite Egypt, his reunification of west Asian Islam was under the banner of Sunnite orthodoxy. And most difficult of all, while still fighting the Crusaders he won their reluctant admiration and respect. When he took Jerusalem in 1187, ripping the great gold cross off the crown of the Dome of the Rock, he was unusually merciful for his time. He allowed Crusaders, who had entered it in a bloodbath, to leave the city in peace—no massacre, reprisals, or pillage—but not without great pain. Of some nine thousand Christian refugees stranded in fallen Jerusalem, only seven thousand were able to raise gold ransom and the poorest two thousand were apparently sold into slavery.[41]

The third period of the age of the Crusades (1187–1291) was a century of downward spiraling, abortive attempts by the Latin West to revive the spirit and successes of the First Crusade. But never again until the twentieth century, except for the strangely paradoxical laymen's Crusade of Frederick II in 1228—"alone of all crusades it was not blessed but cursed by the papacy"[42]—did the forces of Christendom seriously threaten Islam's control of western Asia.

NOTES

1. Al-Qahir (932–934), al-Mutaqqi (940–944), and al-Mustakfi (940–946); see T. W. Arnold, *The Caliphate* (Oxford: Clarendon, 1924), 60.

2. *World Christian Encyclopedia*, 25.

3. Scholars argue about whether religion, ethnic nationalism, power poli-

tics, or economics was the decisive factor in the 'Abbasid revolution and its fall. Wellhausen argues for Iranian nationalism (*Das Arabische Reich und sein Sturz* [Berlin, 1902]); B. Lewis calls for more consideration of the role of the Arabs (*Islam from the Prophet Muhammad to the Capture of Constantinople* [New York: Harper & Row, 1974]); H. A. R. Gibb points out the importance of the rival religious polemics of Shi'ite and Sunnite theories of the caliphate (*Studies on the Civilization of Islam* [Boston: Beacon, 1962], 141–50); and W. B. Bishai stresses economics (*Islamic History of the Middle East* [Boston: Allyn and Bacon, 1968]). For a detailed account of the historical and religious background of the first 'Abbasids see F. Omar, *The 'Abbasid Caliphate, 132/750–170/786* (Baghdad: Univ. of Baghdad, 1969), esp. 136, 138f.

4. Quoted by P. K. Hitti, *History of the Arabs from Earliest Times to the Present* 5th ed. (New York: Macmillan, 1951), 441, who cites ibn-al Jawzi, an eleventh-century Arab historian.

5. On the origin of the Sunnite-Shi'ite schism, see chap. 16, pp. 334f.

6. The first four caliphs after the death of Muhammad, the "orthodox" or "patriarchal" caliphs, were not dynastic.

7. See chap. 16, pp. 340f., 347f.

8. Lewis, *Islam*, xvf. He distinguishes the periods more by the social dominance of language—Arabic, new Persian, and Turkish—than by chronology.

9. See G. E. von Grunebaum, *Classical Islam: A History 600–1258* (London: Allen and Unwin, 1970), 107; Hitti, *History of the Arabs*, 106f.

10. The blinded caliph was al-Mustakfi (944–946). He was succeeded by al-Muti' (946–974) and an unhappy procession of three other powerless caliphs.

11. Hitti, *History of the Arabs*, 471f.

12. L. E. Browne, *The Eclipse of Christianity in Asia* (Cambridge: Cambridge Univ. Press, 1933), 60, quoting from Mari, and citing Bar Hebraeus. See also Hitti, *History of the Arabs*, 440.

13. The patriarchs under the Buyids were Emmanuel (938–960), Israel (962), Ebedyeshu I (963–986), Mares (987–1001), John V (1001–1011), John VI (1013–1020) Yeshuyab IV (1021–1025), Elias I (1028–1049), John VII (1050–1057). See A. R. Vine, *The Nestorian Churches* (London: Independent, 1937), 138, for comparison with other suggested dates, as by J. E. T. Wiltsch and L. E. Browne and A. Fortescue, and W. G. Young.

14. J. M. Neale, *A History of the Holy Eastern Church* (London: Masters, 1847), 1:143. Innocent III was pope from 1198 to 1216.

15. A. S. Atiya, *A History of Eastern Christianity* (London: Methuen, 1968), 260.

16. See chap. 15, pp. 302f.

17. *Imam* is a Shi'ite title for a ruler descended from the family of Muhammad; *caliph* is a title for ruler more generally preferred by Sunnites. The Fatimids used both titles. See Hitti, *History of the Arabs*, 618.

18. Hitti, *History of the Arabs*, 360, citing the tenth-century Arab geographer Ibn al-Faqi's *Kitab al-Buldan*.

19. B. Spuler, "The Disintegration of the Caliphate in the East," in P. M. Holt, et al., *Cambridge History of Islam*, vol. 1 (Cambridge: Cambridge Univ. Press, 1970), 154. He notes elsewhere that Christians then were "incomparably more numerous than today" (p. 144).

20. Hitti, *History of the Arabs*, 620, 627; A. S. Tritton, *The Caliphs and Their Non-Muslim Subjects* (London: F. Cass, 1970), 54.

21. Browne, *Eclipse of Christianity*, 60f. It was the destruction by Hakim of the sacred Church of the Holy Sepulchre in Jerusalem that was later to be a major motivating factor in arousing Europe to the Great Crusades.

22. *Cambridge Medieval History*, vol. 5, ed. J. B. Bury et al., reprint of corrected 1929 edition (Cambridge: Cambridge Univ. Press, 1957), 256.

23. Hitti, *History of the Arabs*, says 992.

24. The founder of the Sufi community of Balkh was probably Ibrahim ibn Adham, an eighth-century prince of that famous once-Buddhist city who renounced his throne to take on the coarse woolen robes of a Sufi and invite ridicule, beatings, and abuse. On Sufism see A. Schimmel, *Mystic Dimensions of Islam* (Chapel Hill: Univ. of North Carolina, 1975); and R. A. Nicholson, *The Mystics of Islam* (London: Bell, 1914). Nicholson argues for early Christianity as at least a strong secondary influence on the development of Sufism, both in the style of dress adopted by the dervishes and the frequent references to Jesus and Christian ascetics in the early writings (10ff.). But this connection, though not unreasonable, has been hotly debated. The general conclusion is that Sufism is genuinely Islamic in origin, but inevitably rooted in many religious soils, including Christianity. On theories of Sufi origins see A. J. Arberry, *An Account of the Mystics of Islam* (London: 1950); and Schimmel, 10ff.

25. Nicholson, *Mystics*, 164f., citing a commentary on Niffari.

26. Hitti, *History of the Arabs*, 474 n. 2.

27. Hitti, *History of the Arabs*, 475.

28. The numbering of the crusades varies, but for convenience I will append one commonly used pattern:

First Crusade (1095–1099). The French capture Jerusalem in 1099 and establish a string of Christian Latin kingdoms from Edessa to Antioch and Jerusalem. But Saladin ousts the Fatimids from Egypt, unites the Muslims in Syria, and counterattacks for Islam. Edessa falls in 1144.

Second Crusade (1147–1149). Preached by Bernard of Clairvaux but Germans and French fail to cooperate; a failure.

Third Crusade (1189–1192). The "great alliance" of Richard the Lion-heart of England, Philip II of France, and Frederick Barbarossa, Holy Roman Emperor, fails against Saladin who had recaptured Jerusalem in 1187.

Fourth Crusade (1202—1204). Pope Innocent calls Europe to another crusade but excommunicates the Crusaders when they storm Christian Constantinople instead of Muslim Jerusalem.

Fifth Crusade (1218–1221). Attacks Egypt to reach Jerusalem but fails.

Sixth Crusade (1228–1229). Frederick II launches a lay crusade and is excommunicated by the pope but negotiates a treaty of peace with Saladin's nephew and crowns himself king in Jerusalem; Muslims retake Jerusalem in 1244.

Seventh Crusade (1243–1254). King Louis IX of France attacks Cairo and is taken prisoner.

Eighth Crusade (1270–1271). Led by Louis IX of France and Edward I of England; last of the Crusades; Acre falls to Islam in 1291.

29. On the Franco-'Abbasid treaty see F. W. Buckler, *Harunu'l-Rashid and Charles the Great* (Cambridge, MA: Mediaeval Academy of America, 1931), answering some questions raised by W. W. Barthold. At the time the treaty was made, of course, both Charlemagne and 'Abbasid Baghdad opposed the Umayyad dynasty in Muslim Spain. True or not (the treaty is not mentioned in Arab sources), its existence was widely accepted in the West and Christian pilgrims in fact were admitted to Jerusalem.

30. There were important exceptions, such as Godfrey, Duke of Bouillon, who sold his own inherited lands to pay his way for the crusade, and when elected king after the capture of Jerusalem, chose rather to be called Baron of the Holy Sepulchre than by the high title of King of Jerusalem. *Cambridge Medieval History,* 5:274, 300.

31. See the discussion of the number of Crusaders in the First Crusade by W. B. Stevenson in *Cambridge Medieval History,* 297f.

32. This is corroborated by an interesting and admittedly tentative attempt to calculate the proportional rate of Christian conversion to Islam in the medieval Middle East, at least among the patrician classes, by an analysis of the biographical dictionaries that survive from that period. It suggests that whereas "the primary conversion process in Iran was earlier, subsiding by the middle of the 9th century, and in Iraq and Syria at the end of the 10th, in Syria the converts to Islam were at least a century later to take their place in the established Islamic religious and intellectual life of society." R. W. Bulliet, *Conversion to Islam in the Medieval Period* (Cambridge, MA, and London: Harvard Univ. Press, 1979), esp. the charts, pp. 8, 23, 82, 104.

33. Usamah ibn Munqidh (1095–1188), cited in F. Gabrielli, *Arab Historians of the Crusades* (Berkeley: Univ. of California Press, 1969), 76f.

34. A. Maalouf, *The Crusades Through Arab Eyes,* trans. J. Rothschild (New York: Schocken, 1985), 39, also citing the chronicler Usamah (or Usama) ibn Munqidh.

35. See B. Hamilton, *The Latin Church in the Crusader States; The Secular Church* (London, 1980), esp. 217ff., 310ff.

36. See K. S. Salibi, "The Maronite Church in the Middle Ages," in *Oriens*

Christianus 42 (1958): 92–104, cited by K. M. Setton et al., eds., *A History of the Crusades,* 2d ed., 25 vols. (Madison: Univ. of Wisconsin Press, 1969–1985), 5:235. M. Moosa, *The Maronites in History* (Syracuse, NY: Syracuse Univ. Press, 1986), 195–232.

37. C. R. Condor, *The Latin Kingdom of Jerusalem* A.D. *1099 to 1291* (London: Palestine Exploration Fund, 1897), 219. On the subject of the Latin reestablishment during the Crusades, which is somewhat peripheral to the focus of this history, see the more definite treatments of W. Hotzelt, *Kirchengeshichte Palastinas im Zeitalter der Kreuzzuge 1099–1291* (Cologne, 1940), and Hamilton, *Latin Church.*

38. Setton, *Crusades,* 5:70. Armenians, who had negotiated better treatment in Asia Minor from Constantinople and who considered the Franks to be the allies of Byzantium, were more openly welcoming of the Crusaders than the Syrians. But all "quickly learned to detest their Frankish overlords" (1:160, 408).

39. See K. S. Latourette, *A History of the Expansion of Christianity* (New York: Harper, 1938, 1939), 2:321, 324–29.

40. "Egypt and Spain" by B. Lewis from Holt, *Cambridge History of Islam,* 1:199.

41. Holt, *Cambridge History of Islam,* 1:616.

42. Frederick, Holy Roman Emperor though excommunicated by the pope, preferred the way of peaceful negotiation with the Muslim sultan of Egypt, al-Kamil, rather than military confrontation. It was surprisingly effective. Jerusalem was transferred to Christian rule and in 1229 Frederick crowned himself king of Jerusalem. The terms of the treaty granted him a ten-year peace with territorial rights to sacred sites from Jerusalem and Bethlehem to Nazareth, and the fortresses of Jaffa, Caesarea, and Sidon. Jerusalem by agreement was left unwalled. Rome wisely rewarded his success and in 1230 he was absolved from excommunication (though tensions between pope and emperor were long to continue). "The last year of the emperor's truce," writes Condor, "was the last of Christian peace and prosperity in Syria." Condor, *Latin Kingdom,* 311–15; Setton, *Crusaders,* 5:357–69.

PART III

The Pax Mongolica: From Genghis Khan to Tamerlane

Chapter *18*
The Mongols and the Recovery of Asian Christianity

"For several years I put off reporting this event. I found it terrifying and felt revulsion at recounting it. . . . If anyone were to say that at no time since the creation of man by the great God had the world experienced anything like it, he would only be telling the truth. In fact nothing comparable is reported in past chronicles. The worst they recall is the treatment of the Israelites and the destruction of Jerusalem by Nebuchadnezzar. But what is Jerusalem compared with the areas destroyed by these monsters . . .? It may well be that the world from now until its end . . . will not experience the like of it again, apart from Gog and Magog. Dadjdjal [the Muslim Antichrist] will at least spare those who adhere to him, and will only destroy his adversaries. [The Mongols], however, spared none. They killed women, men and children, ripped open the bodies of the pregnant and slaughtered the unborn . . ."

—Ibn al-Athir (1160–1234),
Chronicon. Translated by B.
Spuler, *History of the Mongols*, 29f.

IT seems absurd to link the names of Genghis Khan and Tamerlane—as merciless a pair of warriors as the world has ever known—to peace. But there is a reason for the title which prefaces this part of the history, "The Pax Mongolica: From Genghis Khan to Tamerlane." Like other ages of revolutionary change, "it was the best of times; it was the worst of times."

Genghis Khan, no man of peace, nevertheless laid the foundations of a temporary interlude in the turbulent history of thirteenth-century Asia, a short period of relative peace and continental unity and religious toleration that, like the *pax romana* centuries earlier, prepared the way for the expansion of Christianity. And it was Tamerlane a century and a half later who put an abrupt end to that time of Christian hope and progress.

Christian Keraits and Shamanist Mongols

Only a few years before the caliph of Cairo destroyed the Church of the Holy Sepulchre in Jerusalem and thereby loosed emotions that later erupted into the Crusades, thousands of miles to the east in the heart of Asia, unknown Nestorian lay missionaries, Christian merchants engaged in trade with the restless tribes of the Mongolian steppes, began to convert a Turko-Mongolian tribe called the Keraits (or Kereyid). The only account that survives is that of the thirteenth-century historian, the Jacobite maphrian of the East, Gregory Bar Hebraeus. "At that time the king of a people called Keraith" lost his way while hunting in the high mountains. "When he had abandoned all hope, a saint appeared in a vision and said 'If you will believe in Christ I will lead you lest you perish.'" He returned home safely and remembered the vision when he met some Christian merchants, so he questioned them about their faith. They said, "You cannot be saved unless you are baptized," and urged him to send a message to Ebedyeshu, the Nestorian metropolitan of Merv, asking for "priests and deacons to baptize him and his tribe."[1] Bar Hebraeus goes on to quote a letter from Ebedyeshu to the Nestorian patriarch John VI in Baghdad, dated 1009, which reports that as a result of the mission that followed, the Kerait prince and two hundred thousand of his tribesmen accepted baptism.[2]

Whether the remembered details and numbers are authentic or not, the fact remains that for the next two hundred years the Keraits were known as a Christian Nestorian tribe of ever-increasing importance.[3] By the twelfth or thirteenth century the whole tribe was considered Christian and—what was of great import for the future—had become the first of all the Turko-Mongol tribes to befriend and protect a petty chieftain of an insignificant Mongol subclan. The chief was named Yesugei, the father of Temujin who is better known as Genghis Khan.[4]

The Keraits were one of a cluster of hunting tribes beginning to settle down on the banks of the rivers east and south of Lake Baikal. The principal tribes evangelized there by the Nestorians were the Naiman,[5] the Merkit, and the Kerait (see map pp. xxiv–xxv). To their south and west were the more cultured and stable communities of the Uighurs, who had been reached three centuries earlier in China by the Nestorians of the T'ang dynasty[6] and who have been described as "the educators of the Turco-Mongol world,"[7] but who had been scattered and driven west by the fall of their Uighur "empire" in the ninth century. As they moved west, Uighur culture changed from a mixture of shamanism, Manichaeanism, and Christianity to one more Buddhist and Christian but was eventually dominated by Islam.[8] The Uighur script, which had been created for them by Syrian Nestorians and transmitted by Nestorian and Manichaean missions was in turn passed on to Mongols farther east who still had no written language.[9]

Toward the end of the twelfth century, the Christian chief of the Keraits, Toghrul Wang-Khan (his title indicates a position of some prominence both in Chinese and Mongol politics),[10] became patron of the young Temujin (later known as Genghis Khan ca. 1162–1227). It may have been reports of this Mongol Christian ruler, the Kerait Wang-Khan, that gave rise in the West to the various legends about a "Christian king of Asia, Prester John," who was said to be a disciple of the Nestorians.[11]

However, it was not the Christian Toghrul who was to change Asian history, but his fiery young protégé whose ambition and organizing skills soon absorbed not only his protectors and principal allies, the Keraits, into his own rising orbit, but crushed other semievangelized tribes as well, such as the more powerful Merkit, the Naiman, and the Ongut, and began to unite them into the most warlike empire the world has ever known. It was in this period that the Mongols first became a political entity, and in the organization of the confederation the Keraits, though subdued by Genghis, were greatly influential.

A. Lobanov-Rostovsky credits Nestorians with shaping parts of Genghis Khan's written law, the *yasa* (or *yasak*), which became as sacred to Mongol rulers as the Ten Commandments to Christians. Among the most important of the laws was, "All men are to believe in one God, Creator of Heaven and earth." Other laws forbade adul-

tery and exempted clergy, whether Christian, Buddhist, or shamanist, from taxation. But the *yasa* are a curious mixture of basics and
trivia, of superstition and religious toleration, of morality and lenience. One even permitted a measure of drunkenness: "Get drunk
only three times a month; it would be better not to do so at all, but
who can abstain altogether."[12]

Another avenue of Kerait influence at the Mongol court was
through royal marriage. Genghis Khan, in order to strengthen his
position as ruler, used a simple method of making alliances without
losing control. He married or had his sons marry the daughters of
powerful tribal leaders, and if any of his new relatives challenged his
authority, he destroyed them. Toghrul Wang-Khan was an example.
When it was reported to Genghis that his chief protector, the Wang-
Khan of the Keraits, was plotting against him, Genghis rode the
Keraits down, but even as he crushed them, he cannily took the
eldest daughter of the brother of the fallen chief to wife. At the same
time he gave her younger sister as wife to his fourth son, Tolui (ca.
1190–1231/32), whom he appointed head of the center army under
his own command in the ensuing great campaigns.[13]

Genghis's new daughter-in-law, the Nestorian Kerait princess,
was Sorkaktani-beki (or Sorghaghtani),[14] a name worth remembering. She was one of three Christian sisters each of whom played a
noteworthy part in the history of the Mongol empire. The eldest,
Ibaka-beki, became the wife of Genghis Khan; the second, Bek-
tutmish, was the senior wife of Genghis's oldest son, Jochi.[15] But
Sorkaktani, who married the fourth son, Tolui, was destined for yet
greater things. She became the Christian mother of three imperial
sons, an emperor (Great Khan) of the Mongols, an emperor of
China, and an emperor (ilkhan) of Persia, as we shall see.

When Genghis had thus, about 1206, subdued or allied himself
with the most powerful of the Mongol tribes, he called a meeting of
the chiefs, and there in the frozen north on the lonely banks of the
Onon River, where it begins to run from the mountains eastward
toward China, they proclaimed him "World-Ruler" and "Great Khan
of the Mongols."[16] The world took little notice of the occasion, but
it was the first tremor of an earthquake that rippled out from that
edge of nowhere to shake the whole earth.

The east felt it first. Genghis Khan rode against the Tangut dynasty of the Hsi-Hsia (Xixia), Tibetan Buddhists who controlled the
eastern approach of the Old Silk Road into northwest China. Then
to protect his rear, he moved still farther east against a Manchurian
dynasty, the Chin (or Jin), which had wrested northern China from
the imperial Sung (Song) dynasty. The Mongols captured and

burned the Chin capital, Yenching (now Peking), but at that point, with all China relatively helpless before them, they unexpectedly halted their eastward march into the empire and turned fatefully west, over the high mountains of the Altai Range toward Lake Balkash and on into the fertile valleys and great cities between the Oxus and the Jaxartes. The sudden change of direction may have been triggered by the report of a treacherous murder of Mongol trade ambassadors who had been dispatched to a Muslim border principality between China and Persia, the Kara-Khitai "empire."

There were at that time two such border nations that protected the 'Abbasid caliphate of Persia against the increasing pressure of the Mongol tribes of central Asia. Nearest to the advancing Mongols was the Kara-Khitai kingdom composed largely of Muslim Turks but ruled since the twelfth century by an earlier Mongol tribe that had granted shelter around the Turfan oasis to great numbers of Uighurs, among them many Nestorian Christians, as they were pushed west by other Mongols. In Genghis's time, still another Mongol wave seized the kingdom. It was led by a nominally Nestorian prince of the Naiman, named Kuchlug, fleeing west from a defeat by Genghis. He was violently and brutally anti-Muslim. Under Kuchlug, "for the first and last time since Islam was introduced into Central Asia, this religion suffered persecution," writes W. Barthold.[17] But Kuchlug was curiously indifferent about the alternatives to Islam he was willing to approve, and Muslim historians contend that as ruler in Kara-Khitai he became either Buddhist or Confucian. He offered Muslims a choice between Christianity, Buddhism, or simply an exchange of their Muslim dress for Chinese. It is little wonder that when after seven short years of rule (1211–1218) he was defeated by a general of Genghis, Muslims and Christians alike welcomed his overthrow by the less intolerant forces of the Great Khan.[18]

Genghis Khan's next objective was the other border state, nearer Persia, the luxury-loving realm of the rich and sophisticated shah of Khwarazmia whose Muslim rulers had displaced the Shamanist Kara-Khitai (map, pp. xxiv–xxv).[19] As Genghis himself, with his son Tolui leading the center, advanced west against the Khwarazmian empire, "for the first time the Mongol military machine was set in motion against a Muslim state."[20] In three fierce, bloody years the Mongols overran both border kingdoms, and in 1220 Genghis captured his greatest prize, beautiful Bokhara (Bukhara), "the Baghdad of the East," "the cupola of Islam."[21] It was said that when the Mongols entered Khwarazmia it was "the garden of Asia"; they left it "an empire of the dead." Crossing the Oxus, the Mongols moved into Persia. Their legions, wrote Bar Hebraeus, "exceeded the locusts and ants in number,"[22] spreading death, terror, and despair. Tolui captured Merv, seat of the Nestorian bishop, and in the fall of that one city, seven hundred thousand men, women, and children were butchered, according to Ibn al-Athir, whose reaction to the utter ruthlessness of the Mongols is quoted on the title page of this chapter.[23]

Nishapur, the capital of Persia's rich eastern province of Khurasan and last governmental center of the Khwarazmian empire, fell to Tolui in 1221. This was the Mongols' farthest major thrust to the west under Genghis Khan. His generals continued their raids as far as Georgia. Genghis, however, with Tolui, who seems to have been his favorite son,[24] turned back eastward across what is now Afghanistan and fought his way south to the banks of the Indus River. But there at the edge of great India, again he stopped. From that time on he did little further fighting himself, leaving that to his sons and generals, until he died. Instead he contented himself mainly with hunting, and trying to maintain order among the turbulent Mongols. It is said that he turned philosophical, asking questions about the nature of the world and of its religions. Concerning the latter, he was skeptical and tolerant of them all, including Nestorian Christianity. His people remained basically shamanist. Genghis Khan was buried in 1227 with shamanist Mongol ceremonies that included the sacrifice of forty young women and forty horses.[25]

The Mongol Empire

Genghis Khan had four sons by his first wife—Jochi, Chagatai, Ogetai, and Tolui—and through laws of descent and tradition through these four, the Mongol empire developed its line of authority and rule. It is astounding how quickly illiterate[26] but by no means unintelligent nomads who were unaccustomed to settled government managed to organize and stabilize the succession to the rule of half of Asia.[27] The empire was divided into four units, one for each of the sons, and these units were under the titular rule of one of them, a Great Khan elected by royal family council.

The first son, Jochi (d. 1227), had never been on good terms with his father and died before him. He was bypassed for the succession to the title of Great Khan, but his son Batu's military conquests in Europe earned the house of Jochi the rule of Russia and the northwest. This came to be called the territory of the Golden Horde. Batu's brother and later successor became the first of the Mongol khans to turn Muslim.

The second son, Chagatai (d. 1242), did not contest his father's judgment that a younger brother was better fitted to succeed him and received as his territory central Asia east of the house of Jochi, which included Transoxiana and Turkestan as far as the borders of Mongolia. He was the most traditionally Mongolian of the sons and the most harshly anti-Muslim,[28] yet from the house of Chagatai sprang the longest enduring of the Genghisid Muslim powers, the moghuls of north India.

It was the third son, Ogetai (d. 1241), who was elected to succeed his father as the second Great Khan. His title was greater than his territory and his line did not even hold the title very long, but he was a good ruler, tolerant of Christians, and holding the family together from his center above and to the east of Lake Balkash.

The youngest principal son, Tolui (d. 1232), was given, by Mongol custom, the rule of the family heartland, and it was through the line of this fourth son that Asia's church history was most directly open to and influenced by Christianity. Immediately after Genghis's death and pending the affirmation by the family council of Ogetai as his successor, Tolui ruled the empire as interim regent from 1227 to 1229. Ogetai then ruled as Great Khan from 1229 for eleven years and was succeeded by his son Kuyuk as the third Great Khan in 1246. But upon the death of Kuyuk a momentous dynastic change in succession brought to the Mongol throne as the fourth Great Khan, Mongke (or Mangu), grandson of Genghis through the line of Tolui and the Christian princess Sorkaktani.[29] This was a palace revolution that was to have great consequences, not so much for the history of Christianity in Mongolia, where little came of it, but most significantly in China and in Persia. The Christian princess's second son, Hulegu (or Hulagu), conquered Muslim Persia, and her third and greatest son, Kublai, as all know, became emperor of China.

It is not far wrong to call this period the *pax Mongolica*, an Asian counterpart, in a way, to the Western *pax Romana* of the first century A.D. And like that Roman peace it was more often violent than peaceful. But for the first and only time in history it gave Asia a continental unity, a short-lived but immensely powerful trans-Eurasian empire that stretched Mongol authority from the shores of the Pacific to the gates of Constantinople and from the Korean border to Moscow and the edge of Poland.

The First Franciscan Missions to the Mongols

As the *pax Romana* had prepared the way for the work of the apostles in the first century, so now in the thirteenth a *pax Mongolica* opened doors for Catholic missions across Asia to the half of the world beyond Constantinople. Never once in the century and a quarter from the first Catholic mission to Mongolia in 1245 to the fall of the Mongol dynasty in 1368 was there not at least one cross-Asiatic artery open for trade and cultural interchange between East and West. Whether by the Old Silk Road through Mongol Persia, or the two northern routes across Mongol Russia, or by sea around India, the Far East was nearer to Europe than it had ever been before.[30]

Innocent IV was the pope (1243–1254) who dispatched the first Catholic missionary to the Mongols in 1245, choosing a Franciscan for the task, John of Plano Carpini (or Pian di Carpina), one of Francis of Assisi's direct disciples and an early organizer of the order in western Europe. Providentially, missionary revival had already begun in the Roman church. Two potentially great new missionary societies had recently been founded, the Franciscans and the Dominicans. They were called the mendicant orders, taking vows of poverty and adding, as a new dimension to traditional monasticism, an explicit insistence on preaching and mission to those outside the church. They were missionary and evangelistic.

The pope was still recovering from the shock of the second Mongol invasion, the campaigns against Europe of 1236–1241. All Christendom trembled as the Golden Horde of Genghis Khan's grandson, Batu, swept across Russia. He destroyed Kiev, the mother of Russian Christianity, and put all its people to the sword. He laid eastern Europe utterly waste from the Baltic to the Danube. Then as suddenly as they had appeared, the Mongols withdrew. Batu's uncle, the Great Khan Ogetai, died, and the death of a khan in far-off Mongolia once again saved Europe.

In the respite that followed, the pope determined to learn more about the intentions of the fierce Eastern nomads whose brutal advance was alternately terrorizing and tantalizing Europe. Reports of its irresistible ferocity were frightful, yet the possibility of an alliance, far East and far West against the Muslim center, held out such hope of a last, great victorious Crusade that the wish proved stronger than the counsels of reality.

The first papal missions to east Asia were therefore as much political as religious. The missionaries were given two commissions: a political one, to avert further onslaughts on Christendom by the invaders, and a spiritual one, to preach Christianity to them that they might be converted. So in the next hundred years, from 1242 to 1342, seven or eight different Catholic missions were dispatched on the long and difficult journey across Asia. Most of the missionaries were Franciscan, with a scattering of Dominicans. "'Tis worthy of the grateful remembrance of all Christian people," wrote Ricold of Montecroce, "that just at the time when God sent forth into the eastern parts the Tartars to slay and to be slain, He also sent forth in the west his faithful and blessed servants Dominic and Francis, to enlighten, instruct and build up in the faith."[31]

Here is a listing of the first major missionary ventures of the friars into oriental Asia in the more than a century that the way remained open:

1. Friar John of Plano Carpini (1245–1247), Franciscan.
2. Friar Lawrence of Portugal (1245 ?), Franciscan.[32]
3. Friar Anselm of Lombardy (1247–1250), Dominican.
4. Friar Andrew of Longumeau (1249–1251), Dominican.
5. Friar William of Rubruck (1253–1255), Franciscan.
6. The Polo brothers:
     First journey, without missionaries (1260–1269).
     Second journey, with Marco and missionaries (1271–1295).
7. John of Montecorvino (1291–1328), Franciscan.
8. Reinforcements for the Franciscan mission (1307, 1311).
9. Friar Odoric of Pordenone (1322–1328), Franciscan.
10. John of Marignolli (1342–1346), Franciscan.

John of Plano Carpini,[33] was the first to reach Mongolia. With a companion, Benedict the Pole[34], he took the northern route to the Far East through what is now the Ukraine to deliver his papal letter to the chief Mongol prince in Russia. This was Batu, conqueror of eastern Europe, son of Genghis Khan's eldest son, and ruler of the Golden Horde, the far western division of the Mongols. Two weeks beyond Kiev,[35] in territory where the two travelers had been told that not even their horses could live and that they must have Mongol horses that could find fodder under the snow if they hoped to survive, they were suddenly halted by Mongols who "rushed upon us in a horrible manner."[36] They were taken to Batu's great camp on the Don.[37] Batu refused the letter and ordered them to deliver it to the Great Khan in Mongolia.

Plano Carpini had already been traveling for nine months and every mile was torture for the brave, fat friar jolting his way at full speed across Asia perched precariously on top of a wild, short-legged Mongol pony. "We started out most tearfully," he wrote, "not knowing whether we were going to life or death, [and] . . . so feeble that we could hardly ride; during the whole of that Lent our only food had been millet with salt and water . . ., nor had we anything else to drink but snow melted in the kettle."[38]

It was another five months of agony before they at last reached the court of Kuyuk (Guyug), grandson of Genghis by his second son, who was about to be elected third of the Great Khans. On arrival at what must have seemed the end of the world, the good Catholic was astounded to find himself surrounded by Nestorian Christians. The khan's personal clerks were Nestorians, and a Nestorian chapel, placed in front of the royal tent, resounded with the sound of public chants and the beating of tablets loudly announcing the appointed hours of Christian worship. Some of the Mongol Christians were even claiming that the Great Khan himself was about to become a Christian.[39]

After the enthronement, which the two plain friars attended along with four thousand other envoys and ambassadors including a Seljuk sultan, Grand Prince Jaroslav of Russia (the father of Alexander Nevski), and princes from China and Korea, they were at last brought before the Great Khan to deliver the pope's letter. But the Khan kept them waiting another month for his answer. When finally they were allowed to begin their long journey home they had spent four months in the center of the Mongol empire.

The Khan proposed sending Mongol ambassadors back with them, but Carpini discreetly discouraged this. His reasons are revealing. First, he said, "we were afraid lest, seeing the dissensions and wars which are rife among us, they might be all the more encouraged to attack us." Second, "we feared that their real purpose might be to spy out our land." And third, "we were apprehensive that they might be killed, for our people are for the most part arrogant and proud."[40] The weaknesses of the West, the missionaries feared, were better not exposed to outsiders.

They returned to the pope in Lyons with optimistic news concerning the possibility of converting the Mongols.[41] Unknown to them, the Great Khan's reply held out no such hope. It was a chilling warning of precisely the opposite. Perhaps because of its negative nature it was never made public and was unknown to historians until the nineteenth century. It reads, in part, as follows:

> We, by the power of the eternal heaven, Khan of the Great Nations: This is a decree sent to the great Pope . . . [Y]ou have sent us an offer of subordination which we have accepted. . . . You have said it would be well for us to become Christians. . . . This your request we cannot understand. Furthermore you have written me these words: "You have attacked all the territories of the Magyars and other Christians. . . . Tell me what was their crime?" These your words we likewise cannot understand. . . . Those [Hungarians and Christians] of whom you speak showed themselves highly presumptuous and slew our envoys. Therefore, in accordance with the commands of the Eternal Heaven they have been slain. . . .
>
> And when you say, "I am a Christian. I pray to God. I arraign and despise others," how do you know who is pleasing to God and to whom he allots his grace? . . .
>
> Thanks to the power of the Eternal Heaven, all lands have been given us from sunrise to sunset. . . . Now . . ., you in person at the head of the monarchs, all of you without exception, must come to tender us service and pay us homage.[42]

This does not sound like the reply of a king about to become a Christian. It shocked the pope but it did not stop the missionaries.

WILLIAM OF RUBRUCK

About seven years later, in 1253, a second Roman Catholic envoy, William of Rubruck,[43] reached the court at Karakorum in central Mongolia to find a new Great Khan of a new line of descent from Genghis on the throne. Kuyuk Khan had died, and the succession to the khanate was bitterly disputed. Batu, khan of the Russian steppes, whose father, the eldest son of Genghis, had died early and had been bypassed in the succession,[44] allied himself with the Princess Sorkaktani, widow of Tolui, to whom Genghis had bequeathed the Mongolian homeland, and together they effected the election of the princess's first son, Mongke,[45] as the fourth Great Khan of the Mongols.

This Christian Kerait princess, so cavalierly taken from a defeated tribe and given to the Conqueror's son, had proved to be a woman of iron will, great courage, and remarkable political shrewdness. Bar Hebraeus, who lived in that same period, writing about her, uses terms of praise about a woman as are not often found in the writings of thirteenth-century bishops, much less in the mouth of a Monophysite writing about a Nestorian woman:

> Now this queen had four sons [Mongke, Kublai, Hulegu, and Arikbuka] . . . and trained her sons so well that all the princes marvelled at her power of administration. And she was a Christian, sincere and true like Helena [wife of Constantine]. And it was in respect of her that a certain poet said, "If I were to see among the race of women another woman like this, I should say that the race of women was far superior to that of men."[46]

Rubruck was terrified by reports of the territory he must cross. At Batu's camp the Mongols told him that Karakorum was still four months away, and the passes are so high that "stones and trees are split by the cold."[47] Reaching the Khan's capital exhausted, he was disappointed to discover it was not as full of Christians as the report of Plano Carpini might have led him to expect. There were, he said, twelve heathen temples (probably Buddhist), two Muslim mosques, and one Nestorian church.[48] Moreover, the Great Khan Mongke (Mangu),[49] gave no sign of adherence to his mother's Nestorian faith or evidence of the baptism allegedly performed by an Armenian (and therefore Monophysite) bishop in 1253 during a visit by the Christian King Haithon I of Armenia to the Mongol court.[50] But he did note the presence of a number of prominent Nestorians at the court, including the Great Khan's mother, Sorkaktani, and his chief counselor, Bulgai.[51]

Rubruck also thought that Mongke Khan's first wife (Kutuktei, or Qutuqtai),[52] and eldest son (Baltu),[53] and his youngest brother, Arikbuka (Arikh-Boke), might be Christians, which would be a significant core of Christian influence in the very highest court circles. He quotes Arikbuka as rebuking a Muslim with the words, "We know that the Messiah is God."[54] Rubruck's comments on the religion of the Mongol royal family are extremely important, but not always completely reliable. He was not aware, for example, that the first Mongol prince he had met on his journey, Sartak, was a Christian, the eldest son and heir of Batu, khan of the Golden Horde.[55] But he did report the highly significant fact that another Mongol prince of the Golden Horde, Berke, brother of Batu and uncle of Sartak, had converted to Islam. Berke was therefore the first of the Mongols of the line of Genghis Khan to become a Muslim.[56] He hid the occurrence of his conversion for some time, which indicates that Mongols in general at this early stage, about 1253, still reacted far more negatively against Islam than toward Christianity. H. H. Howorth informs us that when Berke, who had been converted by Muslim traders from Bokhara, made known his conversion, some of his generals sought to depose him in favor of Hulegu, who was considered to be leaning toward Christianity.[57] Such a move could have united Russian and Persian "Mongolia" in one great empire with possible religious consequences of continental significance, for it was the rivalry of the northwestern Mongols of Berke's Islamized Golden Horde against the somewhat pro-Christian early ilkhans of the line of Hulegu that irreparably destroyed the unity of the Mongol empire in the west and saved Muslim Egypt.[58]

Rubruck's description of Nestorian Christianity under the Mongols is devastating, but it should be held in mind that it was biased. To him, Nestorians were heretics. He found this ancient faith spread widely through Asia from the camps of the Golden Horde near the Don to the court of Mongke and beyond. Near Lake Balkash he passed through a village inhabited entirely by Nestorians. This was in the territory between Russia proper and Mongolia, which was given to Genghis Khan's second son, Chagatai. Chagatai was known to be friendly toward Christians but strongly opposed to the spread of Islam.[59]

Rubruck names four important central Asian tribes as Christian: the Uighurs (in part), the Naimans, the Keraits (Crits, he called them), and the Merkits.[60] The Uighurs he described as a tribe of idolaters east of the Ili valley containing a large mixture of Nestorians and Muslims. Of their Christianity, however, he had a low opinion. Their only article of Christian faith, he wrote, seemed to be that of belief in one God. Their priests dressed like Buddhists, denied that God ever took upon him human nature, and filled the churches with felt images of the dead.[61] They rebaptized Christians from other communions, ate meat on Fridays, did not practice confession, and recited the offices in Syriac, a language they did not understand.[62]

There is undoubtedly considerable truth in this unflattering description of tribal faith on the steppes, a Christianity weakened by isolation, superstition, and syncretism. But it must be compared with and perhaps modified by the far more favorable example of two more famous Uighur Nestorians, Sauma and Mark, who journeyed west and made contact with Western Christianity only twenty or so years later, which will be reported in another chapter.[63]

Though scornful of their theology, Rubruck did find the Nestorians at the court better grounded than the Uighur Nestorians he had passed on his journey. They were thoroughly familiar with the biblical account of sacred history from creation to the death of Christ, though they slighted the significance of his death, he felt. He also detected Manichaean heresy in their doctrine and was horrified to find how greatly the dark shadow of shamanist superstitions had clouded their practice of the gospel. Nestorian priests not only failed to condemn sorcery and divination, but even practiced it themselves, professing to heal the sick with swords and ashes, giving their followers charms, and engaging in various forms of divination.[64]

But his greatest contempt was reserved for the morals of the Nestorians. He called them corrupt, liars, usurers, simoniacs, and polygamists,[65] and he wrote of swarms of "[Nestorian] priests singing with great howling in their drunkenness." The Buddhist priests, he reluctantly confessed, were more respectable than the Nestorians.[66]

In all of Rubruck's contacts with the Khan, notably in a famous debate held by command of the Khan between Manichaeans, Muslims, Nestorians, and Rubruck representing Roman Catholicism, the Khan was steadfastly tolerant, took no sides, and declared no winner. The Buddhist spokesman clashed with Rubruck's doctrine of one, omnipotent God, "Fools say there is only one God, but the wise say there are many. Are there not many lords in your country, and is not [Mongke Khan] a greater lord?" Rubruck replied, "You choose a foolish example . . ., there is no comparison between man and God . . ."; he asked the Buddhist, "Is any God omnipotent?" "No," said the Buddhist. "Then," said Rubruck, "no one of your gods can save you from every peril, for occasions may arise in which he has no power. Furthermore, no man can serve two masters." This he said remembering that the Great Khan, though not present, would be following the debate. "So how can you serve so many gods in heaven and earth?" he concluded. The Buddhist refused to reply, perhaps fearing he had compromised his loyalty to the Khan, and Rubruck had won the first stage of the debate.[67]

But as a missionary he was not satisfied. The Christian mission is not a debate with the world's religions. It is not even a dialogue, though that too must enter into it. Its aim is not to defeat an enemy or simply to explore the world of ideas as in dialogue. Its primary purpose is to share whatever truth the human mind and heart can know and to witness to that truth in Christ. So as the day ended, Rubruck rather sadly noted:

> They all listened . . ., but no one said, "I believe; I want to become a Christian." [And] when it was over, the Nestorians as well as the Saracens sang with a loud voice while the [Buddhists] kept silence, and after that they all drank deeply.

Later the Great Khan called Rubruck in for a remarkable interview that has no parallel in any other surviving accounts of personal

Christian conversation with the great Mongol khans. There in his huge royal tent Mongke candidly confided to the missionary his own religious faith:

> We . . . believe there is only one God . . . but as God gives us the different fingers of the hand, so he gives to men diverse ways . . .

He then added in what was a strong indication that his personal convictions remained proudly Mongolian and shamanist,

> God gave you the Scriptures, and you do not keep them; he gave us diviners [shamans]; we do what they tell us, and we live in peace.[68]

Soon after, he spoke of his intention to allow Rubruck to begin his journey home, and the missionary never again found the opportunity to speak to this powerful Asiatic ruler about the Christian faith. Rubruck wistfully concludes this part of his journal, "If I had had the power by signs and wonders to work like Moses, perhaps he would have humbled himself [and believed]."

Nevertheless he was able to leave cheered by the knowledge that during his stay at the court he had been able to baptize six Christian captives held by the Mongols.[69] So on 10 July 1253, he left Karakorum for the camp of Batu, and then down the Volga and along the west coast of the Caspian Sea and over the Caucasus Mountains through Armenia and Turkey to Syria.

The record of Rubruck's journey is the earliest accurate description of the Asiatic heartland, its peoples, and its religions to reach the West.[70] Its highly critical appraisal of the theology and practice of the Far Eastern Nestorians, however biased it may be, throws light on at least one of the various reasons that must be considered in any discussion of the disappearance of Nestorian Christianity from central Asia after the fourteenth century.

When he reached Syria Rubruck found the last of the Christian Crusaders holding onto a narrow footing along the coast. They had already lost Jerusalem and were not to hold much longer the rest of the territory they had so painfully wrested from the Muslims in two hundred years of war. Not long after Rubruck's return, the southwestern edges of the Mongolian military explosion across Asia at last reached the Mediterranean. The great Saracen stronghold of Damascus, which had once been Saladin's headquarters in his wars against the Franks, fell to the invaders in 1260, and the Christian beachheads on the coast braced themselves for attack. Some of their forts did indeed fall to the Mongols, but, surprisingly, the Mongol general who marched out of Damascus to continue the invasion was a Christian, and his advance was not so much against the thin line of Latin states clinging to the Mediterranean coast as against the Mameluke rulers of Muslim Egypt.

The Crusaders survived in Asia for another thirty years. But victory for the Christians of Damascus lasted only a week. They poured into the streets in unchristian acts of vengeance against their former Muslim rulers and soon regretted it. As it turned out, the Christian Mongol general marched south from Damascus not to victory but to a defeat that changed the entire history of the Middle East with sober consequences for the church in Asia. At Ain Jalut he met the Egyptians and a Muslim Mameluke destroyed a Mongol army led by a Christian, as we shall see in the next chapter. It happened in Galilee, only a few miles from a little town called Nazareth.[71]

NOTES

1. Bar Hebraeus, *Chronicon ecclesiasticum,* ed. and trans. J. B. Abbeloos and T. J. Lamy, 3 vols. (Paris and Louvain: Maisonneuvre, Peeters, 1872–1877), vol. 3, cols. 280–82. Merv had been the seat of a bishop of the Church of the East (Nestorian) since the fourth century, 334. Samarkand, northeast of the Oxus, had been a bishopric since the sixth century. Bar Hebraeus's great work is more correctly entitled the *Chronography* and is divided in three parts: (1) History of the World; (2) History of the Church, to 1286; and (3) History of the Eastern Church, from St. Thomas. Part 1 contains a short reference to the account above taken from Part 3. See E. A. W. Budge's English translation, *The Chronography . . . First Part* (London: Oxford Univ. Press, 1932), 184.

2. R. Grousset, *The Empire of the Steppes* (New Brunswick, NJ: Rutgers Univ. Press, 1970), 191.

3. See, for example, the description by the most trustworthy fourteenth-century Persian historian Rashid al-Din, "the Keraits had for a long time been Christians," and "the Keraits had their own rulers and professed the Christian faith" (French translation of Rashid's *Jami 'al-Tawarikh* [Paris 1836, reprint 1968], 94, 95). And W. Barthold, *Zur Geschichte des Christentums in Mittel-Asien bis zur mongolischen Eroberung,* trans. R. Stube (Tubingen and Leipzig: Mohr, 1901), 2nn, 14, 16, 51, 56f.

4. "A compact made [about 1167] between the two men [Toghril, chief of the Keraits and Yesugai (sic)] . . . in the Black Wood by the banks of the Tula river may be considered the first of the alliances contracted by the house of Chingis with the Turkish peoples of the Eurasian steppes," J. J. Saunders, *The History of the Mongol Conquests* (London: Routledge & Kegan Paul, 1971), 47. Mongols and Turks, it should be remembered, are related tribal groups distinguished principally by language differences.

5. On Christianity among the Naiman, see M. Haydar (fourteenth-century), *Tarik-i-Rashidi: A History of the Moghuls of Central Asia,* ed. N. Elias and trans. by E. D. Ross (1895; reprint, Delhi, India: Renaissance Publishing Co., 1986), 290.

6. See chap. 15, pp. 299, 303.

7. Saunders, *Mongol Conquests*, 34.

8. On the Keraits, see H. H. Howorth, *History of the Mongols from the Ninth to the Nineteenth Century*, 5 vols. (1876; reprint, Taiwan: Ch'eng Wen, 1970), 1:534–57. On the Uighurs of this period (the twelfth and thirteenth century, in which their Kocho kingdom around Turfan was absorbed first by the Muslim Karakhanids, then briefly by Mongol Kara-Khitai, and finally by Genghis Khan), see Barthold, *Geschichte*, 47ff.; J. Dauvillier, *Histoire et institutions des Eglises orientales au Moyen Age* (London: Variorum, 1983), 1:307f.; and Grousset, *Empire*, 120–26, map 164, and 165, 180, 189f.

9. Bar Hebraeus, *Chronography*. B. Spuler, *History of the Mongols* (London: Routledge and Kegan Paul, 1972), 39, translates a passage from pt. III, 411ff.

10. Wang is Chinese, Khan is Turkic for "king" or "prince."

11. There have been many conflicting attempts to identify the origin of the legend of "Prester John" since it was first mentioned to Western readers about 1146 in the *Chronicon* by the royal-born German historian Otto of Freising (d. 1158). See, for example, the opposing opinions of Oppert and Howorth. Gustav Oppert (*Der Presbyter Johannes in Sage und Geschichte*, 2d ed. [Berlin, 1870], 167–79), like Otto of Freising, identified Prester John as a possible reference to Yeh-lu Ta-Shih, Gur-Khan of the twelfth-century Kara-Khitai empire around Bokhara and Samarkand and a tolerant Buddhist protector of Nestorians. Howorth's *History of the Mongols* (pt. 1, 535–45) on the other hand defends the view that Prester John was a Kerait prince from farther east. Even more exhaustive and carefully critical are the articles of F. Zarncke on "Der Priester Johannes" in *Proceedings* of the Saxon Academy (Leipzig, 1879, 1883). See also the recent comments of Saunders (*Mongol Conquests*, 40 and n.), who suggests that Otto's immediate reference may well have been to the Gur-Khan. Nevertheless, Howorth's argument is compelling that as a Christian prince of a Christian Asian tribe, Toghrul of the Keraits more clearly resembles the mythical Prester John than the Gur-Khan. Bar Hebraeus specifically identifies him as "Ung Khan, that is John, king of the Christians . . . reigning over a certain tribe of the [Huns] called Krit [Kerait]," *Chronography*, pt. 1 (Budge trans.), 352f.

12. See A. Lobanov-Rostovsky, *Russian and Asia* (New York: Macmillan, 1933), 17; and the more scholarly study by V. A. Riasanovsky, *Fundamental Principles of Mongol Law* (The Hague, 1965). Bar Hebraeus on the Christian side (*Chronography*, pt. 1, p. 418, Budge trans.), and Rashid and Juvaini, thirteenth-century Muslim historians, give somewhat different versions of the *yasa*. Saunders (*Mongol Conquests*, 69) comments, "Copies of the code in Uighur script were traced out on great sheets of parchment, and kept in the treasuries of the Mongol princes, to be taken out and consulted as need arose", but notes that no complete text of the code survives.

13. B. Spuler, 22, 32, 45. Spuler transliterates the name Toghrul as To'oril, and Wang-Khan as Ong Khan. For an accurate interpretation and concise account of the early Mongol campaigns against the borders of Islam, I rely on Saunders, *Mongol Conquests*, 52–70.

14. She was the daughter of Jagambu and niece of Wang-Khan. Her name has a bewildering variety of transliterations: Sorkaktani (Saunders), Sorghaghtani (*Encyclopedia of Asian History*), Sorkhakhtani or Seyurkhokhataitai (Spuler), Ssorqoqtani (Boyle), Sorghaqtani (Grousset), Sorhatani (Moule), Siurkukteni (Howorth), or simply Sorocan (Latin), with the subscriptive title *-beg* or *-beki*. I will arbitrarily use Sorkaktani. Her official imperial name in Chinese was Hsien-i-chuang-sheng (Moule, *Christians in China* [London: Society for Promoting Christian Knowledge, 1930], 224n; but see p. 132n, which from another source gives Pieh-chi as her name as dowager empress).

15. J. A. Boyle, *The Successors of Genghis Khan, Translated from the Persian of Rashid al-Din* (New York and London: Columbia Univ. Press, 1971), 99. Boyle romanizes the names as Ibaqa Beki, Bek-Tutmish Fujin and Sorqoqtani Beki.

16. The details of these early years are from the semihistorical, semilegendary *Secret History of the Mongols* (*Yuan Ch'ao pi-shih*), which centers on the life of Genghis Khan. On its date and composition see Saunders, *Mongol Conquests*, appendix 1, 192ff. B. Spuler collects some useful selections from it in his *History of the Mongols*, 17–26, but see the more complete English translation by F. W. Cleaves, *The Secret History of the Mongols* (Cambridge, MA: Harvard Univ. Press, 1982). See also H. D. Martin, *The Rise of Chingis Khan and his Conquest of North China* (Taipeh, Taiwan: Rainbow-Bridge Press, 1950; reprint 1971).

17. W. Barthold, *Four Studies on the History of Central Asia*, 3 vols. (Leiden: Brill, 1952–1956), 1:35.

18. Barthold, *Central Asia*, 1:34f.

19. For more detail see Barthold, *Central Asia*, 1:30ff., 34ff.

20. Saunders, *Mongol Conquests*, 55.

21. B. Spuler, 32ff., using Boyle's translation of Juvaini, *History of the World Conqueror*, pp. 97–108. See Martin, *The Rise of Chingis Khan*, 326-34.

22. Bar Hebraeus, *Chronography*, (Budge trans.), 1:376.

23. Saunders, *Mongol Conquests*, 60. Saunders notes one historically significant pocket of survivors. "[A] small clan of nomad Turks, who grazed their flocks on the pastures just outside Merv, fled westwards through Irak into Asia Minor, where they were granted asylum by the Seljuk princes there and became the progenitors of the Ottoman Turks."

24. Of all his sons, only Tolui was with him at his death. Howorth, *History of the Mongols*, 1:103.

25. According to Rashid al-Din, in Howorth, *History of the Mongols*, 1:105.

26. So described by the Armenian historian Heython (or He'tum) in 1307. See *Hetoum, A Lytell Cronycle: Richard Pynson's Translation (c. 1520) of La Fleur des histoires de la terre d'Orient (c 1307)* (Toronto: Univ. of Toronto Press, 1988), 32f.

27. The stabilization of course was only partial, as the subsequent civil wars revealed, but the empire lasted for a century and a half. On the succession, see Boyle, *Successors of Genghis Khan.*

28. See Saunders, *Mongol Conquests,* 74.

29. In the chart below of the family relationships of the line of Genghis through his four principal sons, the succession to the Great Khanate is marked by names in italics: 1) *Genghis,* 2) *Ogetai,* 3) *Kuyuk,* 4) *Mongke,* and 5) *Kublai.*

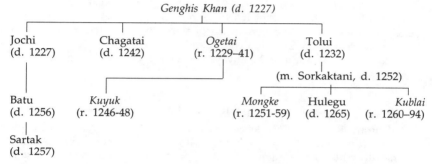

Genghis Khan (d. 1227)

| Jochi | Chagatai | *Ogetai* | Tolui |
| (d. 1227) | (d. 1242) | (r. 1229–41) | (d. 1232) |

(m. Sorkaktani, d. 1252)

| Batu | *Kuyuk* | *Mongke* | Hulegu | *Kublai* |
| (d. 1256) | (r. 1246-48) | (r. 1251-59) | (d. 1265) | (r. 1260–94) |

Sartak
(d. 1257)

Note that the first and second sons were skipped in the succession to the Great Khanate, but Jochi's descendants ruled much of what is now Russia, and Chagatai's heirs controlled much of Central Asia. Hulegu, though never Great Khan, became ilkhan of Persia.

30. See T. T. Allsen, "Mongol Empire," in *Encyclopedia of Asian History,* 3:28.

31. Quoted in H. Yule, *Cathay and the Way Thither,* 1:155. Ricold, "one of the most learned of the monk travelers of the age," died in 1309 and had himself traveled east as far as Baghdad (p. 170).

32. Lawrence may have been sent before Plano Carpini but probably reached only the Mongol encampments north of the Caspian. Little more is known about him. See W. W. Rockhill, *The Journey of William of Rubruck to the Eastern Parts* (London: Hakluyt Society, 1900), xxii–xxiv.

33. The full text of John of Plano Carpini's *History of the Mongols* is translated into English by "a nun of Stanbrook Abbey" in *Mission to Asia: Narratives and Letters of the Franciscan Missionaries in Mongolia and China in the Thirteenth and Fourteenth Centuries,* ed. Christopher Dawson (New York: Harper Torchbooks, 1966, reprinted from the 1955 edition titled *The Mongol Mission* [London: Sheed and Ward]). I refer to this below as, "Plano Carpini (Dawson)." The text of the Latin original is edited by A. van den Wyngaert, *Sinica Franciscana,* vol. 1: *Itinera et Relationes Fratrum Minorum saec. XIII et XIV* (Quarracchi-Firenze: Franciscan Press, 1929), 1–86. A shorter version with map and extensive notes, to which I refer as "Plano Carpini (Rockhill)," is appended by W. W. Rockhill to his edition of the *Journal of William of Rubruck,* 1–32.

34. See Benedict the Pole's short *Narrative* of the account in Dawson, *Mission to Asia*, 79–84, and Rockhill, *Rubruck*, 33–39.

35. "While the Golden Horde endured Asia began at the southern outskirts of Kiev," Grousset, *Empire*, 346.

36. Plano Carpini (Dawson), 52f.

37. They thought it was the Volga.

38. Plano Carpini (Rockhill), 11.

39. Plano Carpini (Dawson), 68. "Christians . . . are constantly with him [the Khan]. The Christians of his household also told us that they firmly believed he was about to become Christian and they have clear evidence of this, for he maintains Christian clerics and provides them with supplies of Christian things; in addition he always has a chapel of the Christians before his big tent . . ."

40. Plano Carpini (Dawson), 68.

41. Plano Carpini was later appointed archbishop of Antivari.

42. M. Prawdin, in his *The Mongol Empire, Its Rise and Legacy*, trans. E. and P. Cedar (London: Allen and Unwin, 1940), 280f. Compare with the more technically critical translation from the Persian in B. Spuler (following P. Pelliot), *History*, 68f.

43. See William of Rubruck, *The Journey of William of Rubruck to the Eastern Parts, 1253–55, as Narrated by Himself, with Two Accounts of the Earlier Journey of John of Pian de Carpine*, trans. and ed. W. W. Rockhill (London: Hakluyt Society, 1900), ix–lvi, 40–304, referred to in the notes as *Rubruck* (Rockhill).

44. Batu, whose territory stretched from the Don to the Ili, was only in nominal subjection to the Great Khan. By Western standards, as the principal heir of Genghis's eldest son, he would himself have been Great Khan, but the Mongols chose their ruler by election from the whole royal family.

45. Who was, as we have noted, a direct grandson of Genghis through his fourth son, Tolui. For the details of the struggle over the succession see Howorth, *History of the Mongols*, 1:170ff.

46. Bar Hebraeus, *Chronography*, Budge trans., 1:398. Plano Carpini had described her as "among the Tartars this lady is the most renowned, with the exception of the Emperor's mother, and more powerful than anyone else except [Batu]," the Khan of the Golden Horde and ruler of what is now western Russia, (Plano Carpini Dawson), 26. She was as respected by Muslim historians as by Christian monks. Rashid al-Din, a generation later, wrote of her: "She was extremely intelligent and able and towered above all the women in the world. . . . [W]hen her sons were left by their father [Tolui died in 1232/33], some of them still children, she went to great pains in their education, teaching them various accomplishments and good manners and never allowing the slightest sign of strife to appear amongst them. She caused their wives also to have love in their hearts for one another. . . . There is no doubt that it was through her intelligence and ability that she

raised the station of her sons above that of their cousins and caused them to attain the ranks of qa'ans [khans] and emperors," Rashid al-Din, *Jami' al-Tawarikh [Compendium of Histories]*, vol. 2, *The Successors of Genghis Khan*, trans. J. A. Boyle (New York and London: Columbia Univ. Press, 1971), 168–70.

47. Rubruck (Rockhill), 128.

48. Rubruck (Rockhill), 213, 221.

49. Mongke is the Mongol form of the name, but many early Western writers used the Turkic form, Mangu.

50. See J. A. Boyle, "The journey of Het'um I, King of Little Armenia, to the Court of the Great Khan Mongke," in *Central Asia Journal* vol. 9, no. 3 (Wiesbaden, 1964); and also Rockhill (*Journey*, 239), who vigorously disputes the claim concerning the baptism.

51. Bulgai (or Bolgai) was not only Mongke's chancellor but also had charge of finances and the department of home affairs, Rockhill, *Journey*, 182. Saunders describes him as "secretary of state," (*Mongol Conquests*, 104).

52. Rubruck (Rockhill) calls her Cotota Caten, 184.

53. On Baltu, see Boyle, *Successors of Genghis Khan*, 197n.

54. It is noteworthy that these three, that is, Mongke's first wife, first son, and younger brother, were allied together after Mongke's death in Arikbuka's unsuccessful five-year contest against Khublai Khan for the Khanate. Rubruck (Rockhill), 184, 224, 189. See also Howorth, *History of the Mongols*, 216ff.

55. Rubruck denied the report that Sartak was a Christian, accepting the word of some of his retainers that "he is not a Christian but a Mongol." But better informed thirteenth-century historians witness to the contrary as Grousset rightly observes (*Empire*, 396), citing Bar Hebraeus the Syrian Jacobite, Kirakos the Armenian, and two Muslim historians, Juvaini (*History of the World Conqueror*, trans. Boyle) and Juzjani (*Tabaqat-i Nasiri*, trans. H. G. Raverty, 1881).

56. Rubruck (Rockhill), 117.

57. Howorth, *History of the Mongols*, 2:105f. See also Barthold, *Central Asia*, vol. 1, pt. 2, "History of Semirechye," 116.

58. See Saunders, *Mongol Conquests*, 169, for other possible consequences.

59. Barthold, *Central Asia*, 1:116.

60. Rubruck's description of the Naimans as Christian has been strongly challenged. Plano Carpini had flatly stated that they were pagan (Rockwell, 17), and Howorth agrees, "It seems almost incredible to suppose that the Naimans were Christian" (*History of the Mongols*, 1:540ff.). But there is some wisdom in the suggestion that if their Christianity was no better than that of the Uighurs as Rubruck saw them, it might easily be mistaken for paganism. See Moule, *Christians in China*, 216f., 234n; and Rubruck (Rockhill), 110.

61. Rubruck (Rockhill), 141–50.

62. Rubruck (Rockhill), 143ff., 158, 213, 217ff. See p. 214 for his description of a Nestorian mass.

63. See chap. 19, pp. 430ff.; and Moule, *Christians in China*, 94ff. Mark may have been an Ongut.

64. Rubruck (Rockhill), 228–32, 195, 219, 242ff.

65. To him, marrying again after the death of the first wife was bigamy.

66. "They are absolutely depraved. In the first place they are usurers and drunkards; some even among them who live with the Tartars have several wives like them. . . . The bishop rarely visits these parts, hardly once in fifty years. When he does, they have all the male children, even those in the cradle, ordained priests, so nearly all the males among them are priests. Then they marry, which is clearly against the statutes of the fathers, and they are bigamists, for when the first wife dies these priests then take another. They are all simoniacs, for they administer no sacrament gratis. They are solicitous for their wives and children, and are consequently more intent on the increase of their wealth than of the faith. And so those of them who educate some of the sons of the noble [Mongols], though they teach them the Gospel and the articles of the faith, through their evil lives and their stupidity estrange them from the Christian faith, for the lives that the [Mongols] themselves and the Tuins [Buddhist priests, bonzes] or idolaters lead are more innocent than theirs," Rubruck (Rockhill), 153f.; and Rubruck (Dawson), 144f.

67. Rubruck (Rockhill), 230–35.

68. Rubruck (Rockhill), 235f.

69. Rubruck (Rockhill), 239, 254.

70. History has been unkind to Rubruck. Marco Polo who followed him some twenty years later became famous overnight for travel records more complete but no better than Rubruck's, yet except for a brief notice in Roger Bacon's *Opus Majus* (1264), Rubruck's journey was ignored for almost 250 years. Richard Hakluyt published the first 28 chapters in 1589; the complete work appeared first in *Pilgrimes*, by Purchas, in 1625.

71. See Below, chap. 19, pp. 423ff.

Chapter *19*
The Mongols and the Church in Persia

"And in the year fifteen hundred and seventy-six of the Greeks [1265] . . . Hulabu [Hulegu], King of Kings, departed from this world. The wisdom of this man, and his greatness of soul, and his wonderful actions are incomparable. And in the days of summer Tokuz Khatun, the believing queen, departed and great sorrow came to all the Christians throughout the world because of the departure of these two great lights, who made the Christian religion triumphant."

—Bar Hebraeus (ca. 1286)

THE history of the church in Asia in the thirteenth and fourteenth centuries outside the subcontinent of India to the south is dominated by the political power and traditions of three great Mongol conquerors, Hulegu, Kublai, and Timur the Great (better known as Tamerlane). The first two were brothers, sons of the Nestorian Princess Sorkaktani.[1] The third, Tamerlane, was an outsider, not of royal Mongol blood and more Turk than Mongol. Hulegu and Kublai protected Christians; Tamerlane destroyed them.

But for the space of about forty-five years—from the accession of Genghis Khan's grandson Mongke as Great Khan in 1251 to the conversion to Islam of Genghis's great-great-great-grandson Ghazan,[2] ilkhan of Persia, in 1295—Asia, though hesitant and wary, seemed at times to be on the brink of adopting the Christian faith as the religion of a continental empire.

Hulegu and the Christians

In 1251 when Mongke was raised to the Mongol throne as the fourth Great Khan, he announced that it was his will to complete the conquest of the world begun by his victorious grandfather, Genghis, and that Mongols would ride again to the attack. He himself intended to lead one army east against China, but left most of the actual warfare there to his brother Kublai. It was Mongke who received the Franciscan missionary William of Rubruck so kindly in 1253.

The war against the West he entrusted to his other brother, Hulegu (ca. 1217–1265).[3] Hulegu began at once, sending out a special column of his best troops under his most gifted general to lead the way across the Oxus into Persia. Thus commenced the historic Mongol invasion that destroyed the 'Abbasid caliphate, captured Baghdad, and came so close to taking Egypt that the future of Islam in Asia hung for a few months by a thread. The commander of the Mongol army's vanguard was a Nestorian Christian named Ked-Buka, "the Bull."[4] Hulegu's queen, Dokuz, was also a Christian, so zealous in her faith that she rarely traveled without a portable Nestorian chapel on an accompanying wagon.[5] Moreover, as the Mongol armies moved west, increasing numbers of troops from the Christian tribes of central Asia and southern Russia joined them. The Nestorians, remarks J. J. Saunders, were returning to their homeland in Syria and Persia.[6] It was the beginning of the most memorable, the briefest, and the last real renaissance of the ancient Nestorian "Church of the East."

When Hulegu[7] joined his vanguard with a great army and stormed Baghdad in 1258, the Nestorian patriarch was Makika II. His predecessors had ruled the churches of most of Asia from that city for almost five hundred years (since 762) but always under the shadow of Muslim control. Now, for the first time in half a millennium, Christians in the Middle East faced the prospect of life free from the pressures of an officially hostile, always discriminatory, though sometimes lenient government.

As the Mongols approached his Persian capital, the 'Abbasid caliph made a fatal mistake. Arrogant but powerless, he tried to outbluster the invading "barbarians." To Hulegu's demand for surrender he foolishly replied, "Young man . . . , drunk with a ten-day success [who] believe yourself superior to the whole world, do you not know that from the East to the Maghreb (Morocco), all the worshipers of Allah, whether kings or beggars, are slaves of mine, and that I can command them to muster?"[8] The Mongols simply surrounded the city, the defense faltered, and the caliph sent a group of envoys, including the Nestorian patriarch[9] to sue for peace. Hulegu gave the Persians one more chance, unconditional surrender. The caliph refused. The result, as Mongol military tradition demanded, was annihilation. They cut the caliph's troops to pieces, drove almost the entire population out of the city, and massacred them by the thousands. Only the Christians who took refuge in one of the churches of the Nestorian patriarch were spared,[10] perhaps because the patriarch had been willing to serve as negotiator or perhaps because of Hulegu's family connection with Christianity. His queen, Dokuz, personally managed to ransom the lives of many of her fellow believers.[11] The caliph, still proud but very pale, was brought before Hulegu, who handed him over to the soldiers with the reminder that royal blood must not be spilled on the ground. They rolled the last of the 'Abbasid caliphs in a rug and trampled him under their horses' feet.[12] "And so," as Muir concludes his history of the caliphate, "suffering a fate similar to that which five centuries before it had itself inflicted on the [Umayyads], the 'Abbasid dynasty came to a violent and untimely end."[13]

A year later the victorious Hulegu invaded Syria, with the Christian general Ked-Buka again leading the vanguard; and it was Ked-Buka who triumphantly received the surrender of Damascus in 1260 and prepared to march on Egypt. Two Christian rulers of principalities carved out of the Mediterranean coast by the Crusaders rode with him, King Hethoum of Lesser Armenia and Count Bohemund of Antioch. It is painful to have to record the reaction of some of Damascus's Christians to their liberation from Muslim rule. This is how the Mameluke historian Maqrizi (d. 1442) described it about a century and a half later:

> They produced a diploma of [Hulegu] guaranteeing express protection and the free exercise of their religion. They drank wine freely in the month of Ramazan and spilt it in the open streets, on the clothes of the Mussulmans and the doors of the mosques. When they traversed the streets they compelled the merchants to rise and ill-treated those who refused. . . . When the Mussulmans complained, they were treated with indignity by the governor appointed by [Hulegu], and several of them were by his orders bastinadoed. He [Hulegu] visited the Christian church and paid deference to their clergy.[14]

At this point, however, fortune suddenly turned against the invaders. Four important factors checked the Mongol advance. The first was the unexpected death of the Great Khan Mongke. At the news, Hulegu abruptly departed for Mongolia to take part in the election of a new Great Khan, taking most of the army with him. He left Ked-Buka with only ten to twenty thousand troops. The result was momentous, as Saunders observes. "The death of Ogetai in 1241 saved Christian Europe; the death of Mongke in 1259 was to save Muslim Asia."[15]

A second factor was the loss of Mongol unity in a series of debilitating disputes over the succession to the title of Great Khan of the Mongols. The beginnings of this trace back to the death of Genghis, who had bypassed his first son, Jochi, and designated his third son, Ogetai, as principal heir, with the significant proviso that on matters of major import he should consult with the fourth son, Tolui, husband of the Christian princess Sorkaktani.[16] Division was accentuated at the death of Ogetai in 1241 when the houses of Genghis's four sons (Jochi, Chagatai, Ogetai, and Tolui) openly quarreled for four years before grudgingly accepting the election in 1246 of Ogetai's eldest son, Kuyuk, as Great Khan of an empire that stretched from Hungary to the Pacific. But Kuyuk died scarcely two years later, throwing the succession once more into doubt, and the empire split down the middle—the first and fourth sons' lines (Jochid and Toluid) against the second and third sons' heirs (the Chagatid and Ogetid lines).

Despite the rivalries, for a few brief years between 1251 and 1256 when the Christian Sorkaktani's son Mongke became Great Khan, his brother Kublai Khan was conquering China, his uncle Batu, khan of the Russian steppes, died and was succeeded by his Christian son Sartak, and his other brother Hulegu, with his Christian queen, was subduing Persia, it almost seemed that the heart of Asia might sud-

denly turn Christian.[17] Instead the next decades saw the empire be-
gin to disintegrate. Kublai in the east fought his rebellious brother
Arikabuka for control of Mongolia and China; and the khans of the
Golden Horde in Russia warred against the ilkhans in Persia.

Still a third factor was the ambivalent attitude of the Crusaders.
At first they welcomed the Mongols. Then, when a nephew of the
Christian Mongol general Ked-Buka tried to restrain them from plundering, they turned and began to help their former foes, the Muslim
armies of Egypt.

The fourth factor that drove the Mongols out of Syria and back
into Persia was the emergence of a new military power in Egypt. Its
army was no longer led by Kurd or Arab or Persian or even Egyptian
officers, but by Mamelukes, a Turkish dynasty founded by rebelling
slave-warriors with whom Egypt's ineffective sultans, after the death
of Saladin, had filled their armies. Unlike other opponents against
whom the all-conquering Mongols had fought, this new race of pro-
fessional soldier-rulers had been trained themselves in the arts of
Mongol warfare. Their general, in fact, was racially Mongol, a
Kipchak Tartar sold as a slave when the Mongols conquered southern Russia.[18]

At the Springs of Goliath (Ain Jalut) near Nazareth, the Muslim
army met the elite but now outnumbered Mongols and destroyed
them. Ked-Buka died rather than retreat. At the end, he is said to
have faced the Muslim general without fear, reminding him contemptuously of his Mameluke Turkic slave origins. As for me, he
said, "From my birth I have been the slave of the King. I am not like
you, a traitor and murderer of my master."[19] The surviving Mongols,
bereft of their greatest field commander, Ked-Buka, and without
their ilkhan, Hulegu, who had left for the election in Mongolia, were
driven out of Syria and back across the Euphrates. Never again were
they seriously to threaten Syria, but for nearly a hundred more years
(1261–1369) Hulegu's heirs ruled a Persian empire that stretched, like
Old Persia, from the Euphrates to beyond the Oxus and from Ankara
in present-day Turkey to Kandahar in Afghanistan.

Ilkhans and Patriarchs in Mongol Persia

When Hulegu returned to Persia and the election in Karakorum gave
the throne of the Mongol empire to his older brother Kublai, he
placed his capital at Maragheh, north of Baghdad in Azerbaijan territory near Lake Urmia, and appointed the tolerant Persian historian

Juvaini (d. 1283) governor of Baghdad. Those first thirty-seven years of Mongol rule in Persia, from the fall of Baghdad in 1258 to the conversion of Hulegu's great-grandson Ghazan to Islam in 1295, were the last short years of flowering for the Nestorian church. We have already seen how the Nestorian patriarch Makika II (or Machicha)[20] was favorably treated and how with the help of Hulegu's Christian wife rescued his Christian community from at least some of the bloody massacre that followed the sack of Baghdad. Hulegu even turned over a palace of the fallen 'Abbasid caliph to the Christian patriarch.

It was also reported that Hulegu was about to be baptized. Both the Muslim historian Rashid al-Din and the Armenian Christian chronicler Vartan attest to Hulegu's openness to Christianity. Rashid wrote:

> To please his princess [Dokuz] Hulegu heaped favors upon [the Christians] and gave them every token of his regard so that new churches were continually being built and at the gate of Doquz-khatun's *ordu* there was always a chapel where bells were rung.[21]

Vartan, who was at the court of Hulegu in 1264, noted the presence there of the Christian kings of Little Armenia and Georgia and the Crusader prince of Antioch and was given a private interview with the ilkhan in which Hulegu told him "that his mother [Sorkaktani] was a Christian and that he felt much attached to the Christians."[22]

However, the more sober realities affecting the Mongol court in Persia were less promising for Christianity than such indications might have suggested. When the Christians of Tagrit, north of Baghdad and seat of the Jacobite metropolitan, rioted against the Muslim part of town, with typical Mongol ferocity Hulegu simply ordered all the Christians there killed except for the very old and very young, and he turned their cathedral over to the Muslims.[23]

Hulegu was probably always, to the end of his life, no candidate for baptism but an eclectic shamanist who may even have finally turned Buddhist,[24] rather than Christian. The favor he showed to Christians, apart from a desire to please his wife, was undoubtedly due to his need for Christian allies against the rising tide of Islam encircling him on three sides—Mameluke Egypt and Syria in the west, spreading conversions to the Muslim faith among his cousins of the Golden Horde on the north, and the Chagatai khanate emerging on his northeast frontier in central Asia. "We love the Christians," he said to Vartan, "and their religion is popular in our palace, whereas they [my cousins] favor Muslims."[25]

The death of both Hulegu and his Christian princess Dokuz in 1265, the same year that the Nestorian patriarch Makika II also died, brought mourning and a sense of foreboding to Christians all through the Middle East. Even in Baghdad the power of Islam was on the rise again. The new patriarch, Denha I, soon found himself fleeing from an outbreak of Muslim violence that had erupted in protest against his baptizing of a convert from Islam. He was saved only by the kindness of the Muslim historian and governor of Baghdad, Juvaini, who offered him refuge in his own home. Denha felt it prudent soon thereafter to move for a time from Baghdad to the old Nestorian stronghold of Arbela, modern Erbil.[26]

However protective of Christianity Mongol tolerance proved to be through the short eighty years of the ilkhans' rule in Persia, the Nestorian community lived always with fragile confidence in the court and with the wary vulnerability of any Asian religious minority anywhere. Change was to be hoped for, but also to be feared. J. M. Fiey, in the title headings of his chapters on the history of these times,[27] dramatically highlights the alternating moods of optimism and despair in the church as one ilkhan succeeded another:

The New Constantine: Hulegu (1256–1265)
Collaboration: Abaka (1265–1282)
First Warning: Teguder-Ahmad (1282–1284)
The Climax [of Hope]: Arghun (1284–1291)
Interlude: Kaikhatu (1291–1295)
Ambivalence (Evasion): Baidu (1295)
Black Clouds: Ghazan (Mahmud) (1295–1304)

The new ilkhan, Hulegu's son Abaka, who ruled for the next seventeen years (1265–1282), proved to be as protective of Christians as his father, and probably for the same motives—fear of encirclement by Islam. In fact, to ensure himself of Christian allies in the West, he married Mary, the daughter of the Byzantine emperor of Constantinople, Michael Paleologus, and sent envoys to the pope in Rome, to James of Aragon, and to Edward I of England, suggesting an alliance against the Mamelukes in Egypt and Syria, but nothing came of all the diplomatic maneuvering, save for the baptism of three Mongol messengers in Rome and Rome's dispatch of two friars in 1278 on a fruitless mission to baptize the ilkhan of Persia.[28]

The ilkhan Abaka's wife Kotai (Kutui?) was a Christian, and in general his reign was just and favorable to Christians. When Muslims accused the Christian provincial governor in Mosul, and the governor's Uighur assistant who was also a Christian, of mismanagement, he ordered an investigation, and when the charges proved false, executed the accuser.[29] On another occasion when Muslims threatened to prevent the annual Epiphany ceremony of the blessing of the waters of the river at Maragheh, northern seat of the Nestorian patriarch, the ilkhan's wife, Kotai, intervened and "told the Christians to fasten crosses on the end of their spears and proceed to the river." They did so, and the wintry cold subsided and the ice melted. "And the Mongols [rejoiced that the grass grew for feeding their horses] and the Christians [rejoiced] at the triumph of their faith," wrote Bar Hebraeus.[30]

Bar Hebraeus and the Jacobites

Bar Hebraeus (1226–1286), like most of the scholars of his age, was sometimes uncritical and somewhat credulous but he was superbly equipped and well connected for writing the history of those times, and he is unequalled as an eyewitness source of information from a Christian perspective about the church in Persia under the Mongols.[31] As his name indicates, he was the son of a Jewish physician living in Melitene (now Malatya in eastern Turkey) and his mother may have been Arabic, for he also had an Arab name, Abu'l Faraj.[32] The father must have been a man of considerable reputation. When the terrors of the Mongol invasion reached Melitene, the commander of that part of the attacking army fell sick and asked for a physician; it was Bar Hebraeus's father who was brought to treat him. The general[33] recovered and insisted on taking the family with him to Antioch, where the son was able to study under both Jacobite and Nestorian teachers.[34] This interweaving of interracial, interdenominational, linguistic, and intercultural influences in his background, combined with the political advantage of his family's felicitous connection with the Mongol high command, formed the base upon which Bar Hebraeus was to build a remarkably effective Christian ministry in the chaotic world of the thirteenth-century Middle East.

At about age seventeen Bar Hebraeus became a Jacobite monk and all his life strove to moderate the personal and theological jealousies that separated the two major branches of early Asiatic Christianity, Nestorian (Dyophysite) and Jacobite (Monophysite).[35]

His calling to wider leadership in the Asian church came very suddenly. When he was scarcely twenty years old the Jacobite patriarch of Antioch, Ignatius II, summoned him from the monastery and consecrated him a bishop. From the isolation of his studies he now found himself thrust into the murky world of Eastern church politics. The Jacobites, split and embarrassed by rival patriarchs in their own church, discovered that their young bishop was a superb negotiator who could move with ease and integrity between the political factions of the Mongols, Arabs, and Persians; and as an irenic Christian he could deal equably not only with historically hostile Nestorians, but also with his own quarreling Jacobite colleagues. He was soon promoted, first to the prominent episcopal diocese of Aleppo, and then in 1264 to the position of maphrian of the East, which was, next to the patriarchate, the second highest post in the world of Syrian orthodoxy.

As maphrian he became the head of all the Monophysite churches of Asia east of the Euphrates. He found his flock leaderless and in great distress. The ancient center of the Monophysite hierarchy outside Syria was in Tagrit, on the Tigris, but he discovered that no maphrian had even visited Tagrit for sixty years.[36] Wars, persecutions, and massacres, he wrote, had left his church in the east "a widow."[37] For the next two decades he worked indefatigably at three great tasks. First he had to bring hope and confidence to his people and rebuild their shattered Jacobite churches. Equally important in the long run was to ensure their continued welfare by winning the confidence of the Mongol court. By 1284 he had restructured the hierarchy and consecrated twelve new Jacobite bishops in the east.[38] By then he had also moved his residence from Mosul (near ancient Nineveh), to Maragheh where the Mongol ilkhans were wont to settle their shifting residence.

His third goal was to mend as best he could the divisions that tore apart the unity of the churches of Asia. From the beginning he had recognized how seriously rivalry between the two Christian minorities (Nestorian and Jacobite) had weakened their reputation and witness in a non-Christian culture. One of his early acts as maphrian was to entreat the Nestorian patriarch Denha I (1265–1281) to agree not to "engage in quarrels before the barbarian Huns" lest this should "lower our dignity in their eyes but that we should settle [our quarrels] among ourselves." The Nestorian was hesitant, for Nestorians were the dominant Christian group in Persia. He did not take kindly to advice from Jacobites. But Bar Hebraeus persisted in his efforts to improve inter-Christian relationships. Later, in 1279, when Denha found himself facing a revolt in his own Nestorian community stirred up by a bishop he had recently ordained as the "metropolitan of the Chinese," the patriarch must have been grateful for the period of more friendly interchurch relations Bar Hebraeus had provided.[39]

But in the midst of all this ecumenicity, he wisely respected the principle that ordered peace among differing communions must begin with truth and order and peace in one's own. When his Jacobite patriarchate in thirteenth-century Antioch assumed more authority than belonged to it, Bar Hebraeus spoke up like Paul against Peter in New Testament Antioch and boldly defended the rights of his churches in oriental Asia. He was adamant that the election of a patriarch of Antioch was invalid without the participation of the maphrian of the East.[40]

His life was a mixture of fragile successes and many disappointments, but it demonstrates how in the most impossible of situations—a Jacobite bishop in Nestorian territory, a Christian in Muslim Persia, and a member of a vanquished race under Mongol conquerors—one persistent witness and example can bring to light moments of Christian unity out of dark divisions. As at his installation in 1264, so also at his funeral ceremonies in 1286 representatives of many different bickering communions gathered to honor this learned historian and peace-loving churchman. Even Edward Gibbon in his *Decline and Fall of the Roman Empire*, which is not uniformly kind to Christians, writes admiringly of Bar Hebraeus:

> In his death his funeral was attended by his rival Nestorian patriarch, with a train of Greeks and Armenians, who forgot their disputes and mingled their tears on the grave of an enemy.[41]

The Travels of the "Monks of Kublai Khan"

The Nestorians in Persia, despite their recurring inner frictions, had always been the dominant Christian community east of the Euphrates. When their patriarch Denha died in 1281, there opened up before them what must have seemed an unprecedented and providential opportunity for even greater, higher standing, an opportunity to revitalize their ancient communion not simply as preeminent among the religious minorities (*melets*) of the land, but to take their long-desired place as the faith of the whole empire, as once long before in the West the church had become in Europe the Church of Rome and in Byzantium the Church of the New Rome, Constantinople. Could not now, at last, Nestorians, under an emerging *pax mongolica*, become in reality as well as in name the "Church of the East"?

It never quite happened. But for that story we must retrace our steps back to the time when, in 1251, the three brothers, Mongke, Hulegu, and Kublai, grandsons of Genghis Khan and sons of the Christian princess Sorkaktani, began their separate careers in Mongolia, Persia, and China.

Some time around 1245 a godly Nestorian archdeacon in the Chinese province west of Peking now called Shansi bore a son,

Mark, who when he was twenty-three gave away all his possessions, became a monk, and was ordained by the Nestorian metropolitan in Peking. There, in Kublai Khan's new capital,[42] he had met another Mongol Christian, Sauma,[43] who at first had discouraged him from entering the priesthood in order to test the strength of his calling. Sauma was a Uighur born in Peking;[44] Mark was probably an Ongut.[45]

When Mark was about thirty, the two young Mongol monks left Peking for a pilgrimage to Jerusalem. The ease and rapidity with which they crossed the thousands of miles of war-troubled Mongol territory suggests that they traveled with permits from the Great Khan himself. At Mark's home, on their way, two Mongol princes, sons-in-law of Kuyuk Khan and Kublai Khan, respectively,[46] begged them to stay in their territory but sent them on their way when they insisted, and provided for their journey. They reached Khotan halfway across the great desert and found Christian communities here and there, but at that point fighting blocked their way and delayed their progress. This part of the journey took them eight months. Once on their way again they came to Kashgar on the western edge of the desert, the seat of a Nestorian metropolitanate, only to find the city looted and empty.[47] They pressed on over the high ranges that divide Asia east and west and on the Persian side were welcomed by a friendly Nestorian bishop in a Christian monastery near Meshed who sent them on to Patriarch Denha. In those uncertain years the patriarch was often forced to leave the traditional seat of authority in Baghdad and, like the restless Mongol ilkhans, temporarily fix his headquarters elsewhere. Denha was then at Maragheh in Azerbaijan, seventy miles from the ilkhan Abaka's occasional capital at Tabriz.

The two pilgrims had not anticipated that war between Persia and Egypt would keep them from proceeding on to their spiritual goal, Jerusalem, but were not at all averse to spending more time in Persia, visiting the great Christian holy places of Baghdad, Seleucia-Ctesiphon, Arbela, Nisibis, and Nineveh (Mosul). They were amazed at the many churches, sacred relics, and the numbers of Christians in the churches and monasteries. They decided to enter a monastery near Arbela while waiting for the road to Jerusalem to open, but the patriarch urged them instead to return to China and offered to consecrate Mark as metropolitan "of Cathay and Ong."[48]

This was in 1280, and Mark was thirty-five years old, but the "young, handsome, dagger-bearded prelate" was destined never to see his homeland again. For more than two years he tried to cross the high roads of Asia but wars blocked his passage. In the meantime the patriarch, Denha, had died, and unexpectedly the high council of Nestorian bishops chose as his successor the young stranger from far-off China. He was shocked. "I cannot even speak Syriac [the language of the Nestorian church]," he said. But the wise Nestorians, who had lived successively under Roman, Persian, and Arab conquerors, knew that in the thirteenth century it was the Mongols who ruled the world, and they were therefore determined for good political reasons to have a Mongol patriarch. He was enthroned in the church in Mar Koka near Baghdad late in the year 1281 as Mar Yaballaha III.[49]

Their wisdom was soon apparent. The ilkhan Abaka was favorably impressed with the new patriarch of the Nestorians, and the Christians in turn praised the ilkhan for what his contemporary the Jacobite bishop Bar Hebraeus described as God-given "understanding, and wisdom, and . . . good disposition, and mercifulness." But scarcely a year later Abaka died. Only a few days earlier, he had attended Easter Sunday services "to rejoice at the festival with the Christians,"[50] and when Christians received the word that his uncle Teguder (Ahmad) would succeed him, they ceased their rejoicing, for Teguder was a convert to Islam.[51]

The new ilkhan, third of the line of Hulegu to rule Persia,[52] represented an abrupt and unpopular reversal of the policies of his two predecessors. As the son of a Nestorian Christian mother, the princess Kutai, Teguder had been baptized a Christian, receiving the Christian name Nicholas, according to the Armenian chronicler Haithon.[53] But at his enthronement he publicly announced his conversion to Islam and took the Muslim name Ahmad. A considerable number of his Mongol commanders took offense at the sudden change, which disturbed them both religiously and politically, for they still bore bitter memories of their defeat by Muslims at Ain Jalut some twenty years earlier. So when the late ilkhan Abaka's eldest son, Prince Arghun, disputed his uncle's succession and rebelled, they rallied around him as being more truly Mongol than the Muslim.[54] Teguder was captured and executed in the royal Mongol fashion by breaking his back to avoid spilling his blood. He had ruled less than two years, and once again Christians hoped for better things. Arghun ruled for the next seventeen years, from 1284 to 1291.

One of the early acts of Teguder had been to imprison Mark, the Nestorian patriarch Yaballaha III, for forty days, on charges trumped up against him by a rival bishop seeking political favor for himself. The accusation was that the patriarch was supporting Arghun in the rebellion.[55] The charges were dismissed, and when Arghun triumphed, the report of the imprisonment only increased the church leader's favor with the new regime. But in speaking of Mongol favor for any religion, it must be remembered that it was the kind of favor that protected against persecution and injustice. It did not extend to an endorsement by the state that would give preference to any one religion, such as Christianity, over others. It was hard, calculating, often brutal, and sometimes avaricious, but it did try to be fair by the standards of the times. Bar Hebraeus, who from 1264 until his death in 1286 was maphrian (Primate) of all the Monophysites (Jacobites) in Persia and the East, gives us this pithy summary of Mongol religious policy in those years:

> With the Mongols there is neither slave nor free man; neither believer nor pagan; neither Christian nor Jew; but they regard all men as belonging to the one and the same stock. . . . All they demand is strenuous service and submission [which] is beyond the power of man to deliver.[56]

Ilkhan Arghun now seriously considered pursuing the on-again, off-again negotiations that for more than a quarter of a century had explored possibilities of an alliance between Christian Europe and Mongol Asia against the Muslim Middle East. This time, in a major reversal of the initiative, the feelers came from Asia, not the West. With the consent of Khublai Khan, as the documents indicate, the ilkhan Arghun dispatched an official ambassador in 1287 to the pope and the Christian courts of Europe. His choice for the post was Sauma, now a bishop, the pilgrim companion of Mark who had been made patriarch.[57]

At Rome the Mongol diplomat and priest was examined carefully on his theology, for Nestorians were considered heretical, and was asked why the Mongols had chosen a Christian priest for the mission. His reply, as recorded, was in part:

> St. Thomas, St. Adai and St. Mares evangelized our country and the rites which they taught us we still observe.
>
> You must know that many of our fathers have gone to the lands of the Mongols, the Turks and the Chinese, and have taught them. Today many Mongols are Christians; there are princes and queens who have been baptized and confess Christ. They have churches with them in the camp, and show great honor to the Christians, and there are many converts among them. . . .
>
> No one has been sent to us Orientals from the Pope. The holy Apostles aforesaid taught us and we still hold today what they handed down to us. . . .
>
> I am come from distant lands not to discuss or to teach my belief, but to pay my respects to my lord the Pope and to the relics of the

Saints, and to deliver the messages of the king and of the Catholicos [Patriarch]. If you please let us have done with discussion.

The only further request he made was for a guide to show him the churches and tombs of the saints in Rome.[58]

From Rome he went to Paris where Philip the Fair received him royally and dazzled him with a display of relics, including the crown of thorns and a piece of the cross, and also promised support for the ilkhan's crusade. The embassy then traveled from Paris to Gascony where the English King, Edward I, was holding court. Edward, too, at the mention of Jerusalem, promised his sword for the Crusade, and asked Sauma to celebrate mass—an English king receiving Communion from a Nestorian bishop. Upon their return to Rome, Sauma asked and was granted permission by Pope Nicholas IV to celebrate a Nestorian mass there too, and the people marveled at the sight. "The language is different," they said, "but the rite is the same."[59]

When Sauma returned to Persia in 1288 he was received with great honor by the ilkhan. Arghun went so far as to promise to build a church for him at the gate of his palace in which, he said to Sauma, "you may say your services and prayers."[60] Others reported that the ilkhan had given permission for the baptism of his son, Kharbanda; and that at the consecration of a Nestorian church by the patriarch and twelve bishops, the ilkhan himself carried the wooden gong, which Nestorians used for a bell, and joined the procession, ordering everyone to receive the patriarchal blessing.[61]

Twice more, in 1289 and in 1290, Arghun sought in vain for an alliance with Christian Europe against Muslim Egypt. The Mongolian text of his first letter still survives. It called on the pope and Edward I of England to honor their previous offers of support and promised in return, "Praying to Heaven, we shall take the field in [January 1291] . . . and if blessed by good fortune . . . we shall give you Jerusalem." His next and last embassy to the West was entrusted to a high Mongolian officer, Chaghan, who had converted to Christianity.[62] The latter embassy returned only after Arghun died and like the others brought back assurances but no results. The Crusades of the West were over. Acre, the last citadel of the Crusaders' Latin kingdom of Jerusalem, fell to the Egyptians in 1291.

The reign of Arghun was the last high plateau in the history of the Nestorians in Asia. Their Mongol patriarch, Mark (Yaballaha III), exercised ecclesiastical sovereignty over more of the earth's surface than even the pontiff in Rome, and after his death the Nestorian catholicate, despite the calamities that began to befall it, continued to be the dominant branch of the faith east of the Euphrates for another hundred years. The thirteenth century can with some justification, therefore, be called the years when Christians spread the faith more widely in Asia that at any time in the first millennium and a half of church history. Not until 1492 and 1498, when the explorers and navigators of the Age of Discovery began to open up new chapters in that history, would the broad extent of the expansion of the Nestorians be surpassed.

Intimations of Weakness in Persian Christianity

If this period is indeed the time when Christianity in Persia was at its prime, as so many indications suggest, how is it that it collapsed so suddenly—within two generations, as we shall see? It had disappeared once before in China three hundred years earlier in the tenth century. Will the same reasons apply to explain its decline and fall in most of Asia at the end of the fourteenth?

Looking back, in chapter 15 we gave four possible reasons for the collapse of T'ang-dynasty Christianity. The first reason was theological. It was charged that the Nestorians overly adjusted to the indigenous Chinese religions and succumbed to syncretism. They were too Chinese. The second charge concerned organization, and the argument is precisely the opposite. They were not Chinese enough. The Nestorian priests in China then were apparently almost all Persian, not Chinese. A third charge was that the social and cultural level of the church was inferior to that of China's intellectual and political leadership and therefore failed to promise effective improvement for the life of the masses. The fourth charge was that the church was far too subservient to and dependent upon the state and therefore fell with the dynasty.

How do these factors relate to the Nestorians in Persia at their height in the thirteenth century? To put it briefly, the first two charges do not seem applicable. In Persia the church was exclusive, and not syncretistic. Unlike the church in seventh- and eighth-century China, Christianity under the Muslims in Persia was so sharply defined as *non*-Muslim that crossing that line except by conversion was legally prohibited. It might be argued that some aspects of the Nestorianism under the invading Mongols, as described by Rubruck, for example, were dangerously similar to the animistic beliefs of Mongol shamanism and were an open invitation to syncretism. But the history of missions has almost universally demonstrated that in animistic societies such similarities often prove to be as much a bridge toward conversion to Christianity, as from a more primitive to a more intellectually credible faith, than a downward spiral toward syncretism. In fact, so it proved to be in the early contacts of Christians with the Mongols in central Asia.

The second criticism, which is that Christianity was too foreign and Western, is likewise not so arguable in the case of Persia. Nestorianism in Persia had always carefully separated itself from the charge of being Roman, though it never quite escaped from its vulnerability to attack as a Syrian religion or a Byzantine fifth column. But to the Mongols, it was as Persian as Persia, and its Christians and priests and patriarchs were far more to be trusted than the Muslim population.

So, though signs of syncretism and foreignness were never altogether absent, at least in this period we must rather look more closely for an explanation of the calamities that befell the church to the other two reasons: a failure of intellect and dependence upon government.

But before that, we must move in the final two chapters of this volume, to what was happening to the church in the thirteenth- and fourteenth-century Chinese empire of the Mongols of Kublai Khan; and in a very different vein, we must note the omens of a Christian disaster brewing in central Asia.

NOTES

1. See genealogical chart chap. 18, n. 29.

2. The line descended as follows: Genghis (d. 1227), Tolui (d. 1232), Hulegu (r. 1261–1265), Abaka (r. 1265–1282), Arghun (r. 1284–1291), Ghazan (r. 1295–1304).

3. Bar Hebraeus, *Chronography*, trans. E. A. W. Budge (London: Oxford Univ. Press, 1932), 417f.; and Rashid al-Din (Boyle translation as *The Successors of Genghis Khan*, trans. into English by J. A. Boyle, New York: Columbia University, 1971), 222ff., 246ff. On Hulegu, see also H. H. Howorth *History of the Mongols from the Ninth to the Nineteenth Century*, 5 vols. (1876, reprint, Taiwan: Ch'eng Wen, 1970), 3:90–217, and J. A. Boyle, *The Saljuq and Mongol Periods*, vol. 5 in *The Cambridge History of Iran* (Cambridge: Cambridge Univ. Press, 1968), 340–55. On the religious situation, the two best thirteenth-century historians of this period in Persia were the Christian Bar Hebraeus and the Muslim Rashid al-Din, both reputedly of Jewish descent.

4. The name is also spelled Ket-Buka (*Cambridge*), Kitbuka, or Kitubuka (Howorth). He is variously identified as a Naiman or a Kerait. Howorth, *History of the Mongols*, 1:210; J. J. Saunders, *The History of the Mongol Conquests* (Lon-

don: Routledge and Kegan Paul, 1971), 108; Boyle, *Saljuq and Mongol* 342ff., *passim*. The sometimes too credulous Armenian prince and historian Haithon (Heythum), who visited the Mongol court in 1299, wrote of Ked-Buka (whom he calls Guiboga), "[He] loved the Christians for he belonged to the race of the three kings who went to worship Our Saviour at his nativity," Howorth, *History of the Mongols*, 3:150, referring to Haithon's *Chronicle*, 30.

5. Howorth, *History of the Mongols*, 1:542, quotes the Persian historian Rashid al-Din's *Jami' al-Tawarikh* on Dokuz Khatun. She had been one of Hulegu's father's wives, which was not unusual among royal Mongols, and was therefore also his stepmother. Dokuz should perhaps more properly be called a princess rather than queen, since the Mongol ilkhans of Persia recognized the nominal headship of the Great Khans in Mongolia. But in Persia she was a queen.

6. Among the ethnic groups other than Uighurs, Naimans, and Keraits which he names were the "Turks, Georgians, Alans and Armenians." Saunders, *Mongol Conquests*, 108.

7. For greater detail on the campaign against 'Abbasid Persia, and the rule of Hulegu's successors to the death of Ghazan, see Howorth, *History of the Mongols*, 3:90–532; and for a briefer, systematic and critical perspective, Boyle, *Saljuq and Mongol*, 340–421. Both rely heavily on the primary authority for the period, the *Jami' al-Tawarikh* , or *Compendium of Histories*, of the Muslim-Jewish historian Rashid al-Din (d. 1318) who was a personal adviser to the ilkhans; and on the work of his contemporary Christian (Jacobite) historian of the period, Bar Hebraeus, *Chronography* (trans. Budge), and *Chronicon ecclesiasticum* (ed. Abbeloos and Lamy, 1872–77).

8. R. Grousset, *Empire of the Steppes* (New Brunswick, NJ: Rutgers Univ. Press, 1970), 355, citing Rashid al-Din in d'Ohsson, *Histoire des Mongols*, 3:217.

9. J. M. Fiey, "Chrétiens Syriaques sous les Mongols," CSCO, vol. 362, t. 44 (Louvain, 1975), 21ff.; Howorth, *History of the Mongols*, 3:123.

10. Howorth, *History of the Mongols*, 3:126; Boyle, *Saljuq and Mongol*, 348.

11. Fiey, "Chrétiens Syriaques," 22.

12. Howorth, *History of the Mongols*, 3:129, citing Kirakos (Guiragos), the Georgian of Ganja, in *Journal Asiatique*, 5th series, vol. 11 (1858), p. 491. Howorth gives several other reported versions of the caliph's death, 127ff.

13. Muir, *The Caliphate, Its Rise, Decline, and Fall*, rev. ed. (Edinburgh: Grant, 1924), 592.

14. As cited by Howorth, *History of the Mongols*, 3:150, referring to [Maqrizi], 1. 98.

15. Saunders, *Mongol Conquests*, 114.

16. Moses and S. A. Halkovic, Jr., *Introduction to Mongolian History and Culture* (Bloomington, IN: Indiana Univ. Uralic and Altaic Series, 1985), vol. 149, p. 52.

17. See chap. 18, *passim.*

18. Bibars (or Baybars), the Mameluke general, shortly thereafter deposed the last of the Saladin line of sultans and founded the Mameluke dynasty, which ruled Egypt from 1260 to 1517. See C. Brockelmann, *History of the Islamic Peoples* (New York: Capricorn, 1960), 238ff., 250f., 288f.

19. Howorth, *History of the Mongols*, 3:169, citing Quatremere's translation of Rashid al-Din. Rashid was pro-Mongol. See also "Ayn Jalut: Mamluk Success or Mongol Failure?" in *Harvard Journal of Asiatic Studies*, 44:2 (Dec. 1984), 307-45.

20. The name is variously transliterated: Makika (Howorth), Machicha (J. A. Assemani, *De Catholicis* . . .), and Makikha (French).

21. Cited by Grousset, *Empire*, 357.

22. J. M. Fiey, "Chrétiens Syriaques," 24f.; Howorth, *History of the Mongols*, 3:206. Less authentic was the report circulating in the West that Pope Alexander VI in 1261 had been so impressed with news brought by a Hungarian "envoy" from Hulegu announcing the ilkhan's readiness for Catholic baptism, that he responded with a letter urging him to make arrangements for it with the Catholic patriarch (Howorth, *ibid.*, 210).

23. Bar Hebraeus, *Chronography* (trans. Budge), 434. See Fiey, "Chrétiens Syriaques," 35ff., for numerous instances of friction between Christians and Muslims in Persia during this period.

24. See A. Bausani, "Religion Under the Mongols," in *Cambridge History of Iran*, 5:540ff., 540f.

25. E. Dulaurier, "Les Mongols d'après les Histoires Arméniens," *Journal Asiatique*, 2 (1860): 304.

26. Bar Hebraeus, *Chronography* (trans. Budge), 419f.; and Grousset, *Empire*, 367, citing Barthold's article "Dzuwaini," in *Encyclopedie de l'Islam*, p. 1100.

27. Fiey, "Chrétiens Syriaques."

28. On the correspondence between Abaka and Christian rulers in Europe, see Howorth, *History of the Mongols*, 3:278ff.; and Fiey, *Chrétiens Syriaques*, 34ff.

29. Bar Hebraeus, *Chronography* (trans. Budge), 459f., 462.

30. Bar Hebraeus, *Chronography* (trans. Budge), 460. The helpful princess was probably Abaka's first wife and mother of his son Teguder. See Fiey, *Chrétiens Syriaques*, 38. Howorth (*History of the Mongols*, 3:212, 265) suggests as a less likely identification Abaka's second wife Tukuri, niece of Hulegu's queen, Dokuz.

31. On his writings, see E. A. W. Budge, *The Chronography of Gregory Abu'l Faraj* . . . *Commonly known as Bar Hebraeus*, vol. 1 (London and Oxford: Oxford Univ. Press, 1932), xxxii–xliii. The most important is his *Political History of the World (Chronicon Ecclesiasticum* . . .), ed. J. B. Abbeloos and T. J. Lamy (Latin trans., 1872); of which Budge has published an English translation of

pt. I as *The Chronography* . . ., from the Nestorian Syriac text which is Budge's vol. 2. Bar Hebraeus wrote in Jacobite Syriac.

32. On his life, see Budge, *Chronography,* 1:xv–xxxi.

33. Shawer Nawin.

34. His primary connection was with the Jacobite patriarch, but he also studied rhetoric under a Nestorian named Yakub. As a linguist he was fluent in Hebrew, Syriac, and Arabic and apparently also knew Greek, Armenian, Uighur, and even some Chinese. Budge, *Chronography,* 1:xvif., xlivff.

35. See chap. 9 for the origins of this "great schism."

36. Budge, *Chronography,* 1:xxiv.

37. Budge, *Chronography,* 1:xx, citing *Chronicon Ecclesiasticum* 2, cols. 432f.

38. Budge, *Chronography,* 1:xxvii.

39. Budge, *Chronography,* 1:xxii–xxiv.

40. "From ancient times," he wrote, "the holy fathers have laid it down that a Maphrian cannot be established without a Patriarch, and a Patriarch cannot be established without a Maphrian." Budge, *Chronography,* 1:xxvi.

41. Budge, *Chronography,* 1:xx, xxixf., xliv, citing Smith's edition, vol. 6, p. 55.

42. Peking is Cambaluc or Khan-baliq in Turkic, sometimes called the "Xanadu" of Coleridge's poem: "In Xanadu did Kublai Khan, a stately pleasure dome decree, where Alph the sacred river ran, through caverns measureless to man, down to a sunless sea." The more accurate reference is Shangtu, the summer capital.

43. The primary source on the two travelers is the edition by Paul Bedjan, *Histoire de Mar Jabalaha, patriarche, et de Rabban Cauma* [Syriac text], 2d ed. (Leipzig, 1895). An important French translation is by J. B. Chabot, *Histoire de Mar Jabalaha III et du moine Rabban Cauma* (extracted from the *Revue de l'Orient Latin,* t. 1 and 2, Paris, 1895). The most complete English translation is by E. A. W. Budge, *The Monks of Kublai Khan* (London: Religious Tract Society, 1928). See Budge's review of the surviving Syriac, Persian, and Arabic manuscripts, pp. 3–7.

44. Sauma is also written Sawma, or Barsauma, or Rabban Sauma, and Çauma in French.

45. Bar Hebraeus, who was the first in west Asia to mention Sauma and Mark, calls them both Uighurs (*Chronicon Ecclesiasticum,* ed. Abbeloos and Lamy, vol. 3, col. 4410). But see the critical notes on the monks' backgrounds in Moule, *Christians in China* (London: Society for Promoting Christian Knowledge, 1930), 94; and Budge, *Monks,* 1–3.

46. See Moule, *Christians in China,* 8 n. 6. Chabot and Budge both describe them as sons-in-law of Kublai. One of them, Aibuga, was the father of King George, who figured prominently in the later history of Christianity in Peking under Kublai Khan.

47. Some seventy years earlier the Nestorian patriarch Elias III (1176–1190) had made Kashgar the seat of a metropolitan, with jurisdiction north to Lake Balkash and the Tokmak cemeteries. W. Barthold, *Four Studies on the History of Central Asia,* 3 vols. (Leiden: Brill, 1952–56), 1:105f.

48. That is, "Cathay and the Onguts," Budge, *Monks,* 142–148; and Moule (following Chabot), *Christians in China,* 101–103.

49. Moule, *Christians in China,* 104. Moule notes that the first Yaballaha had served as patriarch 416–420, the second 1190–1221.

50. Bar Hebraeus, *Chronography* (trans. Budge), 455, 466.

51. It is true that the Christian historian Bar Hebraeus chose not to mention Teguder's defection to Islam and diplomatically wrote that "he looked upon all peoples with a merciful eye, and especially on the heads of the Christian Faiths, and . . . freed all the churches, and the religious houses, and the priests and monks from taxation." However, of Teguder's death he wrote, "there was gladness for all the Christians" (*Chronography* [Budge trans.], 1:467, 472). And elsewhere he reported that Teguder ordered the Buddhist temples and Christian churches converted into mosques and vowed to behead Christians who refused to convert to Islam (Howorth, *History of the Mongols,* 3:288, citing Bar Hebraeus, *Chron. Syr.,* 614–15).

52. Teguder (Takudar) was the seventh and eldest surviving son of Hulegu and brother of Abaka. He had taken the Muslim name Ahmad upon his conversion.

53. Haithon refers to him as "Tangader-Mahomet," *A Lytell Cronycle (ca. 1307),* 48f. The Princess Kutai (Qutui) was from the Kunkurat tribe. See also Howorth (*History of the Mongols,* 3:212f.) for the tangled list of Hulegu's six wives and twelve concubines and on Teguder's baptism (285). His rival Arghun was descended from Hulegu through a wife of the Suldus tribe, and tribal jealousies may have contributed to the friction between the uncle, Teguder, and his nephew, Arghun, who overthrew him.

54. Howorth quotes the Mongol general Buka as saying "Ahmad has determined to exterminate the descendants of [Genghis] Khan. . . . he favors the Mussulmans," *History of the Mongols,* 3:304.

55. Moule, *Christians in China,* 105. Thereafter Yaballaha chose to live in Maragheh, in the north.

56. Bar Hebraeus, *Chronography* (trans. Budge), 1:490.

57. See J. B. Chabot, *Mar Jabalaha, passim.* A concise summary of the mission, based on Chabot, is in Moule, *Christians in China,* 105–17. Chabot reports the possibility of an earlier mission, in 1285 (pp. 185–93). See also Howorth, *History of the Mongols,* 3:348f.

58. Moule, *Christians in China,* 107f.

59. Moule, *Christians in China,* 110f.

60. Chabot, *Mar Jabalaha,* 3.

61. The report of the baptism is not necessarily false, though it says the

baptism was Catholic not Nestorian. The ilkhan was seeking Catholic allies. His participation in the consecration would not be at all out of place for a tolerant Mongol ruler. See Howorth, *History of the Mongols*, 3:355.

62. J. A. Boyle, "The Ilkhans of Persia and the Princes of Europe," *Central Asia Journal* 20, no. 1–2: 34–37.

Chapter 20
Christianity in
Mongol China

"Naian [cousin and rival of Kublai Khan] was a baptized Christian and in this battle he had the Cross of Christ on his standard . . . but it availed them nothing. . . . And after the great Kaan [Kublai] had . . . won this battle, many . . . made fun of the Cross . . . and spoke against the Christians who were there. . . . Then [Kublai] . . . begins to comfort them and says If the Cross of your God has not helped Naian it has done very right. . . . Naian who came against his lord was both disloyal and treacherous, and so there is great right in that which is happened to him and the Cross of your God did well if it does not help him against right. . . ."

—Marco Polo, ca. 1300 writing
about a rebellion against Kublai
Khan in 1287. Translated by
Moule

Sorkaktani and the Line of Dynastic Succession

"Kublai is more like his mother's people [the Keraits]," said Genghis Khan one day as he was watching his grandson play. "He is dark, not ruddy like our side of the family."[1] But in fact Kublai Khan (1215–1294)[2] owed much to both sides of his lineage. He had something of the same world-conquering ambition of Genghis and the love of combat for which his father, Tolui, was famed. He also had a good measure of the political wisdom and religious fair-mindedness of his mother, the Christian princess Sorkaktani. He was the greatest of the Mongol rulers of China in the short Yuan dynasty (1260–1368),[3] and the most powerful man in the world of his time.

Sorkaktani died in 1252. She lived just long enough to see her first son, Mongke, succeed to the title Great Khan first borne by her father-in-law Genghis, Great Khan of the Mongols, but not long enough to rejoice in the elevation of her third son, Hulegu, to the Persian throne as ilkhan in 1261.[4] Nor did she live to see her second son, Kublai, carry the line of Genghis to its greatest heights. She died while Kublai was still fighting his way to imperial power in China, the "center of the world." But her influence on her sons' character and policies was widely credited as the shaping factor in the ultimate success of this remarkable family of rulers of Asia.

Her husband, Tolui, had died twenty years earlier when only forty-two years old, a brilliant but alcoholic general of the Mongol center army and regent of the empire for two years after the death of his father, Genghis Khan. His brother, Ogetai, who succeeded Genghis as the second Great Khan, proposed that the widow marry his son, her nephew Kuyuk, who would later become the third Great Khan, but Sorkaktani discreetly declined. "I must raise my four sons to be men," she said; and so greatly was she respected that neither Ogetai nor Kuyuk held the refusal against her. In fact, Ogetai granted her territory in north China when shortly thereafter he over-threw the Chin dynasty, and she, finding that her new subjects were Chinese farmers not Mongol nomads, wisely refrained from trying to change them into hunters and horsemen. Instead she took an un-usual course for a Mongol; she encouraged them in what they did best, agriculture.[5]

Later, the third ruling Mongol emperor of China, a grandson of Kublai, acknowledged the dynasty's debt to Sorkaktani, and in 1310 posthumously granted her the title of "empress." The elaborate cer-emonies included a Nestorian mass celebrated probably before her imperial portrait in her own tablet halls, one in far northwestern China[6] and another near the new capital at Peking (Khanbalik).

Like his mother Kublai Khan was a friend of the Christians, but unlike her he was not a Christian himself. He once told Marco Polo, or at least gave him the impression, that he fully intended to become a Christian,[7] but as we have seen before, this was standard political practice for a Mongol ruler. As H. H. Howorth remarks, "With Khubilai, as with his predecessors, religion was treated as a political matter. The Khakan [Great Khan] must be obeyed; how man shall worship God is indifferent."[8]

It was in this third generation after Genghis Khan, however, following the death of Kuyuk Khan, son of Ogetai, that dynastic rivalries within the house of Genghis, brother against brother and cousin against cousin, began to chip away at the authority of the Great Khan and ultimately destroyed the Mongol hegemony over Asia. We have already noted the conflict between Mongol Russia (the line of Genghis's first son, Jochi) and Mongol Persia (the line of his fourth son, Tolui). Now the line of Genghis's grandsons by Tolui and Princess Sorkaktani began to unravel. Her eldest son, the Great Khan Mongke died in 1259. Her third son, Hulegu, ruler of Persia, was occupied with his own wars against the Muslims in the south and with the threat of civil war with the Golden Horde in the north. But in the far east, after the death of their brother Mongke, both her second son, Kublai, and her fourth son, Arikbuka, claimed the right of prime succession. Kublai felt the Great Khanate belonged to him because of his military successes in north China, and Arikbuka felt it was his because, like his father, Tolui, he had inherited the rule of the Mongolian heartland on the steppes.

Their civil war lasted four years (1260–1264).[9] Given the prevailing syncretistic tolerance of the Mongols, religion probably had nothing to do with the rupture, but it is worth noting that Arikbuka was drawn more closely to his mother's Christianity than any of his brothers. He was also supported against Kublai by a powerful group of Mongol Christians and Christian allies that included the late Great Khan Mongke's first wife, the dowager Kutuktei, whose preparation for Nestorian baptism Rubruck believed he had witnessed in Karakorum in 1253,[10] and Mongke's chancellor and principal adviser, Bulgai, who was, like Sorkaktani, a Nestorian Kerait. Moreover, Kublai's defeat of Arikbuka was not the only instance of a Christian connection to a losing cause in the tangled course of dynastic rebellions that plagued Kublai throughout his Great Khanate (1260–1294). Another was the rebellion of Nayan in 1287 which we will consider later.

It must be remembered that what we know of the Christians and churches in China during this period comes for the most part from non-Chinese sources, and these are very few. For any descriptive details we must rely on the reports of Western visitors and traders like the Polos and the letters of the missionary bishops of the first Franciscan missions in China. References in Chinese sources in the hundred years of Mongol rule are rare and tantalizingly brief, but, such as they are, they do confirm the existence of a fairly widespread Christian presence at the Mongol court and irregularly throughout the empire, most notably in the northwest and east.[11]

The Polos at the Court of Kublai Khan (1266–1292)

The Polo brothers and their famous son and nephew, Marco, were not missionaries, but Marco Polo's account of his journey to Mongol China and of the Christians he found there is one of the most important pieces of information that has come down to us about Nestorianism in China in the thirteenth century.[12] Moreover, on the second Polo journey—the older Polos had made the trip once before in 1260–1269 without Marco—two Dominican missionaries, Nicholas of Vicenza and William of Tripoli, were assigned by the pope to accompany the merchants but dropped out on the way.

On their earlier journey the Polo brothers became the first known Europeans to reach China. Travelers and missionaries to the East before that had not been able to penetrate beyond the Mongol capital in Mongolia. But by 1265/66 when the two merchants reached Kublai's summer capital at Shangtu, ten days by horse north of Peking, the Mongol Khan was already master of all north China and had won his first important battle against the failing Sung emperor in the south. North China at that time, though heavily outnumbering Mongolia in population, had only an estimated ten to fifteen million inhabitants and was vastly dwarfed by south China's four or five times as many people.[13]

Kublai not only welcomed the Westerners warmly, asking them innumerable questions about their kings and countries, but also expressed much interest in their religion, Christianity. He even asked them to return to Europe with letters from the Khan to the pope asking for a hundred missionaries:

> Wise men of learning in the Christian religion and doctrine . . . who should know also the seven arts and be fitted to teach his people and who should know well how to argue and to show plainly to him and to the idolaters and to the other classes of people . . . that all their religion was erroneous . . . and who should know well how to show

clearly by reason that the Christian faith and religion is better than theirs and more true than all the other religions; and if they proved this, that he [Kublai] and all his potentates would become men of the Church . . .[14]

Kublai Khan may have been more interested in the "seven arts," that is, in Western science and learning, and in possible political alliances than in the Christian faith, but received a disappointing reply. When the Polos were finally able to deliver Kublai's letters to the new pope, Gregory X, he had other matters on his mind. He asked the brothers, now joined by seventeen-year-old Marco, to take back with them not a hundred missionaries, but only two Dominicans who, unfortunately, were so dismayed by the outbreak of war in central Asia that they turned home, leaving the three Polos to reach China in 1275 without benefit of clergy. Had they exhibited more missionary courage and availed themselves of the advantage of the Polos' prestige with the Great Khan, there is no telling what an impact a strong Catholic mission with wide Western contacts might have had in the expanding early years of the Mongol dynasty before it began to decline after 1280.[15] By the time the first Catholic mission reached Peking in 1294, the great emperor, Kublai Khan, overlord of Asia from Korea to the Euphrates and south to Hanoi and Burma, had just died.

Despite its minor inaccuracies and although it was first greeted in Europe with wide disbelief, Marco Polo's report of his incredible sixteen or seventeen years in China slowly changed the West's vague images of the Far East as a land of ill-taught, savage barbarians. Its tempting tales of great riches and magnificent cities loosened the purses of Western rulers and opened the doors to the "age of discovery." Columbus possessed a copy of the book and used it in planning his first voyage. He carried a "letter of credence" from Ferdinand and Isabella for presentation to "the Great Cam [Khan]."[16] That the great explorer missed the Great Khan by a whole dynasty and ten thousand miles or more was not Polo's fault.

Of higher interest to Western Christians were Polo's references to widespread Nestorian communities scattered across the fabled empire of China, the first eyewitness description of a country that ruled Asia from the great northern desert of central Asia to the Great Ocean and from Yunnan on modern China's Burma-Vietnam border to the Great Wall. He took reports back to Europe of Christian communities in the great ports of the Pacific numbering as many as seven hundred thousand secret Christians altogether. At Fugiu (Foochow, Fuzhou), for example, a Muslim told the Polos that:

in the city is a certain manner of people whose religion no one understands. For it is not idolatry because they keep no idols, they do not worship fire [and so are not Zoroastrians]; it does not profess Mahomet; nor does it seem to have the Christian rule . . .

The Polos tracked these believers down and concluded they were indeed Christians.

"For they had books, and Masters Mafeu and Marc reading in them began to interpret the writing . . . so that they found it to be the words of the Psalter. They asked them whence they had that religion and rule. And they answered and said, From our ancestors. And thus they had in a certain temple of theirs three figures painted, who had been three apostles of the seventy who had gone preaching throughout the world, and they said that those had taught their ancestors in that religion long ago, and that that faith had already been preserved among them for seven hundred years, but for a long time they had been without teaching and so were ignorant of the chief things."[17]

The figure of seven hundred thousand believers is, of course, wildly exaggerated. But who were these people "whose religion no one understands"? Is it possible that the reference to their seven-hundred-year-old tradition indicates that they might have been surviving descendants of T'ang-dynasty Christians in the line of Alopen? Some have thought so and point to the possibility that the "three apostles" they commemorated were the three earliest leaders of pre-Nestorian Edessene Christianity, Addai, Aggai, and Mari. The point is highly debatable, and a more realistic conclusion is that they could have been either Nestorian or Manichaean, and not nearly so numerous as described.[18]

Polo also reports Christians and Nestorian churches in at least eleven other Chinese cities.[19] The largest concentrations were those he found in the northwest along the Old Silk Road. He called them "Turks," describing the believers by their ethnic origin. Their principal Christian centers there were at Kashgar, which in his time was the seat of a Nestorian metropolitan bishop,[20] and at Kanchou (Canpicion), soon to become the capital of Kansu province, where there were "three churches large and beautiful." One of these was probably the Nestorian monastery in which Sorkaktani, mother of Kublai Khan, was buried.[21] He mentions Camul (Hami) but apparently did not visit it, nor did he note that it was the seat of a Nestorian bishop who had attended the consecration of the Nestorian patriarch Denha in Persia in 1266.[22]

Another area with many Christians was on the southeast China coast in the provinces of what are now Chekiang and Fukien from

Hangchow and Foochow to Amoy.[23] There was also a Christian community in China at that time that Polo barely mentions, but one about which we know more than about any other sizable concentration of Christians in thirteenth-century China. It was a Nestorian center at Chinkiang between Nanking and Shanghai where the Yangtze River intersects with the Grand Canal.[24] The city circuit, with its population of between 400,000 and 700,000, had a Christian population of not more than 2,421. At one time the Nestorians had seven monasteries in and around the city, all of them founded about the year 1279 by Mar Sargis,[25] a devout governor of the city, whose influence was augmented by the fact of his descent from Christian physicians to both Genghis Khan and his son Tolui.

In the years that followed, the Christian community benefited from the appointment to that district by Tolui's son Kublai Khan of a succession of Christian governors and assistant governors. But not many years after Kublai's death, between 1309 and 1333, Buddhist pressures at the imperial court compelled the Christians to surrender the monasteries, one after another, to jealous and angry Buddhists.[26]

Nestorian Church Organization

Marco Polo made no attempt to attribute any central hierarchical organization to the Nestorian communities except for one tantalizing reference to "a certain man who was head of the Christians at the court of the Great Kaan." When the community at Foochow, asked Marco's uncles for advice they said, "[You should] explain to him your state, that he may come to know you and you may be able freely to keep your religion and rule."[27] This is probably a reference to the Nestorian metropolitan in Peking, but if so, it raises the question why, if they were really Nestorian Christians, they were not already in touch with him. The answer may be either that, contrary to what the Polos thought, they were Manichaeans or that, if they were Chinese Nestorian survivors from the T'ang dynasty, they might have been wary of revealing themselves to the new wave of Yuan-dynasty Mongol Nestorians.[28]

By this time, near the end of the thirteenth century, the Nestorian patriarchate in Baghdad, taking advantage of the *pax mongolica*, was seeking to reestablish and extend its hierarchical network of missionary bishoprics across central Asia to the Pacific. The precise shape, locations, and numerical strength of Nestorian organization can no longer be traced with any credible assurance. Some episcopal dioceses were planted for a time and disappeared. The episcopal seats of some bishops appointed to nomadic tribes were probably only tent chapels mounted on wagons, movable "cathedrals," as it were.

Marco Polo has little to say about any of the non-Catholic Asian Christians and what he does say is not flattering:

> They are called Nestorian and Jacobite and Armenians and they are the worst heretics. . . . They have a great Patriarch [who] makes archbishops, bishops and abbots and all other prelates and priests and clerics and sends them everywhere to preach, into all the parts of Indie and to the Catai [China], and into Baudac [Baghdad] . . .; and heretics make heretics . . .[29]

But from the records of the Nestorian synods in Persia and from various sometimes conflicting sources, it is possible to discern a general outline of the building blocks of the Nestorian church in this its transient period of widest glory.

The foundations for Asian medieval Nestorianism in its expansion across the continent were laid as early as the patriarchate of the great Timothy I toward the end of the eighth century. In the interests of greater internal administrative regularity and more efficient evangelistic outreach, he reorganized the upper echelon of the episcopate, the metropolitans, into two classes, electoral metropolitans and missionary metropolitans.[30] Electoral metropolitans were dominant in the domestic administration of the church, but always in obedience to the patriarch. In the interval following the death of a patriarch, it was the council of domestic, electoral metropolitans who controlled the process of choosing a new patriarch. Missionary metropolitans (more accurately designated as "metropolitans of the exterior") were located too far away to take part in elections and in effect were virtually independent of the control of the home church in Persia.

The major metropolitanates of the exterior were Ray (near what is now Teheran) and two older metropolitanates that were shifted by Timothy's reorganization from electoral to missionary status, namely Rewardashir (on the road to India) and Merv (on the road to China). Timothy created also new missionary metropolitans for Tibet and for Sarbaziyeh, farther southeast beyond Rewardashir toward India. In the Mongol period five metropolitans were created along the Old Silk Road (Herat, Samarkand, Kashgar, Almalik [or Tangut], and Navekath), the last of which was in Uighur territory north of Kashgar.[31] A glance at the map on pp. xxiv–xxv will confirm that the Nestorian church in this period was persistently expanding east and south, toward India and China, and supporting its growth with a structure of highly independent Nestorian missionary episcopates.[32] Finally, in the reign of Kublai Khan, a metropolitanate was created for the new Mongol capital of China at Peking. Missionary metropolitans were empowered to consecrate new bishops in their territories, and missionary bishops were entitled to be assisted by one or more archdeacons who were usually chosen from the indigenous clergy.[33]

Prince George of the Onguts

Polo was impressed and excited by his discovery of a Christian kingdom in the region around the great northern loop of the Yellow River (Hwang Ho). In what is now Inner Mongolia just north of the upper borders of Shensi he found a whole province, which he called "Tenduc," where "the greater part of the people . . . are Christians." It was ruled by a Christian "king" named George, sixth in descent, as Polo asserted, from the legendary Prester John.[34]

He was mistaken, but not far wrong. The Christian ruler[35] he thus described was an Ongut, whereas any connection with the dubious Prester John legend would more likely have to be through the Keraits.[36] But Keraits and Onguts were close neighbors on the endless Mongolian plains, and in the tribal battles by which the great Genghis had consolidated his empire, he owed as much to the Onguts as to the Keraits. And just as the Keraits were rewarded by the marriage of the Great Khan's son Tolui to a Kerait Christian princess, Sorkaktani, so to a Christian Ongut prince, the father of George, was given a daughter of Genghis Khan in marriage.[37]

It was from the Ongut tribe that Mark, the "monk of Kublai Khan," came to Peking and joined the Uighur Sauma[38] on their great journey to the West, described above. Two Ongut princes speeded them on their way, Kumbuga, son-in-law of the Great Khan Kuyuk, and Aibuka, son-in-law of Kuyuk's successor Kublai Khan. So when in 1281 in faraway Baghdad, Mark was elevated to the patriarchate as Mar Yaballaha III, he represented far more than the Onguts. Symbolically he knit together both the Turkic and Mongol elements of the empire of Genghis Khan, as well as the Persian and Chinese and east Asia and central Asia. He was the patriarch of all Asia. It was an unexpected coincidence that while two Ongut monks, Nestorians, were bringing Eastern Christians into contact with the West, three Italian Catholic merchants, the Polos, were strengthening ties in the other direction, from west to east.

Prince George (d. 1299)[39] and his Christian Onguts occupied the territory of their ancestors just outside the Great Wall north of the ancient capital Chang'an and due west of Peking. Prince George had married the daughter of Kublai's eldest and favorite son; and after she died early he married the daughter of Kublai's principal grandson, Timur, who became the second reigning Mongol emperor of China (1294–1307).[40] These were political connections of the highest order and made the Christian prince a figure to be reckoned with in the empire. He was a distinguished general, a highly literate aristocrat well versed in the Confucian classics, and a devout Christian.[41]

It is not altogether surprising, therefore, that when the arrival of Franciscan missionaries after Kublai Khan's death ended the Nestorians' six hundred years and more of uncontested primacy of Christian presence in China proper, Prince George became the center of an ecclesiastical tug-of-war. Impressed by the new arrivals, George became a Catholic and built for the missionaries the first Catholic church in China. But that occurred after Kublai Khan's death and must be discussed later.[42]

Prince George died in 1298 or 1299, bravely commanding the armies of Kublai's grandson and successor, the emperor Timur. He was taken prisoner in a battle on the Mongolian border by an invading army of Kublai's old rival, Kaidu,[43] and was executed by the rebels when they were defeated and fled back into central Asia.[44]

The Religious Policies of Kublai Khan

True to the tradition of the Mongols, Kublai Khan's tolerance of all religions was pragmatic and political. Like that of his royal ancestors before him his religious base was shamanist. Marco Polo describes him officiating in the great annual ceremony of the white mare's milk at the summer capital in Shandu in which the emperor took part with the shamans to appease the spirits of earth and air and bring blessing on his reign.[45] He once even brought a Korean shaman, a woman, as were most shamans in Korea, all the way to the Chinese court for a special ceremony.[46] Instances like this of special prominence given the shamans indicate Kublai's concern lest the attention he gave to Chinese and foreign religions offend the more primitive religious sensibilities of his own Mongol warriors, many of whom, as he knew, were becoming increasingly troubled by the sedentary tendencies of imperial life in China.

But very early, even before he became Great Khan in 1260, he had begun to exhibit a special affinity toward Buddhism. This is generally attributed to the powerful influence of his primary wife and queen, Chabi, a devout Buddhist, but equally significant was the role played by the Tibetan monk, the 'Phags-pa Lama (1235–1280), who was invited by Kublai to the court in 1253 and soon became the Khan's most trusted religious adviser.[47] In fact, as a recent biography relates, "When Khubilai received private religious instruction from the lama, he would sit on a lower platform than the Tibetan cleric," a remarkably generous gesture for a Mongol khan.[48]

So it was no surprise that a few years later when violent disputes between Taoists and Buddhists threatened the stability of Mongol-ruled north China and Kublai was ordered by his older brother, the Great Khan Mongke, to organize a meeting between the two warring Chinese religions and settle their charges and countercharges by a debate, Kublai as judge ruled in favor of the Buddhists. The penalties against the losers—humiliation of Taoist leaders and the return of Buddhist temples seized by them—were the only significant instance of religious persecution condoned by Kublai Khan. They were more symbolic than harsh and in no way stamped out Taoism as a continuing influence in Chinese history.

Kublai was much less personally committed and more careful in his treatment of Confucianism. He never quite trusted the loyalty of the powerful Chinese bureaucracy, which was overwhelmingly Confucianist, though some of his earliest chief advisers were Confucian. Nor could he read Chinese, and his inability to read the Confucian classics made him uncomfortable in discussions of Confucianism. He turned again, therefore, to his more comfortable association with the Buddhists and ordered his Tibetan adviser, the monk 'Phags-pa, to devise a phonetic alphabet somewhat like his own Mongolian script but more like the related Tibetan written language that might be used to transcribe Chinese characters, the ideographs, into a readily pronounceable language. The result pleased Kublai immensely and added to the Buddhist lama's power but never proved able to replace the Chinese ideographs.[49]

However, Kublai Khan knew well that China could never be governed long without the cooperation of the Confucian bureaucracy. To the Confucianists Buddhism was not only superstition and unacceptable intellectually, it was a foreign religion and unacceptable culturally. Accordingly Kublai built Confucian temples in his capitals and encouraged the veneration of ancestors, including of course his own. One of his earliest advisers, a Confucianist, noting the rising influence of Buddhism at the court, convinced the Khan that Confucianists too could be trusted and the Khan promptly added twenty Confucian scholars to the inner advisory group of his administration. He also appointed Chinese scholars as principal tutors for his son and designated heir, the son whose early death bitterly saddened the emperor and deprived the dynasty of a ruler whose solid acculturation to Chinese society and civilization might have stabilized and prolonged the Mongol rule of China. But history does not follow the rule of what might have been. In history as it is, the emperor's son died, and the principal Confucian adviser, who had risen to the rank of chief administrator, foolishly implicated himself in a Chinese-led rebellion and was executed;[50] and in history as it actually is, the Mongols, losing the support of traditionally Confucian Chinese, fell in less than seventy years to a thoroughly Chinese dynasty, the Ming.

Islam was another strong influence in the Yuan-dynasty government. Through his brother Hulegu, ilkhan of Persia, Kublai Khan was well acquainted with the power of Islam and of its potential threat to the Mongol rule of Asia. He was also able, like Hulegu, to take advantage of knowledge and advice of Muslims without surrendering to them his own control of the government and the military. Kublai did not hesitate to add Muslims to the Buddhists, Confucianists, and Christians already in his inner circle.[51] Their presence was particularly powerful in the field of finance and tax collection, but their connection with the raising of government revenues also led to their undoing. Sometimes the fault was theirs. Money is corrupting. But just as often, since tax collecting is never welcome, the Muslim financial advisers were made the government's scapegoats in times of economic hardship. Except on the central Asiatic borders, Islam was never a popular influence in Mongol China.

The position of Christianity under Kublai Khan is a mixture of considerable visibility but fluctuating influence. It benefited of course from its widely recognized reputation as the faith of his mother, Princess Sorkaktani, but this must not be overestimated. Much closer to him as emperor and far more effective was the influence of his principal wife, Chabi, the Buddhist. Nevertheless, Christian advisers too were well known at the court. The Nestorians, expelled after the fall of the T'ang dynasty in the tenth century, now reentered China in the thirteenth century with a more visible and better recognized status than they had ever achieved under the T'ang.

The father of the monk Sauma, mentioned in the account of the travels of the two Mongol monks to the West, is probably the same Siban who is described as one of Kublai Khan's earliest Christian advisers.[52]

A far more powerful adviser was another Nestorian named Ai-hsueh (or Ai-se) from "Fu-lin" (Syria), who was so esteemed by the

Great Khan that he rose rapidly from posts as court physician and astronomer to even higher honors. When, in 1289, Kublai Khan created a department[53] of the Chinese government to deal with the affairs of the increasing numbers of Christians in his empire, the Nestorian physician Ai-hsueh was named its president, with nineteen officers and staff under him. Later he was made president of the famous Han-lin Academy, which over the centuries became the heart and center of academic prestige in all China. His five sons, all of whom bore Christian names—Elijah, Denha, Issa, George, and Luke—likewise rose to high rank. Ai-hsueh became well known for his sage advice to the emperor against extravagance and in favor of mercy (as when he won a pardon for Kublai's most famous general, Bayan). He once persuaded Kublai to cut short the personal pleasure of a hunting trip and to give priority instead to the country's struggling farmers. And when a later empress ordered him to "consult the secret courses of the stars" like an astrologer, he had the courage to refuse.[54]

Kublai's vulnerable situation as a foreign Mongol ruler of a conquered but thickly populated and highly civilized Chinese nation led him to adopt a strategy of governing through intermediates. This in turn tended to enlarge the powers of foreign advisers, including Christians, far more than their small numbers warranted. Mongol tolerance for religious differences did not extend to race, at least not to Chinese.[55] In part because of his suspicions concerning the loyalty of the Chinese and probably in part due to a feeling of Mongol superiority engendered by the worldwide victories of his family, Kublai divided his empire into four categories. At the top were the Mongols who were always given preference in appointments. Next were the "aliens," his other non-Chinese subjects and advisers, western central Asiatics, Persians, and even Westerners like the Polos. These two classes were at the top. The Chinese were in two lower classes officially. Northern Chinese, including Manchurians, were rated higher than the southern Chinese, who had been the last to submit to his rule. There were Christians in both the top two social classifications, but very few if any in the lower two.[56]

One of the Khan's Western advisers, and the only European, was, of course, Marco Polo, who reached the Chinese court in the same year that the Khan's two Mongol envoys, the Nestorian monks Sauma and Mark, were leaving on their journey that carried them to the royal courts of Persia and Europe.[57] Marco Polo's highest office in China was that of governor of a district on the Grand Canal for about three years, but his position as the only European in the

Khan's confidence made him uniquely useful as a window to the West for the Mongol ruler.

Better than anyone else, Polo has described Kublai Khan's personal reactions to Christianity. In the latter years of Kublai's reign he was troubled by an outbreak of revolts on the fringes of his empire from Tibet to Manchuria. Added to the overriding central dynastic challenge to the throne from his cousin Kaidu in Mongolia, these lesser rebellions could not be taken lightly.

One of the most serious came from the northeast, from the Korean borderlands in Manchuria, and because it involved the rebellion of a Christian Mongol prince it is of particular relevance to the study of Christianity under Kublai Khan. Prince Naian, a junior cousin of Kublai through a stepbrother of the great Genghis, joined in rebellion the more powerful Prince Kaidu, who was ruler in fact if not in name (for Kublai was still Great Khan) of all central Asia. They denounced Kublai as a sinicized, overcivilized traitor to the frontier-fighting traditions of real Mongols. Sensing the danger in such half-true criticisms, the aging Kublai rose to the challenge and led an imperial counterattack in person.

The religious overtones to this rebellion and Kublai's reaction are important. Naian was a Nestorian, secretly baptized but more superstitious than actually practicing "the works of a Christian," as Marco Polo comments in his vivid description of the ensuing battle.[58] He rode into battle under the banner of the cross, a proud young man only thirty years old and already commander of four hundred thousand horsemen (another of Polo's exaggerations). Kublai, the emperor, was overweight and seventy-four years old, but with four awesome battle elephants lumbering across the plains and surrounded by swarms of imperial troops he was still more than a match for the overconfident prince. Naian was captured and executed, wrapped tightly in a carpet and trampled and tumbled to death.

Asia never produced a Constantine or a Clovis. The defeat of Naian is another example of a recurring, melancholy pattern in the history of Christianity in Asia. A Christian victory won by force of arms under the cross is a tarnished victory, but a victory nevertheless, and such victories have changed the course of whole continents' cultures, as in Europe and Latin America. But a Christian defeat, lost under the same standard, can turn the tide almost irreversibly in the other direction.

Kublai Khan's actions after the battle commend him even more than his courage in the field. Polo tells how at the court, when the victorious Mongols began to deride the Christians and taunt them about the failure of their powerless God, Kublai rebuked them, observing with some severity that it was not the Christian God's lack of power but his regard for justice that led to the Christian defeat. The cross, he said, does not help the disloyal but the righteous.[59]

As if to emphasize the point that he was not anti-Christian, he interrupted the feasting that later celebrated the victory at his capital and on Easter called the Christians of the capital to come and bring him the book of the four Gospels and "with great ceremony, kissed it devoutly, and desired that all his barons and lords who were present should do the same."

But this was what he was careful to do for all the religions of his empire, Christian, Buddhist, Muslim, or Jewish. Polo believed, contrary to the weight of other contemporary evidence against it, that the Great Khan was convinced that the Christian faith was the best of all the religions and that only the low level of learning he found among the Nestorians and his fear that adherence to any one religion would divide the people and set the other religions against the government, prevented him from being baptized.[60] This was patently not true. It was the Buddhist faith that Kublai favored and that benefited most from Mongol rule. Moreover the form of that faith the Mongols favored was not classic Mahayana Buddhism, but its more superstitious and esoteric Tibetan variety, Tantric Buddhism. Nevertheless the Yuan dynasty marked the turning point when Buddhism, after more than a thousand years of missionary effort, began to be accepted by most of the Chinese people (though not by the Confucian literati) as a Chinese religion and no longer foreign. This was the crucial step that the Christianity in China at that time, for all its occasional signs of public success, proved itself unable to accomplish.

John of Montecorvino and the Roman Catholics

The first of the Roman Catholic missionaries[61] to reach China, as distinct from Mongolia, was John of Montecorvino (1246/47-ca. 1330), who had served the emperor Frederic II as soldier, magistrate, and physician until, at age twenty-six, he entered the Franciscan order.[62] About eight years later in 1280 he was sent by the order on a mission to Mongol Persia. This was late in the ilkhanate of Abaka, son of Hulegu. Not long after his return to Italy, about 1290, the Franciscans organized their missions to the East into two vicariates: northern Tartary and eastern Tartary,[63] and it was to the latter, to the mission farthest east, that John was sent on a second mission, a long, arduous journey by way of India to Peking (Cambaluc), which he reached probably just after the death of Kublai Khan in 1294.[64] He was received courteously by the new emperor, Timur (Oljeitu), Kublai's grandson.

The Nestorians were not so courteous. They were most unhappy at the arrival of Roman Catholics whom they feared not only as rivals but as schismatics. And when, shortly after his arrival, he achieved what must have seemed an astounding success, the conversion to Roman Catholicism of the highest-ranking Nestorian Christian in the empire, Prince George of the Onguts, they were furious. They made John of Montecorvino's first five years miserable with bitter charges and deadly threats. They charged that he was no representative of the pope but "a spy, magician, and deceiver of men."

Through it all, with the help of Prince George, the doughty friar persevered. He was permitted to build a church in Peking in 1299, and the prince built it for him "on a scale of royal magnificence." By the year 1305 he could report that he had won as many as six thousand converts, "and if there had not been the above-named slanders," he wrote, "I should have baptized more than thirty thousand." The next year he began to build a second church and organized a small school. He "bought one after another forty boys, the sons of pagans," between seven and eleven years old. He baptized them and began to teach them Latin and the Roman services and hymns. The emperor, he wrote,

> is greatly delighted with their chanting. I strike the bells at all the hours, and perform the divine Office with a congregation of babes and sucklings. But we sing by heart because we have no service-book with notes.[65]

He was proud of his second church, with its "red cross planted aloft" and its large compound "only a stone's throw" from the emperor Timur's gate. The chapel could seat two hundred, and other buildings and offices enabled him to move half the boys from the first church choir to form another school.[66]

When the news of John's success reached Europe it created a sensation, and in 1307 the pope, Clement V,[67] appointed him archbishop of Peking (Cambaluc), and primate of all the Far East with the authority of a patriarch.[68] But that encouraging word was long in reaching him. For eleven years John of Montecorvino labored alone ("old . . . and white more from toils and troubles than from age, for

I am fifty-eight years old") with no word from the pope or the Franciscans at home. The journey, he wrote wistfully, would take only five or six months by land, but that route was closed by wars, and the sea route would require at least two years.

At last, about the year 1313,[69] John received the reinforcements for which he longed, seven bishops with the authorization to consecrate him as archbishop and if necessary as many other bishops as might be needed for the establishment of a full episcopate in China. Only three of the seven survived the journey. Four were martyred on the way by Muslims in India near Bombay.[70]

The leader of the new group was Andrew of Perugia, who became bishop of a Franciscan community in central China centered around the busy port city of Zaitun (Ch'uanchou near Amoy). It was noted for fine porcelain and shipbuilding. The Muslim traveler Ibn Batuta, who visited it in the 1340s, described China as "the safest as well as the pleasantest of all the regions on earth for the traveler" and Zaitun as "the greatest harbor in the world."[71] He found many Persian Muslims in the city but does not mention the Christians of Bishop Andrew's well-established, active diocese there. Andrew was the third bishop of Zaitun.[72] His cathedral church had been given and endowed by an Armenian woman of the city to the Catholics. She was undoubtedly Armenian Orthodox, which suggests that Western Christian divisions meant less to the Western missionaries in China than their continuing abrasive relationship with the more indigenously Eastern Nestorians. Both, however, were considered foreign by the Chinese, to whom Nestorianism was Mongol and Catholicism was European.

About 1322 the monks at Zaitun welcomed a visitor, a fellow Franciscan, Odoric of Pordenone (ca. 1265–1331), who had reached southern China on a long voyage from Europe by way of India. The account of his travels[73] written on his return in 1330 was soon almost as popular in medieval Europe as Marco Polo's. Leaving Zaitun on his way to the mission in Peking, he also visited the missionaries in Hangchow (Quinsai), largest city in the world, a hundred miles in circumference, he said, "and there is not in it a span of ground which is not well peopled." The men there in southern China (which he called "upper India") were "colourless," but as for the women, "they are the most beautiful in the world."[74] The good friar's book abounds in superlatives and deals more with the Mongol court and Chinese customs than with the church, but in Peking, where he lived for three years, he noted that of the Great Khan's four hundred personal physicians, eight were Christian and only one was Muslim.[75]

It may have been from Odoric that a contemporary writer, John of Cara, archbishop of Sultania in Persia, received the information, true or untrue, that at that time, in 1330, there were thirty thousand Nestorians in China. Odoric had stopped in Sultaniyeh on his way to China and quite probably returned through it. The archbishop added, "These Nestorians are very rich and . . . have very handsome and devoutly ordered churches with crosses and images in honour of God and the saints. They hold sundry offices under the emperor and have great privileges from him."[76]

But for the Catholics the situation was not so promising. Bishop Andrew wrote home a little sadly in a letter dated 1326 that he was "sound of body and as far as length of age allows, vigorous and active having indeed none of the defects, accidents, and properties of old age except white hair," and that he was generously supported with funds by the emperor himself. With those funds he built another monastery, "convenient and beautiful" in a grove outside the walls. He was also grateful for the religious toleration of the Mongol regime, which "allowed to all and each to live according to his sect . . . We are able to preach freely and unmolested. But," he adds on a gloomier note, "of the Jews and Saracens none is converted. Of idolaters [Buddhists] a very large number are baptized, but having been baptized they do not walk straight in the path of Christianity."[77] That rather discouraging word is just about all the knowledge that survives about the final years of the Franciscans of Zaitun except for one last notice of the murder of a "James of Florence, Archbishop of Zaitun, somewhere in Central Asia in 1362."[78]

The Outer Limits of Nestorian Advance

Various claims have been made as to just how far Nestorian missionaries actually carried the Christian faith across Asia during the *pax mongolica*. Did it reach Korea, for example, while that country was occupied by the Mongols? Are reports to be believed of Nestorian beachheads in Japan and the Philippines in the thirteenth to the fifteenth centuries or in Java and along the southeast fringes of the Mongol empire in Burma and the Thai-Vietnam peninsula in this period? The short answer is, probably not. The longer one is that we cannot be sure.

The Japanese scholar P. Y. Saeki, who gave much of his life to the collection and study of Nestorian source materials, makes no claim that the Nestorian faith was ever planted in Japan. He found only two possible indications that Nestorians even reached the islands, and neither was in Christian mission. One such piece of evidence is a steel Mongol helmet on display in the Mongolian Invasion Museum in Fukuoka, bearing a cross etched in silver above the outline of a heart. It could be taken as proof that a rather high-ranking Mongol soldier in Kublai Khan's second invasion of Japan in 1281 was a Christian, perhaps an Ongut or Uighur. But a dead officer is not a Christian community. Saeki also conjectures that one of the envoys in the embassy that had been sent by the Khan to Japan the year before, 1280, may have been a Christian. The secretary to the embassy was a Uighur, a man named Kuo, and Kublai's court was full of Christian secretaries, Ongut and Uigur.[79] But Christian or not, just as dead officers do not plant churches, neither do executed ambassadors. When the Mongol chief envoy arrogantly demanded a Japanese surrender, all members of the embassy were executed. It was this insult that led Kublai Khan to launch the gigantic, failed invasion by sea the next year.

In recent years, some have revived apocryphal stories of even less credible and mysterious traces of Nestorianism in Japan. One such story declares that after his resurrection Jesus was seen in Japan, which sounds like a variation of the imaginative cultic Muslim report of his reappearance in southcentral Asia. Another tells of the coming of a Nestorian physician and some missionaries to Japan during the reign of Emperor Shomu (724–728) and of "apparently Syriac" inscriptions found on the beams of the ancient Horyuji temple, the oldest Buddhist temple in Japan, near seventh-century Nara. The whole city of Nara was built after the model of the T'ang-dynasty capital, Chang'an. Since there were Nestorian missionaries in Chang'an in that period, a posssible connection has been conjectured. But all this is pure speculation.[80]

References to early Christianity in Southeast Asia before the West's "Age of Discovery"—in Burma, Thailand, the kingdoms of the Cambodia/Vietnam peninsula, Java, and the Philippines—are even less verifiable. Burma was temporarily conquered by the Mongol armies of Kublai Khan in 1277 and 1283, as vividly described by Marco Polo, and the city of Pegu northeast of present-day Rangoon was sometimes referred to late in the fifteenth century as a Christian center. DaGama in India said he had heard that it was a Christian country, and a visitor there in 1496 speaks of finding "a ruined church" but no visible Christians. A few years later another traveler, Louis of Varthema, made the questionable claim that he found a thousand Christians in the service of the king in Pegu. He may well have mistaken chanting Buddhists for Nestorians. But if, as he says, he was traveling in the company of Nestorian merchants, surely they should have known the difference between Nestorians and Buddhists.

His traveling companions, the Nestorian merchants, were from the capital of Siam (Sornau), he says. Two northern Thai kingdoms, Chiengmai and Sukhotai, had become dependencies of the Mongol empire in 1294. About 1350 a powerful new kingdom was founded farther south at Ahudya just north of present-day Bangkok. It welcomed traders from China and Persia, some of them perhaps Nestorian, like those Varthema met a hundred and fifty years later.[81] But there is no record of Christian churches there.

Were there Christians in Sumatra or Java before the coming of the Western explorers? That is even more doubtful, but not impossible. The island was briefly subdued by Kublai's naval forces in 1293, but there is no mention of Nestorians there in any account of the venture. The only reference to a possible Christian community that early in Indonesia is a tantalizing remark by John of Marignolli, who says that on his way home from China, after he had stopped in India to see St. Thomas's tomb near Madras, he sailed in 1348 or 1349 to a great island called Sabah, where there were "a few Christians." A number of writers identify this with Java, as does H. Yule, but only after giving up hope of a better solution "in something like despair," for there is still no convincing evidence available for anything but a guess.[82]

Early Catholics in the Philippines found old images that might have been pre-Catholic Christian, and it has been argued that an earlier Nestorian presence must have been the reason for the rapid growth and widespread acceptance of the Roman Catholic Christianity that followed it. But none of these claims can be historically verified.[83]

As for Korea, the evidence of at least one possible ancient Nestorian community at its northern border is more convincing, but as in the case of Indonesia, it depends on a question of location. In 1927 a Japanese team excavated an old tomb near Anshan in what is now southern Manchuria about a hundred miles from the present Korean border, on the railroad line up the Liaotung peninsula to Shenyang (Mukden). They found the remains of seven bodies and at the head of each a clay cross, only one of which was still in perfect condition. They were able to date the grave at between 998 and 1006 by Chinese coins of the Sung dynasty left with the bodies. As Saeki points out this is striking evidence of the existence of a strong Nestorian family in the Liaoyang area.[84]

The question remains, was Anshan in Korea or Manchuria at the beginning of the tenth century? In the seventh century the Liaotung peninsula was Korean, under the rule of Koguryo, the northernmost of the three Korean kingdoms before their unification. But by about 1000, the apparent date of the burial, the Korean border had been pushed south to the Yalu, and a Manchurian tribe, the Liao (or Ch-'itan Liao), had taken that part of the northeast from the Chinese Sung emperor.[85] All we can say with certainty, therefore, is that as early as 1000 there were Nestorian Christians in what had not long before been Korean territory.[86]

NOTES

1. Rashid al-Din in J. A. Boyle, *Successors of Genghis Khan, Translated from the Persian of Rashid al-Din [Jami' al-Tawarikh]* (New York and London: Columbia Univ. Press, 1971), 241 (adapted).

2. The best biography by far is M. Rossabi, *Khubilai Khan: His Life and Times* (Berkeley: Univ. of California Press, 1988).

3. Mongol history backdates the dynasty to Genghis Khan in 1206; and official Chinese history begins it only with the final fall of the southern Sung in 1279/80. But Kublai was already ruler of most of China by 1260.

4. He was ruler of Persia in fact, if not yet in Baghdad, as early as 1256 (see J. A. Boyle, ed., *The Saljuk and Mongol Periods*, vol. 5 in *The Cambridge History of Iran* (Cambridge: Cambridge Univ. Press, 1968), 345f.

5. Ogetai, her brother-in-law, the second Great Khan, had already recognized the need for encouraging agriculture. L. Moses and S. A. Halkovic, Jr., *Introduction to Mongolian History and Culture* (Bloomington, IN: Univ. of Indiana Press), 6ff. See also Rossabi, *Khubilai*, 11–13.

6. See A. C. Moule, *Christians in China* (London: Society for Promoting Christian Knowledge, 1930), 132n, 224–25. Moule conjectures that the more distant hall was in the Kansu corridor that brings the Old Silk Road out of central Asia into northwestern China, perhaps at Kanchou, south of the Jade Gate (Yumen), and not far outside the Great Wall. Sorkaktani's imperial name was Pieh-chi (her posthumous title was Hsien-i-chuang-sheng). See also Rossabi, *Khubilai*, 19.

7. A. C. Moule and P. Pelliot, *Marco Polo: The Description of the World*, 2 vols. (London: Routledge & Sons, 1938), 1:202.

8. H. H. Howorth, *History of the Mongols from the Ninth to the Nineteenth Century*, 5 vols. (1876; reprint, Taiwan: Ch'eng Wen, 1970), 272f. (citing Yule's Marco Polo, 1, 311).

9. Many histories follow C. M. d'Ohsson, *Histoire des Mongols* (The Hague, 1834–35) in dating Arikbuka's submission to 1266; but P. Pelliot corrects this

to 1264; P. Pelliot, *Recherches sur les Chrétiens d'Asie Centrale et d'Extrême-Orient*, vol. 1 (Paris: Imprimerie Nationale, 1973), 4.

10. See W. W. Rockhill, *The Journey of William of Rubruck to the Eastern Parts* (London: Hakluyt Society, 1900), 184 and n., 189, 224. "All the Nestorian priests assembled before dawn in the chapel, beat the board and solemnly sang matins; they put on their church vestments, and prepared a censer and incense. And as they thus waited in the court of the church, the first wife, called Cotota Caten [Kutuktai Khatun] . . . entered the chapel with several other ladies, and her first-born son called Baltu . . . and they prostrated themselves the forehead to the ground according to the fashion of the Nestorians, and after that they touched all the images with their right hand, always kissing their hand after touching them. . . . Then the priests sang a great deal, putting incense in the lady's hand; and she put it on the fire. . . . After that when it was already bright day she began taking off her headdress . . . and I saw her bare head, and then she told us to leave, and as I was leaving, I saw a silver bowl brought in. Whether they baptized her or not, I know not."

11. For a catalogue and summary of the more important Chinese references, see Moule, *Christians in China*, and Ch'en Yuan, *Western and Central Asians in China under the Mongols* (Los Angeles: Univ. of California, 1966).

12. The best English translations and editions of Marco Polo's travels (his *Description of the World*) are A. C. Moule and P. Pelliot, *Marco Polo: The Description of the World*, 2 vols. (London: Routledge, 1938), in which the first volume is Moule's translation; and the H. Cordier revision of H. Yule, *The Book of Ser Marco Polo*, 3d ed., rev., 2 vols. (London: Murray, 1903). I will refer to them as Polo (*Description*) and Polo (Yule). Moule has made Polo's references to Christianity more easily accessible by collecting them separately as part of his *Christians in China*, to which, in this chapter, I will refer as Polo (Moule).

13. See Moses and Halkovic, *Mongolian History and Culture*, 62; and W. Eberhard, *History of China*, 3d ed., rev. (Berkeley: Univ. of California Press, 1969), 236. Moses and Halkovic estimate by people; Eberhard numbers by families.

14. Polo (*Description*), 79; and Polo (Moule), 129.

15. See Rossabi, *Khubilai*, 206ff.

16. The title "El Gran Cam" was left blank for Columbus to verify and fill in correctly. S. E. Morison, *Journals and Other Documents on the Life and Voyages of Christopher Columbus* (New York, 1963), 30f. and n. The voyage by sea around the New World continents would, of course, stretch far beyond a straight line ten-thousand miles.

17. Polo (*Description*), 347f.

18. See chap. 3, pp. 48ff., 78f. on Addai, Aggai, and Mari. Moule leaned toward an identification as Christian (*Christians in China*, 143n); Pelliot toward a Manichaean connection ("Les traditions manichéennes au Fou-kien," *T'oung Pao* 23 [1923]:193).

19. Polo usually calls the Christians Turks; the more accurate word would be Turko-Mongol. The first cities with Christians on the Mongolian side of the mountains were *Kashgar* (Cascar), in which he found "Turks who are Nestorian Christians who have churches of their own, and they are mixed and dwell with the inhabitants as the Jews in these parts live with Christians" (Polo, *Description*, 143); *Yarkand*, with some Nestorian and Jacobite Christians, "but not a great number" (p. 146); *Barkul?* (Ghinghintalas; p. 156); *Shachau* (Succiu) near Tun-huang, "all idolators [Buddhists], though it is true there are some Turks [Uighurs and Tanguts] who hold the religion of Nestorian Christians" (p. 150f.); *Kanchou* (p. 158); *Karakorum* (p. 169); *Yunchang?* (Ergiuul), "many Nestorian Christians" (p. 178); *Hsiningchou* (Silingui) (p. 179); *Ninghsia* (Calacian), "three very beautiful churches" (p. 181).

20. Polo (Yule), 1:183n.

21. Polo (*Description*), 158; Moule, *Christians in China*, 132n.

22. Polo (Yule), 1:211n.

23. Hangchow he calls Quinsai; Fuchou is Polo's Fugui; and Amoy is near Polo's Zaitun (now Ch'uanchou). There is no unanimous agreement on these identifications. See Polo (Yule), 220–45, with maps; and Moule, *Christians in China*, 141–43.

24. Polo spells it Quengianfu (Polo, *Description*, 263). A far more important independent Chinese text on the city's population and Christians is the *Chih shun chen chiang chih*, written about 1333 and found in 1795; see Moule's notes and translation of important passages, with notes, in *Christians in China*, 145–65.

25. His Chinese name was Hsieh-li-chi-ssu; Polo calls him Marsarchis. On his title and the question of his dates as governor, see Moule, *Christians in China*, 147, 148 n. 4, 156 n. 29.

26. See Moule, *Christians in China*, 151–55 nn. 20–26.

27. Polo (*Description*), 350.

28. As in Japan centuries later, the surviving hidden Catholics of the "years of silence" after the sixteenth-century persecutions were extremely reluctant to expose themselves to the incoming priests of the nineteenth century.

29. Polo (*Description*), 100.

30. The metropolitanate had been recognized since the First Synod (of Isaac in 410), which established its order of precedence as: (1) Beit Lapat (Gundishapur), (2) Nisibis (capital of Beit 'Arbaye), (3) Basra (Perath de Maysan), (4) Arbela (capital of Adiabene), and (5) Beit Selokh (Kirkuk, capital of Beit Garmai, east of the Tigris). The Seventh Synod (of Joseph in 554) added two more: (6) Rewardashir, and (7) Merv. Another: (8) Holwan (Halah) was added by the Synod of Ishoyabh II, in 642. At various times some changes were made. See J. Dauvillier, *Histoire et institutions des Églises orientales au Moyen Age*, (London: Variorum Reprints, 1983), a collection of his journal articles; and P. Pelliot, *Recherches sur les Chrétiens d'Asie Centrale et d'Extrême-*

Orient, 2 vols., ed. J. Dauvillier and L. Hambis (Paris: Imprimerie Nationale, 1973, 1983), a posthumous edition of three of his writings.

31. See map, pp. xxiv—xxv. For the various permutations of location and relationship among these dioceses, see Dauvillier, *Histoires et institutions,* 1:268ff., 288–95, 304ff.; 7:27–32; and Pelliot, *Recherches,* 5–12. Jacobite bishoprics are mentioned in Herat, Segestan, and Khorasan, and in two locations in Chinese Turkestan, Yarkand and Barkul (Polo's Ghingintalas).

32. Pelliot (*Recherches,* 1:8f.) warns against some exaggerations of how far Nestorians had planted their churches across Asia in the Middle Ages, as in C. E. Bonin, "Note sur les anciennes chrétientés nestoriennes de l'Asie centrale," *Journal Asiatique,* series 9, tome 15 (14), 1 (1900); 584–92, which has misled a number of later writers and mapmakers.

33. Dauvillier, *Histoires et institutions,* 7:28f.

34. Polo (*Description*), 181ff. The capital of the province, now part of Inner Mongolia, was probably the present Tokto or Tung-sheng, says Moule, *Christians in China,* 134n.

35. On this important leader, see Moule, *Christians in China,* 234–40, and from Chinese sources, see Ch'en Yuan, *Western and Central Asians,* 55–57. Ch'en believes the prince was a first-generation Christian.

36. See chap. 18, n. 11.

37. Prince George, however, was not a grandson of Genghis, for the Great Khan's daughter was childless. But the close family relationship continued. George's father, Prince Aibuka, married Kublai Khan's daughter, and George himself was twice married into the Genghis line, both times to granddaughters of Kublai Khan. See R. Grousset, *Empire of the Steppes* (New Brunswick, NJ: Rutgers Univ. Press, 1970), 301f.

38. Sauma was called "bishop" by Pope Nicholas IV, and Howorth reports he was consecrated bishop of the Uighurs (Howorth, *History of the Mongols,* 3:283), but see Moule's notes, *Christians in China,* 103, 115, 118.

39. The prince's Nestorian name of George, when transmitted through the Mongol language into Chinese characters emerged as a clumsy K'uo-li-ki-ssu. He is mentioned briefly by Rashid al-Din as Korguz Kuregen. Rashid al-Din, in Boyle, *Successors,* 286.

40. Known also as Oljeitu Temur, his dynastic title is Cheng-tsung.

41. See Ch'en Yuan, *Western and Central Asians,* 54f. Cf. Moule, *Christians in China,* 239 n. 38.

42. See, p. 457.

43. Kaidu, grandson of Ogetai, the second Great Khan, had never willingly recognized the displacement of his family line in the royal succession by the line of Ogetai's younger brother Tolui and Tolui's two sons Mongke and Kublai. He had won fame as a very young prince fifty years earlier by conquering Poland, Prussia, and Moravia in the great Mongol invasion of Europe in 1241.

44. Grousset, *Empire*, 294.

45. Polo (*Description*), 188.

46. Rossabi, *Khubilai*, 174. His note 85 cites J.-P. Roux, "Le chaman gengiskhanide," *Anthropos* 54, no. 3–4, pp. 401–32.

47. See A. Wright, *Buddhism in Chinese History* (Stanford, CA: Stanford Univ. Press, 1959).

48. Rossabi, *Khubilai*, 41. In public court appearance, however, Kublai returned to proper Confucian ritual etiquette and the lama was restricted to a lower seat.

49. Rossabi, *Khubilai*, 154–60. But P. Pelliot suggests that the influence of 'Phags-pa may be overestimated. See his "Les systemes d'ecriture chez les anciens Mongols," in *Asia Major* (1925): 284–88.

50. On Kublai and the Confucianists see Rossabi, *Khubilai*, 15f., 65f., 131–41.

51. Rossabi, *Khubilai*, 141f.; Howorth, *History of the Mongols*, 3:243.

52. Moule, *Christians in China*, 94n; and Rossabi, *Khubilai*, 16, citing P. Pelliot, *Recherches*, 1:247.

53. Called *chung-fu-ssu* in Chinese.

54. P. Pelliot, "Chretiens d'Asie Centrale," *T'oung Pao* (Shanghai, 1914): 640, (1927): 159; and Moule, *Christians in China*, 225–33.

55. J. J. Saunders (*History of the Mongol Conquests* [London: Routledge and Kegan Paul, 1971], 124) notes that Chinese were forbidden to learn the Mongol language, intermarry with Mongols, or carry arms.

56. See Rossabi's discussion (*Khubilai*, 71ff.) of the administrative structure of the Mongol dynasty. In the reign of Kublai's successor, Timur Oljeitu, the Muslim historian Rashid al-Din noted that Christians were entitled to rank among the ruling classes, as of second civil rank: "It is the custom in the Great Divan [Council] to have four *finjans* [ministers and viziers] from amongst the great emirs of the various groups, Taziks, Khitayans, Uighurs, and Christians." The highest civil rank was *chingsang* [vizier or minister], and the highest military rank was *taifu* [army commander] which was, however, secondary to *chingsang*. (Rashid al-Din, in Boyle, *Successors*, 278f.) See also Howorth, *History of the Mongols*, 1:252–58.

57. See above, pp. 445ff.

58. See the excerpt on the title page of this chapter, taken from Polo's account of the rebellion in his *Description*, 192–201. For more on Naian, see H. Franke's review of E. P. J. Mullie, "De Mongoolse Prins Nayan," in *Asia Major*, new series 12, pt. 1 (1966): 130–31; and Polo (Yule), 1:334 n. 4.

59. Polo (*Description*), 1:200. See the quotation at the heading of this chapter.

60. Polo (*Description*), 201f. On one occasion he was asked why he did not become a Christian and, if the biographer of Marco Polo, Ramusio, is not embroidering the story, replied, "How would you have me become a Christian? You see that the Christians of these parts are so ignorant that they

achieve nothing, whilst you see the idolaters can do anything they please." They work miracles, he continued. They move cups of wine on the table without touching them; they control storms; their idols speak. Ask your pope to send a hundred men skilled in your Christian law who could show the idolaters that "they too have known how to do such things but will not, because they are done by the help of the devil," and then, "I will receive baptism . . . and in the end there will be more Christians here than exist in your part of the world."

61. The primary source on these first Franciscan missions in China are the letters of John of Montecorvino and Andrew of Perugia, first published by the seventeenth-century Franciscan historian L. Wadding, *Annales Minorum*, t. 3 (1657). See also the translations of letters from both John and Andrew by Moule, *Christians in China*, 166–217.

62. A. Thomas, *Histoire de la Mission de Pekin* (Paris: Louis-Michaud, 1923), 56. The classic history of the early years of the Franciscan order is L. Wadding's seventeenth-century *Annales Ordinis Minorum*, 8 vols.; see the 1931–35 edition.

63. S. Delacroix, *Histoire Universelle des Missions Catholiques* (Paris: Librairie Grund, n.d.), 1:181. In 1320 a third vicariate was added, that of Cathay.

64. He left Europe in 1291 and might possibly have reached Peking earlier, Delacroix, *Histoire Universelle*, 172n.

65. Letter from John in Peking dated 8 January 1305, trans. Moule, *Christians in China*, 172–74. See also K. S. Latourette, *History of Christian Missions in China* (New York: Macmillan, 1929), 68–72.

66. Letter of John of Montecorvino, February 1306, in H. Yule, ed. H. Cordier, *Cathay and the Way Thither*, 4 vols. (London: Hakluyt Society, 1913–16), 3:51–58. See also Moule, *Christians in China*, 177–81.

67. Who had recently excommunicated Robert the Bruce of Scotland.

68. License, Pope Clement to Brother John, with letter dated 23 July 1307, in Moule, *Christians in China*, 188. The license "grants him all his authority that, as the lord Pope presides in the Western and Latin Church as chief Pontiff over all Bishops and Prelates as vicar of the blessed Peter, so also may Brother John preside as Archbishop over all Bishops and Prelates in those parts, with this agreement and understanding that he always confesses himself subject to the Roman Pontiff."

69. The date of arrival is variously given and ranges from 1308 to 1318. See Moule's note, *Christians in China*, 191f.

70. Moule, *Christians in China*, 191–95.

71. Yule (Cordier), *Cathay*, 4:118f. See his translation and notes of Ibn Batuta's travels in Bengal and China, 4:1–166. Cordier identifies Zaitun as Tswan-chau, not Ch'uanchou (p. 117 n. 1).

72. His predecessors were Bishop Gerard and Bishop Peregrine.

73. Translated into English by Yule as vol. 2 of *Cathay and the Way Thither*

(ed. Cordier, with extensive notes); and excerpts in Moule, *Christians in China*, 241–47.

74. Yule, *Cathay*, 2:179, 192f.

75. Yule, *Cathay*, 2:226.

76. John of Cara, *The Book of the Estate of the Great Kaan*, English trans. Yule, *Cathay*, 3:89–103, esp. 100ff.

77. Yule, *Cathay*, 191–94.

78. Yule, *Cathay*, 197.

79. Saeki, *The Nestorian Documents and Relics in China*, 2d ed. (Tokyo: Maruzen, 1951), 444–47.

80. Dauvillier, for example, dismisses any claim that Nestorians even indirectly influenced Japan, "Les Provinces Chaldeennes 'de l'Exterieur' au Moyen Age," 1:310, in *Histoire et institutions*. For these and other speculations and unvalidated claims, see J. Stewart, *Nestorian Missionary Enterprise* (Edinburgh: Clark, 1928), 187ff. The Nestorian physician's name is given as Li-mi-i, and one of the wonders he allegedly performed was the conversion of the empress Komyo. These latter items Saeki wisely deleted in the two revisions (1937 and 1951) of his first work, *The Nestorian Monument in China* (1916). See also the convenient outline and careful assessment of these and other references to early Christians outside China in J. C. England, "The Earliest Christian Communities in Southeast and Northeast Asia," *Missiology* (Scottdale, PA), vol. 19, no. 2 (April 1991): 203–15.

81. Yule, *Cathay*, 1:123 n. 1; 4:201 n. 2; and Varthema's report has been edited by C. Scheffer as *Les Voyages de Ludovic de Varthema (1502–1508)*, trans. J. Balarin de Racoins (Paris, 1888). Yule notes that travelers frequently confused Buddhists and Nestorians. See also F. Nau, "L'Expansion Nestorienne en Asie," *Conferences au Musee Guimet*, 277f. For Thai history see D. K. Wyatt, *Thailand: A Short History* (1984).

82. Yule, *Cathay*, 3:191–96.

83. See K. S. Latourette, *A History of the Expansion of Christianity*, 7 vols. (New York: Harper, 1937, 1945), 2:333; and Stewart, *Missionary Enterprise*, 100n.

84. Saeki (1951), 440f.

85. See maps and chronology in M. Penkala, *A Correlated History of the Far East* (Rutland VT/Tokyo: Charles Tuttle, 1966), 34, 40–43.

86. Farther south, in indisputably Korean territory at Kyungju, the ancient capital of unified Korea, the historian Kim Yang-Sun discovered what appears to be a stone cross being used by Buddhist monks at Pusoksa, Korea's most famous temple, as a charm to aid in childbirth. It is now kept at the Christian Museum of Soongsil University in Seoul. But there is no way to date it or even to determine whether it is indeed an ancient Christian cross

or a cross-shaped pediment used for architectural purposes, which because of its unusual form was regarded as endowed with religious power. See Kim Yang-Sun, *History of the Korean Church in the Ten Years since Liberation (1945–1955)*, trans. A. D. Clark. Seoul, Korea: privately published, ca. 1956 and *Catalogue of the Soongsil University Museum*, Seoul Soongsil University, 1988.

Chapter *21*
The Eclipse of
Christianity in Asia

"The history of the Mongols is necessarily a 'drum
and trumpet history.' It deals chiefly with the
conquests of great kings and the struggles of rival
tribes . . . It is . . . the story of one of those hardy,
brawny races cradled amidst want and hard
circumstances, in whose blood there is a good
mixture of iron, which are sent periodically to
destroy the luxurious and the wealthy . . ."

—H. H. Howorth, *History of the*
Mongols, 1:x

"To this ferocity Tamerlane added a taste for
religious murder. He killed from piety. He represents
a synthesis, probably unprecedented in history, of
Mongol barbarity and Muslim fanaticism, and
symbolizes that advanced form of primitive slaughter
which is murder committed for the sake of abstract
ideology, as a duty and a sacred mission."

—Rene Grousset, *The Empire of the*
Steppes, 434

LIKE a sun in eclipse, Christianity in Asia moved so abruptly, yet so imperceptibly, from its peaks of expansion down into the shadows of history, that it is difficult to pinpoint any precise moment at which progress turned into decline. L. E. Browne, in the book from which the title of this chapter is borrowed,[1] begins his analysis of the decline as far back as Muhammad, for there is no question that the rise of Islam is the first decisive turning point in Asian church history. But it was not the last. In Muhammad's own lifetime Asian Christianity launched its most vigorous missions of expansion. For six hundred years and more it pushed on across Asia, though not without other nearly fatal defeats, and did not reach its widest extent and nearest approach to continental acceptance until the *pax mongolica* of the thirteenth century, as we have seen.

It could be argued that the definitive turning point was not reached until 1294 in east Asia and 1295 in west Asia. In the space of one year the emperor Kublai Khan, protector of the church in China died, and in Persia the ilkhan Ghazan announced his conversion to Islam. The death of Kublai, last of the truly great Khans, signaled the approaching dissolution of the Mongolian empire in the Far East. Ghazan's conversion turned the Persian sector of that empire irreversibly Muslim and carried with it into the world of Islam most of Asia from the western end of the Great Wall to the Euphrates. The protecting continental umbrella of the *pax mongolica* was folded and withdrawn. It had never been much of a peace, but it had not completely collapsed even under the battering of the persistent civil wars among its four major sectors (after 1259): China (including Mongolia), central Asia, Persia, and Russia. All four were then still nominally united under the fifth Great Khan of the Mongols, Kublai. But never again was so much of the Asian continent to be so nearly united.[2] In the next one hundred years the religious tolerance of Mongol imperial rule gave way to a new destructive wave of widespread Mongolian ferocities fueled by conquering Muslim zeal, and the shattered remnants of Asian Christianity were left isolated in ever smaller pockets of desperation.

The Second Disappearance of the Church in China

Kublai Khan's death in 1294 did not, however, immediately worsen the position of the Chinese churches under the Mongol dynasty. In fact, as we have seen in chapter 20, John of Montecorvino, the greatest of Catholic missionaries of his generation, reached China only after Kublai had died but was well received. A modern historian, K. S. Latourette, has paid the Franciscan this tribute: "almost single-handedly [he] established the Roman Catholic faith in the capital of the mightiest empire of his time and to do so had journeyed farther from his home than ever any missionary of any religion is known to have done before him."[3] He was the first Catholic archbishop in China and the last until modern times.

Prospects for Roman Catholic expansion throughout the Mongol realms still seemed so bright, however, that in 1318 Pope John XXII divided Asia into two missionary districts, one for China under the jurisdiction of the Franciscans, the other for the ilkhanate of Persia under the Dominicans. Montecorvino remained as missionary archbishop at the Yuan-dynasty capital of Cambaluc (Peking), and a new archbishopric was created for the Dominicans at the newly built Persian capital of Sultaniyeh.[4]

But by the time of Montecorvino's death, sometime between 1328 and 1333, the Mongol dynasty that had given him such liberty to preach and plant churches was disintegrating, and when it finally fell about forty years later, the Chinese churches disappeared, not only his own Roman Catholics but also his rivals, the more indigenous Nestorians. Just so had the church of the T'ang dynasty disappeared four hundred years before when an empire fell. Asian church history is discouragingly cyclical.

From Kublai's death to the end of the dynasty, nine Mongol emperors ruled China, each one seemingly more ineffective than his predecessor. The first was Kublai's grandson Timur Oljeitu (1294–1307), who was wise and tolerant enough to recognize his need for support from all available religious and ethnic quarters in the administration of the empire his Mongols had conquered and were trying to rule. His great generals were Mongols like Prince George, the Ongut Christian, who guarded the dangerous northern frontier. Concerned about the spreading Islamization of his rivals in central Asia, Timur received non-Muslims gladly to his capital and encouraged the Italian Franciscan mission to build its first church. He also worked to gain the confidence of the Chinese Confucian bureaucracy, which disapproved of his family's Buddhist leanings, and for them he built a temple in honor of Confucius. But his own preference, like that of his grandfather, remained Buddhist.

No successor reached China to replace Montecorvino for more than ten years. A professor at the University of Paris named Nicholas was appointed but never reached Peking.[5] So in the early years of the long reign of the last Mongol emperor, Toghan Timur (Shun-ti, 1333–1368), the emperor's guard of Alans, white Christians from the Caucasus mountains, sent word to Rome that the church had been left "without a governor and without spiritual guidance" since the death of the archbishop. The emperor himself attached a letter of approval confirming the request for more missionaries and added a suggestion that "horses and other wonderful things" would be welcome. But it was six years before a bishop arrived, John of Marignolli, who left for Asia in 1338 and appeared in Peking in 1342 with handsome gifts and a retinue of thirty-two people. He wrote that "the Great Kaan, when he saw the warhorses, and the Pope's presents and . . . the gold . . . rejoiced with great joy." But after the impressive entrance Marignolli stayed not more than three years, and though his account of his mission tells of "a great harvest of souls" there is little supporting evidence to confirm this.[6] He was the last resident Catholic bishop in Peking until the end of the Middle Ages.[7]

Throughout the final decades of the dynasty as the power of the Mongols declined, so also, it appears, did the faith of some of the most prominent Christian Mongols. Records of a Nestorian Christian family of Onguts who entered northwest China late in the eleventh century tell of their acculturation to Chinese ways and of how they took the Chinese name of Ma, which means "horse," as they moved eastward to Kaifeng. In seven Christian generations they rose to high rank in the service of the expanding Mongol empire. But the same records show that in the next two generations, beginning perhaps about 1300, when the family had reached the height of its influence as magistrates and scholars and had become more Chinese than Mongol, they turned from their original Nestorian faith. Most of them embraced Confucianism, a few Taoism.[8]

Even more abrupt was the defection of another powerful Ongut Christian family, the Chao. Its most famous member, Chao Shih-yen was "duke of the state of Lu" and "chief councilor of Szechwan province" under several of Kublai Khan's successors. He early left the faith of his Christian father for Confucian studies and later, according to his Confucian critics, fell into cultic Taoism and debauchery.[9]

The Mongol emperor who had welcomed Marignolli to the court in 1342 ruled for another quarter of a century (1333–1368). Toghan Timur was only thirteen when he became emperor. He was a fifth-generation descendant of Kublai Khan and reigned longer than any Mongol in China since his great ancestor. A long rule usually implies strength and stability in the empire, but not in his case. This fourteenth and last of a line of Great Khans that stretched back through a hundred and fifty years of Mongol victories to Genghis, the greatest conqueror of them all, grew "to middle age rather than man-hood." He was "foolish, lazy and indecisive."[10] His prime minister was openly anti-Chinese. Farmers rebelled against the rich; Chinese rose against the Mongols; the south invaded the north under the anti-Mongol slogan, "These barbarians are created to obey and not to command a civilised nation."[11]

Had the Mongols pulled themselves together and united their warriors from the steppes into the fearful three-pronged assaults against the enemy for which their ancestors were famous, they could have stopped the rebellion in its tracks. But the Mongol armies who came out of the north to the aid of the dynasty, instead of attacking the rebels, revived the old rivalries of the descendants of Ogetai, Genghis's third son, against the house of Tolui, the fourth son, from whom the Yuan emperors descended, and in so doing fatally split into civil war, one Mongol army against another. Toghan Timur abandoned Peking in panic. The Chinese kept advancing. They de-feated, pursued, and butchered the Mongols all across north China and into central Asia. They burned their palaces and tore down the walls of Peking, which had been Mongol for a hundred and fifty years. They turned the north over to their soldiers to loot, kill, and destroy all trace of the barbarians. China, as it has so often done, turned away from the world and turned in upon itself. The new China was to be isolationist, nationalist, and orthodox Confucian, ruled by a completely China-centered dynasty, the Ming (1368–1644).

It is no surprise that the church fell with the old dynasty. This was the pattern of past Chinese history. But the Christians of the Yuan dynasty compounded the errors of their forerunners under the T'ang who had disappeared with their imperial patrons four hun-dred years before. That earlier Christianity had at least been unitedly Nestorian. The China of the fourteenth century, however, could not but fail to note the enmity between Nestorians and their newly ar-rived rivals, the Catholics, and both were considered foreign by the Chinese. Compounding the handicap this imposed on the church, the Mongol dynasty itself was foreign. So to the Chinese, Christi-anity appeared as a foreign religion protected and supported by a foreign government. Catholic missions gave the impression of being even more foreign than the Nestorians, who were almost entirely Mongol, for they received far more visible support from outside China than ever was true of the Nestorians either in the ninth or fourteenth century. The Catholic cathedral in Zaitun was built and endowed by the wealthy wife of an Armenian trader. An Italian trader, Peter of Lucalongo, bought the land for John of Montecorvino's church in Peking.[12] The largest single community of Christians in Peking in these later years of the dynasty may well have been the emperor's guard of Alans.[13]

With the defeat of the Mongols, China turned Chinese in religion also, but there is little evidence of direct religious persecution. Later writers have assumed that the foreign protégés of the Mongols, whether Christian or Muslim, were massacred with their patrons, that their bishops were killed, their churches demolished, and their cemeteries obliterated.[14] It is a natural assumption and may be true, but if so, the sufferings of little Christian communities went unnoticed amidst the chaos of the fall of the world conquerors, the Mongols. It is just as likely that Nestorians and foreigners were killed indiscriminately in the pursuit of the Mongols, and that without foreign support a church that had become dependent upon it withered away.[15] And because its withering was so undramatic, China lost even the memory of its passing. This was the second disappearance of Christianity in China, and when it returned two hundred years later, the next wave of Christians seemed largely unaware that there had ever been Christians there before them.

The Conversion of the Persian Ilkhanate to Islam

As long as the Great Khan Kublai lived, the Mongol rulers of Persia gave lip service, at least, to his primacy as lord of the *kuriltai* (*quriltai*), the family assembly of the Genghisid khans. Hulegu, conqueror of Persia, was his younger brother, and the title he took when he proclaimed himself master of the Persian empire was ilkhan, which means "subordinate khan." In 1294 at Kublai's death, the reigning ilkhan was Geikhatu (1291–1295), brother of Arghun, the fourth ilkhan and grandson of Hulegu. He was a disaster as ruler, but like his brother he befriended Christians, visiting the great new church built by his fellow Mongol, the patriarch Mar Yaballaha, in the ilkhan's northern capital of Maragheh.[16] But his mismanagement of finances triggered a rebellion and he was strangled.

His short-lived successor, a first cousin named Baidu, was even more inclined to Christianity. In fact the *Chronography* of Bar Hebraeus, as continued after his death by an anonymous writer, declares that the ilkhan personally claimed to be Christian and wore a cross around his neck but, for fear of the Muslims, felt he must hide it, telling Christians he was Christian and Muslims that he had converted to Islam. His fears were well-founded. Retaliating for the

favors he showed in appointing Christians to important government
positions, the Muslims persuaded Arghun's son, Ghazan, a Buddhist, who had been bypassed in the succession, to turn Muslim and
rally the Persian population, which had been basically Muslim for
centuries, against the pro-Christian Baidu. The strategy was successful, and Baidu lasted less than a year.[17]

Since the defeat of the Crusaders and the fall of Acre in 1291,
Mongol enthusiasm for an alliance with the Christian world against
the world of Islam had begun to wane. The more worldly and the
more superstitious among them murmured that perhaps the Allah of
Islam was stronger than the Christians' God after all.

Ghazan (1295–1304), the seventh ilkhan and the first to rule as
a Muslim, was the ablest since his great-grandfather Hulegu, but for
Christians he was the angel of doom. In his history of Syriac Christians under the Mongols, the French historian J. M. Fiey bleakly
titles the chapter on Ghazan, "Black Clouds."[18] His first decree ordered the destruction of all churches, synagogues, and Buddhist
temples throughout the land. Gone was his Mongol tolerance for all
religions. "Thus, after a lapse of some seventy years, Islam again
became the official religion of Iran."[19]

The *Chronography* describes the plight of the Christians in the
days that followed:

> No Christian dared to appear in the streets (or market), but the women
> went out and came in and bought and sold, because they could not be
> distinguished from the Arab women, and could not be identified as
> Christians, though those who were recognized as Christians were dis-
> graced, and slapped, and beaten and mocked.[20]

Much of the venom exhibited against Christians may have been
due to the fanaticism of Ghazan's Muslim general, Nauruz, and
much was simply naked greed. In many instances persecutors were
only too happy to be bought off, for as the Christian narrator observed, "they were far more anxious to collect money than to destroy
the churches."[21] But churches were destroyed nevertheless, notably
in Arbela, Baghdad, Hamadan, Tabriz, and Maragheh (Maragha).

Not even the influence of their Mongol patriarch, the Ongut
monk Yaballaha III, could protect the church from Muslim reprisals,
for in truth when Christians were in favor too many had shown
themselves to be not averse to harassing Muslims. In the capital at
Maragheh Muslims broke into the palace of the Nestorian patriarch,
seventy-third in a line that stretched back a thousand years to Papa
bar-Aggai.[22] They beat him, tied him up naked, hung him head
downward, stuffed his mouth with ashes, and hit him, according to

his biographer, crying, "Abandon your faith; turn Muslim and you will be saved." When he refused to apostatize, only after more abuse did they agree to a costly ransom.[23]

Not until the ilkhan himself, irritated by Muslim extremists, intervened to restore order and stop the looting, did the persecution abate. Ghazan brought the shaken patriarch, Yaballah, to the palace and restored him to some of his former honor, reissuing the golden seal of royal recognition given the patriarch by the Great Khan Mongke in 1281.[24] At the same time he began to lose confidence in the chief persecutor, his Muslim general Nauruz, who had pressed him to leave Buddhism for Islam. He now discovered that Nauruz had been plotting behind his back with Muslim Egypt against the Mongols in Persia. The hated Nauruz was executed in 1297 and Christians rejoiced.[25]

Thereafter the ilkhan showed himself more lenient toward Christians though no less immovably Muslim. Two years after his accession to the throne Ghazan and all his highest nobles publicly and ritually "exchanged their broad-brimmed Mongol hats for the Muslim turban."[26]

Sporadic persecution of Christians continued throughout his reign, and though Yaballaha was allowed to build a great monastery at the capital, the patriarchate never completely regained either its former power or its assurance of government support. Only occasionally, as when the ilkhan threatened to destroy the citadel of Arbela, birthplace of Persian Christianity, because of continuing troubling outbursts of violence there between Muslims and Christians, was the patriarch effective in changing the strongman's mind. Perhaps it was Yaballaha's despairing remark that if such an outrage occurred he would be driven to return home to imperial Mongol China or find a place to die in dignity in Christian France that persuaded him not to carry out the threat.[27] It was a none too subtle reminder to the ilkhan that Persia's major allies east and west against Muslim Egypt were either Christian or tolerantly protective of Christians. In fact in 1299 Ghazan mounted another attack against Egyptian Syria and invited the Christian princes of the West to join him, a plea that even the irenic missionary to Islam, Raymond Lull, supported in vain.[28] Despite the failure to form such an alliance, in the last years of his reign the ilkhan showed more favor and bestowed such rich treasures upon the Christian patriarch that even the Christians mourned the death in 1304 of the ilkhan who made Persia definitively Muslim.[29]

Hopes of more security for the Christian community seemed about to blossom again when, at Ghazan's death he was succeeded as ilkhan by his brother Oljeitu (1304–1316), for Oljeitu had been baptized as an infant by his Christian mother, the Kerait princess Uruk-khatun, a niece of Hulegu's powerful Christian queen.[30] Throughout this whole span of Mongol royal history, the major channel of continuous Christian influence, apart from the patriarchate itself, runs through the blood of royal women from Sorkaktani to Uruk-khatun.

The patriarch Yaballaha had known the new ilkhan as a child and visited him at once. He was received with "due honour" his biographer wrote, "though not heartily." This was a warning, for far from being a Christian, Oljeitu had turned Muslim and soon displayed all the personal animosity so frequently found in converts against their former faith. Though he was often outwardly friendly and sometimes generous, "there was found in him a kind of hatred of the Christians."[31] If the reign of Ghazan was a "black cloud" portending affliction, Oljeitu's twelve years on the throne brought in "the tempest."[32]

He first ordered the Nestorian patriarch to give up his magnificent new monastery in Maragheh and the church in Tabriz to be converted into mosques and was dissuaded from this only with great difficulty by his uncle, a Naiman or Kerait prince, who argued that it would be unnecessarily provocative.[33] A few years later, in 1307 he ordered the Christian king of Georgia and all his people to renounce the Christian faith and give up their churches to be destroyed.[34] It may have been the courage of the Georgian Christians in resisting this decree that so impressed one of the Mongol generals named Choban, who was sent to enforce it, that later, though always a zealous Muslim, he became known as a protector of the Christians. By then he had risen to the highest military position in the ilkhan Oljeitu's army as "amir of amirs" (commander-in-chief), a son-in-law of one ilkhan (Oljeitu) and brother-in-law of another (Abu Sa'id).[35]

The atrocity for which Oljeitu's melancholy reign is best remembered is the massacre at Arbela in 1310. When the Christian fortress was attacked by angry Kurds and Arabs, the ilkhan weakly vacillated between promising protection to the Christians and ordering them all executed as rebels, depending on whose advice he had listened to last. Famine weakened the defenders:

> The wheat was already finished. . . . As for salt, who could find any? They had already finished the asses, the dogs and the ferrets, and no old leather objects were left. . . . Widows stretched out their hands and wept. . . . And there was absolutely no one to bury the dead. . . .
>
> And the people of the Arabs went up to the fortress . . . and they

conquered it. And they slew everyone . . . and spared none, and everyone they saw they carried off into captivity . . .[36]

The patriarch Yaballaha, who for five months, at risk of his life, had worked tirelessly to make peace and save lives, asked for an audience with the ilkhan, but when they met, the king made him no greeting, and the old patriarch, weary and heartbroken, did not dare to speak first and left brokenhearted, saying he would never go to the court again, "I am wearied with the service of the Mongols."[37] Seven years later he died, in November 1517. Two incidents somewhat brightened his last years. An old friend, Prince Irnadjin and his wife, the daughter of Ilkhan Ghazan, visited him and left the almost penniless Yaballaha rich gifts; and in 1312 the council of the ilkhan's *amirs* brought his case to the attention of the court and Oljeitu granted him "an annuity of 5,000 *dinars,* and the revenues of certain villages near Baghdad."[38] Not many remember the names of the patriarchs of the East who came after him.

The latest recorded synod of the Church of the East (Nestorian) met in 1318 for the last public enthronement of a patriarch in Persia.[39] The bishops chose for the post the brave metropolitan of stricken Arbela. Joseph was a just and honest man. He took the name Timothy II perhaps to remind his people in their dark days of how the great Timothy I had brought luster to the name of Christ in just such troubled times under Muslim rule a half a millennium earlier. He sorrowed for his stricken people, but like his contemporary, the unknown historian who chronicled the life of Yaballaha, he candidly and realistically admitted that among his followers at Arbela were many who claimed to be Christians but did not act like Christians and had brought down on their own heads the disaster at Arbela.[40]

Abu Sa'id (1316–1335), the twelve-year-old son of Oljeitu, succeeded his father as the seventh and last of the ilkhans. Seven was a lucky number, remarks H. H. Howorth, and great things were expected from his reign. Instead his greatest generals quarreled and intrigued and split his armies; his two highest civil administrators tore the government apart in a vicious and fatal feud;[41] his cousin khans of the Russian steppes invaded from the northwest, while the khans of the rival line of Genghis's son Chagatai invaded from central Asia and Egypt's Sunnite sultan threatened him from the south. The great Choban, "last protector of the Christians,"[42] who had become in effect if not in name the real ruler of Persia, now found himself caught in a tangled web of political and military jealousies. The utter profligacy of his own son further undermined his reputation in the eyes of the ilkhan. Slandered, rebellious, and betrayed, he was executed in 1327, but not without honor paid to his fifty years of loyal service through tumultuous times.[43]

Deprived of its best civil and military leadership, the ilkhanate slid into disintegration. It split up into roughly five rival principalities dominated by local warlords. The line of Hulegu was ended, and with it ended all hopes of further friendly relations between Europe and Mongol Asia. A fitting epitaph might be a comment of J. A. Boyle: "the Middle East would today bear an altogether different aspect if the House of Hulegu had retained its full vigour for a decade or two longer."[44]

Tamerlane, "Scourge of God and Terror of the World"

In the year that the last effective ilkhan, Abu Sa'id, died, a Mongol infant was born on the ancient border between Persia and Turkestan who was destined to rival even the world-conqueror Genghis as a destroyer of kingdoms. Both were militarily merciless, but whereas the victories of the religiously tolerant Genghis opened up Asia to Christian missions, the return of Mongol power under the fiercely Muslim Tamerlane brought unparalleled destruction of churches, synagogues, and temples all across Asia from the western edge of China to the Christian fortress of Smyrna on the Aegean Sea and as far south as Indian Delhi.[45]

This was the second wave of Mongol conquest. The first wave, that of Genghis Khan and his sons and sons' sons of the *pax mongolica,* had rolled through Asia for a hundred and fifty years or more, only to collapse in a sea of alcohol, high living, family strife, and political disintegration. First to disappear in 1335, after six generations, was the Persian ilkhanate of the line of Genghis's fourth son Tolui, through Hulegu.[46] Next was the khanate in central Asia of his second son, Chagatai, which fell in 1338 after seven generations. In 1357 the line of the Conqueror's first son, in Russia, ended in six generations (after Genghis).[47] Last of all and greatest of them all, the Chinese empire of Kublai Khan survived to the seventh generation but fell more spectacularly than any of them in 1368.[48]

The new wave, like the first, came from central Asia. Its roots traced indirectly back to Genghis through Chagatai, who like his older brother had been bypassed in the succession to the Great Khanate. Unlike its cousin khanates of Persia and Russia and to an even greater degree Yuan-dynasty China, the Chagatai Mongols of the great steppes at first remained nomadic, roaming the grasslands, dominating the caravan routes between East and West, and ruling their more settled Turkic-speaking town centers with the arrogant, arbitrary power of country-bred and city-suspicious warriors.[49]

In 1269 the central Asiatic khanate split into two parts, roughly corresponding to east and west Turkestan.[50] The eastern part, under Prince Kaidu, whom we noted above for his revolt against Kublai Khan, clung longer to the traditional, proud nomad-warrior ways and the religious shamanism of their Mongol ancestors. Kaidu protected both Christians and Muslims with the typical religious tolerance of the first three or four generations of the Genghis clan. Though almost constantly at war with his cousin Kublai Khan, he graciously received Sauma and Mark, the two monks from Kublai's Peking, and sent them on their way to Persia with letters of safe passage.[51]

The western part of the khanate (west Turkestan), remained under the line of Chagatai, whose successors centered their rule more and more around the highly civilized Muslim cities of Tashkent, Bokhara, and especially Samarkand. Administration they turned over to Muslim governors and found it pleasant to adjust to the life and religion of their Muslim subjects.[52] The area had been Muslim since the ninth century, long before the coming of the Mongols. Of the minority religions that remained, Jews outnumbered Christians in the larger cities, but the tenth-century ruins of a large Nestorian monastery have been found south of Samarkand, and there are passing notices of many towns with Christian churches from that time on.[53]

Before the division of Turkestan, the sixth khan, Mubarak (in 1266), had professed Islam in Tashkent, the first of the Chagatai line to do so.[54] But his conversion was superficial. Mongols still spurned Arabic and governed themselves not by the Koran but by Mongol law, the *yasa* of Genghis.

As the pressures of economics and administration mounted, however, Mongol tradition proved ill-suited to peace. In everything but war they found themselves prisoners of their own non-Mongol, increasingly Muslim, bureaucracy.[55] After the death of Kaidu in 1301 the more Mongolian eastern division of Turkestan was absorbed back into the western khanate, and Christians increasingly felt the pressures of Muslim intolerance. Taliku (1308–1309), the twelfth khan in the west, was criticized by his Mongol warriors for overfavoritism toward Muslims; and Kebek, the fourteenth khan (1318–1326), protected the Muslims of west Turkestan and northern Afghanistan from the enmity of his more fervent shamanist followers.

Under the fifteenth khan, Elchigidei (or Ilchigedai), there seems to have been a brief revival of Christian activity. He welcomed a visit in 1326 from a Dominican missionary, Thomas of Mancasol, and, according to Thomas, sent him back to the pope in Avignon with the news, true or not, that he would grant permission for the building of a church dedicated to John the Baptist in Samarkand. Pope John XXII, greatly encouraged, appointed Thomas bishop of Samarkand and dispatched him back to central Asia, but the journey was too long, the khan had died, and his brother who succeeded him was no friend of Christians.[56]

The seventeenth khan, Tamashirin (1326–1334), was zealously Islamic and took the Arabic name 'Ala al-Din ("Greatness of the Faith"). After him no ruler of the Chagatai domain dared publicly profess any faith but that of Islam. As B. Spuler points out, "The religion founded by Muhammad thus [had] won over the three western Mongol courts" in Russia, Persia, and central Asia.[57]

Even under Muslim rulers some freedom remained for Christian missionary outreach. Buzan, who ruled briefly in 1334, allowed Nestorian Christians to rebuild their churches and Jews their synagogues. He permitted Roman Catholics of the Franciscan order to move their missionary episcopate to his capital at Almalik (Kuldja), and Archbishop Nicholas,[58] a professor of divinity at the University of Paris, who had been appointed to China, apparently settled instead in Almalik, which had been a bishopric since 1320. The last Chagatai khan, Chingshi (or Jenkshi, 1334–1338), was a Muslim but no friend of Islam, according to Muslim writers. He even allowed his seven-year-old son to be educated and baptized by the Franciscans, which may be the reason his own brother assassinated him. After his death a massacre of Christians swept through the streets of the capital. Marignolli, who passed through Almalik on his way to Peking the next year, was the first to report the "glorious martyrdom" of the bishop of Almalik, Richard, and six Franciscan missionary priests. Another list of martyrs includes the name of "Master John of India, a black man belonging to the third order of St. Francis," who had been converted by Franciscans in India. The persecution was violent and ruthless but mercifully short. By the time Marignolli arrived, he was able to build a church and baptize and preach openly for some months before proceeding on his way to China.[59]

There is very little other mention of Christians in Chagatai territory, though among their subjects were numbers of Uighurs, who had once been part Buddhist, part Christian.[60] Late in the nineteenth century, however, two medieval Christian graveyards were discovered in the heart of Chagatai territory near Issyk-kul, a hot salt lake described as the "Dead Sea" of southern Siberia. Inscriptions on the tombstones in Syriac and Turkic date back to the thirteenth century, from 1249 to 1345, and prove the existence in that period of a sizable community of Turkic Nestorian Christians not far from one of the Chagatai capitals at Frunze.[61] A. Mingana counts the names of "nine archdeacons, eight doctors of ecclesiastical jurisprudence and of biblical interpretation, twenty-two visitors, three commentators, forty-six scholastics, two preachers and an imposing number of priests" in the inscriptions reported by D. A. Chwolson. Christians in central Asia were in sufficient numbers and well enough known to compel one popular Nestorian hymn writer named Khamis to compose a hymn for them. It begins, "The Son of Mary is born to us" and was written with alternate stanzas in Syriac and Mongolian.[62]

Rivalry between Muslim and Mongol factions again split the realm in 1346. The Mongol line of Chagatai in the more sedentary western capital softened and was displaced by Muslim Turkic governors. Kaidu's successors in the Ogetai line of eastern Turkestan failed to match him in Mongol leadership. The later princes of both lines took Muslim names and, like the 'Abbasids of earlier Persia, became the puppets of their Turkic governors. The rule was in Muslim hands, whether in the Turkic west or the still more shamanist Mongol east, which came to be called Moghulistan. As the Muslim historian Mirza Haydar describes it, "Although [the Khans] had become Mussulmans, neither these Khakans nor the Moghul people had a knowledge of the . . . 'True Road to Salvation' . . . and they continued in the road that leads to Hell."[63] Both eastern and central Asia were torn by poverty and savage civil disorder from the 1360s into the 1370s, Turkestan against Moghulistan, Samarkand against the Mongolian steppes. Huge areas, probably including the Christian communities of the cemeteries uncovered around Lake Issyk-kul, were virtually depopulated.[64]

It was in this time of bitterness that a new conqueror arose who brought a spark of hope for a revival of Mongol greatness, perhaps even a new *pax mongolica*. He brought no peace, however, only the sword. He was Timur the Great, known to history as Tamerlane (1336–1405),[65] a tiger born in the Year of the Mouse. He dreamed of reviving an Islamic caliphate that would again crush the infidels as in its glory days of seven hundred years before. Instead, while trampling Asian Christianity, he still further divided Islam. He boasted that he would make Samarkand the capital of all Asia. Instead he snapped the last threads of the Old Silk Road that had given Asia its only tangible symbols of a continental identity. He destroyed but could not plant, tore down but failed to build.[66]

Tamerlane came from a well-born military family in west-central Asia (west Turkestan) near Samarkand that had fallen on hard days in the anarchy of the times and had taken to banditry. Their enemies called them "sheep stealers." His father, disillusioned with such a life, had retreated to a Muslim monastery.[67] Tamerlane, however, reverted to the family's military tradition, rising through the ranks, and switching with opportunistic ease from one rival regional victor to the next. When a Turkic warlord from his native west Turkestan faltered, he offered his services to a Mongol invader from east Turkestan.[68] Two reasons may have made the betrayal easy for him. The first was religious. The new ruler was a Muslim like himself, not shamanist, who had recently converted to Islam amidst the applause of his people, a hundred and sixty thousand of whom became Muslim with him.[69] The second consideration was political. The invader was of the line of Chagatai, and all his life Tamerlane strove to legitimize his claim to rule in Mongol territory by the use of nominal Chagatid "khans." The thought may have occurred to him that the invader had rendered a great service by reuniting Turkestan, east and west, and that what one warrior had won by conquest another might win from him. At any rate, in a very few years it was the Turk Tamerlane who was ruling Samarkand, and a Mongol "khan" was his puppet. Tamerlane zigzagged his way upward by cunning, courage, deceit, and terror. Twenty years later he was master of all of western central Asia.

First he drove the Chagatai Mongols out of the rich valleys of Samarkand and Bokhara back into the desert. Then he turned north against the lower flank of the Golden Horde in Mongol Russia. Then, striking south against his own brother-in-law, through the Iron Gates, the famous mountain pass separating Transoxiana from Bactria, he conquered Afghanistan and crowned himself khan in Balkh. From north to south his new empire slashed diagonally through all the major land trade routes that connected Europe, Syria, and Persia in the West to China in the East. Before he died, this son of small tribal sheep stealers, this Machiavellian prince who fought like a common soldier hand-to-hand in battle with his troops, had conquered and murdered and pillaged his way from Turfan to Damascus and from Delhi almost to Moscow and Constantinople. He had subdued both of the great powers of western Asia—Persia and the fast-rising Ottoman Empire of the Turks. He had defeated Egypt in Syria, the White Horde in Russia, and the sultanate of northern India. Still unsatisfied at age seventy-one, he was gathering a mighty force to invade Ming-dynasty China when, in January 1405, he died. Then, within a single generation, this vast expanse of military dominance shattered, and in two generations it shriveled back into the shell of its origins in eastern Persia and west Turkestan.[70] He ploughed deep but left no seed in the furrows, only death. Even the great jade slab on his tomb in Samarkand is cracked.

Did the churches he destroyed so zealously die with him? True, he massacred Christians with cold-blooded, calculated ferocity. He declared a holy war against the Georgians of the Caucasus, clapped their Christian ruler and his family into chains, and forced the king to a public acceptance of Islam, which the king promptly recanted as soon as Tamerlane withdrew. After fifteen more years and four more holy wars Tamerlane was still brutally trying to separate the stubborn Georgian highlanders of the little kingdom from their Christian faith. He destroyed seven hundred large villages, wiped out the inhabitants, and reduced all the Christian churches of Tiflis to rubble.[71]

Again, at the sack of the Christian stronghold of Smyrna, famous since the days of the apostles as a symbol of courage and martyrdom,[72] Tamerlane personally directed the slaughter as his warriors systematically collected Christian heads as souvenirs.[73] At Tana on the Black Sea, Muslims in the city were spared, while the Christians were killed, sent into slavery, or ransomed at enormous price.[74]

There is a chilling irony hidden in this popular picture of Tamerlane as the all-conquering champion of Islam against the Christian infidels. The irony lies in the fact that for every massacre of Christians, Muslims have recorded many more numerous and frightening accounts of his slaughter of his fellow believers in the brotherhood of Islam. "He was one of the worst enemies to whom Islamic civilization ever fell a victim" is the verdict of B. Spuler, a distinguished historian of the Mongol period.[75] Muslim historians, notably Ibn Arabshah (d. 1401), have questioned whether he was truly a Muslim at all, and at best many have accepted him only with half-praise as "semi-Muslim." He kept Sunnite Muslims and their eastern rivals the Shi'ites guessing as to his own preference. Generally he was Sunnite, but in practice he was "more light," a Muslim who claimed personal revelations from Allah by which he could sanction the ferocity he vented against the less enlightened who dared oppose him. He destroyed "infidels because they were not Muslims and Muslims because they were not faithful."[76] When more light leads to darkness, "how great is that darkness."

At times, when it suited him he was not above seeking Christian alliances and posing as a friend to Christians. The Spanish ambassador from Castile, Clavijo, left a record of a long journey and a year as a guest at Tamerlane's court (1403–1406). He reported back to the

Christian West, with something less than the whole truth, that Tamerlane's severe treatment of Christians was due to the conqueror's anger at greedy Genoese and Venetians who helped Christian allies of the Ottoman Turks escape across the Bosphorus into Constantinople after his great victory over the Ottoman emperor in 1402.[77]

Sometimes, when Christians did not oppose him, Tamerlane could treat them with great courtesy. One of his rules of conduct at court, for example, forbade Muslims to drink wine, save at important celebrations, yet permitted Christians to drink it at his table, "but not after dinner." The Dominican John II, missionary archbishop of Sultaniyeh, who reported this to his sovereign, Charles VI of France, was given considerable freedom in his work and further asserted that, "He [Tamerlane] does not harm Christians—especially Latins [Catholics]—and receives them well; merchants in particular are allowed to go about their business and worship as if they were in Christiandom" [sic].[78] Samarkand, Tamerlane's main capital, always had a sprinkling of Christians. They were, however, mostly traders and prisoners, and there is no mention of an organized church. There were probably more Nestorians there than Jacobites, and to a lesser extent Orthodox and Roman Catholics, particularly among the unransomed prisoners who were commonly turned either into slaves or craftsmen.

As for the larger church outside the Turkestan center, Asiatic Christianity began to disappear even where it had been strongest. In Persia, says B. Spuler, "he (Tamerlane) systematically decimated the Christians."[79] But, except for those few already mentioned, it is difficult to find specific evidence of killings directed solely against the Christians. Viewed against the frightful background of flaming cities, rivers of blood, and pyramids of skulls with which Tamerlane marked his line of march, who could distinguish a Christian corpse from a Muslim in "a tower of two thousand live men laid one upon the other and smothered with clay and . . . brick"?[80] In India he ordered a hundred thousand Hindu prisoners killed to free his warriors for the advance on Delhi.[81] Compared with such horrors, the miseries inflicted upon the little communities of Christians here and there in his vast empire could easily pass unnoticed.

One clear measure of the devastation of the church in this its time of greatest suffering in Asia are the melancholy gaps in the list of patriarchs and metropolitans in the fourteenth and fifteenth centuries. Browne, following 'Amr and Assemani, notes a vacancy of nine years (1369–1378) in the Nestorian list and twenty-five years (1379–1404) for the Jacobites, and suspects many more such vacancies went unrecorded.[82] A. R. Vine measures the decline by counting churches whose names cease to appear in the records: six in important Nestorian centers after 1318 and two more by 1360. Twenty years later when Tamerlane swept through Persia, Vine writes, "we can only say with certainty that there were churches at Baghdad, Mosul, Erbil, Nisibis, Bakerda (Gezira), Tabriz and Maragheh."[83] This list of seven compares with twenty-four cities known to have had churches when Hulegu captured Baghdad in 1238, and sixty-eight in the year 1000. He rightly concludes that it may not have been Tamerlane alone who wiped out the church in Persia; it had been eroding steadily ever since the Muslim conquest.

Toward the end of the fifteenth century (Tamerlane died in 1405), the situation of the Nestorians had become so precarious that they resorted to making the patriarchate hereditary, uncle to nephew, rather than by election in a council of bishops. This ensured that the sometimes troublesome matter of succession could be kept simpler, less noticeable, and better protected from outside manipulation.[84] It also meant the end of a nationally effective church organization east of the Euphrates. The Church of the East (Nestorian), which had once directed a continental network of Christian influence and expansion from its first tentative beginnings in Edessa, later in Seleucia-Ctesiphon, and finally in Baghdad, was left without a home on earth. Baghdad was no refuge. The continuation of Bar Hebraeus's *Chronography* lamented:

> And in those days the foreign peoples [the Mongols] stretched out their hands to Tabriz, and they destroyed all the churches which were there and there was great sorrow among the Christians in all the world. The persecutions, and disgrace, and mockings and ignominy which the Christians suffered at this time, especially in Baghdad, words cannot describe.[85]

Bar Hebraeus is referring here to the time of the Muslim ilkhan Gazan, but it became yet more true of the devastations of Tamerlane, which though less directly anti-Christian were indiscriminately and more thoroughly brutal. In Tamerlane's general massacre of the inhabitants of Baghdad in 1401 it is said that ninety thousand people were killed. Each of his soldiers was ordered to bring him one head (another historian says two heads).[86] Who knows which were Christian, which were Muslim?

Before the century was ended Tamerlane's successors proved completely unable to hold the empire together. Persians took back Iran from the Mongols and a shah of Persia made a drinking cup out of the skull of a Mongol khan. The last central Asiatic ruler of the line of Tamerlane in Samarkand was defeated by the Uzbeks in 1500. In

Mongolia the twenty-seventh successor of Genghis Khan died and left the Mongolian east in anarchy in 1467. And by then a Chinese dynasty, the Ming, had been ruling once-Mongol China for more than a hundred years. They had made it the richest country in the world. As the Mongols faded away, all Asia north of the Himalayas was once more either Muslim or Chinese. If there were any Christians left, here and there, no one noticed them.

NOTES

1. L. E. Browne, *The Eclipse of Christianity in Asia* (Cambridge: Cambridge Univ. Press, 1933), is the best single survey of the decline of the Nestorians from the seventh to the fourteenth century.

2. For a careful analysis of the fragile nature of Mongol imperial unity in this period, see P. Jackson, "The Dissolution of the Mongol Empire," *Central Asia Journal* 23, no. 3–4 (1978): 188–244.

3. K. S. Latourette, *History of Christian Missions in China* (New York: Macmillan, 1929), 71. He adds, "[Montecorvino] is by no means the greatest of Christian apostles, but for single-hearted devotion and quiet persistence he deserves to be ranked with the foremost pioneers of all faiths and times."

4. J. Schmidlin, *Catholic Mission History,* trans. M. Braun (Techny, IL: Mission Press, 1933), 237.

5. See below, p. 482.

6. See A. C. Moule, *Christians in China* (London: Society for Promoting Christian Knowledge, 1930), 252–64; Latourette, *Missions in China,* 72f.

7. The papacy continued the title through a succession of nonresident titular bishops for a hundred years or more. The most complete listing is in Joseph de Moidrey, "La hierarchie catholique en Chine, en Coree, et au Japon (1307–1914)," in *Varietes sinologiques,* no. 38 (Shanghai, 1914). See also a listing from 1307 to 1483 in H. Yule, ed. H. Cordier, *Cathay and the Way Thither,* 4 vols. (London: Hakluyt Society, 1913–16), 3:14n; and Latourette, *Missions in China,* 72f.

8. Ch'en Yuan, *Western and Central Asians in China Under the Mongols* (Los Angeles: Univ. of California, 1966), 41–53, 110–19. The original Ma's Mongolian name was transcribed Ho-lu-mi-ssu in Chinese. *Ma* may have been a corruption of the Syriac *Mar.* See P. Y. Saeki, *The Nestorian Documents and Relics in China* (Tokyo: Maruzen, 1951), 480–88, who summarizes two Ma family inscriptions. He transcribes the name of the first Ma as Ho-lu-ch'ih-ssu.

9. Ch'en Yuan, *Western and Central Asians,* 3, n. 9, 112–19. Chao Shih-yen died in 1336.

10. J. J. Saunders, *The History of the Mongol Conquests* (London: Routledge and Kegan Paul, 1971), 151.

11. M. Prawdin, *The Mongol Empire: Its Rise and Legacy* (London: Allen and Unwin, 1940), 386.

12. Moule, *Christians in China*, 192; and Yule (Cordier), *Cathay*, 3:55.

13. On the Alans in Peking see particularly Yule (Cordier), *Cathay*, 3:179–87, 210; and Moule, *Christians in China*, 252–64. John of Marignolli, reporting on his mission in Peking from 1342 to about 1345, said there were then thirty thousand Alans in the emperor's service. Exaggeration or not, the figure implies an unusually large presence.

14. See, for example, Prawdin, *Mongol Empire*, 388.

15. See Latourette, *Missions in China*, 74f.

16. R. Grousset, *Empire of the Steppes* (New Brunswick, NJ: Rutgers Univ. Press, 1970), 377, citing Chabot, in *Revue de l'Orient latin* (1894), pp. 127–28.

17. Bar Hebraeus, *Chronography*, vol. 1, ed. E. A. W. Budge (London: Oxford Univ. Press, 1932), 505.

18. J. M. Fiey, "Chrétiens Syriaques sous les Mongols" in *CSCO*, vol. 362, pp. 66–73.

19. A. Bausani, "Religion Under the Mongols," in J. A. Boyle, ed., *Cambridge History of Iran*, vol. 5 (Cambridge: Cambridge Univ. Press, 1968), 542.

20. Bar Hebraeus, *Chronography* (Budge), 507.

21. Bar Hebraeus, *Chronography* (Budge), 507.

22. Papa (ca. 315) was the first bishop of a united Persian church; Isaac was declared catholicos in 410; and Dadyeshu (421–426) was the first patriarch.

23. *Histoire de Yaballaha*, in E. A. W. Budge, *The Monks of Kublai Khan* (London: Religious Tract Society, 1928), 210–25.

24. Fiey, "Chrétiens Syriaques," citing J. Hamilton, "Le text turc en caracteres syriaques du grand sceau cruciforme de Mar Yahbalaha III," in *Journal Asiatique* 260 (1972): 155–70.

25. Bar Hebraeus, *Chronography* (Budge), vol. 2, appendix 28. See also Boyle, *Cambridge History of Iran*, 382f.

26. Boyle, *Cambridge History of Iran*, 384. Ghazan's continued war against Egypt, which carried him victorious as far as Damascus, and his letters to Pope Boniface VIII, Edward I of England, and James II of Aragon, which included an offer to turn Christian in exchange for an alliance with Europe against Egypt, reveal how completely political was his religion, whether Buddhist, Muslim, or potentially Christian (386ff.); and see H. H. Howorth, *History of the Mongols*, 5 vols. (1876; reprint, Taiwan: Ch'eng Wen, 1970), pt. 3, 488f., citing Remusat.

27. *Histoire de Yaballaha*, in Budge, *Monks of Kublai Khan*, 231–39.

28. Fiey, "Chrétiens Syriaques," 70f.

29. Fiey, "Chrétiens Syriaques," 240–54. Christians lamented "the bitter, horrible and truly evil report of the death of the victorious King Kazan. . . .

And all the inhabitants of the countries of his great dominions mourned for him," as the biography of the patriarch records the event.

30. On Uruk-khatun, see Howorth, *History of the Mongols*, 3:360, 535. She was the widow of the ilkhan Arghun, "a Kerait, and doubtless a Christian." Hulegu's queen was Dokuz-khatun, a cousin or niece of Sorkaktani. See above, chap. 19, pp. 422, 427.

31. Howorth, *History of the Mongols*, 3:256.

32. This is the title Fiey gives to his chapter on Oljeitu (Oldjaitu), "Chrétiens Syriaques," 74–79. See also the *Histoire de Yaballaha* in Budge, *Monks of Kublai Khan*, 254–302; and Howorth, *History of the Mongols*, 3:534–84.

33. *Histoire*, in Budge, *Monks*, 257.

34. One account says the order was enforced; another that the people protested so bravely they were spared. See Browne, *Eclipse*, 169.

35. On Choban (or Djoban), see Howorth, *History of the Mongols*, 3:543f., 555, 567, 570, 585ff., 604ff. He claimed descent from a Crimean warrior who had once saved Genghis Khan's life (p. 610). He was also a faithful Sunnite Muslim who refused to turn Shi'ite with the ilkhan Oljeitu (p. 559).

36. *Histoire*, in Budge, *Monks*, 297, 301.

37. *Histoire*, in Budge, *Monks*, 304.

38. *Histoire*, in Budge, *Monks*, 88.

39. There is no certain list of the later patriarchs. The most complete is in J. A. Assemani, *De Catholicis . . . Chaldaeorum et Nestorianorum* (Rome, 1775; reprint, Farnborough, Eng.: Gregg, 1969). He in turn relies greatly upon a list by the fourteenth-century Nestorian historian 'Amr.

40. "The hearts of the inhabitants of the Fortress . . . had become hard. They had forsaken the way of Christianity; they had treated wholly with contempt the divine law, and scoffed at recluses, and the priests, and robbed each other, and they had broken through the fences of the laws of our Lord. . . . Hatred had waxed great among them, envy had seized their hearts, they brought accusations against each other, and they oppressed, and smote, and persecuted and defrauded and plundered . . .," *Histoire*, in Budge, *Monks*, 262, 272f.

41. One of whom was the great historian Rashid al-Din, a convert from Judaism to Islam. Howorth, who disputes his Jewish origin, calls him "the greatest vizier of the Ilkhan empire and one of the greatest men the East has produced" (*History of the Mongols*, 3:589). On recent scholarship confirming his Jewish descent, see Boyle, *Cambridge History of Iran*, 407.

42. Fiey, "Chrétiens Syriaques," 81.

43. Boyle, *Cambridge History of Iran*, 409f.

44. Boyle, in *The Cambridge History of Iran*, 417. The end of the house of Hulegu, however, was not quite the end of the line of Hulegu's father and mother, the Tolui-Sorkaktani line. A strong old-line Mongol, a prince of the

blood, named Arpa (Arpagaon), was elected to succeed Abu Sa'id. He was descended from Hulegu's and Khublai's rebellious younger brother Arik-buka (Arigh Boke), and by sheer military audacity and decisiveness almost succeeded in pulling the empire back together. But by then the realm had splintered beyond repair, and he failed (p. 413).

45. The dramatic phrase in the title of the section, of course, is from Christopher Marlowe's *Tamburlaine the Great* (1587).

46. See chap. 19.

47. Jochi died before his father, Genghis, and the first khan of the Golden Horde was his son Batu. But in modern Russia the line is known by the name of Batu's great-greatgrandson Uzbek, the ninth khan (1313–1341), and survives in the name of the Uzbek Soviet Socialist Republic (now Uzbekistan).

48. See chap. 20.

49. On Chagatai, see N. Elias's introduction to the *Tarikh-i-Rashidi* of Mirza Haydar, trans. D. Ross (1895; reprint, Delhi, India: Renaissance Publishing House, 1986), 28–50. Also W. Barthold, *Four Studies on the History of Central Asia,* 3 vols. (Leiden: Brill, 1952–56), 1:114ff.; 2:8–12, 26, 30; and Howorth, *History of the Mongols,* 1:171, 174, 218.

50. The complicated rivalries of the sibling clans of Genghis's sons need not detain us, save to note that the house of Chagatai was almost destroyed by the rise of the houses of Jochi in Russia, and Tolui in Persia and China. It was resurrected by the fifth Chagatid khan in 1260 and under the sixth khan, Mubarak, began to turn Muslim, ibid.; see also Grousset, *Empire,* 326–46.

51. By Mongol law Kaidu, as grandson of the second Great Khan Ogetai, had as much of a right to the primacy as Kublai, but elections then as now were sometimes ruled as much by politics as by law. See chap. 18, pp. 404f. and for more on Kaidu see Howorth, *History,* 1:173–81; Barthold, *Four Studies,* 1:124ff.; and Moule, *Christians in China,* 101. He was a military genius and unlike most of his cousins an able administrator. Barthold remarks, "It is noteworthy that this son and grandson of drunkards was perhaps the only Chingizid [i.e. prince of the house of Genghis] who never touched [alcohol]." Mongol Shamanist though Kaidu remained, Muslim writers commend him for protecting Islam.

52. Barthold, 1:125ff.

53. As the journeys of Plano Carpini, Rubruck, and the two Mongol monks Sauma and Mark testify. See also Barthold, *Four Studies,* 1:15f., 88.

54. Barthold, *Four Studies,* 1:125. Mubarak was also the first Mongol khan to declare himself ruler without the consent of the Great Khan (who at that time was Kublai). The present Muslim ruler of Egypt takes his name from this khan.

55. See Grousset, *Empire,* 326ff.; Howorth, *History,* 3:228, 618, 680.

56. Barthold, *Four Studies,* 1:52, 2:7f. Delacroix, *Histoire Universelle des Missions Catholiques* (Paris: Librairie Grund, n.d.), 191.

57. B. Spuler, *The Muslim World, Part II, The Mongol Period*, trans. F. R. C. Bagley (Leiden: Brill, 1960), 45.

58. But A. Thomas, *Histoire de la Mission de Pekin* (Paris: Louis-Michaud, 1923), 64, gives the name as Jean de Botras.

59. The most complete account of the Catholic work and massacre in Al-malik is by a late fourteenth-century Franciscan, Bartholomew of Pisa, whose writing borders on the hagiographic. See Yule's translation, *Cathay*, 3:11–13, 31–35f.; and on Marignolli's report, 212f.; also Spuler, *Central Asia*, 1:135f.

60. The last of the Uighurs in Turfan, at the eastern edge of the Great Desert, were forced to convert en masse to Islam around 1390, "so that at the present time it is called 'Dar-al-Islam' (Seat of Islam)," wrote the Muslim historian Mirza Haydar in the fifteenth century (*Tarikh-i-Rashidi*, 52).

61. The larger cemetery is ten miles south of Tokmak on the River Chu. The primary source references are D. A. Chwolson in three articles, "Syrische Grabinschriften aus Semirjetschie," in *Memoires de l'Academie imp. des Sciences de Saint-Petersbourg*, series 8, vol. 34, no. 4 (1886), 37 no. 8 (1890), and "Syrisch-nestorianische Grabinschriften aus Semirjetschie, Neue Folge" (1897). See also F. Nau, "Les pierres tombales nestoriennes du Musee Guimet," in *Revue de l'Orient chretien* 18, no. 1 (1913); and A. Mingana, "Early Spread of Christianity in Central Asia and the Far East," *Bulletin of the John Rylands Library* 9, no. 2 (1925): 334–46.

62. Mingana, "Early Spread," 334–38. He quotes from one tombstone, dated about 1322 (Seleucid year 1627): "This is the grave of Shliha, the celebrated commentator and teacher, who illuminated all the monasteries with light; son of Peter the august commentator of Wisdom. His voice rang as high as the sound of a trumpet." But Chwolson reads too much into the evidence of a total of only about 630 tombstones. He speaks rashly of a possible "million" Christians among the Turkish tribes of the Chagatai khanate.

63. Mirza Haydar, *Tarikh-i-Rashidi*, 3.

64. See Barthold, *Four Studies*, 1:137ff.

65. The English name Tamerlane derives from Timur-i-lenk, which means Timur the Lame. No one called him that to his face. How he got the name is obscure, which suggests it may not have come from battle.

66. On Tamerlane, see principally Grousset, *Empire*; and H. Hookham, *Tamburlaine the Conqueror* (London: Hodder and Stoughton, 1962). Uncritical original sources include the untranslated Persian *Zafar Nama* of Nizam-i-Shams (ca. 1404), and its later rewritten edition by Ali of Yazd (Sherif ad-din), which is translated into French by Petis de la Croix as *l'Histoire de Timur-bec* (1722), and into English (London, 1723). For color and drama combined with fairly careful attention to the sources, there is also H. Lamb's *Tamerlane the Earth Shaker* (New York: McBride, 1928). The *Memoirs of Timur* (*Mulfuzat Timury*) are not now considered genuine.

67. On the family background see Barthold, *Four Studies*, 2:14ff.; and Hookham, *Tamburlaine*, 41ff.

68. Tughlugh-Timur.

69. Mirza Haydar, *Tarikh-i-Rashidi*, 12–15.

70. His sons and grandsons fought each other into oblivion over the pieces, as it divided into Afghanistan, east Persia, and Transoxiana. See the genealogical chart in B. Spuler, *Muslim World*, 2:103.

71. The first in 1386; other campaigns in 1393, 1396, 1399 (the "campaign of extermination"), and 1403. See chronology of Tamerlane's life, in Hookham, *Tamburlaine*, 313ff.; and Grousset, *Empire*, 433f.

72. "To the angel of the church in Smyrna write: . . . 'I know your tribulation. . . . Do not fear what you are about to suffer. . . . Be faithful unto death, and I will give you the crown of life" (Rev., 2:8–11).

73. The Christian historian is compelled to balance this picture of Muslim ferocity with the reminder that Christians of the time were not without blemish. About a hundred years earlier a Dominican bishop of Smyrna, William Adam, a former missionary to Persia, had written a book with the violently inflammatory title *On a Method of Exterminating the Saracens*. Delacroix, *Histoire Universelle*, 193; and R. Waterfield, *Christians in Persia* (London: Allen and Unwin, 1973), 53.

74. Grousset, *Empire*, 442.

75. B. Spuler, "The Disintegration of the Caliphate in the West," in P. M. Holt, et al., *Cambridge History of Islam*, vols. 1 and 2 (Cambridge: Cambridge Univ. Press, 1970), 1:170.

76. Barthold, *Four Studies*, 2:22–24; and Hookham, *Tamburlaine*, 79, which contains the quotation.

77. R. G. de Clavijo, *Narrative of the Embassy to the Court of Tamerlane at Samarcand, A.D. 1403–1406*, trans. G. le Strange (London, 1928), cited by Hookham, 253f.

78. John of Sultaniyeh, in H. Moranville, *Memoire sur Tamerlan et Sa Cour par un Dominicain en 1403*, Bibliotheque de l'ecole de Chartres, vol. 55 (Paris, 1894), quoted by Hookham, *Tamburlaine*, 75, 258.

79. Spuler, "Disintegration," *Cambridge History of Islam*, 1:170.

80. See Barthold, *Four Studies*, 2:39f.

81. A hundred years earlier the Hindus had set a precedent by trampling Mongol prisoners under their elephants' feet. Grousset, *Empire*, 340, 444.

82. Browne, *Eclipse*, 172. He records one further instance of specific persecution of Christians. "At Tur 'Abdin, once the great centre of the Jacobites, the Christians were hunted out, and those who took refuge in underground caves were suffocated with smoke."

83. A. R. Vine, *Nestorian Churches* (London: Independent, 1937), 159. I have altered a few transliterations. He adds that there may have been others

around Mosul and Nisibis, and perhaps churches at Amadia, Urmi, Mardis, Amida (Diabekr), and Maiperkat.

84. A. R. Vine, *Nestorian Churches*, 123f., 158f.

85. *The Chronography of Bar Hebraeus* (Budge), p. 507.

86. Grousset, *Empire*, 434f.

Chapter 22
The Church in the Shadows

"Beset by an advancing Islam in the East, having lost the larger proportion of its wide-flung communities in Asia, and suffering from corruption and indifference in the Church which represented it in the West, in 1500 Christianity did not seem to face a promising future. The coming centuries might well have appeared to belong to Islam. . . . Moslem merchants were in charge of most of the trade routes to the Malay Peninsula and the islands of the East. Christianity was slowly yielding its remaining footholds in Asia and was confined almost entirely to Europe . . ."

—Kenneth Scott Latourette, *The History of the Expansion of Christianity*, vol. 2, p. 341

AFTER fifteen hundred years, the story of Christianity in Asia beyond the Euphrates nearly ends about where it began, in two small circles of survival. In earlier chapters we traced the beginnings of its expansion outside the Roman Empire to two pockets of Christians, one in the northern hills of eastern Syria, and the other in India.

A millennium and a half later the same two pockets are all that is left of an Asian church that once spread all across the continent from Mesopotamia to the Pacific. The Syrian center had shifted only slightly eastward from Edessa on the Upper Euphrates to a village called Gagarta on the Upper Tigris, which today is called Cisre, a staging area for Kurdish refugees.[1] About two and a half thousand miles away in India the St. Thomas Christians on the Malabar Coast still held to their beachhead in South Asia and their memories of "the apostle to Asia." Little else remained of the church in Asia at the end of the sixteenth century. But for a brief moment in approximately 1499 the two circles touched, then separated. When they came together again, the whole world was changing around them. The black ships of the barbarians from the other side of the earth had entered the Indian seas.

The contrast at this point between Eastern and Western church history is startling. What was it about the Asian branch of Christianity that makes its record of expansion and subsequent decline so somberly different from the dramatic triumph of the faith that conquered Europe? The West in 1500 was exploding into global mission. Spain drove out the last of the Moors; the pope sent Columbus to convert the ends of the earth; Loyola would soon organize the greatest missionary society Christianity had ever known; Russia pushed the Mongols east and replaced a Muslim khan with a Christian czar; and the Holy Roman Emperor proclaimed an age of "Perpetual Peace."

Not so in Asia. At the turn of the century in 1500 the situation facing Asia's Christians resembled more the end of hope than the beginning of perpetual peace. The Crusaders had long lost Jerusalem and Antioch. The Ottoman Turks, who ruled western Asia for the next four hundred and fifty years, had recently (1454) stormed across the Bosphorus to capture Constantinople and turn its thousand-year-old churches into Sunnite Muslim mosques. Persia was recovering its sense of national identity after centuries of foreign rule. Its new dynasty, the Safavids (1499–1736), claimed descent from the Sassanian shahs of Persia's glory days and continued the Muslim pressures on Christians that had driven the Nestorian patriarchate out of Baghdad and Maragheh to seek safety in the Kurdish hills. In far-off

India, the Thomas Christians had nearly lost their tenuous links with the Persian patriarchate and were adjusting themselves to life as an isolated Christian caste within a Hindu society. In Ming-dynasty China, Christians had simply disappeared once more. Few would have denied the obvious: Asian Christianity was on the verge of extinction.

What were the causes of its decline?

The Middle East

Mesopotamia, ancient homeland of the Church of the East, contained what was probably the largest surviving communities of Asian Christians east of the Mediterranean coast. There the Nestorians, along with smaller pockets of Syrian Jacobites, found that they had outlasted the fury of Tamerlane's Mongols only to be engulfed in the emerging empire of the Turks. The Nestorian patriarchate in Baghdad found itself caught in the middle of a Muslim war, Sunnite Turks against Shi'ite Persians. Baghdad was sometimes Turkish, sometimes Persian, but in either case militantly Islamic. Devastated by the border wars, oppressed by the Muslim population, and with its once-great tradition of missionary outreach dulled by centuries of failing hopes, the Nestorian remnants slowly retreated from the cities into the wild hills and valleys of Kurdistan, Azerbaijan, Armenia, and northwestern Iran.

The national structure of the church collapsed. Most of its records have disappeared. Even the names and dates of the Nestorian patriarchs in these years are uncertain, though lists have been carefully reconstructed by later writers. The surviving bishops were forced to protect the patriarchal succession by abandoning attempts at public episcopal election, and the headship of the church almost by default became hereditary.[2] The greater number of Syrian and Persian Christians simply disappeared, merging into the Muslim culture of the conquerors. Only very infrequently are there any references to an occasional nationally visible patriarchal residence in Baghdad, and Baghdad itself faded in importance as the Turks proudly poured their wealth into an Islamic restoration of the glories of once-Christian Constantinople.

One of the last credible glimpses of the patriarchate in this melancholy period tells of the unexpected arrival of two Christians who had come all the way from India to the mountain village of Gagarta, northwest of Mosul, to seek an audience with the Nestorian patriarch Shimon V. Their urgent purpose, they said, was to plead for bishops who could restore communion between the Syrian church in Persia and its far-off sister community on the Malabar Coast.

This eventful meeting of leaders from the two major Christian communities in oriental Asia that survived the Middle Ages, Nestorians in Persia and St. Thomas Christians in India, demands a final look at what had been happening in India while Islam was reestablishing its dominance of the Middle East.

St. Thomas Christians in the Middle Ages

East of Mesopotamia, the only other large and undoubtedly the least disturbed community of Asian Christians on the eve of the age of Western expansion was in southern India. Islam's conquests penetrated India only from the northwest and did not greatly disturb the subcontinent until about the year 1000 when Mahmud of Ghazna invaded and ruled the Punjab, as we have seen.[3] A second invasion in the late twelfth century by the central Asiatic Turko-Afghan armies of Muhammad Ghuri established permanent Muslim rule in northern India under what is loosely called the Delhi sultanates (from the thirteenth to the sixteenth century), but again the south was spared. The St. Thomas Christians of the Syrian colony in what is now the southern province of Kerala suffered not at all, so far as we know.

As with their earlier history,[4] what records remain of this period in the life of the Thomas Christians exist only in widely separated fragments and small clusters, which only accentuate the prevailing silence of evidence.[5] For all intents and purposes, reliable written records of Christians in India trace back no further than the eighth or ninth century, and even these are still subject to differing interpretations. The most important are the famous Kerala copper plates, probably about a thousand or more years old.

Five of the plates survive; two are lost. They contain "the earliest details concerning the Christian community in India from India itself." The date is probably around 850. They mention a grant of land, "marked by walking a she-elephant with earth and water around the property," and describe special privileges accorded to the "Tarisa" church and community of Christians at Quilon.[6] Another copper plate, usually considered somewhat older, describes a community at Cranganore a few miles farther north. It records a grant in perpetuity by an Indian king of personal honors and commercial rights to the head of the community, a man named Ravi-Korran. The plate does not directly identify the group as Christian but several indications seem to support that conclusion. For example, Cranganore is the traditional site of the landing of the apostle Thomas; it is the old home of the extensive Christian community that still claims him as its founder; and some find a Christian connection in one or two of the inscribed names on the plate.[7]

To the evidence of the plates must be added the five stone "St. Thomas" crosses of south India, four in Kerala and one on the east coast at the traditional tomb of Thomas near Madras. The lettering around three of the crosses is in Pahlavi (ancient Persian) and adds another link to the connection between the St. Thomas Christians and the Nestorian Persian church. If the paleographic experts are correct, some of the crosses may belong to the seventh or eighth century, which would make them even earlier than the copper plates. One of the inscriptions quotes Paul's words in Galatians 6:14, "Let me not glory save in the cross of our Lord Jesus Christ."[8] The design is very like the T'ang-dynasty cross carvings of the Nestorians of the same period in China, but with a subtle difference. Both combine the Christian symbol of the cross with a lotus flower design popular in Buddhism at the base. The Chinese Christian cross, however, stands on the lotus as its base and the petals flow both up and down, whereas in India, as G. M. Moraes notes, the "St. Thomas cross is mounted on Calvary and the petals, as it were, issue from the cross at its base," flowing downward.[9] It is tempting but entirely speculative to read a theological meaning into the difference.

These, then, are the only contemporary Indian sources that have survived to throw light upon the first Christians of the subcontinent, but about four hundred years later, another cluster of reports opens up a little more of the lost history of the ancient Thomas Christians. They come from Westerners, mostly Catholic missionaries, who about the end of the thirteenth century either journeyed to India to preach there or passed through on their way to and from China.

On his way to Cathay in 1291, John of Montecorvino[10] became the first Roman Catholic priest to set foot in India. He stayed thirteen months, visited the tomb of St. Thomas near Madras, where, he wrote, he baptized about a hundred people. But a later visitor to the tomb, the energetic traveler Odoric of Pordenone in 1324, found no Catholics there, only a Nestorian church ministering to fifteen families of "vile and pestilent heretics." In an earlier letter, copied and forwarded by a Dominican monk in Italy, Montecorvino had added that there were very few Christians and Jews in India and that the Christians were much persecuted.[11] Later, when John was made archbishop of Peking, Rome included India as part of his Catholic jurisdiction.[12]

If the Franciscan Montecorvino was the first Catholic priest in India, a Dominican, Jordanus,[13] could be called the first intentionally resident Catholic missionary. He was a French Dominican who had been a missionary for a while in Persia at Tabriz as a member of the Society of Wanderers for Christ, which focused on Dominican missions to Muslims. His introduction to India in 1321 was shattering. Scarcely had he reached Thana, in Muslim territory near Bombay, than he was called to bury the bodies of four martyred Dominican missionaries who had stopped in India on their way to China.[14] Three years later Odoric of Pordenone, who was passing through India on his way to China, gives a highly dramatic but untrustworthy description of the martyrdoms of the four: the elderly Thomas of Tolentino, a former missionary to the Mongols who may have known John of Montecorvino in Peking and is described as somewhat overzealous, James of Padua, Peter of Siena, and a Georgian lay brother named Demetrius. The emotionally intemperate Thomas was no model for the Christian mission if, as Odoric asserts, he really answered his Muslim judge's question, "What do you say of Muhammad?" with "He is the son of perdition and has his place in hell." Perhaps that is why the church apparently never beatified him. Or was that due to an earlier incident in which he had the temerity to dispute the authority of the pope to relax the Franciscan rule of poverty?[15]

Odoric dug up the bones of the martyrs, wrapped them in a sack, and carried them with him to China where he gave the relics to the Catholic mission at Zaitun.[16]

Despite the inauspicious beginning, Jordanus continued resolutely with his mission and went about the region of Gujerat, preaching and baptizing—ninety baptisms in one town, twenty in another, and thirty-five in a third.[17] He was so encouraged that he wrote home pleading urgently for more missionaries, "for there are three places that I know where they might reap great harvest." Two and a half years later he was not so optimistic. No recruits had come for the work, he writes in a second letter (1324); he was lonely and sick, "tortured by pains sometimes in the head, sometimes in the chest, in the stomach, or in all my limbs in turn . . ."; and he was deeply troubled by "a horrid schism among the people in reference to me." This veiled report of disagreement in the Christian community over his ministry suggests a possible rift between the older Thomas Christians and the incoming Catholics, much as occurred in Peking when Montecorvino about the same time found Nestorians already well established there under Kublai Khan. Jordanus begs for more friars, "but they must be ready to bear all things with patience, and martyrdom with gladness."[18]

Shortly thereafter he returned to Italy to seek in vain for the volunteers he had hoped for. In 1328 he was consecrated bishop of Columbum (Quilon in Kerala) by Pope John XXII with an impossible double mission. He was to convert the Muslims and reunite the Nestorians ("Nazarenes") with "the true church."[19] Jordanus may have set out for a return to India in 1330, but, if so, he never reached his goal.

In summary, these reports, plates, and crosses form the slender but significant pillars of historical evidence from within India before the coming of the Portuguese that confirm the fact that the St. Thomas Christians did indeed maintain their identity throughout the Middle Ages. How much more evidence was destroyed by the Muslim conquests in the eleventh century, the Turko-Afghan sultanate in the thirteenth to the sixteenth century, and finally and most devastatingly by the Portuguese after 1498, who can tell? Taken together with the indelible St. Thomas traditions handed down for generations, there is proof enough of a very ancient Christian community tracing its roots with complete confidence to an apostolic origin, welcoming and absorbing Syrian traders, refugees, priests, and bishops, growing in wealth, attaining some measure of social prestige by the seventh or eighth century, and perhaps even receiving some form of independent political recognition[20] by the tenth century.

Moreover, as early as the sixth century and perhaps even before that, India's Christian community had maintained a conscious connection with the authority of the Persian patriarch and with the Syriac language and theology of the Nestorian church.[21] In the seventh century this dependence took on a measure of structural independence when the Nestorian patriarch granted the metropolitan (archbishop) in India freedom from the jurisdiction of a Persian metropolitan.[22] From that time on India's ecclesiastical ties with the Baghdad patriarchate became more and more intermittent. No continuous succession of resident metropolitans in India can be traced with any reliability, and it is thought that during vacancies in the see, a local archdeacon assumed temporary authority. By the end of the fifteenth century, as the Persian patriarchate shrank back from the cities into the hills, India's ecclesiastical ties with any church outside India had all but reached the vanishing point. The community of Thomas Christians maintained ever fainter but never quite extinguished loyalties to the Persian church but were becoming, as K. Menon has described them, "Hindu in culture, Christian in religion and oriental in worship."[23]

A Syriac document, translated by A. Mingana, describes the last meeting, referred to above, of a Nestorian patriarch with the St. Thomas Christians of India before the coming of the Portuguese:

> In the year [1490], three believing Christian men came from the remote countries of India to the Catholicos Mar Simeon, Patriarch of the East, in order to bring bishops to their countries . . . and two of them reached the Catholicos alive. . . . The Catholicos who was then in the town of Gazarta of Beith Zabdai . . . ordained both of them priests . . . and took two monks [from a monastery there] and ordained both of them bishops. . . . After having prayed for them, and blessed them, he despatched them to India in the company of the Indians. By the assistance of Christ, our Lord, the four of them reached there alive.
>
> The faithful were greatly pleased with them, went to meet them joyfully with Gospel, Cross, thurible and candells, and ushered them in with great pomp, with psalms and canticles. They consecrated altars and ordained many priests, because the Indians were for a long time without bishops. Bishop John remained in India, and Bishop Thomas, his companion, returned after a short time to the Catholicos.
>
> [But the Catholicos Simon had died]. He was succeeded by Mar Elijah, the Catholicos and Patriarch, who also took from the monastery of St. Eugenius [in Gazarta] three pious monks, one of whom . . . he ordained Metropolitan and re-named Mar Yahb Alaha; the next one . . . he ordained bishop, and re-named Mar Jacob. He ordained all of them . . . in the year [1503], and he sent them to the country of India, to the islands of the sea which are inside Java, and to China. The four of them reached there in peace and safety, by the assistance of Christ their Lord, and they saw Mar John, bishop of India alive.[24]

Mingana appropriately calls this document, "the swan song of the Nestorian Church before . . . western missionaries made themselves felt on Indian soil."

In the absence of the St. Thomas pilgrims on their long journey from the Malabar Coast to the Tigris River and back to India, strange ships had landed on their home coast at Calicut in Kerala. The year was 1498; the strangers were Portuguese; and Vasco da Gama's discovery of a new sea route from Lisbon around Africa to India changed the history of the world, and not least the history of the St. Thomas Christians in India. But that story must wait for another volume, for only in the sixteenth century does that ancient church emerge with any clarity of detail from its largely unrecorded past.

So we end in Asia about where we began, with India and the memory of "the apostle to Asia," St. Thomas. In most of Asia, it was a time of disappointment and near despair for Christians. What had more than once appeared to be a Christendom in Asia with the potential of matching its expanding medieval European counterpart, now withered away again, as it had so many times before, into harassed and isolated pockets.

Conclusion

Why did Asian Christianity come so near to extinction just as the Christianity of the West was about to circle the globe? What differences, East and West, between the character of the Christians, or the nature of their faith, or the structure of their churches, or the social and political environment in which they grew or declined led to such surprisingly contrary consequences on the two continents?

Of the reasons this survey has from time to time suggested for the turbulence of the course of Asian church history—its sudden disappearances, its equally surprising reappearances—the most reasonable perhaps are these seven: geographical isolation, chronic numerical weakness, persecution, the encounter with formidable Asian religions, ethnic introversion, dependence upon the state, and the church's own internal divisions. Much debated and often cited is another, eighth factor, the theological. The relative weight of each can be debated, but historians can at least demonstrate that all were significant at various times and in different places.

Isolation was a far greater factor in Asia than in Europe. In its earliest period, which this survey calls the Syrian period (up to A.D. 225), Edessa was separated from the rest of Christendom by the Roman border, and when Rome absorbed Edessa, it separated Edessene Christianity from the church in Persia.

The very geography of Asia contributed immensely to the isolation. Comparatively speaking, Europe is a mere peninsula; Asia is the continent from which the peninsula protrudes. Rome to London, for example, is only about a thousand miles. But in Asia in the church's Persian period (up to 635), to travel from the Nestorian patriarch's seat in Seleucia-Ctesiphon to China was a journey of more than five thousand rough, winding, and frightening miles. When Pope Gregory the Great wrote from Rome to his missionary bishop in Canterbury in 600, he expected a reply. When the first known Nestorian missionary to China, Alopen, reached the Chinese capital in 635, there is no evidence that his patriarch, who died in 643, ever even knew that he had a missionary in China. The communication factor across the vast spaces and thin lines of Nestorian expansion prevented the Church of the East, despite its continental growth, from becoming an effectively cohesive continental community.

The second factor was numerical. There was a far smaller ratio of Christians to population in Asia than in Europe. Excluding the Greco-Roman Mediterranean coast, which is outside the scope of this study, oriental Asian Christianity never planted a large enough critical mass of Christians in any Asian national culture sufficient to change the course of its history as decisively as Catholicism and Orthodoxy changed Europe.

Estimates vary wildly but by the close of the third century when persecution ended in the West and Rome began to turn Christian, Christians may already have been an important twelve percent of the population of the empire.[25] From then on, the numbers climbed swiftly. By the year 1000, according to another estimate, there may have been some thirty-eight million Christians within the borders once ruled by Rome. But in Asia beyond the Euphrates, which then as now was by far the most populous of continents, the same estimate for the same year counts at most only twelve million Nestorians,[26] which may be too high. There is little hard evidence on which to base any numbering of Christians there in that period. The only certainty is that by then the number was declining, not increasing.

A third reason, which many believe was the single most important cause of the failure of Christianity in Asia, if failure it was, was Persia's persecution of Christians in the fourth century, which surpassed in number of martyrs and in intensity of religious hatred anything suffered in the West under three hundred years of pagan Roman emperors. Muslim persecution after the conquest in the seventh century was less intense than many have supposed, but nothing in Western history, with its centuries of almost unchallenged Christian command of a continent's culture, can compare with the paralyzing effect of Islam's complete dominance of the Middle Eastern heart and center of the Church of the East throughout those same centuries. The church might better have withstood violence. Sharp persecution breaks off only the tips of the branches; it produces martyrs and the tree still grows. Never-ending social and political repression, on the other hand, starves the roots; it stifles evangelism and the church declines. Such was the history of the church in Asia under Islam until, at the beginning of the fifteenth century, Tamerlane swept the continent with the persecution to end all persecutions, the wholesale massacres that gave him the name of "the exterminator" and gave Asian Christianity what appeared to be its final, fatal blow.

A fourth element checking Christianity's advance was its en-counter with other Asian religions. The pagan religions of the West were already crumbling when Christianity entered Europe, but in its birthplace, Asia, religion constituted a formidable obstacle to Chris-tian expansion. Its missionaries met head-on some of the most pow-erful religions the world has ever known: Persian Zoroastrianism, Indian Hinduism, Chinese Buddhism, Confucianism, and Arabic Is-lam. Not surprisingly they resisted.

All of the religions mentioned, with the possible exception of Confucianism, at one time or another persecuted Christians. But more serious were the social, intellectual, and religious barriers that these strong national faiths created against conversion to Christian-ity. From the outset, the disadvantage was with the foreign-sounding, politically powerless gospel of the Christian missionaries.

The surprise is that at several moments in Asian history Chris-tianity seemed almost ready to break through the barriers of religion and culture into national acceptance and influence. This happened once in Edessa in the late second century.[27] It never quite happened in India or Sassanid Persia or the Islamic caliphates. But once again during the *pax mongolica*, had Asian history shifted and changed as Western history did under Constantine, the world might have been given an Eastern Christendom to add a global dimension and an enriching balance to the Christendom that emerged in the West.

But Asia never produced a Constantine. Was that the pivotal difference between Asian and European Christian history? In Asia, it never emerged from politically dependent minority status under absolute non-Christian monarchies. Asia had a Gundaphar in India and an Abgar VIII in Edessa, but unlike Constantine neither one provides unequivocal evidence of conversion to the Christian faith. Pre-Islamic Arabia had a Christian queen, Mawiyya of the western Tanukhs, and a reportedly Christian king, al-Numan of Lakhmid Hirta in the east, but it was Muslim central Arabia that conquered the Middle East. Sassanid Persia had a Christian queen, Sirin, but it was her husband, Chosroes II, who ruled. Had the Mongol princess Sorkaktani been a man instead of a woman, there at last Asia might have found its Constantine. But Nestorian Christian though she was, not one of her three imperial sons—Mongke, Great Khan of Mongolia, Hulegu, ruler of the Persian Empire, or Kublai Khan, em-peror of China—followed her into the Christian faith. In Asia, Chris-tianity never won more than a temporary touch of imperial favor.

Instead, for most of their first fifteen hundred years the Asian churches were compelled to rely on the fitful tolerance of non-

Christian rulers whose power of life or death over their subjects was unlimited. Dependence upon political power is always perilous to religious integrity and is not an unfamiliar phenomenon in Western church history. But in Asia, where dependence was extreme, the damage was extreme. It lasted longer, for one thing. With the partial exception of the religiously tolerant Mongol period of little more than one century (1240–1368), in all of Asia's history from the time of Yazdegerd I in early fifth century Persia down to the defeat of the Ottoman Turks in the twentieth century, the Christians of the non-Hellenic Middle East were never free from severe religious discrimination.

The empires of Asia, except for the early Mongol domains, were not only non-Christian, they were usually anti-Christian. More debilitating than outright persecution was the Middle Eastern pattern of state control of a religious minority, whether Christian or Jewish, as developed first by Persia and then by the victorious Arabs. The *melet* system of the Sassanids and the socially harassed, separated ghettos, or *dzimmis*, of the Muslim caliphates have been described in previous chapters. How could churches so insulated from society, so crippled politically and financially, so despised by the culture around them even survive, much less advance? And yet, out of the Persian monasteries, which were themselves *melets*, the Nestorians reached forth as far as China, and out of the Christian *dzimmis* in the caliphate Nestorian missionaries were sent to convert Mongol tribes in central Asia.

A case could be made that in Asia, as everywhere, Christians have always been their own worst enemies. In the final analysis, the deadliest obstacle to any community of Christians is to be found not outside it but within it. This is the seventh, and least excusable of the roots of failure. The School of Nisibis, for example, was almost destroyed not by Zoroastrian priests but by dissension in its own Christian faculty. Pride and rivalry among quarreling bishops were as much to blame for state interference in the government of the church as the ambition of Zoroastrian shahs and Muslim caliphs to control it. The lives and untrained minds of the Nestorian priesthood in isolated medieval central Asia, however much the reports of discreditable behavior may have been exaggerated by Catholic missionaries, cannot but have increased the tendency of Mongol princes to moderate the initial favor with which they viewed Christianity. Almost to a man, every ruling Mongol prince, however much he might show political favors to the church, remained personally uncommitted and unconverted.

It has also sometimes been suggested that the theologians of the Asian church were of an intellectual caliber inferior to the apologists of the West, such as Clement of Alexandria or Tertullian, and were no match for the later great church fathers like the Cappadocians and Augustine. That may be true. The East never did give the Christian world an Augustine. But the West itself produced only one of his stature in its own first millennium. There is a touch of Western bias in the charge of theological mediocrity brought against the early Asian Christians. It traces back perhaps to the schisms that split Christendom apart in the fifth century. Ever since those divisions and until very recently Nestorians and Monophysites have been scorned by the West as heretical and therefore unworthy. Protestants, in turn, have criticized the early Persian missionaries in China for their apparent failure to translate the New Testament into Chinese, thereby depriving the church of the T'ang dynasty of the indispensable foundation for a Christian theology in its own language.

Recent scholarship, however, has begun to moderate these judgments. The discovery of Nestorius's own defense, *The Bazaar of Heracleides*, uncovered a Nestorius nearer to Chalcedonian orthodoxy than would have been believed a century ago. The surviving fragments of T'ang-dynasty Nestorian writings in China are too slender a base for hasty judgments about the theology of eighth-century Christianity in China. We can say with certainty that at least some selected portions of the New Testament were translated and much more may have disappeared.[28] The Nestorian monument and the documents that remain contain at least the bare basics of historic Christianity, written in Chinese. It is true that the language often reveals a vulnerability to syncretism in its use of terms borrowed from Chinese religions. This, however, might be due more to translation difficulties than to theological compromise. Or the Persian priests might have used Buddhist and Taoist phrases in a commendable but overzealous attempt to communicate their Christian faith cross-culturally. It is no easy task to transfer the religious concepts of one culture's faith into the language of another civilization and other faiths. The attempt to blame the disappearance of early Christianity in China on the supposed defects of Nestorian theology is difficult to substantiate.

It is also true that Asian Christian witness in the Nestorian heartland, Mesopotamia, did not meet quite the same unique level of intellectual challenge as that presented in the West by Greek philosophy. The early Persian and Arabic challenges to Christianity were essentially either religious or political, not philosophical, and the response was accordingly not so precisely and academically articulated. Later, by the time Arab philosophy began to acquire Greek learning from the Nestorians, the pressures of religious discrimination had all but closed the once-famous Nestorian schools both to theological inquiry and to the stimulation of intellectual debate. The Christian ghettos were as much theological prisons as social dead ends.

Finally, perhaps it was the introverting pressure of those same ghettos that, fairly or not, stamped Christianity as ethnic and foreign to most of Asia's peoples and nations. This was more true of west and south Asia than of the Far East, but throughout Asia its small Christian minorities tended to become isolated not only by religion but also by national or racial origin. In India the Christians were called Syrians and became a strong but separated, castelike community in south India. In Persia, where Christianity took deeper national roots than anywhere else in Asia, Christians were also at first considered Syrians because of their liturgical use of Syriac. And by the time they had become thoroughly Persian, it was their religion, not their race that, through no fault of their own, arbitrarily separated them, first from a Zoroastrian populace and then from the Muslim national culture. In T'ang-dynasty China the earliest name given to the Christian religion was "the Syrian religion." Later it was changed to "Persian," and the leadership of the church apparently remained almost entirely Persian, not Chinese. On the Mongolian steppes Christianity was considered Persian, or tribal, such as Kerait or Ongut. And in the China of Kublai Khan, the conquered Chinese associated the church with the conquering Mongols.

Those early Christian communities of Asia, though they were themselves Asian and for centuries were planted by Asian missionaries, nevertheless found it difficult to break through the barriers of their own ethnic differences and take root in the social fabric of other Asian peoples. Where they met advanced civilizations and the higher religions they were still regarded as foreigners for a thousand years and more. The coming of the Christian West to Asia in the sixteenth century did not change this; it only accentuated it.

This suggests the possibility that in the early spread of Christianity across Asia, instead of adapting too much or too little to new contexts, the Nestorians might have indigenized at the wrong levels. Theological integrity does not preclude ethnic and social adaptation. Ethnic pride is a powerful force for survival, but it is essentially self-centered, separating the missionary church from other national cultures and limiting its evangelistic effectiveness. Social adaptation is indispensable for cross-cultural communication but may become an invitation to religious pluralism.

It is easier and self-satisfying to seek for external reasons for decline, when the failure is within. What finally withered the proud advance of Christianity across Asia was not the persecution of a Tamerlane, though the permanent effects of that ravaging destruction still linger. More crippling than any persecution was the church's own long line of decisions, traceable as far back as the Persian *melets* of the sixth century, to compromise evangelistic and missionary priorities for the sake of survival. It did survive, but it was no longer a whole Church.

Must we end in this depressing fashion, searching inconclusively for more reasons to explain the decline of Christianity in Asia, asking why it came so perilously close to utter failure on the great continent? No single one of the above reasons can be taken by itself as a definitive answer, and not even all of them taken together are sufficient. The human Christian weaknesses they describe, though obviously contributing to the equally human failures of the church, are no more limited to Asia than to any other part of the world.

There are times when history can only be described, not explained, and perhaps the history of Christianity in Asia is best left as one of the mysteries of the providence of God, whose ways, as seen from a Christian perspective, are not our ways; nor are his purposes ever entirely made known. But from that same Christian perspective, history does not end with despair but with hope.

Allow us, therefore, to close this part of the history with words from a later missionary to Asia who said at a time when his own prospects never seemed darker, "The future is as bright as the promises of God."[29] Who would have dared to predict in 1500 that before another five hundred years had passed the Christians of Asia, revived and renewed, would emerge from the shadows and begin again to outpace the West in the growth of the church and in mission to the world?

NOTES

1. Gagarta (Jezira, the modern Cisre) is a village on the upper Tigris in far eastern Turkey where the borders of Iraq, Syria, and Turkey meet.

2. G. D. Malech lists the fourteenth- and fifteenth-century Nestorian patriarchs as Timothy II (1318), Denha II (1328–1359), Denha III (1359–1368), Shimon or Simeon II (1368–1375), Shimon III (1385–1405), Elias IV (1405–1433), Shimon IV (1433–1472), Shimon V (1472–1502). See his *History of the*

Syrian Nation and the Old Evangelical Apostolic Church of the East (Minneapolis, MN: privately printed, 1910), 11ff.

3. See chap. 17, p. 375.

4. See chap. 14.

5. See chaps. 2 and 13.

6. M. K. Kuriakose, *History of Christianity in India: Source Materials* (Madras, India: Christian Literature Society, 1982), 10–12. Noting the difficulty of translation, he cites translations from two of the plates. A few excerpts: "The church and land shall be protected." "Slave tax shall not be imposed on the slaves bought by the church."

7. For an account of the discovery of the copper plates in 1806/7, see C. Buchanan, *Christian Researches in Asia*, 2d ed. (Boston: Armstrong, 1811), 113ff. For a sympathetic outside critique and a summary of different opinions on the date of the inscriptions, ranging all the way from 230, to 774, 880, and as late as 1300, see S. Neill, *History of Christianity in India* (Cambridge: Cambridge Univ. Press, 1984), 1:10f., and especially 388–90, noting his sources: *Epigraphica India*, 4:290ff., and *Indian Antiquary*, vol. 3 (1924), reprinted as *Dissertations on the Copper Plates in the Possession of the St. Thomas Christians* (Bombay, 1925). Cf. C. B. Firth, *Introduction to Indian Church History* (Madras: Christian Literature Society, 1961), 29ff. For Indian Christian analyses, see S. G. Pothan, *The Syrian Christians of Kerala* (Bombay and London: Leaders, 1963), 32–35, 102–105; and C. V. Cheriyan, *A History of Christianity in Kerala* (Kottayam, India: C. M. S. Press, 1973), 112ff. These plates should not be confused with the so-called "Thomas of Cana plates," which no longer exist, if they ever did, though they are often quoted to describe the Syrian Christian community in Kerala in the fourth century (see chap. 13, p. 267).

8. See Kuriakose, *Christianity in India*, 9f.; A. Mingana, "The Early Spread of Christianity in India," *Bulletin of the John Rylands Library* 10, no. 2 (July 1926): 73f.; Firth, *Introduction*, 33; F. E. Keay, *A History of the Syrian Church in India*, 2d ed. (Kanpur, India: S.P.C.K., 1951), 27–29.

9. G. M. Moraes, *History of Christianity in India*, vol. 1 (Bombay: Manaktalas, 1964), 78.

10. See chap. 20, pp. 456f.

11. See H. Yule, ed. H. Cordier, *Cathay and the Way Thither*, 4 vols. (London: Hakluyt Society, 1913–16), 3:45, 63 for the letters of Montecorvino; and 2:141f. for Odoric.

12. A. M. Mundadan, *History of Christianity in India*, vol. 1, *From the Beginning* (Bangalore: Church History Association of India, 1984), 126.

13. On Jordanus see A. C. Moule, "Brother Jordan of Sévérac," *Journal of the Royal Asiatic Society* (London, 1928): 349–76.

14. Yule (Cordier), *Cathay*, 3:75ff.

THE CHURCH IN THE SHADOWS

15. Yule (Cordier), *Cathay,* 2:119ff, 126n; and J. Foster, "The Four Martyrs of Thana, 1321," *International Review of Missions* (April, 1956): 204–208.

16. On the Zaitun mission, see chap. 20, pp. 458f.

17. Yule, *Cathay,* 3:76; and Neill, *History,* 73. Neill suspects with some reason that he may have been baptizing members of Nestorian families who had been long isolated from the services of a priest and might not know the difference between Nestorians and Catholics.

18. Yule (Cordier), *Cathay,* 3:78–80.

19. Firth, *Introduction,* 38–41.

20. One tradition, which is difficult to accept, even claims the existence for a time in the tenth century of a Christian kingdom recognized by Hindu rajahs and a Christian king (Villiarvattam, or Belliarte), a descendant of Thomas of Cana, who represented all the Christians of Kerala from his seat at Udayamperur (Diamper) near Cochin. Perhaps it was this tradition that led Pope Eugenius IV in 1439 to dispatch a letter "To my most beloved son in Christ, Thomas, the most illustrious lord (*dominus*) of the Indians. . . . There has reached us a constant rumour that Your Serenity and all who are subjects of your kingdom are true Christians." See Moraes, *History,* 1:68ff. But were there actually such a head of the Christians in Kerala at that time, he would undoubtedly have been a Nestorian ecclesiastic, a bishop, or an archdeacon, or perhaps a Christian chief merchant.

21. E. Tisserant, *Eastern Christianity in India* (Westminster, MD, 1957), 17f., leans toward tracing the Indian Nestorian connection back to the end of the fifth century. Two synods called then by the patriarch Babai (497–502/3) reasserted the basic tenets of Nestorian theology and acknowledged the preeminence of the bishop of Seleucia-Ctesiphon as patriarch of "all the East." This presumably included India, but the Synod of 497, however, did not mention it (See J. B. Chabot, *Synodicon Orientale on Recueil de Synodes Nestoriens* [Paris: Klincksieck, 1902], 310–17). See also Mundadan, who gives some weight to the Thomas of Cana tradition and to the tradition of two Armenian brothers, Sapor and Prat, as the roots of India's connection with Seleucia-Ctesiphon (*History of Christianity,* 90ff., 103ff.). These latter two traditions, however, survive only as filtered through later Portuguese reports.

22. See chap. 13, pp. 269f. The Nestorian canonist Ibn at-Tayyib (d. 1043) attributes the formation of a metropolitanate for India to the patriarch Yeshuyab, probably Yeshuyab III (650–660) according to W. G. Young (*Handbook of Source Materials for Students of Church History* [Madras: Christian Literature Society, 1969], 21, 319), although Mingana ("Early Spread in India," 64) attributes this to Yeshuyab II (628–643).

23. K. P. Kesava Menon, in foreword to A. C. Perumalil and E. R. Hambye, eds., *Christianity in India* (Alleppey, India: Prakasam, 1972), 7.

24. J. S. Assemani, *Bibliotheca Orientalis Clementino-Vaticana.* vol. 3, p. 590, trans. A. Mingana, "*Early Spread of Christianity in India,*" 36–42. The manu-

script (*Vat. Syr. 204*) is dated 1504 in another mss. copy in Paris (Syr. 25) and was brought to the Vatican from Asia in 1718–1721. See Tisserant, *Eastern Christianity*, 24f., citing Assemani vol. 2a, pp. 590–99.

25. See K. S. Latourette, *A History of the Expansion of Christianity*, 1:108. A high proportion of that number was in Asia, but in Greco-Roman Asia, not oriental Asia

26. These figures, which must be regarded with due caution, are adapted from statistics in Barrett, *World Christian Encyclopedia* (New York, Oxford: Oxford Univ. Press, 1980), 3, 25. The estimate does not include the once-Roman west Syrian coast.

27. Interestingly, Edessa reappears during the Crusades as the Christian citadel of the Christian county of Edessa (1098–1144), but it was one of the first of those ephemeral Crusader fiefdoms to slip from dependence on Christian militancy into the bruising embrace of a more successfully militant Islam.

28. See P. Pelliot, *Recherches sur les Chrétiens d'Asie Centrale et d'Extrême-Orient*, vol. 2, 1 (Paris: La Fondation Singer-Polignac, 1983), 19.

29. Adoniram Judson, missionary to Burma (1813–1850).

Appendix:
The Nestorian
Monument's
Theological
Introduction

MY only additions to the text (P. Y. Saeki's translation)[1] will be to outline its logical order by bracketed subject headings, and to use italics to draw attention to possible borrowing from Chinese religious concepts:

[GOD] "Behold! there is One who is true and firm, who, being Uncreated, is the Origin of Origins; who is ever Incomprehensible and Invisible, yet ever mysteriously existing to the last of the lasts; who, holding the Secret Source of Origin, created all things, and who, surpassing all the Holy Ones, is the only unoriginated Lord of the Universe—is not this our *Aloha*,[2] the Triune, mysterious person, the unbegotten and true Lord?

[CREATION] "Dividing the *Cross*,[3] He determined *the four cardinal points*.[4] Setting in motion the primordial spirit [wind], He produced *the two principles of nature*.[5] The dark void was changed, and Heaven and Earth appeared. The sun and moon revolved, and day and night began. Having designed and fashioned all things, He then created the first man . . .

[MAN] "and bestowed on him an excellent disposition superior to all others, and gave him to have dominion over the Ocean of created things. The original nature of Man was pure, and void of all selfishness, unstained and unostentatious, his mind was free from inordinate lust and passion.

[SIN] "When, however, Satan employed his evil devices on him, Man's pure and stainless (nature) was deteriorated; what is just and noble was eliminated from that which is called right on the one hand, and what is fundamentally identical (with wickedness) was abstracted from that which is named wrong on the other. . . .[6]

"In consequence of this, three hundred and sixty-five (spiritual beings) with different seeds (of error) arose in quick succession and left deep furrows behind. They strove to weave nets of the laws wherewith to ensnare the innocent.[7]

"Some pointing to natural objects pretended that they were the right objects to worship; others got hold of (the idea that) *nonexistence* (lit., emptiness) *and existence* (are alike after all).[8] Some sought to call down blessings . . . by means of prayers and sacrifices; others again boasted of their own goodness, and held their fellows in contempt. (Thus) the intellect and the thoughts of Men fell into hopeless confusion . . . but all their travail was in vain. The heat of their distress became a scorching flame; and self-blinded, they increased the darkness still more; and losing their path for a long while they went astray and became unable to return home again.

[INCARNATION] "Whereupon one person of our Trinity,[9] the Messiah, who is the Luminous Lord of the Universe, folding up

514

Himself and concealing His true Majesty, appeared upon earth as a man. Angels proclaimed the Glad Tidings. A virgin gave birth to the Holy One in Ta-ch'in [Syria]. A bright star announced the blessed event. Persians saw the splendour and came forth with their tribute.

[SALVATION] "Fulfilling the old Law as it was declared by the twenty-four Sages,[10] He (the Messiah) taught *how to rule both families and kingdoms*[11] according to His own great Plan. *Establishing His New Teaching of Nonassertion*[12] which operates silently through the Holy Spirit, another Person of the Trinity, He formed in man the capacity for well-doing through the Right Faith. Setting up the standard of the *eight cardinal virtues,*[13] He purged away the dust from human nature and perfected a true character. Widely opening the Three Constant Gates,[14] He brought Life to light and abolished Death. *Hanging up the bright Sun*[15] He swept away the abodes of darkness. All the evil devices of the devil were thereupon defeated and destroyed. He then took an oar in the *Vessel of Mercy*[16] and ascended to the Palace of Light. *Thereby all rational beings were conveyed across the Gulf.*[17] His mighty work being thus completed, He returned at noon to His original position (in Heaven).

[THE SCRIPTURES] "The twenty-seven standard works of His Sutras were preserved.[18]

[THE MEANS OF GRACE and THE CHRISTIAN LIFE] "The Great Means of Conversion (or leavening, i.e., transformation) were widely extended, and the sealed Gate of the Blessed Life was unlocked.

[*Baptism*] "His law is to bathe with water and the Spirit, and thus to cleanse from all vain delusions and to purify men until they regain the whiteness of their nature.

[*Evangelism*] "(His ministers) carry the Cross with them as a Sign. They travel about wherever the sun shines and try to reunite those that are beyond the pale (i.e., those that are lost).

[*The Ministry*] "Striking the wood[19] they proclaim the Glad Tidings (lit., "joyful sounds") of Love and Charity. They turn ceremoniously to the East, and hasten in the Path of Life and Glory. They preserve the beard to show that they have outward works to do, whilst they shave the crown (tonsure) to remind themselves that they have no private selfish desires.

[*Conduct*] "They keep neither male nor female slaves. Putting all men on an equality, they make no distinction between the noble and the mean. They neither accumulate property nor wealth; but giving all they possess, they set a good example to others.

[*Worship: Fasting, Prayer and Eucharist*] "They observe fasting in order that they may subdue 'the knowledge' (which defiles the mind). They keep the vigil of silence and watchfulness so that they may observe "the Precepts." Seven times a day they meet for worship and praise, and earnestly they offer prayers for the living as well as for the dead. Once in seven days, they have 'a sacrifice without the animal' (i.e., a bloodless sacrifice). Thus cleansing their hearts, they regain their purity.

[*The Name of the "Way"*] "This ever True and Unchanging *Way*[20] is mysterious, and is almost impossible to name. But its meritorious operations are so brilliantly manifested that we make an effort and call it by the name of 'The Luminous Religion.'"

NOTES

1. P. Y. Saeki, *The Nestorian Documents and Relics in China*, 2d. rev. and enlarged (Tokyo: Maruzen, 1951), 54–56.

2. The Chinese characters are a transcription of the Syriac word for "God," but they are borrowed from a Buddhist word for an *arhat*, which in classical Buddhism is one who has achieved enlightenment and in popular Buddhism is an angel-like spirit with magical powers.

3. The crosslike Chinese character for "ten" was often used by the Nestorians to refer to the Christian cross.

4. The concept of the four directions of the compass is powerful in Chinese geomancy and is not biblically related to the cross but is in no way limited to religious superstition. J. Foster (*The Church of the T'ang Dynasty* [London: SPCK, 1939], 135) sees here a reference to St. Basil's exposition of Isaiah 11:12, "He will raise an ensign for the nations . . . and gather the dispersed of Judah from the four corners of the earth."

5. The "yin and yang" of Taoism and Chinese Confucian cosmology.

6. For other translations of this difficult passage see A. Wylie, "Nestorian Monument at Si-gnan Fu, China," *Missionary Review* 8, no. 3 (Princeton, May–June 1885): 186; Foster, *Church*, 135; and A. C. Moule, *Christians in China Before the Year 1550* (London: 1930), 35f.

7. Cf. Wylie's translation of this difficult text: "hence 365 sects followed each other in continuous trace, inventing every species of doctrinal complexity." ("Nestorian Monument," 186f.).

8. Perhaps an allusion to the Taoist concept of "nameless nothingness" as the original, eternal principle.

9. Wylie's translation gives a significantly different nuance: "Thereupon our Trinity being divided in nature. . . ." And Moule carries it a step further: "Upon this the divided Person of our Three in One, the brilliant and reverend Messiah. . . ." He adds that "divided body (Person)" (*fen shen* in Chi-

nese is regularly used when a spiritual being appears to two or more places, making clear that it is a reference not to the whole Trinity but to the second Person of the Trinity." Wylie, "Nestorian Monument," 187; Moule, *Christians in China*, 36, n. 19. This may be an instance of what is called "the Nestorian heresy," the division of the "person," not just the "nature" of Christ. The Council of Chalcedon insisted that the "person" is undivided, though there are "two natures, human and divine." See J. M. L. Young's discussion of the Christology of the monument inscription ("The Theology and Influence of the Nestorian Mission to China," *Reformed Bulletin of Missions* 2 [April 1970]: 7–12).

10. The writers of the Old Testament according to some rabbinical traditions.

11. A core Confucian phrase, as in the "Great Learning" of the *Book of Rites*.

12. A Taoist principle, but it has its Christian parallels.

13. A Buddhist formula, but one that might by some counts refer as well to the Beatitudes.

14. Faith, hope, and love?

15. A phrase occasionally found in Buddhism, but more probably referring to the crucifixion. See Moule, *Christians in China*, 37 n. 20.

16. Cf. the Amitabha Buddha's boat to paradise, or Kuan-yin who is called the goddess or "boat" of mercy.

17. J. Legge (*The Nestorian Monument of Hsi-an Fu in Shen-hsi* [London: Trubner, 1888], 7) detects a reference here to the 63rd hexagram of the Confucian (and Taoist) *Book of Changes* (the *I Ching*).

18. The New Testament. No satisfactory explanation has yet been given as to how the orthodox Western canonical number of twenty-seven is used here instead of the Syriac canonical number of twenty-two (and in some cases a few more but never twenty-seven). By 781, the date of the monument, it is quite possible that Nestorian standards of canonicity, always somewhat vague, were, particularly in missionary outreach, gradually enlarging to increase the earlier authorized number. The Syriac Peshitta of 420 recognized only the four Gospels, Acts, fourteen Epistles of Paul, James, 1 Peter, and 1 John. See P. Pelliot, *Recherches sur les Chrétiens*, 2:19; A. R. Vine, *Nestorian Christianity*, 188.

19. The Nestorian practice, brought from Persia, of using a wooden board instead of a bell. Moule (*Christians in China*, 37 n. 31) cites a reference in the ninth-century *Book of Governors* (II, p. 224). The following reference to "turning to the East" was also ancient Nestorian practice noted in the fourth-century Syriac *Teaching of the Apostles* from Edessa.

20. The "Way" as a description of the truth in life and thought is, of course, as Christian as it is Taoist.

Bibliography

AB. Analecta Bollandiana. Brussels, 1882ff.

Abbeloos, J. B. "Acta Sancta Maris, Assyriae, Babyloniae, ac Persidis secula I Apostoli . . ." in *Analecta Bollandiana.* Brussels, 1885. Tom. 4, pp. 43–138.

———, and T. J. Lamy. *See* Bar Hebraeus Chronicon.

Abbott, E. A. "Light on the Gospel from an Ancient Poet," *Diatessarica,* vol. 9. Cambridge: Cambridge Univ. Press, 1912.

Abramowski, Luise. "Ein unbekanntes Zitat aus *Contra Eunomium* des Theodor von Mopsueste." *Le Muséon* 7 (1958).

———. "Zur Theologie Theodors von Mopsuestia." *Zeitschrift für Kirkengeshichte* 72 (Gotha-Stuttgart, 1961).

———. *Untersuchungen zum Liber Heraclidis des Nestorius.* CSCO, [242] subsidia 22. Louvain, 1963.

———, and Alan E. Goodman. *A Nestorian Collection of Christological Texts: Cambridge University Library ms. 1319.* Cambridge: Cambridge Univ. Press, 1972.

———, and Alan E. Goodman. *A Nestorian Collection of Christological Texts,* vol 2. *Introduction, Translation and Indices.* Cambridge: Cambridge Univ. Press, 1972.

Abu'l Faraj, Gregory. *See* Bar Hebraeus.

Acta Apostolicae Sedis. Citta del Vaticano, Italy.

"Acta Sancta Maris. . . ." *See* Abbeloos, J. B.

"Acts of Aqiba-shima." *See* P. Bedjan, *Acta Martyrum et Sanctorum,* ii, in Syriac. Paris, 1891; reprint, Hildesheim, 1968.

"Acts of Miles of Susa." *See* Miles of Susa.

"Acts of Sharbil." *See* W. Cureton, *Ancient Syriac Documents,* pp. 41–62.

Acts of Thomas, See A. F. J. Klijn, *The Acts of Thomas* (Leiden: Brill, 1962); and G. Bornkamm, "The Acts of Thomas" in E. Hennecke, *New Testament Apocrypha,* vol. 2, English ed. by R. McL. Wilson (London: Lutterworth, 1965); and M. R. James, "The Acts of Thomas," in *The Apocryphal New Testament* (Oxford: Clarendon, 1924).

Addai (Addaeus). "Doctrine of Addai." *See* W. Cureton, *Ancient Syriac Documents,* pp. 6–23; and G. Phillips, *The Doctrine of Addai the Apostle* (London, 1876).

Africanus, Julius. "Kestoi" (Latin). In M. Thevenot, *Veterum Mathematicorum opera*. Paris, 1693. Pp. 300ff.

Agapius of Hierapolis (Mabbug). "Kitab-al-'Unwan." 2 vols. Edited and translated into Latin by A. Vasiliev. *PO* 7. Paris, 1911. Pp. 457–591.

Alexander Mar Thoma. *The Mar Thoma Church: Heritage and Mission*. Tiruvalla, India: Ashram, 1985.

Altaner, B., *Patrology*, English translation by H. C. Graef. New York: Herder and Herder, 1958.

Ammianus, Marcellinus. *Rerum Gestarum Libri*. English translated by John G. Rolfe as *Ammianus Marcellinus*. . . . 3 vols. Cambridge, MA: Harvard Univ. Press, 1963–64.

'Amr ibn Matta. *De Patriarchis nestorianorum commentaria (History of the Nestorian Patriarchs)*. Edited and translated into Latin by H. Gismondi. *Maris, Amri et Slibae, De Patriarchis*. . . . 2 vols. Berlin, 1896, 1899.

Andrae. Tor. *Muhammed sein Leben und Glaube*. Gottingen, 1932. Translated by T. Menzel. *Mohammed, The Man and His Faith*. New York: Scribner, 1955.

Aphrahat (Aphraates) the Persian. *Demonstrations*. Translated by John Gwynn in *Nicene and Post-Nicene Fathers*, second series, vol. 13 (*Demonstrations* 1, 5, 6, 8, 10, 17, 21). Translated by J. Neusner in *Aphrahat and Judaism* (*Demonstrations* 11, 12, 13, 15, 16, 17, 18, 19, 21, 23). Translated by F. H. Hallock in *Journal of the Society of Oriental Research*, vol. 14 (1930 *Demonstrations* 2, 23); Translated by R. H. Connolly in "Aphraates and Monasticism" in *JTS*, vi, 1905 (portions of *Demonstrations* 7)

Aprem, Mar. *The Chaldaean Syrian Church in India*. Trichur, Kerala, India: Mar Narsai, 1977.

———. *The Council of Ephesus of 431*. Trichur, India: Mar Narsai, 1978.

Arberry, A. R. *An Account of the Mystics of Islam*. London: 1950.

Arnold, T. W., *The Caliphate*. Oxford: Clarendon, 1924.

Asmussen, Jes P. "Christians in Iran." *Cambridge History of Iran*, vol. 3. Cambridge: Cambridge Univ. Press, 1983. Pp. 924–48.

———. *Manichaean Literature*. Delmar, New York, 1975.

———. "The Sogdian and Uighur-Turkish Christian Literature in Central Asia before the Real Rise of Islam: A Survey." *Indological and Buddhist Studies*. Edited by L. A. Hercus, et al. Canberra, Australia: Faculty of Asian Studies, 1982. Pp. 11–30.

———. *XuASTVANIFT: Studies in Manichaeism*. Vol. 7 in *Acta Theologica Danica*. Copenhagen: Munksgaard, 1965.

Assemani, Joseph A. [Guiseppe L.]. *De Catholicis seu Patriarchis Chaldaeorum et Nestorianorum, Commentarius Historico-Chronologicus*. Rome, 1775. Reprint. Farnborough, Eng.: Gregg International, 1969.

Assemani, J. [Guiseppe S.], ed. *Bibliotheca Orientalis Clementino-vaticano* (Syriac Mss., Italian). 4 vols. Rome: Sacra Congregatio Propaganda Fide, 1719–28.

Atiya, Aziz S. *A History of Eastern Christianity*. London: Methuen, 1968.

Ayer, J. C. *Source-book for Ancient Church History*. New York: Scribner, 1913.

Ayyer, L. K. Anantakrishna. *Anthropology of the Syrian Christians*. Ernakulam: Cochin Goverment Press, 1926.

Babai the Great. *Book of the Union [of Christ's Two Natures]. Liber de unione*.

In *CSCO, Scriptores Syri* [33], Syriac text [34]. Latin translation by A. Vaschalde. Series 2, t. 61, 1915.

Bailey, Sir Harold W. "Saka Studies: The Ancient Kingdom of Khotan." *Iran: Journal of the British Institute of Persian Studies* 8 (1970).

————. *Zoroastrian Problems in the Ninth Century Books*. Oxford: Clarendon, 1943, reprint 1971.

al-Baladhuri, Ahmad ibn-Yahya ibn-Jabir. *The Origins of the Islamic State (Kitab Futuh al-Buldan)*. Vol. 1. English translation by Philip Hitti. New York: Columbia Univ. Press, 1916.

Bar-Koni, Theodore. *Livre des Scolies (Liber Scoliorum* or "Religious Encyclopedia"). French translation by R. Hespel and R. Draguet. In *CSCO* [431,432], *Scriptores Syri*, t. 187,188 (1981,1982). See also "Theodore Bar Khoni . . . On Mani's Teachings. . . ." English translation by A. V. W. Jackson. In *Researches in Manichaeism*. New York: Columbia Univ. Press, 1932. Pp. 221–54.

Bardaisan. *The Book of the Laws of Countries: Dialogue on Fate of Bardaisan of Edessa*. Translated and edited by H. J. W. Drijvers. Semitic Texts with Translations. Vol 3. Assen: Van Gorcum, 1965.

Bardy, G. "Tatian." In *Dictionnaire de Théologie Catholique*. Paris, 1903.

————. *Ecclesiastical Chronicle (Gregorii Barhebraei Chronicon Ecclesiasticum . . .)*. Edited by J. B. Abbeloos and T. J. Lamy in *Analecta Bollandiana*. Vol. 4. Pp. 43–138 Brussels, 1885.

Barhadbesabba 'Arbaia. "Cause de la fondation des écoles." French translation by A. Scher in *PO*, IV, 4. Paris: 1908. Pp. 315–404.

————. *Histoire ecclésiastique*. In two parts. Edited and translated into French by F. Nau. Pt. I in *PO* 23, 2 (1932), pp. 179–340; Pt. II in *PO* 9, 5 (1913), pp. 488–631.

Bar Hebraeus (Abu'l Faraj, Gregory). *Chronography*. Edited by E. A. W. Budge as *The Chronography of Abul Faraj. . . .* Vol. 1 (English translation). London: Oxford Univ. Press, 1932.

————. *Gregorii Barhebraei, Chronicon ecclesiasticum quod e codice musei Britannica . . . .* 3 vols. Edited and translated into Latin from the Syriac by J. B. Abbeloos and T. J. Lamy. Paris and Louvain: Maisonneuve; Peeters, 1872–77). Esp. vol. 3.

Barrett, David. *World Christian Encyclopedia*. New York, Oxford: Oxford Univ. Press, 1980.

Barthold, Wilhelm [Vasilii V. Bartol'd]. *Turkestan Down to the Mongol Invasion*. English translation of the Russian 3d ed. 1963.

————. *Four Studies on the History of Central Asia*. 3 vols. Vol. 1, *A Short History of Turkestan*. Vol. 2, *Ulugh-Beg*. Vol. 3, *Mir 'Ali-Shir and a History of the Turkman People*. English translation from the Russian by V. and T. Minorsky. Leiden: Brill, 1952–56.

————. *Histoire des Turcs d'Asie Centrale*. French translation of the German edition of 1935. Paris: 1945.

————. *Zur Geschichte des Christentums in Mittel-Asian bis zur Mongolischen Eroberung*. German translation by R. Stube from the Russian original. Tubingen and Leipzig: Mohr, 1901.

Basham, A. L. *The Wonder That Was India*. 3d ed. London: Sidgwick & Jackson, 1967.

————, ed. *A Cultural History of India*. Oxford: Clarendon, 1975.

Battles, Floyd L., *The Sermons of Nestorius*. English translation from the

French text of F. Loof and F. Nau. Third printing. Pittsburgh: Battles, 1973.

Bauer, Walter. *Rechtglaubigkeit und Ketzerei im altesten Christentum.* Tubingen, 1934. *Orthodoxy and Heresy in Earliest Christianity.* Philadelphia: Fortress, 1972. English translation by R. A. Kraft et al. from 2d ed., enlarged.

Baumstark, Anton. *Geschichte der Syrischen Literatur.* Bonn: Markus und Weber, 1922.

―――. "Iwannis von Dara über Bardaisan." *Oriens Christianus,* dritte Serie, 8 (1933): 62–71.

Baur, P. V. C., H. I. Rostovtzeff, et al. *The Excavations at Dura-Europos.* 10 vols. New Haven, CT: Yale Univ. Press, 1929–52.

Beck, E. "Das heiligen Ephraem des Syrers Hymnen Contra Haereses." In *CSCO* (1957). See Ephraem Syrus.

Beckingham, C. F. *The Achievements of Prester John: An Inaugural Lecture.* London: School of Oriental and African Studies, 1966.

Bedjan, P., ed. *Acta Martyrum et Sanctorum.* 7 vols. Esp. vol 2, *Martyres Chaldaei et Persae,* in Syriac. Paris, 1890–97.

Bell, Richard. *The Origin of Islam in Its Christian Environment.* London: Frank Cass, 1926; reprint, 1968.

Belyaev, E. A. *Arabs, Islam and the Arab Caliphate in the Early Middle Ages.* English translation from Russian by A. Goveritch. London and New York: Pall Mall and Praeger, 1969.

Bernard, Henri. *Aux portes de la Chine: les missionaires du seizième siècle, 1514–1588.* Tientsin, China: Hautes Études, 1933.

―――. *La Découverte de nestoriens Mongols aux Ordos et l'histoire ancienne du Christianisme en extrême-orient. . . .* Tientsin, China, 1935.

Bethune-Baker, J. F. *An Introduction to the Early History of Christian Doctrine to the Time of the Council of Chalcedon.* 3d ed. London: Methuen, 1933.

―――. *Nestorius and His Teaching, A Fresh Examination of the Evidence.* Cambridge: Cambridge Univ. Press, 1908.

Bickell, G. *St Ephraemi Syri Carmina Nisibena.* In Latin. Leipzig: Bruckhaus, 1866.

Bidawid, Raphael J. *Les Lettres du Patariarche Nestorien Timothee I (Studi e Testi, 187).* Vatican City: Bibliotheca Apostolica Vaticana, 1956.

Bishai, Wilson B. *Islamic History of the Middle East: Backgrounds, Development, and Fall of the Arab Empire.* Boston: Allyn and Bacon, 1968.

BJRL. Bulletin of the John Rylands Library. (Manchester, England).

Blackman, E. C., *Marcion and His Influence.* London: SPCK, 1948.

Blum, Georg G. "Rabbula von Edessa, der Christ, der Bischof, der Theolog." In *CSCO* [300], subsidia 34 (1969), pp. 1–215.

Book of Chastity. Le livre de la chasteté composé par Jesusdenah évêque de Bacra. Edited by J. B. Chabot. In *Mélanges d'archeologie et d'histoire,* no. 16 (Paris, 1896).

Book of Degrees. Liber Graduum. Edited by Michael Kmosko. PS III, Pt. 1, t. 3. Paris, 1926.

Book of the Himyarites. See A. Moberg.

Bornkamm, G. *See Acts of Thomas.*

Boyce, Mary. *A Catalogue of the Iranian Manuscripts in Manichaean Script in the German Turfan Collection.* Berlin, 1960.

————. *The Letter of Tansar.* Rome: Instituto Italiano per il Media ad Estrema Oriente, 1968.

————. *Zoroastrians: Their Religious Beliefs and Practices.* London: Routledge and Kegan Paul, 1979.

Boyle, John A. *History of the World Conqueror, Translated from the Persian of Juvaini, Tarikh-i jahan gusha.* 2 vols. Manchester: Manchester Univ. Press, 1958.

————. "The Journey of Het'um I, King of Little Armenia, to the Court of the Great Khan Mongke." *Central Asia Journal* 9, no. 3 (The Hague/Wiesbaden, 1964): 175–89.

————. "Kirakos of Ganjak on the Mongols." *Central Asia Journal* 8, no. 3 (The Hague/Weisbaden, 1963): 199–215.

————. *The Successors of Genghis Khan, Translated from the Persian of Rashid al-Din (Jami' al-Tawarikh).* Pt. I. New York and London: Columbia Univ. Press, 1971.

Braun, Francois M. "L'Énigme des Odes de Salomon," *Revue de Théologie et des questions religieuses.* 57 (Montauban: Imprimerie Cooperative, 1957): 597–625.

————. *Jean le théologien et son évangile dans l'église ancienne.* Paris: Libre Lecoffre, 1959.

Brock, S. P. "Early Syrian Asceticism." *Numen* 20 (Leiden, 1973): 1–19.

————. "A Martyr of the Sassanid Court Under Vahran II: Candida." *Analecta Bollandiana,* t. 96, fasc. 1–2 (1978): 167–81.

Brockelmann, Carl. *History of the Islamic Peoples.* Translated by J. Carmichael and M. Perlmann from the German. 1939. New York: Capricorn, 1960.

Brooks, E. W. "The Emperor Zeno and the Isaurians." *English Historical Review* 8 (London, 1893): 209–38.

————. *Lives of the Eastern Saints. PO,* vols. 17–19 (1923–26).

Brown, L. W. *The Indian Christians of St. Thomas.* Cambridge: Cambridge Univ. Press, 1956.

Brown, Peter. *Augustine of Hippo: A Biography.* Berkeley: Univ. of California Press, 1967.

Browne, Edward G. *A Literary History of Persia. . . .* Vol. 1. London and Leipzig: Fisher Unwin, 1909.

Browne, Laurence E. *The Eclipse of Christianity in Asia from the Time of Muhammad till the Fourteenth Century.* Cambridge: Cambridge Univ. Press, 1933.

Bruce, F. F. *The New Testament Documents.* 5th ed. Leicester: Inter-Varsity, 1960.

BSOAS. *Bulletin of the School of Oriental and Asian Studies.* London.

Buchanan, Claudius. *Christian Researches in Asia: With Notices of the Translation of the Scriptures into the Oriental Languages.* 2d ed. Boston: Armstrong, Cornhill, 1811.

Buckler, F. W. *Harunu'l-Rashid and Charles the Great.* Cambridge, MA: Medieval Academy of America, 1931.

Budge, Ernest A. Wallis. *The Book of Governors: The Historia Monastica of Thomas, Bishop of Marga,* A.D. *840.* 2 vols. English translation in vol. 2. London: Kegan Paul, Trench, Trubner, 1893.

————. *The Chronography of Gregory Abul Faraj . . . commonly known as Bar*

Hebraeus, being the first part of his political history of the world. . . . 2 vols. English translation in vol. 1. Oxford: Oxford Univ. Press, 1932.
_____, ed. and trans. *The Discourses of Philoxenus, Bishop of Mabbogh*, A.D. *485–519.* 2 vols. London: Asher, 1894.
_____. *The Monks of Kublai Khan Emperor of China, or the history of the life and travels of Rabban Sawma . . . and Markos . . . Yabhallaha III . . . patriarch of the Nestorian church in Asia.* London: Religious Tract Society, 1928.
al-Bukhari. *Al-Jami as-Sahih.* Edited by Krehl et Juynboll. Leiden, 1862–1908). French translation by O. Hondas and W. Marcais. *El-Bokhari: les Traditions Islamigres.* 4 vols. Paris: 1903–1914.
Bulliet, Richard W. *Conversion to Islam in the Medieval Period: An Essay in Quantitative History.* Cambridge, MA, and London: Harvard Univ. Press, 1979.
Burkitt, F. C. *Early Eastern Christianity Outside the Roman Empire.* London: Murray, 1904.
_____. *Evangelion da-Mepharreshe, ii.* Cambridge: Cambridge Univ. Press, 1904.
The Cambridge History of the Bible. Edited by P. R. Ackroyd and C. F. Evans. Cambridge: Cambridge Univ. Press, 1970.
The Cambridge History of China. Edited by Denis Twitchett and John K. Fairbank. Cambridge: Cambridge Univ. Press, 1979. Vol. 3, *Sui and T'ang China,* Pt. I. (1979).
The Cambridge History of India. Vol. 1. Edited by E. J. Rapson. Cambridge: Cambridge Univ. Press, 1922.
The Cambridge History of Iran. Vol. 4, *The Seleucid, Parthian and Sasanian Periods,* Edited by E. Yarshater. Vol. 5, *The Saljuq and Mongol Periods.* Edited by J. A. Boyle. Cambridge: Cambridge Univ. Press, 1968.
The Cambridge History of Islam. Vols. 1 and 2. Edited by P. M. Holt et al. Cambridge: Cambridge Univ. Press, 1970.
Carrington, Phillip. *The Early Christian Church.* Cambridge: Cambridge Univ. Press, 1957.
Casartelli, L. C. "Sassanians." In *Hastings Encyclopedia of Religion and Ethics.* Vol. 11.
Casey, R. P., ed. *Quantulacumque: Studies Presented to Kirsopp Lake.* . . . London, Baltimore: Waverly, 1937.
Central Asiatic Journal. Wiesbaden.
Chabot, J. B., ed. *Chronique de Michel le Syrien.* . . . 2 vols. Paris, 1901. Reprint Brussels, 1963.
_____. "L'École de Nisibe, Son Histoire, Ses Statuts." Extrait du *Journal Asiatique,* 9, ser. vii, 1896. In *Varia Syriaca* 1 (Paris, 1897): 55 pp.
_____. *Histoire de Mar Jabalaha III et du moine Rabban Cauma.* Extracted from the *Revue de l'Orient Latin,* t. 1 and 2. Paris, 1895.
_____, ed. "Le livre de la chasteté composé par Jesusdenah évêque de Bacra." *Mélanges d'archéologie et d'histoire,* no. 16 (Paris, 1896).
_____. *Littérature Syriaque.* In *Bibliotheque Catholique des Sciences Religieuse.* Paris, Blond et Gay, 1934.
_____. *Synodicon Orientale ou Recueil de Synodes Nestoriens.* Paris: Imprimerie Nationale, Klincksieck, 1902.
Chadwick, Henry. *The Early Church.* Vol. 1, *Pelican History of the Church.* Harmondsworth, England: Penguin, 1967.

————. "Some Reflections on the Character and Theology of the Odes of Solomon." In P. Granfield and J. A. Jungmann, eds., *Kuriakon*, vol. 1. Munster: Aschendorff, 1971.

Chan Hok-Lam and William T. De Bary, eds. *Yuan Thought: Chinese Thought and Religion Under the Mongols*. New York: Columbia Univ. Press, 1982.

Charles, R. H. "A Church Hymnal of the First Century." *The Times Literary Supplement* 430 (7 April 1910).

Charlesworth, J. H. *The Odes of Solomon: Syriac Texts Edited with Translation and Notes*. Oxford: Clarendon, 1973. Reprint with corrections and added indices. Missoula, MT: Scholars Press, 1977.

————. "Les Odes de Solomon et les manuscrites de la Mer Morte." *Revue Biblique*, 77 (October 1970): 522–49.

Charpentier, J. "Die ethnographische Stellung der Tocharer." *Zeitschrift der deutschen morgenländischen Gesellschaft* 71 (1917): 347–88.

Chase, Frederic H., Jr., trans. *Saint John of Damascus, Writings*. Trans. Vol. 37 of *The Fathers of the Church*. New York: Fathers of the Church, Inc., 1958.

Chaumont Marie-Louise. "Les Sassanides et la christianisation de l'empire iranien au IIIe siècle. . . ." in *Revue de l'Histoire des Religions* 165 (Paris: Universitaires de France, 1964): 165–202.

————. L'inscription de Kartir a la 'Ka'bah de Zoroastre." *Journal Asiatique* (Paris, 1960): 339–80.

Chavannes, E. *Les mémoires historiques de Se-ma Ts'i'en*. Vol. l. Selected passages only. Paris: Leroux, 1895.

————"Trois généreaux chinois de la dynastie des Han" (Biographies of Pan Ch'ao, Pan Yung, and Liang K'in). *T'oung Pao*, series II, vol. 7 (Shanghai, 1906): 210–69.

Ch'en, Kenneth K. S. *Buddhism in China: A Historical Survey*. Princeton, NJ: Princeton Univ. Press, 1964.

Ch'en Yuan, *Western and Central Asians in China Under the Mongols*. Monumenta Serica Monograph 15. Translated and annotated by Chien Hsing-hai and L. C. Goodrich. Los Angeles: Monumenta Serica at the University of California, 1966.

Cheriyan, C. V. *A History of Christianity in Kerala*. Kottayam, India: Kerala Historical Society C. M. S. Press, 1973.

Ch'ien, Ssu-ma. *Shi-chi*. For English translations of selected passages *see* Chavannes, E., and Watson, Burton.

Christensen, A. *L'Iran sous les Sassanides*. Copenhagen: Levin and Munksgaard, 1936.

Chronicle of Arbela, Historie de l'Église d'Adiabene sous les Parthes et Sassanides. Edited by A. Mingana. *Sources Syriaques*. Vol. 1, *Msiha-zkha*. Leipzig: Harrasowitz, 1907. See also C. E. Sachau for German edition and translation.

Chronicle of Seert, or *Histoire Nestorienne*. Edited and translated from Arabic into French by Addai Scher. *PO* reprint, t. 4, f. 3, no. 17 (1971); t. 5, f. 2 (1950); t. 7, f. 2 (1950); t. 13, f. 4, no. 65 (1973). Paris and Turnhout, Belgium, 1973.

Chronicon anonymum. Edited by I. Guidi. In *CSCO, Scriptores Syri*, series 3, vol. 4. *Chronica minora* (Louvain, 1903): 13–32.

Chronicon Edessenum. Edited by I. Guidi. In *CSCO, Scriptores Syri*, series 3, vol. 4 (Paris, 1903). English translation in *Journal of Sacred Literature and Biblical Record*, new series, vol. 5 (London, 1864): 28–45. (NB: volume numbering and date of some issues is often incorrect.)

Clement of Alexandria. *Stromata*. In *Ante-Nicene Fathers*, vol. 2. New York, 1903. Reprint. Grand Rapids: Eerdmans, 1983. Pp. 299–568.

Clementine Recognitions. In Migne, *PG*, vol. 14. Paris, 1845.

Colledge, M. A. R. *The Parthians*. London: Thames and Hudson, 1967.

Conder, C. R. *The Latin Kingdom of Jerusalem* A.D. *1099 to 1291*. London: Palestine Exploration Fund, 1897.

Connolly, R. H., "Aphraates and Monasticism." *Journal of Theological Studies* 6 (Oxford and London, July 1905): 522–39.

_____. *Didascalia Apostolorum: The Syriac Version Translated and Accompanied by the Verona Latin Fragments*. Oxford: Clarendon Press, 1929.

_____. "Liturgical Homilies of Narsai." *Texts and Studies* 8 (Cambridge: Cambridge Univ. Press, 1909): i–lxxvf.

_____. "On Aphraates' Hom. 1:19." *Journal of Theological Studies* 9 (Oxford and London, 1908): 572–76.

CSCO. *Corpus Scriptorum Christianorum Orientalium*. Paris, 1903. Esp. *Scriptores Syri*. Paris, 1903. Revision of volume numbering indicated by brackets [ ].

Cosmas Indicopleustes. *Christian Topography*. 3 vols. Edited and translated into French by Wanda Wolska-Conus. In *Sources Chretiennes*. Paris: 1968, 1970, 1973. Also, edited with English translations by J. M. McCrindle. London: Hakluyt Society, 1897. And by E. O. Windstedt. Cambridge, 1909.

Couling, Charlotte Eliza. *The Luminous Religion, a Study of Nestorian Christianity in China*. . . . London: Carey, 1925.

Cragg, Kenneth. *Muhammad and the Christian: A Question of Response*. London: Darton, Longman, Todd; Maryknoll, NY: Orbis, 1984.

Cureton, W. *Ancient Syriac Documents Relative to the Earliest Establishment of Christianity in Edessa and the Neighboring Countries*. . . . London, 1864. Reprint. Amsterdam: Oriental Press, 1967.

Dahlmann, J. *Die Thomas Legende*. Freiburg, 1912.

Daniel, David. *The Orthodox Church of India (History and Faith)*. Vol. 1. *History*. New Delhi: Printaid, 1972.

Danielou, J. "Odes de Soloman." In *Dictionnaire de la Bible*, suppl. 6 (1960).

_____. *The Theology of Jewish Christianity*. Vol. 1 in *History of Early Christian Doctrine*, English translation by J. A. London: Darton, Longman, and Todd, 1964.

Dauvillier, Jean. *Histoire et institutions des Églises orientales au Moyen Age*. London: Variorum Reprints, 1983.

Dennett, Daniel Clement. *Conversion and the Poll Tax in Early Islam*. Cambridge, MA: Harvard Univ. Press, 1950.

Devreese, R. *Essai sur Theodore de Mopsueste*. Vatican City, 1948.

DeVries, S., T. Luykx, and W. O. Henderson. *An Atlas of World History*. London: Nelson, 1965.

de Zwaan, J. "The Edessene Origin of the Odes of Solomon." *Quantulacumque. Studies Presented to Kirsopp Lake*. . . . Edited by R. P. Casey. London and Baltimore: Waverly, 1937.

Dictionnaire de Théologie Catholique (Paris: 1905–1908).

Didascalia Apostolorum (Syriac). Edited and translated by William Cureton in *Ancient Syriac Documents* (London, 1864; reprint, Amsterdam: Oriental Press, 1967), pp. 24–35; also R. H. Connolly, *Didascalia Apostolorum: The Syriac Version Translated and Accompanied by the Verona Latin Fragments* . . . (Oxford, 1929); and Arthur Voobus trans., *The Didascalia Apostolorum in Syriac, I, Chapters I–IX*, in *CSCO, Scriptores Syri* (Louvain, 1979).

Doctrine of Addai. See Addai.

Doresse, Jean. *The Secret Books of the Egyptian Gnostics . . . with English Translation and Critical Evaluation of the Gospel According to Thomas.* English translation by P. Mairet. London: Hollis and Carter, 1960.

Dorner, I. A. *The Development of the Doctrine of the Person of Christ.* Div. I. 2 vols. English translation by W. L. Alexander and D. W. Swann. Edinburgh, 1891.

Drijvers, H. J. W. *Bardaisan of Edessa.* English translation by G. E. von Baaren-Pape. Assen: Van Gorcum, 1966.

————, ed. *The Book of the Laws of Countries: Dialogue on Fate of Bardaisan of Edessa.* Semitic Texts with Translations, vol. 3. Assen: Van Gorcum, 1965.

————. *Cults and Beliefs at Edessa.* In *Études Preliminaires aux Religions Orientales dans l'Empire Romain.* Vol. 82. Leiden: Brill, 1980.

————. "Quq and the Quqites," *Numen* 14 (Leiden, 1967): 104–29.

Driver, G. R. and L. Hodgson. *Nestorius, The Bazaar of Heracleides.* Edited and translated into English from the Syriac. Oxford: Clarendon, 1925.

Duchesne, Louis. *Early History of the Christian Church.* Translated from 4th ed. by Jenkins. Vols. 2, 3. London: Murray, 1912, 1924.

Dulaurier, E., "Les Mongols, d'apres les Historiens Arméniens: Fragments traduits sur les textes originaux," *Journal Asiatique*, 5th series, vol. 16 (1860) 2:304.

Duncan, Edward J. *Baptism in the Demonstrations of Aphraates, the Persian Sage.* In *Catholic University of America Studies in Christian Antiquity*, vol. 8. Washington, DC: Catholic Univ. of America, 1945.

Dunlop, Douglas. "The Karaits of Eastern Asia." *Bulletin of the School of Oriental and African Studies, London University* 11 (1943–46): 276–89.

Duval, Rubens. *Historie politique, religieuse et littéraire d'Edesse jusqu'a la première croisade.* Paris, 1892.

————. *Isho'yabh III Patriarcha, Liber Epistularum.* Latin translation in *CSCO* [11,12], series 2, t. 64 (1904), pp. 8–216.

————. *Littérature-syriaque.* Paris: Lecoffre, 1899.

Elia Bar Sinaya. *Opus Chronologicum.* Edited by E. W. Brooke in *CSCO, Scriptores Syri*, 3d series, vol. 7 (Rome: 1910).

Elia Bar Sinaya (Pseudo). Prefix to the *Opus Chronologicum.*

Encyclopedia of Asian History. 4 vols. New York, London: Scribner, Collier Macmillan, 1988.

Encyclopedia of Islam. Leiden: Brill, 1913–36ff.

Englert, Donald M.C. *The Peshitto of Second Samuel. Journal of Biblical Literature Monograph Series*, vol. 3. Philadelphia: Society of Biblical Literature and Exegesis, 1949.

Ephrem the Syrian. *Carmina Nisibena.* Edited with Latin translation by G. Bickell. Leipzig: Bruckhaus, 1866.

_____. *Des heiligen Ephraem des Syrers Hymnen contra Haereses.* Edited and translated into German by E. Beck, in *CSCO* [169], *Scriptores Syri,* t. 76, 77. Louvain, 1957.

_____. *S. Ephraim's Prose Refutations of Mani, Marcion and Bardaisan.* London: Williams and Norgate for the Text and Translation Society, 1912–21.

Epiphanius of Salamis. *Panarion.* Edited by K. Holl. *Die Griechischen christlichen Schriftstellen der ersten drei Jahrhundert.* Leipzig: J. C. Hinrichs'sche, 1915–33; English translation Bk. 1, Sections 1–46 by Frank Williams in *Nag Hammadi Studies,* vol. 35 (Leiden, New York: Brill, 1987).

Eusebius Pamphilius of Caesarea. *Ecclesiastical History.* 3 vols. Greek text and English translation. London and New York: Loeb Classical Library, 1926–32.

_____. *Life of Constantine.* Edited and translated by E. C. Richardson. New York: Christian Literature, 1890.

_____. *Orations (De laudibus Constantini).* English translation by H. A. Drake. Berkeley: Univ. of California Press, 1976.

Fan Yeh. *Annals of the Later Han.* See translation of parts relating to the West in F. Hirth. *China and the Roman Orient.* Leipzig and Shanghai, 1885.

Farquhar, J. N. "The Apostle Thomas in North India." *Bulletin of the John Rylands Library* 10, no. 1 (January 1926): 80–111.

_____. "The Apostle Thomas in South India." *Bulletin of the John Rylands Library* 11 (1927): 20–50.

Fiey, J. M. "Auteur et date de la chronique d'Arbeles." *L'Orient Syrien* 12 (1967): 265–302.

_____. "Chrétiens Syriaques sous les Abbasides, surtout à Bagdad (749–1258)." *CSCO* [420] Subsidia 59 (Louvain, 1980).

_____. "Chrétiens Syriaques sous les Mongols (Il-Khanat de Perse XIIIe–XIVe s.)." *CSCO* [362] Subsidia 44 (Louvain, 1975), pp. i–x; 1–112.

_____. "Nisibis, metropole syriaque orientale et ses suffragants des origines à nos jours." *CSCO* [388] subsidia 54 (Louvain, 1977).

Fihrist. See al-Nadim.

Firth, Cyril Bruce. *An Introduction to Indian Church History.* Madras: Christian Literature Society, 1961.

Fischer, R. H. *A Tribute to Arthur Voobus: Studies in Early Christian Literature and Its Environment, Primarily in the Syrian East.* Chicago: Lutheran School of Theology, 1977.

Fitzgerald, Charles Patrick. *The Empress Wu.* 2d ed. Reprint. Taiwan: Rainbow Bridge, 1968.

_____. *Son of Heaven.* Cambridge: Cambridge Univ. Press, 1933.

_____. "Sino-Western Contacts Under the Mongol Empire." *Journal of the Royal Asiatic Society, Hong Kong Branch* 6 (1966): 49–72.

Fleet, J. F. "Saint Thomas and Gondophernes." *Journal of the Royal Asiatic Society* (London, 1905): 223–36.

Foakes-Jackson, F. J., *History of the Church . . . to A.D. 461.* 4th ed. Cambridge: Hall, 1905.

Fortescue, Adrian. *The Lesser Eastern Churches.* London: Catholic Truth Society, 1913.

Foster, John. *The Church of the T'ang Dynasty.* London: SPCK, 1939.

———. "The Four Martyrs of Thana, 1321." *International Review of Missions* 45 (London, April 1956): 204–208.

Foucher, A. *L'Art Greco-Bouddique du Ganhara.* Vol. 2. Paris: Leroux, 1905–23.

Franke, Herbert. Review of E. P. J. Mullie, *De Mongoolse Prins Nayan.* In *Asia Major,* new series 12, pt. 1 (1966): 130–132.

Franke, Wolfgang. *China and the West: The Cultural Encounter, Thirteenth to Twentieth Centuries.* English translation by R. A. Wilson. New York: Harper & Row, 1967.

Frend, W. H. C. *Martyrdom and Persecution in the Early Church.* New York: New York Univ. Press, 1963.

———. *The Rise of the Monophysite Movement: Chapters in the History of the Church in the Fifth and Sixth Centuries.* Cambridge: Cambridge Univ. Press, 1972.

Frye, R. N. *The Heritage of Persia,* 2d ed. London: Cardinal, 1976.

von Gabain, Annemarie, "Vorislamische alttürkische Litteratur." *Handbuch der Orientalistik* 5.1 (Leiden/Koln, 1963): 207–28.

Gabrieli, Francesco. *Arab Historians of the Crusades.* Translated from Italian by E. J. Costello. Berkeley: Univ. of California Press, 1969.

Garbe, Richard. *Indien und das Christentum.* Tubingen, 1914. English translation by Lydia G. Robinson. *India and Christendom: The Historical Connections Between their Religions.* LaSalle, IL: Open Court, 1959.

Gardener, Percy. *The Coins of the Greek and Scythic Kings of Bactria and India in the British Museum.* London: British Museum Trustees, 1886.

Gavin, Frank. "Aphraates and the Jews: A Study of the Controversial Homilies of the Persian Sage in their Relation to Jewish Thought." Toronto: Trinity College, 1923. Reprint of Columbia Univ. Ph.D. diss. in *Journal of the Society of Oriental Research,* Toronto, 7, no. 3, 4.

Gelazius of Cyzicus. *Ecclesiastical History.* In Migne, *PG,* tome 65, col. 1342ff. An unofficial collection of the acts of the Council of Nicaea.

Ghirshman, Roman. *Iran: Parthians and Sassanians.* English translation by S. Gilbert and J. Emmons. London: Thames and Hudson, 1962.

Gibb, H. A. R. *The Arab Conquests in Central Asia.* London, 1923.

———. "Chinese Records of the Arabs in Central Asia." in *BSOS,* 2 (1922): 613–22.

———. *Studies on the Civilization of Islam.* Boston: Beacon, 1962.

———, and J. H. Kraemer, eds. *Shorter Encyclopedia of Islam.* Leiden: Brill, 1953.

Gismondi, H. *Maris, Amri et Slibae, De Patriarchis nestorianorum commentaria.* 2 vols. Berlin, 1896, 1899. Vol. 1, Mari; vol. 2, 'Amr and Saliba.

Glassé, Cyril. *The Concise Encyclopedia of Islam.* San Francisco; Harper & Row, 1989.

Goldziher, Ignaz. *Mohammedanische Studien.* 2 vols. Halle: Niemeyer, 1889.

The Gospel of Thomas. In *The Nag Hammadi Library.* Edited by James Robinson. English translation by T. O. Lambdin. San Francisco: Harper & Row, 1977.

de Gouvea, Antoine. *Jornado do Arcebispo Dom. Meneses . . .,* French translation of the Portuguese by J. B. Glen *Histoire Orientale, des grans progrès de l'Eglise Catholique Apostolique et Romaine. . . .* Anvers: Verdussen, 1609.

Graf, G. *Geschichte der christlichen arabischen Literatur*. Vol. 2. Studi e testi, 133. Vatican City, 1947.

Gregorios, Mar Paulos. *The Orthodox Church in India: An Overview*. Delhi and Kottayam: Sophia Publications, 1982.

Gregory of Tours. *De gloria martyrum*. In Migne, *PL*, tome 81.

Grillmeier, Aloys. *Christ in the Christian Tradition*. Vol. 1, *From the Apostolic Age to Chalcedon*. 2d ed. rev. English translation by J. Bowden. London and Oxford: Mowbray, 1975.

Grousset, Rene. *The Empire of the Steppes: A History of Central Asia*. Translated by N. Walford. New Brunswick, NJ: Rutgers Univ. Press, 1970.

von Grunebaum, G. E. *Classical Islam: A History 600–1258*. English translation from the German ed. of 1963 by K. Watson. London: Allen and Unwin, 1970.

Guidi, I., ed. *Chronicon Edessenum*, in *CSCO*, 3d ser., *Scriptores Syri*, vol. 4. Paris, 1903.

Guillaume, Alfred. *Islam*. 2d rev. ed. London: Cassell, 1963.

_____. *The Life of Muhammed: A Translation of Ishaq's Sirat Rasul Allah*. Oxford: Oxford Univ. Press, 1955.

von Gutshmid, A. *Untersuchungen über die Geschichte des Konigreiches Osrhoene*. Memoires de l'Academie imperiale des Sciences de S. Petersburg, series 7, vol. 35.1 (1887).

Gwynn, John. *The Apocalypse of St. John in a Syriac Version Hitherto Unknown*. Dublin and London: Hodges, Figgis, 1897.

_____. *Aphrat', Demonstrations in Nicene and Post Nicene Fathers*, 13. Grand Rapids: Eerdmans.

Hage, Wolfgang. "Early Christianity in Mesopotamia: Some Remarks Concerning the Authenticity of the Chronicle of Arbela." in *The Harp*, vol. 1. Kottayam, 1988.

_____. *Introduction, and Select Demonstrations of Aphrahat the Persian*. In *Nicene and Post-Nicene Fathers*, 2d series, vol. 13. Reprint. Grand Rapids: Eerdmans, 1983. Pp. 152–62; 345–412.

Haithon. *See* Hethum.

Hallier, Ludwig. *Untersuchungen über die Edessenische Chronik, mit dem Syrischen Text und einer Übersetzung*. Leipzig: Heinrichs'sche, 1892.

Hallock, F. H. "De Caritate." Aphrahat's second *Demonstration*. Translated into English, in *JSOR*, 14 (1930): 18–32.

Hambye, E. R. "Saint Thomas and India." *Clergy Monthly* 16, 1952: 363–75.

Handbuch der Orientalistik. Two series. Leiden/Koln: Brill, 1952–.

von Harnack, A. *Marcion, das Evangelium vom fremden Gott*. In *Texte und Untersuchungen zur Geschichte der alt-christlichen Literatur*, vol. 45, 2d ed. Leipzig: Hinrichs, 1924. *See also* English translation by J. F. Streeter and L. D. Bierma, *Marcion: The Gospel of the Alien God*, Durham, NC: Labyrinth Press, 1990.

Harris, J. R. *The Odes and Psalms of Solomon: Now First Published from the Syriac Version*. 2d ed. rev. Cambridge: Cambridge Univ. Press, 1911.

al-Hashimi 'abd Allah, *Dialogue islamo-chrétien sous le caliphe Al-Mamun (813–834): les épitres d'Al Hashimi et d'Al-Kindi*. Translated into French and edited by Georges Tarter. Paris: Nouvelles editions latines, 1985.

Hastings Encyclopedia of Religion and Ethics. 13 vols. New York: Scribner, 1910–27.

Haydar, Mirza Muhammad. *The Tarikh-i-Rashidi: A History of the Moghuls of Central Asia.* Edited by N. Elias and translated into English by E. D. Ross. 1895. Reprint. Delhi, India: Renaissance Publishing House, 1986.

Heimbucher, M. *Die Orden und Kongregationen der katholischen Kirche.* 2d ed. 3 vols. Paderborn: Schoningh, 1907.

Heissig, Walther. *The Religions of Mongolia.* Translated by G. Samuel. Berkeley: Univ. of California Press, 1980.

Heller, J. E. *Das Nestorianische Denkmal in Singan fu.* Budapest, 1897.

Hennecke, E. *New Testament Apocrypha.* Vol. 1. Edited by W. Schneemelcher; Eng. tr. by A. J. B. Higgins etc. and ed. by R. McL. Wilson (London: Lutterworth, 1963–66). Also published by Philadelphia: Westminster, 1964.

Heras, Henry. *The Two Apostles of India.* Trichinopoly: Catholic Truth Society of India, 1944.

Herodotus. *The Persian Wars.* Translated by H. Cary. London: Ball & Sons, Bohn's Classical Library, 1894.

Herzfeld, E. "Sakastan." *Archaeologische Mitteilungen aus Iran* 4 (Berlin, 1931–32): 1–116.

Hethum (Hetoum, Het'um, Haithon, or Haytonus). *Hetoum, A Lytell Cronycle: Richard Pynson's Translation (c. 1520) of La Fleur des histoires de la terre d'Orient (1307).* Edited by G. Burger. Toronto, Buffalo, London: Univ. of Toronto Press, 1988. The Latin text, *Flos Historiarum Terrae Orientis,* is in *Recueil des Historiens des Croisades, Documents arméniens.* Paris, 1906.

Higgins, M. J. "Chronology of the Fourth-Century Metropolitans of Seleucia-Ctesiphon." *Traditio* 9 (1953): 45–100.

———. "Aphraates' Dates for Persian Persecution." *Byzantische Zeitschrift* 44 (Munich, 1951): 265–71.

———. "Date of Martyrdom of Simeon bar-Sabba'e." *Traditio* 11 (1955): 1–17.

Hilgenfeld, A. *Bardesanes, der letzte Gnostiker.* Leipzig: Weigel, 1864.

Hippolytus. *Philosophoumena (Refutatio).* Edited by P. Wendland. In *Die griechischen christliche Schrifstellen der ersten Jahrhundert,* 26. Leipzig, 1916.

———. *Refutatio omnium haeresium.* Edited by M. Marcovich. New York, Berlin: DeGruyter, 1986. English translation by J. H. MacMahon in *Ante-Nicene Fathers.* Vol. 5 Reprint. Grand Rapids: Eerdmans, 1981. Pp. 9–153.

Hirth, F. *China and the Roman Orient, Researches into Their Ancient and Medieval Relations as Reprinted in Old Chinese Records.* Leipzig and Shanghai: Hirth, and Kelly and Walsh, 1885.

———. "The Story of Chang K'ien: A Translation of Chapter 123 of the Shi-ki of Ssu-ma Ch'ien." *Journal of the American Oriental Society* 37 (1917).

Histoire de Jaballaha (Yabalaha). Syriac text, ed. by P. Bedjan, *Histoire de Mar Jab-Alaha, patriarche, et de Rabban Cauma* (Paris 1888; enlarged ed. Leipzig, 1895); French translation by J. B. Chabot, *Histoire de Jabalaha III et du moine Rabban Cauma,* extract from *Revue de l'Orient,* I, II

(Paris, 1895); English translation by E. A. W. Budge, *The Monks of Kublai Khan* (London, 1928).

Histoire Nestorienne. See Chronicle of Seert.

Hitti, Philip, K. *History of the Arabs from the Earliest Times to the Present.* 5th ed. New York: Macmillan, 1951.

_____. *Origins of the Islamic State. See al-Baladhuri.*

Honigmann, Ernest. "La hiérarchie monophysite au temps de Jacques Baradée (542–578)." In *CSCO* [127], subsidia v.2 (Louvain, 1951), pp. 156–286.

Hookham, Hilda. *Tamburlaine the Conqueror.* London: Hodder and Stoughton, 1962.

Hosten, H. *Antiquities from San Thome and Mylapore.* Madras: Mylapore Diocese, 1936.

Howorth, Henry H. *History of the Mongols from the Ninth to the Nineteenth Century.* 5 vols. 1888. Reprint. Taiwan: Ch'eng Wen, 1970.

Hughes, T. P., ed. *Dictionary of Islam.* Lahore: Premier Book House, 1885. Reprint, 1964.

ibn-Ishaq, Muhammad. *Sirat Rasul Allah ("of the Messenger of God").* English translation of ibn-Hisham's edition, by A. Guillaume as *The Life of Muhammed.* London: Oxford University Press, 1955.

Indian Church History Review. Bangalore.

Indological and Buddhist Studies: Volume in Honour of Prof. J. W. de Jong. Edited by L. A. Hercus, et al. Canberra, Australia: Faculty of Asian Studies, 1982.

Isho'dad of Merv. *The Commentaries.* Edited by M. D. Gibson as *The Commentaries of Isho'dad of Merv.* In *Horae Semiticae.* Vols. 5, 6, 7, 10, 11, 2 parts. Cambridge, 1911–16.

Isho'yabh III, of Arbela. *Pastoral Epistles.* Edited by Philip Scott-Moncrieff as *The Book of Consolations, or the Pastoral Epistles of Mar Ish-yabh of Kuphlana in Adiabene.* Pt. I, the Syriac text. London: Luzac, 1904.

Iso'dena of Basra. See *Book of Chastity.*

Jackson, A. V. Williams. *Researches in Manichaeism, with Special Reference to the Turfan Fragments.* New York: Columbia Univ. Press, 1932.

Jackson, P. "The Dissolution of the Mongol Empire." *Central Asiatic Journal* 22, no. 3–4 (1978): 186–244.

Jacob of Edessa. "Two epistles of Jacob of Edessa." Edited by W. Wright. *Journal of Sacred Literature and Biblical Record.* New series, vol. 6 (1867): 430ff.

Jargy, S. "Les 'fils et filles du pacte' dans la littérature monastique syriaque." *Orientalia Christiana Periodica* (1951): 304–20.

Jiang Wen-Han. *Ancient Chinese Christianity and the Jews of Kaifeng.* Shanghai: Zhi Shi Press, 1982.

Jerome. *Epistola LXX ad Magnum oratorem urbis Romae,* in Migne, *PL* vol. 22, c. 667.

_____. *Liber de Viris Illustribus,* in Migne, *PL* vol. 36, c. 681–82.

_____. *Epistola LIX ad Marcellam,* in Migne, *PL* vol. 22, c. 589.

John of Cara. *The Book of the Estate of the Great Kaan* (attributed). English translation by H. Yule in vol. 3 of *Cathay and the Way Thither.* London: Hakluyt & Society, 1915. Pp. 89–103.

John of Damascus. *Writings.* Translated by Frederic H. Chase, Jr. Vol. 37 of *The Fathers of The Church.* New York: Fathers of the Church, Inc., 1958.

————. *Barlaam and Joasaph.* Translated by C. R. Woodward and H. Mattingly. London: Heinemann, 1914.

John of Ephesus. *Vita Baradaei* (in Syriac). Edited by J. P. N. Land. In *Analecta Syriaca.* Vol 2. Leiden, 1862–75. Also *PO,* vol. 18, pp. 600–607 in John's *Eastern Saints.*

Johnson, Paul. *A History of Christianity.* London: Weidenfeld and Nicolson, 1976.

Jones, Bayard H. "The History of the Nestorian Liturgies." *Anglican Theological Review* 46 (Evanston, IL, 1964): 155–76.

Joseph, T. K. "Constantine and the Indias." *Journal of Indian History* 18 (1950).

————. *The Malabar Christians and Their Ancient Documents.* Trivandrum, India, 1929.

JSOR. Journal of the Society of Oriental Research.

JTS. Journal of Theological Studies. Oxford.

Juhanon Mar Thoma. *Christianity in India and a Brief History of the Mar Thoma Syrian Church.* 4th ed. rev. and enlarged. Madras, India: Cherian, 1952.

Julius Africanus, Sextus. *Kestoi.* In M. Thevenot, *Veterum Mathematicorum Opera.* Paris, 1693. And in J. R. Viellefond, *Fragments des Cestes.* 1932.

Justin Martyr. *Dialogue with Trypho.* In A. Roberts and J. Donaldson, eds. *The Ante-Nicene Fathers.* New York: Scribner, 1903. Vol. 1, pp. 194–270.

————. *First Apology.* In Roberts and Donaldson. *Ante-Nicene Fathers.* Pp. 163–87.

————. *The Discourse to the Greeks.* In Roberts and Donaldson. *Ante-Nicene Fathers.* Pp. 271–89.

Juvaini, 'Ala al-din 'Ata-Malik. *The History of the World Conqueror (Tarikh-i Jahan gusha).* 2 vols. English translation from the Persian by John A. Boyle. Manchester, Eng.: Manchester Univ. Press, 1958.

Kaufhold, Hubert. *Die Rechtssammlung des Gabriel von Basra und ihr Verhaltnis zu den anderen Juristischen Sammelwerken der Nestorianer.* Syriac with German translation. Berlin: Schweitzer, 1976.

Keay, F. E. *A History of the Syrian Church in India.* 2d ed. Kanpur, India: SPCK, 1951.

Kelly, John N. D., *Early Christian Creeds.* 3d ed. New York: McKay, 1972.

————. *Early Christian Doctrines.* New York: Harper, 1959.

Kephalaia. Edited by C. Schmidt Stuttgart: Kohlhammer, 1935. Paul McGruckin. *Symeon, the New Theologian.* Kalamazoo, MI: Cistercian Publications, 1982.

Kidd, B. J. *The Churches of Eastern Christendom from A.D. 451 to the Present.* London: The Faith Press, 1927.

————. *A History of the Church to A.D. 461.* 3 vols. Oxford: Clarendon, 1922.

Kim, Yang-Sun. *History of the Korean Church in the Ten Years since Liberation (1945–1955.)* Seoul: mimeographed, ca. 1956.

al-Kindi, Abd al-Masih. *Dialogue islamo-chretien sous le calife Al-Mamun (813–834): les épitres d'Al-Hashimi et d'Al Kindi.* Translated into French by Georges Tartar. Paris: Nouvelles editions latines, 1985.

al-Kindi, Abu Umar Muhammad ibn Yusuf. *The History of the Governors of Egypt (Kitab al Umara).* New York: Columbia Univ. Press, 1908.

al-Kindi, Yakub ibn Ishak ibn Subbah. *Die philoshischen Abhandlungen des Jaqub ban Ishaq al-Kindi*. Edited by Albino Nagy. Munster: Ashendorff, 1897.

Kirakos of Ganjak. See French translation by M. J. Brosset. *Deux historiens arméniens Kirakos de Gantzag, Oukhtanes d'Ourha*. St. Petersburg, 1870–71. Extracts translated by Dulaurier. "Les Mongols d'apres les historiens arméniens." in *Journal Asiatique*, 5th series, vol. 11, pp. 192–255, 426–473, 481–508. And J. A. Boyle. "Kirakos of Ganjak on the Mongols." *Central Asiatic Journal* 9 (1964): 175-89.

Klijn, A. F. J. *The Acts of Thomas: Introduction, Text and Commentary*. Leiden: Brill, 1962.

_____. *Die Stadt des Apostels Thomas: Das Alteste Christentum in Syrien*. Giessen: Neukirchener Verlag des Erzeihungsverein, 1965.

Klima, O. *Mazdak*. (Prague: Nakladatelstvi akademie ved, 1957.

_____. *Manis Zeit und Leben*. Prague: Tschechoslowakischen Akademie der Wissenschaften, 1962.

Koester, Helmut, "Introduction to the Gospel of Thomas." In the *Nag Hammadi Library*. Edited by James Robinson. San Francisco: Harper & Row, 1977.

Konow, Sten, "Kalawan Copper-plate Inscription of the Year 134." *Journal of the Royal Asiatic Society*, new series, vol. 63 (London, 1932): 949ff., esp. 957.

Koran (al-Qur'an). In English translation: A. Yusuf Ali. *The Meaning of the Glorious Quran: Text, Translation and Commentary*. Cairo, Beirut, and Lahore, 1938ff. And A. J. Arberry. *The Koran Interpreted*. Oxford, London and New York: Oxford Univ. Press, 1964.

Kritzek, James. *Sons of Abraham: Jews, Christians and Moslems*. Baltimore and Dublin: Helicon, 1965.

Kruger, Paul. "Ein Missionsdokument aus Fruh Christlicher Zeit," *Zeitschrift fur Missionswissenschaft und Religionswissenschaft* 42 (1958): 271–91.

Kung, Tien Min. *Christianity in the T'ang Dynasty*. In Chinese. Hong Kong: Council on Christian Literature for Overseas Chinese, 1960.

Kuriakose, M. K. *History of Christianity in India: Source Materials*. Indian Theological Library, No. 9. Madras: Christian Literature Society, 1982.

Kuruvilla, K. K. *A History of the Mar Thoma Church and Its Doctrines*. Indian Research Series No. 5. Madras: Christian Literature Society for India, 1951.

Kwanten, Luc Herman M. *Imperial Nomads: A History of Central Asia, 500–1500*. Philadelphia: Univ. of Pennsylvania Press, 1979.

Kyriakon: Festschrisft Johannes Quasten. 2 vols. Edited by P. Granfield and J. A. Jungmann. Munster: Aschendorff, 1971.

Labourt, J. *Le Christianisme dans l'Empire Perse sous le dynastie Sassanide, 224–632*. Paris: Lecoffre, 1904.

Lamb, Harold. *Genghis Khan: Emperor of All Men*. New York: McBride, 1927.

_____. *Tamerlane: The Earth Shaker*. New York: McBride, 1928.

Lammens, Henri. "Le Chantre des Omiades, Notes biographiques et littéraires sur le poete Arabe Chrétien Ahtal." *Journal Asiatique* Neuvieme serie 4 (Paris, 1894): 94–176, 193–241, 381–459.

Langlois, John D., ed. *China Under Mongol Rule*. Princeton, NJ: Princeton Univ. Press, 1981.

Latourette, Kenneth Scott. *The Chinese: Their History and Culture*. 2d ed., rev. New York: Macmillan, 1941.

———. *A History of Christian Missions in China*. New York: Macmillan, 1929.

———. *A History of the Expansion of Christianity*. Vol. 1, *The First Five Centuries*. Vol. 2, *The Thousand Years of Uncertainty*. New York: Harper, 1937, 1938.

Ledyard, Gari. "The Mongol Campaigns in Korea and the Dating of the *Secret History of the Mongols*." *Central Asiatic Journal* 9 (1964): 1–22.

Lee, Shiu-Keung. *The Cross and the Lotus*. Hong Kong: Christian Study Centre on Chinese Religion and Culture, 1971.

Legge, Francis. *Forerunners and Rivals of Christianity, from 330 B.C. to A.D. 330*. Vol. 2. New Hyde Park, NY: University Books, 1964.

Legge, James. *The Nestorian Monument of Hsi-an Fu in Shen-hsi, China, Relating to the Diffusion of Christianity in China. . . .* London: Trubner, 1888.

Le Quien, Michel. *Oriens Christianus*. In *Quatuor Patriarchatus. . . .* Paris: Typographia Regia, 1740. Reprint. Graz: Akademische Druck-und Verlagstanstalt, 1958. 3 vols.

Leslie, Donald. *The Survival of the Chinese Jews: The Jewish Community of Kaifeng*. Leiden: Brill, 1972.

Le Strange, Guy. *Baghdad During the 'Abbasid Caliphate*. Oxford: Clarendon Press, 1924.

———. *Lands of the Eastern Caliphate; Mesopotamia, Persia and Central Asia; from the Muslim Conquest to the Time of Timur*. Cambridge, [Eng.]: University Press, 1905.

Lewis, Bernard. *The Arabs in History*. London, 1950.

———, and P. M. Holt, eds. *Historians of the Middle East*. London: Oxford Univ. Press, 1962.

———. *Islam from the Prophet Muhammad to the Capture of Constantinople*. Vol. 2, *Religion and Society*. New York: Harper & Row, 1974.

Liber Graduum (or *Book of Degrees*). Edited by M. Kmosko. *PS*, 3. Paris, 1926.

Lietzmann, H. *A History of the Early Church*. English translation by B. Lee Wolf. 4 vols. London: Lutterworth, 1937–51.

Lieu, S. N. C. *The Religion of Light: An Introduction to the History of Manichaeism in China*. Hong Kong: Centre of Asian Studies, Univ. of Hong Kong, 1979.

Loofs, F. *Nestorius and His Place in the History of the Christian Doctrine*. Cambridge: Cambridge Univ. Press, 1914. Reprint, New York: B. Franklin, 1975.

Ludemann, Gerd. "The Successors of Pre-70 Jerusalem Christianity: A Critical Evaluation of the Pella Tradition." in E. P. Sanders, ed. *Jewish and Christian Self-Definition*. Philadelphia: Fortress, 1980. Pp. 161–73.

Maalouf, Amin. *The Crusades Through Arab Eyes*. Translated by J. Rothschild. New York: Schocken, 1985.

MacGowan, J. *The Imperial History of China*. 2d ed. Shanghai: American Presbyterian Mission Press, 1906.

Mackerras, Colin. *The Uighur Empire According to the T'ang Dynastic Histories: A Study in Sino-Uighur Relations 744–840*. Canberra: Centre of Oriental Studies, Australian National University, 1968, and Columbia, SC: Univ. of South Carolina Press, 1980.

Maclean, Arthur John, and William Henry Browne. *The Catholicos of the East and His People*. London: SPCK, 1892.

Maenchen-Helfen, Otto J. *The World of the Huns: Studies in Their History and Culture*. Edited by Max Knight. Berkeley: Univ. of California Press, 1973.

_____. "Manichaeans in Siberia." In *Semitic and Oriental Studies Presented to William Popper*. Berkeley: Univ. of California Press, 1951.

Magie, David. *Roman Rule in Asia Minor to the End of the Third Century*. Princeton, NJ: Princeton Univ. Press, 1950.

Majumdar, R. C., ed. *The History and Culture of the Indian People*. Vol. 2. *The Age of Imperial Unity*. Bombay: Bharatiya Vidya Bhavan, 1951.

Malcolm, Sir John. *The History of Persia from the Most Early Period to the Present Time*. . . . 2 vols. London: Murray, 1815.

Malech, G. D. *History of the Syrian Nation and the Old Evangelical-Apostolic Church of the East*. Minneapolis: private, 1910.

Mar Aprem. *See* Aprem, Mar.

Mar Thoma, Alexander. *See* Alexander Mar Thoma.

Mar Thoma, Juhanon. *See* Juhanon Mar Thoma.

Marco Polo. *See* Polo, Marco.

Mari ibn Suleiman. *Liber Turris (Book of the Tower)*. Edited and translated into Latin by H. Gismondi. *Maris, Amri et Slibae, De Patriarchis nestorianorum commentaria*. 2 vols. Rome: C. de Luigi, 1896, 1899.

Maris, Amri et Slibae. *See* Mari ibn Suleiman, 'Amr ibn Matta and Saliba ibn Johannan.

Martin, F., ed. "Homélie de Narses sur les trois docteurs nestoriens." In *Journal Asiatique*, ser. 9, vol. 14 (1899): 446–92.

McCrindle, J. W., ed. and trans. *The Christian Topography of Cosmas, an Egyptian Monk*. London: Hakluyt Society, 1897.

McCullough, W. Stewart. *A Short History of Syriac Christianity to the Rise of Islam*. Chico, CA: Scholars Press, 1982.

McGiffert, A. C. *A History of Christian Thought*. Vol. 1. New York: Scribner, 1932.

McNamara, K. "Theodore of Mopsuestia and the Nestorian Heresy." *Irish Theological Quarterly* 19 (1952): 254–78; 20 (1953): 172–91.

McVey, Kathleen E., translated and intro. *Ephrem the Syrian: Hymns*. New York: Paulist Press, 1989.

_____. "A Memra on the Life of Severus of Antioch . . . by George, Bishop of the Arab Tribes". Ph.D. dissertation, Harvard, 1977.

Medleycott, A. E. *India and the Apostle Thomas, an Inquiry, with a Critical Analysis of the Acta Thomae*. London: David Nutt, 1905.

Metzger, Bruce M. *Early Versions of the New Testament, Their Origin, Transmission, and Limitations*. Oxford: Clarendon, 1977.

_____. "Seventy or Seventy-Two Disciples?" In *Historical and Literary Studies: Pagan, Jewish, and Christian*. Leiden: Brill, 1968. Pp. 67–76.

_____. *The Text of the New Testament, Its Transmission, Corruption, and Restoration*. 2d ed. New York: Oxford Univ. Press, 1968.

_____. "Witnesses to Tatian's Diatessaron." In *Chapters in the History of New Testament Textual Criticism*. Grand Rapids: Eerdmans, 1963.

Michael I, the Syrian. *Chronique de Michel le Syrien*. . . . 2 vols. Edited by J. B. Chabot. Paris, 1901. Reprint. Brussels, 1963.

Migne, J. P. *Patrologia Cursus Completus Series Graeca (PG)*. Greek texts with Latin translations. Paris, 1857–1912.

————. *Patrologia Cursus Completus Series Latina (PL)* Latin texts. Paris, 1844–64.

Miles of Susa, "Acts" (attributed). Edited and translated into Latin by S. E. Assemani in *Acta MM orientalium et occidentalium*. Vol. 1. Rome, 1748.

Mingana, A. "The Early Spread of Christianity in Central Asia and the Far East." *Bulletin of the John Rylands Library* 9, no. 2 (Manchester, July 1925): 297–371. Reprint with additions, 1925.

————. "The Early Spread of Christianity in India." *Bulletin of the John Rylands Library* 10, no. 2 (Manchester, July 1926): 435–510.

————. ed. and trans. *Sources Syriaques*. Vol. 1, *Msiha-zkha, Texte et Traduction* or *Historie de l'Église d'Adiabene*. Leipzig: Harrasowitz, 1907.

————. ed. and trans. *Job of Edessa, Encyclopedia of Philosophical and Natural Sciences as taught in Baghdad about 817 A.D., or Book of Treasures,* Woodbrooke Scientific Publications, vol. 1 (Cambridge: W. Heffer, 1932).

————. ed. and trans. *ali Tabari, The Book of Religion and Empire (Kitab al-din wal-dawlah)*. Manchester: Manchester Univ. Press, 1922.

————, ed. and trans. *Theodore of Mopsuestia on the Nicene Creed*. No. 5, Woodbrooke Studies. Cambridge: Heffer, 1932.

————, ed. and trans. *The Apology of Timothy the Patriarch before the Caliph Mahdi*. No. 3, Woodbrooke Studies, *Bulletin of the John Rylands Library* (Manchester, 1928): 137–298.

Moberg, Axel, ed. and trans. *The Book of the Himyarites*. London and Oxford: H. Milford, and Oxford University Press, 1924.

Moffatt, James. *The First Five Centuries of the Christian Church*. London: Univ. of London Press and Hodder and Stoughton, 1938.

Moidrey, Joseph de. "La hiérarchie catholique en Chine, en Corée, et au Japon (1307–1914)." *Variétés sinologique*, no. 38 (Shangai, 1914).

Mommsen, Theodore. *The Provinces of the Roman Empire*. Vol. 2. Translated by W. Dickson. London: Bentley, 1886.

Montgomery, James A., trans. and ed. *The History of Yaballaha III, Nestorian Patriarch, and of his Vicar, Bar Sauma, Mongol Ambassador to the Frankish Courts at the End of the Thirteenth Century*. New York: Columbia Univ. Press, 1927.

Mooker, George. "A Reappraisal of Nestorianorism." *Bangalore Theological Forum* 1 (Bangalore, India, 1967): 52–72.

Moraes, G. M. *A History of Christianity in India*. Vol. 1. Bombay: Manaktalas, 1964.

Mosheim, J. L. *Ecclesiastical History*. Translated by A. Maclaine. New York: Harper, 1879.

Moule, Arthur Christopher. *Christians in China Before the Year 1550*. London: Society for Promoting Christian Knowledge, 1930.

————. "Brother Jordan of Sévérac." *Journal of the Royal Asiatic Society*. New Series. Vol. 60 (London, 1928): 349–76.

————, and Paul Pelliot. *Marco Polo: The Description of the World*. 2 vols. London: Routledge, 1938.

————. *Nestorians in China, Some Corrections and Additions*. London: China Society, 1940.

Mourret, F., and N. Thompson. *History of the Catholic Church*. Vol. 2. St. Louis and London: Herder, 1935.

Msiha-zkha. *Histoire de l'Église d'Adiabene*. See A. Mingana, *Sources Syriaques*.

Muir, William. *The Life of Mohammed*. Edinburgh: Grant, 1923.

_____. *The Caliphate, Its Rise, Decline and Fall*. Rev. ed. Edinburgh: Grant, 1924.

Mundadan, A. Mathias. *History of Christianity in India*. Vol. 1, *From the Beginning up to the Middle of the Sixteenth Century (to 1542)*. Bangalore, India: Church History Association of India, 1984.

_____. *Indian Christians: Search for Identity and Struggle for Autonomy*. Bangalore, India: Dharmaram Publications, 1984.

_____. "Indian Church and the East Syrian Church: Part I, The East Syrian Church; Part II, Relations Before the Sixteenth Century." *Indian Church History Review* 6, no. 1 (Bangalore, June 1972): 23–42.

_____. *Sixteenth-Century Traditions of St. Thomas Christians*. Bangalore, India: Dharmaram College, 1970.

Murray, Robert. *Symbols of Church and Kingdom: A Study in Early Syriac Tradition*. Cambridge: Cambridge Univ. Press, 1975.

Nicene and Post-Nicene Fathers, First Series, Grand Rapids: Eerdmans, 1983.

Nicene and Post-Nicene Fathers, Second Series, Grand Rapids: Eerdmans, 1983.

al-Nadim, Muhammad ibn-Ishaq. *Fihrist*. Edited and German translation by G. Flugel. 1862. *The Fihrist of al-Nadim: a Tenth Century-Survey of Muslim Culture*. Edited and English translation by Bayard Dodge. New York: Columbia Univ. Press, 1970.

Narain, A. K. *The Indo-Greeks*. Oxford: Clarendon, 1957.

Narsai. "Les Homélies sur la Creation." Edited and translated by P. Gignoux, in *PO*, vol. 34, pp. 430–58.

_____. "Liturgical Homilies of Narsai." Edited with introduction by R. H. Connolly. In *Texts and Studies* 8 (Cambridge: Cambridge Univ. Press, 1909): 1–lxxvi, 1–84.

_____. *On the Three Doctors (Homélie de Narses sur les trois docteurs nestoriens)*. Edited and translated into French by F. Martin in *Journal Asiatique*, ser. 9, vol. 14 (1899), and in *Varia Syriaca*, vol. 1 (1900): 1–106.

_____. *Narsai doctorii syri homiliae et carmina*. 2 vols. Edited by A. Mingana. Mausilii: Typis Fratrum Praedicatorum, 1905.

_____. *Statutes of the School of Nisibis*. Edited and translated by A. Voobus. *Papers of the Estonian Theological School in Exile*, 12 (Stockholm, 1958).

Nasrallah, Joseph. *Saint Jean de Damas, Son époque, sa vie, son oeuvre*. Paris: Office des Éditions Universitaires, 1950.

Nau, F. *Une Biographie Inédité de Bardesane l'Astrologue; Tirée de l'histoire de Michel le Grand, Patriarche d'Antioche, 1126–1199*. Paris, 1897.

_____. *La première partie de l'histoire de Barhadbesabba 'Arbaia*. Syriac text and translation, *PO* 9, 23 (Paris, 1913, 1932).

_____. "Life of Maruta" by Denha. Edited by F. Nau in his "Histoires d'Ahoudemmeh et de Marouta. . . ." Introduction in French, text in Syriac. *PO*, 3 (1905).

————. "Life of Dioscurus by Theophistus." Translated into French in *Journal Asiatique*, series 10, vol. 1 (1903).

Nautin, Pierre. "L'auteur de la 'Chronique de Séert': Iso'denah de Basra." *Revue de l'Histoire des Religions* 185 (Paris, 1974): 113–26.

Neale, John Mason. *A History of the Holy Eastern Church: The Patriarchate of Alexandria.* Vol. 1. London: Masters, 1847.

Neill, Stephen. *A History of Christianity in India.* Vol. 1, *The Beginning to* A.D. *1707.* Cambridge: Cambridge Univ. Press, 1984.

Nestorius. *Bazaar of Heracleides.* Translated into English by anonymous author [R. H. Connolly] in J. F. Bethune-Baker, *Nestorius and His Teachings.* And by G. R. Driver and L. Hodgson. *Nestorius, The Bazaar of Heracleides.* 1925.

Neusner, Jacob. *Aphrahat and Judaism: The Christian-Jewish Argument in Fourth-Century Iran.* Studia Post-Biblica, no. 19. Leiden: Brill, 1971.

————. "The Conversion of Adiabene to Christianity." *Numen,* no. 13 (Leiden, 1966): 144–50.

————. "The Conversion of Adiabene to Judaism." *Journal of Biblical Literture* 83, no. 1 (1964): 60–66.

————. *A History of the Jews in Babylonia.* Vol. 1, *The Parthian Period.* Vols. 2–5, *The Sassanian Period.* Studia Post-Biblica, nos. 9, 11–12, 14–15. Leiden, 1966–70.

Nicene and Anti-Nicene Fathers. Grand Rapids: Eerdmans, 1952ff.

Nicholson, Reynold A. *The Mystics of Islam.* London: Bell, 1914.

Nock, A. D. "Gnosticism." In *Arthur Darby Nock: Essays on Religion and the Ancient World.* Edited by Z. Stewart. Vol 2. Oxford: Clarendon, 1972.

Omar, Farouk. *The 'Abbasid Caliphate, 132/750–170/786.* Baghdad: Univ. of Baghdad, 1969.

Orosius. *Historiae (The Seven Books of History against the Pagans).* English translation by R. J. Deferrari. Washington, DC: Catholic Univ. of America Press, 1964. Esp. Book 7.

Ostrogorsky, G. *History of the Byzantine State.* Translated from German by J. M. Hussey. New Brunswick, NJ: Rutgers Univ. Press, 1957.

PG Patrologia . . . Graeca, ed. Migne.

PL Patrologia . . . Latina, ed. Migne.

PO Patrologia Orientalis.

PS Patrologia Syriaca.

Pan Ku. *Annals of the Former Han, Ch'ien han shu.* Translated by A. Wylie. "Notes on the Western Regions: Translation of Chapter 96, pt. 2 of the *Ch'ien han-shu*," *Journal of the Anthropological Institute,* vol. 11 (1882).

Panikkar, K. M. *Studies in Indian History.* Bombay: Asia Publishing House, 1963.

Parisot, Jean, ed. Aphrahat, *Demonstrations,* 1–22 in *PS* vol. 1 (1894); *Demonstration* 23, in vol. 2 (1907), pp. 1–1050; Preface, pp. ix–xl.

Parrinder, Geoffrey. *Jesus in the Qur'an.* London: Shedon, 1965.

Pass, H. L. "The Creed of Aphraates." *Journal of Theological Studies* 9 (Oxford and London, 1908).

Patrologia . . . Graeca. 162 vols. Greek text, Latin translation, edited by J. P. Migne. Paris, 1857–1912.

Patrologia . . . Latina. 221 vols. Latin texts edited by J. P. Migne. Paris, 1844–1864.

Patrologia Orientalis. Vols. 1–34, Paris, 1966; vols. 35–43, Turnhout, 1969–1986.

Patrologia Syriaca. 3 vols. Paris, 1893–1926. Vol. 2 edited by O. de Urbina. Rome, 1965.

Peeters, P. "La date du martyre de S. Symeon, archevêque de Seleucia-Ctesiphon." *Analecta Bollandiana* 56 (Brussels, 1938): 118–43.

Pelliot, Paul. "Chrétiens de l'Asie Centrale et d'Extrême-Orient." *T'oung Pao* 15 (Shanghai/Leiden: Brill, 1914): 623–44; (1927): 159.

————. "Le vrai nom de 'Seroctan.'" *T'oung Pao* 29 (1932): 43–54.

————. "Les traditions manichéennes au Fou-kien." *T'oung Pao* 23 (1923): 193–208.

————. *Notes on Marco Polo.* 2 vols. Paris: Adrien-Maisonneuve, 1949.

————. *Recherches sur les Chrétiens d'Asie Centrale et d'Extrême-Orient,* 2 vols. Vol. 1, in 3 parts: "Jean du Plan Carpin; Guillaume de Rubrouck; Mar Ya(h)b'allaha, Rabban Suma et les princes Ongut chrétiens." Paris: Imprimerie Nationale, 1973. Vol. 2 "La Stèle de Si-Ngan-Fou." Paris: Fondation Singer-Polignac, 1983.

Periplus Maris Erythraei (The Periplus of the Erythraean Sea: Travel and Trade in the Indian Ocean). Edited and translated by W. H. Schoff. New York: Longmans, Green, 1912.

Perowne, Stewart. *Caesars and Saints: The Evolution of the Christian State,* A.D. *180–313.* London: Hodder and Stoughton, 1962.

————, and E. R. Hambye, eds. *Christianity in India: A History in Ecumenical Perspective.* Alleppey, India: Prakasam Publications, 1972.

Philipose, A. *The Apostolic Origin and Early History of the Syrian Church of Malabar.* 1904.

Philipps, W. R. "The Connection of St. Thomas the Apostle with India." Reprint from the *Indian Antiquary* 32 (Bombay, India, 1903): 1–15; 145–60.

Phillips, George, ed. and trans. *The Doctrine of Addai the Apostle.* 1876.

Phillips, E. D. *The Royal Hordes, Nomad Peoples of the Steppes.* London: Thames and Hudson, 1965.

Philostorgius. *Ecclesiastical History.* In Photius, *Bibliotheca, PG,* ci–civ.

Philoxenus of Mabbog. *Discourses of Philoxenus . . . on the Christian Life.* Edited and translated into English by E. A. W. Budge. 2 vols. London, 1893, 1894.

Podipara, Placid J. *The Thomas Christians.* London: Darton, Longman and Tidd, 1970.

Plano Carpini, John of. *Journey. See* W. W. Rockhill; and Christopher Dawson.

Pliny, the Younger. *Letters.* In Loeb Classical Library. New York and London, 1926–32.

Plooij, D. "The Attitude of the Outspread Hands (Orante) in Early Christian Literature and Art." *Expository Times* 22 (Edinburgh, 1912).

Polo, Marco. *The Book of Ser Marco Polo, the Venetian, Concerning the Kingdoms and Marvels of the East.* 2 vols. Translated and edited with notes by Henry Yule. 3d ed. revised by Henri Cordier. London: Murray, 1903.

————. *The Description of the World.* 2 vols. Edited by A. C. Moule and Paul Pelliot. Vol. 1 edited and translated by A. C. Moule. London: Routledge, 1938.

Pothan, S. G. *The Syrian Christians of Kerala.* 4th ed. Madras: K. M. Cherian, 1968.

Prawdin, Michael [Charol]. *The Mongol Empire, Its Rise and Legacy.* Translated from the Russian by Eden and Paul Cedar. London: Allen and Unwin, 1940.

Procopius of Caesarea. *De Bello Persico.* Edited by J. Haury in *Procopius Caesarensis opera.* 3 vols. Leipzig, 1905–13. English translation by H. B. Dewing. New York: Macmillan, 1914–40.

Pseudo-Clementine. *De Virginitate de S. Clement ou de S. Athanase?* Edited by L. Th. Lefort in *Le Museon* 40 (1927).

Pseudo-Elias Damascenus. Edited by J. S. Assemani. *Bibliotheca Orientalis clementino-vaticana.* Vol. 2. Rome, 1721. P. 392.

Pseudo-Elias Nisibenus. Prefix to Elias, *Opus chronologicon.*

Ptolemy. *Geographia.* Translated and edited by Edward Lutha Stevenson as *Geographia of Claudius Ptolemy.* New York: New York Public Library, 1932.

Puech, H. Ch. *Le Manichéisme. Son fondateur, sa doctrine.* Paris, Civilisations du Sud, S.A.E.R., 1949.

Putnam, Hans. *L'Église et l'Islam sous Timothée I (780–823): Étude sur Église Nestorienne au Temps des Premiers Abbasides.* Recherches: l'Institut de lettres Orientales de Beyrouth, Nouvelle Serie, B., *Orient Chrétien,* Tome III. Beirut: Dar el-Machreq, 1975.

Quasten, J. *Patrology.* 3 vols. Utrecht-Antwerp: Spectrum, 1950, 1975.

Quatremere, E. Marc. *Historie des Mongols de la Perse écrite en persan par Raschid-eldin.* Paris: Geuthner, 1836.

Quispel, G. "Gnosticism and the New Testament." In J. P. Hyatt, ed., *The Bible in Modern Scholarship.* London: Kingsgate, 1965. Pp. 252–71.

Rachewiltz, Igor de. *Papal Envoys to the Great Khans.* London: Faber & Faber, 1971.

Rae, G. Milne. *The Syrian Church in India.* Edinburgh, London: Blackwood, 1892.

Rapson, E. J., ed. *The Cambridge History of India.* Vol. 1. Cambridge: Cambridge University Press, 1922.

Rashid al-Din. *Compendium of World Histories (Jami' al-Tawarikh), Part 1.* Translated into English by John A. Boyle as *The Successors of Genghis Khan.* New York and London: Columbia Univ. Press, 1971.

Rawlinson, G. *The Sixth Great Oriental Monarchy, . . . Parthia. . . .* London: Longmans, Green, 1873.

———. *The Seventh Great Oriental Monarchy, . . . Sassanian. . . .* London: Longmans, Green, 1876.

Reischauer, Edwin O., and J. K. Fairbank. *East Asia: The Great Tradition.* Boston: Houghton Mifflin, 1958.

Riasanovsky, V. A. *Fundamental Principles of Mongol Law.* The Hague: 1965.

Ricci, Matteo. *Opera storiche del P. Matteo Ricci.* 2 vols. Edited by Tacchi Venturi. Macerata, 1911, 1913.

Richard, Jean. "La conversion de Berke et les débuts de l'islamisation de la Horde d'Or." *Revue des études islamiques* 35 (1967): 173–84.

Richards, W. J. *The Indian Christians of St. Thomas.* London, 1908.

Robinson, James, ed. *The Nag Hammadi Library.* San Francisco: Harper & Row, 1977.

Rocca, Father. "La leggende de S. Tomaso Apostolo." In *Orientala Christiana*, vol. 32, 89. Rome: Pont. Institutum Orientalium Studiorum, 1938.

Rockhill, William W. *The Journey of William of Rubruck to the Eastern Parts, 1253–55, with Two Accounts of the Earlier Journey of John of Pian de Carpine*. London: Hakluyt Society, 1900.

Rodinson, Maxime. *Mohammed*. English translation from the French by Anne Carter. Harmondsworth, Eng.: Penguin Books, 1971.

Rosenkranz, Gerhard. *Die Alteste Christenheit in China, in den Quellenzeugnissen der Nestorianen.* . . . Berlin: Verlag der Ostasien-Mission, 1938.

Rossabi, Morris, ed. *China Among Equals: The Middle Kingdom and Its Neighbors, Tenth—Fourteenth Centuries*. Berkeley: Univ. of California Press, 1983.

———. *Khubilai Khan: His Life and Times*. Berkeley: Univ. of California Press, 1988.

Rostovtzeff, M. I. *Dura-Europos and Its Art*. Oxford: Clarendon, 1938.

Rubruck, William of. *Journey*. See W. W. Rockhill; and Christopher Dawson.

Rothstein, G. *Die Dynastie der Lahmiden in al-Hira*. Berlin: Rothstein, 1899.

Rucker, Ignaz. *Studien zum Concilium Ephesinum.* . . . Vol. 4. Oxenbrunn: Selbstverlag des Verfassers, 1934.

Rudolph, Kurt R. *The Nature and History of Gnosticism*. San Francisco: Harper & Row, 1982.

Ryckmans, Gonzague. "Une inscription chrétienne sabéenne aux Musees d'Antiquites d'Istanbul." *Le Muséon* 59 (Louvain, 1946): 165–72.

———. *Les Religions arabes pre-islamiques*. 2d ed. Louvain: Publications Universitaires, 1951.

Ryckmans, Jacques. "Le Christianisme en Arabie du Sud pre-islamique." In *L'Orient cristiano nella storia della Civilta*. Rome: Academia nazionale dei Lincei, 1964. Pp. 413–53.

———. *La Persécution des Chrétiens Himyarites au Sixième Siècle*. Istanbul: Nederlands Hist.-Arch. Inst. in het Nabije Oosten, 1956.

Sachau, C. E. *Die Chronik von Arbela: Ein Beitrag zur Kenntnis des altesten Christentums im Orient*. Berlin: konigl preuss. Akademie der Wissenschaft, 1915. See also French translation by A. Mingana. *Sources Syriaque*. 1907.

———. *Zur ausbreitung des Christentums in Asien*. Berlin: Georg Reimer, 1919.

Saeki, P. Yoshiro. *The Nestorian Documents and Relics in China*. 2d ed., rev. and enlarged. Tokyo: Maruzen, 1951.

Sahas, David J. *John of Damascus on Islam: "The Heresy of the Israelites."* Leiden: Brill, 1972.

Saliba (Sliba) ibn Johannan. *De patriarchis nestorianorum commentaria*. Edited by H. Gismondi. *Maris, 'Amr et Slibae.* . . . Rome, 1896–99.

Salibi, Kamal S. "The Maronite Church in the Middle Ages." *Oriens Christianus* 42 (1958): 92–104.

Sanders, E. P. *Jewish and Christian Self-Definition*. Vol. 1, *The Shaping of Christianity in the Second and Third Centuries*. London: SCM, 1980.

Saunders, J. J. *A History of Medieval Islam*. New York: Barnes and Noble, 1965.

————. *The History of the Mongol Conquests.* London: Routledge & Kegan Paul, 1971.

Schaeder, H. H. "Bardesanes von Edessa in der Überlieferung der griecheshen und syrischen Kirche." *Zeitshrift für Kirchengeschichte* 51 (Stuttgart, 1932).

Schafer, Edward H. "Iranian Merchants in T'ang Dynasty Tales." *Univ. of California Publications in Semitic Philology* 11 (Berkeley): 403ff.

Scher, Addai. *See Chronicle de Séert (Histoire Nestorienne).*

Schimmel, Annemarie. *Mystic Dimensions of Islam.* Chapel Hill: Univ. of North Carolina Press, 1975.

Schmidlin, Joseph. *Catholic Mission History.* English translation by M. Braun. Techny, IL: Mission Press, 1933.

Schoff, W. H., ed. and trans. *The Periplus of the Erythraean Sea.* London, New York, Bombay: Longmans, Green, 1912.

Schwartz, E. "Die sogenannten Gegenanathematismen des Nestorius." In *Sitzungsberichte der Bayrischen Akademie der Wissenschaften, philosophisch-philologisch-historische Klasse.* Munich, 1922.

————. "Zur Vorgeschichte des ephesinischen Konzils: Ein Fragment." *Historische Zeitschrift* (Munich, 1914): 237–63.

Schwen, Paul. *Afrahat, seine Person und sein Verständnis des Christentums: Ein Betrag zur Geschichte der Kirche im Osten.* Berlin: Trowitsch, 1907.

Scott-Moncrieff, Philip. *The Book of Consulation, or the Pastorial Epistles of Mar Isho-yabh of Kuphlana in Adiabene.* Pt. 1, the Syrian Text. London: Luzac, 1904.

Scullard, H. H. *From the Gracchi to Nero.* London: Methuen, 1959.

Secret History of the Mongols (Yuan Ch'ao pi-shih). See Francis W. Cleaves; and B. Spuler.

Segal, J. B. *Edessa, The Blessed City.* Oxford: Clarendon, 1970.

————. Review of E. M. Yamauchi's *Gnostic Ethics and Mandaean Origins. Bulletin of the School of Oriental and Asian Studies* 36. London, 1973.

————. Review of A. F. J. Klijn's *The Acts of Thomas. BSOAS* 27 (1965).

Sellers, Robert V. *The Council of Chalcedon, A Historical and Doctrinal Survey.* London: SPCK, 1953.

————. *Two Ancient Christologies: A Study in the Christological Thought of the Schools of Alexandria and Antioch in the Early History of Christian Doctrine* (London: SPCK, 1954).

Setton, Kenneth M., et al., eds. *A History of the Crusades.* 5 vols. Madison: Univ. of Wisconsin Press, 1969–1985.

Shaban, M. A. *Islamic History: A New Interpretation,* A.D. *750–1055 (*A.H. *132–448).* Cambridge: Cambridge Univ. Press, 1976.

Siddiqi, M. Mazheruddin. *Development of Islamic State and Society.* Lahore, Pakistan: Institute of Islamic Culture, 1956.

Smallwood, E. Mary. *The Jews Under Roman Rule: From Pompey to Diocletian.* Leiden: Brill, 1976.

Smith, A. V. *Early History of India.* 4th ed. Oxford, 1924.

Smith, George. *The Conversion of India.* London: Murray, 1893.

Smith, John Masson. "'Ayn Jalut: Mamluk Success or Mongol Failure?" *Harvard Journal of Asiatic Studies* 44, no. 2 (December 1984): 307–45.

Smith, Vincent A. *Catalogue of the Coins in the Indian Museum in Calcutta.* Vol. 1. Oxford: Clarendon, 1906.

Socrates "Scholasticus." *Historia ecclesiastica.* Translation into English with notes by A. C. Zenos in *Nicene and Post-Nicene Fathers,* 2d series, vol. 2, pp. 1–178. Grand Rapids: Eerdmans, 1983.

Sozomen. *Ecclesiastical History.* Translation into English with notes by C. D. Hartranft in Nicene and Post-Nicene Fathers 2, vol. 2, pp. 179–427. Grand Rapids: Eerdmans, 1983.

Spuler, B. "The Disintegration of the Caliphate in the East." In P. M. Holt, et al., eds. *Cambridge History of Islam.* Vol. 1. Cambridge: Cambridge Univ. Press, 1970. Pp. 143–74.

Spuler, B. *History of the Mongols, Based on Eastern and Western Accounts of the Thirteenth and Fourteenth Centuries.* English translation from the German by H. and D. Drummond. London: Routledge and Kegan Paul, 1972.

_____. *Die Morgenlandischen Kirchen,* Handbuch der Orientalistik, Erste Abteilung, Band 8, Abschnitt 2. Leiden, 1961.

_____. *Die Mongolen in Iran.* 3d ed. Berlin, 1968.

_____. *The Muslim World, A Historical Survey.* English translation from the German by F. R. C. Bagley. 3 vols. Pt. 1, "The Age of the Caliphs"; Pt. 2, "The Mongol Period." Leiden: Brill, 1960, 1969.

Stewart, J. *Nestorian Missionary Enterprise: The Story of a Church on Fire.* Edinburgh: Clark, 1928.

Stone, D. *Episcopacy and Valid Orders in the Primitive Church.* London, New York, Bombay: Rising House Occasional Papers, 1910.

Strabo. *Geographica.* London and New York: Loeb Classical Library, 1917.

Strauss, E. "The Social Isolation of Ahl al-Dhimma." In *P. Hirschler Memorial Book.* Budapest, Hungary, 1949. Pp. 73–94. Reprinted under the name of Eliyahu Ashtor in *The Mediaeval Near East,* Variorum Reprints, no. 7, 1978.

Streeter, B. H., *The Primitive Church, Studied with Special Reference to the Origin of the Christian Ministry.* New York: Macmillan, 1929.

Sunquist, Scott. "Narsai and the Persians: A Study in Cultural Contact and Conflict." Diss., Princeton Theological Seminary, 1990.

Suter, R. "The words *san-i-fan-shen* in the inscription on the Nestorian Monument at Hsian-Fu." *Journal of the American Oriental Society* 58 (New Haven, 1938): 384–93.

Swete, H. B. *Theodore of Mopsuestia on the Minor Epistles of St. Paul.* 2 vols. Cambridge, 1880–82.

Sykes, Percy. *A History of Persia.* 3d ed., 2 vols. London: Macmillan, 1951.

Synodicon Orientale ou Recueil de Synodes Nestoriens. Edited and translated into French by J. B. Chabot (Paris: Klincksieck, 1902).

al-Tabari, Abu Ja'far Muhammad. *Annals of the Prophets and Kings (Tarikh al-Rusul wal-Muluk).* Edited by M. J. de Goeje. Leiden, 1879–1901.

al-Tabari, 'Ali ibn Sahl. *The Book of Religion and Empire (Kitab al-din wal-dawlah).* English translation by A. Mingana (Manchester, Eng. Manchester Univ. Press, 1922).

_____. *Chronique.* 4 vols. French translation by Herman Zotenbert. Paris: Imprimerie Nationale, 1867–74.

Taggart, Frederick. *Rome and China: A Study in Correlations in Historical Events.* (Berkeley: Univ. of California Press, 1939).

T'ang Dynasty Histories: *Chiu T'ang shu,* ca. 941 (Peking, 16 vols., 1975); *Hsin T'ang shu,* 11th c. (Peking, 20 vols, 1975); *Tzu-chi t'ing-chien,* by Ssu-ma Kuang, 11th c.; *T'ang hui yao,* 9th or 10th c. (Shanghai, 1936).

Tarik-i-Rashidi. See Haydar, Mirza Muhammad.

Tarn, W. W. *The Greeks in Bactria and India.* 2d ed. Cambridge: Cambridge Univ. Press, 1951.

Tartar, Georges. *Dialogue Islamo-Chrétien sous le calife Al-Ma'mun (813–834): les épitres d'Al-Hashimi et d'Al-Kindi.* Paris: Nouvelles Editions Latines, 1985.

Tatian. "Address to the Greeks." Chap. 42. English translation in *The Ante-Nicene Fathers.* Vol. 3. New York: Scribner, 1903.

Telfer, W. *The Office of a Bishop.* London: Darton, Longman & Todd, 1962.

Testuz, M. *Papyrus Bodmer. 10–12.* Cologny-Geneve: Bibliotheca Bodmeriana, 1959.

Thapar, Romila. *A History of India.* Vol. 1. Harmondsworth, Eng.: Penguin, 1966.

———. *Asoka and the Decline of the Mauryas.* Oxford: Clarendon, 1961.

Theodoret of Cyrrhus. *Ecclesiastical History.* English translation with introduction and notes by Bloomfield Jackson in *Ante-Nicene Fathers,* 2d series, vol. 3. Grand Rapids: Eerdmans, 1983. Pp. xi–159.

———. *History of the Syrian Monks.* 2 vols. Edited by Pierre Canivet and Alice Leroy-Mohlingen in French in *Sources Chrétiennes.* Vols. 234, 257. Paris: 1977, 1979.

Thomas, A. *Histoire de la Mission de Pékin, depuis les origines jusqu'à l'arrivée des Lazaristes.* Paris: Louis-Michaud editeur, 1923.

Thomas of Marga. *See* E. A. W. Budge, *Book of Governors.*

Thomas, F. W., "The Date of Kaniska." *Journal of the Royal Asiatic Society* (London, 1913): 627–50.

Timothy I. *Apology. See* A. Mingana, *The Apology of Timothy.*

———. *Letters.* Edited by O. Braun as *Timothei Patriarchae I epistolae* (letters 21 and 39), in *CSCO, Scriptores Syri,* series 2a, t. 57 (1914–15).

Tisserant, E. *Eastern Christianity in India: A History of the Syro-Malabar Church from the Earliest Time to the Present Day.* Translated and edited by E. R. Hambye. Westminster, MD: Newman Press, 1957.

Tixeront, L. J. *Les Origines l'église d'Édesse et la légende d'Abgar.* Paris: Maisonneuve et Ch. Le Clerc, 1888.

Tonneau, R. Devreesse. "Les homélies catéchetiques de Théodore de Mopsueste." *Studi e Testi,* no. 45 (Citta del Vaticano, 1949).

Torrance, Thomas. *China's First Missionaries: Ancient "Israelites."* 2d ed. rev. Chicago: Daniel Shaw, 1988.

Trimingham, J. Spencer. "Mawiyya: The First Christian Arab Queen." *The Near East School of Theology Theological Review* 1, no. 1 (Beirut, 1978): 3–10.

———. *Christianity Among the Arabs in Pre-Islamic Times.* London and New York/Beirut: Longman/Librairie du Liban, 1979.

Tritton, A. S. *The Caliphs and Their Non-Muslim Subjects: A Critical Study of the Covenant of 'Umar.* London: Frank Cass, 1930; reprint 1970.

Tucci, Giuseppe. *Die Religionen Tibets.* Stuttgart, 1970. English translation by G. Samuel as *The Religions of Tibet.* London: Routledge and Kegan Paul, 1980, and Berkeley, CA: Univ. of California Press, 1980.

Turner, H. E. W., *The Pattern of Christian Truth: A Study in the Relation Between Orthodoxy and Heresy in the Early Church* London: Mowbray, 1954.

Unvala, J. M. *Observations on the Religion of the Parthians.* Bombay: private, 1925.

Van den Eynde, C. "Isho'dad of Merv, Commentary on the Old Testament." In *CSCO, Scriptores Syri*, vol. 30, p. 97. Louvain, 1963.

Van der Ploeg, J. P. M. *The Christians of St. Thomas in South India and Their Syriac Manuscripts.* Bangalore, India: Dharmaram Publications, 1983.

Van Lohuizen-De Leeuw, J. "The Scythian Period." Diss., Leiden, 1949.

Varaghese, V Titus, and P. P. Philip. *Glimpses of the History of the Christian Churches in India.* Madras, India: Christian Literature Society, 1983.

Vasiliev, Alexander A. *History of the Byzantine Empire, 324–1453.* 2 vols. Translated from the Russian. Madison: Univ. of Wisconsin Press, 1958.

Vine, Aubrey R. *An Approach to Christology: An Interpretation and Development of Some Elements in the Metaphysic and Christology of Nestorius.* London: Independent Press, 1948.

_____. *The Nestorian Churches: A Concise History of Nestorian Christianity in Asia from the Persian Schism to the Modern Assyrians.* London: Independent Press, 1937.

Voobus, Arthur. *Celibacy, A Requirement for Admission to Baptism in the Early Syrian Church.* Papers of the Estonian Theological Society in Exile. Stockholm, 1951.

_____. *Early Versions of the New Testament. . . .* Papers of the Estonian Theological Society in Exile. Stockholm, 1954.

_____. *History of Asceticism in the Syrian Orient.* 2 vols. In *CSCO*, vols. 184, 197, Subsidia t. 14, 17 (Louvain: 1958, 1960).

_____. *History of the School of Nisibis.* In *CSCO*, vol. 266, Subsidia t. 26 (Louvain, 1965).

_____. "Investigations into the Text of the New Testament Used by Rabbula of Edessa." In *Contributions of the Baltic Univ.* 59 (Pinneberg, 1947).

_____. "A Letter of Ephrem to the Mountaineers." In *Contributions of the Baltic Univ.* 51 (Pinneberg, 1947).

_____. *Peschitta und Targumim des Pentateuchs: Neues Licht zur Frage der Herkunft der Peschitta aus dem altpalastinischen Targum.* Handschriftstudien. Papers of the Estonian Theological Society in Exile. Vol. 9. Stockholm, 1957.

_____. *Statutes of the School of Nisibis,* Papers of the Estonian Theological Society in Exile. Vol. 12. Stockholm, 1962.

_____. *Studies in the History of the Gospel Text in Syriac.* In *CSCO* [128], subsidia t. 3. Louvain, 1951. Pp. 1–xxv, 1–201.

_____. "Un vestige d'une lettre de Narsai et son importance historique." *L'Orient Syrien* 11 (1964): 515–23.

Waddell, Helen. *The Desert Fathers.* London: Constable, 1936.

Warmington, E. H. *The Commerce Between the Roman Empire and India.* 2d ed. London and New York: Curzon and Octagon, 1974.

Waterfield, Robin E. *Christians in Persia, Assyrians, Armenians, Roman Catholics and Protestants.* London: Allen and Unwin, 1973.

Watt, W. Montgomery. *Muhammed at Mecca.* Oxford: Clarendon, 1953.

_____. *Muhammed at Medina.* Oxford: Clarendon, 1956.

Weinstein, Stanley. "Imperial Patronage in the Formation of T'ang

Buddhism." In A. F. Wright and D. Twitchett. *Perspectives on the T'ang.* Taiwan: Rainbow Bridge, 1973.

Widengren, George. *Mani and Manichaeanism.* English translation by Charles Kessler. London: Trinity Press, 1966.

Wiessner, Gernot. "Untersuchungen zu einer Gruppe syrischer Martyrakten aus der Christenverfolgung Schapurs II." Doctoral diss., Wurzburg, 1962.

Wigram, W. A. *History of the Assyrian Church* A.D. *100–640.* London: SPCK, 1910.

Wilson, R. McL. *The Gnostic Problem.* London: Mowbray, 1958.

Wiltsch, J. E. T. *Handbuch der kirchlichen geographie und statistik.* Berlin: H. Schultz, 1846.

Wolska-Conus, Wanda. *Cosmas Indicopleustes.* In *Sources Chrétiennes.* Paris, 1968, 1970, 1973.

Woodcock, George. *The Greeks in India.* London: Faber and Faber, 1966.

Woodward, E. L. *Christianity and Nationalism in the Later Roman Empire.* London: Longmans, Green, 1916.

Workman, H. B. *The Evolution of the Monastic Ideal. . . .* London: Epworth, 1913.

Wright, Arthur F., and Denis Twitchett. *Perspectives on the T'ang.* Taiwan: Rainbow Bridge, 1973.

Wright, W., ed. "Two Epistles of Jacob of Edessa." Syriac text and notes in *Journal of Sacred Literature,* N Series, X (London, 1867): 430–60.

———. *A Short History of Syriac Literature.* London: Black, 1894.

———. "Syriac Literature." In *Encyclopedia Britannica,* 9th ed.

Wylie, A. "Nestorian Monument at Si-ngan Fu, China." *The Missionary Review* 8, no. 3 (Princeton, May–June 1885): 184–87.

XuASTVANIFT: Studies in Manichaeism. Edited by J. P. Asmussen. Copenhagen: Munksgaard, 1965.

Yarshater, Ehsan. "Manichaeism and Its Iranian Background." In *Cambridge History of Iran.* Vol. 3. 1983. Pp. 965–90.

Young, John M. L. "The Theology and Influence of the Nestorian Mission to China, 635–1036," in 2 parts. *Reformed Bulletin of Missions* 5, no. 1 (Philadelphia, November 1969): 1–18, and no. 2 (April 1970): 1–20.

Young, William G. "The Church of the East in 650 A.D. Patriarch Ishv'-Yabh [Yeshvyah] III and India." *Indian Church History Review,* 2, no. 1 (1988): 55-71. *Handbook of Source Materials for Students of Church History Indian Theological Library No. 2.* Madras: Christian Literature Society, 1969.

———. *Patriarch, Shah and Caliph.* Rawalpindi, India: Christian Study Center, 1974.

Yule, Henry, trans. *The Book of Ser Marco Polo, the Venetian, Concerning the Kingdoms and Marvels of the East.* 2 vols., 3d. ed. rev. by Henri Cordier (London: John Murray, 1903).

———. Edited by H. Cordier. *Cathay and the Way Thither,* 4 vols. London: Hakluyt Society, 1913–16. Republished in 2 vols. Taipei, Taiwan: Ch'eng-Wen, 1966.

Zachariah of Mitylene. *Ecclesiastical History.* Edited by E. W. Brooks. In *CSCO,* series 3, vols. 5–6 (Paris, 1917, 1921). Translated into English by F. J. Hamilton and E. W. Brooks as *The Syrian Chronicle,* vol. 10, no. 12. London: Methuen, 1899.

Zaehner, Robert Charles. *The Teaching of the Magi, A Compendium of Zoroastrian Beliefs.* London: Allen and Unwin; and New York: Macmillan, 1950.

————. *Zurvan, A Zoroastrian Dilemma.* Oxford: Clarendon, 1955.

Zurcher, E. *The Buddhist Conquest of China: The Spread and Adoption of Buddhism in Early China.* Leiden: Brill, 1959. Vol. 11 in *Sinica Leidensia* (Institutum Sinologica Lugduno-Batavum).

de Zwann, J., "The Edessene Origin of the Odes of Solomon." In *Quantulacumque: Studies presented to Kirsopp Lake. . . .* Edited by R. P. Casey. London, Baltimore: Waverly Press, 1937.

Zwemer, Samuel M. *Arabia: The Cradle of Islam.* New York: Revell, 1900.

————. *The Moslem Christ, An Essay on the Life, Character and Teachings of Jesus Christ According to the Koran and Orthodox Tradition.* New York: American Tract Society, 1912.

Index

Acknowledgment is made for permission to reprint material from the following sources:

Excerpts from C. S. Lewis, "Evil and Good," *The Spectator,* Vol. 166 (Feb. 7, 1941). Copyright 1941 by *The Spectator.* Reprinted by permission of *The Spectator;* from *Christ in the Christian Tradition, Volume 1, From the Apostolic Age to Chalcedon,* second edition revised, by Aloys Grillmeier. English translation © 1975 by J. Bowden. Reprinted by permission of Mowbray's, a division of Cassel PLC; from *The Odes of Solomon,* reprint © 1977 by J. H. Charlesworth. Reprinted by permission of Scholars Press in conjunction with the Society for Biblical Literature; from *Orthodoxy and Heresy in Earliest Christianity,* second edition, by Walter Bauer. Translation © 1971 by R. A. Kraft. Reprinted by permission of Fortress Press; from *The Journey of William of Rubruck to the Eastern Parts, 1253–1255, as narrated by himself with two accounts of the Earlier Journey of John of Pian de Carpini,* Copyright 1900 by William W. Rockhill. Reprinted by permission of the Hakluyt Society; from *The Book of the Laws of Countries: Dialogue on Fate of Bardaisan of Edessa, Semitic texts with translations III.* Copyright 1965 by H. J. W. Drijvers. Reprinted by permission of Van Gorcum Publishers; from *"L'inscription de Kartir a la 'Ka'bah de Zoroastre"* by Marie-Louise Chaumont in the Tome CCXLVIII, Fascicule 3. Copyright 1960 by the Journal Asiatique; from *History of the Arabs from the Earliest Times to the Present.* Copyright 1951 by Philip K. Hitti. Reprinted by permission of Macmillan Publishing Company.

From *History of the Assyrian Church 100–640 A.D.* Copyright 1910 by W. A. Wigram. Reprinted by the Society for the Publication of Christian Knowledge; from *The Council of Chalcedon: A Historical and Doctrinal Survey.* Copyright 1953 by Robert V. Sellers. Reprinted by the Society for the Publication of Christian Knowledge; from *East Asia: The Great Tradition.* Copyright 1958 by Edwin O. Reischauer and J. K. Fairbank. Reprinted by permission of Houghton Mifflin Company; from William G. Young, *Handbook of Source Materials for Students of Church History,* copyright 1969 by the Christian Literature Society Indian Theological Library. Used by permission; from *The Life of Muhammed: A Translation of Isag's Sirat Rasul Allah.* Copyright 1955 by Alfred Guillaume. Reprinted by permission of Oxford University Press; from J. Labourt, *Le Christianisme dans l'Empire Perse sous le Dynastie Sassanide.* Copyright 1904 by Victor Le Coffre, Publishers. Used by permission; from *The Heritage of Persia,* second edition. Copyright 1984 by R. N. Frye. Reprinted by permission of Weidenfeld & Nicholson, Limited; from *The Empire of the Steppes: A History of Central Asia,* by Rene Grousset. Translation Copyright 1970 by Naomi Walford. Reprinted by permission of Rutgers University Press; from *Saint John of Damascus, Writings,* vol. 37 of *The Fathers of the Church.* Translation by Frederick H. Chase, Jr. Copyright 1958 by Fathers of the Church. Used by permission; from *Didascalia Apostolorum: The Syriac Version, Translated and accompanied by the Verona Latin Fragments.*